Why Do You Need this New Edition?

The requirements, strategies, and tools for college writing assignments have changed in many ways since the last edition of *The Longman Writer* was published, so make sure you're up to date! If you're still wondering why you should buy this new edition, here are a few more great reasons:

1. New Process Diagrams spotlight each step of the writing process to **help you see how to break down your writing assignments into manageable tasks** (Chs. 2–9).
2. New Development Diagrams highlight distinctive features of different patterns of development for writing, summarizing chapter content to **help you find key concepts quickly** (Chs. 10–18).
3. New guidance on creating and following a writing schedule combined with new tips for more efficient online research **help you make the most of your time when writing research papers** (Ch. 19).
4. New advice on evaluating, using, and citing electronic sources explains **how to use the most current online information sources—like blogs and wikis—credibly** (Ch. 19).
5. New visual source samples show you where in books, online periodicals, and subscription databases you can **find all the information you need to cite your sources in research papers** (Ch. 20).
6. New Essay Structure Diagrams outline the structure of professional readings to **help you use the reading as a pattern for your own writing** (Chs. 10–18).
7. New sample student essays written in both MLA and APA formats are annotated to offer **guidance and models for writing research papers in the academic style required by your course** (Ch. 20).
8. Eleven new readings have been added in chapters 10–18 on current topics such as slang, high school football, and e-mail style that are **models for the different patterns of writing that you'll be learning and practicing.**
9. A new appendix, "A Guide to Avoiding Plagiarism," provides the concrete **guidelines you need to avoid unintentional plagiarism and its consequences.**
10. **And now—use *The Longman Writer* alongside Pearson's unique MyCompLab and find a world of resources developed specifically for you!**

About the Authors

Judith Nadell was until several years ago Associate Professor of Communications at Rowan University (New Jersey). During her eighteen years at Rowan, she coordinated the introductory course in the Freshman Writing Sequence and served as Director of the Writing Lab. In the past several years, she has developed a special interest in grassroots literacy. Besides designing an adult-literacy project, a children's reading-enrichment program, and a family-literacy initiative, she has worked as a volunteer tutor and a tutor trainer in the programs. A Phi Beta Kappa graduate of Tufts University, she received a doctorate from Columbia University. She is the author of *Becoming a Read-Aloud Coach* (Townsend Press) and coauthor of *Doing Well in College* (McGraw-Hill), *Vocabulary Basics* (Townsend Press), and *The Longman Reader*. The recipient of a New Jersey award for excellence in the teaching of writing, Judith Nadell lives with her coauthor husband, John Langan, near Philadelphia.

John Langan has taught reading and writing at Atlantic Cape Community College near Atlantic City, New Jersey, for more than twenty-five years. Before teaching, he earned advanced degrees in writing at Rutgers University and in reading at Rowan University. Coauthor of *The Longman Reader* and author of a series of college textbooks on both reading and writing, he has published widely with McGraw-Hill Book Company, Townsend Press, and Longman. Through Townsend Press, his educational publishing company, he has developed the nonprofit "Townsend Library"—a collection of more than fifty new and classic stories that appeal to readers of any age.

Eliza A. Comodromos has taught composition and developmental writing in the English Departments of both Rutgers University and John Jay College of Criminal Justice. After graduating with a B.A. in English and in French from La Salle University, she did graduate work at the City University of New York Graduate School and went on to earn an advanced degree at Rutgers University, New Brunswick. A freelance editor and textbook consultant, Eliza has delivered numerous papers at language and literature conferences around the country. She lives with her husband, Paul Langan, and daughters, Anna Maria and Sophia Mae, near Philadelphia.

THE LONGMAN WRITER

RHETORIC, READER, AND RESEARCH GUIDE

SEVENTH EDITION

BRIEF EDITION

JUDITH NADELL

JOHN LANGAN
Atlantic Cape Community College

ELIZA A. COMODROMOS

Longman

New York San Francisco Boston
London Toronto Sydney Tokyo Singapore Madrid
Mexico City Munich Paris Cape Town Hong Kong Montreal

Acquisitions Editor:	Lauren A. Finn
Senior Development Editor:	Anne Brunell Ehrenworth
Senior Supplements Editor:	Donna Campion
Senior Media Producer:	Stefanie Liebman
Senior Marketing Manager:	Sandra McGuire
Production Manager:	Eric Jorgensen
Project Coordination, Text Design, and Electronic Page Makeup:	Elm Street Publishing Services
Senior Cover Design Manager:	Nancy Danahy
Photo Researcher:	Photosearch, Inc.
Senior Manufacturing Buyer:	Dennis J. Para
Printer and Binder:	Worldcolor Book Services/Taunton
Cover Printer:	Coral Graphic Services, Inc.

For permission to use copyrighted material, grateful acknowledgment is made to the copyright holders on pp. 729–730, which are hereby made part of this copyright page.

Library of Congress Cataloging-in-Publication Data

Nadell, Judith.
The Longman writer: rhetoric, reader, research guide, handbook/Judith Nadell, John Langan, Eliza A. Comodromos.—7th ed.
p. cm.
Includes bibliographical references and index.
ISBN-13: 978-0-205-73997-4
ISBN-13: 978-0-205-73999-8 (brief edition)
1. English language—Rhetoric. 2. English language—Grammar—Handbook, manuals, etc. 3. College readers. 4. Report writing. I. Langan, John, 1942– II. Comodromos, Eliza A. III. Title.

PE1408.N19 2007
808'.0427—dc22 2007041534

This book includes 2009 MLA guidelines.

3 4 5 6 7 8 9 10—QWT—12 11 10

Longman
is an imprint of

PEARSON

ISBN-13: 978-0-205-73997-4 (Full edition)
ISBN-10: 0-205-73997-0 (Full edition)
ISBN-13: 978-0-205-73999-8 (Brief edition)
ISBN-10: 0-205-73999-7 (Brief edition)

www.ablongman.com/nadell

Contents

Preface

Since the publication of the first edition of *The Longman Writer*, the college classroom has made tremendous technological advances, affecting the way we teach. Not only has the electronic world evolved to the point where nearly all communication can be conducted virtually, but also we have formed an unprecedented reliance on the Internet as our means of acquiring and communicating information. Despite all these technological leaps, students still need to learn how to write well. The new edition of *The Longman Writer: Brief Edition* continues its mission of teaching students how to develop sound writing skills.

Like the long version, the seventh edition of *The Longman Writer: Brief Edition's* approach is eclectic; we bring together the best from often conflicting schools of thought and blend in our own class-tested strategies. The result is a balanced text that is equal parts product and process. We describe possible sequences and structures to stress the connection between reading and writing and emphasize that these steps and formats should be viewed as strategies, not rigid prescriptions, for helping students discover what works best for them. This flexibility ensures that *The Longman Writer: Brief Edition* can fit a wide range of teaching philosophies and learning styles.

The Longman Writer: Brief Edition includes everything that students and instructors need in a one- or two-semester, first-year composition course: (1) a comprehensive *rhetoric*, including chapters on each stage of the writing process and discussions of the exam essay and literary paper; (2) a *reader* with thirty-four *professional selections* and twelve *student essays* integrated into the rhetoric; and (3) a *research guide*, with in-depth information on writing and properly documenting a research paper. The *Brief Edition* thus contains everything that's in the long version except for the Handbook. In those classes where students are likely to have purchased a separate English handbook, the *Brief Edition* is especially appropriate.

Throughout the text, we aim for a supportive, conversational tone that inspires students' confidence without being patronizing. Numerous *activities* and *writing assignments—more than 350 in all*—develop awareness of rhetorical choices and encourage students to explore a range of composing strategies.

WHAT'S NEW IN THE SEVENTH EDITION?

The seventh edition of *The Longman Writer: Brief Edition* has been fully updated to reflect the way students compose and present their work—electronically. In addition, we have provided more advice on the writing process, more in-depth coverage of the research process, and more examples of student writing throughout.

- **In Chapters 2–9, new Process Diagrams highlight each step of the writing process in detail**, showing students how every stage of composing an essay is integral in crafting an effective piece of writing. In response to reviewers' requests for more visuals on the writing process, each chapter in Part II, which discusses a step of the writing process, contains a Process Diagram with two columns. The left column lists the steps of the writing process, highlighting the particular step discussed in the corresponding chapter; the right column details the integral components of that step, guiding students as they prewrite (Ch. 2), identify a thesis (Ch. 3), find evidence (Ch. 4), organize their evidence (Ch. 5), write a first draft (Ch. 6), revise their paragraphs (Ch. 7) and sentences (Ch. 8), and edit and proofread their final draft (Ch. 9).
- **In Chapters 2–9, the featured student's work**, traced from initial prewriting phase to completed essay, **better reflects how students are writing in today's technological environment**. In Chapter 2, Harriet Davids's journal entries, subject narrowing, brainstorming, freewriting, mapping, and thesis creation have been updated. Her topic outline (Ch. 5), first draft (Ch. 6), peer reviewed draft (Ch. 7), and proofread paper (Ch. 9) include references that students can relate to (listening to MP3 players, talking on cell phones and texting, using computers to IM and play video games).
- **In Chapters 10–18, new professional selections** are included on timely and interesting topics: David Helvarg's "The Storm This Time," a descriptive essay in Chapter 10 about Hurricane Katrina that uses visuals to illustrate its supporting details; Charmie Gholson's "Charity Display?," a narrative essay in Chapter 11 about one woman's humiliating yet humbling experience as the recipient of another's good will; Leslie Savan's "Black Talk and Pop Culture," an illustrative essay in Chapter 12 on slang influences on the English language; David Brooks's "Psst! 'Human Capital'," a division-classification essay in Chapter 13 on the reasons why our successes and failures have less to do with the skills and knowledge we acquire and more to do with how we are raised; David Shipley's "Talk About Editing," a process analysis essay in Chapter 14 about the steps one major newspaper takes in editing the work of others; Eric Weiner's "Euromail and Amerimail," a comparison-contrast essay in Chapter 15 that contains comical observations on the differences between email in America and overseas; Buzz Bissinger's "Innocents Afield," a cause-effect essay in Chapter 16 on high school football and the game's loss of innocence; Natalie Angier's "The Cute Factor," a definition essay in Chapter 17 about the biological basis for our concept of "cuteness"; Stanley Fish's "Free-Speech Follies," an argumentation-persuasion essay in Chapter 18 on the true definition of First Amendment rights; Roberto

Rodriguez's "The Border on Our Backs," and Star Parker's "*Se Habla* Entitlement," a pair of argumentation-persuasion essays in Chapter 18 presenting conflicting views on the subject of immigration.

- **In Chapters 10–18, new Development Diagrams discuss each pattern of development in detail**, highlighting the distinctive features of each type of writing. In response to reviewers' requests for visuals that aid in explaining the patterns of development, each chapter in Part III, which discusses a particular pattern, contains a Development Diagram with two columns. The left column lists the steps of the writing process; the right column details the integral components of the steps in the writing process as it relates to a particular pattern, guiding students as they write essays within that pattern.
- **In Chapters 10–18, new Essay Structure Diagrams outline a professional reading in each chapter.** To better help students see how a reading is organized and supported, each diagram identifies the reasons why the reading exemplifies a particular pattern of development and provides a model for students to refer to in their own writing. Diagrams include Maya Angelou's "Sister Flowers" in Chapter 10; Audre Lorde's "The Fourth of July" in Chapter 11; Kay Hymowitz's "Tweens: Ten Going on Sixteen" in Chapter 12; William Lutz's "Doublespeak" in Chapter 13; Clifford Stoll's "Cyberschool" in Chapter 14; Toni Morrison's "A Slow Walk of Trees" in Chapter 15; Stephen King's "Why We Crave Horror Movies" in Chapter 16; K. C. Cole's "Entropy" in Chapter 17; and Stanley Fish's "Free-Speech Follies" in Chapter 18.
- **In Chapter 19, "Locating, Evaluating, and Integrating Research Sources," there are three new series of screen shots**, showing detailed online searches using the Library of Congress' catalog, a library subscription service, and a search directory. With the increasing shift of source materials from print to online, many students do not know how to perform library searches. These examples demonstrate the process in a step-by-step format, showing students how they can obtain the right sources for their research papers.
- **In Chapter 19, "Locating, Evaluating, and Integrating Research Sources,"** there is guidance for students on creating and following a writing schedule, making the most of their online time searching for potential research sources, and evaluating and using blogs and wikis in research papers.
- **In Chapter 20, "Writing the Research Paper," there are three new, full-color source samples** that vividly illustrate how to correctly cite books, online periodicals, and articles from a library subscription service. By providing original sources, the text shows students how they can locate the components for any citation.
- **In Chapter 20, "Writing the Research Paper," MLA and APA documentation sections contain the latest information on citing online and electronic sources** such as blogs, wikis, and podcasts. Students can look to these models when citing similar sources in their papers.
- **In Chapter 20, "Writing the Research Paper," there is a new, complete, and fully documented student essay in MLA format, and a new documented**

student essay in APA format. Both essays are annotated and provide models that students can refer to as they write their own research papers.

- **A new appendix, "A Guide to Avoiding Plagiarism,"** summarizes the key points students need in order to avoid unintentional plagiarism. This coverage serves as a supplement to *The Longman Writer: Brief Edition's* exhaustive coverage of this very important topic.

THE BOOK'S PLAN

Gratified by the first six editions' enthusiastic reception by instructors and students, we've maintained the *Longman Writer: Brief Edition's* essential structure. The book's format is as follows:

Part I, "The Reading Process," provides guidance in a three-step process for reading, in which students learn the importance of developing critical reading skills.

Part II, "The Writing Process," takes students, step-by-step, through a multistage composing sequence. Each chapter presents a stage of the writing process and includes:

- *Checklists* that summarize key concepts and keep students focused on the essentials as they write.
- *Diagrams* that encapsulate the writing process, providing at-a-glance references as students compose their own essays.
- *Activities* that reinforce pivotal skills and involve students in writing from the start, showing them how to take their papers through successive stages in the composing process.

Part III, "The Patterns of Development," covers nine patterns: description, narration, illustration, division-classification, process analysis, comparison-contrast, cause-effect, definition, and argumentation-persuasion. Each chapter contains a detailed explanation of the pattern, as well as:

- *Checklists* for prewriting and revising that summarize key concepts and keep students focused on the essentials as they write.
- *Diagrams* that encapsulate the patterns of development, providing at-a-glance references as students compose their own essays.
- *Annotated student essays* that clearly illustrate each pattern of development. Commentary following each essay points out the blend of patterns in the paper and identifies both the paper's strengths and the areas that need improvement.
- *Prewriting* and *Revising Activities* that help students appreciate the distinctive features of the pattern of development being studied. Prewriting Activities ask students to generate raw material for an essay and help them to see that the essay may include more than one pattern of development. Revising Activities allow students, working alone or in groups, to rework and strengthen paragraphs and examine and experiment with rhetorical options and composing techniques.

- *Professional selections* that represent not only a specific pattern of development, but also showcase a variety of subjects, tones, and points of view. Selections include tried-and-true classics such as George Orwell's "Shooting an Elephant" and contemporary pieces such as Leslie Savan's "Black Talk and Pop Culture" and Eric Weiner's "Euromail and Amerimail." An extensive instructional apparatus accompanies each professional selection:
  - *Biographical notes* that provide background on every professional author and create an interest in each piece of writing.
  - *Pre-Reading Journal Entries* that prime students for each professional selection by encouraging them to explore, in an unpressured way, their thoughts about an issue. These entries motivate students to read each professional piece with extra care, attention, and personal investment.
  - *Diagrams* that outline the essay structure of one professional reading per chapter, providing students with an easy reference for identifying and emulating each pattern of development.
  - *Questions for Close Reading* that help students to interpret each selection, while *Questions About the Writer's Craft* ask students to analyze a writer's use of patterns in the piece.
  - *Writing Assignments* that ask students to write essays using the same pattern as in the selection, to write essays that make connections to other patterns and selections, and to conduct library or Internet research. In addition, one assignment asks students to develop the ideas explored in their Pre-Reading Journal Entry into a full-length essay.
- End-of-chapter *General Assignments* and *Assignments with a Specific Purpose, Audience, and Point of View* that provide open-ended topics for students to explore and applications of rhetorical context to real-world settings.

Part IV, "The Research Paper," discusses how to locate, evaluate, integrate, and document electronic and print sources for a research paper and includes:

- *Checklists* that summarize key concepts of writing a research paper and keep students focused on the essentials as they select a research topic, evaluate sources, write and revise a research paper, and create and refine a bibliography.
- *Source Samples* that provide concrete examples of how students can locate all the necessary components of an MLA citation (for a book, online periodical, and subscription database) by presenting the actual source and its corresponding citation.
- *Activities* that ensure mastery of key research skills.

Part V, "The Literary Paper and Exam Essay," shows students how to adapt the composing process to fit the requirements of two highly specific writing situations and includes:

- *Checklists* that summarize key concepts of analyzing literary works, revising a literary analysis, and preparing for an exam essay.

- *Student essays* that provide solid models of writing and commentary that analyzes each piece of writing, indicating the reasons why each essay is exemplary.
- *Writing Assignments* and *Activities* that encourage students to write their own essays, using the skills they have learned in each chapter.

Marginal icons throughout alert both students and instructors to unique elements of this book:

- In Part II, student writing-in-progress is indicated with .
- In Part III, cross-references to other professional selections are indicated with .
- In Part III, assignments that are conducive to using the library or Internet are indicated with .
- In Parts II–V, ethical issues are indicated with .
- In Parts II, III, and V, combined patterns of development are indicated with .

TEACHING SUPPLEMENTS

A comprehensive Instructor's Manual to accompany *The Longman Writer: Brief Edition,* Seventh Edition, includes: a thematic table of contents; pointers about using the book; suggested activities; a detailed syllabus, and in-depth responses to the end-of-chapter activities, Questions for Close Reading, and Questions about the writer's Craft.

MyCompLab (www.mycomplab.com)

MyCompLab is a Web application that offers comprehensive and integrated resources for every writer. With MyCompLab, students can access a dynamic E-book version of *The Longman Writer: Brief Edition;* learn from interactive tutorials and instruction; practice and develop their skills with grammar, writing, and research exercises; share and collaborate their writing with peers; and receive comments on their writing from instructors and tutors. Go to http://mycomplab.com to register for these premiere resources and much more!

ACKNOWLEDGMENTS

Throughout our teaching and certainly in writing this book, we've drawn upon the expertise and wisdom of many composition scholars and practitioners. Although we cannot list all those who have influenced us, we owe a special debt to James Britton, Kenneth Bruffee, Frances Christensen, Edward P. J. Corbett, Peter Elbow, Janet Emig, Linda Flower, Donald Hall, Ken Macrorie, James Moffett,

Donald Murray, Frank O'Hare, Mina Shaughnessy, Nancy Sommers, and W. Ross Winterowd.

Over the years, many writing instructors have reviewed *The Longman Writer*. These colleagues' hard-hitting, practical comments guided our work every step of the way. To the following reviewers we are indeed grateful: John C. Baker, Concord College; Thomas G. Beverage, Coastal Carolina Community College; Barry Brunetti, Gulf Coast Community College; Joyce L. Cherry, Albany State University; Tony C. Clark, Scottsdale Community College; Bruce Coad, Mountain View College; Michael Cronin, Northern Oklahoma College; Beatrice I. Curry, Columbia State Community College; Juanita Davis, Columbia State Community College; William Dyer, Mankato State University; Jo Nell Farrar, San Jacinto College Central; Adam Fischer, Coastal Carolina Community College; Andrea Glebe, University of Nevada, Las Vegas; Linda Hasley, Redlands Community College; Kathryn Henkins, Mt. San Antonio College; Gretel Hichman, Kaskaskia College; M. Jean Jones, Columbia State Community College; Rowena R. Jones, Northern Michigan University; Leela Kapai, University of the District of Columbia; Tamara M. Karn, Chapman University; Kenneth Kerr, Frederick Community College; Sara Kinsey, Tarrant County College; Anne M. Kuhta, Northern Virginia Community College; William B. Lalicker, West Chester University of Pennsylvania; David Landis, James Sprunt Community College; Joe Law, Wright State University; Carol Owen Lewis, Trident Technical College; James L. Madachy, Gallaudet University; Jeffrey Maxson, Rowan University; Nancy McGee, Detroit College of Business; Rita M. Mignacca, State University of New York at Brockport; Margaret Kissam Morris, Mercy College; Betty P. Nelson, Volunteer State Community College; Douglas L. Okey, Spoon River College; Doris Osborn, Northern Oklahoma College; Mack A. Perry, Jackson State Community College; John S. Ramsey, State University of New York at Fredonia; Clay Randolph, Oklahoma City Community College; Gladys C. Rosser, Fayetteville Technical Community College; Peggy Ruff, DeVry Institute of Technology; Elizabeth Sarcone, Delta State University; Laura A. Scibona, State University of New York at Brockport; Marilyn Segal, California State University at Northridge; Rodger Slater, Scottsdale Community College; Richard Stoner, Broome Community College; Austin Straus, Mt. San Antonio College; Ellen K. Straw, Mt. San Antonio College; Elizabeth Stringer, East Mississippi Community College; Martha Coultas Strode, Spoon River College; Carole F. Taylor, University of Dayton; Ellen Tiedrich, Gloucester County College; Delores Waters, Delgado Community College; Wendy F. Weiner, Northern Virginia Community College; Carol Wershoven, Palm Beach Community College; Stephen Wilhoir, University of Dayton; Gene Young, Morehead State University; B. J. Zamora, Cleveland Community College; and Richard C. Zath, DeVry Institute of Technology.

For help in preparing the seventh edition, we owe thanks to the perceptive comments of these reviewers: Donna Armentrout, Potomac State College of West Virginia University; Carmen Christopher, Sampson Community College; Christine Hubbard, Tarrant County College; Lori Hughes, Montgomery College; Ronald Hulewicz, Broward Community College; Holly L. Norton, University of

Northwestern Ohio; J. J. Sheeran, Westwood College—Ft. Worth Campus; Anne Slater, Frederick Community College; and Laura Swartley, ITT Tech.

At Longman, many thanks go to our editor Lauren Finn for her fresh perspective and sound guidance as she shepherded the latest edition of our book. We're also indebted to Anne Brunell Ehrenworth at Longman and to Heather Johnson at Elm Street Publishing Services for skillfully handling the complex details of the production process.

Perhaps most of all, we're indebted to Linda Stern, who provided invaluable judgment and expertise helping us conceptualize and execute many features new to this edition, particularly the graphic diagrams and the revamped research chapters. Her intimate knowledge of the book and composition classroom has served us—and our readers—very well, and we thank her sincerely.

Several individuals from our in-home office deserve thanks. Beth Johnson and Joan Dunayer provided valuable assistance with the instructional apparatus following the reading selections. And Janet M. Goldstein shared with us her cartoon-excavation expertise as well as her fine editorial eye in refining the visual-writing assignments.

Of course, much appreciation goes to our families. To both sides of Judy Nadell and John Langan's family go affectionate thanks for being so supportive of our work. To Eliza Comodromos's husband, Paul Langan, and their daughters, Anna Maria and Sophia Mae, much love and gratitude for their plentiful supply of patience, encouragement, support—and laughter.

Finally, we're grateful to our students. Their candid reactions to various drafts of the text sharpened our thinking and kept us honest. We're especially indebted to the students whose work is included in this book. Their essays illustrate dramatically the potential and the power of student writing.

Judith Nadell, John Langan, Eliza A. Comodromos

PART I

THE READING PROCESS

1

Becoming a Strong Reader

"Dad, can you read?"

More than two hundred years ago, essayist Joseph Addison commented, "Of all the diversions of life, there is none so proper to fill up its empty spaces as the reading of useful and entertaining authors." Addison might have added that reading also challenges our beliefs, deepens our awareness, and stimulates our imagination.

Why, then, don't more people delight in reading? After all, most children feel great pleasure and pride when they first learn to read. As children grow older, though, the initially magical world of books is increasingly associated with homework, tests, and grades. Reading turns into an anxiety-producing chore. Also, as demands on a person's time accumulate throughout adolescence and adulthood, reading often gets pushed aside in favor of something that takes less effort. It's easier simply to switch on the television and passively view the ready-made images that flash across the screen. In contrast, it's almost impossible to remain passive while reading. Even a slick best-seller requires that the reader decode, visualize, and interpret what's on the page. The more challenging the materials, the more actively involved the reader must be.

The essays we selected for Part III of this book call for active reading. Representing a broad mix of styles and subjects, the essays range from the classic to the contemporary. They contain language that will move you, images that will enlarge your understanding of other people, ideas that will transform your views on complex issues.

The selections in Part III serve other purposes as well. For one thing, they'll help you develop a repertoire of reading skills—abilities that will benefit you throughout life. Second, as you become a better reader, your own writing style will become more insightful and polished. Increasingly, you'll be able to draw on the ideas presented in the selections and employ the techniques that professional writers use to express such ideas. As novelist Saul Bellow has observed, "A writer is a reader moved to emulation."

In the pages ahead, we outline a three-stage approach for getting the most out of this book's selections. Our suggestions will enhance your understanding of the book's essays, as well as help you read other material with greater ease and assurance.

STAGE 1: GET AN OVERVIEW OF THE SELECTION

Ideally, you should get settled in a quiet place that encourages concentration. If you can focus your attention while sprawled on a bed or curled up in a chair, that's fine. But if you find that being very comfortable is more conducive to day-dreaming and dozing off than it is to studying, avoid getting too relaxed.

Once you're settled, it's time to read the selection. To ensure a good first reading, try the following hints.

FIRST READING: A CHECKLIST

- ☐ Get an overview of the essay and its author. Start by reading the biographical note that precedes the selection. By providing background information about the author, the note helps you evaluate the writer's credibility as well as his or her slant on the subject. For example, if you know that William Lutz is a widely published professor of English at Rutgers University, you can better assess whether he is a credible source for the analysis he presents in his essay "Doublespeak" (see page 288).
- ☐ Do the *Pre-Reading Journal Entry* assignment, which precedes the selection. This assignment "primes" you for the piece by helping you to explore—in an easy, unpressured way—your thoughts about a key point raised in the selection. By preparing the journal entry, you're inspired to read the selection with special care, attention, and personal investment. (For more on pre-reading journal entries, see pages 15–18.)

- ☐ Consider the selection's title. A good title often expresses the essay's main idea, giving you insight into the selection even before you read it. For example, the title of Stanley Fish's essay, "Free Speech Follies," suggests the piece will explore the issue of First Amendment rights. A title may also hint at a selection's tone. The title of Robert Barry's piece, "Becoming a Recordoholic," (the student essay in Chapter 14) points to an essay that's light in spirit, whereas George Orwell's "Shooting an Elephant" (Chapter 11) suggests a piece with a serious mood.
- ☐ Read the selection straight through purely for pleasure. Allow yourself to be drawn into the world the author has created. Just as you first see a painting from the doorway of a room and form an overall impression without perceiving the details, you can have a preliminary, subjective feeling about a reading selection. Moreover, because you bring your own experiences and viewpoints to the piece, your reading will be unique. As Ralph Waldo Emerson said, "Take the book, my friend, and read your eyes out; you will never find there what I find."
- ☐ After this initial reading of the selection, focus your first impressions by asking yourself whether you like the selection. In your own words, briefly describe the piece and your reaction to it.

STAGE 2: DEEPEN YOUR SENSE OF THE SELECTION

At this point, you're ready to move more deeply into the selection. A second reading will help you identify the specific features that triggered your initial reaction.

There are a number of techniques you can use during this second, more focused reading. You may, for example, find it helpful to adapt some of the strategies that Mortimer Adler, a well-known writer and editor, wrote about in his 1940 essay "How to Mark a Book." There, Adler argues passionately for marking up the material we read. The physical act of annotating, he believes, etches the writer's ideas more sharply in the mind, helping readers grasp and remember those ideas more easily. And "best of all," Adler writes, the "marks and notes . . . stay there forever. You can pick up the . . . [material] the following week or year, and there are all your points of agreement, doubt, and inquiry. It's like resuming an uninterrupted conversation."

Adler goes on to describe various annotation techniques he uses when reading. Several of these techniques, adapted somewhat, are presented in the following checklist.

SECOND READING: A CHECKLIST

Using a pen (or pencil) and highlighter, you might . . .

- ☐ Underline or highlight the selection's main idea, or thesis, often found near the beginning or end. If the thesis isn't stated explicitly, write down your own version of the selection's main idea.
- ☐ Locate the main supporting evidence used to develop the thesis. Place numbers in the margin to designate each key supporting point.
- ☐ Circle or put an asterisk next to key ideas that are stated more than once.
- ☐ Take a minute to write "Yes" or "No" beside points with which you strongly agree or disagree. Your reaction to these points often explains your feelings about the aptness of the selection's ideas.
- ☐ Return to any unclear passages you encountered during the first reading. The feeling you now have for the piece as a whole will probably help you make sense of initially confusing spots. However, this second reading may also reveal that, in places, the writer's thinking isn't as clear as it could be.
- ☐ Use your dictionary to check the meanings of any unfamiliar words.
- ☐ Ask yourself if your initial impression of the selection has changed in any way as a result of this second reading. If your feelings *have* changed, try to determine why you reacted differently on this reading.

STAGE 3: EVALUATE THE SELECTION

Now that you have a good grasp of the selection, you may want to read it a third time, especially if the piece is long or complex. This time, your goal is to make judgments about the essay's effectiveness. Keep in mind, though, that you shouldn't evaluate the selection until after you have a strong hold on it. Whether positive or negative, any reaction is valid only if it's based on an accurate reading.

At first, you may feel uncomfortable about evaluating the work of a professional writer. But remember: Written material set in type only *seems* perfect; all writing can be finetuned. By identifying what does and doesn't work in others' writing, you're taking an important first step toward developing your own power as a writer. You might find it helpful at this point to get together with other students to discuss the selection. Comparing viewpoints often opens up a piece, enabling you to gain a clearer perspective on the selection and the author's approach.

To evaluate the essay, ask yourself the following questions.

EVALUATING A SELECTION: A CHECKLIST

- ☐ *Where does support for the selection's thesis seem logical and sufficient? Where does support seem weak?* Which of the author's supporting facts, arguments, and examples seem pertinent and convincing? Which don't?
- ☐ *Is the selection unified? If not, why not?* Where does something in the selection not seem relevant? Where are there any unnecessary digressions or detours?
- ☐ *How does the writer make the selection move smoothly from beginning to end?* How does the writer create an easy flow between ideas? Are any parts of the essay abrupt and jarring? Which ones?
- ☐ *Which stylistic devices are used to good effect in the selection?* Which pattern of development or combination of patterns does the writer use to develop the piece? Why do you think those patterns were selected? How do paragraph development, sentence structure, and word choice (diction) contribute to the piece's overall effect? What tone does the writer adopt? Where does the writer use figures of speech effectively? (The terms *patterns of development, sentence structure, diction,* and the like are explained in Chapter 2.)
- ☐ *How does the selection encourage further thought?* What new perspective on an issue does the writer provide? What ideas has the selection prompted you to explore in an essay of your own?

It takes some work to follow the three-stage approach just described, but the selections in Part III make it worth the effort. Bear in mind that none of the selections you'll read in Part III sprang full-blown from the pen of its author. Rather, each essay is the result of hours of work—hours of thinking, writing, rethinking, and revising. As a reader, you should show the same willingness to work with the selections, to read them carefully and thoughtfully. Henry David Thoreau, an avid reader and prolific writer, emphasized the importance of this kind of attentive reading when he advised that "books must be read as deliberately and unreservedly as they were written."

To illustrate the multi-stage reading process, we've annotated the professional essay that follows: Ellen Goodman's "Family Counterculture." Note that annotations are provided in the margin of the essay as well as at the end of the essay. As you read Goodman's essay, try applying the three-stage sequence. You can measure your ability to dig into the selection by making your own annotations on Goodman's essay and then comparing them to ours. You can also see how well you evaluated the piece by answering the preceding five questions and then comparing your responses to ours on pages 8–10.

ELLEN GOODMAN

The recipient of a Pulitzer Prize, Ellen Goodman (1941–) worked for *Newsweek* and *The Detroit Free Press* before joining the staff of *The Boston Globe* in the mid-1970s. A resident of the Boston area, Goodman writes a popular syndicated column that provides insightful commentary on life in the United States. Her pieces have appeared in a number of national publications, including *The Village Voice* and *McCall's*. Collections of her columns have been published in *Close to Home* (1979), *Turning Points* (1979), *At Large* (1981), *Keeping in Touch* (1985), *Making Sense* (1989), and *Value Judgments* (1993). Most recently, she authored *Team of Rivals* (2005), a book that examines the life of Abraham Lincoln. The following selection is from *Value Judgments*.

Pre-Reading Journal Entry

Television is often blamed for having a harmful effect on children. Do you think this criticism is merited? In what ways does TV exert a negative influence on children? In what ways does TV exert a positive influence on youngsters? Take a few minutes to respond to these questions in your journal.

FAMILY COUNTERCULTURE

Interesting take on the term *counterculture*

Time frame established

Light humor. Easy, casual tone

Sooner or later, most Americans become card-carrying members of the 1
counterculture. This is not an underground holdout of hippies. No beads are required. All you need to join is a child.

Time frame picked up

Thesis, developed overall by cause-effect pattern

At some point between Lamaze and the PTA, it becomes clear that one of 2
your main jobs as a parent is to counter the culture. What the media delivers to children by the masses, you are expected to rebut one at a time.

First research-based example to support thesis

The latest evidence of this frustrating piece of the parenting job descrip- 3
tion came from pediatricians. This summer, the American Academy of Pediatrics called for a ban on television food ads. Their plea was hard on the heels of a study showing that one Saturday morning of TV cartoons contained 202 junk-food ads.

The kids see, want, and nag. That is, after all, the theory behind advertis- 4
ing to children, since few six-year-olds have their own trust funds. The end result, said the pediatricians, is obesity and high cholesterol.

Their call for a ban was predictably attacked by the grocers' association. 5
But it was also attacked by people assembled under the umbrella marked "parental responsibility." We don't need bans, said these "PR" people, we need parents who know how to say "no."

6 Well, I bow to no one in my capacity for naysaying. I agree that it's a well-honed skill of child raising. By the time my daughter was seven, she qualified as a media critic.

Relevant paragraph? Identifies Goodman as a parent, but interrupts flow

7 But it occurs to me now that the call for "parental responsibility" is increasing in direct proportion to the irresponsibility of the marketplace. Parents are expected to protect their children from an increasingly hostile environment.

Transition doesn't work but would if ¶6 cut.

8 Are the kids being sold junk food? Just say no. Is TV bad? Turn it off. Are there messages about sex, drugs, violence all around? Counter the culture.

Series of questions and brief answers consistent with overall casual tone

9 Mothers and fathers are expected to screen virtually every aspect of their children's lives. To check the ratings on the movies, to read the labels on the CDs, to find out if there's MTV in the house next door. All the while keeping in touch with school and, in their free time, earning a living.

Brief real-life examples support thesis.

Fragments

10 In real life, most parents do a great deal of this monitoring and just-say-no-ing. Any trip to the supermarket produces at least one scene of a child grabbing for something only to have it returned to the shelf by a frazzled parent. An extraordinary number of the family arguments are over the goodies—sneakers, clothes, games—that the young know only because of ads.

More examples

11 But at times it seems that the media have become the mainstream culture in children's lives. Parents have become the alternative.

Another weak transition—no contrast

Restatement of thesis

12 Barbara Dafoe Whitehead, a research associate at the Institute for American Values, found this out in interviews with middle-class parents. "A common complaint I heard from parents was their sense of being overwhelmed by the culture. They felt their voice was a lot weaker. And they felt relatively more helpless than their parents.

Second research-based example to support thesis

Citing an expert reinforces thesis.

13 "Parents," she notes, "see themselves in a struggle for the hearts and minds of their own children." It isn't that they can't say no. It's that there's so much more to say no to.

Restatement of thesis

14 Without wallowing in false nostalgia, there has been a fundamental shift. Americans once expected parents to raise their children in accordance with the dominant cultural messages. Today they are expected to raise their children in opposition.

Comparison-contrast pattern—signaled by *Today, Once,* and *Now*

15 Once the chorus of cultural values was full of ministers, teachers, neighbors, leaders. They demanded more conformity, but offered more support. Now the messengers are Ninja Turtles, Madonna, rap groups,

and celebrities pushing sneakers. Parents are considered "responsible" only if they are successful in their resistance.

Restatement of thesis → 16 It's what makes child raising harder. It's why parents feel more isolated. It's not just that American families have less time with their kids. It's that we have to spend more of this time doing battle with our own culture.

Conveys the challenges that parents face

17 It's rather like trying to get your kids to eat their green beans after they've been told all day about the wonders of Milky Way. Come to think of it, it's exactly like that.

Thesis: First stated in paragraph 2 (" . . . it becomes clear that one of your main jobs as a parent is to counter the culture. What the media delivers to children by the masses, you are expected to rebut one at a time.") and then restated in paragraphs 11 ("the media have become the mainstream culture in children's lives. Parents have become the alternative."); 13 (Parents are frustrated, not because " . . . they can't say no. It's that there's so much more to say no to."); and 16 ("It's not just that American families have less time with their kids. It's that we have to spend more of this time doing battle with our own culture.").

First Reading: A quick take on a serious subject. Informal tone and to-the-point style get to the heart of the media vs. parenting problem. Easy to relate to.

Second and Third Readings:

1. Uses the findings of the American Academy of Pediatrics, a statement made by Barbara Dafoe Whitehead, and a number of brief examples to illustrate the relentless work parents must do to counter the culture.
2. Uses cause-effect overall to support thesis and comparison-contrast to show how parenting nowadays is more difficult than it used to be.
3. Not everything works (reference to her daughter as a media critic, repetitive and often inappropriate use of *but* as a transition), but overall the essay succeeds.
4. At first, the ending seems weak. But it feels just right after an additional reading. Shows how parents' attempts to counter the culture are as commonplace as their attempts to get kids to eat vegetables. It's an ongoing and constant battle that makes parenting more difficult than it has to be and less enjoyable than it should be.
5. Possible essay topics: A humorous paper about the strategies kids use to get around their parents' saying "no" or a serious paper on the negative effects on kids of another aspect of television culture (cable television, MTV, tabloid-style talk shows, and so on).

The following answers to the questions on page 5 will help crystallize your reaction to Goodman's essay.

1. **Where does support for the selection's thesis seem logical and sufficient? Where does support seem weak?** Goodman begins to provide evidence for her thesis when she cites the American Academy of Pediatrics's call for a "ban on television food ads" (paragraphs 3–5). The ban followed a study showing that kids are exposed to 202 junk-food ads during a single Saturday morning of television cartoons. Goodman further buoys her thesis with a list of brief "countering the culture" examples (8–10) and a slightly more detailed example (10) describing the parent-child conflicts that occur on a typical trip to the

supermarket. By citing Barbara Dafoe Whitehead's findings (12–13) later on, Goodman further reinforces her point that the need for constant rebuttal makes parenting especially frustrating: Because parents have to say "no" to virtually everything, more and more family time ends up being spent "doing battle" with the culture (16).

2. **Is the selection unified? If not, why not?** In the first two paragraphs, Goodman identifies the problem and then provides solid evidence of its existence (3–4, 8–10). But Goodman's comments in paragraph 6 about her daughter's skill as a media critic seem distracting. Even so, paragraph 6 serves a purpose because it establishes Goodman's credibility by showing that she, too, is a parent and has been compelled to be a constant naysayer with her child. From paragraph 7 on, the piece stays on course by focusing on the way parents have to compete with the media for control of their children. The concluding paragraphs (16–17) reinforce Goodman's thesis by suggesting that parents' struggle to counteract the media is as common—and as exasperating—as trying to get children to eat their vegetables when all the kids want is to gorge on candy.

3. **How does the writer make the selection move smoothly from beginning to end?** The first two paragraphs of Goodman's essay are clearly connected: The phrase "sooner or later" at the beginning of the first paragraph establishes a time frame that is then picked up at the beginning of the second paragraph with the phrase "at some point between Lamaze and the PTA." And Goodman's use in paragraph 3 of the word *this* ("The latest evidence of *this* frustrating piece of the parenting job description . . .") provides a link to the preceding paragraph. Other connecting strategies can be found in the piece. For example, the words *Today, Once,* and *Now* in paragraphs 14–15 provide an easy-to-follow contrast between parenting in earlier times and parenting in this era. However, because paragraph 6 contains a distracting aside, the contrast implied by the word *But* at the beginning of paragraph 7 doesn't work. Nor does Goodman's use of the word *But* at the beginning of paragraph 11 work; the point there emphasizes rather than contrasts with the one made in paragraph 10. From this point on, though, the essay is tightly written and moves smoothly along to its conclusion.

4. **Which stylistic devices are used to good effect in the selection?** Goodman uses several patterns of development in her essay. The selection as a whole shows the *effect* of the mass media on kids and their parents. In paragraphs 3 and 12, Goodman provides *examples in the form of research data* to support her thesis, while paragraphs 8–10 provide a series of *brief real-life examples.* Paragraphs 12–15 use a *contrast,* and paragraph 17 makes a *comparison* to punctuate Goodman's concluding point. Throughout, Goodman's *informal, conversational tone* draws readers in, and her *no-holds-barred style* drives her point home forcefully. In paragraph 8, she uses a *question and answer format* ("Are the kids being sold junk food? Just say no.") and *short sentences* ("Turn it off" and "Counter the culture") to illustrate how pervasive the situation is.

And in paragraph 9, she uses *fragments* ("To check the ratings . . ." and "All the while keeping in touch with school . . .") to focus attention on the problem. These varied stylistic devices help make the essay a quick, enjoyable read. Finally, although Goodman is concerned about the corrosive effects of the media, she leavens her essay with dashes of *humor.* For example, the image of parents as card-carrying hippies (1) and the comments about green beans and Milky Ways (17) probably elicit smiles or gentle laughter from most readers.

5. **How does the selection encourage further thought?** Goodman's essay touches on a problem most parents face at some time or another—having to counter the culture in order to protect their children. Her main concern is how difficult it is for parents to say "no" to virtually every aspect of the culture. Although Goodman offers no immediate solutions, her presentation of the issue urges us to decide for ourselves which aspects of the culture should be countered and which should not.

If, for each essay you read in this book, you consider the preceding questions, you'll be able to respond thoughtfully to the *Questions for Close Reading* and *Questions About the Writer's Craft* presented after each selection. Your responses will, in turn, prepare you for the writing assignments that follow the questions. Interesting and varied, the assignments invite you to examine issues raised by the selections and encourage you to experiment with various writing styles and organizational patterns.

Following are some sample questions and writing assignments based on the Goodman essay; all are similar to the sort that appear later in this book. Note that the final writing assignment paves the way for the successive stages of a student essay presented in Part II, "The Writing Process." (The final version of the essay appears on pages 144–145.)

Questions for Close Reading

1. According to Goodman, what does it mean to "counter the culture"? Why is it harder now than ever before?
2. Which two groups, according to Goodman, protested the American Academy of Pediatrics's ban on television food ads? Which of these two groups does she take more seriously? Why?

Questions About the Writer's Craft

1. What audience do you think Goodman had in mind when she wrote this piece? How do you know? Where does she address this audience directly?
2. What word appears four times in paragraph 16? Why do you think Goodman repeats this word so often? What is the effect of this repetition?

Writing Assignments

1. Goodman believes that parents are forced to say "no" to almost everything the media offer. Write an essay supporting the idea that not everything the media present is bad for children.
2. Goodman implies that, in some ways, today's world is hostile to children. Do you agree? Drawing upon but not limiting yourself to the material in your pre-reading journal, write an essay in which you support or reject this viewpoint.

The benefits of active reading are many. Books in general and the selections in Part III in particular will bring you face to face with issues that concern all of us. If you study the selections and the questions that follow them, you'll be on your way to discovering ideas for your own papers. Part II offers practical suggestions for turning those ideas into well-organized, thoughtful essays.

PART II

THE WRITING PROCESS

2

Getting Started Through Prewriting

"I have a lot of really good ideas, but I just can't get them down on paper."

www.CartoonStock.com

OBSERVATIONS ABOUT THE WRITING PROCESS

Not many people retire at age thirty-eight. But Michel Montaigne, a sixteenth-century French attorney, did exactly that. Montaigne retired at a young age because he wanted to read, think, and write about all the subjects that interested him. After spending years getting his ideas down on paper, Montaigne finally published his short prose pieces. He called them *essais*—French for "trials" or "attempts."

In fact, all writing is an attempt to transform ideas into words, thus giving order and meaning to life. By using the term *essais*, Montaigne acknowledged that a written piece is never really finished. Of course, writers have to stop at some point, especially if they have deadlines to meet. But, as all experienced writers know, even after they dot the final *i*, cross the final *t*, and say "That's it," there's always something that could have been explored further or expressed a little better.

When we read a piece of writing, we see only the finished product. Not being privy to the writer's effort to convey meaning, we may hold a romanticized notion of what it means to be a writer. We may imagine the writer transported by flashes of creativity, polished prose appearing—as if by magic—on the page. In practice, though, most writers do anything but pour out well-formed thoughts. Rather, they stare into space, dash off a few pages, crumple them up, and start all over. Even E. B. White, the American essayist celebrated for his eloquent, seemingly effortless prose, confessed, "Writing . . . is a hell of a chore for me, closely related to acid indigestion."

If White, who made his living as a writer, admitted such anxiety, you shouldn't be surprised if you feel some apprehension when it's time to write a paper. Your uneasiness may stem in part from your belief that some people are born writers, others are not—and that you're one of the latter. Some people *do* seem to be born with a gift for language, just as some people seem to be born with a gift for athletics or music. But with practice, just about anyone can learn to play a solid game of tennis or to sing on key. And that's what most of us are aiming for—not to be the Venus Williamses, the Pavarottis, or the E. B. Whites of the world, but to perform skillfully and confidently.

As with singing or playing tennis, learning to write well is a challenge. Shaky starts and changes in direction aren't uncommon. Although there's no way to eliminate the work needed to write effectively, certain approaches can make the process more manageable and rewarding. In Chapters 2–9, we describe a sequence of steps for writing essays. Each step is presented in a full-color graphic "process diagram" so you can see clearly each step of the writing process. Familiarity with a specific sequence develops your awareness of strategies and choices, making you feel more confident when it comes time to write. You're less likely to look at a blank piece of paper and think, "Help! Now what do I do?" During the sequence, you do the following:

- Prewrite
- Identify your thesis
- Support the thesis with evidence
- Organize the evidence
- Write the paragraphs of the first draft
- Revise meaning, structure, and paragraph development
- Revise sentences and words
- Edit and proofread

Even though we present the sequence as a series of steps, it's not a rigid formula that you must follow step by unchanging step. Somewhere in school we were taught that a straight line is the shortest distance between two points. But writing isn't as simple or tidy as that. Most people develop personalized approaches to the writing process. Some writers mull over a topic in their heads and then move quickly into a promising first draft; others outline their essays in detail before beginning to write. Between these two extremes are any number of effective approaches.

Most of us tend to be creatures of habit; we feel secure and comfortable doing things the way we always have. You've probably approached writing in much the same way for many years. At first, you may be reluctant to try the techniques we describe here and in the following chapters. That's understandable. But we urge you to experiment with the strategies we present. Try them, use what works, discard what doesn't. And always feel free to streamline or alter the steps in the sequence to suit your individual needs and the requirements of specific writing assignments.

USE PREWRITING TO GET STARTED

Prewriting refers to strategies you can use to generate ideas *before* starting the first draft of a paper. (See Figure 2.1 below.) Prewriting techniques are like the warm-ups you do before going out to jog—they loosen you up, get you moving, and help you to develop a sense of well-being and confidence. Since prewriting techniques encourage imaginative exploration, they also help you discover what interests you most about your subject. Having such a focus early in the writing process keeps you from plunging into your initial draft without first giving some thought to what you want to say. Prewriting thus saves you time in the long run by keeping you on course.

Prewriting can help in other ways, too. When we write, we often sabotage our ability to generate material because we continually critique what we put down

FIGURE 2.1
Process Diagram: Prewriting

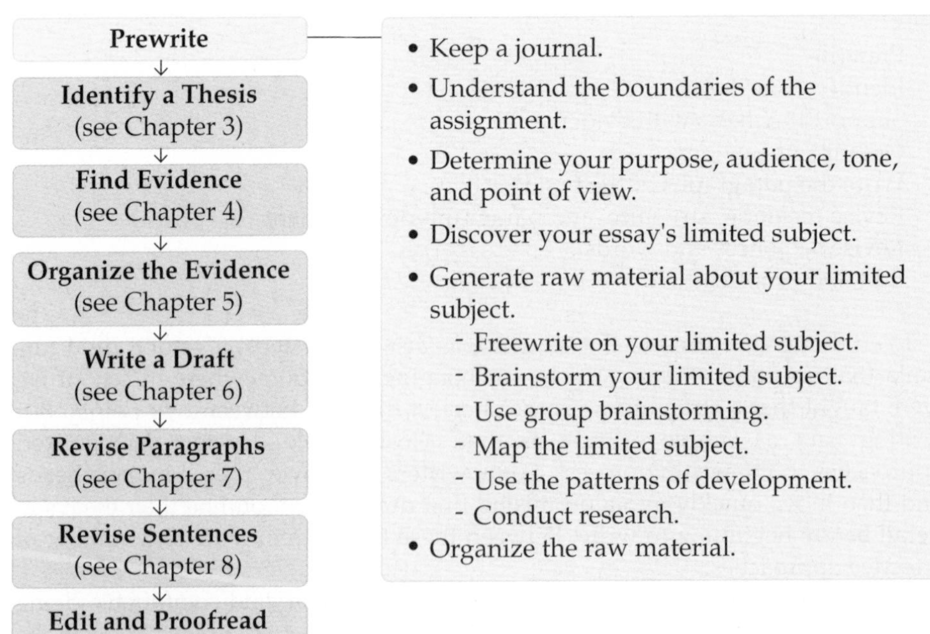

on paper. "This makes no sense," "This is stupid," "I can't say that," and other critical thoughts pop into our minds. Such negative, self-critical comments stop the flow of our thoughts and reinforce the fear that we have nothing to say and aren't very good at writing. During prewriting, you deliberately ignore your internal critic. Your purpose is simply to get ideas down on paper or on a computer screen *without evaluating* their effectiveness. Writing without immediately judging what you produce can be liberating. Once you feel less pressure, you'll probably find that you can generate a good deal of material. And that can make your confidence soar.

One final advantage of prewriting: The random associations typical of prewriting tap the mind's ability to make unusual connections. When you prewrite, you're like an archaeologist going on a dig. On the one hand, you may not unearth anything; on the other hand, you may stumble upon one interesting find after another. Prewriting helps you appreciate—right from the start—this element of surprise in the writing process.

Keep a Journal

Of all the prewriting techniques, keeping a **journal** (daily or almost daily) is the one most likely to make writing a part of your life. If you prefer keeping a handwritten journal, consider using a small notebook that you can carry with you for on-the-spot writing. If you feel more comfortable working at a computer, keep your journal printouts in a loose-leaf notebook. No matter how you proceed, be sure to date all entries.

Some journal entries focus on a single theme; others wander from topic to topic. Your starting point may be a dream, a snippet of overheard conversation, a video on YouTube, a political cartoon, an issue raised in class or in your reading—anything that surprises, interests, angers, depresses, confuses, or amuses you. You may also use a journal to experiment with your writing style—say, to vary your sentence structure if you tend to use predictable patterns.

Here is a fairly focused excerpt from a student's journal:

Today I had to show Paul around school. He and Mom got here at 9. I didn't let on that this was the earliest I've gotten up all semester! He got out of the car looking kind of nervous. Maybe he thought his big brother would be different after a couple of months of college. I walked him around part of the campus and then he went with me to Am. Civ. and then to lunch. He met Greg and some other guys. Everyone seemed to like him. He's got a nice, quiet sense of humor. When I went to Bio., I told him that he could walk around on his own since he wasn't crazy about sitting in on a science class. But he said "I'd rather stick with you." Was he flattering me or was he just scared? Anyway it made me feel good. Later when he was leaving, he told me he's definitely going to apply. I guess that'd be kind of nice, having him here. Mom thinks it's great and she's pushing it. I don't know. I feel kind of like it would invade my privacy. I found this school and have made a life for myself here. Let him find his own school! But it could be great having my kid brother here. I guess this is a classic case of what my psych teacher calls ambivalence. Part of me wants him to come, and part of me doesn't. (November 10)

The journal is a place for you to get in touch with the writer inside you. Although some instructors collect students' journals, you needn't be overly concerned with spelling, grammar, sentence structure, or organization. While journal writing is typically more structured than freewriting (see pages 26–27), you don't have to strive for entries that read like mini-essays. On the contrary, sometimes you may find it helpful to use a simple list (see the journal entry on page 17) when recording your thoughts about a subject. You may leave loose ends, drift to new topics, and evoke the personal and private without fully explaining or describing. The most important thing is to let your journal writing prompt reflection and insights.

Writing openly and fluently doesn't happen overnight; you need to keep at it. Try to complete a page-long journal entry three to five times a week. It's also a good idea to reread each week's entries to identify recurring themes and concerns. Keep a list of these issues at the back of your journal, under a heading like "Possible Essay Subjects." Here, for instance, are a few topics suggested by the preceding journal entry: deciding which college to attend, leaving home, sibling rivalry. Each of these topics could be developed in a full-length essay.

Using the journal to identify potential essay subjects helps you see that everyday life can be the source of meaningful writing. Most of us have become so accustomed to the routines of our lives that we cannot see the interesting in the ordinary. In *Walden,* a collection of journal entries, Henry David Thoreau wrote that our lives would be enriched immeasurably if we "employ[ed] a certain portion of each day looking back upon the time which has passed and in writing down . . . [our] thoughts and feelings." Keeping a journal does indeed foster an awareness of our own lives. It prevents us from thinking of ourselves as dull, dreary people to whom nothing happens. And it provides a wealth of material to draw on in our writing.

The Pre-Reading Journal Entry

To reinforce the value of journal writing, we've included a journal assignment before every selection in the book. This assignment, called the *Pre-Reading Journal Entry,* gets you ready for the piece by encouraging you to explore—in a tentative fashion—your thoughts about an issue that will be raised in the selection.

Here, once again, is the *Pre-Reading Journal Entry* assignment that precedes Ellen Goodman's "Family Counterculture" (see page 6):

> Television is often blamed for having a harmful effect on children. Do you think this criticism is merited? In what ways does TV exert a negative influence on children? In what ways does TV exert a positive influence on youngsters? Take a few minutes to respond to these questions in your journal.

The following journal entry shows how one student, Harriet Davids, responded to the journal assignment. A thirty-eight-year-old college student and mother of two young teenagers, Harriet was understandably intrigued by the assignment. As you'll see, Harriet used a listing strategy to prepare her journal entry. She found that lists were perfect for dealing with the essentially "for or against" nature of the journal assignment.

TV's Negative Influence on Kids	TV's Positive Influence on Kids
Teaches negative behaviors (violence, sex, swearing, drugs, alcohol, etc.)	Teaches important educational concepts (*Sesame Street*, shows on The Learning Channel, etc.)
Cuts down on imagination and creativity	Exposes kids to new images and worlds (*Dora the Explorer*, *Mister Rogers' Neighborhood*)
Cuts down on time spent with parents (talking, reading, playing games together)	Can inspire important discussions (about morals, sexuality, drugs, etc.) between kids and parents
Encourages parents' lack of involvement with kids	Gives parents a needed break from kids
Frightens kids excessively by showing images of real-life violence (terrorist attacks, war, murders, etc.)	Educates kids about the painful realities in the world
Encourages isolation (watching screen rather than interacting with other kids)	Creates common ground among kids, basis of conversations and games
De-emphasizes reading and creates need for constant stimulation	Encourages kids to slow down and read books based on a TV series or show (the *Arthur* and the *Clifford, the Big Red Dog* series, *The Bookworm Bunch*, etc.)
Promotes materialism (commercials)	Can be used by parents to teach kids that they can't have everything they see

The journal assignment and subsequent journal entry do more than prepare you to read a selection with extra care and attention; they also pave the way to a full-length essay. Here's how. The final assignment following each selection is called *Writing Assignment Using a Journal Entry as a Starting Point.* This assignment helps you to translate the raw material in your journal entry into a thoughtful, well-considered essay. By the time you get to the assignment, the rough ideas in your journal entry will have been enriched by your reading of the selection. (For an example of a writing assignment that draws upon material in a pre-reading journal entry, turn to page 167.)

As you've just seen, journal writing can stimulate thinking in a loose, unstructured way; journal writing can also prompt the focused thinking required by a specific writing assignment. When you have a specific piece to write, you should approach prewriting in a purposeful, focused manner. You need to:

- Understand the boundaries of the assignment
- Determine your purpose, audience, tone, and point of view
- Discover your essay's limited subject
- Generate raw material about your limited subject
- Organize the raw material

We'll discuss each of these steps in turn. But first, here's a practical tip: If you don't use a computer during the prewriting stage, try using a pencil and scrap paper. They reinforce the notion that prewriting is tentative and exploratory.

Understand the Boundaries of the Assignment

Most likely, you'll find considerable variety in your college writing assignments. Sometimes a professor will indicate that you can write on a topic of your own choosing; other times you may be given a highly specific assignment. Most assignments, though, will fit somewhere in between. In any case, you shouldn't start writing a paper until you know what's expected. First, clarify the *kind of paper* the instructor has in mind. Assume the instructor asks you to discuss the key ideas in an assigned reading. What exactly does the instructor want you to do? Should you include a brief summary of the selection? Should you compare the author's ideas with your own view of the subject? Should you determine if the author's view is supported by valid evidence? If you're not sure about an assignment, ask your instructor—not the student next to you, who may be as confused as you—to make the requirements clear. Most instructors are more than willing to provide an explanation. They would rather take a few minutes of class time to explain the assignment than spend hours reading dozens of student essays that miss the mark.

Second, find out *how long* the paper is expected to be. Many instructors will indicate the approximate length of the papers they assign. If no length requirements are provided, discuss with the instructor what you plan to cover and indicate how long you think your paper will be. The instructor will either give you the go-ahead or help you refine the direction and scope of your work.

Determine Your Purpose, Audience, Tone, and Point of View

Once you understand the requirements for a writing assignment, you're ready to begin thinking about the essay. What is its *purpose?* For what *audience* will it be written? What *tone* and *point of view* will you use? Later on, you may modify your decisions about these issues. That's fine. But you need to understand the way these considerations influence your work in the early phases of the writing process.

Purpose

Start by clarifying to yourself the essay's broad **purpose.** What do you want the essay to accomplish? The papers you write in college are usually meant to *inform* or *explain,* to *convince* or *persuade,* and sometimes to *entertain.*

In practice, writing often combines purposes. You might, for example, write an essay trying to *convince* people to support a new trash recycling program in your community. But before you win readers over, you most likely would have to *explain* something about current waste-disposal technology.

When purposes blend in this way, the predominant one influences the essay's content, organization, pattern of development, emphasis, and language. Assume you're writing about a political campaign. If your primary goal is to *entertain,* to take a gentle poke at two candidates, you might use the comparison-contrast pattern to organize your essay. You might, for example, start with several accounts of one candidate's "foot-in-mouth disease" and then describe the attempts of the other candidate, a multimillionaire, to portray himself as an average Joe. Your language, full of exaggeration, would reflect your objective. But if your primary purpose is to *persuade* readers that the candidates are incompetent and shouldn't be elected, you might adopt a serious, straightforward style. Selecting the argumentation-persuasion pattern to structure the essay, you might use one candidate's gaffes and the other's posturings to build a case that neither is worthy of public office.

Audience

Writing is a social act and thus implies a reader or an **audience.** To write effectively, you need to identify who your readers are and to take their expectations and needs into account. An essay about the artificial preservatives in the food served by the campus cafeteria would take one form if submitted to your chemistry professor and a very different form if written for the college newspaper. The chemistry paper would probably be formal and technical, complete with chemical formulations and scientific data: "Distillation revealed sodium benzoate particles suspended in a gelatinous medium." But such technical material would be inappropriate in a newspaper column intended for general readers. In this case, you might provide specific examples of cafeteria foods containing additives—"Those deliciously smoky cold cuts are loaded with nitrates and nitrites, both known to cause cancer in laboratory animals"—and suggest ways to eat more healthfully—"Pass by the deli counter and fill up instead on vegetarian pizza and fruit juices."

If you forget your readers, your essay can run into problems. Consider what happened when one student, Roger Salucci, submitted a draft of his essay to his instructor for feedback. The assignment was to write about an experience that demonstrated the value of education. Here's the opening paragraph from Roger's first draft:

> When I received my first page as an EMT, I realized pretty quickly that all the weeks of KED and CPR training paid off. At first, when the call came in, I was all nerves, I can tell you. When the heat is on, my mind tends to go as blank as an unplugged computer screen. But I beat it to the van right away. After a couple of false turns, my partner and I finally got the right house and found a woman fibrillating and suffering severe myocardial arrhythmia. Despite our anxiety, our heads were on straight; we knew exactly what to do.

Roger's instructor found his essay unclear because she knew nothing about being an EMT (emergency medical technician). When writing the essay, Roger neglected to consider his audience; specifically, he forgot that college instructors are no more knowledgeable than anyone else about subjects outside their specialty. Roger's instructor also commented that she was thrown off guard by the paper's casual, slangy approach ("I was all nerves, I can tell you"; "I beat it to the van right away"). Roger used a breezy, colloquial style—almost as though he were chatting about the experience with friends—but the instructor had expected a more formal approach.

The more you know about your readers, the more you can adapt your writing to fit their needs and expectations. The accompanying checklist will help you analyze your audience.

☑ ANALYZING YOUR AUDIENCE: A CHECKLIST

- ☐ What are my readers' age, sex, and educational levels? How do these factors affect what I need to tell and don't need to tell my readers?
- ☐ What are my readers' political, religious, and other beliefs? How do these beliefs influence their attitudes and actions?
- ☐ What interests and needs motivate my audience?
- ☐ How much do my readers already know about my subject? Do they have any misconceptions?
- ☐ What biases do they have about me, my subject, and my opinion?
- ☐ How do my readers expect me to relate to them?
- ☐ What values do I share with my readers that will help me communicate with them?

Tone

Just as your voice may project a range of feelings, your writing can convey one or more **tones,** or emotional states: enthusiasm, anger, resignation, and so on. Tone isn't a decorative adornment tacked on as an afterthought. Rather, tone is integral to meaning. It permeates writing and reflects your attitude toward yourself, your purpose, your subject, and your readers.

In everyday conversation, vocal inflections, facial expressions, and body gestures help convey tone. In writing, how do you project tone without these aids? You pay close attention to *sentence structure* and *word choice.* In Chapter 8, we present detailed strategies for finetuning sentences and words during the revision stage. Here we simply want to help you see that determining your tone should come early in the writing process because the tone you select influences the sentences and words you use later.

Sentence structure refers to the way sentences are shaped. Although the two paragraphs that follow deal with exactly the same subject, note how differences in sentence structure create sharply dissimilar tones:

> During the 1960s, many inner-city minorities considered the police an occupying force and an oppressive agent of control. As a result, violence grew against police in poorer neighborhoods, as did the number of residents killed by police.

> An occupying force. An agent of control. An oppressor. That's how many inner-city minorities in the '60s viewed the police. Violence against police soared. Police killings of residents mounted.

Informative in its approach, the first paragraph projects a neutral, almost dispassionate tone. The sentences are fairly long, and clear transitions ("During the 1960s"; "As a result") mark the progression of thought. But the second paragraph, with its dramatic, almost alarmist tone, seems intended to elicit a strong emotional response; its short sentences, fragments, and abrupt transitions reflect the turbulence of earlier times.

Word choice also plays a role in establishing the tone of an essay. Words have **denotations,** neutral dictionary meanings, as well as **connotations,** emotional associations that go beyond the literal meaning. The word *beach,* for instance, is defined in the dictionary as "a nearly level stretch of pebbles and sand beside a body of water." This definition, however, doesn't capture individual responses to the word. For some, *beach* suggests warmth and relaxation; for others, it calls up images of hospital waste and sewage washed up on a once-clean stretch of shoreline.

Since tone and meaning are tightly bound, you must be sensitive to the emotional nuances of words. Think about some of the terms denoting *adult human female: woman, chick, broad, member of the fair sex.* While all of these words denote the same thing, their connotations—the pictures they call up—are sharply different. Similarly, in a respectful essay about police officers, you wouldn't refer to *cops, narcs,* or *flatfoots;* such terms convey a contempt inconsistent with the tone intended. Your words must also convey tone clearly; otherwise, meaning is lost. Suppose you're writing a satirical piece criticizing a local beauty pageant.

Dubbing the participants "livestock on view" leaves no question about your tone. But if you simply referred to the participants as "attractive young women," readers might be unsure of your attitude. Remember, readers can't read your mind, only your paper.

Point of View

When you write, you speak to your audience as a unique individual. **Point of view** reveals the person you decide to be as you write. Like tone, point of view is closely tied to your purpose, audience, and subject. Imagine you want to convey to students in your composition class the way your grandfather's death—on your eighth birthday—impressed you with life's fragility. To capture that day's impact on you, you might tell what happened from the point of view of a child: "Today is my birthday. I'm eight. Grandpa died an hour before I was supposed to have my party." Or you might choose instead to recount the event speaking as the adult you are today: "My grandfather died an hour before my eighth birthday party." Your point of view will obviously affect the essay's content and organization.

The most strongly individualized point of view is the **first person** (*I, me, mine, we, us, our*). Because it focuses on the writer, the first-person point of view is appropriate in narrative and descriptive essays based on personal experience. It also suits other types of essays (for example, causal analyses and process analyses) when the bulk of evidence presented consists of personal observation. In such essays, avoiding the first person often leads to stilted sentences like "There was strong parental opposition to the decision" or "Although Organic Chemistry had been dreaded, it became a passion." In contrast, the sentences sound much more natural when the first person is used: "*Our* parents strongly opposed the decision" and "Although *I* had dreaded Organic Chemistry, it became *my* passion."

Like many students, you may feel that a lightning bolt will strike you if you use the first person when writing. Indeed, in high school, you may have been warned away from (even forbidden to use) the first person. And it does have its dangers. For one thing, in essays voicing an opinion, most first-person expressions ("I believe that . . ." and "In my opinion . . .") are unnecessary; the point of view stated is assumed to be the writer's unless another source is indicated. Second, in a paper intended to be an objective presentation of an issue, the first person distracts from the issue by drawing unwarranted attention to the writer: "I think it's important to realize that most violent crime in this country is directly related to substance abuse." By way of contrast, note how the matter under discussion is clearly highlighted when the first person is omitted: "Most violent crime in this country is directly related to substance abuse."

In some situations, writers use the **second person** (*you, your, yours*), alone or in combination with the first person. In fact, we frequently use forms of *you* in this book. For instance, we write, "If *you're* the kind of person who doodles while thinking, *you* may want to try mapping . . ." rather than "If a *writer* is the kind of person who doodles while thinking, *he* or *she* may want to try mapping. . . ." As you can see, the second person simplifies style and involves the reader in a more personal way. You'll also find that the *imperative* form of the verb ("*Send* letters of protest to the television networks") engages readers in much the same way. The implied *you* speaks to the audience directly and lends immediacy to the directions. Despite these advantages, the second-person point of view often isn't appropriate in many college courses where more formal, less conversational writing is called for.

The **third-person** point of view is by far the most common in academic writing. The third person gets its name from the stance it conveys—that of an outsider or "third person" observing and reporting on matters of primarily public rather than private importance: "The international team of negotiators failed to resolve the border dispute between the two nations." In discussions of historical events, scientific phenomena, works of art, and the like, the third-person point of view conveys a feeling of distance and objectivity. When you write in the third person, though, don't adopt such a detached stance that you end up using a stiff, artificial style: "On this campus, approximately two-thirds of the student body is dependent on bicycles as the primary mode of transportation to class." Aim instead for a more natural and personable quality: "Two-thirds of the students on campus ride their bikes to class." (For a more detailed discussion of levels of formality, see pages 124–127 in Chapter 8.)

Discover Your Essay's Limited Subject

Once you have a firm grasp of the assignment's boundaries and have determined your purpose, audience, tone, and point of view, you're ready to focus on a **limited subject** of the general assignment. Because too broad a subject can result in a diffuse, rambling essay, be sure to restrict your general subject before starting to write.

The following examples show the difference between general subjects that are too broad for an essay and limited subjects that are appropriate and workable. The examples, of course, represent only a few among many possibilities.

General Subject	Less General	Limited Subject
Education	Computers in education	Computers in elementary school arithmetic classes
	High school education	High school electives
Transportation	Low-cost travel	Hitchhiking
	Getting around a metropolitan area	The transit system in a nearby city
Work	Planning for a career	College internships
	Women in the work force	Women's success as managers

How do you move from a general to a narrow subject? Imagine that you're asked to prepare a straightforward, informative essay for your writing class.

The assignment, prompted by Ellen Goodman's essay "Family Counterculture" (page 6), is an extension of the journal-writing assignment on page 11.

> Goodman implies that, in some ways, today's world is hostile to children. Do you agree? Drawing upon but not limiting yourself to the material in your pre-reading journal, write an essay in which you support or reject this viewpoint.

You might feel unsure about how to proceed. But two techniques can help you limit such a general assignment. Keeping your purpose, audience, tone, and point of view in mind, you may **question** or **brainstorm** the general subject. These two techniques have a paradoxical effect. Although they encourage you to roam freely over a subject, they also help restrict the discussion by revealing which aspects of the subject interest you most.

Question the General Subject

One way to narrow a subject is to ask a series of *who, how, why, where, when,* and *what* questions. The following example shows how Harriet Davids, the mother of two young teenagers, used this technique to limit the Goodman assignment.

You may recall that, before reading Goodman's essay, Harriet had used her journal to explore TV's effect on children (see page 17). After reading "Family Counterculture," Harriet concluded that she essentially agreed with Goodman; like Goodman, she felt that parents nowadays are indeed forced to raise their children in an "increasingly hostile environment." She was pleased that the writing assignment gave her an opportunity to expand preliminary ideas she had jotted down in her journal.

Harriet realized that she had to narrow the Goodman assignment. She started by asking a number of pointed questions about the general topic. As she proceeded, she was aware that the same questions could have led to different limited subjects—just as other questions would have.

General Assignment: We live in a world that is difficult, even hostile toward children.

Question	**Limited Subject**
Who is to blame for the difficult conditions under which children grow up?	Parents' casual attitude toward child rearing
How have schools contributed to the problems children face?	Not enough counseling programs for kids in distress
Why do children feel frightened?	Divorce
Where do kids go to escape?	Television, which makes the world seem even more dangerous
When are children most vulnerable?	The special problems of adolescents

What dangers or fears should parents discuss with their children?	AIDS, drugs, alcohol, war, terrorism, school shootings

Brainstorm the General Subject

Another way to focus on a limited subject is to list quickly everything about the general topic that pops into your mind. Working vertically down a page of paper or computer screen, note brief words, phrases, and abbreviations that capture your free-floating thoughts. Writing in complete sentences will slow you down. Don't try to organize or censor your ideas. Even the most fleeting, random, or seemingly outrageous thoughts can be productive.

Here's an example of the brainstorming that Harriet Davids decided to do in an effort to gather even more material for the Goodman assignment:

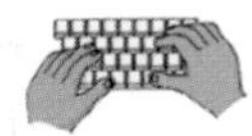

General Subject: We live in a world that is difficult, even hostile toward children.

```
TV—shows corrupt politicians, casual sex, sexually explicit
videos, drugs, alcohol, foul language, violence
Real-life violence on TV, esp. terrorist attacks, war, and
school shootings, scares kids—have nightmares!
Kids babysat by TV
Not enough guidance from parents
Kids raise selves
Too many divorces
Parents squabbling over material goods in settlements
Money too important
Kids feel unimportant
Families move a lot
I moved in fourth grade—hated it
Rootless feeling
Nobody graduates from high school in the same district in
which they went to kindergarten
Drug abuse all over, in little kids' schools
Pop music glorifies drugs
Kids not innocent—know too much
Single-parent homes
Day-care problems
Abuse of little kids in day care
TV coverage of day-care abuse frightens kids
Perfect families on TV make kids feel inadequate
```

As you can see, questioning and brainstorming suggest many possible limited subjects. To identify especially promising ones, reread your material. What arouses your interest, anger, or curiosity? What themes seem to dominate and cut to the heart of the matter? Star or circle ideas with potential. Be sure to pay close attention to material generated at the end of your questioning and brainstorming. Often your mind takes a few minutes to warm up, with the best ideas popping out last.

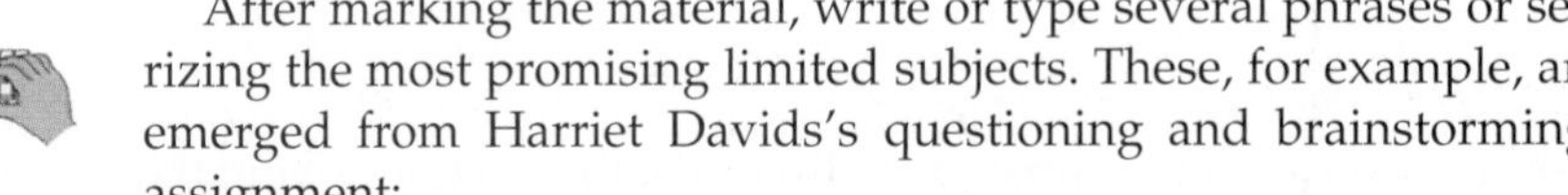

After marking the material, write or type several phrases or sentences summarizing the most promising limited subjects. These, for example, are just a few that emerged from Harriet Davids's questioning and brainstorming the Goodman assignment:

TV partly to blame for children having such a hard time

Relocation stressful to children

Schools also at fault

The special problems that parents face raising children today

Harriet decided to write on the last of these limited subjects. This topic, in turn, is the focus of our discussion on the pages ahead.

Generate Raw Material About Your Limited Subject

When a limited subject strikes you as having possibilities, your next step is to begin generating material about that topic. If you do this now, in the prewriting stage, you'll find it easier to write the paper later on. Since you'll already have amassed much of the material for your essay, you'll be able to concentrate on other matters—say, finding just the right words to convey your ideas. Taking the time to sound out your limited subject during the prewriting stage also means you won't find yourself halfway through the first draft without much to say.

To generate raw material, you may use *freewriting, brainstorming, mapping,* and other techniques.

Freewrite on Your Limited Subject

Although freewriting can help you narrow a general subject, it's more valuable once you have limited your topic. **Freewriting** means jotting down (whether on paper or on a computer) in rough sentences or phrases everything that comes to mind. Although freewriting looks like regular prose because it is recorded horizontally, from margin to margin, it's much more fragmented. As you freewrite, you get swept along and go wherever your thoughts take you. You may skip back and forth between ideas, taking off in a more focused manner when you stumble across something interesting.

To capture this continuous stream of thought, write or type nonstop for ten minutes or more. Don't censor anything; put down whatever pops into your head. Don't reread, edit, or pay attention to organization, spelling, or grammar. If your mind goes blank, repeat words until another thought emerges.

Consider part of the freewriting that Harriet Davids generated about her limited subject, "The special problems that parents face raising children today":

Parents today have tough problems to face. Lots of dangers. The Internet first and foremost. Also crimes of violence against kids. Parents also have to keep up with cost of living, everything costs more, kids want and expect more. Television? Another thing is *Playboy, Penthouse*. Sexy ads and videos on TV, movies deal with sex. Kids grow up too fast, too fast. Drugs and alcohol. Witness real-life violence on TV, like terrorist attacks and school shootings. Little kids can't handle knowing too much at an early age. Both parents at work much of the day. Finding good day care a real problem. Lots of latchkey kids. Another problem is getting kids to do homework, lots of other things to do. Especially like going to the mall or chatting with friends online! When I was young, we did homework after dinner, no excuses accepted by my parents.

Brainstorm Your Limited Subject

Let your mind wander freely, as you did when narrowing your general subject. This time, though, list every idea, fact, and example that occurs to you about your limited subject. Use brief words and phrases, so you don't get bogged down writing full sentences. For now, don't worry whether ideas fit together or whether the points listed make sense.

To gather additional material on her limited subject for the Goodman assignment ("The special problems that parents face raising children today"), Harriet brainstormed the following list:

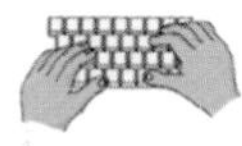

Trying to raise kids when both parents work

Prices of everything outrageous, even when both parents work

Commercials make everyone want <u>more</u> of everything

Clothes so important

Day care not always the answer—cases of abuse

Day care very expensive

Sex everywhere—TV, movies, magazines, Internet

Sexy clothes on little kids. Absurd!

Sexual abuse of kids

Violence on TV, esp. images of real-life terrorist attacks and school shootings—scary for kids!

Violence against kids when parents abuse drugs

Acid, Ecstasy, heroin, cocaine, AIDS

Schools have to teach kids about these things

Schools doing too much—not as good as they used to be

Not enough homework assigned—kids unprepared

Distractions from homework—Internet, TV, cellphones, MP3s, computer games, malls

Use Group Brainstorming

Brainstorming can also be conducted as a group activity. Thrashing out ideas with other people stretches the imagination, revealing possibilities you may not have considered on your own. Group brainstorming doesn't have to be conducted in a formal classroom situation. You can bounce ideas around with friends and family anywhere—over lunch, at the student center, and so on.

Map the Limited Subject

If you're the kind of person who doodles while thinking, you may want to try **mapping,** sometimes called **diagramming** or **clustering.** Like other prewriting techniques, mapping proceeds rapidly and encourages the free flow of ideas.

Begin by expressing your limited subject in a crisp phrase and placing it in the center of a blank sheet of paper. As ideas come to you, put them along lines or in boxes or circles around the limited subject. Draw arrows and lines to show the relationships among ideas. Don't stop there, however. Focus on each idea; as subpoints and details come to you, connect them to their source idea, again using boxes, lines, circles, or arrows to clarify how everything relates.

Figure 2.2 is an example of the kind of map that Harriet Davids could have drawn to generate material for her limited subject based on the Goodman assignment.

FIGURE 2.2
Mapping the Limited Subject

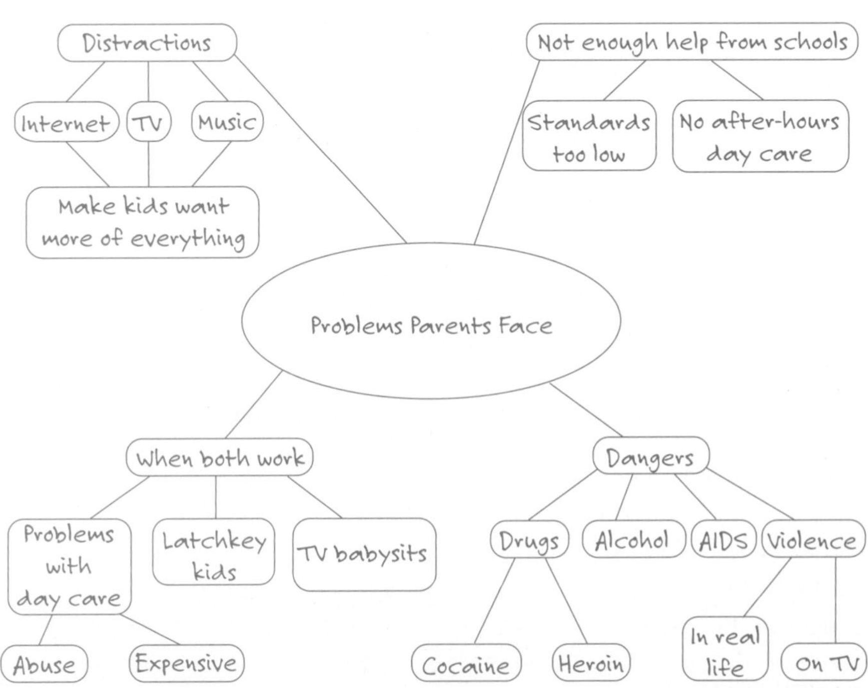

There's no right or wrong way to do mapping. Sometimes you'll move from the limited subject to a key related idea and all the details it prompts before moving to the next key idea; other times you'll map all the major divisions of a limited subject before mapping the details of any one idea.

Use the Patterns of Development

Throughout this book, we show how writers use various **patterns of development,** singly or in combination, to develop and organize their ideas. Because each pattern has its own distinctive logic, the patterns encourage you to think about a limited subject in surprising new ways.

The various patterns of development are discussed in detail in Chapters 10–18 of Part III. At this point, though, you should find the following chart helpful. It not only summarizes the broad purpose of each pattern but also shows the way each pattern could generate different raw material for the limited subject of Harriet Davids's essay.

Limited Subject: The special problems that parents face raising children today.

Pattern of Development	Purpose	Raw Material
Description	To detail what a person, place, or object is like	Detail the sights and sounds of a glitzy mall that attracts lots of kids
Narration	To relate an event	Recount what happened when neighbors tried to forbid their kids from going online
Illustration	To provide specific instances or examples	Offer examples of family arguments nowadays: Can a friend known to use drugs visit? Will permission be given to go to a party where alcohol will be served? Can parents outlaw certain websites on the Internet?
Division-classification	To divide something into parts or to group related things into categories	Identify the components of a TV commercial that distorts kids' values Classify the kinds of commercials that make it difficult to teach kids values
Process analysis	To explain how something happens or how something is done	Explain step by step how family life can disintegrate when parents have to work all the time to make ends meet
Comparison-contrast	To point out similarities and/or dissimilarities	Contrast families today with those of a generation ago

(Continued)

Pattern of Development	Purpose	Raw Material
Cause-effect	To analyze reasons and consequences	Explain why parents are not around to be with their kids: industry's failure to provide day care and its inflexibility about granting time off for parents with sick kids Explain the consequences of absentee parents: Kids feel unloved; they spend long hours on the Internet; they turn to TV for role models; they're undisciplined; they take on adult responsibility too early
Definition	To explain the meaning of a term or concept	What is meant by "tough love"?
Argumentation-persuasion	To win people over to a point of view	Convince parents that they must work with the schools to develop programs that make kids feel safer and more secure

(For more on ways to use the patterns of development in different phases of the writing process, see pages 39, 46–48, 55, and Part III.)

Conduct Research

Some limited subjects (for example, "Industry's day-care policies") can be developed only if you do some research. You may conduct **primary research,** in which you interview experts, conduct your own studies, compile your own statistics, and the like. Or you may conduct **secondary research,** in which you visit the library and/or go online to identify books and articles about your limited subject. (See pages 529–532 in Part IV on how to conduct research.) At this point, you don't need to read closely the material you find. Just skim and perhaps take a few brief notes on ideas and points that could be useful.

In researching the Goodman assignment, for instance, Harriet Davids could look under the following headings and subheadings:

- Day care
- Drug abuse
- Family
- Parent-child relationship
  - Child abuse
  - Children of divorced parents
  - Children of working mothers
- School and home

Organize the Raw Material

Some students prefer to wait until after they have formulated a thesis to shape their prewriting material. (For information on thesis statements, see Chapter 3.) But if you find that imposing a preliminary order on your prewriting provides the focus needed to devise an effective thesis, you'll probably want to prepare a **scratch list** or **outline** at this point. In Chapter 5, we talk about the more formal outline you may need later on in the writing process (pages 58–61). Here we show how a rough outline or scratch list can help shape the tentative ideas generated during prewriting.

As you reread your exploratory thoughts about the limited subject, keep the following questions in mind: What *purpose* have you decided on? What are the characteristics of your *audience?* What *tone* will be effective in achieving your purpose with your audience? What *point of view* will you adopt? Record your responses to these questions at the top of your prewriting material.

Now go to work on the raw material itself. Cross out anything not appropriate for your purpose, audience, tone, and point of view; add points that didn't originally occur to you. Star or circle compelling items that warrant further development. Then draw arrows between related items, your goal being to group such material under a common heading. Finally, determine what seems to be the best order for the headings.

By giving you a sense of the way your free-form material might fit together, a scratch outline makes the writing process more manageable. You're less likely to feel overwhelmed once you actually start writing because you'll already have some idea about how to shape your material into a meaningful statement. Remember, though, the scratch outline can, and most likely will, be modified along the way.

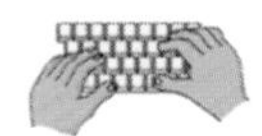

Harriet Davids's handwritten annotations on her brainstormed list (page 32) illustrate the way Harriet began shaping her raw prewriting material. Note how she started by recording at the top her limited subject as well as her decisions about purpose, audience, tone, and point of view. Next, she crossed out the material she didn't want to use. For instance, Harriet decided that the example of violence, such as terrorism, on TV was too complex to include it in her essay, so she crossed it out. Note how clear supporting points emerged after she grouped together similar ideas.

```
Purpose: To inform

Audience: Instructor as well as class members, most of
whom are 18-20 years old

Tone: Serious and straightforward

Point of view: Third person (mother of two teenage
girls)

Limited subject: The special problems that parents face
raising children today
```

① Day Care

Trying to raise kids when both parents work
~~Prices of everything outrageous, even when both parents work~~
~~Commercials make everyone want more of everything~~
~~Clothes so important~~
Day care ~~not always the answer—cases of abuse~~ problems—before and after school
Day care very expensive

③ Sexual material everywhere

Sex everywhere—Internet, TV, movies, magazines
~~Sexy clothes on little kids. Absurd!~~
~~Sexual abuse of kids~~

④ Dangers

~~Violence on TV, esp. images of real life terrorist attacks and school shootings—scary for kids!~~
Violence against kids when parents abuse drugs
Acid, Ecstasy, heroin, cocaine, AIDS—also drinking
~~Schools have to teach kids about these things~~
~~Schools doing too much—not as good as they used to be~~
~~Not enough homework assigned—kids unprepared~~

② Homework distractions

Distractions from homework—Internet, TV, cellphones, MP3s, computer games, malls

The following scratch outline shows how Harriet began to shape her prewriting into a more organized format. (If you'd like to see Harriet's more formal outline and her first draft, turn to pages 60–61 and 86–87.)

Purpose: To inform

Audience: Instructor as well as class members, most of whom are 18-20 years old

Tone: Serious and straightforward

Point of view: Third person (mother of two teenage girls)

Limited subject: The special problems that parents face raising children today

1. Day care for two-career families
   - Expensive
   - Before-school problems
   - After-school problems
2. Distractions from homework
   - Internet, televisions, MP3s, cellphones
   - Places to go—malls, movies, fast-food restaurants
3. Sexually explicit materials
   - Internet
   - Magazines

```
      • Television shows
      • Movies
   4. Life-threatening dangers
      • Drugs
      • Drinking
      • AIDS
      • Violence against children (by sitters, in day care, etc.)
```

Continues on page 38

The prewriting strategies described in this chapter provide a solid foundation for the next stages of your work. But invention and imaginative exploration don't end when prewriting is completed. As you'll see, remaining open to new ideas is crucial during all phases of the writing process.

ACTIVITIES: GETTING STARTED THROUGH PREWRITING

1. Number the items in each set from 1 (*broadest subject*) to 5 (*most limited subject*):

Set A	**Set B**
Abortion	Business majors
Controversial social issue	Students' majors
Cutting state abortion funds	College students
Federal funding of abortions	Kinds of students on campus
Social issues	Why students major in business

2. Which of the following topics are too broad for an essay of two to five typewritten pages: soap operas' appeal to college students; day care; trying to "kick" junk food; male and female relationships; international terrorism?

3. Assume you're writing essays on two of the topics below. For each one, explain how you might adapt your purpose, tone, and point of view to the audiences indicated in parentheses. (You may find it helpful to work with others on this activity.)

   a. Overcoming shyness (ten-year-olds; teachers of ten-year-olds; young singles living in large apartment buildings)
   b. Telephone solicitations (people training for a job in this field; homeowners; readers of a humorous magazine)
   c. Smoking (people who have quit; smokers; elementary school children)

4. Choose one of the following general topics for a roughly five-hundred-word essay. Then use the prewriting technique indicated in parentheses to identify several limited topics. Next, with the help of one or more patterns of development, generate raw material on the limited subject you consider most interesting.

a. Friendship (*journal writing*)
b. Malls (*mapping*)
c. Leisure (*freewriting*)
d. Television (*brainstorming*)
e. Required courses (*group brainstorming*)
f. Manners (*questioning*)

5. For each set of limited subjects and purposes that follows, determine which pattern(s) of development would be most useful. (Save this material so you can work with it further after reading the next chapter.)

a. The failure of recycling efforts on campus
Purpose: to explain why students and faculty tend to disregard recycling guidelines
b. The worst personality trait that a teacher, parent, boss, or friend can have
Purpose: to poke fun at this personality trait
c. The importance of being knowledgeable about national affairs
Purpose: to convince students to stay informed about current events

6. Select *one* of the following limited subjects. Then, given the purpose and audience indicated, draft a paragraph using the first-, second-, or third-person point of view. Next, rewrite the paragraph two more times, each time using a different point of view. What differences do you see in the three versions? Which version do you prefer? Why?

a. American action movies like *Mission Impossible* and *Oceans Eleven*
Purpose: to defend the enjoyment of such films
Audience: those who like foreign "art" films
b. Senioritis
Purpose: to explain why high school seniors lose interest in school
Audience: parents and teachers
c. Television commercials aimed at teens and young adults
Purpose: to make fun of the commercials' persuasive appeals
Audience: advertising executives

7. Select *one* of the following general subjects. Keeping in mind the indicated purpose, audience, tone, and point of view, use a prewriting technique to limit the subject. Next, by means of another prewriting strategy, generate relevant information about the restricted topic. Finally, shape your raw material into a scratch outline—crossing out, combining, and adding ideas as needed. (Save your scratch outline so you can work with it further after reading the next chapter.)

a. Hip-hop music
   Purpose: to explain its attraction
   Audience: classical music fans
   Tone: playful
   Writer's point of view: a hip-hop fan
b. Becoming a volunteer
   Purpose: to recruit
   Audience: ambitious young professionals
   Tone: straightforward
   Writer's point of view: head of a volunteer organization
c. Sexist attitudes in music videos
   Purpose: to inform
   Audience: teenagers of both sexes
   Tone: objective but with some emotion
   Writer's point of view: a teenage male
d. Major problems in high school education
   Purpose: to create awareness of the problems
   Audience: teachers
   Tone: serious and concerned
   Writer's point of view: a former high school student

For additional writing, reading, and research resources, go to **www.mycomplab.com** and choose **Nadell/Langan/Comodromos'** ***The Longman Writer,*** **7/e.**

Identifying a Thesis

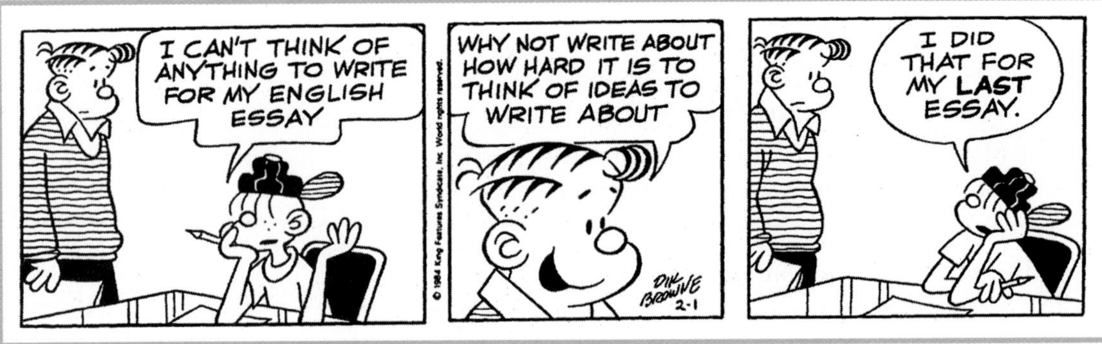

The process of prewriting—discovering a limited subject and generating ideas about it—prepares you for the next stage in writing an essay: identifying the paper's *thesis,* or controlling idea.

What Is a Thesis?

Presenting your position on a subject, the **thesis** should focus on an interesting and significant issue, one that engages your energies and merits your consideration. You may think of the thesis as the essay's hub—the central point around which all the other material revolves. Your thesis determines what does and does not belong in the essay. The thesis, especially when it occurs early in an essay, also helps focus the reader on the piece's central point and thus helps you achieve your writing purpose.

FINDING A THESIS

Sometimes the thesis emerges early in the prewriting stage, particularly if a special angle on your limited topic sparks your interest or becomes readily apparent. Often, though, you'll need to do some work to determine your thesis. For some topics, you may need to do some library research. For other subjects, the best way to identify a promising thesis is to look through your prewriting and ask yourself questions like these: What statement does all this prewriting support? What aspect of the limited subject is covered in most detail? What is the focus of the most provocative material? (See Figure 3.1.)

For a look at the process of finding the thesis within prewriting material, glance back in Chapter 2 at the annotated brainstorming (pages 31–32) and the resulting scratch outline (page 33) that Harriet Davids prepared for her limited subject, "The special problems that parents face raising children today." Harriet eventually devised the following thesis to capture the focus of her prewriting: "Being a

FIGURE 3.1
Process Diagram: Identifying a Thesis

Process	
Prewrite (see Chapter 2)	
Identify a Thesis	• Develop a point of view or attitude about your limited subject. • Write a statement expressing your limited subject and point of view. • Think of patterns of development that best serve your purpose. • Optional: Include a plan of development presenting the essay's main points. • Avoid thesis statements that are - Highly opinionated statements. - Neutral announcements. - Simply factual statements. - Broad statements. • Find an effective placement for your thesis statement: - At the middle or end of the introductory paragraph for most essays. - After background paragraphs if your subject is complex. - Early on, for a direct approach.
Find Evidence (see Chapter 4)	
Organize the Evidence (see Chapter 5)	
Write a Draft (see Chapter 6)	
Revise Paragraphs (see Chapter 7)	
Revise Sentences (see Chapter 8)	
Edit and Proofread (see Chapter 9)	

parent today is much more difficult than it was a generation ago." (For more on how Harriet arrived at her thesis, see pages 41–42.)

Sometimes the thesis won't be easy to pinpoint. Indeed, you may find that you need to refocus your thesis as you move through the stages of the writing process. To see how this progressive clarification might work, imagine you're writing a paper about adjusting to the academic demands of college life. After looking over your prewriting, you might identify this preliminary thesis: "Many college students flounder during the first semester because they have trouble adjusting to the amount of work required by their professors." However, once you start writing the essay, you might realize that students' increased personal freedom, not their increased workload, is the primary problem. You would revise your thesis accordingly: "Many college students flounder the first semester because they become so distracted by new freedoms in their personal lives that they don't give enough attention to academics."

WRITING AN EFFECTIVE THESIS

What makes a thesis effective? Generally expressed in one or two sentences, a thesis statement often has two parts. One part presents your paper's *limited subject;* the other presents your *point of view,* or *attitude,* about that subject. Here are some examples of the way you might move from general subject to limited subject to thesis statement. In each thesis statement, the limited subject is underlined once and the attitude twice.

General Subject	**Limited Subject**	**Thesis Statement**
Education	Computers in elementary school arithmetic classes	Computer programs in arithmetic can individualize instruction more effectively than the average elementary school teacher can.
Transportation	A metropolitan transit system	Although the city's transit system still has problems, it has become safer and more efficient in the last two years.
Work	College internships	The college internship program has had positive consequences for students.
Our anti-child world	Special problems that parents face raising children today	Being a parent today is much more difficult than it was a generation ago.

(*Reminder:* The last of these thesis statements is the one that Harriet Davids devised for the essay she planned to write in response to the assignment on page 17.

Harriet's prewriting appears on pages 17 and 24–28. You can find her first draft on pages 86–87.)

Tone and Point of View

An effective thesis establishes a tone and point of view suitable for a given purpose and audience. If you're writing an essay arguing that multimedia equipment can never replace a live teacher in the classroom, you need to frame a thesis that matches your and your readers' concerns about the subject. Instead of breezily writing, "Parents, school boards, principals: ditch the boob tube and the cutesy interactive computer and put the bucks where it counts—in teachers," you would aim for a more thoughtful and serious tone: "Education won't be improved by purchasing more electronic teaching tools but by allocating more money to hire and develop good teachers."

Implied Pattern of Development

On page 19, we show how an essay's purpose may suggest a pattern of development. In the same way, an effective thesis may point the way to a pattern of development that would be appropriate for developing the essay. Consider the thesis statements in the preceding list. The first thesis might use *comparison-contrast;* the second *illustration;* the third *cause-effect;* and the fourth *argumentation-persuasion.* (For more information about the relationship between an essay's purpose and its pattern of development, see the chart on pages 29–30.)

Including a Plan of Development

Sometimes a thesis will include a **plan of development:** a concise *overview of the essay's main points in the exact order* in which those points will be discussed. To incorporate a plan of development into your thesis, use single words or brief phrases that convey—in a nutshell—your essay's key points; then add those summarized points to the end of the thesis, being sure to present them in the order they will appear in the essay. Note, for example, the way a plan of development (in italics) is included in the following thesis: "Baseball's inflated salaries hurt *the fans, the sport, and most of all, the athletes.*"

A thesis with a plan of development is an effective strategy for keeping readers focused on an essay's main points. If you decide to prepare such a thesis, be careful not to overload it with too much information. Rather than writing, "An after-school job can promote a sense of responsibility in young people, teach important human-relations skills, and create awareness of career options," tighten the plan of development so it reads more crisply: "An after-school job develops responsibility, human-relations skills, and an awareness of career options."

If the essay's key points resist your efforts to reduce them to crisp phrases, you can place the plan of development in a separate sentence, directly *after* the thesis. Consider the plan of development (in italics) that comes after the following thesis: "Many parents have unrealistic expectations for their children. These parents want their children to *accept their values, follow their paths, and succeed where they have failed.*" Note that the points in a plan of development are expressed in grammatically parallel terms: The plan of development for the paper on baseball salaries contains nouns in series ("the fans," "the sport," "the athletes"), while the plan of development for the paper on parental expectations contains verb phrases ("accept their values," "follow their paths," "succeed where they have failed").

Because preparing an effective thesis is such a critical step in writing a sharply focused essay, you need to avoid the following four common problems.

1. Don't Write a Highly Opinionated Statement

Although your thesis should express your attitude toward your subject, don't go overboard and write a dogmatic, overstated thesis: "With characteristic clumsiness, campus officials bumbled their way through the recent budget crisis." A more moderate thesis can make the same point, *without alienating readers:* "Campus officials had trouble managing the recent budget crisis effectively."

2. Don't Make an Announcement

Some writers use the thesis statement merely to announce the limited subject of their paper and forget to indicate their attitude toward the subject. Such statements are announcements of intent, not thesis statements.

Compare the following three announcements with the thesis statements beside them:

Announcement	**Thesis Statement**
My essay will discuss whether a student pub should exist on campus.	This college should not allow a student pub on campus.
Handgun legislation will be the subject of my paper.	Banning handguns is the first step toward controlling crime in America.
I want to discuss cable television.	Cable television has not delivered on its promise to provide an alternative to network programming.

3. Don't Make a Factual Statement

Your thesis and thus your essay should focus on an issue capable of being developed. If a fact is used as a thesis, you have no place to go; a fact generally doesn't invite much discussion.

Notice the difference between the following factual statements and thesis statements:

Factual Statement	**Thesis Statement**
Many businesses pollute the environment.	Tax penalties should be levied against businesses that pollute the environment.
Movies nowadays are often violent.	Movie violence provides a healthy outlet for aggression.
America's population is growing older.	The aging of the American population will eventually create a crisis in the delivery of health-care services.

4. Don't Make a Broad Statement

Avoid stating your thesis in vague, general, or sweeping terms. Broad statements make it difficult for readers to grasp your essay's point. Moreover, if you start with a broad thesis, you're saddled with the impossible task of trying to develop a book-length idea in an essay that runs only several pages.

The following examples contrast thesis statements that are too broad with effectively focused statements:

Broad Statement	**Thesis Statement**
Nowadays, high school education is often meaningless.	High school diplomas have been devalued by grade inflation.
Newspapers cater to the taste of the American public.	The success of *USA Today* indicates that people want newspapers that are easy to read and entertaining.
The computer revolution is not all that we have been led to believe it is.	Home computers are still an impractical purchase for many people.

ARRIVING AT AN EFFECTIVE THESIS

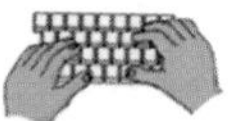

On pages 36–37, we discussed the basic process for finding a thesis; we also pointed out how Harriet Davids—after reviewing her prewriting—identified her paper's thesis: "Being a parent today is much more difficult than it was a generation ago." But Harriet didn't discover her thesis immediately; she went through several stages before she came up with the final wording. The following paragraph describes the steps Harriet took when formulating her essay's central point. In all likelihood, you too will need to experiment a bit before arriving at an effective thesis.

Starting with her limited subject ("The special problems that parents face raising children today"), Harriet at first worded her thesis to read, "My essay will show that raising children today is a horror show compared to how it was when my parents raised me." As soon as she read what she had written, Harriet saw that she had prepared an *announcement* rather than a thesis. Rephrasing the statement to do away with the announcement, she next wrote, "Raising children today is a horror show compared to how it was when my parents raised me." When Harriet read this version out loud, she was pleased to hear that the rewording eliminated the announcement—but she was surprised to discover that the rephrasing highlighted two problems she hadn't detected earlier. For one thing, her statement was *highly opinionated* and *slangy* ("horror show"). Second, the statement *misrepresented* what she intended to do by suggesting—incorrectly—that she was going to (1) discuss the child-rearing process and (2) contrast her parents' and her own child-raising experiences. She planned to do neither. Instead, she intended to (1) emphasize parenthood's challenges and (2) address—in a general way—the difference between parenting today and parenting years ago. So, recasting her statement one more time to eliminate these problems, Harriet arrived at the final wording of her thesis: "Being a parent today is much more difficult than it was a generation ago."

Continues on page 49

PLACING THE THESIS IN AN ESSAY

The thesis is often located in the middle or at the end of the introduction. But considerations about audience, purpose, and tone should always guide your decision about its placement. You may, for example, choose to delay the thesis if you feel that background information needs to be provided before readers can fully understand your key point—especially if the concept is complex and best taken in slowly. Similarly, if you sense your audience is resistant to your thesis, you may choose to lead readers to it gradually. Conversely, if you feel that readers would appreciate a direct, forthright approach, you might place the thesis early in the essay—perhaps even at the very beginning of the introduction.

Sometimes the thesis is reiterated—using fresh words—in the essay's conclusion or elsewhere. If done well, this repetition keeps readers focused on the essay's key point. You may even leave the thesis implied, relying on strong support, tone, and style to convey the essay's central idea.

One final point: Once you start writing your first draft, some feelings, thoughts, and examples may emerge that modify, even contradict, your initial thesis. Don't resist these new ideas. Keep them in mind as you revise the thesis and—in the process—move toward a more valid and richer view of your subject.

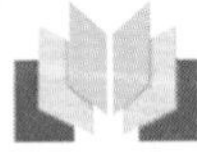

ACTIVITIES: IDENTIFYING A THESIS

1. For each of the following limited subjects, four possible thesis statements are given. Indicate whether each thesis is an announcement (A), a factual statement (FS), too broad a statement (TB), or an acceptable thesis (OK).

Revise the flawed statements. Then, for each effective thesis statement, identify a possible purpose, audience, tone, and point of view.

a. *Limited subject:* The ethics of treating severely disabled infants
   - Some babies born with severe disabilities have been allowed to die.
   - There are many serious issues involved in the treatment of newborns with disabilities.
   - The government should pass legislation requiring medical treatment for newborns with disabilities.
   - This essay will analyze the controversy surrounding the treatment of severely disabled babies who would die without medical care.

b. *Limited subject:* Privacy and computerized records
   - Computers raise some significant questions for all of us.
   - Computerized records keep track of consumer spending habits, credit records, travel patterns, and other personal information.
   - Computerized records have turned our private lives into public property.
   - In this paper, the relationship between computerized records and the right to privacy will be discussed.

2. Turn back to activity 5 on page 34. For each set of limited subjects listed there, develop an effective thesis. Select *one* of the thesis statements. Then, keeping in mind the purpose indicated and the pattern of development you identified earlier, draft a paragraph developing the point expressed in the thesis. (Save the paragraph so you can work with it further after reading the next chapter.)

3. Following are four pairs of general and limited subjects. Generate an appropriate thesis for each pair. Select one of the thesis statements, and determine which pattern of development would support the thesis most effectively. Use that pattern to draft a paragraph developing the thesis. (Save the paragraph so you can work with it further after reading the next chapter.)

General Subject	**Limited Subject**
Psychology	The power struggles in a classroom
Health	Doctors' attitudes toward patients
The elderly	Television's depiction of the elderly
Work	Minimum-wage jobs for young people

4. Each set that follows lists the key points for an essay. Based on the information provided, prepare a possible thesis for each essay. Then propose a possible purpose, audience, tone, and point of view.

Set A

- One evidence of this growing conservatism is the re-emerging popularity of fraternities and sororities.
- Beauty contests, ROTC training, and corporate recruiting—once rejected by students on many campuses—are again popular.

- Most important, many students no longer choose possibly risky careers that enable them to contribute to society but instead select safe fields with money-making potential.

Set B

- We do not know how engineering new forms of life might affect the earth's delicate ecological balance.
- Another danger of genetic research is its potential for unleashing new forms of disease.
- Even beneficial attempts to eliminate genetic defects could contribute to the dangerous idea that only perfect individuals are entitled to live.

5. Keep a journal for several weeks. Then reread a number of entries, identifying two or three recurring themes or subjects. Narrow the subjects and, for each one, generate possible thesis statements. Finally, using an appropriate pattern of development, draft a paragraph for one of the thesis statements. (Save the paragraph so you can work with it further after reading the next chapter.)

6. Select a broad topic—either your own or one of the following: animals, popularity, the homeless, money, fashion trends, race relations, parties. Working with a partner, use a prewriting technique to narrow the topic so that it's suitable for an essay of two to five typed pages. Using another prewriting strategy, generate details on the limited topic. Next, examine the material and identify at least two possible thesis statements. Then, for each thesis, reshape your prewriting, determining which items are appropriate, which are not, and where more material is needed.

7. Return to the scratch outline you prepared in response to activity 7 on page 35. After examining the outline, identify a thesis that conveys the central idea behind most of the raw material. Then, ask others to evaluate your thesis in light of the material in your scratch outline. Finally, keeping the thesis—as well as your purpose, audience, and tone—in mind, refine the scratch outline by deleting inappropriate items, adding relevant ones, and indicating where more material is needed. (Save your refined scratch outline and thesis so you can work with them further after reading the next chapter.)

For additional writing, reading, and research resources, go to **www.mycomplab.com** and choose **Nadell/Langan/Comodromos'** ***The Longman Writer, 7/e***.

Supporting the Thesis with Evidence

PEANUTS reprinted by permission of United Features Syndicate, Inc.

After identifying a preliminary thesis, you should develop the evidence needed to support that central idea. This supporting material grounds your essay, showing readers you have good reason for feeling as you do about your subject. Your evidence also adds interest and color to your writing.

In college essays of 500 to 1,500 words, you usually need at least three major points of evidence to develop your thesis. These major points—each focusing on related but separate aspects of the thesis—eventually become the supporting paragraphs (see pages 66–78) in the body of the essay.

What is Evidence?

By **evidence,** we mean a number of different kinds of support. *Reasons* are just one option. To develop your thesis, you might also include *examples, facts, details, statistics, personal observation* or *experience, anecdotes,* and *expert opinions* and *quotations* (gathered from books, articles, interviews, documentaries, and the like). Imagine you're writing an essay with the thesis, "People normally unconcerned about the environment can be galvanized to constructive action if they feel personally affected by an environmental problem." You could support this thesis with any combination of the following types of evidence:

- *Reasons* why people become involved in the environmental movement: they believe the situation endangers the health of their families; they fear the value of their homes will plummet; they feel deceived by officials' assurances that there's nothing to worry about.
- *Examples* of neighborhood recycling efforts succeeding in communities once plagued by trash-disposal problems.

- *Facts* about residents' efforts to preserve the quality of well water in a community undergoing widespread industrial development.
- *Details* about the specific steps the average person can take to get involved in environmental issues.
- *Statistics* showing the growing number of Americans concerned about the environment.
- A *personal experience* telling about the way you became involved in an effort to stop a local business from dumping waste into a neighborhood stream.
- An *anecdote* about an ordinarily apathetic friend who protested the commercial development of a wooded area where he jogs.
- A *quotation* from a well-known scientist about the considerable impact that well-organized, well-informed citizens can have on environmental legislation.

HOW DO YOU FIND EVIDENCE?

Where do you find the examples, anecdotes, details, and other types of evidence needed to support your thesis? As you saw when you followed Harriet Davids's strategies for gathering material for an essay (pages 24–33), a good deal of information is generated during the prewriting stage. In this phase of the writing process, you tap into your personal experiences, draw upon other people's observations, perhaps interview a person with special knowledge about your subject. The library and the Internet, with their abundant material, are another rich source of supporting evidence. (For information on using the library and the Internet, see Chapter 19.) In addition, the various patterns of development are a valuable source of evidence. (See Figure 4.1 on page 48).

How the Patterns of Development Help Generate Evidence

In Chapter 2, we discussed how the patterns of development could help generate material about Harriet Davids's limited subject (pages 29–30). The same patterns also help develop support for a thesis. The chart on page 47

Pattern of Development	Evidence Generated
Description	Details about a child who, while being babysat, was badly hurt playing on a backyard swing.
Narration	Story about the time a friend babysat a child who became seriously ill and whose condition was worsened by the babysitter's remedies.
Illustration	Examples of potential babysitting problems: an infant who rolls off a changing table; a toddler who sticks objects into an electric outlet; a school-age child who is bitten by a neighborhood dog.
Division-classification	A typical babysitting evening divided into stages: playing with the kids; putting them to bed; dealing with their nighttime fears once they're in bed.
	Classify kids' nighttime fears: of monsters under their beds; of bad dreams; of being abandoned by their parents.
Process analysis	Step-by-step account of what a babysitter should do if a child becomes ill or injured.
Pattern of Development	Evidence Generated.
Comparison-contrast	Contrast between two babysitters: one well-prepared, the other unprepared.
Cause-effect	Why children have temper tantrums; the effect of such tantrums on an unskilled babysitter.
Definition	What is meant by a *skilled* babysitter?
Argumentation-persuasion	A proposal for a babysitting training program to be offered by the local community center.

shows how they generate evidence for this thesis: "To those who haven't done it, babysitting looks easy. In practice, though, babysitting can be difficult, frightening, even dangerous." (For further discussion of ways to use the patterns of development in different phases of the writing process, see pages 29–30, 39, 55 and 69–70.)

CHARACTERISTICS OF EVIDENCE

No matter how it is generated, all types of supporting evidence share the characteristics described in the following sections. You should keep these characteristics in mind as you review your thesis and scratch list. That way, you can make the changes needed to strengthen the evidence gathered earlier. As you'll see shortly, Harriet Davids focused on many of these issues as she worked with the evidence she collected during the prewriting phase.

FIGURE 4.1
Process Diagram: Finding Evidence

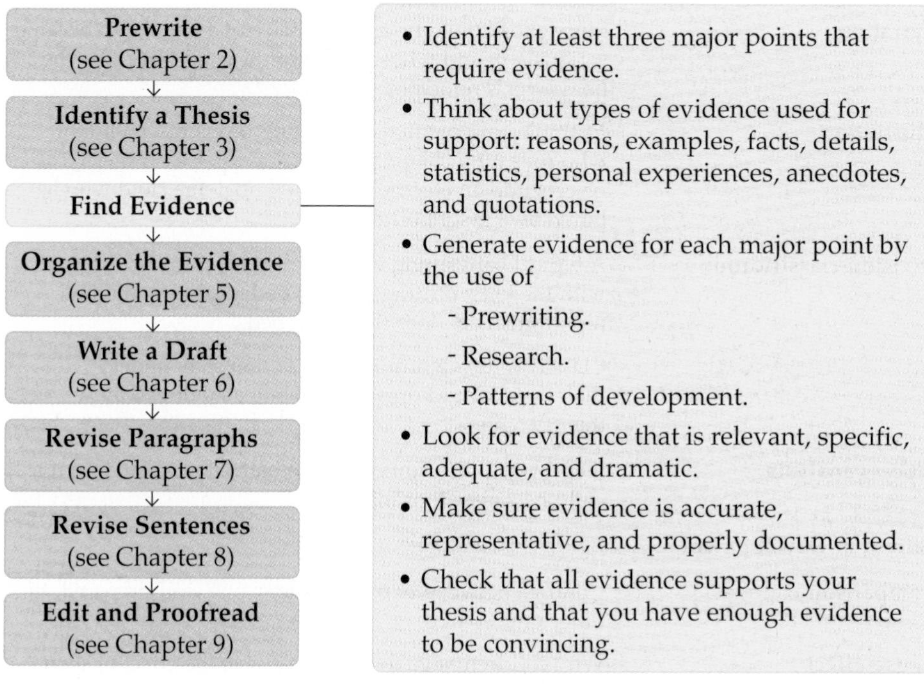

The Evidence Is Relevant and Unified

All the evidence in an essay must clearly support the thesis. It makes no difference how riveting material might be; if it doesn't *relate directly* to the essay's central point, the evidence should be eliminated. Irrelevant material can weaken your position by implying that no relevant support exists. It also distracts readers from your controlling idea, thus disrupting the paper's overall unity.

Suppose you want to write an essay with the thesis, "Fairly fought arguments can strengthen relationships." To support your thesis, you could adapt prewriting material about an argument you had with a friend: how the disagreement started, how you and your friend worked out your differences, how your friendship deepened because of what you learned about each other. Also to the point would be statements from your sister who found, after reading a book on conflict management, that her relationship with her co-workers improved significantly. Similarly relevant would be an account of a conflict-ridden family whose tensions eased once a counselor taught them how to air their differences. It would *not* serve your thesis, however, to include details about the way negotiating strategies can backfire. This material wouldn't be appropriate because it contradicts the point you want to make.

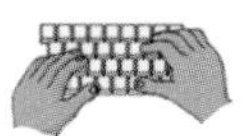

Early in the writing process, Harriet Davids was aware of the importance of relevant evidence. Take a moment to review Harriet's annotated prewriting (page 32). Even though Harriet hadn't yet identified her thesis, she realized she should delete a number of items on the reshaped version of her brainstormed list—for example, "prices of everything outrageous . . . " and "Not enough homework assigned—kids unprepared." Harriet eliminated these points because they weren't consistent with the focus of her limited subject.

The Evidence Is Specific

When evidence is vague and general, readers lose interest in what you're saying, become skeptical of your ideas' validity, and feel puzzled about your meaning. In contrast, *specific, concrete evidence* provides sharp *word pictures* that engage your readers, persuade them that your thinking is sound, and clarify meaning.

Consider a paper with this thesis: "College students should not automatically dismiss working in fast-food restaurants; such jobs can provide valuable learning experiences." Here's how you might go wrong trying to support the thesis: Suppose you begin with the broad claim that these admittedly lackluster jobs can teach students a good deal about themselves. In a similarly abstract fashion, you go on to say that such jobs can affect students' self-concepts in positive ways. You end by declaring that such changes in self-perception lead to greater maturity.

To prevent readers from thinking "Who cares?" or "Who says?" you need to replace these vague generalities with specific, concrete evidence. For example, focusing on your own experience working at a fast-food restaurant, you might start by describing how you learned to control your sarcasm; such an attitude, you discovered, alienated co-workers and almost caused your boss to fire you. You could also recount the time you administered the Heimlich maneuver to a choking customer; your quick thinking and failure to panic increased your self-esteem. Finally, you could explain that the job encouraged you to question some of your values; you became close friends with a bookish, introspective co-worker—the kind of person you used to spurn. This specific, particularized evidence would support your thesis and help readers "see" the point you're making. (Pages 71–73 describe strategies for making evidence specific.)

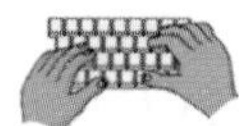

At this point, it will be helpful to look once again at the annotations that Harriet Davids entered on her prewriting material (page 32). Note the way she jotted down new details to make her prewriting more specific. For instance, to the item, "Distractions from homework," she added the example "malls." And once Harriet arrived at her thesis ("Being a parent today is much more difficult than it was a generation ago"), she realized that she needed to provide even more specifics. With her thesis firmly in mind, she expanded her prewriting material—for instance, the point about sexuality on television. To develop that item, she specified three kinds of TV programming that depict sexuality offensively: soap operas, R-rated comedians, R-rated cable movies. And, as you'll soon discover, Harriet added many more specific details when she prepared her final outline (pages 60–61) and her first and final drafts (pages 86–87 and 144–145).

The Evidence Is Adequate

Readers won't automatically accept your thesis; you need to provide *enough specific evidence* to support your viewpoint. On occasion, a single extended example will suffice. Generally, though, you'll need a variety of evidence: facts, examples, reasons, personal observations, expert opinion, and so on.

Assume you want to write an essay arguing that "college students living on campus should register and vote where they attend school." Hoping the essay will be published in the campus newspaper, you write it in the form of an open letter to the student body. One reason in support of your thesis strikes you immediately: that eighteen-year-olds should act as the adults they are and become involved in the electoral process. You also present as evidence a description of how good you felt during the last election when you walked into the voting booth set up in the student center. If this is all the support you provide, students probably won't be convinced; you haven't offered *sufficient* evidence. You need to present additional material—statistics on the shockingly low number of students registered to vote at your school; an account of a voter-registration drive at a nearby university that got students involved in the community and thus reduced traditional "town-gown" tensions; quotations from several students who voted against an anti-student housing ordinance and saw the ordinance defeated; an explanation of how easy it is to register.

Now take a final look at Harriet's annotations on her prewriting (page 32). As you can see, Harriet realized she needed more than one block of supporting material to develop her limited subject; that's why she identified four separate blocks of evidence (day care, homework distractions, sexual material, and dangers). As soon as Harriet formulated her thesis, she reexamined her prewriting to see if it provided sufficient support for her essay's central point. Luckily, Harriet recognized that these four blocks of evidence needed to be developed further. She thus decided to enlarge the "Distractions from homework" block by drawing upon her daughters' love affair with the Internet and the "Life-threatening dangers" block by including details about the way peer pressure to experiment with drugs and alcohol endangers young people. Harriet's final outline (pages 60–61) reflects these decisions. When you look at the outline, you'll also note that Harriet ended up eliminating one of the four blocks of evidence ("Day care") she had identified earlier. But she added so many specific and dramatic details when writing her first and final drafts (pages 86–87 and 144–145) that her evidence was more than sufficient.

Continues on page 60

The Evidence Is Dramatic

The most effective evidence enlarges the reader's experience by *dramatizing reality.* Say you plan to write an essay with the thesis, "People who affirm the value of life refuse to wear fur coats." If, as support, you state only that most animals killed for their fur are caught in leg-hold traps, your readers will have little sense of the suffering involved. But if you write that steel-jaw, leg-hold traps snap shut on an animal's limb, crushing tissue and bone and leaving the animal to die, in severe pain, from exposure or starvation, your readers can better envision the animal's plight.

The Evidence Is Accurate

Make your evidence as dramatic as you can, but be sure it is *accurate*. When you have a strong belief and want readers to see things your way, you may be tempted to overstate or downplay facts, disregard information, misquote, or make up details. Suppose you plan to write an essay making the point that dormitory security is lax. You begin supporting your thesis by narrating the time you were nearly mugged in your dorm hallway. Realizing the essay would be more persuasive if you also mentioned other episodes, you decide to invent some material. Perhaps you describe several supposed burglaries on your dorm floor or exaggerate the amount of time it took campus security to respond to an emergency call from a residence hall. Yes, you've supported your point—but at the expense of truth.

The Evidence Is Representative

Using *representative* evidence means that you rely on the *typical*, the *usual*, to show that your point is valid. Contrary to the maxim, exceptions don't prove the rule. Perhaps you plan to write an essay contending that the value of seat belts has been exaggerated. To support your position, you mention a friend who survived a head-on collision without wearing a seat belt. Such an example isn't representative because the facts and figures on accidents suggest your friend's survival was a fluke.

Borrowed Evidence Is Documented

If you include evidence from outside sources (books, articles, interviews), you need to *acknowledge* where that information comes from. If you don't, readers may consider your evidence nothing more than your point of view, or they may regard as dishonest your failure to cite your indebtedness to others for ideas that obviously aren't your own.

The rules for crediting sources in informal writing are less established than they are for formal research. Follow any guidelines your instructor provides, and try to keep your notations, like those that follow, as simple as possible.

Business Life (March 16, 2005) reports that corporate wrongdoing has led to a rash of consumer protests.

Science writer Natalie Angier believes that private zoos may be the only hope for some endangered species.

In formal research, you need to provide much more detailed documentation of sources. For information on formal documentation, see Chapter 20.

Strong supporting evidence is at the heart of effective writing. Without it, essays lack energy and fail to project the writer's voice and perspective. Such lifeless writing is also more apt to put readers to sleep than to engage their interest and convince them that the points being made are valid. Taking the time to accumulate solid supporting material is, then, a critical step in the writing process. (If you'd like to read more about the characteristics of strong evidence, see pages 71–74. If you'd like suggestions for organizing an essay's evidence, see the diagram on page 85.)

ACTIVITIES: SUPPORTING THE THESIS WITH EVIDENCE

1. Imagine you're writing an essay with the following thesis in mind. Which of the statements in the list support the thesis? Label each statement acceptable (OK), irrelevant (IR), inaccurate (IA), or too general (TG).

Thesis: Colleges should put less emphasis on sports.

a. High-powered athletic programs can encourage grade fixing.
b. Too much value is attached to college sports.
c. Athletics have no educational value.
d. Competitive athletics can lead to extensive and expensive injuries.
e. Athletes can spend too much time on the field and not enough on their studies.
f. Good athletic programs create a strong following among former undergraduates.

2. For each of the following thesis statements, list at least three supporting points that convey vivid word pictures.

a. Rude behavior in movie theaters seems to be on the rise.
b. Recent television commercials portray men as incompetent creatures.
c. The local library fails to meet the public's needs.
d. People often abuse public parks.

3. Turn back to the paragraphs you prepared in response to activity 2, activity 3, or activity 5 in Chapter 3 (pages 43 and 44). Select one paragraph and strengthen its evidence, using the guidelines presented in this chapter.

4. Choose one of the following thesis statements. Then identify an appropriate purpose, audience, tone, and point of view for an essay with this thesis. Using freewriting, mapping, or the questioning technique, generate at least three supporting points for the thesis. Last, write a paragraph about one of the points, making sure your evidence reflects the characteristics discussed in this chapter. Alternatively, you may go ahead and prepare the first draft of an essay having the selected thesis. (If you choose the second option, you may want to turn to page 85 to see a diagram showing how to organize a first draft.) Save whatever you prepare so you can work with it further after reading the next chapter.

a. Winning the lottery may not always be a blessing.
b. All of us can take steps to reduce the country's trash crisis.
c. Drug education programs in public schools are (or are not) effective.

5. Select one of the following thesis statements. Then determine your purpose, audience, tone, and point of view for an essay with this thesis. Next, use the patterns of development to generate at least three supporting points for the thesis. Finally, write a paragraph about one of the points, making sure that your evidence demonstrates the characteristics discussed in this chapter. Alternatively, you may go ahead and prepare a first draft of an essay having the thesis selected. (If you choose the latter option, you may want to turn to page 85 to see a diagram showing how to organize a first draft.) Save whatever you prepare so you can work with it further after reading the next chapter.

a. Teenagers should (or should not) be able to obtain birth-control devices without their parents' permission.
b. The college's system for awarding student loans needs to be overhauled.
c. E-mail has changed for the worse (or the better) the way Americans communicate with each other.

6. Look at the thesis and refined scratch outline you prepared in response to activity 7 in Chapter 3 (page 44). Where do you see gaps in the support for your thesis? By brainstorming with others, generate material to fill these gaps. If some of the new points generated suggest that you should modify your thesis, make the appropriate changes now. (Save this material so you can work with it further after reading the next chapter.)

(For more activities on generating evidence, see pages 89–93 in Chapter 6 as well as pages 135–138 in Chapter 8.)

For additional writing, reading, and research resources, go to **www.mycomplab.com** and choose **Nadell/Langan/Comodromos'** ***The Longman Writer,*** **7/e**.

Organizing the Evidence

"Let me just make a little note of that. I never seem to get anything done around here unless I make little notes."

Once you've generated supporting evidence, you're ready to *organize* that material. Even highly compelling evidence won't illustrate the validity of your thesis or achieve your purpose if it isn't organized properly. Some writers can move quickly from generating support to writing a clearly structured first draft. (They usually say they have sequenced their ideas in their heads.) Most, however, need to spend some time sorting out their thoughts on paper before starting the first draft; otherwise, they tend to lose their way in a tangle of ideas.

When moving to the organizing stage, you should have in front of you your scratch list (see pages 31–33) and thesis, plus any supporting material you've accumulated since you did your prewriting. To find a logical framework for all this material, you'll need to (1) determine which pattern of development is implied in your evidence, (2) select one of four basic approaches for organizing your evidence, and (3) outline your evidence. These issues are discussed in the following sections.

USE THE PATTERNS OF DEVELOPMENT

As you saw on pages 29–30 and 46–48, the patterns of development (definition, narration, process analysis, and others) can help you develop prewriting material and generate evidence for a thesis. In the organizing stage, the patterns provide frameworks for presenting the evidence in an orderly, accessible way. Here's how.

Each pattern of development has its own internal logic that makes it appropriate for some writing purposes but not for others. (You may find it helpful at this point to turn to pages 29–30 so you can review the broad purpose of each pattern.) Imagine that you want to write an essay *explaining why* some students drop out of college during the first semester. If your essay consisted only of a lengthy narrative of two friends floundering through the first month of college, you wouldn't achieve your purpose. A condensed version of the narrative might be appropriate at some point in the essay, but—to meet your objective—most of the paper would have to focus on *causes* and *effects.*

Once you see which pattern (or combination of patterns) is implied by your purpose, you can block out your paper's general structure. For instance, in the preceding example, you might organize the essay around a three-part discussion of the key reasons that students have difficulty adjusting to college: (1) they miss friends and family, (2) they take inappropriate courses, and (3) they experience conflicts with roommates. As you can see, your choice of pattern of development significantly influences your essay's content and organization.

Some essays follow a single pattern, but most blend them, with a predominant pattern providing the piece's organizational framework. In our example essay, you might include a brief *description* of an overwhelmed first-year college student; you might *define* the psychological term *separation anxiety;* you might end the paper by briefly explaining a *process* for making students' adjustment to college easier. Still, the essay's overall organizational pattern would be *cause-effect* because the paper's primary purpose is to explain why students drop out of college. (See pages 69–70 for more information on the way patterns often mix.)

Although writers often combine the patterns of development, your composition instructor may ask you to write an essay organized according to a single pattern. Such an assignment helps you understand a particular pattern's unique demands. Keep in mind, though, that most writing begins not with a specific pattern but with a specific *purpose.* The pattern or combination of patterns used to develop and organize an essay evolves out of that purpose.

SELECT AN ORGANIZATIONAL APPROACH

No matter which pattern(s) of development you select, you need to know four general approaches for organizing the supporting evidence in an essay: chronological, spatial, emphatic, and simple-to-complex. (See Figure 5.1 on page 56.)

FIGURE 5.1
Process Diagram: Organizing the Evidence

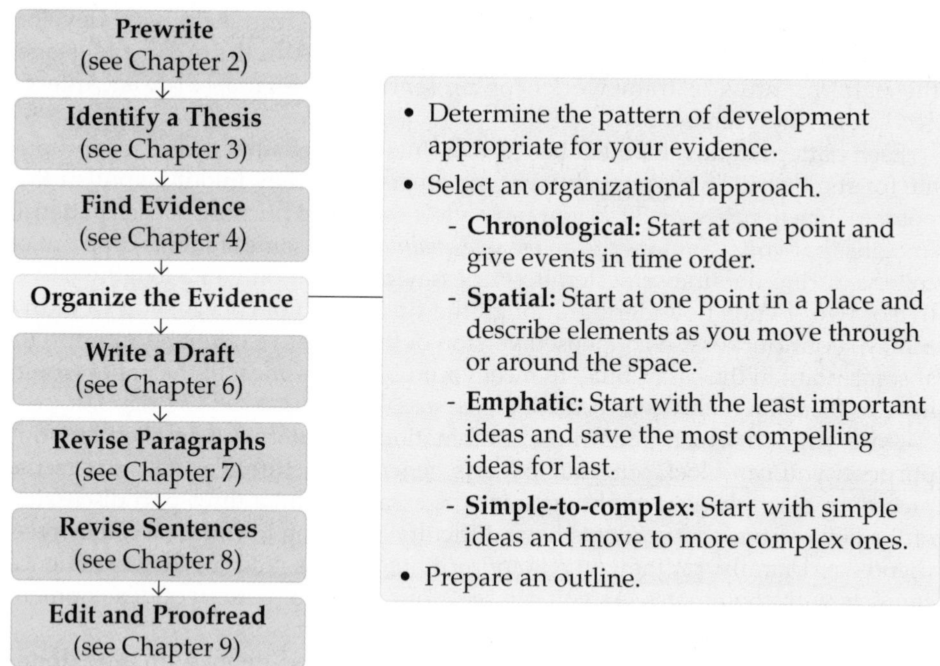

Chronological Approach

When an essay is organized **chronologically,** supporting material is arranged in a clear time sequence, usually starting with what happened first and ending with what happened last. Occasionally, chronological arrangements can be resequenced to create flashback or flashforward effects, two techniques discussed in Chapter 11 on narration.

Essays using narration (for example, an experience with prejudice) or process analysis (for instance, how to deliver an effective speech) are most likely to be organized chronologically. The paper on public speaking might use a time sequence to present its points: how to prepare a few days before the presentation is due; what to do right before the speech; what to concentrate on during the speech itself. (For examples of chronologically arranged student essays, turn to pages 203–204 in Chapter 11 and pages 319–321 in Chapter 14.)

Spatial Approach

When you arrange supporting evidence **spatially,** you discuss details as they occur in space, or from certain locations. This strategy is particularly appropriate for description. Imagine that you plan to write an essay describing the joyous times you spent as a child playing by a towering old oak tree in the neighborhood park. Using spatial organization, you start by describing the rich animal life (the plump earthworms, swarming anthills, and numerous animal tracks) you observed while hunkered down *at the base* of the tree. Next, you re-create the contented feeling you experienced sitting on a branch *in the middle* of the tree. Finally, you describe the glorious view of the world you had *from the top* of the tree.

Although spatial arrangement is flexible (you could, for instance, start with a description from the top of the tree), you should always proceed systematically. And once you select a particular spatial order, you should usually maintain that sequence throughout the essay; otherwise, readers may get lost along the way. (A spatially arranged student essay appears in Chapter 10 on pages 160–162.)

Emphatic Approach

In **emphatic** order, the most compelling evidence is saved for last. This arrangement is based on the psychological principle that people remember best what they experience most recently. Emphatic order has built-in momentum because it starts with the least important point and builds to the most significant. This method is especially effective in argumentation-persuasion essays, in papers developed through examples, and in pieces involving comparison-contrast, division-classification, or causal analysis.

Consider an essay analyzing the negative effect that workaholic parents can have on their children. The paper might start with a brief discussion of relatively minor effects, such as the family's eating mostly frozen or take-out foods. Paragraphs on more serious effects might follow: children get no parental help with homework; they try to resolve personal problems without parental advice. Finally, the essay might close with a detailed discussion of the most significant effect—children's lack of self-esteem because they feel unimportant in their parents' lives. (The student essays on pages 242–243 in Chapter 12, pages 357–359 in Chapter 15, and pages 429–430 in Chapter 17 all use an emphatic arrangement.)

Simple-to-Complex Approach

A final way to organize an essay is to proceed from relatively **simple** concepts to more **complex** ones. By starting with easy-to-grasp, generally accepted evidence, you establish rapport with your readers and assure them that the essay is firmly grounded in shared experience. In contrast, if you open with difficult or highly technical material, you risk confusing and alienating your audience.

Assume you plan to write a paper arguing that your college has endangered students' health by not making an all-out effort to remove asbestos from dormitories and classroom buildings. It probably wouldn't be a good idea to begin with a medically sophisticated explanation of precisely how asbestos damages lung tissue. Instead, you might start with an observation that is likely to be familiar to your readers—one that is part of their everyday experience. You could, for example, open with a description of asbestos—as readers might see it—wrapped around air ducts and furnaces or used as electrical insulation and fireproofing material. Having provided a basic, easy-to-visualize description, you could then go on to explain the complicated process by which asbestos can cause chronic lung inflammation. (See pages 395–397 in Chapter 16 for an example of a student essay using the simple-to-complex arrangement.)

Depending on your purpose, any one of these four organizational approaches might be appropriate. For example, assume you planned to write an essay developing Harriet Davids's thesis: "Being a parent today is much more difficult than it was a generation ago." To emphasize that the various stages in children's lives present parents with different difficulties, you'd probably select a *chronological* sequence. To show that the challenges parents face vary depending on whether children are at home, at school, or in the world at large, you'd probably choose a *spatial* sequence. To stress the range of problems that parents face (from less to more serious), you'd probably use an *emphatic* sequence. Finally, to illustrate today's confusing array of theories for raising children, you might take a *simple-to-complex* approach, moving from the basic to the most sophisticated theory.

Prepare an Outline

Do you, like many students, react with fear and loathing to the dreaded word *outline?* Do you, if asked to submit an outline, prepare it *after* you've written the essay? If you do, we hope to convince you that having an outline—a skeletal version of your paper—*before* you begin the first draft makes the writing process much more manageable. The outline helps you organize your thoughts beforehand, and it guides your writing as you work on the draft. Even though ideas continue to evolve during the draft, an outline clarifies how ideas fit together, which points are major, which should come first, and so on. An outline may also reveal places where evidence is weak, prompting you to eliminate the material altogether, retain it in an unemphatic position, or do more prewriting to generate additional support.

Like previous stages in the writing process, outlining is individualized. Some people prepare highly structured, detailed outlines; others make only a few informal jottings. Sometimes outlining will go quickly, with points falling easily into place; at other times you'll have to work hard to figure out how points are related. If that happens, be glad you caught the problem while outlining, rather than while writing or revising.

To prepare an effective outline, you should reread and evaluate your scratch list and thesis as well as any other evidence you've generated since the prewriting stage. Then decide which pattern of development (description, cause-effect, and so on) seems to be suggested by your evidence. Also determine whether your evidence lends itself to a chronological, a spatial, an emphatic, or a simple-to-complex order. Having done all that, you're ready to identify and sequence your main and supporting points.

The amount of detail in an outline will vary according to the paper's length and the instructor's requirements. A scratch outline consisting of words or phrases (such as the one on page 33 in Chapter 2) is often sufficient, but for longer papers, you'll probably need a more detailed and formal outline. In such cases, the suggestions in the accompanying checklist will help you develop a sound plan. Feel free to modify these guidelines to suit your needs.

OUTLINING: A CHECKLIST

- ☐ Write your purpose, audience, tone, point of view, and thesis at the top of the outlining page.
- ☐ Below the thesis, enter the pattern of development that seems to be implied by the evidence you've accumulated.
- ☐ Record which of the four organizational approaches would be most effective in sequencing your evidence.
- ☐ Reevaluate your supporting material. Delete anything that doesn't develop the thesis or that isn't appropriate for your purpose, audience, tone, and point of view.
- ☐ Add any new points or material.
- ☐ Group related items together. Give each group a heading that represents a main topic in support of your thesis.
- ☐ Label these main topics with roman numerals (I, II, III, and so on). Let the order of numerals indicate the best sequence.
- ☐ Identify subtopics and group them under the appropriate main topics. Indent and label these subtopics with capital letters (A, B, C, and so on). Let the order of the letters indicate the best sequence.
- ☐ Identify supporting points (often reasons and examples) and group them under the appropriate subtopics. Indent and label these supporting points with arabic numbers (1, 2, 3, and so on). Let the numbers indicate the best sequence.
- ☐ Identify specific details (secondary examples, facts, statistics, expert opinions, quotations) and group them under the appropriate supporting points. Indent and label these specific details with lowercase letters (a, b, c, and so on). Let the letters indicate the best sequence.
- ☐ Examine your outline, looking for places where evidence is weak. Where appropriate, add new evidence.
- ☐ Double-check that all main topics, subtopics, supporting points, and specific details develop some aspect of the thesis. Also confirm that all items are arranged in the most logical order.

The sample outline on pages 60–61 develops the thesis, "Being a parent today is much more difficult than it was a generation ago." You may remember that this is the thesis that Harriet Davids devised for the essay she planned to write in response to the assignment on page 24. Harriet's scratch list, based on her brainstorming, appears on page 33. (You may want to review

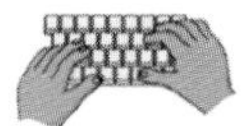

page 33 to see how Harriet later reconsidered material on the scratch list in light of her thesis.) When you compare Harriet's scratch list and outline, you'll find some differences. On the one hand, the outline tends to contain more specifics (for instance, the details about sexually explicit materials—on the Internet, in magazines, in movies, and on television). On the other hand, the outline doesn't include all the material in the scratch list. For example, after reconsidering her purpose, audience, tone, point of view, and thesis, Harriet decided to omit from her outline the section on day care and the point about AIDS.

Harriet's outline is called a **topic outline** because it uses phrases, or topics, for each entry. (See pages 317–318, 356–357, and 480–481 for other examples of topic outlines.) For a more complex paper, a **sentence outline** might be more appropriate (see pages 236–237 and 614–616). You can also mix phrases and sentences (see pages 393–394), as long as you are consistent about where you use each.

In Harriet's outline, note that indentations signal the relationships among the essay's points and that the same grammatical form is used to begin each entry on a particular level. For instance, since a noun phrase ("Distractions from homework") follows Roman numeral I, noun phrases also follow subsequent Roman numerals. Such consistency helps writers see if items at a particular level are comparable.

Purpose: To inform

Audience: Instructor as well as class members, most of whom are 18-20 years old

Tone: Serious and straightforward

Point of view: Third person (mother of two teenage girls)

Thesis: Being a parent today is much more difficult than it was a generation ago.

Pattern of development: Illustration

Organizational approach: Emphatic order

I. Distractions from homework
   A. At home
      1. MP3 players
      2. Computers--Internet, computer games
      3. Television
   B. Outside home
      1. Malls
      2. Movie theaters
      3. Fast-food restaurants
II. Sexually explicit materials
   A. Internet
      1. Easy-to-access adult chat rooms
      2. Easy-to-access pornographic websites

```
      B. In print and in movies
         1. Sex magazines—Playboy, Penthouse
         2. Casual sex
      C. On television
         1. Soap operas
         2. R-rated comedians
         3. R-rated movies on cable

  III. Increased dangers
      A. Drugs—peer pressure
      B. Alcohol—peer pressure
      C. Violent crimes against children
```

(If you'd like to see the first draft that resulted from Harriet's outline, turn to pages 86–87. Hints for moving from an outline to a first draft appear on pages 64–66. For additional suggestions on organizing a first draft, see the diagram on page 85.)

Before starting to write your first draft, show your outline to several people (your instructor, friends, classmates). Their reactions will indicate whether your proposed organization is appropriate for your thesis, purpose, audience, tone, and point of view. Their comments can also highlight areas needing additional work. After making whatever changes are needed, you're in a good position to go ahead and write the first draft of your essay.

ACTIVITIES: ORGANIZING THE EVIDENCE

1. The following thesis statement is accompanied by a scrambled list of supporting points. Prepare a topic outline for a potential essay, being sure to distinguish between major and secondary points.

   Thesis: Our schools, now in crisis, could be improved in several ways.

   Certificate requirements for teachers
   Schedules
   Teachers
   Longer school year
   Merit pay for outstanding teachers
   Curriculum
   Better textbooks
   Longer school days
   More challenging course content

2. For each of the following thesis statements, there are two purposes given. Determine whether each purpose suggests an emphatic, chronological, spatial,

or simple-to-complex approach. Note the way the approach varies as the purpose changes.

a. *Thesis:* Traveling in a large city can be an unexpected education.

   Purpose 1: To explain, in a humorous way, the stages in learning to cope with the city's cab system

   Purpose 2: To describe, in a serious manner, the vastly different sections of the city as viewed from a cab

b. *Thesis:* The student government seems determined to improve its relations with the college administration.

   Purpose 1: To inform readers by describing efforts that student leaders took, month by month, to win administrative support

   Purpose 2: To convince readers by explaining straightforward as well as intricate pro-administration resolutions that student leaders passed

c. *Thesis:* Supermarkets use sophisticated marketing techniques to prod consumers into buying more than they need.

   Purpose 1: To inform readers that positioning products in certain locations encourages impulse buying

   Purpose 2: To persuade readers not to patronize those chains using especially objectionable sales strategies

3. Return to the paragraph or first draft you prepared in response to activity 4 or activity 5 in Chapter 4 (pages 52–53). Applying the principles discussed in Chapter 5, strengthen the organization of the evidence you generated. (If you rework a first draft, save the draft so you can refine it further after reading the next chapter.)

4. Each of the following brief essay outlines consists of a thesis and several points of support. Which pattern of development would you probably use to develop the overall organizational framework for each essay? Which pattern(s) would you use to develop each point of support? Why?

a. *Thesis:* Friends of the opposite sex fall into one of several categories: the pal, the confidante, or the pest.

   Points of Support

   - Frequently, an opposite-sex friend is simply a "pal."
   - Sometimes, though, a pal turns, step by step, into a confidante.
   - If a confidante begins to have romantic thoughts, he or she may become a pest, thus disrupting the friendship.

b. *Thesis:* What happens when a child gets sick in a two-income household? Numerous problems occur.

   Points of Support

   - Parents often encounter difficulties as they take steps to locate a babysitter or make other child-care arrangements.

- If no child-care helper can be found, a couple must decide which parent will stay at home—a decision that may create conflict between husband and wife.
- No matter what they do, parents inevitably will incur at least one of several kinds of expenses.

5. For one of the thesis statements given in activity 4, identify a possible purpose, audience, tone, and point of view. Then, use one or more patterns to generate material to develop the points of support listed. Get together with someone else to review the generated material, deleting, adding, combining, and arranging ideas in logical order. Finally, make an outline for the body of the essay. (Save your outline. After reading the next chapter, you can use it to write the essay's first draft.)

6. Look again at the thesis and scratch outline you refined and elaborated in response to activity 6 in Chapter 4 (page 53). Reevaluate this material by deleting, adding, combining, and rearranging ideas as needed. Then, in preparation for writing an essay, outline your ideas. Consider whether an emphatic, chronological, spatial, or simple-to-complex approach will be most appropriate. Finally, ask at least one other person to evaluate your organizational plan. (Save your outline. After reading the next chapter, you can use it to write the essay's first draft.)

Writing the Paragraphs in the First Draft

After prewriting, deciding on a thesis, and developing and organizing evidence, you're ready to write a first draft—a rough, provisional version of your essay. Some people work slowly as they prepare their drafts, while others quickly dash off their drafts. No matter how you proceed, you should concentrate on providing paragraphs that support your thesis. Also try to include all relevant examples, facts, and opinions, sequencing this material as effectively as you can.

Because of your work in the preceding stages, the first draft may flow quite smoothly. But don't be discouraged if it doesn't. You may find that your thesis has to be reshaped, that a point no longer fits, that you need to return to a prewriting activity to generate additional material. Such stopping and starting is to be expected. Writing the first draft is a process of discovery, involving the continual clarification and refining of ideas.

How to Move from Outline to First Draft

There's no single right way to prepare a first draft. With experience, you'll undoubtedly find your own basic approach, adapting it to suit each paper's length, the time available, and the instructor's requirements. Some writers rely heavily on their scratch lists or outlines; others glance at them only occasionally. Some people write the first draft in longhand; others use a computer.

However you choose to proceed, consider the suggestions in the following checklist when moving from an outline or scratch list to a first draft.

TURNING OUTLINE INTO FIRST DRAFT: A CHECKLIST

- ☐ Make the outline's *main topics* (I, II, III) the *topic sentences* of the essay's supporting paragraphs. (Topic sentences are discussed later in this chapter.)
- ☐ Make the outline's *subtopics* (A, B, C) the *subpoints* in each paragraph.
- ☐ Make the outline's *supporting points* (1, 2, 3) the *key examples* and *reasons* in each paragraph.
- ☐ Make the outline's *specific details* (a, b, c) the *secondary examples*, facts, statistics, expert opinion, and quotations in each paragraph.

(To see how one student, Harriet Davids, moved from outline to first draft, turn to pages 86–87.)

GENERAL SUGGESTIONS ON HOW TO PROCEED

Although outlines and lists are valuable for guiding your work, don't be so dependent on them that you shy away from new ideas that surface during your writing of the first draft. It's during this time that promising new thoughts often pop up; as they do, jot them down. Then, at the appropriate point, go back and evaluate them: Do they support your thesis? Are they appropriate for your essay's purpose, audience, tone, and point of view? If so, go ahead and include the material in your draft.

It's easy to get stuck while preparing the first draft if you try to edit as you write. Remember: A draft isn't intended to be perfect. For the time being, adopt a relaxed, noncritical attitude. Working as quickly as you can, don't stop to check spelling, correct grammar, or refine sentence structure. Save these tasks for later. One good way to help remind you that the first draft is tentative is to prepare it in longhand, using scrap paper and pencil. Writing on alternate lines also underscores your intention to revise later on, when the extra space will make it easier to add and delete material. Similarly, writing on only one side of the paper can prove helpful if, during revision, you decide to move a section to another part of the paper.

IF YOU GET BOGGED DOWN

All writers get bogged down now and then. The best thing to do is accept that sooner or later it will happen to you. When it does, keep calm and try to write something—no matter how awkward or imprecise it may seem. Just jot a reminder to yourself in the margin ("Fix this," "Redo," or "Ugh!") to finetune the section later. Or leave a blank space to hold a spot for the right words when they finally break loose. It may also help to reread—out loud is best—what you've already written. Regaining a sense of the larger context is often enough to get you moving again. You might also try talking your way through a troublesome section. Like most people, you probably speak more easily than you write; by speaking aloud, you tap this oral fluency and put it to work in your writing.

If a section of the essay strikes you as particularly difficult, don't spend time struggling with it. Move on to an easier section, write that, and then return to the challenging part. If you're still getting nowhere, take a break. Watch television, listen to music, talk with friends. While you're relaxing, your thoughts may loosen up and untangle the knotty section. If, on the other hand, an obligation such as a class or an appointment forces you to stop writing when the draft is going well, jot down a few notes in the margin to remind yourself of your train of thought. The notes will keep you from getting stuck when you pick up the draft later.

A SUGGESTED SEQUENCE FOR WRITING THE FIRST DRAFT

Because you read essays from beginning to end, you may assume that writers work the same way, starting with the introduction and going straight through to the conclusion. Often, however, this isn't the case. In fact, since an introduction depends so heavily on everything that follows, it's usually best to write the introduction *after* the essay's body. (See Figure 6.1 on page 67.)

When preparing your first draft, you may find it helpful to follow this sequence:

1. Write the essay's supporting paragraphs.
2. Write the other paragraphs in the essay's body.
3. Write the introduction.
4. Write the conclusion.

Write the Supporting Paragraphs

Before starting to write the essay's **supporting paragraphs,** enter your thesis at the top of the page. You might even underline key words in the thesis to keep yourself focused on the central ideas you plan to develop. Also, now that you've planned the essay's overall organization, you may want to add to your thesis a **plan of development:** a brief *overview* of the essay's *major points in the exact order* in which you will discuss those points. (For more on plans of development, see pages 39–40.)

Not every essay needs a plan of development. In a brief paper, readers can often keep track of ideas without this extra help. But in a longer, more complex essay, a plan of development helps readers follow the progression of main points

FIGURE 6.1
Process Diagram: Writing a Draft

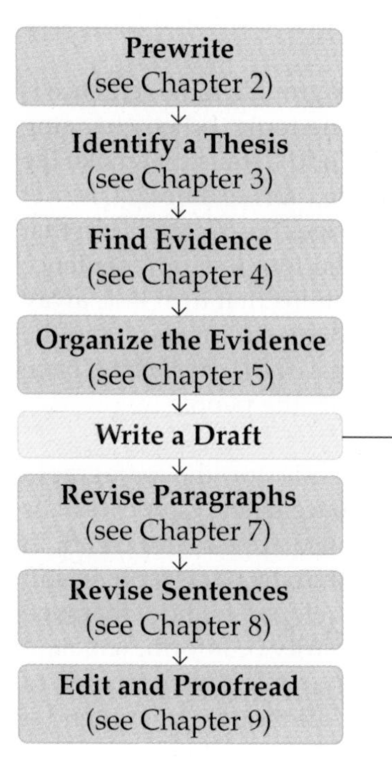

- Write the supporting paragraphs.
  - Use topic sentences.
  - Use patterns of development.
  - Make paragraphs unified.
  - Make paragraphs specific.
  - Provide adequate support.
  - Use signal devices—transitions, bridging sentences, repeated words, synonyms, and pronouns—to make paragraphs coherent.
- Write background and transitional paragraphs.
- Write the introduction, which may include:
  - A broad statement narrowing to a limited subject.
  - A brief anecdote.
  - The opposite of the idea you actually develop.
  - A series of short questions.
  - A quotation.
  - Some brief background.
  - Refutation of a common belief.
  - A dramatic fact or statistic.
- Write the conclusion; include a summary, prediction, quotation, statistic, or call for action.

in the supporting paragraphs. Whether or not you include a plan of development, always keep in mind that writing the draft often leads to new ideas; you may have to revise your thesis, plan of development, and supporting paragraphs as the draft unfolds.

Drawn from the main sections in your outline or scratch list, each supporting paragraph should develop an aspect of your essay's thesis or plan of development. Although there are no hard-and-fast rules, strong supporting paragraphs are (1) often focused by topic sentences, (2) organized around one or more patterns of development, (3) unified, (4) specific, (5) adequately supported, and (6) coherent. Aim for as many of these qualities as you can in the first draft. The material on the following pages will help keep you focused on your goal. But don't expect the draft paragraphs to be perfect; you'll have the chance to revise them later on.

Use Topic Sentences

Frequently, each supporting paragraph in an essay is focused by a **topic sentence.** This sentence usually states a main point in support of the thesis. In a formal outline, such a point customarily appears, often in abbreviated form, as a *main topic* marked with a roman numeral (I, II, III).

The transformation of an outline's main topic to a paragraph's topic sentence is often a matter of stating your attitude toward the outline topic. When changing from main outline topic to topic sentence, you may also add details that make the topic sentence more specific and concrete. Compare, for example, Harriet Davids's outline on pages 60–61 with her first draft on pages 86–87. You'll see that the outline entry "I. Distractions from homework" turned into the topic sentence "Parents have to control all the new distractions/temptations that turn kids away from schoolwork" (paragraph 2). The difference between the outline topic and the topic sentence is thus twofold: The topic sentence has an *element of opinion* ("have to control"), and it is focused by *added details* (in this case, the people involved—parents and children).

The topic sentence functions as a kind of mini-thesis for the paragraph. Generally one or two sentences in length, the topic sentence usually appears at or near the beginning of the paragraph. However, it may also appear at the end, in the middle, or—with varied wording—several times within the paragraph. In still other cases, a single topic sentence may state an idea developed in more than one paragraph. When a paragraph is intended primarily to clarify or inform, you may want to place its topic sentence at the beginning; that way, readers are prepared to view everything that follows in light of that main idea. If, though, you intend a paragraph to heighten suspense or to convey a feeling of discovery, you may prefer to delay the topic sentence until the end.

Regardless of its length or location, the topic sentence states the paragraph's main idea. The other sentences in the paragraph provide support for this central point in the form of examples, facts, expert opinion, and so on. Like a thesis statement, the topic sentence *signals the paragraph's subject* and frequently *indicates the writer's attitude* toward that subject. In the topic sentences that follow, the subject of the paragraph is underlined once and the attitude toward that subject is underlined twice:

Topic Sentences

Some students select a particular field of study for the wrong reasons.

The ocean dumping of radioactive waste is a ticking time bomb.

Several contemporary rock groups show unexpected sensitivity to social issues.

Political candidates are sold like slickly packaged products.

As you work on the first draft, you may find yourself writing paragraphs without paying too much attention to topic sentences. That's fine, as long as you remember to evaluate the paragraphs later on. When revising, you can provide a topic sentence for a paragraph that needs a sharper focus, recast a topic sentence for a paragraph that ended up taking an unexpected turn, even eliminate a topic sentence altogether if a paragraph's content is sufficiently unified to imply its point.

With experience, you'll develop an instinct for writing focused paragraphs without having to pay such close attention to topic sentences. A good way to develop such an instinct is to note how the writers in this book use topic sentences to shape paragraphs and clarify meaning. (If you'd like some practice in identifying topic sentences, see pages 88–89.)

Use the Patterns of Development

As you saw on page 55, an entire essay can be organized around one or more patterns of development. These patterns can also provide the organizational framework for an essay's supporting paragraphs. Assume you're writing an article for your town newspaper with the thesis, "Year-round residents of an ocean community must take an active role in safeguarding the seashore environment." As the following examples indicate, your supporting paragraphs could develop this thesis through a variety of patterns, with each paragraph's topic sentence suggesting a specific pattern or combination of patterns.

Topic Sentence	Possible Pattern of Development
In a nearby ocean community, signs of environmental damage are everywhere.	*Description* of a seaside town with polluted waters, blighted trees, and diseased marine life
Typically, residents blame industry or tourists for such damage.	*Narration* of a conversation among seaside residents
Residents' careless behavior is also to blame, however.	*Illustrations* of residents' littering the beach, injuring marine life while motor boating, walking over fragile sand dunes
Even environmentally concerned residents may contribute to the problem.	*Cause-effect* explanation of the way Styrofoam packaging and plastic food wrap, even when properly disposed of in a trash can, can harm scavenging seagulls
Fortunately, not all seaside towns are plagued by such environmental problems.	*Comparison-contrast* of one troubled shore community with another more ecologically sound one
It's clear that shore residents must become "environmental activists."	*Definition* of an *environmental activist*
Residents can get involved in a variety of pro-environmental activities.	*Division-classification* of activities at the neighborhood, town, and municipal levels
Moreover, getting involved is an easy matter.	*Process analysis* of the steps for getting involved at the various levels
Such activism yields significant rewards.	A final *argumentation-persuasion* pitch showing residents the benefits of responsible action

Of course, each supporting paragraph in an essay doesn't have to be organized according to a different pattern of development; several paragraphs may use the same pattern. Nor is it necessary for any one paragraph to be restricted to a single pattern; supporting paragraphs often combine patterns. For example, the topic sentence "Fortunately, not all seaside towns are plagued by such environmental problems" might be developed primarily through *comparison-contrast*, but the paragraph would need a fair amount of *description* to clarify the differences between towns. (For more on the way the patterns of development come into play throughout the writing process, see pages 29–30, 39, 46–48, and 55.

Make the Paragraphs Unified

Just as overall evidence must support an essay's thesis (pages 45–46), the facts, opinions, and examples in each supporting paragraph must have *direct bearing* on the paragraph's topic sentence. If the paragraph has no topic sentence, the supporting material must be *consistent* with the paragraph's *implied focus.* A paragraph is **unified** when it meets these requirements.

Consider the following sample paragraph, taken from an essay illustrating recent changes in Americans' television-viewing habits. The paragraph focuses on people's reasons for switching from network to cable television. As you'll see, though, the paragraph lacks unity because it contains points (underlined) unrelated to its main idea. Specifically, the criticism of cable's foul language contradicts the paragraph's topic sentence, "Many people consider cable TV an improvement over network television." To present a balanced view of cable versus network television, the writer should discuss these points, but in *another paragraph.*

Nonunified Support

Many people consider cable TV an improvement over network television. For one thing, viewers usually prefer the movies on cable. Unlike network films, cable movies are often only months old, they have not been edited by censors, and they are not interrupted by commercials. Growing numbers of people also feel that cable specials are superior to the ones the networks grind out. Cable viewers may enjoy such performers as U2, Madonna, or Chris Rock in concert, whereas the networks continue to broadcast tired, look-alike reality shows and boring awards ceremonies. <u>There is, however, one problem with cable comedians. The foul language many of them use makes it hard to watch these cable specials with children. The networks, in contrast, generally present "clean" shows that parents and children can watch together</u>. Then, too, cable TV offers viewers more flexibility since it schedules shows at various times over the month. People working night shifts or attending evening classes can see movies in the afternoon, and viewers missing the first twenty minutes of a show can always catch them later. It's not surprising that cable viewership is growing while network ratings have taken a plunge.

Make the Paragraphs Specific

If your supporting paragraphs are vague, readers will lose interest, remain unconvinced of your thesis, even have trouble deciphering your meaning. In contrast, paragraphs filled with **concrete, specific details** engage readers, lend force to ideas, and clarify meaning.

Following are two versions of a paragraph from an essay about trends in the business community. Although both paragraphs focus on one such trend—flexible working hours—note how the first version's vague generalities leave meaning unclear. *What,* for example, is meant by "flex-time scheduling"? *Which* companies have tried it? *Where,* specifically, are these companies located? *How,* exactly, does flex-time increase productivity, lessen conflict, and reduce accidents? The second paragraph answers these questions with specifics and, as a result, is more informative and interesting.

Nonspecific Support

More and more companies have begun to realize that flex-time scheduling offers advantages. Several companies outside Boston have tried flex-time scheduling and are pleased with the way the system reduces the difficulties their employees face getting to work. Studies show that flex-time scheduling also increases productivity, reduces on-the-job conflict, and minimizes work-related accidents.

Specific Support

More and more companies have begun to realize that flex-time scheduling offers advantages over a rigid 9-to-5 routine. Along suburban Boston's Route 128, such companies as Compugraphics and Consolidated Paper now permit employees to schedule their arrival any time between 6 a.m. and 11 a.m. The corporations report that the number of rush-hour jams and accidents has fallen dramatically. As a result, employees no longer arrive at work weighed down by tension induced by choking clouds of exhaust fumes and the blaring horns of gridlocked drivers. Studies sponsored by the journal *Business Quarterly* show that this more mellow state of mind benefits corporations. Traffic-stressed employees begin their workday anxious and exasperated, still grinding their teeth at their fellow commuters, their frustration

```
often spilling over into their performance at work. By contrast,
stress-free employees work more productively and take fewer days
off. They are more tolerant of co-workers and customers, and less
likely to balloon minor irritations into major confrontations.
Perhaps most important, employees arriving at work relatively
free of stress can focus their attention on working safely. They
rack up significantly fewer on-the-job accidents, such as falls
and injuries resulting from careless handling of dangerous
equipment. Flex-time improves employee well-being, and as well-
being rises, so do company profits.
```

Five Strategies for Making Paragraphs Specific. How can you make the evidence in your paragraphs specific? The following techniques should help.

1. **Provide examples that answer *who, which, what,* and similar questions.** In contrast to the vague generalities in the first paragraph on flex-time scheduling, the second paragraph provides examples that answer a series of basic questions. For instance, the general comment "Several companies outside Boston" (*which* companies?) is replaced by "Compugraphics and Consolidated Paper." The vague phrase "difficulties their employees face getting to work" (*what* difficulties?) is dramatized with the examples "rush-hour jams and accidents." Similarly, "work-related accidents" (*which* accidents?) is illustrated with "falls and injuries resulting from careless handling of dangerous equipment."
2. **Replace general nouns and adjectives with precise ones.** In the following sentences, note how much sharper images become when exact nouns and adjectives replace imprecise ones:

General	More Specific	Most Specific
A *man* had trouble lifting the *box* out of the *old* car.	A *young man, out of shape,* struggled to lift the *heavy crate* out of the *beat-up sports car.*	*Joe, only twenty years old but more than fifty pounds overweight,* struggled to lift the *heavy wooden crate* out of the *rusty* and *dented Mustang.*

3. **Replace abstract words with concrete ones.** Notice the way the example on the right, firmly grounded in the physical, clarifies the intangible concepts in the example on the left:

Abstract	Concrete
The fall day had great *beauty,* despite its *dreariness.*	*Red, yellow,* and *orange* leaves *gleamed wetly* through the *gray mist.*

(For more on making abstract language concrete, see pages 127–128 in Chapter 8.)

4. **Use words that appeal to the five senses (sight, touch, taste, smell, sound).** The sentence on the left lacks impact because it fails to convey any sensory

impressions; the sentence on the right, though, gains power through the use of sensory details:

Without Sensory Images	**With Sensory Images**
The computer room is eerie.	In the computer room, keys *click* and printers *grate* while row after row of students stare into screens that *glow without shedding any light.* (sound and sight)

(For more on sensory language, see pages 156–158 in Chapter 10.)

5. **Use vigorous verbs.** Linking verbs (such as *seem* and *appear*) and *to be* verbs (such as *is* and *were*) paint no pictures. Strong verbs, however, create sharp visual images. Compare the following examples:

Weak Verbs	**Strong Verbs**
The spectators *seemed* pleased and *were* enthusiastic when the wheelchair marathoners *went* by.	The spectators *cheered* and *whistled* when the wheelchair marathoners *whizzed* by.

(For more on strong verbs, see pages 128–130 in Chapter 8.)

Provide Adequate Support

Each supporting paragraph should also have **adequate support** so that your readers can see clearly the validity of the topic sentence. At times, a single extended example is sufficient; generally, however, an assortment of examples, facts, personal observations, and so forth is more effective.

Following are two versions of a paragraph from a paper showing how difficult it is to get personal, attentive service nowadays at gas stations, supermarkets, and department stores. Both paragraphs focus on the problem at gas stations, but one paragraph is much more effective. As you'll see, the first paragraph starts with good specific support, yet fails to provide enough of it. The second paragraph offers additional examples, descriptive details, and dialog—all of which make the writing stronger and more convincing.

Inadequate Support

Gas stations are a good example of this impersonal attitude. At many stations, attendants have even stopped pumping gas. Motorists pull up to a combination convenience store and gas island where an attendant is enclosed in a glass booth with a tray for taking money. The driver must get out of the car, pump the gas, and walk over to the booth to pay. That's a real inconvenience, especially when compared with the way service stations used to be run.

Adequate Support

Gas stations are a good example of this impersonal attitude. At many stations, attendants have even stopped pumping gas. Motorists pull up to a combination convenience store and gas island where an attendant is enclosed in a glass booth with a tray for taking money. The driver must get out of the car, pump the gas, and walk over to the booth to pay. Even at stations that still have "pump jockeys," employees seldom ask, "Check your oil?" or wash windshields, although they may grudgingly point out the location of the bucket and squeegee. And customers with a balky engine or a nonfunctioning heater are usually out of luck. Why? Many gas stations have eliminated on-duty mechanics. The skillful mechanic who could replace a belt or fix a tire in a few minutes has been replaced by a teenager in a jumpsuit who doesn't know a carburetor from a charge card and couldn't care less.

Make the Paragraphs Coherent

A jigsaw puzzle with all the pieces heaped on a table remains a baffling jumble unless it's clear how the pieces fit together. Similarly, paragraphs can be unified, specific, and adequately supported, yet—if internally disjointed or inadequately connected to each other—leave readers feeling confused. Readers need to be able to follow with ease the progression of thought within and between paragraphs. One idea must flow smoothly and logically into the next; that is, your writing must be **coherent.**

The following paragraph lacks coherence for two main reasons. First, it sequences ideas improperly. (The idea about toll attendants' being cut off from co-workers is introduced, dropped, then picked up again. References to motorists are similarly scattered throughout the paragraph.) Second, it doesn't indicate how individual ideas are related. (What, for example, is the connection between drivers who pass by without saying anything and attendants who have to work at night?)

Incoherent Support

Collecting tolls on the turnpike must be one of the loneliest jobs in the world. Each toll attendant sits in his or her booth, cut off from other attendants. Many drivers pass by each booth. None stays long enough for a brief "hello." Most don't acknowledge the attendant at all. Many toll attendants work at night, pushing them "out of sync" with the rest of the world. The attendants have to deal with rude drivers who treat them like non-people, swearing at them for the long lines at the tollgate.

Attendants dislike how cut off they feel from their co-workers. Except for infrequent breaks, they have little chance to chat with each other and swap horror stories—small pleasures that would make their otherwise routine jobs bearable.

Coherent Support

Collecting tolls on the turnpike must be one of the loneliest jobs in the world. First of all, although many drivers pass by the attendants, none stays long enough for more than a brief "hello." Most drivers, in fact, don't acknowledge the toll collectors at all, with the exception of those rude drivers who treat the attendants like non-people, swearing at them for the long lines at the tollgate. Then, too, many toll attendants work at night, pushing them further "out of sync" with the rest of the world. Worst of all, attendants say, is how isolated they feel from their co-workers. Each attendant sits in his or her booth, cut off from other attendants. Except for infrequent breaks, they have little chance to chat with each other and swap horror stories—small pleasures that would make their otherwise routine jobs bearable.

To avoid the kinds of problems found in the incoherent paragraph, use—as the revised version does—two key strategies: (1) a clearly *chronological, spatial,* or *emphatic order* ("*Worst of all,* attendants say . . . ") and (2) *signal devices* ("*First of all,* although many drivers pass by . . . ") to show how ideas are connected. The following sections discuss these two strategies.

Chronological, Spatial, and Emphatic Order. As you learned in Chapter 5, an entire essay can be organized using chronological, spatial, or emphatic order (pages 55–57). These strategies can also be used to make a paragraph coherent.

Imagine you plan to write an essay showing the difficulties many immigrants face when they first come to this country. Let's consider how you might structure the essay's supporting paragraphs, particularly the way each paragraph's organizational approach can help you arrange ideas in a logical, easy-to-follow sequence.

One paragraph, focused by the topic sentence, "The everyday life of a typical immigrant family is arduous," might be developed through a **chronological** account of the family's daily routine: purchasing, before dawn, fruits and vegetables for their produce stand; setting up the stand early in the morning; working there for ten hours; attending English class at night. Another paragraph might develop its topic sentence,"Many immigrant families get along without the technology that others take for granted," through **spatial** order, taking readers on a brief tour of an immigrant family's rented home: the kitchen lacks a dishwasher or microwave; the living room has no stereo, computer, or VCR, only a small black-and-white TV; the basement has just a washtub and clothesline instead of a washer and dryer. Finally, a third paragraph with the topic sentence, "A number of worries typically beset immigrant families," might use an **emphatic** sequence, moving from less significant concerns (having to wear old, unfashionable clothes) to more critical issues (having to deal with isolation and discrimination).

Signal Devices. Once you determine a logical sequence for your points, you need to make sure that readers can follow the progression of those points within and between paragraphs. **Signal devices** provide readers with cues, reminding them where they have been and indicating where they are going.

Try to include some signals—however awkward or temporary—in your first draft. If you find you *can't,* that's probably a warning that your ideas may not be arranged logically—in which case, it's better to find that out now rather than later on.

Useful signal devices include *transitions, bridging sentences, repeated words, synonyms,* and *pronouns.* Keep in mind, though, that a light touch should be your goal with such signals. Too many call attention to themselves, making the essay mechanical and plodding.

1. **Transitions.** Words and phrases that ease readers from one idea to another are called **transitions.** The following chart lists a variety of such signals. (You'll notice that some transitions can be used for more than one purpose.)

TRANSITIONS

Time

first	immediately	afterward
before	at the same time	after
earlier	simultaneously	finally
next	in the meantime	later
then	meanwhile	eventually
now	subsequently	

Addition (or Sequence)

moreover	one . . . another	next
also	and	finally
furthermore	also	last
in addition	too	
first, . . . second, . . . third	besides	

Space

above	next to
below	behind

Examples

for instance	specifically
for example	namely
to illustrate	

Contrast

but
however
yet
in contrast
on the contrary
although
otherwise
conversely
despite
even though
on the one (other) hand
still
whereas
nevertheless
nonetheless

Comparison

similarly
in the same way
also
likewise
too
in comparison

Cause or Effect

because
as a result
consequently
therefore
then
so
since

Summary or Conclusion

therefore
thus
in short
in conclusion

Note how the underlined transitions in the following paragraph provide clear cues to readers, showing how ideas fit together:

Although the effect of air pollution on the human body is distressing, its effect on global ecology is even more troubling. In the Bavarian, French, and Italian Alps, for example, once magnificent forests are slowly being destroyed by air pollution. Trees dying from pollution lose their leaves or needles, allowing sunlight to reach the forest floor. During this process, grass prospers in the increased light and pushes out the native plants and moss that help hold rainwater. The soil thus loses absorbency and becomes hard, causing rain and snow to slide over the ground instead of sinking into it. This, in turn, leads to erosion of the soil. After a heavy rain, the eroded land finally falls away in giant rockslides and avalanches, destroying entire villages and causing life-threatening floods.

2. **Bridging sentences.** Although **bridging sentences** may be used within a paragraph, they are more often used to move readers from one paragraph to the next. Look again at the first sentence in the preceding paragraph on pollution. Note that the sentence consists of two parts: The first part reminds readers that the previous discussion focused on pollution's effect on the body; the second part tells readers that the focus will now be pollution's effect on ecology.

3. **Repeated words, synonyms, and pronouns.** The **repetition** of important words maintains continuity, reassures readers that they are on the right track, and highlights key ideas. **Synonyms**—words similar in meaning to key words or phrases—also provide coherence, while making it possible to avoid unimaginative and tedious repetitions. Finally, **pronouns** (*he, she, it, they, this, that*) enhance coherence by causing readers to think back to the original word (antecedent) the pronoun replaces. When using pronouns, however, be sure there is no ambiguity about antecedents.

   The following paragraph uses repeated words (underlined once), synonyms (underlined twice), and pronouns (underlined three times) to integrate ideas:

   > Studies have shown that color is also an important part of the way people experience food. In one study, individuals fed a rich red tomato sauce didn't notice it had no flavor until they were nearly finished eating. Similarly, in another experiment, people were offered strangely colored foods: gray pork chops, lavender mashed potatoes, dark blue peas, dessert topped with yellow whipped cream. Not one of the subjects would eat the strange-looking food, even though it smelled and tasted normal.

Write Other Paragraphs in the Essay's Body

Paragraphs supporting the thesis are not necessarily the only kind in the body of an essay. You may also include paragraphs that give background information or provide transitions.

Background Paragraphs

Usually found near the essay's beginning, **background paragraphs** provide information that doesn't directly support the thesis but that helps the reader understand or accept the discussion that follows. Such paragraphs may consist of a definition, brief historical overview, or short description. For example, in the student essay "Salt Marsh" on pages 160–162 the paragraph following the introduction defines a salt marsh and summarizes some of its features. This background information serves as a lead-in to the detailed description that makes up the rest of the essay.

Because you don't want to distract readers from your essay's main point, background paragraphs should be kept as brief as possible. In a paper outlining a program that you believe your college should adopt to beautify its grounds, you would probably need a background paragraph describing typical campus eyesores. Too lengthy a description, though, would detract from the presentation of your step-by-step program.

Transitional Paragraphs

Another kind of paragraph, generally one to three sentences long, may appear between supporting paragraphs to help readers keep track of your discussion.

Like the bridging sentences discussed earlier in the chapter, **transitional paragraphs** usually sum up what has been discussed so far and then indicate the direction the essay will take next.

Although too many transitional paragraphs make writing stiff and mechanical, they can be effective when used sparingly, especially in essays with sharp turns in direction. For example, in a paper showing how to purchase a car, you might start by explaining the research a potential buyer should do beforehand: Consult publications like *Consumer Reports;* check performance records published by the automotive industry; call several dealerships for price information. Then, as a transition to the next section—how to negotiate at the dealership—you might provide the following paragraph:

> Once you have armed yourself with the necessary information, you are ready to meet with a salesperson at the showroom. Your experience at the dealership should not be intimidating as long as you follow the guidelines below.

Write the Introduction

Many writers don't prepare an **introduction** until they have started to revise; others feel more comfortable if their first draft includes in basic form all parts of the final essay. If that's how you feel, you'll probably write the introduction as you complete your first draft. No matter when you prepare it, keep in mind how crucial the introduction is to your essay's success. First impressions count heavily. More specifically, the introduction serves three distinct functions: It arouses readers' interest, introduces your subject, and presents your thesis.

Introductions are difficult to write—so difficult, in fact, that you may be tempted to take the easy way out and use a stale beginning like, "According to Webster, . . . " Equally yawn-inducing are sweeping generalizations that sound grand but say little: "Throughout human history, people have waged war" or "Affection is important in all our lives." Don't, however, go too far in the other direction and come up with a gimmicky opening: "I don't know about you, but in my life, love is the next best thing to being there. Where? Heaven, that's where!" Contrived and coy, such introductions are bound to be inconsistent with your essay's purpose, tone, and point of view. Remember, the introduction's style and content should flow into the rest of the essay.

The length of your introduction will vary according to your paper's scope and purpose. Most essays you write, however, will be served best by a one- or two-paragraph beginning. To write an effective introduction, use any of the following methods, singly or in combination. The thesis statement in each sample introduction is underlined. Note, too, that the first thesis includes a plan of development, whereas the last thesis is followed by a plan of development (see pages 39–40).

Broad Statement Narrowing to a Limited Subject

For generations, morality has been molded primarily by parents, religion, and schools. Children traditionally acquired their ideas about what is right and wrong, which goals are important in life, and how others should be treated from these three sources collectively. But in the past few decades, a single force—television—has undermined the beneficial influence that parents, religion, and school have on children's moral development. Indeed, <u>television often implants in children negative values about sex, work, and family life</u>.

Brief Anecdote

At a local high school recently, students in a psychology course were given a hint of what it is like to be the parents of a newborn. Each "parent" had to carry a raw egg around at all times to symbolize the responsibilities of parenthood. The egg could not be left alone; it limited the "parents'" activities; it placed a full-time emotional burden on "Mom" and "Dad." This class exercise illustrates a common problem facing the majority of new mothers and fathers. <u>Most people receive little preparation for the job of being parents</u>.

Starting with an Idea That Is the Opposite of the One Actually Developed

We hear a great deal about divorce's disastrous impact on children. We are deluged with advice on ways to make divorce as painless as possible for youngsters; we listen to heartbreaking stories about the confused, grieving children of divorced parents. Little attention has been paid, however, to a different kind of effect that divorce may have on children. <u>Children from divorced families may become skilled manipulators, playing off one parent against the other, worsening an already painful situation</u>.

Series of Short Questions

What happens if a child is caught vandalizing school property? What happens if a child goes for a joyride in a stolen car and accidentally hits a pedestrian? Should parents be liable for their children's mistakes? Should parents have to pay what might be hundreds of thousands of dollars in damages? Adults have begun to think seriously about such questions because the laws concerning the limits of parental responsibility are changing rapidly. With unfortunate frequency, courts have begun to hold parents legally and financially responsible for their children's misbehavior.

Quotation

Educator Neil Postman believes that television has blurred the line between childhood and adulthood. According to Postman, "All the secrets that a print culture kept from children . . . are revealed all at once by media that do not, and cannot, exclude any audience." This media barrage of information, once intended only for adults, has changed childhood for the worse.

Brief Background on the Topic

For a long time, adults believed that "children should be seen, not heard." On special occasions, youngsters were dressed up and told to sit quietly while adults socialized. Even when they were alone with their parents, children were not supposed to bother adults with their concerns. However, beginning with psychologist Arnold Gesell in the 1940s, child-raising experts began to question the wisdom of an approach that blocked communication. In 1965, Haim Ginott's ground-breaking book *Between Parent and Child* stressed the importance of conversing with children. More recently, two of Ginott's disciples, Adele Sager and Elaine Mazlich, wrote a book on this subject: *How to Talk So Children Will Listen and Listen So Children Will Talk*. These days, experts agree, successful parents are those who encourage their children to share their thoughts and concerns.

Refutation of a Common Belief

Adolescents care only about material things; their lives revolve around brand-name sneakers, designer jeans, the latest fad in electronics. They resist education, don't read, barely know who is president, mainline rock 'n' roll, experiment with drugs, and exist on a steady diet of Ring-Dings, nachos, and beer. This is what many adults, including parents, seem to believe about the young. The reality is, however, that young people today show more maturity and common sense than most adults give them credit for.

Dramatic Fact or Statistic

Seventy percent of the respondents in a poll conducted by columnist Ann Landers stated that, if they could live their lives over, they would choose not to have children. This startling statistic makes one wonder what these people believed parenthood would be like. Many parents have unrealistic expectations for their children. Parents want their children to accept their values, follow their paths, and succeed where they failed.

Write the Conclusion

You may have come across essays that ended with jarring abruptness because they had no conclusions at all. Other papers may have had conclusions, but they sputtered to a weak close, a sure sign that the writers had run out of steam and wanted to finish as quickly as possible. Just as satisfying closes are an important part of everyday life (we feel cheated if dinner doesn't end with dessert or if a friend leaves without saying goodbye), a strong **conclusion** is an important part of an effective essay.

However important conclusions may be, they're often difficult to write. When it comes time to write one, you may feel you've said all there is to say. To prevent such an impasse, you can try saving a compelling statistic, quotation, or detail for the end. Just make sure that this interesting item fits in the conclusion and that the essay's body contains sufficient support without it.

Occasionally, an essay doesn't need a separate conclusion. This is often the case with narration or description. For instance, in a narrative showing how a crisis can strengthen a faltering friendship, your point will probably be made with sufficient force without a final "this is what the narrative is all about" paragraph.

Usually, though, a conclusion is necessary. Generally one or two paragraphs in length, the conclusion should give the reader a feeling of completeness and finality. One way to achieve this sense of "rounding off" is to return to an image, idea, or anecdote from the introduction.

Because people tend to remember most clearly the points they read last, the conclusion is also a good place to remind readers of your thesis, phrasing this central idea somewhat differently than you did earlier in the essay. You may also use the conclusion to make a final point about your subject. This way, you leave your readers with something to mull over. Be careful, though, not to open an entirely new line of thought at the essay's close. If you do, readers may feel puzzled and frustrated, wishing you had provided evidence for your final point. And, of course, always be sure that concluding material fits your thesis and is consistent with your purpose, tone, and point of view.

In your conclusion, it's best to steer away from stock phrases like "In sum," "In conclusion," and "This paper has shown that . . . " Also avoid lengthy conclusions. As in everyday life, prolonged farewells are tedious.

Following are examples of some of the techniques you can use to write effective conclusions. These strategies may be used singly or in combination. The first strategy, the *summary conclusion,* can be especially helpful in long, complex essays since readers may appreciate a review of your points. Tacked onto a short essay, though, a summary conclusion often seems boring and mechanical.

Summary

Contrary to what many adults think, most adolescents are not only aware of the important issues of the times but also deeply concerned about them. They are sensitive to the plight of the homeless, the destruction of the environment, and the pitfalls of rampant materialism. Indeed, today's young people are not less mature and sensible than their parents were. If anything, they are more so.

Prediction

The growing tendency on the part of the judicial system to hold parents responsible for the actions of their delinquent children can have a disturbing impact on all of us. Parents will feel bitter toward their own children and cynical about a system that holds them accountable for the actions of minors. Children, continuing to escape the consequences of their actions, will become even more lawless and destructive. Society cannot afford two such possibilities.

Quotation

The comic W. C. Fields is reputed to have said, "Anyone who hates children and dogs can't be all bad." Most people do not share Fields's cynicism. Viewing childhood as a time of purity, they are alarmed at the way television exposes children to the seamy side of life, stripping youngsters of their innocence and giving them a glib sophistication that is a poor substitute for wisdom.

Statistic

Granted, divorce may, in some cases, be the best thing for families torn apart by parents battling one another. However, in longitudinal studies of children from divorced families, psychologist Judith Wallerstein found that only 10 percent of the youngsters felt relief at their parents' divorce; the remaining 90 percent felt devastated. Such statistics surely call into question parents' claims that they are divorcing for their children's sake.

Recommendation or Call for Action

It is a mistake to leave parenting to instinct. Instead, we should make parenting skills a required course in schools. In addition, a nationwide hotline should be established to help parents deal with crises. Such training and continuing support would help adults deal more effectively with many of the problems they face as parents.

Write the Title

Some writers say that they often begin a piece with only a title in mind. But for most, writing the **title** is the finishing touch. Although creating a title is usually one of the last steps in writing an essay, it shouldn't be done haphazardly. It may take time to write an effective title—one that hints at the essay's thesis and snares the reader's interest.

Good titles may make use of the following techniques: *repetition of sounds* ("The Plot Against People"), *humor* ("Neat People Versus Sloppy People"), and *questions* ("Am I Blue?"). More often, though, titles are straightforward phrases derived from the essay's subject or thesis: "Shooting an Elephant" and "Why We Crave Horror Movies," for example.

PULLING IT ALL TOGETHER

Now that you know how to prepare a first draft, you might find it helpful to examine Figure 6.2 to see how the different parts of a draft can fit together. Keep in mind that not every essay you write will take this shape. As your purpose, audience, tone, and point of view change, so will your essay's structure. An introduction or conclusion, for instance, may be developed in more than one paragraph; the thesis statement may be implied or delayed until the essay's middle or end; not all paragraphs may have topic sentences; and several

FIGURE 6.2
Structure of an Essay

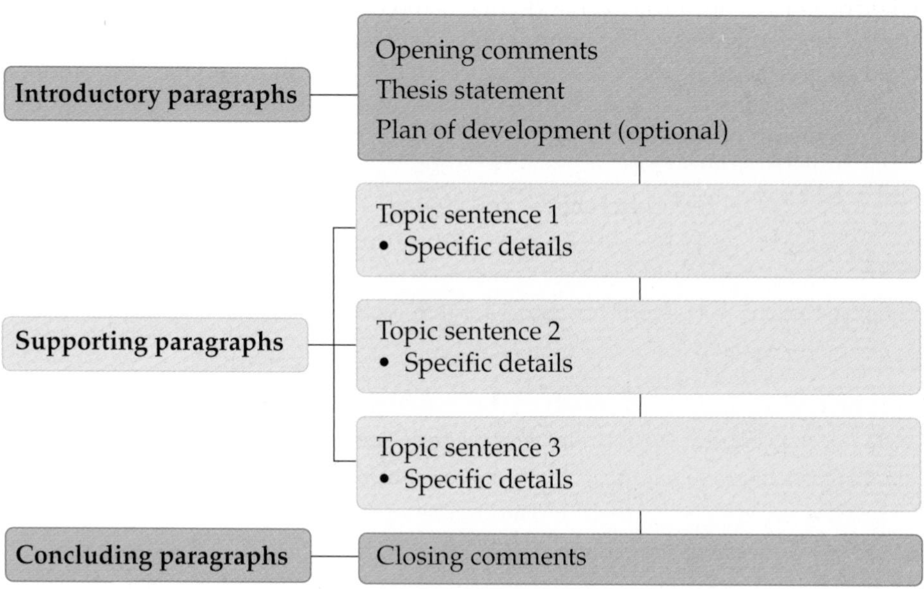

supporting paragraphs may be needed to develop a single topic sentence. Even so, the basic format presented here offers a strategy for organizing a variety of writing assignments—from term papers to lab reports. Once you feel comfortable with the structure, you have a foundation on which to base your variations. (This book's student and professional essays illustrate some possibilities.) Even when using a specific format, you always have room to give your spirit and imagination free play. The language you use, the details you select, the perspective you offer are uniquely yours. They are what make your essay different from anyone else's.

SAMPLE FIRST DRAFT

Here is the first draft of Harriet Davids's essay. (You saw Harriet's prewriting scratch list on page 33, her thesis on page 38, and so on.) Harriet wrote the draft in one sitting. Working at a computer, she started by typing her thesis at the top of the first page. Then, following the guidelines on pages 64–65, she moved the material in her outline (page 60) to her draft. (See page 68 for an explanation of the differences between her outline and draft.) Harriet worked rapidly; she started with the first body paragraph and wrote straight through to the last supporting paragraph.

By moving quickly, Harriet got down her essay's basic text rather easily. Once she felt she had captured in rough form what she wanted to say, she reread her draft to get a sense of how she might open and close the essay. Then she drafted her introduction and conclusion; both appear here, together with the body of the essay. The commentary following the draft will give you an even clearer sense of how Harriet proceeded. (Note that the marginal annotations reflect Harriet's comments to herself about areas she needs to address when revising her first draft.)

Challenges for Today's Parents
by Harriet Davids

Thesis: Being a parent today is much more difficult than it was a generation ago.

Raising children used to be much simpler in the '50s and '60s. I remember TV images from that era showing that parenting involved simply teaching kids to clean their rooms, do their homework, and ______. But being a parent today is much more difficult because nowadays parents have to shield/protect kids from lots of things, like distractions from schoolwork, from sexual material, and from dangerous situations.

ADD SPECIFICS

Parents have to control all the new distractions/temptations that turn kids away from schoolwork. These days many kids have MP3 players, computers, and televisions in their rooms. Certainly, my girls can't resist the urge to watch TV and go online, especially if it's time to do homework. Unfortunately, though, kids aren't assigned much homework and what is assigned is too often busywork. And there are even more distractions outside the home. Teens no longer hang out/congregate on the corner where Dad and Mom can yell to them to come home and do homework. Instead they hang out at the mall, in movie theaters, and at fast-food restaurants. Obviously, parents and school can't compete with all this.

WEAK TRANS.

Also, parents have to help kids develop responsible sexual values even though sex is everywhere. It's too easy for kids to access chat rooms and websites dealing with adult, sometimes pornographic material. Kids see sex magazines in convenience stores where they used to get candy and comic books. And instead of the artsy nude shots of the past, kids see ronchey, explicit shots in *Playboy* and *Penthouse*. And movies have sexy stuff in

SP?

them today. People treat sex casually/as a sport. Not exactly traditional values. TV is no better. Kids see soap-opera characters in bed, sexy music videos, and cable shows full of nudity by just flipping the channel. The situation has gotten so out of hand that maybe the government should establish guidelines on what's permissible.

Worst of all are the life-threatening dangers that parents must help children fend off over the years. With older kids, drugs fall into place as a main concern. Peer pressure to try drugs is bigger to kids than their parents' warnings. Other kinds of warnings are common when children are small. Then parents fear violence since news shows constantly report stories of little children being abused. And when kids aren't much older, they have to resist the pressure to drink. (Alcohol has always attracted kids, but nowadays they are drinking more and this can be deadly, especially when drinking is combined with driving.)

AWK

WRONG WORD

ADD SPECIFICS

REDO

Most adults love their children and want to be good parents. But it's difficult because the world seems stacked against young people. Even Holden Caufield had trouble dealing with society's confusing pressures. Parents must give their children some freedom but not so much that the kids lose sight of what's important.

SP?

Commentary

As you can see, Harriet's draft is rough. Because she knew she would revise later on (pages 106 and 135), she "zapped out" the draft in an informal, colloquial style. For example, she occasionally expressed her thoughts in fragments ("Not exactly traditional values"), relied heavily on "and" as a transition, and used slangy expressions such as "kids" and "lots of things." She also used slashes between alternative word choices and left a blank space when wording just wouldn't come. Then, as Harriet reviewed the printed copy of this rough draft, she made handwritten marginal notes to herself in capital letters: "AWK"or "REDO" to signal awkward sentences; "ADD SPECIFICS" to mark overly general statements; "WRONG WORD" after an imprecise word; "SP?" to remind herself to check spelling in the dictionary; "WEAK TRANS." to indicate where a stronger signaling device was needed. (Harriet's final draft appears on pages 144–145.)

Continues on page 106

Writing a first draft may seem like quite a challenge, but the tips offered in this chapter should help you proceed with confidence. Indeed, as you work on the draft, you may be surprised by how much you enjoy writing. After all, this is your chance to get down on paper something you want to say.

ACTIVITIES: WRITING THE PARAGRAPHS IN THE FIRST DRAFT

1. For each paragraph that follows, determine whether the topic sentence is stated or implied. If the topic sentence is explicit, indicate its location in the paragraph (beginning, end, middle, or both beginning and end). If the topic sentence is implied, state it in your own words.

    a. In 1902, a well-known mathematician wrote an article "proving" that no airplane could ever fly. Just a year later, the Wright brothers made their first flight. In the 1950s, a famed British astronomer said in an interview that the idea of space travel was "utter bilge." Similarly, noted scholars in this country and abroad claimed that automobiles would never replace the trolley car and that the electric light was an impractical gimmick. Clearly, being an expert doesn't guarantee a clear vision of the future.

    b. Motorists in Caracas, Venezuela, must follow an odd/even license-number system for driving their cars on any given day. Cars with license plates ending in even numbers can drive downtown only on even-numbered days. Similarly, in Los Angeles several summers ago, an experimental program required businesses with more than one hundred employees to form "Don't drive to work" programs. Such programs established ride-sharing schedules and offered employees incentives for using mass transportation. Even more extreme is Singapore's method for limiting downtown traffic—most private vehicles are completely banned from central sections of the city.

    c. A small town in Massachusetts that badly needed extra space for grade school classes found it in an unlikely spot. Most of the town's available buildings were too far from the main school or too small. One building, however, was nearby and spacious; it even offered excellent lunchroom and recreation facilities. Despite some objections, the building was chosen—a former saloon, complete with bar, bar stools, cocktail lounge, and pool hall.

    d. The physical complaints of neurotics—people who are exceptionally anxious, pessimistic, hostile, or tense—were once largely ignored by physicians. Many doctors believed that neurotics' frequent health complaints simply reflected their emotional distress. New research, though, shows that neurotics are indeed likely to have physical problems. Specifically, researchers have found that neurotics stand a greater chance of suffering from arthritis, asthma, ulcers, headaches, and heart disease. In addition, there is growing evidence that people who were chronically anxious or depressed in their teens and twenties are more likely to become ill, even die, in their forties.

e. Many American companies have learned the hard way that they need to know the language of their foreign customers. When Chevrolet began selling its Nova cars in Latin America, hardly anyone would buy them. The company finally realized that Spanish speakers read the car's name as the Spanish phrase "no va," meaning "doesn't go." When Pepsi-Cola ran its "Pepsi gives you life" ads in China, consumers either laughed or were offended. The company hadn't translated its slogan quite right. In Chinese, the slogan came out "Pepsi brings your ancestors back from the dead."

2. Using the strategies described on pages 72–73, strengthen the following vague paragraphs. Elaborate each one with striking specifics that clarify meaning and add interest. As you provide specifics, you may need to break each paragraph into several.

a. Other students can make studying in the college library difficult. For one thing, they take up so much space that they leave little room for anyone else. By being inconsiderate in other ways, they make it hard to concentrate on the task at hand. Worst of all, they do things that make it almost impossible to find needed books and magazines.

b. Some people have dangerous driving habits. They act as though there's no one else on the road. They also seem unsure of where they're going. Changing their minds from second to second, they leave it up to others to figure out what they're going to do. Finally, too many people drive at speeds that are either too slow or too fast, creating dangerous situations for both drivers and pedestrians.

c. Things people used to think were safe are now considered dangerous. This goes for certain foods that are now considered unhealthy. Similarly, some habits people thought were harmless have been found to be risky. Even things in the home, in the workplace, and in the air have been found to cause harm. So much has been discovered in recent years about what is harmful that it makes you wonder: What additional dangers lurk in the environment?

d. Society encourages young people to drink. For one thing, youngsters learn early that alcohol plays a prominent role in family and business celebrations. Children also see that liquor is an important part of adults' celebration of national holidays. But the place where youngsters see alcohol depicted most enticingly is on TV. Prime-time shows and beer commercials imply that alcohol is an essential part of a good life.

3. Using the designations indicated in parentheses, identify the flaw(s) in the development of each of the following paragraphs. The paragraphs may lack one or more of the following: unity (U), specific and sufficient support (S), coherence (C). The paragraphs may also needlessly repeat a point (R). Revise the paragraphs, deleting, combining, and rearranging material. Also, add supporting evidence and signal devices where needed.

a. Studies reveal that individuals' first names can influence other people's perceptions. Some names reflect favorably on individuals. For example, a survey conducted by Opinion Masters, Inc., showed that male business executives thought the names *Dorothy* and *Katherine* conveyed competence and professionalism. And participants in a British study reported that names like *Richard* and *Charles* commanded respect and sounded "classy." Of course, participants' observations also reflect the fairly rigid stratification of British society. Other names, however, can have a negative impact. In one study, for instance, teachers gave lower grades to essays supposedly written by boys named *Hubert* and *Elmer* than to the very same essays when credited to boys with more popular names. Another study found that girls with unpopular names (like *Gertrude* or *Gladys*) did worse on tests than girls with more appealing names. Such findings underscore the arbitrary nature of the grading process.

b. This "me first" attitude is also behind the cheating that seems prevalent nowadays. School is perhaps the first place where widespread cheating occurs, with students devising shrewd strategies to do well—often at the expense of others. And since schools are reluctant to teach morality, children grow up with distorted values. The same exaggerated self-interest often causes people, once they reach adulthood, to cheat their companies and co-workers. It's no wonder American business is in such trouble.

c. Despite widespread belief to the contrary, brain size within a species has little to do with how intelligent a particular individual is. A human brain can range from 900 cubic centimeters to as much as 2,500 cubic centimeters, but a large brain does not indicate an equally large degree of intelligence. If humans could see the size of other people's brains, they would probably judge each other accordingly, even though brain size has no real significance.

d. For the 50 percent of adult Americans with high cholesterol, heart disease is a constant threat. Americans can reduce their cholesterol significantly by taking a number of easy steps. Since only foods derived from animals contain cholesterol, eating a strict vegetarian diet is the best way to beat the cholesterol problem. Also, losing weight is known to reduce cholesterol levels—even in those who were as little as ten pounds overweight. Physicians warn, though, that quick weight loss almost always leads to an equally rapid regaining of the lost pounds. For those unwilling to try a vegetarian diet, poultry, fish, and low-fat dairy products can substitute for such high-cholesterol foods as red meat, eggs, cream, and butter. Adding oat bran to the diet has been shown to lower cholesterol. The bran absorbs excess cholesterol in the blood and removes it from the body through waste matter.

4. Strengthen the coherence of the following paragraphs by providing a clear organizational structure and by adding appropriate signal devices. To improve the flow of ideas, you may also need to combine and resequence sentences.

I was a camp counselor this past summer. I learned that leading young children is different from leading people your own age. I was president of my high school Ecology Club. I ran it democratically. We wanted to bring a speaker to the school. We decided to do a fund-raiser. I solicited ideas from everybody. We got together to figure out which was best. It became obvious which was the most profitable and workable fund-raiser. Everybody got behind the effort. The discussion showed that the idea of a raffle with prizes donated by local merchants was the most profitable.

I learned that little kids operate differently. I had to be more of a boss rather than a democratic leader. I took suggestions from the group on the main activity of the day. Everyone voted for the best suggestion. Some kids got especially upset. There was a problem with kids whose ideas were voted down. I learned to make the suggestions myself. The children could vote on my suggestions. No one was overly attached to any of the suggestions. They felt that the outcome of the voting was fair. Basically, I got to be in charge.

5. For an essay with the thesis shown here, indicate the implied pattern(s) of development for each topic sentence that follows.

Thesis: The college should make community service a requirement for graduation.

Topic Sentences

a. "Mandatory community service" is a fairly new and often misunderstood concept.
b. Certainly, the conditions in many communities signal serious need.
c. Here's the story of one student's community involvement.
d. There are, though, many other kinds of programs in which students can become involved.
e. Indeed, a single program offers students numerous opportunities.
f. Such involvement can have a real impact on students' lives.
g. This is the way mandatory community service might work on this campus.
h. However, the college could adopt two very different approaches—one developed by a university, the other by a community college.
i. In any case, the college should begin exploring the possibility of making community service a graduation requirement.

6. Select one of the topic sentences listed in activity 5. Use individual or group brainstorming to generate support for it. After reviewing your raw material, delete, add, and combine points as needed. Finally, with the thesis in mind, write a rough draft of the paragraph.

7. Imagine you plan to write a serious essay on one of the following thesis statements. The paper will be read by students in your composition class. After determining your point of view, use any prewriting techniques you want to identify the essay's major and supporting points. Arrange the points in order and determine where background and/or transitional paragraphs might be helpful.

   a. Society needs stricter laws against noise pollution.
   b. The traditional lecture format used in many large colleges and universities discourages independent thinking.
   c. Public buildings in this town should be redesigned to accommodate the disabled.
   d. Long-standing discrimination against women in college athletics must stop.

8. Use any of the techniques described on pages 79–84 to revise the opening and closing paragraphs of two of your own papers. When rewriting, don't forget to keep your purpose, audience, tone, and point of view in mind.

9. Reread Harriet Davids's first draft on pages 86–87. Overall, does it support Harriet's thesis? Which topic sentences focus paragraphs effectively? Where is evidence specific, unified, and coherent? Where does Harriet run into some problems? Make a list of the draft's strengths and weaknesses. Save your list for later review. (In the next chapter, you'll be asked to revise Harriet's draft.)

10. Freewrite or write in your journal about a subject that's been on your mind lately. Reread your raw material to see what thesis seems to emerge. What might your purpose, audience, tone, and point of view be if you wrote an essay with this thesis? What primary and secondary points would you cover? Prepare an outline of your ideas. Then draft the essay's body, providing background and transitional paragraphs if appropriate. Finally, write a rough version of the essay's introduction, conclusion, and title. (Save your draft so you can revise it after reading the next chapter.)

11. If you prepared a first draft in response to activity 3 in Chapter 5 (page 62), work with at least one other person to strengthen that early draft by applying the ideas presented in this chapter. (Save this stronger version of your draft so you can refine it further after reading the next chapter.)

12. Referring to the outline you prepared in response to activity 5 or activity 6 in Chapter 5 (page 63), draft the body of an essay. After reviewing the draft, prepare background and transitional paragraphs as needed. Then draft a rough introduction, conclusion, and title. Ask several people to react to what you've prepared, and save your draft so you can work with it further after reading the next chapter.

For additional writing, reading, and research resources, go to **www.mycomplab.com** and choose **Nadell/Langan/Comodromos'** ***The Longman Writer, 7/e***.

Revising Overall Meaning, Structure, and Paragraph Development

By now, you've probably abandoned any preconceptions you might have had about good writers sitting down and creating a finished product in one easy step. Alexander Pope's comment that "true ease in writing comes from art, not chance" is as true today as it was more than two hundred years ago. Writing that seems effortlessly clear is often the result of sustained work, not of good luck or even inborn talent. And much of this work takes place during the final stage of the writing process, when ideas, paragraphs, sentences, and words are refined and reshaped.

You've most likely seen cartoons picturing writers plugging away at their typewriters, filling their wastebaskets with sheet after sheet of crumpled paper. It's true. Professional writers—novelists, journalists, textbook authors—seldom submit a piece of writing that hasn't been revised. They recognize that rough, unpolished work doesn't do them justice. What's more, they often look forward to revising. Columnist Ellen Goodman puts it this way: "What makes me happy is rewriting. . . . It's like cleaning house, getting rid of all the junk, getting things in the right order, tightening up."

In a sense, revision occurs throughout the writing process: At some earlier stage, you may have dropped an idea, overhauled your thesis, or shifted paragraph order. What, then, is different about the rewriting that occurs in the revision stage? The answer has to do with the literal meaning of the word ***revision***—reseeing, or seeing again. Genuine revision involves casting clear eyes on your work, viewing it as though you're a reader rather than the writer. Revision is not, as some believe, simply touch-up work—changing a sentence here, a word there, eliminating spelling errors, typing a neat final copy. Revision means that you go through your paper looking for trouble, ready to pick a fight with your own writing. And then you must be willing to sit down and make the changes needed for your writing to be as effective as possible.

Throughout this book, we emphasize that everyone approaches early stages in the writing process differently. The same is true for the revision stage. Some people dash off a draft, knowing they'll spend hours reworking it later. Others find that writing the first draft slowly yields such good results that wholesale revision isn't necessary. Some writers revise neatly, while others fill their drafts with messily scribbled changes. Then there are those who find that the more they revise, the more they overcomplicate their writing and rob it of spontaneity. So, for each writer and for each piece of writing, the amount and kind of revision will vary.

Because revision is hard work, you may resist it. After putting the final period in your first draft, you may feel done and have trouble accepting that more work remains. Or, as you read the draft, you may see so many weak spots that you view revision as punishment for not getting things right the first time. And, if you feel shaky about how to proceed, you may be tempted to skip revising altogether.

If all this sounds as though we're talking about you, don't give up. Here are five strategies to help you get going if you balk at or feel overwhelmed by revising.

FIVE STRATEGIES TO MAKE REVISION EASIER

Keep in mind that the revision strategies discussed here should be adapted to each writing situation. Revising an answer on an essay exam is quite different from revising a paper you've spent several weeks preparing. Other considerations include your professor's requirements and expectations, the time available, and the paper's bearing on your grade. In any case, the following strategies will help you approach revision more confidently. (See Figure 7.1 on page 97.)

Set Your First Draft Aside for a While

When you pick up your draft after having set it aside for a time, you'll approach it with a fresh, more objective point of view. How much of an interval to leave depends on the time available to you. In general, though, the more time between finishing the draft and starting to revise, the better.

FIGURE 7.1
Process Diagram: Revising Paragraphs

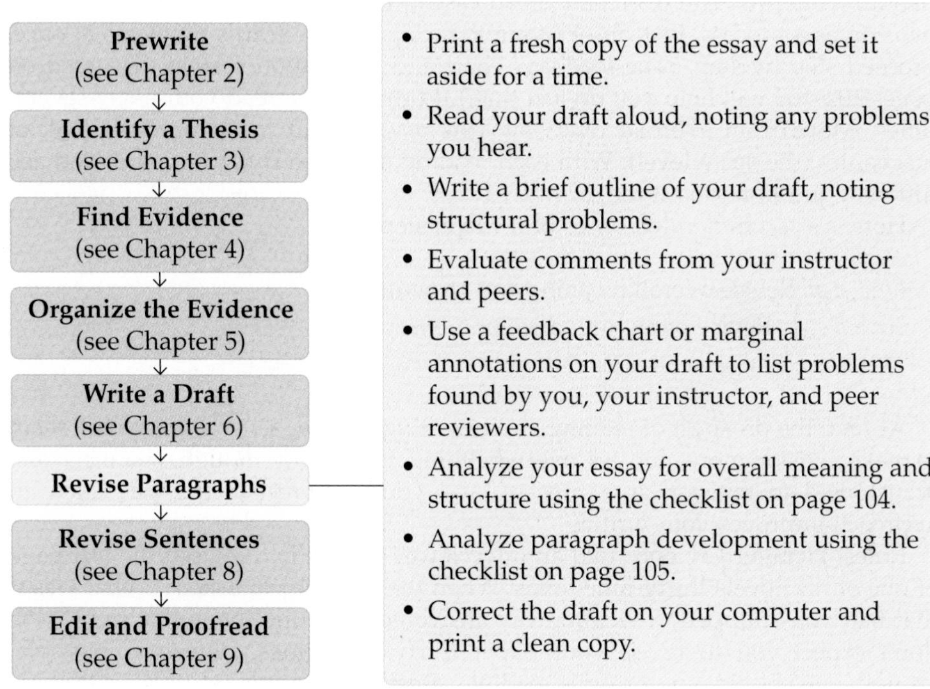

Work from Printed Text

Working with an essay in impersonal printed form, instead of in your own familiar handwriting, helps you see the paper impartially, as if someone else had written it. Each time you make major changes, try to retype your essay so that you can see it anew. Using a word processor makes it easy to prepare successive copies. If, however, you work from handwritten drafts, don't boldly strike out or erase as you revise. Instead, lightly cross out material, in case you want to retrieve it later on.

Read the Draft Aloud

Hearing how your writing sounds helps you pick up problems that might otherwise go undetected: places where sentences are awkward, meaning is ambiguous, words are imprecise. Even better, have another person read your draft aloud to you. The thought of this probably makes you shudder, but it's worth the risk. Someone else doesn't have—as you do—a vested interest in making your writing sound good. If a reader slows to a crawl over a murky paragraph or trips over a convoluted sentence, you know where you have to do some rewriting.

View Revision as a Series of Steps

Like many students, you may find the prospect of revising your draft to be a daunting one. You can overcome a bad case of revision jitters simply by viewing revision as a process. Instead of trying to tackle all of a draft's problems at once, proceed step by step. (The feedback chart and annotation system discussed on pages 102–103 will help you do just that.) If time allows, read your essay several times. Move from a broad overview (the *macro* level) to an up-close look at mechanics (the *micro* level). With each reading, focus on different issues and ask different questions about the draft.

Here is a recommended series of revision steps:

First step: Revise overall meaning and structure.

Second step: Revise paragraph development.

Third step: Revise sentences and words.

At first, the prospect of reading and rewriting a paper several times may seem to make revision more, not less, overwhelming. Eventually, though, you'll become accustomed to revision as a process, and you'll appreciate the way such an approach improves your writing.

Ernest Hemingway once told an interviewer that he had revised the last page of one of his novels thirty-nine times. When the interviewer asked, "What was it that had you stumped?", Hemingway answered, "Getting the words right." We don't expect you to revise your paper thirty-nine times. Whenever possible, though, you should aim for three readings. Resist the impulse to tinker with, say, an unclear sentence until you're sure the essay as a whole makes its point clearly. After all, it can be difficult to rephrase a muddy sentence until you have the essay's overall meaning well in hand.

Remember, though: There are no hard-and-fast rules about the revision steps. For one thing, there are bound to be occasions when you have time for, at best, only one quick pass over a draft. Moreover, as you gain experience revising, you'll probably streamline the process or shift the steps around. Assume, for example, that you get bogged down trying to recast the thesis so it more accurately reflects the draft's overall meaning (the first step). You might take a break by fastforwarding to the final stage and using the dictionary to check the spelling of several words. Or, while reorganizing a paragraph (the second step), you might realize you need to rephrase some sentences (the third step).

Evaluate and Respond to Instructor Feedback

Often, instructors collect and respond to students' first drafts. Like many students, you may be tempted to look only briefly at your instructor's comments. Perhaps you've "had it" with the essay and don't want to think about revising it to reflect the instructor's remarks. But taking your instructor's comments into account when revising is often what's needed to turn a shaky first draft into a strong final draft.

When an instructor returns a final draft graded, you may think that the grade is all that counts. Remember, though: Grades are important, but comments are even more so. They can help you *improve* your writing—if not in this paper, then in the next one. If you're reading or listening to your instructor's feedback, pay close attention and take notes. Then use a modified version of the feedback chart or a system of marginal annotations (see pages 102–103) to help you evaluate and react to the instructor's comments. If you don't understand or don't agree with the instructor's observations, you shouldn't hesitate to request a conference. Be sure to go to the conference prepared. You might, for example, put a check next to the instructor's comments you want to discuss. Your instructor will appreciate your thoughtful planning; getting together gives both you and the instructor a chance to clarify your respective points of view.

Peer Review: An Additional Revision Strategy

Many instructors include in-class or at-home peer review as a regular part of a composition course. Peer review—the critical reading of another person's writing with the intention of suggesting constructive changes—accomplishes several important goals. First, peer review helps you gain a more objective perspective on your work. When you write something, you're often too close to what you've prepared to evaluate it fairly; you may have trouble seeing where the writing is strong and where it needs to be strengthened. Peer review supplies the fresh, neutral perspective you need. Second, reviewing your classmates' work broadens your own composing options. You may be inspired to experiment with a technique you admired in a classmate's writing but wouldn't have thought of on your own. Finally, peer review trains you to be a better reader and critic of your *own* writing. When you get into the habit of critically reading other students' writing, you become more adept at critiquing your own.

The revision checklists on pages 104, 105, 124, and 134–135 of this book will help focus your revision—whether you're reworking your own paper or responding to a peer's. Your instructor may have you respond to all questions on the checklist or to several selected items. What follows is a peer review worksheet that Harriet Davids's instructor prepared to help students respond to first drafts based on the assignment on page 11. Wanting students to focus on four areas (thesis statement, support for thesis statement, overall organization, and signal devices), the instructor drew upon relevant sections from the revision checklists. With this customized worksheet in hand, Harriet's classmate Frank Tejada was able to give Harriet constructive feedback on her first draft (see page 100). (*Note:* Because Harriet didn't want to influence Frank's reaction, the draft she gave him didn't include her marginal notations to herself.)

As the peer review worksheet shows, Frank flagged several areas that Harriet herself also noted needed work. (Turn to pages 86–87 to see Harriet's marginal comments on her draft.) But he also commented on entirely new areas (for example, the sequence problem in paragraph 4), offering Harriet a fresh perspective on what she needed to do to polish her draft. To see which of Frank's suggestions

Peer Review Worksheet

Essay Author's Name: Harriet Davids Reviewer's Name: Frank Tejada

1. What is the essay's thesis? Is it explicit or implied? Does the thesis focus on a limited subject and express the writer's attitude toward that subject?

   Thesis: "Being a parent today is much more difficult [than it used to be]." The thesis is limited and expresses a clear attitude. But the sentence the thesis appears in (last sentence of para. 1) is too long because it also contains the plan of development. Maybe put thesis and plan of development in separate sentences.

2. What are the main points supporting the thesis? List the points. Is each supporting point developed sufficiently? If not, where is more support needed?

   (1) Parents have to control kids' distractions from school.
   (2) Parents have to help kids develop responsible sexual values despite sex being everywhere.
   (3) Parents have to protect kids from life-threatening dangers.

   The supporting points are good and are explained pretty well, except for a few places. The "Unfortunately" sentence in para. 2 is irrelevant. Also, in para. 2, you use the example of your girls, but never again. Either include them throughout or not at all. In para. 3, the final sentence about the government guidelines opens a whole new topic; maybe steer away from this. The items in para. 4 seem vague and need specific examples. In the conclusion, omit Holden Caulfield; since he was from an earlier generation, this example undermines your thesis about parenting today.

3. What overall format (chronological, spatial, emphatic, simple-to-complex) is used to sequence the essay's main points? Does this format work? Why or why not? What organizational format is used in each supporting paragraph? Does the format work? Why or why not?

   The paper's overall emphatic organization seems good. Emphatic order also works in para. 3, and spatial order works well in para. 2. But the sentences in para. 4 need rearranging. Right now, the examples are in mixed-up chronological order, making it hard to follow. Maybe you should reorder the examples from young kids to older kids.

4. What signal devices are used to connect ideas within and between paragraphs? Are there too few signal devices or too many? Where?

   The topic sentence of para. 3 needs to be a stronger bridging sentence. Also, too many "and's" in para. 3. Try "in addition" or "another" in some places. I like the "worst of all" transition to para. 4.

Harriet followed, take a look at her feedback chart on page 102, at her final draft on pages 144–145, and at the "Commentary" following the essay.

Becoming a Skilled Peer Reviewer

Even with the help of a checklist, preparing a helpful peer review is a skill that takes time to develop. At first, you, like many students, may be too easy or too critical. Effective peer review calls for rigor and care; you should give classmates the conscientious feedback that you hope for in return. Peer review also requires tact and kindness; feedback should always be constructive and include observations about what works well in a piece of writing. People have difficulty mustering the energy to revise if they feel there's nothing worth revising.

If your instructor doesn't include peer review, you can set up peer review sessions outside of class, with classmates getting together to respond to each other's drafts. Or you may select non-classmates who are objective (not a love-struck admirer or a doting grandparent) and skilled enough to provide useful commentary.

To focus your readers' comments, you may adapt the revision checklists that appear throughout this book, or you may develop your own questions. If you prepare the questions yourself, be sure to solicit *specific* observations about what does and doesn't work in your writing. If you simply ask, "How's this?" you may receive a vague comment like "It's not very effective." What you want are concrete observations and suggestions: "I'm confused because what you say in the fifth sentence contradicts what you say in the second." To promote such specific responses, ask your readers targeted (preferably written) questions like, "I'm having trouble moving from my second to my third point. How can I make the transition smoother?" Such questions require more than "yes" or "no" responses; they encourage readers to dig into your writing where you sense it needs work. (If it's feasible, encourage readers to *write* their responses to your questions.)

If you and your peer reviewer(s) can't meet in person, **e-mail** can provide a crucial means of contact. With a couple of clicks, you can simply send each other computer files of your work. Before you do so, determine whether your word-processing software is compatible; if so, you'll be able to send each other your computerized drafts as file attachments. If not, you can copy the text of your paper and paste it into the e-mail message box. (You'll likely lose the paper's format features, but the content is what matters most during peer review.) You and your reviewer(s) also need to decide exactly how to exchange comments about your drafts. You might conclude, for example, that you'll use MS Word's "Track Changes" feature or type your responses, perhaps in bold capitals, into the file itself. Or you might decide to print out the drafts and reply to the comments in writing, later exchanging the annotated drafts in person. No matter what you and your peer(s) decide, you'll probably find e-mail an invaluable tool in the writing process.

Evaluate and Respond to Peer Review

Accepting criticism isn't easy (even if you asked for it), and not all peer reviewers will be tactful. Even so, try to listen with an open mind to those giving you feedback. Take notes on their oral observations and/or have them fill out the checklist described above. Later, when you're ready to revise your paper, reread your notes. Which reviewer remarks seem valid? Which recommendations are workable? Which are not? In addition, try using a feedback chart or a system of marginal annotations to help you evaluate and remedy any perceived weaknesses in your draft.

Here's how to use a three-column **feedback chart.** In the first column, list the major problems you and your readers see in the draft. Next, rank the problems, designating the most critical as "1." Then in the second column, jot down possible solutions—your own as well as your readers'. Finally, in the third column, briefly describe what action you'll take to correct each problem. Here is the chart that Harriet Davids composed following Frank Tejada's review of her first draft (the draft appears on pages 86–87; the peer review worksheet appears on page 100):

Problems	Suggestions	Decisions
(1) Thesis is too long	Break into two sentences.	Break after "difficult" and add "than it was a generation ago."
(4) Irrelevant "Unfortunately" sentence in para. 2	Make sentence relevant or delete.	Delete sentence.
(3) Abandoned example of my girls after para. 2	Either include throughout or delete everywhere.	Omit references to my girls.
(2) In para. 3, final sentence opens new topic	Steer away from new topic.	Delete sentence.
(6) Vague items in para. 4	Give more specific examples.	Provide more specifics on violence against children and peer pressure.
(5) Sentences in para. 4 need rearranging	Reorder examples from young kids to older kids.	Begin with small kids, then older kids, then teens.
(7) Weak transitions in para. 3	Strengthen topic sentence; replace "and"s with other transitions.	Create stronger bridging sentence for para. 3. Substitute other transitions for "and"s.

Whether or not you decide to use a feedback chart, be sure to enter **marginal annotations** on your draft (preferably a clean copy of it) before revising it. In the margins, jot down any major problems, numbered in order of importance, along with possible remedies. Marking your paper this way, much as an instructor might, helps you view your paper as though it were written by someone else. (To see how such marginal annotations work, turn to page 106 or look at the sample first drafts of student essays in Chapters 10–18.) Then, keeping the draft's problems in mind, start revising.

If you've been working on a computer, type in your changes, or handwrite changes directly on the draft above the appropriate line. (Rework extensive sections on a separate sheet of paper.) When revising, always keep in mind that you may not agree with every reviewer suggestion. That's fine. It's *your* paper, and it's *your* decision to implement or reject the suggestions made by your peers.

The remainder of this chapter discusses the first and second steps in the revision process—revising overall meaning and structure and paragraph development. Chapter 8 focuses on the third step—revising sentences and words.

REVISING OVERALL MEANING AND STRUCTURE

During this first step in the revision process, you (and any readers you may have) should read the draft quickly to assess its *general effect* and *clarity.* Does the draft accomplish what you set out to do? Does it develop a central point clearly and logically? Does it merit and hold the reader's attention?

It's not uncommon when revising at this stage to find that the draft doesn't fully convey what you had in mind. Perhaps your intended thesis ends up being overshadowed by another idea. (If that happens, you have two options: (1) you may pursue the new line of thought as your revised thesis, or (2) you may bring the paper back into line with your original thesis by deleting extraneous material.) Another problem might be that readers miss a key point. Perhaps you initially believed the point could be implied, but you now realize it needs to be stated explicitly.

Preparing a *brief outline* of a draft can help evaluate the essay's overall structure. Either you or a reader can prepare the outline. In either case, your thesis, reflecting any changes made during the first draft, should be written at the top of the outline page. Then you or your readers jot down in brief outline form the paper's basic structure. With the draft pared down to its essentials, you can see more easily how parts contribute to the whole and how points do or do not fit together. This bare-bones rendering often reveals the changes needed to remedy any fuzziness or illogic in the development of the draft's central idea and key supporting points.

The following checklist is designed to help you and your readers evaluate a draft's overall meaning and structure. As with other checklists in the book, you may either use all the checklist questions or focus only on those especially relevant to a particular essay. (Activities at the end of the chapter will refer you to this checklist when you revise several essays.) To see how one student used the checklist when revising, turn to page 106.

REVISING OVERALL MEANING AND STRUCTURE: A CHECKLIST

- ☐ What is your initial reaction to the draft? What do you like and dislike?
- ☐ What audience does the essay address? How suited to this audience are the essay's purpose, tone, and point of view?
- ☐ What is the essay's thesis? Is it explicit or implied? Does it focus on a limited subject and express the writer's attitude toward that subject? If not, what changes need to be made?
- ☐ What are the points supporting the thesis? List them. If any stray from or contradict the thesis, what changes need to be made?
- ☐ According to which organizing principle(s)—spatial, chronological, emphatic, simple to complex—are the main points arranged? Does this organizational scheme reinforce the thesis? Why or why not?
- ☐ Which patterns of development (narration, description, comparison-contrast, and so on) are used in the essay? How do these patterns reinforce the thesis?
- ☐ Where would background information, definition of terms, or additional material clarify meaning?

You are now ready to focus on the second step in the revising process.

REVISING PARAGRAPH DEVELOPMENT

After you use feedback to refine the paper's fundamental meaning and structure, it's time to look closely at the essay's paragraphs. At this point, you and those giving you feedback should read the draft more slowly. How can the essay's paragraphs be made more unified (see pages 70–71) and more specific (pages 71–72)? Which paragraphs seem to lack sufficient support (pages 73–74)? Which would profit from more attention to coherence (pages 74–75)?

At this stage, you may find that a paragraph needs more examples to make its point or that a paragraph should be deleted because it doesn't develop the thesis. Or perhaps you realize that a paragraph should be placed earlier in the essay because it defines a term that readers need to understand from the outset.

Here's a strategy to help assess your paragraphs' effectiveness. In the margin next to each paragraph, make a brief notation that answers these two questions: (1) What is the paragraph's *purpose?* and (2) What is its *content?* Then skim the marginal notes to see if each paragraph does what you intended.

REVISING PARAGRAPH DEVELOPMENT: A CHECKLIST

- ☐ In what way does each supporting paragraph develop the essay's thesis? Which paragraphs fail to develop the thesis? Should they be deleted or revised?
- ☐ What is each paragraph's central idea? If this idea is expressed in a topic sentence, where is this sentence located? Where does something stray from or contradict the paragraph's main idea? How could the paragraph's focus be sharpened?
- ☐ Where in each paragraph does support seem irrelevant, vague, insufficient, inaccurate, nonrepresentative, or disorganized? What could be done to remedy these problems? Where would additional sensory details, examples, facts, statistics, expert authority, and personal observations be appropriate?
- ☐ By which organizational principle (spatial, chronological, or emphatic) are each paragraph's ideas arranged? Does this format reinforce the paragraph's main point? Why or why not?
- ☐ How could paragraph coherence be strengthened? Which signal devices are used to connect ideas within and between paragraphs? Where are there too few signals or too many?
- ☐ Where do too many paragraphs of the same length dull interest? Where would a short or a long paragraph be more effective?
- ☐ How could the introduction be strengthened? Which striking anecdote, fact, or statistic elsewhere in the essay might be moved to the introduction? How does the introduction establish the essay's purpose, audience, tone, and point of view? Which strategy links the introduction to the essay's body?
- ☐ How could the conclusion be strengthened? Which striking anecdote, fact, or statistic elsewhere in the essay might be moved to the conclusion? Would echoing something from the introduction help round off the essay more effectively? How has the conclusion been made an integral part of the essay?

During this stage, you should also examine the *length of your paragraphs.* Here's why.

You know how boring it can be to travel long stretches of unvarying highway. Without interesting twists and turns, sweeping views, and occasional rest stops, you struggle to stay awake. The same is true in writing. Paragraphs all the same length dull your readers' response, while variations encourage them to sit up and take notice. (We imagine, for example, that the two-sentence paragraph above got your attention.)

If your paragraphs tend to run long, try breaking some of them into shorter, crisper chunks. Be sure, however, not to break paragraphs just anywhere. To preserve the paragraphs' logic, you may need to reshape and add material, always keeping in mind that each paragraph should have a clear and distinctive focus.

However, don't go overboard and break up all your paragraphs. Too many short paragraphs become as predictable as too many long ones. An abundance of brief paragraphs also makes it difficult for readers to see how points are related. (In such cases, you might combine short paragraphs containing similar ideas.) Furthermore, overreliance on short paragraphs may mean that you haven't provided sufficient evidence for your ideas. Finally, a succession of short paragraphs (as in a newspaper article) encourages readers to skim when, of course, you want them to consider carefully what you have to say. So use short paragraphs, but save them for places in the essay where you want to introduce variation or achieve emphasis.

The checklist on page 105 is designed to help you and your readers evaluate a draft's paragraph development. (Activities at the end of the chapter will refer you to the checklist when you revise several essays.) To see how a student used the checklist when revising, see below.

SAMPLE STUDENT REVISION OF OVERALL MEANING, STRUCTURE, AND PARAGRAPH DEVELOPMENT

The introduction to Harriet Davids's first draft that we saw in Chapter 6 (pages 86–87) is reprinted here with Harriet's revisions. In the margin, numbered in order of importance, are the problems with the introduction's meaning, structure, and paragraph development—as noted by Harriet's peer reviewer, Frank, and other classmates. (The group used the checklists on pages 104 and 105 to focus their critique.) The above-line changes show Harriet's first efforts to eliminate these problems through revision.

② Take out personal reference

In the '50s and '60s, parents had it easy. TV comedies of that period show the
~~Raising children used to be much simpler in the 50s and 60s. I~~

③ Give specific TV shows

Cleavers scolding Beaver about his dirty hands
~~remember TV images from that era showing that parenting involved~~

and the Nelsons telling Ricky to clean his room.
~~simply teaching kids to clean their rooms, do their homework,~~

① Thesis too long. Make plan of development separate sentence.

~~and~~ __________. ~~But~~ ~~b~~B eing a parent today is much more difficult.

~~because~~ ~~n~~N owadays parents ~~have to shield/~~ must protect ~~kids~~ their children from ~~lots of~~ many

things ~~like~~ —from a growing number of distractions ~~from schoolwork~~, from sexual ly explicit material, and

from dangerous situations.

(If you'd like to see Harriet's final draft, turn to page 144.)

Continues on page 135

There's no doubt about it: As Harriet's reworked introduction shows, revision is challenging. But once you learn how to approach it step by step, you'll have the pleasure of seeing a draft become sharper and more focused. The rather global work you do early in the revision process puts you in a good position to concentrate on sentences and words—our focus in the following chapter.

ACTIVITIES: REVISING OVERALL MEANING, STRUCTURE, AND PARAGRAPH DEVELOPMENT

An important note: When revising essay drafts in activities 1–3, don't worry too much about sentence structure and word choice. However, do save your revisions so you can focus on these matters after you read the next chapter.

1. Look at the marginal notes and above-line changes that Harriet Davids added to her first draft introduction on page 106. Now look at the draft's other paragraphs on pages 86–87 and identify problems in overall meaning, structure, and paragraph development. Working alone or in a group, start by asking questions like these: "Where does the essay stray from the thesis?" and "Where does a paragraph fail to present points in the most logical and compelling order?" (The critique you prepared for activity 9 in Chapter 6 should help.) For further guidance, refer to the checklists on pages 104 and 105. Summarize and rank the perceived problems in marginal annotations or on a feedback chart. Then type your changes or handwrite them between the lines of the draft (work on a newly typed copy, a photocopy, or the textbook pages themselves). Don't forget to save your revision.

2. Retrieve the draft you prepared in response to activity 12 in Chapter 6 (page 94). Outline the draft. Does your outline reveal any problems in the draft's overall meaning and structure? If it does, make whatever changes are needed. The checklists on pages 104 and 105 will help focus your revising efforts. (Save your revised draft so you can work with it further after reading the next chapter.)

3. Following is the first draft of an essay advocating a longer elementary school day. Read it closely. Are tone and point of view consistent throughout? Is the thesis clear? Is the support in each body paragraph relevant, specific, and adequate? Are ideas arranged in the most effective order? Working alone or in a group, use the checklists on pages 104 and 105 to identify problems with the draft's overall meaning, structure, and paragraph development. Summarize and rank the perceived problems on a feedback chart or in marginal annotations. Then revise the draft by typing a new version or by entering your changes by hand (on a photocopy of the draft, a typed copy, or the textbook pages themselves). Don't forget to save your revision.

The Extended School Day

Imagine a seven-year-old whose parents work until five each night. When she arrives home after school, she is on her own. She's a good girl, but still a lot of things could happen. She could get into trouble just by being curious. Or something could happen through no fault of her own. All over the country, there are many "latchkey" children like this little girl. Some way must be found to deal with the problem. One suggestion is to keep elementary schools open longer than they now are. There are many advantages to this idea.

Parents wouldn't have to be in a state of uneasiness about whether their child is safe and happy at home. They wouldn't get uptight about whether their child's needs are being met. They also wouldn't have to feel guilty because they are not able to help a child with homework. The longer day would make it possible for the teacher to provide such help. Extended school hours would also relieve families of the financial burden of hiring a home sitter. As my family learned, having a sitter can wipe out the budget. And having a sitter doesn't necessarily eliminate all problems. Parents still have the hassle of worrying whether the person will show up and be reliable.

It's a fact of life that many children dislike school, which is a sad commentary on the state of education in this country. Even so, the longer school day would benefit children as well. Obviously, the dangers of their being home alone after school would disappear because by the time the bus dropped them off after the longer school day, at least one parent would be home. The unnameable horrors feared by parents would not have a chance to happen. Instead, the children would be in school, under trained supervision. There, they would have a chance to work on subjects that give them trouble. In contrast, when my younger brother had difficulty with subtraction in second grade, he had to struggle along because there wasn't enough time to give him the help he needed. The longer day would also give children a chance to participate in extracurricular activities. They could join a science club, play on a softball team, sing in a school chorus, take an art class. Because school districts are trying to save money, they often cut back on such extracurricular activities. They don't realize how important such experiences are.

Finally, the longer school day would also benefit teachers. Having more hours in each day would relieve them of a lot of pressure. This longer workday would obviously require schools to increase teachers' pay. The added salary would be an incentive for teachers to stay in the profession.

Implementing an extended school day would be expensive, but I feel that many communities would willingly finance its costs because it provides benefits to parents, children, and even teachers. Young children, home alone, wondering whether to watch another TV show or to wander outside to see what's happening, need this longer school day now.

4. Look closely at your instructor's comments on an ungraded draft of one of your essays. Using a feedback chart, summarize and evaluate your instructor's comments. That done, rework the essay. Type your new version, or make your changes by hand. In either case, save the revision so you can work with it further after reading the next chapter.

5. Return to the draft you wrote in response to activity 10 or activity 11 in Chapter 6 (page 93). To identify any problems, meet with several people and request that one of them read the draft aloud. Then ask your listeners focused questions about the areas you sense need work. Alternatively, you may use the checklists on pages 104 and 105 to focus the group's feedback. In either case, summarize and rank the comments on a feedback chart or in marginal annotations. Then, using the comments as a guide, revise the draft. Either type a new version or do your revising by hand. (Save your revision so you can work with it further after reading the next chapter.)

For additional writing, reading, and research resources, go to **www.mycomplab.com** and choose **Nadell/Langan/Comodromos'** ***The Longman Writer,*** **7/e**.

Revising Sentences and Words

CLOSE TO HOME © 1994 John McPherson. Reprinted with permission of UNIVERSAL PRESS SYNDICATE. All rights reserved.

Revising Sentences

Having refined your essay's overall meaning, structure, and paragraph development, you can concentrate on sharpening individual sentences. Although polishing sentences inevitably involves decisions about individual words, for now focus on each sentence as a whole; you can evaluate individual words later (see Figure 8.1). At this point, work to make your sentences:

- Consistent with your intended tone
- Economical
- Varied in type
- Varied in length
- Emphatic

Make Sentences Consistent with Your Tone

In Chapter 2, we saw how integral **tone** is to meaning (pages 21–22). As you revise, be sure each sentence's **content** (its images and ideas) and **style** (its structure and length) reinforce your intended tone: Both *what* you say and *how* you say it should support the essay's overall mood.

FIGURE 8.1
Process Diagram: Revising Sentences

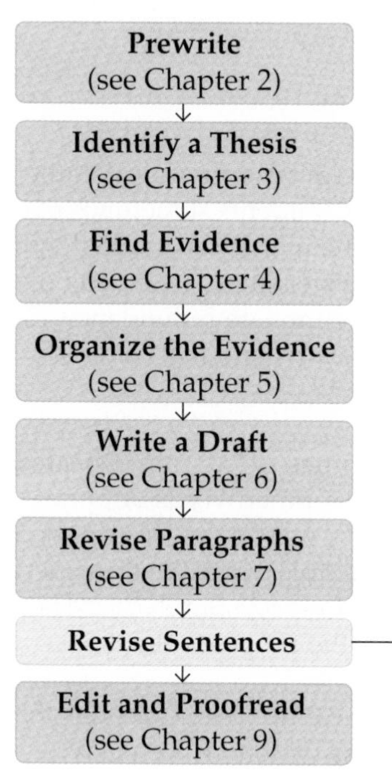

- Review your draft for sentence-level problems.
  - Make sure your tone is consistent.
  - Eliminate redundancies and empty phrases.
  - Vary sentence type—simple, compound, complex, and compound–complex—and length.
  - Make sentences emphatic.
- Review your draft for word-level problems.
  - Use the right level of diction: formal popular, or informal.
  - Watch out for jargon, doublespeak, and euphemism.
  - Use words that are specific and have appropriate connotations.
  - Use strong verbs and avoid unnecessary adverbs.
  - Use effective figures of speech.
  - Avoid sexist vocabulary and pronouns.

Consider the following excerpt from a piece by *Philadelphia Inquirer* columnist Melissa Dribben. Responding to the ongoing debate over gun control, Dribben supports legislation sought by the mayor of Philadelphia to limit handgun purchases to one per person per month. She writes:

> There are people who buy a new toothbrush every month. A new vacuum-cleaner bag. A fresh box of baking soda. A pair of $5 sunglasses. This you understand. You can never have too many.
>
> But when you reach the point where you have a stash of 38-caliber pistols bigger than your supply of clean underwear, you have a problem. And it isn't a shopping addiction.

Dribben's tone here is biting and sarcastic, her attitude exasperated and mocking. She establishes this tone partly through sentence content (what she says). For example, to her it is outrageous that people would want to buy guns more frequently than they purchase basic household and personal necessities. Dribben's style (how she says it) also contributes to her overall tone. The three fragments in the first paragraph convey an attitude of angry disbelief. These fragments, followed by two brief but complete sentences, build to the longer, climactic sentence at the beginning of the second paragraph. That sentence, especially when combined with the crisp last sentence, delivers a final, quick jab to those opposed to the proposed legislation. In short, content and style help express Dribben's impassioned attitude toward her subject.

Make Sentences Economical

Besides reinforcing your tone, your sentences should be **economical** rather than wordy. Use as few, not as many, words as possible. Students sometimes pad their writing because they think the longer a paper is, the higher the grade it will receive. Most instructors, though, are skilled at spotting wordiness intended only to fill pages. Your sentences won't be wordy if you (1) eliminate redundancy, (2) delete weak phrases, and (3) remove unnecessary *who, which,* and *that* clauses.

Eliminate Redundancy

Redundancy means unnecessary repetition. Sometimes words are repeated exactly; sometimes they are repeated by way of *synonyms,* other words or phrases that mean the same thing. When writing is redundant, words can be trimmed away without sacrificing meaning or effect. Why, for example, write "In the expert opinion of one expert" and needlessly repeat the word *expert?* Similarly, "They found it difficult to get consensus or agreement about the proposal" contains an unnecessary synonym (*agreement*) for *consensus.*

Redundancy isn't the same as repetition for dramatic emphasis. Consider the following excerpt from an address to the United Nations by John F. Kennedy:

> Unconditional war can no longer lead to unconditional victory. It can no longer serve to settle disputes. It can no longer be of concern to great powers alone. . . .

Here the repetition of *unconditional* and *can no longer* drives home the urgency of Kennedy's message. Repetition used, in this way, to underscore the relationship among sentences or ideas is called *parallelism.* (For more on parallelism, see pages 121–122.)

When not used as a stylistic device, however, repetition weakens prose. Take a look at the sentence pairs below. Note how the revised versions are clearer and stronger because the redundancy in the original sentences (italicized) has been eliminated:

Original While under the *influence* of alcohol, many people insist they are not under the *influence* and *swear* they are sober.

Revised While under the influence of alcohol, many people insist they are sober.

Original *They designed a computer program* that increased sales by 50 percent. The *computer program they designed* showed how the TRS-80 can be *used* and *implemented* in small *businesses* and *firms.*

Revised Their program, which showed how the TRS-80 computer can be used in small businesses, increased sales by 50 percent.

Delete Weak Phrases

In addition to eliminating redundancy, you can make sentences more economical by **deleting the three types of weak phrases** described here.

1. **Empty Phrases.** In speaking, we frequently use empty phrases that give us time to think but don't add to our message, expressions such as "Okay?" and "You know what I mean?" In writing, though, we have the chance to eliminate such deadwood. Here are some common culprits—expressions that are needlessly awkward and wordy—along with their one-word alternatives:

Wordy Expressions	Revised
due to the fact that	because
in light of the fact that	since
regardless of the fact that	although
in the event that	if
in many cases	often
in that period	then
at the present time	now
at this point in time	now
in the not-too-distant future	soon
for the purpose of	to
has the ability to	can
be aware of the fact that	know
is necessary that	must

Notice the improvement in the following sentences when wordy, often awkward phrases are replaced with one-word substitutes:

Original *It is necessary that* the government outlaw the production of carcinogenic pesticides.
Revised The government *must* outlaw the production of carcinogenic pesticides.

Original Student leaders were upset by *the fact that* no one in the administration consulted them.
Revised Student leaders were upset *because* no one in the administration consulted them.

Some phrases don't even call for concise substitutes. Because they add nothing at all to a sentence's meaning, they can simply be deleted. Here are some examples: "shy *type of* child," "*kind of* person," "*field of* communications," "small *in size*." The revised sentence that follows has exactly the same meaning as the original, but the meaning is expressed without the empty phrase *in color:*

Original The hybrid azaleas were light blue *in color.*
Revised The hybrid azaleas were light blue.

Other times, to avoid an empty phrase, you may need to recast a sentence slightly:

Original The midterm assessment is *for the purpose of letting* students know if they are failing a course.
Revised The midterm assessment *lets* students know if they are failing a course.

2. **Roundabout Openings with *There, It,* and Question Words Like *How* and *What.*** At the beginning of a sentence, you're formulating a new thought, so you may grope around a bit before pinning down what you want to say. For this reason, the openings of sentences are especially vulnerable to unnecessary phrases. Common culprits include phrases beginning with *There* and *It* (when *It* does not refer to a specific noun), and words like *How* and *What* (when they don't actually ask a question). In the following examples, note that trimming away excess words highlights the subject and verb, thus clarifying meaning:

Original It was their belief that the problem had been solved.
Revised They believed the problem had been solved.

Original There are now computer courses offered by many high schools.
Revised Many high schools now offer computer courses.

Original What should be done in this crisis is to transport food to the victims' homes.
Revised Food must be transported to the victims' homes.

Original How to simplify the college's registration process should be a priority.
Revised Simplifying the college's registration process should be a priority.

Of course, feel free to open with *There* or *It* when some other construction would be less clear or effective. For example, don't write "Many reasons can be cited why students avoid art courses" when you can say "There are many reasons why students avoid art courses."

3. **Excessive Prepositional Phrases.** Strings of prepositional phrases (word groups beginning with *at, on,* and the like) tend to make writing choppy; they weigh sentences down and hide main ideas. Note how much smoother and clearer sentences become when prepositional phrases (italicized in the following examples) are eliminated:

Original Growth *in the greenhouse effect* may result *in increases in the intensity of hurricanes.*
Revised The growing greenhouse effect may intensify hurricanes.

Original The reassurance *of a neighbor* who was the owner *of a pit bull* that his dog was incapable *of harm* would not be sufficient to prevent most parents *from calling* the authorities if the dog ran loose.
Revised Despite a neighbor's reassurance that his pit bull was harmless, most parents would call the authorities if the dog ran loose.

These examples show that prepositional phrases can sometimes be eliminated by substituting one strong verb (*intensify*) or by using the possessive form (*neighbor's reassurance, his pit bull*) rather than an *of* phrase.

Remove Unnecessary *Who, Which,* and *That* Clauses

Often *who, which,* or *that* clauses can be removed with no loss of meaning. Consider the tightening possible in these sentences:

Original The townsfolk misunderstood the main point *that the developer made.*
Revised The townsfolk misunderstood *the developer's main point.*

Original The employees *who protested* the restrictions went on strike, *which was a real surprise to management.*
Revised The employees *protesting* the restrictions *surprised management* by going on strike.

Vary Sentence Type

Another way to invigorate writing is to **vary sentence type.** Since the predictable soon becomes dull, try to offer a mixture of simple, compound, complex, and compound-complex sentences.

Simple Sentences

A **clause** is a group of words with both a subject and a verb. Clauses can be **independent** (able to stand alone) or **dependent** (unable to stand alone). A **simple sentence** consists of a single independent clause (whose subject and verb are italicized here):

The *president serves* four years.
Marie Curie investigated radioactivity and *died* from its effects.
Unlike most mammals, *birds* and *fish see* color.

Notice that a simple sentence can have more than one verb (sentence 2) or more than one subject (sentence 3). In addition, any number of modifying phrases (such as *Unlike most mammals*) can extend the sentence's length and add information. What distinguishes a simple sentence is its single *subject-verb combination.*

Simple sentences can convey dramatic urgency:

Suddenly we heard the screech of brakes. Across the street, a small boy lay sprawled in front of a car. We started to run toward the child. Seeing us, the driver sped away.

Simple sentences are also excellent for singling out a climactic point: "They found the solution." In a series, however, they soon lose their impact and become boring. Also, because simple sentences highlight one idea at a time, they don't clarify the relationships among ideas. Consider these two versions of a passage:

Original

> Many first-year college students are apprehensive. They won't admit it to themselves. They hesitate to confide in their friends. They never find out that everyone else is anxious, too. They are nervous about being disliked and feeling lonely. They fear not "knowing the ropes."

Revised

> Many first-year college students are apprehensive, but they won't admit it to themselves. Because they hesitate to confide in their friends, they never find out that everyone else is anxious, too. Being disliked, feeling lonely, not "knowing the ropes"—these are what beginning college students fear.

In addition to sounding repetitive and childish, the simple sentences in the original version fragment the passage into a series of disconnected ideas. In contrast, the revised version includes a variety of sentence types and patterns, all of which are discussed on the pages ahead. This variety clarifies the relationships among ideas, so that the passage reads more easily.

Compound Sentences

Compound sentences consist of two or more independent clauses. There are four types of compound sentences. The most basic type consists of two simple sentences joined by a *coordinating conjunction* (*and, but, for, nor, or, so,* or *yet*). Here's an example:

> Chimpanzees and gorillas can learn sign language, *and* they have been seen teaching this language to others.

Another type of compound sentence has a semicolon (;), rather than a comma and coordinating conjunction, between the two simple sentences:

> Yesterday, editorials attacked the plan; a week ago, they praised it.

A third type of compound sentence links two simple sentences with a semicolon plus a *conjunctive adverb* such as *however, moreover, nevertheless, therefore,* and *thus:*

> Every year billions of U.S. dollars go to researching AIDS; *however,* recent studies show that a large percentage of the money has been mismanaged.

A final type of compound sentence consists of two simple sentences connected by a *correlative conjunction,* a word pair such as *either . . . or, neither . . . nor,* or *not only . . . but also:*

> *Either* the litigants will win the lawsuit, *or* they will end up in debt from court costs.

Compound sentences help clarify the relationship between ideas. Similarities are signaled by such words as *and* and *moreover,* contrasts by *but* and *however,* cause-effect by *so* and *therefore.* When only a semicolon separates the two parts of a compound sentence, the relationship between those two parts is often a contrast. ("Yesterday, editorials attacked the plan; a week ago, they praised it.")

Complex Sentences

In a **complex sentence,** a dependent (subordinate) clause is joined to an independent clause. Sometimes the dependent clause (italicized in the following examples) is introduced by a subordinating conjunction such as *although, because, if, since,* or *when:*

> *Since they have relatively small circulations,* specialty magazines tend to be expensive.

> We knew there had been a power failure *because all the clocks in the building were two hours slow.*

Other dependent clauses are introduced by a relative pronoun such as *that, which,* or *who:*

> Several celebrities revealed *that they have been stalked by delusional fans.*

> Fame and wealth from his writings had little effect on author J. R. R. Tolkien, *who continued to teach until reaching retirement age.*

As you can see, the order of the dependent and independent clause isn't fixed. The dependent clause may come first, last, or even in the middle of the independent clause, as in this example:

> Nurses' uniforms, *although they are no longer the norm,* are still required by some hospitals.

Whether to use a comma between a dependent and an independent clause depends on a number of factors, including the location of the dependent clause and whether it's *restrictive* (essential for identifying the thing it modifies) or *nonrestrictive.*

Because a dependent clause is subordinate to an independent one, complex sentences can clarify the relationships among ideas. Consider the two paragraphs that follow. The first merely strings together a series of simple and compound sentences, all of them carrying roughly the same weight. In contrast, the complex sentences in the revised version use subordination to connect ideas and signal their relative importance.

Original

> Are you the "average American"? Then take heed. Here are the results of a time-management survey. You might want to budget your time differently. According to the survey, you spend six years of your life eating. Also, you're likely to spend two years trying to reach people by telephone, so you should convince your friends to get answering machines. Finally, you may be married and expect long conversations

with your spouse to occur spontaneously, but you'll have to make a special effort. Ordinarily, your discussions will average only four minutes a day.

Revised

If you're the "average American," take heed. After you hear the results of a time-management survey, you might want to budget your time differently. According to the survey, you spend six years of your life eating. Also, unless you convince your friends to get answering machines, you're likely to spend two years trying to reach them by telephone. Finally, if you're married, you shouldn't expect long conversations with your spouse to occur spontaneously. Unless you make a special effort, your discussions will average only four minutes a day.

If you find that the original paragraph resembles your writing more than the revised, don't despair. With experience, you'll develop a strong sense of how to connect and rank ideas through subordination. For now, just remember the following: Expressed as a dependent clause, an idea is relegated to a position of secondary importance; expressed as an independent clause, it's emphasized. So reserve for the independent clause the point you want to highlight.

The following sentences illustrate how meaning shifts depending on what is put in the main clause and what is subordinated:

Although most fraternities and sororities no longer have hazing, pledging is still a big event on many campuses.

Although pledging is still a big event on many campuses, most fraternities and sororities no longer have hazing.

In the first sentence, the focus is on *pledging;* in the second, it is on the *discontinuation of hazing.*

Compound-Complex Sentences

A **compound-complex sentence** connects one or more dependent clauses to two or more independent clauses. In the following example, the two independent clauses are underscored once and the two dependent clauses twice:

The Procrastinators' Club, which is based in Philadelphia, issues a small magazine, but it appears infrequently, only when members get around to writing it.

Go easy on the number of compound-complex sentences you use. Because they tend to be long, a string of them is likely to overwhelm the reader and cloud meaning.

Vary Sentence Length

You've probably noticed that simple sentences tend to be short, compound and complex sentences tend to be of medium length, and compound-complex sentences tend to be long. Generally, by varying sentence type, a writer automatically **varies sentence length** as well. However, sentence type doesn't always determine length. In this example, the simple sentence is longer than the complex one:

Simple Sentence

> Hot and thirsty, exhausted from the effort of carrying so many groceries, I desired nothing more than an ice-cold glass of lemonade.

Complex Sentence

> Because I was hot and thirsty, I craved lemonade.

The difference lies in the number of **modifiers**—words or groups of words used to describe another word or group of words. So, besides considering sentence type, check on sentence length when revising.

Short Sentences

Too many short sentences, like too many simple ones, can sound childish and create a choppy effect that muddies the relationship among ideas. Used wisely, though, a series of short sentences gives writing a staccato rhythm that carries more punch and conveys a faster pace than the same number of words gathered into longer sentences. As you read the two passages that follow, note how the first version's clipped rhythms are more effective for conveying a rush of terrifying events:

> Witches bring their faces close. Goblins glare with fiery eyes. Fiendish devils stealthily approach to claw a beloved stuffed bear. The toy recoils in horror. These are among the terrifying happenings in the world of children's nightmares.

> Witches bring their faces close as goblins glare, their eyes fiery. Approaching stealthily, fiendish devils come to claw a beloved stuffed bear that recoils in horror. These are among the terrifying happenings in the world of children's nightmares.

Brevity also highlights a sentence, especially when surrounding sentences are longer. Consider the dramatic effect of the final sentence in this paragraph:

> Starting in June, millions of Americans pour onto the highways, eager to begin vacation. At the same time, city, state, and federal agencies deploy hundreds, even thousands of workers to repair roads that have, until now, managed to escape bureaucratic attention. Chaos results.

The short sentence "Chaos results" stands out because it's so much shorter than the preceding sentences. The emphasis is appropriate because, in the writer's view, chaos is the dramatic consequence of prolonged bureaucratic inertia.

Long Sentences

Long sentences often convey a leisurely pace and establish a calm tone:

> As I look across the lake, I see the steady light of a campfire at the water's edge, the flames tinting to copper an aluminum rowboat tied to the dock, the boat glimmering in the darkness.

However, as with short sentences, don't overdo it. Too many long sentences can be hard to follow. And remember: A sentence stands out most when it differs in length from surrounding sentences. Glance back at the first paragraph on children's nightmares (page 119). The final long sentence stands in contrast to the preceding short ones. The resulting emphasis works because the final sentence is also the paragraph's topic sentence.

Make Sentences Emphatic

The previous section shows how sentence length affects meaning by highlighting some sentences in a paragraph but not others. Within a single sentence, you can use a number of techniques to make parts of the sentence stand out from the rest. To achieve such **emphasis,** you can: (1) place key ideas at the beginning or end, (2) set them in parallel constructions, (3) express them as fragments, or (4) express them in inverted word order.

Place Key Points at the Beginning or End

A sentence's start and close are its most prominent positions. So, keeping your overall meaning in mind, use those two spots to highlight key ideas.

Let's look first at the **beginning** position. Here are two versions of a sentence; the meanings differ because the openers differ.

> The potentially life-saving drug, developed by junior researchers at the medical school, will be available next month.

> Developed by junior researchers at the medical school, the potentially life-saving drug will be available next month.

In the first version, the emphasis is on the life-saving potential of a drug. Reordering the sentence shifts attention to those responsible for discovering the drug.

An even more emphatic position than a sentence's beginning is its **end.** Put at the close of a sentence whatever you want to emphasize:

> Kindergarten is wasted on the young—especially the co-ed naptime.

Now look at two versions of another sentence, each with a slightly different meaning because of what's at the end:

> Increasingly, overt racism is showing up in—of all places—popular song lyrics.

> Popular song lyrics are showing—of all things—increasingly overt racism.

In the first version, the emphasis is on lyrics; in the second, it's on racism.

Be sure, though, that whatever you place in the climactic position merits the emphasis. The following sentence is so anticlimactic that it's unintentionally humorous:

> The family, waiting anxiously for the results of the medical tests, sat.

Similarly, don't build toward a strong climax only to defuse it with some less important material:

> On the narrow parts of the trail, where jagged cliffs drop steeply from the path, keep your eyes straight ahead and don't look down, toward the town of Belmont in the east.

In the preceding sentence, "toward the town of Belmont in the east" should be deleted. The important point surely isn't Belmont's location but how to avoid an accident.

Use Parallelism

Parallelism occurs when ideas of comparable weight are expressed in the same grammatical form, thus underscoring their equality. Parallel elements may be words, phrases, clauses, or full sentences. Here are some examples:

Parallel Nouns

> We bought *pretzels, nachos,* and *candy bars* to feed our pre-exam jitters.

Parallel Adverbs

> *Smoothly, steadily, quietly,* the sails tipped toward the sun.

Parallel Verbs

> The guest lecturer *spoke* to the group, *showed* her slides, and then *invited* questions.

Parallel Adjective Phrases

> *Playful as a kitten* but *wise as a street Tom,* the old cat played with the string while keeping a watchful eye on his surroundings.

Parallel Prepositional Phrases

> Gloomy predictions came *from political analysts, from the candidate's staff,* and, surprisingly, *from the candidate herself.*

Parallel Dependent Clauses

> *Since our rivals were in top form, since their top player would soon come up to bat,* we knew that all was lost.

As you can see, the repetition of grammatical forms creates a pleasing symmetry that emphasizes the sequenced ideas. Parallel structure also conveys meaning economically. Look at the way the following sentences can be tightened using parallelism:

Nonparallel

> Studies show that most women today are different from those in the past. They want to have their own careers. They want to be successful. They also want to enjoy financial independence.

Parallel

> Studies show that most women today are different from those in the past. They want to have careers, be successful, and enjoy financial independence.

Parallel constructions are often signaled by word pairs (correlative conjunctions) such as *either . . . or, neither . . . nor,* and *not only . . . but also.* To maintain parallelism, the same grammatical form must follow each half of the word pair.

> *Either* professors are too rigorous, *or* they are too lax.
>
> The company is interested in *neither* financing the project *nor* helping locate other funding sources.
>
> When my roommate argues, she tends to be *not only* totally stubborn *but also* totally wrong.

Parallelism can create elegant and dramatic writing. Too much, though, seems artificial, so use it sparingly. Save it for your most important points.

Use Fragments

A **fragment** is part of a sentence punctuated as if it were a whole sentence—that is, with a period at the end. A sentence fragment consists of words, phrases, and/or dependent clauses, *without an independent clause.* Here are some examples:

> Resting quietly.
> Except for the trees.
> Because they admired her.
> A demanding boss who accepted no excuses.

Ordinarily, we advise students to stay clear of fragments. However, like most rules, this one may at times be broken—*if* you do so intentionally and skillfully. To be on the safe side, ask your composition instructor whether an occasional fragment—used as a stylistic device—will be considered acceptable. Here's an example showing the way fragments (underlined) can be used effectively for emphasis:

One of my aunt's eccentricities is her belief that only personally made gifts show the proper amount of love. Her gifts

```
are often strange. Hand-drawn calendars. Home-brewed
cologne that smells like jam. Crocheted washcloths. Frankly,
I'd rather receive a gift certificate from a department
store.
```

Notice how the three fragments focus attention on the aunt's charmingly off-beat gifts. Remember, though: When overused, fragments lose their effect, so draw on them sparingly.

Use Inverted Word Order

In most English sentences, the subject comes before the verb. When you use **inverted word order,** however, at least part of the verb comes before the subject. The resulting sentence is so atypical that it automatically stands out.

Inverted statements, like those that follow, are used to emphasize an idea:

Normal My Uncle Bill is a strange man.
Inverted A strange man is my Uncle Bill.

Normal Their lies about the test scores were especially brazen.
Inverted Especially brazen were their lies about the test scores.

Normal The age-old tree would never again bear fruit.
Inverted Never again would the age-old tree bear fruit.

A note of caution: Inverted statements should be used infrequently and with special care. Bizarre can they easily sound.

Another form of inversion, the question, also acts as emphasis. A question may be a genuine inquiry, one that focuses attention on the issue at hand, as in the following example:

> Since the 1960s, only about half of this country's eligible voters have gone to the polls during national elections. *Why are Americans so apathetic?* Let's look at some of the reasons.

Or a question may be *rhetorical;* that is, one that implies its own answer and encourages the reader to share the writer's view:

> Yesterday, there was yet another accident at the intersection of Fairview and Springdale. Given the disproportionately high number of collisions at that crossing, *can anyone question the need for a traffic light?*

The following checklist is designed to help you and your readers evaluate the sentences in a first draft. (Activities at the end of the chapter will refer you to this checklist when you revise several essays.) To see how one student, Harriet Davids, used the checklist when revising, turn to page 135.

REVISING SENTENCES: A CHECKLIST

- ☐ Which sentences seem inconsistent with the essay's intended tone? How could the problem be fixed?
- ☐ Which sentences could be more economical? Where could unnecessary repetition, empty phrases, and weak openings be eliminated? Which prepositional phrases could be deleted? Where are there unnecessary *who, which*, and *that* clauses?
- ☐ Where should sentence type be more varied? Where would subordination clarify the connections among ideas? Where would simpler sentences make the writing less inflated and easier to understand?
- ☐ Where does sentence length become monotonous and predictable? Which short sentences should be connected to enhance flow and convey a more leisurely pace? Which long sentences would be more effective if broken into crisp, short ones?
- ☐ Where would a different sentence pattern add variety? Better highlight key sentence elements? Seem more natural?
- ☐ Which sentences could be more emphatic? Which strategy would be most effective—expressing the main point at the beginning or end, using parallelism, or rewriting the sentence as a fragment, question, or inverted-word-order statement?

REVISING WORDS

After refining the sentences in your first draft, you're in a good position to look closely at individual words. (Refer back to Figure 8.1 on page 111.) During this stage, you should aim for:

- Words consistent with your intended tone
- An appropriate level of diction
- Words that neither overstate nor understate
- Words with appropriate connotations
- Specific rather than general words
- Strong verbs
- No unnecessary adverbs
- Original figures of speech
- Nonsexist language

Make Words Consistent with Your Tone

Like full sentences, individual words and phrases should also reinforce your intended tone. Reread the Melissa Dribben excerpt on gun control (see page 111). Earlier we discussed how sentence structure and length contribute to the excerpt's biting tone. Word choice also plays an important role. The word *stash* mocks the impulse to hoard guns as if they were essential but depletable goods—like clean underwear. And the specific phrase *.38-caliber pistols* evokes the image of a weapon with frightening lethal power. Such word choices reinforce the overall tone Dribben wants to convey.

Use an Appropriate Level of Diction

Diction refers to the words a writer selects. Those words should be appropriate for the writer's purpose, audience, point of view, and tone. If, for example, you are writing a straightforward, serious piece about on-the-job incompetence, you would be better off saying that people "don't concentrate on their work" and they "make frequent errors," rather than saying they "screw up" or "goof off."

There are three broad levels of diction: *formal, popular,* and *informal.* To describe feelings of pervasive sadness, clinical psychologists might use the highly formal term *dysthymia,* while the popular term for such emotions is *depression.* At the other end of the continuum, someone might use the informal phrase *down in the dumps.* Within each level of diction, there are degrees of formality and informality: *Down in the dumps* and *bummed out* are both informal, but *bummed out* is the slangier expression.

Formal Diction

Impersonal and distant in tone, **formal diction** is the type of language found in scholarly journals. Contractions are rare; long, specialized, technical words are common. Unfortunately, many people mistakenly equate word length with education: The longer the words, they think, the more impressed readers will be. So rather than using the familiar and natural words *improve* and *think,* they thumb through a thesaurus (literally or figuratively) for such fancy-sounding alternatives as *ameliorate* and *conceptualize.* They write, "That is the optimum consequence we have the expectation of attaining" rather than "That is the best result we can expect." Remember: It's a word's ability to convey meaning clearly that counts, not its number of syllables.

Similarly, when writing for a general audience, don't show off specialized knowledge by throwing in **jargon,** insiders' terms from a particular area of expertise (say, a term like *authorial omniscience* from literary theory). Such "shoptalk" should be used only when less specialized words would lack the necessary precision. If readers are apt to be unfamiliar with a term, provide a definition.

Some degree of formality is appropriate—when, for example, you write up survey results for a sociology class. In such a case, your instructor may expect you to avoid the pronoun *I* (see page 22). Other instructors may think it's pretentious for a student to refer to himself or herself in the third person ("The writer observed that . . ."). These instructors may be equally put off by the artificiality of the passive voice (pages 129–130): "It was observed that . . . " To be safe, find out what your instructors expect. If possible, use *I* when you mean "I." Your writing will be no less objective—unless using *I* tempts you to include highly personal remarks and opinions. Even in more formal situations, resist the temptation to dazzle readers by piling up multisyllable words. (For more on avoiding pretentious language, see below.)

Popular Diction

Popular, or **mainstream, diction** is found in most magazines, newspapers, books, and texts (including this one). In such prose, the writer may use the first person and address the reader as "you." Contractions appear frequently; specialized vocabulary is kept to a minimum.

You should aim for popular diction in most of the writing you do—in and out of college. Also keep in mind that an abrupt downshift to slang (*freaked out* instead of *lost control*) or a sudden turn to highly formal language (*myocardial infarction* instead of *heart attack*) will disconcert readers and undermine your credibility.

Informal Diction

Informal diction, which conveys a sense of everyday speech, is friendly and casual. First-person and second-person pronouns are common, as are contractions and fragments. Colloquial expressions (*rub the wrong way*) and slang (*you wimp*) are used freely. Informal diction isn't appropriate for academic papers, except where it is used to indicate *someone else's* speech.

Avoid Words That Overstate or Understate

When revising, be on the lookout for **doublespeak,** language that deliberately overstates or understates reality. Here's an example of each.

In their correspondence, Public Works Departments often refer to "ground-mounted confirmatory route markers"—a grandiose way of saying "road signs." Other organizations go to the other extreme and use **euphemisms,** words that minimize something's genuine gravity or importance. Hospital officials, for instance, sometimes call deaths resulting from staff negligence "unanticipated therapeutic misadventures." When revising, check that you haven't used words that exaggerate or downplay something's significance.

Select Words with Appropriate Connotations

Mark Twain once said, "The difference between the right word and the almost right word is the difference between lightning and the lightning bug." Even two words listed as synonyms in a dictionary or thesaurus can differ in meaning in important ways.

The dictionary meaning of a word is its **denotation.** The word *motorcycle,* for example, is defined as "a two- or three-wheeled vehicle propelled by an internal-combustion engine that resembles a bicycle, but is usually larger and heavier, and often has two saddles." Yet how many of us think of a motorcycle in these terms? Certainly, there is more to a word than its denotation. A word also comes surrounded by **connotations**—associated sensations, emotions, images, and ideas. For some, the word *motorcycle* probably calls to mind danger and noise. For motorcyclists themselves, the word most likely summons pleasant memories of high-speed movement through the open air.

Given the wide range of responses that any one word can elicit, you need to be sensitive to each word's shades of meaning so you can judge when to use it rather than some other word. Examine the following word series to get a better feel for the subtle but often critical differences between similar words:

contribution, donation, handout
quiet, reserved, closemouthed
everyday, common, trite
follower, disciple, groupie

Notice the extent to which words' connotations create different impressions in these two examples:

> The young woman emerged from the interview, her face *aglow.* Moving *briskly* to the coat rack, she *tossed* her raincoat over one arm. After a *carefree* "Thank you" to the receptionist, she *glided* from the room.

> The young woman emerged from the interview, her face *aflame.* Moving *hurriedly* to the coat rack, she *flung* her raincoat over one arm. After a *perfunctory* "Thank you" to the receptionist, she *bolted* from the room.

In the first paragraph, the words *aglow, carefree,* and *glided* have positive connotations, so the reader surmises that the interview was a success. In contrast, the second paragraph contains words loaded with negative connotations: *aflame, perfunctory,* and *bolted.* Reading this paragraph, the reader assumes something went awry.

A thesaurus can help you select words with the right connotations. Just look up any word with which you aren't satisfied, and you'll find a list of synonyms. To be safe, stay away from unfamiliar words. Otherwise, you stand a good chance of using a word incorrectly and creating a howler. Several years ago, one of our students wrote in an essay, "I wanted to *bequeath* the party by midnight." What he meant was that he wanted to "*leave* the party by midnight." He had, though, already used the word *leave* several times, so, looking for a synonym, he turned to the thesaurus, where he came across the word *bequeath.* But writing "I wanted to *bequeath* the party by midnight" doesn't work because *bequeath* means to leave property or goods by means of a will. Our advice? Choose only those words whose nuances you understand.

Use Specific Rather Than General Words

Besides carrying the right connotations, words should be **specific** rather than general. That is, they must avoid vagueness and ambiguity by referring to *particular* people, animals, events, objects, and phenomena. If they don't, readers may misinterpret what you mean.

Assume you're writing an essay about the demise of neighborhood movie houses. If, at one point, you refer to the "theaters' poor facilities," readers may imagine you're referring to faulty sound quality and projection. If you mean the theaters' messy physical surroundings, you need specific language to send the right message: wads of gum stuck under the seats, crushed popcorn tubs everywhere, a sticky film coating the floor. Precise words like these eliminate confusion.

Besides clarifying meaning, specific words enliven writing and make it more convincing. Compare these two paragraphs:

Original

> Sponsored by a charitable organization, a group of children from a nearby town visited a theme park. The kids had a great time. They went on several rides and ate a variety of foods. Reporters and a TV crew shared in the fun.

Revised

> Sponsored by the United Glendale Charities, twenty-five underprivileged Glendale grade-schoolers visited the Universe of Fun Themepark. The kids had a great time. They roller-coastered through a meteor shower on the Space Probe, encountered a giant squid on the Submarine Voyage, and screamed their way past coffins and ghosts in the House of Horrors. At the International Cuisine arcade, they sampled foods ranging from Hawaiian poi to German strudel. Reporters from *The Texas Herald* and a camera crew from WGLD, the Glendale cable station, shared in the fun.

You may have noticed that the specific words in the second paragraph provide answers to "which," "how," and similar questions. In contrast, when reading the first paragraph, you probably wondered, "*Which* charitable organization? *Which* theme park? *Which* rides?" Similarly, you may have asked, "*How* large a group? *How* young were the kids?" Specific language also answers "In what way?" The revised paragraph details *in what way* the children "had a great time." They didn't just eat "a variety of foods." Rather, they "sampled foods ranging from Hawaiian poi to German strudel." So, when you revise, check to make sure that your wording doesn't leave unanswered questions like "How?", "Why?", and "In what way?" (For more on making writing specific, see pages 49 and 71–73.)

Use Strong Verbs

Because a verb is the source of action in a sentence, it carries more weight than any other element. Replacing weak verbs and nouns with **strong verbs** is, then, another way to tighten and energize language. Consider the following strategies.

Replace *To Be* and Linking Verbs with Action Verbs

Overreliance on *to be* verbs (*is, were, has been,* and so on) tends to stretch sentences, making them flat and wordy. The same is true of motionless **linking verbs** such as *appear, become, sound, feel, look,* and *seem.* Since these verbs don't communicate any action, more words are required to complete their meaning and explain what is happening. Even *to be* verb forms combined with present participles (*is laughing, were running*) are weaker than bare **action verbs** (*laughs, ran*). Similarly, linking verbs combined with adjectives (*becomes shiny, seemed offensive*) aren't as vigorous as the action verb alone (*shines, offended*). Look how much more effective a paragraph becomes when weak verbs are replaced with dynamic ones:

Original

> The waves *were* so high that the boat *was* nearly *tipping* on end. The wind *felt* rough against our faces, and the salt spray *became* so strong that we *felt* our breath *would be* cut off. Suddenly, in the air *was* the sound I had dreaded most—the snap of the rigging. I *felt* panicky.

Revised

> The waves *towered* until the boat nearly *tipped* on end. The wind *lashed* our faces, while the salt spray *clogged* our throats and *cut* off our breath. Suddenly, the sound I had dreaded most *splintered* the air—the snap of the rigging. Panic *gripped* me.

The second paragraph is not only less wordy, it's also more vivid.

When you revise, look closely at your verbs. If you find too many *to be* and linking verb forms, ask yourself, "What's happening in the sentence?" Your response will help you substitute stronger verbs that will make your writing more compelling.

Change Passive Verbs to Active Ones

To be verb forms (*is, has been,* and so on) may also be combined with a past participle (*cooked, stung*), resulting in a **passive verb.** A passive verb creates a sentence structure in which the subject is *acted on* and, therefore, is placed in a secondary or passive position. In contrast, the subject of an **active verb** *performs* the action. Consider the following active and passive forms:

Passive	**Active**
A suggestion was made by the instructor that the project plan be revised by the students.	The instructor suggested that the students revise the project plan.
The employees' grievances will be considered by the union-management team when contract terms are being negotiated.	The union-management team will consider employees' grievances when negotiating contract terms.

Although they're not grammatically incorrect, passive verbs generally weaken writing, making it wordy and stiffly formal. Sometimes, though, it makes sense to use the passive voice. Perhaps you don't know who performed an action. ("When I returned to my car, I noticed the door had been dented.") Or you may want to emphasize an event, not the agent responsible for the event. For example, in an article about academic dishonesty on your campus, you might deliberately use the passive voice: "Every semester, research papers are plagiarized and lab reports falsified."

Unfortunately, corporations, government agencies, and other institutions often use the passive voice to avoid taking responsibility for controversial actions.

Notice how easily the passive conceals the agent: "The rabbits were injected with a cancer-causing chemical."

Because the passive voice *is* associated with "official" writing, you may think it sounds scholarly and impressive. It doesn't. Unless you have good reason for deemphasizing the agent, change passive verbs to active ones.

Replace Weak Verb-Noun Combinations

Just as *to be,* linking, and passive verbs tend to lengthen sentences needlessly, so do weak verb-noun combinations. Whenever possible, replace such combinations with their strong verb counterparts. Change "made an estimate" to "estimated," "gave approval" to "approved." Notice how revision tightens these sentences, making them livelier and less pretentious:

Original They *were* of the *belief* that the report was due next week.
Revised They *believed* the report was due next week.

Original The technical adviser *effected a replacement* of the system.
Revised The technical adviser *replaced* the system.

Delete Unnecessary Adverbs

Strong verbs can further tighten your writing by ridding it of unnecessary adverbs. "She *strolled* down the path" conveys the same message as "She *walked slowly* and *leisurely* down the path"—but more economically. Similarly, why write "The crime was *extremely difficult* for the police to solve" when you can simply write "The crime *mystified* the police"?

Adverbs such as *extremely, really,* and *very* usually weaken writing. Although they are called "intensifiers," they make writing less, not more, intense. Notice that the following sentence reads more emphatically *without* the intensifier:

Original Although the professor's lectures are controversial, no one denies that they are *really* brilliant.
Revised Although the professor's lectures are controversial, no one denies that they are brilliant.

"Qualifiers" such as *quite, rather,* and *somewhat* also tend to weaken writing. When you spot one, try to delete it:

Original When planning a summer trip to the mountains, remember to pack warm clothes; it turns *quite* cool at night.
Revised When planning a summer trip to the mountains, remember to pack warm clothes; it turns cool at night.

Use Original Figures of Speech

Another strategy for adding vitality to your writing is to create imaginative, nonliteral comparisons, called **figures of speech.** For example, you might describe midsummer humidity this way: "Going from an air-conditioned building to the street is like being hit in the face with peanut butter." Or you might describe someone's raw, sunburned face by saying it is "as red as a skinned tomato." Notice that in both cases the comparisons yoke essentially dissimilar things (humidity and peanut butter, a face and a tomato). Such unexpected connections surprise readers and help keep their interest.

Figures of speech also tighten writing. Since they create sharp images in the reader's mind, you don't need many words to convey as much information. If someone writes, "My teenage years were like a perpetual root canal," the reader immediately knows how painful and never-ending the author found adolescence.

Similes, Metaphors, Personification

Figures of speech come in several varieties. A **simile** is a direct comparison of two unlike things using the words *like* or *as:* "The moon brightened the yard *like* a floodlight." In a **metaphor,** the comparison is implied rather than directly stated: "The girl's *barbed-wire hair* set off *electric shocks* in her parents." In **personification,** an inanimate object is given human characteristics: "The couple robbed the store without noticing a silent, hidden eyewitness who later would tell all—a video camera." (For more on figures of speech, see page 157.)

Avoid Clichés

Trite and overused, some figures of speech signal a lack of imagination: *a tough nut to crack, cool as a cucumber, green with envy.* Such expressions, called **clichés,** are so predictable that you can hear the first few words (*Life is a bowl of . . .*) and fill in the rest (*cherries*). Clichés lull writer and reader alike into passivity since they encourage rote, habitual thinking.

When revising, either eliminate tired figures of speech or give them an unexpected twist. For example, seeking a humorous effect, you might write, "Beneath his rough exterior beat a heart of lead" (instead of "gold"); rather than, "Last but not least," you might write, "Last but also least."

Two Other Cautions

First, if you include figures of speech, *don't pile one on top of another,* as in the following sentence:

> Whenever the dorm residents prepared for the first party of the season, hairdryers howled like a windstorm, hairspray rained down in torrents, stereos vibrated like an earthquake, and shouts of excitement shook the walls like an avalanche.

Second, guard against *illogical* or *mixed* figures of speech. In the following example, note the ludicrous and contradictory comparisons:

> They rode the roller coaster of high finance, dodging bullets and avoiding ambushes from those trying to lasso their streak of good luck.

To detect outlandish comparisons, visualize each figure of speech. If it calls up some unintentionally humorous or impossible image, revise or eliminate it.

Avoid Sexist Language

Sexist language gives the impression that one gender is more important, powerful, or valuable than the other. You may have noticed such language in certain reading selections in this book—for example, selections that refer to the average person as *he*. Some of these essays were written before people became alert to sexist overtones; others reveal the tenacity of long-standing habits and attitudes. Fortunately, a growing number of writers—female and male—are replacing sexist language with **gender-neutral** or **nonsexist** terms that convey no sexual prejudice. You, too, can avoid sexist language. But to do so, you need to be aware of the situations in which it is apt to occur.

Sexist Vocabulary

Using nonsexist vocabulary means staying away from terms that demean or exclude one of the sexes. Such slang words as *stud, jock, chick,* and *fox* portray people as one-dimensional. Just as adult males should be called *men,* adult females should be referred to as *women,* not *girls.* Similarly, men shouldn't be empowered with professional and honorary titles while professional women are assigned only personal titles. Why, for example, years ago should Ronald Reagan have been referred to as *President* Reagan while the Prime Minister of England, Margaret Thatcher, was called *Mrs.* Thatcher? In addition, consider replacing *Mrs.* and *Miss* with *Ms.;* like *Mr., Ms.* doesn't indicate marital status.

Be alert as well to the fact that words not inherently sexist can become so in certain contexts. Asking "What does the *man* in the street think of the teachers' strike?" excludes the possibility of asking women for their reactions.

Because language in our culture tends to exclude women rather than men, we list here a number of common words that exclude women. When you write (or speak), make an effort to use the more inclusive alternatives given.

Sexist	**Nonsexist**
the average guy	the average person
chairman	chairperson, chair
congressman	congressional representative
fireman	fire fighter
foreman	supervisor
layman	layperson
mailman	mail carrier, letter carrier
mankind, man	people, humans, human beings
policeman	police officer
salesman	salesperson

Sexist	**Nonsexist**
statesman	diplomat
spokesman	spokesperson
workmen	workers

Also, be on the lookout for phrases that suggest a given profession or talent is unusual for someone of a particular sex: *woman judge, woman doctor, male secretary, male nurse.*

Sexist Pronoun Use

Indefinite singular nouns—those representing a general group of people consisting of both genders—can lead to **sexist pronoun use:** "On *his* first day of school, a young child often experiences separation anxiety," or "Each professor should be responsible for monitoring *his* own students' progress." These sentences exclude female children and female professors from consideration, although the situations being described apply equally to them. But writing "On *her* first day of school, a young child often experiences separation anxiety" or "Each professor should be responsible for monitoring *her* own students' progress" is similarly sexist because the language excludes males.

Indefinite *pronouns* such as *anyone, each,* and *everybody* may also pave the way to sexist language. Although such pronouns often refer to a number of individuals, they are considered singular. So, wanting to be grammatically correct, you may write a sentence like the following: "Everybody wants *his* favorite candidate to win." The sentence, however, is sexist because *everybody* is certainly not restricted to men. But writing "Everybody wants *her* candidate to win" is equally sexist because now males aren't included.

Here's one way to avoid these kinds of sexist constructions: Use *both* male and female pronouns, instead of just one or the other. For example, you could write "On *his or her* first day of school, a young child often experiences separation anxiety," or "Everybody wants *his or her* favorite candidate to win." If you use both pronouns, you might try to vary their order; that is, alternate *his or her* with *her or his,* and so on. Another approach is to use the gender-neutral pronouns *they, their,* or *themselves:* "Everybody wants *their* favorite candidate to win." Be warned, though. Some people object to using these plural pronouns with singular indefinite pronouns, even though the practice is common in everyday speech. To be on the safe side, ask your instructors if they object to any of the approaches described here. If not, feel free to choose whichever nonsexist construction seems most graceful and least obtrusive.

If you're still unhappy with the result, two alternative strategies enable you to eliminate the need for *any* gender-marked singular pronouns. First, you can change singular general nouns or indefinite pronouns to their plural equivalents and then use nonsexist plural pronouns:

Original A *workaholic* feels anxious when *he* isn't involved in a task-related project.
Revised *Workaholics* feel anxious when *they're* not involved in task-related projects.

Original *Everyone* in the room expressed *his* opinion freely.
Revised *Those* in the room expressed *their* opinions freely.

Second, you can recast the sentence to omit the singular pronoun:

Original A *manager* usually spends part of each day settling squabbles among *his* staff.
Revised A manager usually spends part of each day settling *staff squabbles.*

Original No *one* wants *his* taxes raised.
Revised No one wants *to pay more taxes.*

The following checklist is designed to help you and your readers evaluate the words in a draft. (Activities at the end of the chapter will refer you to this checklist when you revise several essays.) To see how one student, Harriet Davids, used the checklist when revising, turn to page 135.

REVISING WORDS: A CHECKLIST

- □ Which words seem inconsistent with the essay's tone? What words would be more appropriate?
- □ Which words seem vague and overly general? Where would more specific and concrete words add vitality and clarify meaning?
- □ Where is language overly formal? Which words are unnecessarily long or specialized? Where is language too informal (colloquial or slangy)? Where do unintended shifts in diction level create a jarring effect?
- □ Which words overstate? Which understate? What alternatives would be less misleading?
- □ Which words carry connotations unsuited to the essay's purpose and tone? What synonyms would be more appropriate?
- □ Where could weak verbs be replaced by vigorous ones? Which *to be* and linking verb forms should be changed to action verbs? Which passive verbs could be replaced by active ones? Where could a noun-verb combination be replaced by a strong verb?
- □ Which adverbs, especially intensifiers (*very*) and qualifiers (*quite*), could be eliminated?
- □ Where would original similes, metaphors, and personifications add power? Which figures of speech are hackneyed, illogical, or mixed? How could these problems be fixed?
- □ Where does sexist language appear? What gender-neutral terms could be used instead? How could sexist pronouns be eliminated?

SAMPLE STUDENT REVISION OF SENTENCES AND WORDS

Reprinted here is the introduction to Harriet Davids's first draft—as it looked after she entered on a word processor the changes she made in overall meaning, structure, and paragraph development (see page 106). To help identify problems with words and sentences, Harriet asked someone in her editing group to read the revised version aloud. Then she asked the group to comment on her paper, using the checklists on pages 124 and 134. The marginal notes indicate her ranking of the group's comments in order of importance. The above-line changes show how Harriet revised in response to these suggestions for improving the paragraph's sentences and words.

Reruns of   from the
~~In the 50s and 60s, parents had it easy,~~ TV comedies ~~of that~~
'50s and '60s dramatize the kinds of problems that parents used to have.
~~period show~~ the Cleavers scolding Beaver about his dirty hands,
dock   's allowance because he forgets
the Nelsons ~~telling~~ Ricky to clean his room. Being a parent today
than it was a generation ago.
is much more difficult. Nowadays parents must protect their
children from many things--from a growing number of distractions,
life-threatening
from sexually explicit material, and from ~~dangerous~~ situations.

① Combine into one sentence idea of '50s/'60s parents and TV shows

② Make each family's problems a separate sentence

③ Use stronger verbs (not "telling")

④ Make "dangerous situations" more specific

Once you, like Harriet, have carefully revised sentences and words, your essay needs only to be edited (for errors in grammar, punctuation, and spelling) and proofread. In the next chapter, you'll read about these final steps. You'll also see a student essay that has gone through all phases of the writing process.

Continues on page 144

ACTIVITIES: REVISING SENTENCES AND WORDS

1. Revise the following wordy, muddy sentences, making them economical and clear.

   a. What a person should do before subletting a rental apartment is make sure to have the sublet agreement written up in a formal contract.

   b. In high school, it often happens that young people deny liking poetry because of the fact that they fear running the risk of having people mock or make fun of them because they actually enjoy poetry.

c. In light of the fact that college students are rare in my home neighborhood, being a college student gives me immediate and instant status.
d. There were a number of people who have made the observation that the new wing of the library looks similar in appearance to several nearby buildings with considerable historical significance.
e. It was, in my opinion, an apt comment when the professor noted that most of the students who complain about how demanding the requirements of a course are tend to work at part-time or even full-time jobs.

2. Using only simple or simple and compound sentences, write a paragraph based on one of the following topic sentences. Then rewrite the paragraph, making some of the sentences complex and others compound-complex. Examine your two versions of the paragraph. What differences do you see in meaning and emphasis?

a. The campus parking lot is dangerous at night.
b. Some students have trouble getting along with their roommates.
c. Silent body language speaks loudly.
d. Getting on a teacher's good side is an easily mastered skill.

3. The following sentences could be more emphatic. Examine each one to determine its focus; then revise the sentence, using one of the following strategies: placing the most important item first or last, parallelism, inverted word order, a fragment. Try to use a different strategy in each sentence.

a. The old stallion's mane was tangled, and he had chipped hooves, and his coat was scraggly.
b. Most of us find rude salespeople difficult to deal with.
c. The politician promises, "I'll solve all your problems."
d. We meet female stereotypes such as the gold digger, the dangerous vixen, and the "girl next door" in the movies.
e. It's a wise teacher who encourages discussion of controversial issues in the classroom.

4. The following paragraph is pretentious and murky. Revise to make it crisp and clear.

Since its founding, the student senate on this campus has maintained essentially one goal: to upgrade the quality of its student-related services. Two years ago, the senate, supported by the opinions of three consultants provided by the National Council of Student Governing Boards, was confident it was operating from a base of quality but felt that, if given additional monetary support from the administration, a

```
significant improvement in student services would be facilitated.
This was a valid prediction, for that is exactly what transpired
in the past fifteen months once additional monetary resources
were, in fact, allocated by the administration to the senate and
its activities.
```

5. Write a sentence for each word in the series that follows, making sure your details reinforce each word's connotations:

   a. chubby, voluptuous, portly
   b. stroll, trudge, loiter
   c. turmoil, anarchy, hubbub

6. Write three versions of a brief letter voicing a complaint to a store, a person, or an organization. One version should be charged with negative connotations; another should "soft pedal" the problem. The final version should present your complaint using neutral, objective words. Which letter do you prefer? Why?

7. Describe each of the following in one or two sentences, using a creative figure of speech to convey each item's distinctive quality:

   a. a baby's hand
   b. a pile of dead leaves
   c. a sophisticated computer
   d. an empty room
   e. an old car

8. Enliven the following dull, vague sentences. Use your knowledge of sentence structure to dramatize key elements. Also, replace weak verbs with vigorous ones and make language more specific.

   a. I got sick on the holiday.
   b. He stopped the car at the crowded intersection.
   c. A bird appeared in the corner of the yard.
   d. The class grew restless.
   e. The TV broadcaster put on a concerned air as she announced the tragedy.

9. The following paragraph contains too many linking verbs, passives, adverbs, and prepositions. In addition, noun forms are sometimes used where their verb counterparts would be more effective. Revise the paragraph by eliminating unnecessary prepositions and providing more vigorous verbs. Then add specific, concrete words that dramatize what is being described.

```
  The farmers in the area conducted a meeting during which they
formulated a discussion of the vandalism problem in the county
```

```
in which they live. They made the estimate that, on the average,
each of them had at least an acre of crops destroyed the past
few weekends by gangs of motorcyclists who have been driving
maliciously over their land. The increase in such vandalism has
been caused by the encroachment of the suburbs on rural areas.
```

10. Revise the following sentences to eliminate sexist language.

a. The manager of a convenience store has to guard his cash register carefully.
b. When I broke my arm in a car accident, a male nurse, aided by a physician's assistant, treated my injury.
c. All of us should contact our congressman if we're not satisfied with his performance.
d. The chemistry professors agree that nobody should have to buy her own Bunsen burner.

An important note: When revising essay drafts in activities 11 and 12, don't worry too much about grammar, punctuation, and spelling. However, do save your revisions, so you can focus on these matters after reading the next chapter.

11. In response to activity 1 in Chapter 7 (page 107), you revised the overall meaning, structure, and paragraph development of Harriet Davids's first draft. Find that revision so that you can now focus on its sentences and words. Get together with at least one other person and ask yourselves questions like these: "Where should sentence type, length, or pattern be more varied?" and "Where would more specific and concrete words add vitality and clarify meaning?" For further guidance, refer to the checklists on pages 124 and 134. Summarize and rank any perceived problems in marginal annotations or a feedback chart. Then type your changes into a word processor or enter them between the lines of the draft. (Save your revision so you can edit and proofread it after reading the next chapter.)

12. Return to the draft you prepared in response to activity 2, activity 3, activity 4, or activity 5 in Chapter 7 (pages 107–109). Get together with several people and request that one of them read the draft aloud. Then, using the checklists on pages 124 and 134, ask the group members focused questions about any sentences and words that you feel need sharpening. After evaluating the feedback, revise the draft. Either key your changes into a computer or do your revising by hand. (Save your revision so you can edit and proofread it after reading the next chapter.)

Editing and Proofreading

9

It happens all too often. A student works hard to revise an essay—reading it over, making changes (some of them extensive), refining sentences and words—all to arrive at the best version possible. Then the student types the paper and hands it in without even a glance.

Wanting to get a piece of writing off your desk is a normal human response to so much work. But if you don't edit and proofread—that is, closely check your writing for grammar, spelling, and typographical errors—you run the risk of sabotaging your previous efforts. Readers may assume that a piece of writing isn't worth their time if they're jolted by surface flaws that make it difficult to read. So, to make sure that your good ideas get a fair hearing (and as detailed in Figure 9.1 on page 140), you should do the following:

- Edit
- Use the appropriate manuscript format
- Proofread

FIGURE 9.1
Process Diagram: Editing and Proofreading

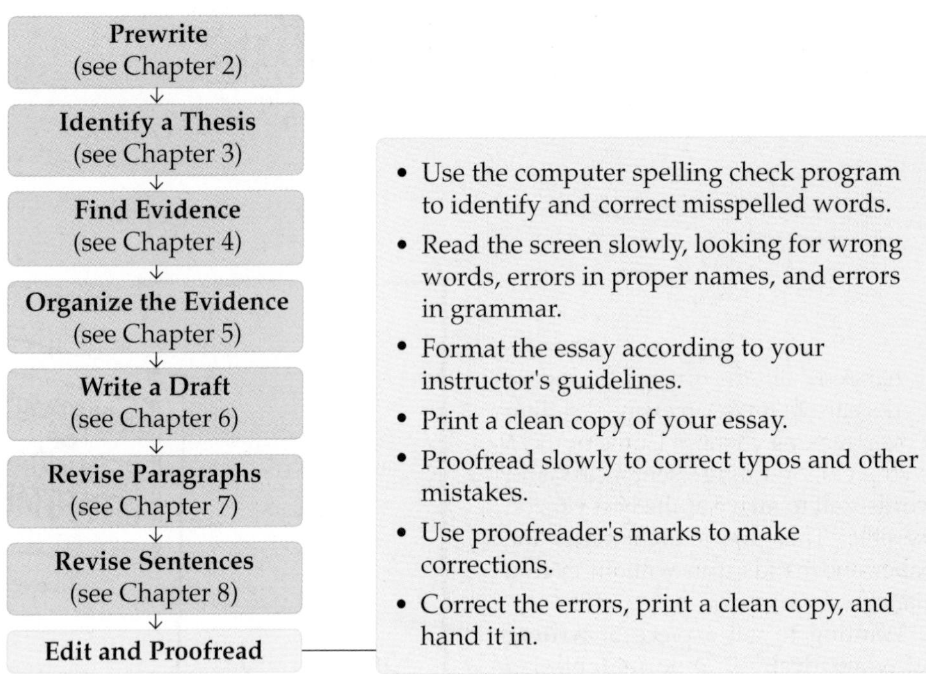

EDIT CAREFULLY

When revising the paper, you probably spotted some errors in grammar, punctuation, or spelling, perhaps flagging them for later correction. Now—after you're satisfied with the essay's organization, development, and style—it's time to fix these errors. It's also time to search for and correct errors that have slipped by you so far.

If you're working with pen and paper or on a printed draft with handwritten annotations, use a different color ink, so your new corrections will stand out. Because most writers find it easier to locate errors on unmarked text, you may want to make changes and corrections you've already noted and then produce a clean copy of your text for editing. If you use a computer, search for errors both on the screen and on a printout. If your software includes a spelling check, your search for misspellings will be greatly simplified. Be aware, however, that such programs may not find errors in the spelling of proper nouns, and that they won't flag errors that constitute legitimate words (for example, *he* when you meant *the* or *their* when you meant *there*).

To be a successful editor of your own work, you need two standard tools: a grammar handbook and a good dictionary. One way to keep track of the errors you're prone to make is to record them on a simple chart. Divide the chart into three columns: (1) *Error,* (2) *Rules for Correcting Error,* and (3) *Error Corrected.* When your instructor returns an essay, copy representative mistakes you've made into the first column. Look up in a handbook the rules that apply and enter them in the second column. Then, in the last column, rewrite the phrase or sentence from your paper with the error corrected. As the semester goes on, you'll develop a *personalized inventory* of writing errors to use in checking your own work.

If you're weak in spelling, make a similar inventory of spelling errors and corrections. Use four columns for this list: (1) *Word Misspelled,* (2) *Part of Word Misspelled,* (3) *Spelling Rule,* and (4) *Word Corrected.*

USE THE APPROPRIATE MANUSCRIPT FORMAT

After correcting all grammar and spelling problems, you're ready to produce the final copy. In doing so, you should follow accepted academic practice, adapted to your instructor's requirements. Most instructors will require that you type your papers. Even if this isn't the case, computer-printed papers look neater, are easier to grade, and show that you have made the transition to college-level format.

The following checklist on manuscript format describes the basic rules for college essays. In addition, check for any specific format preferences your instructor may have.

APPROPRIATE MANUSCRIPT FORMAT: A CHECKLIST

- ☐ Use standard-sized (8½ by 11 inches), white printer paper.
- ☐ Use a standard, text-style font, such as Times Roman or Courier, in 12-point size. Align text at the left only, not at the left and right.
- ☐ Use only black ink for text. Illustrations, such as charts and graphs, may be printed in color.
- ☐ Leave one-inch margins at the top, bottom, left, and right.
- ☐ Double-space all text, including extracts, notes, bibliographies, and Works Cited and References lists.
- ☐ Use the computer's page-numbering feature to add a header, one-half inch from the top of the sheet, that gives your last name followed by a space and then the page number. Do not use "page" or "p." Align the header at the right. The header should appear on all pages of the essay starting with the first page of text. The title page, if you use one, is not numbered and does not have a header.

- ☐ If you include a title page, place the title about one-third of the way down the page. Enter the title, and double-space between lines of the title and your name. Give the course and section, instructor's name, and date on separate lines, double-spaced and centered.
- ☐ If you don't include a title page, use a standard heading, as specified by your instructor, at the top of the first page. One standard format for the heading consists of your name, the instructor's name, the course title, and the date on double-spaced lines in the top left corner of the page.
- ☐ Center the title of your paper one double-space below the heading. Capitalize only the first letter of all main words. Don't use all caps, underlining, quotation marks, or bold type. Double-space a title having more than one line.
- ☐ Double-space between the title and the first paragraph of your essay.
- ☐ Indent the first line of each paragraph one-half inch, the default setting for most word-processing software.
- ☐ Place any illustrations as close as possible to their mention in the text. Position a caption, consisting of "Figure" or "Fig.," a number, and a title or description, below the illustration.
- ☐ Print on only one side of each sheet of paper.
- ☐ Paper-clip or staple the pages, placing the outline wherever your instructor requests. Don't use the "folded corner" method; it doesn't hold, and it spoils the look of a carefully typed paper.
- ☐ Don't use a report cover unless your instructor requests one.
- ☐ If you are sending the essay by e-mail, follow your instructor's directions for naming the file. At the least, the file name should contain your own name and a class identifier—course abbreviation and section number, for example.
- ☐ Keep a backup copy of the essay on a disc or external hard drive.

(For examples of correct MLA and APA manuscript format, see pages 612–628 and 630–631.)

PROOFREAD CLOSELY

Proofreading means checking your final copy carefully for "typos" or other mistakes. One trick is to read your material backward: If you read from the end of each paragraph to the beginning, you can focus on each word individually to make sure no letters have been left out or transposed. This technique prevents you from getting caught up in the flow of ideas and missing small defects, which is easy to do when you've read your own words many times.

What should you do when you find a typo? Simply use a pen with dark ink to make an above-line correction. The following standard proofreader's marks will help you indicate some common types of corrections:

Proofreader's Mark	Meaning	Example
^	insert missing letter or word	telev^ision (i inserted)
(delete mark)	delete	reports the ~~the~~ findings
∼	reverse order	the gang's here all (reversed)
¶	start new paragraph	to dry. ¶Next, put
#	add space	the^#girls
⁀	close up space	boy ⁀ cott

If you make so many corrections on a page that it begins to look like a draft, make the corrections and reprint the page for fresh review.

STUDENT ESSAY: FROM PREWRITING THROUGH PROOFREADING

In the last several chapters, we've taken you through the various stages in the writing process—from prewriting to proofreading. You've seen how Harriet Davids used prewriting (pages 24–32) and outlining (page 33) to arrive at her thesis (pages 38 and 41–42) and her first draft (pages 86–87). You also saw how Harriet's peer reviewer, Frank Tejada, critiqued her first draft (page 100). You then observed how Harriet revised, first, her draft's overall meaning and paragraph development (page 106) and, second, its sentences and words (page 135). In the following pages, you'll look at Harriet's final draft—the paper she submitted to her instructor after completing all the stages of the writing process.

Harriet, a thirty-eight-year-old college student and mother of two teenagers, wanted to write an informative paper with a straightforward, serious tone. While preparing her essay, she kept in mind that her audience would include her course instructor as well as her classmates, many of them considerably younger than she. This is the assignment that prompted Harriet's essay:

> Goodman implies that, in some ways, today's world is hostile to children. Do you agree? Drawing upon but not limiting yourself to the material in your pre-reading journal, write an essay in which you support or reject this viewpoint.

Harriet's essay is annotated so you can see how it illustrates the essay format described in Chapter 6 (page 85). As you read the essay, try to determine how well it reflects the principles of effective writing. The commentary following the paper will help you look at the essay more closely and give you some sense of the way Harriet went about revising her first draft.

Harriet Davids

Professor Kinne

College Composition, Section 203

October 4, 2007

Challenges for Today's Parents

Introduction

Reruns of situation comedies from the 1950s and early 1960s 1
dramatize the kinds of problems that parents used to have with their children. On classic television shows such as *Leave It to Beaver*, the Cleavers scold their son Beaver for not washing his hands before dinner; on *Ozzie and Harriet*, the Nelsons dock little Ricky's allowance because he keeps forgetting to clean his room. But times have changed dramatically. Being a parent today is much more difficult than it was a generation ago. Parents nowadays must protect their children from a growing number of distractions, from sexually explicit material, and from life-threatening situations.

Thesis

Plan of Development

First supporting paragraph

Topic sentence

Today's parents must try, first of all, to control all the 2
new distractions that tempt children away from schoolwork. At home, a child may have a room furnished with an MP3 player, television, and computer. Not many young people can resist the urge to listen to music, watch TV, go online or play computer games and IM their friends—especially if it's time to do schoolwork. Outside the home, the distractions are even more alluring. Children no longer "hang out" on a neighborhood corner within earshot of Mom or Dad's reminder to come in and do homework. Instead, they congregate in vast shopping malls, movie theaters, and gleaming fast-food restaurants. Parents and school assignments have obvious difficulty competing with such enticing alternatives.

Second supporting paragraph

Topic sentence with link to previous paragraph

Besides dealing with these distractions, parents have to 3
shield their children from a flood of sexually explicit materials. Today, children can find pornographic websites and chat rooms on the Internet with relative ease. With the click of a mouse, they can be transported, intentionally or unintentionally, to a barrage of explicit images and conversations. Easily obtainable copies of sex magazines can be found at most convenience stores, many times alongside the candy. Children will not see the fuzzily photographed nudes that a previous generation did but will encounter the hard-core raunchiness of *Playboy* or *Penthouse*. Moreover, the movies young people view often focus on highly

sexual situations. It is difficult to teach children traditional values when films show young people treating sex as a casual sport. Unfortunately, television, with its often heavily sexual content, is no better. With just a flick of the channel, children can see sexed-up music videos, watch reality-TV stars cavorting in bed, or watch cable programs where nudity is common.

4 Most disturbing to parents today, however, is the increase in life-threatening dangers that face young people. When children are small, parents fear that their youngsters may be victims of violence. Every news program seems to carry a report about a school shooting or child predator who has been released from prison, only to repeat an act of violence against a minor. When children are older, parents begin to worry about their kids' use of drugs. Peer pressure to experiment with drugs is often stronger than parents' warnings. This pressure to experiment can be fatal. Finally, even if young people escape the hazards associated with drugs, they must still resist the pressure to drink. Although alcohol has always held an attraction for teenagers, reports indicate that they are drinking more than ever before. As many parents know, the consequences of this attraction can be deadly—especially when drinking is combined with driving.

Third supporting paragraph

Topic sentence with emphasis signal

5 Within a generation, the world as a place to raise children has changed dramatically. One wonders how yesterday's parents would have dealt with today's problems. Could the Nelsons have shielded little Ricky from sexually explicit material on the Internet? Could the Cleavers have protected Beaver from drugs and alcohol? Parents must be aware of all these distractions and dangers yet be willing to give their children the freedom they need to become responsible adults. This is not an easy task.

Conclusion

References to TV shows recall introduction

Commentary

Introduction and Thesis

The opening paragraph attracts readers' interest by recalling some vintage television shows that have almost become part of our cultural heritage. Harriet begins with these examples from the past because they offer such a sharp contrast to the present, thus underscoring the idea expressed in her *thesis:* "Being a parent today is much more difficult than it was a generation ago." Opening in this way, with material that serves as a striking contrast to what follows, is a common and effective strategy. Note, too, that Harriet's thesis states the paper's subject (being a parent) as well as her attitude toward the subject (the job is more demanding than it was years ago).

Plan of Development

Harriet follows her thesis with a *plan of development* that anticipates the three major points to be covered in the essay's supporting paragraphs. When revising her first draft, Harriet followed peer reviewer Frank Tejada's recommendation (page 100) to put her thesis and plan of development in separate sentences. Unfortunately, though, her plan of development ends up being somewhat mechanical, with the major points being trotted past the reader in one long, awkward sentence. To deal with the problem, Harriet could have rewritten the sentence or eliminated the plan of development altogether, ending the introduction with her thesis.

Patterns of Development

Although Harriet develops her thesis primarily through *examples,* she also draws on two other patterns of development. The whole paper implies a *contrast* between the way life and parenting are now and the way they used to be. The essay also contains an element of *causal analysis* since all the factors that Harriet cites affect children and the way they are raised.

Purpose, Audience, Tone, and Point of View

Given the essay's *purpose* and *audience,* Harriet adopts a serious *tone,* providing no-nonsense evidence to support her thesis. Note, too, that she uses the *third-person point of view.* Although she writes from the perspective of a mother of two teenage daughters, she doesn't write in the first person or refer specifically to her own experiences and those of her daughters. You may recall that Frank flagged Harriet's unsustained reference to her children (page 100). In the final draft, Harriet follows his advice and omits mention of her kids. Instead, she adopts an objective stance because she wants to keep the focus on the issue rather than on her family.

What if Harriet had been asked by her daughters' school newspaper to write a humorous column about the trials and tribulations that parents face raising children? Aiming for a different tone, purpose, and audience, Harriet would have taken another approach. Drawing upon her personal experience, she might have confessed how she survives her daughters' nearly nonstop use of the computer, as well as the constant thumping sounds that emanate from the headphones of their MP3s, which seem to be permanently glued to their ears: she cuts off the electricity and hides her daughters' MP3 ear buds. This material—with its personalized perspective, exaggeration, and light tone—would be appropriate.

Organization

Structuring the essay around a series of *relevant* and *specific examples,* Harriet uses *emphatic order* to sequence the paper's three main points: that a growing number of distractions, sexually explicit materials, and life-threatening situations make parenting difficult today. The third supporting paragraph begins with the words, "Most disturbing to parents today . . . ," signaling that Harriet feels particular concern about the physical dangers children face. Moreover, she uses basic organizational strategies to sequence the supporting examples within each paragraph. The details in the first supporting paragraph are organized *spatially,* starting with distractions at home and moving to those outside the home. The second supporting paragraph arranges examples *emphatically.* Harriet starts with sexually explicit materials that can be found on the Internet and ends with the "heavily sexual content" on TV. Note that Harriet follows Frank's peer review advice (page 100) about omitting her first-draft observation that kids don't get enough homework—or that they get too much busy work. The third and final supporting paragraph is organized *chronologically;* it begins by discussing dangers to small children and concludes by talking about teenagers. Again, Frank's advice—to use a clearer time sequence in this paragraph (page 100)—was invaluable when Harriet was revising.

The essay also displays Harriet's familiarity with other kinds of organizational strategies. Each supporting paragraph opens with a *topic sentence.* Further, *signal devices* are used throughout the paper to show the relationship among ideas: *transitions* ("*Instead,* they congregate in vast shopping malls"; "*Moreover,* the movies young people attend often focus on highly sexual situations"); *repetition* ("*sexual* situations" and "*sexual* content"); *synonyms* ("distractions . . . enticing alternatives" and "life-threatening . . . fatal"); *pronouns* ("young people . . . *they*"); and *bridging sentences* ("Besides dealing with these distractions, parents have to shield their children from a flood of sexually explicit materials").

Two Minor Problems

Harriet's efforts to write a well-organized essay result in a somewhat predictable structure. It might have been better had she rewritten one of the paragraphs, perhaps embedding the topic sentence in the middle of the paragraph or saving it for the end. Similarly, Harriet's signal devices are a little heavy-handed. Even so, an essay with a sharp focus and clear signals is preferable to one with a confusing or inaccessible structure. As she gains more experience, Harriet can work on making the structure of her essays more subtle.

Conclusion

Harriet brings the essay to a satisfying *close* by reminding readers of the paper's central idea and three main points. The final paragraph also extends the essay's scope by introducing a new but related issue: that parents have to strike a balance between their need to provide limitations and their children's need for freedom.

Revising the First Draft

As you saw on pages 106 and 135, Harriet reworked her essay a number of times. For a clearer sense of her revision process, compare the final version of her conclusion (on page 145) with the original version reprinted here. Harriet wisely waited to rework her conclusion until after she had fine-tuned the rest of the essay.

The marginal annotations, ranked in order of importance, indicate the problems that Harriet and her editing group detected in the conclusion.

Original Conclusion

① Paragraph seems tacked on

③ Boring sentence—too vague

② Inappropriate reference to Holden

Most adults love their children and want to be good parents. But it's difficult because the world seems stacked against young people. Even Holden Caulfield had trouble dealing with society's pressures. Parents must give their children some freedom but not so much that kids lose sight of what's important.

As soon as Harriet heard her paper read aloud during a group session, she realized her conclusion didn't work at all. Rather than bringing the essay to a pleasing finish, the final paragraph seemed like a tired afterthought. Frank, her peer reviewer, also pointed out that her allusion to *The Catcher in the Rye* misrepresented the essay's focus since Harriet discusses children of all ages, not just teens.

Keeping these points in mind, Harriet decided to scrap her original conclusion. Working at a computer, she prepared a new, much stronger concluding paragraph. Besides eliminating the distracting reference to Holden Caulfield, she replaced the shopworn opening sentence ("Most adults love their children . . . ") with two interesting and rhythmical questions ("Could the Nelsons . . . ? Could the Cleavers . . . ?"). Because these questions recall the essay's main points and echo the introduction's reference to vintage television shows, they help unify Harriet's paper and bring it to a rounded close.

These are just a few of the changes Harriet made when reworking her essay. Realizing that writing is a process, she left herself enough time to revise—and to carefully consider Frank Tejada's comments. Early in her composition course, Harriet learned that attention to the various stages in the writing process yields satisfying results, for writer and reader alike.

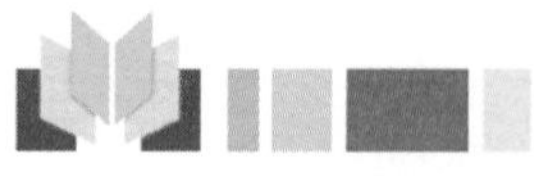

ACTIVITIES: EDITING AND PROOFREADING

1. Applying for a job, a student wrote the following letter. Edit and proofread it carefully, as if it were your own. If you have trouble spotting many grammar, spelling, and typing errors, that's a sign you need to review the appropriate sections of a grammar handbook.

Dear Mr. Eno:

I am a sophomore at Harper College who will be returning home to Brooktown this June, hopefully, to fine a job for the the summer. One that would give me further experience in the retail field. I have heard from my freind, Sarah Snyder, that your hiring college studnets as assistant mangers, I would be greatly intrested in such a postion.

I have quite a bit of experience in retail sales. Having worked after school in a "Dress Place" shop at Mason Mall, Pennsylvania. I started their as a sales clerk, by my second year I was serving as assistant manger.

I am reliable and responsible, and truely enjoy sales work. Mary Carver, the owner of the "Dress Place," can verify my qualifications, she was my supervisor for two years.

I will be visiting Brooktown from April 25 to 30. I hope to have an oppurtunity to speak to you about possible summer jobs at that time, and will be available for interview at your convience. Thank-you for you're consideration.

Sincerley,

Joan Ackerman

Joan Ackerman

2. Retrieve the revised essay you prepared in response to either activity 11 or activity 12 in Chapter 8 (page 138). Following the guidelines described on the preceding pages, edit and proofread your revision. After making the needed changes, prepare your final draft of the essay, using the appropriate manuscript format. Before submitting your paper to your instructor, ask someone to check it for grammar, spelling, and typographical errors that may have slipped by you.

For additional writing, reading, and research resources, go to **www.mycomplab.com** and choose **Nadell/Langan/Comodromos'** ***The Longman Writer, 7/e***.

PART III

THE PATTERNS OF DEVELOPMENT

10 Description

Rudi Von Briel/PhotoEdit Inc.

WHAT IS DESCRIPTION?

All of us respond in a strong way to sensory stimulation. The sweet perfume of a candy shop takes us back to childhood; the blank white walls of the campus infirmary remind us of long vigils at a hospital where a grandmother lay dying; the screech of a subway car sets our nerves on edge.

Without any sensory stimulation, we sink into a less-than-human state. Neglected babies, left alone with no human touch, no colors, no lullabies, become withdrawn and unresponsive. And prisoners dread solitary confinement, knowing that the sensory deprivation can be unbearable, even to the point of madness.

Because sensory impressions are so potent, descriptive writing has a unique power and appeal. **Description** can be defined as the expression, in vivid language, of what the five senses experience. A richly rendered description freezes a subject in time, evoking sights, smells, sounds, textures, and tastes in such a way that readers become one with the writer's world.

HOW DESCRIPTION FITS YOUR PURPOSE AND AUDIENCE

Description can be a supportive technique that develops part of an essay, or it can be the dominant technique used throughout an essay. Here are some examples of the way description can help you meet the objective of an essay developed chiefly through another pattern of development:

- In a *causal analysis* showing the *consequences* of pet overpopulation, you might describe the desperate appearance of a pack of starving stray dogs.
- In an *argumentation-persuasion essay* urging more rigorous handgun control, you might start with a description of a violent family confrontation that ended in murder.
- In a *process analysis* explaining the pleasure of making ice cream at home, you might describe the beauty of an old-fashioned, hand-cranked ice cream maker.
- In a *narrative essay* recounting a day in the life of a street musician, you might describe the musician's energy and the joyous appreciation of passersby.

In each case, the essay's overall purpose would affect the amount of description needed.

Your readers also influence how much description to include. As you write, ask yourself, "What do my particular readers need to know to understand and experience keenly what I'm describing? What descriptive details will they enjoy most?" Your answers to these and similar questions will help you tailor your description to specific readers. Consider an article intended for professional horticulturists; its purpose is to explain a new technique for controlling spider mites. Because of readers' expertise, there would be little need for a lengthy description of the insects. Written for a college newspaper, however, the article would probably provide a detailed description of the mites so student gardeners could spot them with ease.

While your purpose and audience define *how much* to describe, you have great freedom deciding *what* to describe. Description is especially suited to objects (your car or desk, for example), but you can also describe a person, an animal, a place, a time, and a phenomenon or concept. You might write an effective description about a friend who runs marathons (person), a pair of ducks that returns each year to a neighbor's pond (animals), the kitchen of a fast-food restaurant (place), a period when you were unemployed (time), the "fight or flight" response to danger (phenomenon or concept).

Description can be divided into two types: objective and subjective. In an **objective description,** you describe the subject in a straightforward and literal way, without revealing your attitude or feelings. Reporters, as well as technical and scientific writers, specialize in objective description; their jobs depend on their ability to detail experiences without emotional bias. For example, a reporter may write an unemotional account of a township meeting that ended in a fistfight. Or a marine biologist may write a factual report describing the way sea mammals are killed by the plastic refuse (sandwich wrappings, straws, fishing lines) that humans throw into the ocean.

In contrast, when writing a **subjective description,** you convey a highly personal view of your subject and seek to elicit a strong emotional response from your readers. Such subjective descriptions often take the form of reflective pieces or character studies. For example, in an essay describing the rich plant life in an inner-city garden, you might reflect on people's longing to connect with the soil and express admiration for the gardeners' hard work—an admiration you'd like readers to share. Or, in a character study of your grandfather, you might describe his stern appearance and gentle behavior, hoping that the contradiction will move readers as much as it moves you.

The *tone* of a subjective description is determined by your purpose, your attitude toward the subject, and the reader response you wish to evoke. Consider an essay about a dynamic woman who runs a center for disturbed children. If your goal is to make readers admire the woman, your tone will be serious and appreciative. But if you want to criticize the woman's high-pressure tactics and create distaste for her management style, your tone will be disapproving and severe.

The language of a descriptive piece also depends, to a great extent, on whether your purpose is primarily objective or subjective. If the description is objective, the language is straightforward, precise, and factual. Such *denotative* language consists of neutral dictionary meanings. If you want to describe as dispassionately as possible fans' violent behavior at a football game, you might write about the "large crowd" and its "mass movement onto the field." But if you are shocked by the fans' behavior and want to write a subjective piece that inspires similar outrage in readers, then you might write about the "swelling mob" and its "rowdy stampede onto the field." In the latter case, the language used would be *connotative* and emotionally charged so that readers would share your feelings. (For more on denotation and connotation, see pages 21–22 and 126–127.)

Subjective and objective descriptions often overlap. Sometimes a single sentence contains both objective and subjective elements: "Although his hands were large and misshapen by arthritis, they were gentle to the touch, inspiring confidence and trust." Other times, part of an essay may provide a factual description (the physical appearance of a summer cabin your family rented), while another part of the essay may be highly subjective (how you felt in the cabin, sitting in front of a fire on a rainy day).

At this point, you have a good sense of the way writers use description to achieve their purpose and to connect with their readers. Now take a moment to look closely at the photograph at the beginning of this chapter. Imagine you're writing a column, accompanied by the photo, for the local city newspaper. Your purpose is to encourage area businesspeople to provide financial support for the city's mural arts program. Jot down some phrases you might use when *describing* the mural and its impact on the community.

PREWRITING STRATEGIES

The following checklist shows how you can apply to description some of the prewriting strategies discussed in Chapter 2.

DESCRIPTION: A PREWRITING CHECKLIST

Choose a Subject to Describe

- ☐ Might a photograph, postcard, prized possession, or journal entry suggest a subject worth describing?
- ☐ Will you describe a person, animal, object, place, time period, or phenomenon? Is the subject readily observable, or will you have to reconstruct it from memory?

Determine Your Purpose, Audience, Tone, and Point of View

- ☐ Is your purpose to inform or to evoke an emotional response? If you want to do both, which is your predominant purpose?
- ☐ What audience are you writing for? How much does the audience already know about the subject you plan to describe?
- ☐ What tone and point of view will best serve your purpose and make readers receptive to your description?

Use Prewriting to Generate Details About the Subject

- ☐ How could freewriting, journal entries, or brainstorming help you gather sensory specifics about your subject?
- ☐ What relevant details about your subject come to mind when you apply the questioning technique to each of the five senses? What sounds (pitch, volume, and quality) predominate? What can you touch and how does it feel (temperature, weight, texture)? What do you see (color, pattern, shape, size)? What smells (pleasant, unpleasant) can't you forget? What tastes (agreeable, disagreeable) remain memorable?

STRATEGIES FOR USING DESCRIPTION IN AN ESSAY

After prewriting, you're ready to draft your essay. The suggestions in Figure 10.1 (on page 154) and those that follow will be helpful whether you use description as a dominant or supportive pattern of development.

1. **Focus a descriptive essay around a dominant impression.** Like other kinds of writing, a descriptive essay must have a thesis, or main point. In a descriptive essay with a subjective slant, the thesis usually centers on the

FIGURE 10.1
Development Diagram: Writing a Description Essay

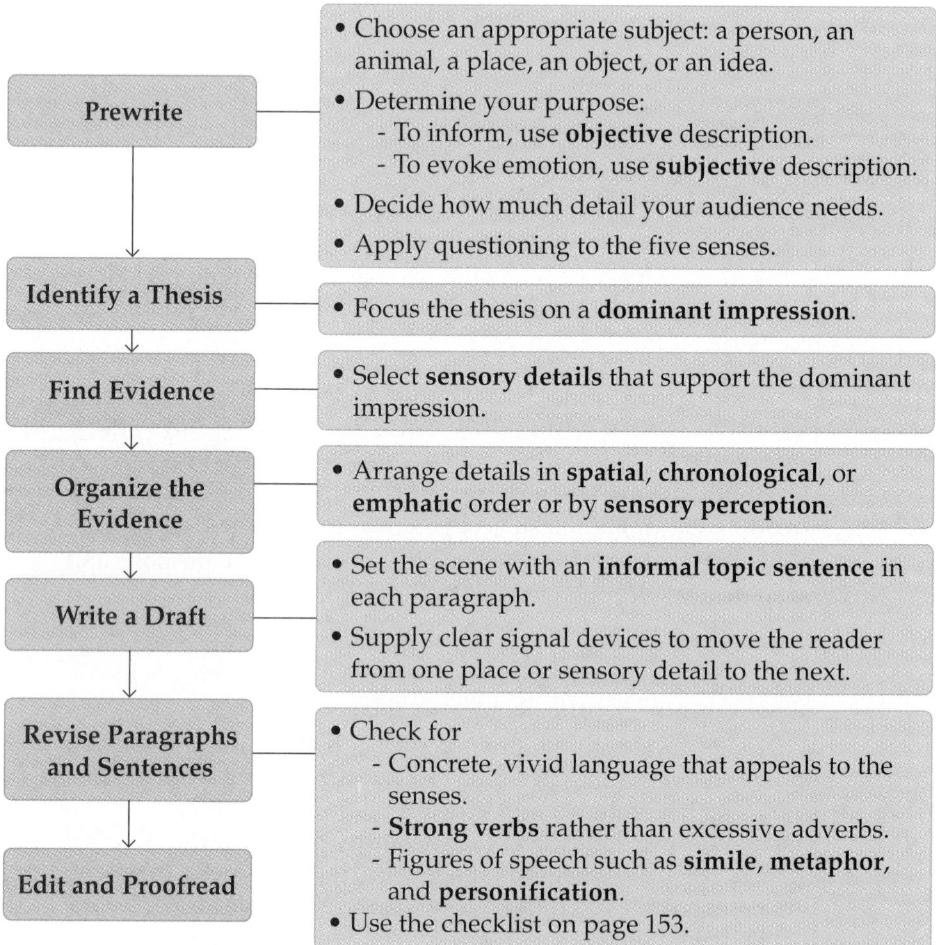

dominant impression you have about your subject. Suppose you decide to write an essay on your ninth-grade history teacher, Ms. Hazzard. You want the paper to convey how unconventional and flamboyant she was. The essay could, of course, focus on a different dominant impression—how insensitive she could be to students, for example. What's important is that you establish—early in the paper—the dominant impression you intend to convey. Although descriptive essays often imply, rather than explicitly state, the dominant impression, that impression should be unmistakable.

2. **Select the details to include.** The prewriting techniques discussed on pages 23–31 can help you develop heightened powers of observation and recall. Practice in noting significant details can lead you to become—in the words of

novelist Henry James—"one of those people on whom nothing is lost." The power of description hinges on your ability to select from all possible details *only those that support the dominant impression.* All others—no matter how vivid or interesting—must be left out. If you were describing how flamboyant Ms. Hazzard could be, the details in the following paragraph would be appropriate:

> A large-boned woman, Ms. Hazzard wore her bright red hair piled on top of her head, where it perched precariously. By the end of class, wayward strands of hair tumbled down and fell into eyes fringed by spiky false eyelashes. Ms. Hazzard's nails, filed into crisp points, were painted either bloody burgundy or neon pink. Plastic bangle bracelets, also either burgundy or pink, clattered up and down her ample arms as she scrawled on the board the historical dates that had, she claimed, "changed the world."

Such details—the heavy eye makeup, stiletto nails, gaudy bracelets—contribute to the impression of a flamboyant, unusual person. Even if you remembered times that Ms. Hazzard seemed perfectly conventional and understated, most likely you wouldn't describe those times because they would contradict the dominant impression.

You must also be selective in the *number of details* you include. Having a dominant impression helps you eliminate many details gathered during prewriting, but there still will be choices to make. For example, it would be inappropriate to describe in exhaustive detail everything in a messy room:

> The brown desk, made of a grained plastic laminate, is directly under a small window covered by a torn yellow-and-gold plaid curtain. In the left corner of the desk are four crumbled balls of blue-lined yellow paper, three red markers (all without caps), two fine-point blue pens, a crumbling pink eraser, and four letters, two bearing special wildlife stamps. A green down-filled vest and an out-of-shape red cable-knit sweater are thrown over the back of the bright blue metal bridge chair pushed under the desk. Under the chair is an oval braided rug, its once brilliant blues and greens spotted by soda and coffee stains.

Readers will be reluctant to wade through such undifferentiated specifics. Even more important, such excessive detailing dilutes the essay's focus. You end up with a seemingly endless list of specifics, rather than with a carefully crafted word picture. In this regard, sculptors and writers are similar—what they take away is as important as what they leave in.

3. **Organize the descriptive details.** It's important to select the organizational pattern (or combination of patterns) that best supports your dominant impression. The paragraphs in a descriptive essay are usually sequenced *spatially* (from top to bottom, interior to exterior, near to far) or *chronologically* (as the subject is experienced in time). But the paragraphs can also be ordered *emphatically* (ending with your subject's most striking elements) or by *sensory impression* (first smell, then taste, then touch, and so on).

   You might, for instance, use a *spatial* pattern to organize a description of a large city as you viewed it from the air, a taxi, or a subway car. A description of your first day on a new job might move *chronologically,* starting with how you felt the first hour on the job and proceeding through the rest of the day. In a paper describing a bout with the flu, you might arrange details *emphatically,* beginning with a description of your low-level aches and pains and concluding with an account of your raging fever. An essay about a neighborhood garbage dump could be organized by *sensory impressions:* the sights of the dump, its smells, its sounds. Regardless of the organizational pattern you use, provide enough *signal devices* (for example, *about, next, worst of all*) so that readers can follow the description easily.

   Finally, although descriptive essays don't always have conventional topic sentences, each descriptive paragraph should have a clear focus. Often this focus is indicated by a sentence early in the paragraph that names the scene, object, or individual to be described. Such a sentence functions as a kind of *informal topic sentence;* the paragraph's descriptive details then develop that topic sentence.

4. **Use vivid sensory language and varied sentence structure.** The connotative language typical of subjective description should be richly evocative. The words you select must etch in readers' minds the same picture that you have in yours. For this reason, rather than relying on vague generalities, you must use language that involves readers' senses. Consider the difference between the following paired descriptions:

Vague	**Vivid**
The food was unappetizing.	The stew congealed into an oval pool of muddy brown fat.
The toothpaste was refreshing.	The toothpaste, minty sweet, tingled against my bare teeth, finally free from braces.
Filled with passengers and baggage, the car moved slowly down the road.	Burdened with its load of clamoring children and bulging suitcases, the car labored down the interstate on bald tires and worn shocks, emitting puffs of blue exhaust and an occasional backfire.

Unlike the *concrete, sensory-packed* sentences on the right, the sentences on the left fail to create vivid word pictures that engage readers. While all good writing blends abstract and concrete language, descriptive writing demands an abundance of specific sensory language. (For more on specific language, see pages 127–128 in Chapter 8.)

Although you should aim for rich, sensory images, avoid overloading your sentences with *too many adjectives:* "A stark, smooth, blinding glass cylinder, the fifty-story skyscraper dominated the crowded city street." Delete unnecessary words, retaining only the most powerful: "A blinding glass cylinder, the skyscraper dominated the street."

Remember, too, that *verbs pack more of a wallop* than adverbs. The following sentence has to rely on adverbs (italicized) because its verbs are so weak: "She walked *casually* into the room and *deliberately* tried not to pay attention to their stares." Rewritten, so that verbs (italicized), not adverbs, do the bulk of the work, the sentence becomes more powerful: "She *strolled* into the room and *ignored* their stares." *Onomatopoetic* verbs, like *buzz, sizzle,* and *zoom,* can be especially effective because their sounds convey their meaning. (For more on vigorous verbs, see pages 128–130 in Chapter 8.)

Figures of speech—nonliteral, imaginative comparisons between two basically dissimilar things—are another way to enliven descriptive writing. *Similes* use the word *like* or *as* when comparing; *metaphors* state or imply that the two things being compared are alike; and *personification* attributes human characteristics to inanimate things. (For further discussion of figures of speech, refer to pages 131–132 in Chapter 8.)

The examples that follow show how effective figurative language can be in descriptive writing:

Simile

> Moving as jerkily as a marionette on strings, the old man picked himself up off the sidewalk and staggered down the street.

Metaphor

> Stalking their prey, the hall monitors remained hidden in the corridors, motionless and ready to spring on any unsuspecting student who tried to sneak into class late.

Personification

> The scoop of vanilla ice cream, plain and unadorned, cried out for hot fudge sauce and a sprinkling of sliced pecans.

(For suggestions on avoiding clichéd figures of speech, see page 131 in Chapter 8.)

Finally, when writing descriptive passages, you need to *vary sentence structure.* Don't use the same subject-verb pattern in all sentences. The second example above, for instance, could have been written as follows: "The hall monitors stalked their prey. They hid in the corridors. They remained motionless and ready to spring on any unsuspecting student who tried to sneak into class late." But the sentence is richer and more interesting when the descriptive elements are embedded, eliminating what would otherwise have been a clipped and predictable subject-verb pattern. (For more on sentence variety, see pages 115–118 in Chapter 8.)

REVISION STRATEGIES

Once you have a draft of the essay, you're ready to revise. The following checklist will help you and those giving you feedback apply to description some of the revision techniques discussed in Chapters 7 and 8.

DESCRIPTION: A REVISION/PEER REVIEW CHECKLIST

Revise Overall Meaning and Structure

- ☐ What dominant impression does the essay convey? Is the dominant impression stated or implied? Where? Should it be made more obvious or more subtle?
- ☐ Is the essay primarily objective or subjective? Should the essay be more personal and emotionally charged or less so?
- ☐ Which descriptive details don't support the dominant impression? Should they be deleted, or should the dominant impression be adjusted to encompass the details?

Revise Paragraph Development

- ☐ How are the essay's descriptive paragraphs (or passages) organized—spatially, chronologically, emphatically, or by sensory impressions? Would another organizational pattern be more effective? Which one(s)?
- ☐ Which paragraphs lack a distinctive focus?
- ☐ Which descriptive paragraphs are mere lists of sensory impressions?
- ☐ Which descriptive paragraphs are too abstract or general? Which fail to engage the reader's senses? How could they be made more concrete and specific?

Revise Sentences and Words

- ☐ What signal devices (such as *above, next, worst of all*) guide readers through the description? Are there enough signals? Too many?
- ☐ Where should sentence structure be varied to make it less predictable?
- ☐ Which sentences should include sensory images?
- ☐ Where should flat verbs and adverbs be replaced with vigorous ones? Where would onomatopoeia enliven a sentence?
- ☐ Where should there be more or fewer adjectives?
- ☐ Do any figures of speech seem contrived or trite? Which ones?

STUDENT ESSAY: FROM PREWRITING THROUGH REVISION

The student essay that follows was written by Marie Martinez in response to this assignment:

> The essay "Sister Flowers" is an evocative piece about a place that had special meaning in Maya Angelou's life. Write an essay about a place that holds rich significance for you, centering the description on a dominant impression.

After deciding to write about the salt marsh near her grandparents' home, Marie used the prewriting technique of *questioning* to gather sensory details about this special place. To enhance her power of recall, she focused, one at a time, on each of the five senses. Then, typing as quickly as she could, she listed the sensory specifics that came to mind.

When Marie later reviewed the details listed under each sensory heading, she concluded that her essay's dominant impression should be the marsh's peaceful beauty. With that dominant impression in mind, she added some details to her prewriting and deleted others. Below is Marie's original prewriting; the handwritten insertions indicate her later efforts to develop the material:

Questioning Technique

See: What do I see at the marsh?

- line of tall, waving reeds bordering the creek
- path—flattened grass
- spring—bright green (brilliant green)
- autumn—gold (tawny)
- winter—gray
- soil—spongy
- dark soil
- birds—little, brown
- low tide—steep bank of creek
- ~~an occasional beer can or potate chip bag~~
- grass under the water—green waves, shimmers
- fish—tiny, with (minnows) silvery sides, dart water and vegetation and underwater tangles
- blue crabs
- creek—narrow, sinuous, can't see beginning or end less than 15' wide
- center of creek—everything water and sky

Hear: How does it sound there?

- chirping of birds ("tweep, tweep")
- splash of turtle or otter
- mainly silent

Smell: Why can't I forget its smell?

- salt
- soil

Feel: How does it feel?

- soil—spongy
- water—warmer than ocean; rub
- my face and neck; mucky and oily
- mud—slimy (through toes)
- crabs brush my legs
- feel buoyant, weightless

When Marie reviewed her annotated prewriting, she decided that, in the essay, she would order her brainstormed impressions by location rather than by sensory type. Using a spatial method of organization, she would present details as she moved from place to place—from her grandparents' home to the creek. The arrangement of details was now so clear to Marie that she felt comfortable moving to a first draft without further shaping her prewriting or preparing an outline. As she wrote, though, she frequently referred to her prewriting to retrieve sensory details about each location.

Now read Marie's paper, "Salt Marsh," noting the similarities and differences between her prewriting and final essay. You'll see that the essay's introduction and conclusion weren't drawn from the prewriting material, whereas most of the sensory details were. Notice, too, that when she wrote the essay, Marie expanded these details by adding more specifics and providing several powerful similes. Finally, consider how well the essay applies the principles of description discussed in this chapter. (The commentary that follows the paper will help you look at the essay more closely and will give you some sense of how Marie went about revising her first draft.)

Salt Marsh

by Marie Martinez

Introduction

In one of his journals, Thoreau told of the difficulty he had escaping the obligations and cares of society: "It sometimes happens that I cannot easily shake off the village. The thought of some work will run in my head and I am not where my body is—I am out of my senses. In my walks I . . . return to my senses." All of us feel out of our senses at times. Overwhelmed by problems or everyday annoyances, we lose touch with sensory pleasures as we spend our days in noisy cities and stuffy classrooms. Just as Thoreau walked in the woods to return to his senses, I have a special place where I return to mine: the salt marsh behind my grandparents' house. 1

Dominant impression (thesis)

Informal topic sentence: Definition paragraph

My grandparents live on the East Coast, a mile or so inland from the sea. Between the ocean and the mainland is a wide fringe of salt marsh. A salt marsh is not a swamp, but an expanse of dark, spongy soil threaded with saltwater creeks and clothed in a kind of grass called salt meadow hay. All the water in the marsh rises and falls daily with the ocean tides, an endless cycle that changes the look of the marsh—partly flooded or mostly dry—as the day progresses. 2

3 Heading out to the marsh from my grandparents' house, I follow a short path through the woods. As I walk along, a sharp smell of salt mixed with the rich aroma of peaty soil fills my nostrils. I am always amazed by the way the path changes with the seasons. Sometimes I walk in the brilliant green of spring, sometimes in the tawny gold of autumn, sometimes in the grayish-tan of winter. No matter the season, the grass flanking the trail is often flattened into swirls, like thick Van Gogh brush strokes that curve and recurve in circular patterns. No people come here. The peacefulness heals me like a soothing drug.

Informal topic sentence: First paragraph in a four-part spatial sequence

Simile

4 After a few minutes, the trail suddenly opens up to a view that calms me no matter how upset or discouraged I might be: a line of tall waving reeds bordering and nearly hiding the salt marsh creek. To get to the creek, I part the reeds.

Informal topic sentence: Second paragraph in the spatial sequence

5 The creek is a narrow body of water no more than fifteen feet wide, and it ebbs and flows as the ocean currents sweep toward the land or rush back toward the sea. The creek winds in a sinuous pattern so that I cannot see its beginning or end, the places where it trickles into the marsh or spills into the open ocean. Little brown birds dip in and out of the reeds on the far shore of the creek, making a special "tweep-tweep" sound peculiar to the marsh. When I stand at low tide on the shore of the creek, I am on a miniature cliff, for the bank of the creek falls abruptly and steeply into the water. Below me, green grasses wave and shimmer under the water while tiny minnows flash their silvery sides as they dart through the underwater tangles.

Informal topic sentence: Third paragraph in the spatial sequence

6 The creek water is often much warmer than the ocean, so I can swim there in three seasons. Sitting on the edge of the creek, I scoop some water into my hand, rub my face and neck, then ease into the water. Where the creek is shallow, my feet sink into a foot of muck that feels like mashed potatoes mixed with motor oil. But once I become accustomed to it, I enjoy squishing the slimy mud through my toes. Sometimes I feel brushing past my legs the blue crabs that live in the creek. Other times, I hear the splash of a turtle or an otter as it slips from the shore into the water. Otherwise, it is silent.

Informal topic sentence: Last paragraph in the spatial sequence

Simile

The salty water is buoyant and lifts my spirits as I stroke through it to reach the middle of the creek. There in the center, I float weightlessly, surrounded by tall reeds that reduce the world to water and sky. I am at peace.

Conclusion

7 The salt marsh is not the kind of dramatic landscape found on picture postcards. There are no soaring mountains, sandy beaches, or lush valleys. The marsh is a flat world that some consider dull and uninviting. I am glad most people do not respond to the marsh's subtle beauty because that means I can be alone there. Just as the rising tide sweeps over the marsh, floating debris out to the ocean, the marsh washes away my concerns and restores me to my senses.

Echo of idea in introduction

Commentary

The Dominant Impression

Marie responded to the assignment by writing a moving tribute to a place having special meaning for her—the salt marsh near her grandparents' home. Like most descriptive pieces, Marie's essay is organized around a *dominant impression:* the marsh's peaceful solitude and gentle, natural beauty. The essay's introduction provides a context for the dominant impression by comparing the pleasure Marie experiences in the marsh to the happiness Thoreau felt in his walks around Walden Pond.

Combining Patterns of Development

Before developing the essay's dominant impression, Marie uses the second paragraph to *define* a salt marsh. An *objective description,* the definition clarifies that a salt marsh—with its spongy soil, haylike grass, and ebbing tides—is not to be confused with a swamp. Because Marie offers such a factual definition, readers have the background needed to enjoy the personalized view that follows.

Besides the definition paragraph and the comparison in the opening paragraph, the essay contains a strong element of *causal analysis:* Throughout, Marie describes the marsh's effect on her.

Sensory Language

At times, Marie develops the essay's dominant impression explicitly, as when she writes "No people come here" (paragraph 3) and "I am at peace" (6). But Marie generally uses the more subtle techniques characteristic of *subjective description* to convey the dominant impression. First of all, she fills the essay with strong *connotative language,* rich with *sensory images.* The third paragraph describes what she smells (the "sharp smell of salt mixed with the rich aroma of peaty soil") and what she sees ("brilliant green," "tawny gold," and "grayish-tan"). In the fifth paragraph, she uses *onomatopoeia* ("tweep-tweep") to convey the birds' chirping sound. And the sixth paragraph includes vigorous descriptions of how the marsh feels to Marie's touch. She splashes water on her face and neck; she digs her toes into the mud at the bottom of the creek; she delights in the delicate brushing of crabs against her legs.

Figurative Language, Vigorous Verbs, and Varied Sentence Structure

You might also have noted that *figurative language, energetic verbs,* and *varied sentence patterns* contribute to the essay's descriptive power. Marie develops a simile in the third paragraph when she compares the flattened swirls of swamp grass to the brush strokes in a painting by Van Gogh. Later she uses another simile when she writes that the creek's thick mud feels "like mashed potatoes mixed with motor oil." Moreover, throughout the essay, she uses lively verbs ("shimmer,""flash") to capture the marsh's magical quality. Similarly, Marie enhances descriptive passages by varying the length of her sentences. Long, fairly elaborate sentences are interspersed with short, dramatic statements. In the third paragraph, for example, the long sentence describing the circular swirls of swamp grass is followed by the brief statement "No people come here." And the sixth paragraph uses two short sentences ("Otherwise, it is silent" and "I am at peace") to punctuate the paragraph's longer sentences.

Organization

We can follow Marie's journey through the marsh because she uses an easy-to-follow combination of *spatial, chronological,* and *emphatic* patterns to sequence her experience. The essay relies primarily on a spatial arrangement since the four body paragraphs focus on the different spots that Marie reaches: first, the path behind her grandparents' house (paragraph 3); then the area bordering the creek (4); next, her view of the creek (5); last, the creek itself (6). Each stage of her walk is signaled by an *informal topic sentence* near the start of each paragraph. Furthermore, *signal devices* (marked by italics here) indicate not only her location but also the chronological passage of time: "*As* I walk along, a sharp smell . . . fills my nostrils" (3); "*After* a few minutes, the trail suddenly opens up . . . " (4); "*Below* me, green grasses wave . . . " (5). And to call attention to the creek's serene beauty, Marie saves for last the description of the peace she feels while floating in the creek.

An Inappropriate Figure of Speech

Although the four body paragraphs focus on the distinctive qualities of each location, Marie runs into a minor problem in the third paragraph. Take a moment to reread that paragraph's last sentence. Comparing the peace of the marsh to the effect of a "soothing drug" is jarring. The effectiveness of Marie's essay hinges on her ability to create a picture of a pure, natural world. A reference to drugs is inappropriate. Now, reread the paragraph aloud, stopping after "No people come here." Note how much more in keeping with the essay's dominant impression the paragraph is when the reference to drugs is omitted.

Conclusion

The concluding paragraph brings the essay to a graceful close. The powerful *simile* found in the last sentence contains an implied reference to Thoreau and to Marie's earlier statement about the joy to be found in special places having restorative powers. Such an allusion echoes, with good effect, the paper's opening comments.

Revising the First Draft

When Marie met with some classmates during a peer review session, the students agreed that Marie's first draft was strong and moving. But they also said that they had difficulty following her route through the marsh; they found her third paragraph especially confusing. Marie reviewed her classmates' peer review worksheets and then entered their comments, numbered in order of importance, in the margin of her first draft. Reprinted here is the original version of Marie's third paragraph, along with her annotations:

Original Version of Third Paragraph

① Chronology is confusing

As I head out to the marsh from the house, I follow a short trail through the woods. A smell of salt and soil fills my nostrils. The end of the trail suddenly opens up to a view that calms me no matter how upset or discouraged I might be: a line of tall, waving reeds bordering the salt marsh creek. Civilization seems far away as I walk the path of flattened grass and finally reach my goal, the salt marsh creek hidden behind the tall, waving reeds. The path changes with the seasons; sometimes I walk in the brilliant green of spring, sometimes in the tawny gold of autumn, sometimes in the gray of winter. In some areas, the grass is flattened into swirls that make the marsh resemble one of those paintings by Van Gogh. No people come here. The peacefulness heals me like a soothing drug. The path stops at the line of tall, waving reeds standing upright at the border of the creek. I part the reeds to get to the creek.

③ Make more specific

② Develop more fully—maybe use a simile

When Marie looked more carefully at the paragraph, she agreed it was confusing. For one thing, the paragraph's third and fourth sentences indicated that she had come to the path's end and had reached the reeds bordering the creek. In the following sentences, however, she was on the path again. Then, at the end, she was back at the creek, as if she had just arrived there. Marie resolved this confusion by breaking the single paragraph into two separate ones—the first describing the walk along the path, the second describing her arrival at the creek. This restructuring, especially when combined with clearer transitions, eliminated the confusion.

While revising her essay, Marie also intensified the sensory images in her original paragraph. She changed the "smell of salt and soil" to the "sharp smell of salt mixed with the rich aroma of peaty soil." And when she added the phrase "thick Van Gogh brush strokes that curve and recurve in circular patterns," she made the comparison between the marsh grass and a Van Gogh painting more vivid.

These are just some of the changes Marie made while rewriting the paper. Her skillful revisions provided the polish needed to make an already strong essay even more evocative.

ACTIVITIES: DESCRIPTION

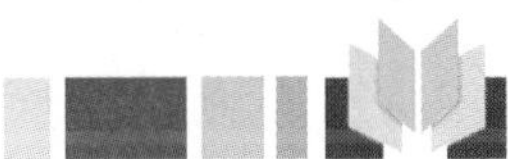

Prewriting Activities

1. Imagine you're writing two essays: One explains how students get "burned out"; the other contends that being a spendthrift is better (or worse) than being frugal. Jot down ways you might use description in each essay.

2. Go to a place on campus where students congregate. In preparation for an *objective* description of this place, make notes of various sights, sounds, smells, and textures, as well as the overall "feel" of the place. Then, in preparation for a *subjective* description, observe and take notes on another sheet of paper. Compare the two sets of material. What differences do you see in word choice and selection of details?

3. Prepare to interview an interesting person by outlining several questions ahead of time. When you visit that person's home or workplace, bring a notebook in which to record his or her responses. During the interview, observe the person's surroundings, voice, body language, dress, and so on. As soon as the interview is over, make notes on these matters. Then review your notes and identify your dominant impression of the person. With that impression in mind, which details would you omit if you were writing an essay? Which would you elaborate? Which organizational pattern (spatial, emphatic, chronological, or sensory) would you select to organize your description? Why?

Revising Activities

4. Revise each of the following sentence sets twice. The first time, create an unmistakable mood; the second time, create a sharply contrasting mood. To convey atmosphere, vary sentence structure, use vigorous verbs, provide rich sensory details, and pay special attention to words' connotations.

a. The card players sat around the table. The table was old. The players were, too.
b. A long line formed outside the movie theater. People didn't want to miss the show. The movie had received a lot of attention recently.
c. A girl walked down the street in her first pair of high heels. This was a new experience for her.

5. The following sentences contain clichés. Rewrite each sentence, supplying a fresh and imaginative figure of speech. Add whatever descriptive details are needed to provide a context for the figure of speech.

a. They were as quiet as mice.
b. My brother used to get green with envy if I had a date and he didn't.
c. The little girl is proud as a peacock of her Girl Scout uniform.
d. The professor is as dull as dishwater.

6. The following descriptive paragraph is from the first draft of an essay showing that personal growth may result when romanticized notions and reality collide. How effective is the paragraph in illustrating the essay's thesis? Which details are powerful? Which could be more concrete? Which should be deleted? Where should sentence structure be more varied? How could the description be made more coherent? Revise the paragraph, correcting any problems you discover and adding whatever sensory details are needed to enliven the description. Feel free to break the paragraph into two or more separate ones.

As a child, I was intrigued by stories about the farm in Harrison County, Maine, where my father spent his teens. Being raised on a farm seemed more interesting than growing up in the suburbs. So about a year ago, I decided to see for myself what the farm was like. I got there by driving on Route 334, a surprisingly easy-to-drive, four-lane highway that had recently been built with matching state and federal funds. I turned into the dirt road leading to the farm and got out of my car. It had been washed and waxed for the occasion. Then I headed for a dirt-colored barn. Its roof was full of huge, rotted holes. As I rounded the bushes, I saw the house. It too was dirt-colored. Its paint must have worn off decades ago. A couple of dead-looking old cars were sprawled in front of the barn. They were dented and windowless. Also by the barn was an ancient refrigerator, crushed like a discarded accordion. The porch steps to the house were slanted and wobbly. Through the open windows came a stale smell and the sound of television. Looking in the front door screen, I could see two chickens jumping around inside. Everything looked dirty both inside and out. Secretly grateful that no one answered my knock, I bolted down the stairs, got into my clean, shiny car, and drove away.

PROFESSIONAL SELECTIONS: DESCRIPTION

MAYA ANGELOU

Born Marguerite Johnson in 1928, Maya Angelou rose from a difficult childhood in Stamps, Arkansas, to become a multitalented performer and writer. A professor at Wake Forest University since 1991, she has danced professionally; starred in an off-Broadway play; acted on television; and become a prolific, highly regarded writer. Her work includes several volumes of poetry, such as *Oh Pray My Wings Are Gonna Fit Me Well* (1975), *Now Sheba Sings the Song* (1988), and *A Brave and Startling Truth* (1995); collections of essays, the latest of which is *Even the Stars Look Lonesome* (1997); children's books, including *Kofi and His Magic* (1996); and a series of autobiographical books, beginning with *I Know Why the Caged Bird Sings* (1969), from which the following selection is taken, through *A Song Flung Up to Heaven* (2002). Raped at the age of eight in St. Louis, Angelou responded by speaking to no one but her brother, Bailey. She and Bailey were soon sent to Stamps to live with their grandmother (Momma), at which point this excerpt begins.

Please note the essay structure diagram that appears following this selection (Figure 10.2 on page 172).

Pre-Reading Journal Entry

Growing up isn't easy. In your journal, list several challenges you've had to face in your life. In each case, was there someone who served as a "life line," providing you with crucial guidance and support? Who was that individual? How did this person steer you through the difficulty?

SISTER FLOWERS

1 For nearly a year [after I was raped], I sopped around the house, the Store, the school and the church, like an old biscuit, dirty and inedible. Then I met, or rather got to know, the lady who threw me my first life line.

2 Mrs. Bertha Flowers was the aristocrat of Black Stamps. She had the grace of control to appear warm in the coldest weather, and on the Arkansas summer days it seemed she had a private breeze which swirled around, cooling her. She was thin without the taut look of wiry people, and her printed voile dresses and flowered hats were as right for her as denim overalls for a farmer. She was our side's answer to the richest white woman in town.

Her skin was a rich black that would have peeled like a plum if snagged, but then no one would have thought of getting close enough to Mrs. Flowers to ruffle her dress, let alone snag her skin. She didn't encourage familiarity. She wore gloves too. 3

I don't think I ever saw Mrs. Flowers laugh, but she smiled often. A slow widening of her thin black lips to show even, small white teeth, then the slow effortless closing. When she chose to smile on me, I always wanted to thank her. The action was so graceful and inclusively benign. 4

She was one of the few gentlewomen I have ever known, and has remained throughout my life the measure of what a human being can be. 5

Momma had a strange relationship with her. Most often when she passed on the road in front of the Store, she spoke to Momma in that soft yet carrying voice, "Good day, Mrs. Henderson." Momma responded with "How you, Sister Flowers?" 6

Mrs. Flowers didn't belong to our church, nor was she Momma's familiar. Why on earth did she insist on calling her Sister Flowers? Shame made me want to hide my face. Mrs. Flowers deserved better than to be called Sister. Then, Momma left out the verb. Why not ask, "How *are* you, *Mrs.* Flowers?" With the unbalanced passion of the young, I hated her for showing her ignorance to Mrs. Flowers. It didn't occur to me for many years that they were as alike as sisters, separated only by formal education. 7

Although I was upset, neither of the women was in the least shaken by what I thought an unceremonious greeting. Mrs. Flowers would continue her easy gait up the hill to her little bungalow, and Momma kept on shelling peas or doing whatever had brought her to the front porch. 8

Occasionally, though, Mrs. Flowers would drift off the road and down to the Store and Momma would say to me, "Sister, you go on and play." As she left I would hear the beginning of an intimate conversation. Momma persistently using the wrong verb, or none at all. 9

"Brother and Sister Wilcox is sho'ly the meanest—" "Is," Momma? "Is"? Oh, please, not "is," Momma, for two or more. But they talked, and from the side of the building where I waited for the ground to open up and swallow me, I heard the soft-voiced Mrs. Flowers and the textured voice of my grandmother merging and melting. They were interrupted from time to time by giggles that must have come from Mrs. Flowers (Momma never giggled in her life). Then she was gone. 10

She appealed to me because she was like people I had never met personally. Like women in English novels who walked the moors (whatever they were) with their loyal dogs racing at a respectful distance. Like the women who sat in front of roaring fireplaces, drinking tea incessantly from silver trays full of scones and crumpets. Women who walked over the "heath" and read morocco-bound books and had two last names divided by a hyphen. It would be safe to say that she made me proud to be Negro, just by being herself. 11

She acted just as refined as whitefolks in the movies and books and she was more beautiful, for none of them could have come near that warm color without looking gray by comparison. 12

It was fortunate that I never saw her in the company of powhitefolks. For since they tend to think of their whiteness as an evenizer, I'm certain that I would have had to hear her spoken to commonly as Bertha, and my image of her would have been shattered like the unmendable Humpty-Dumpty. 13

14 One summer afternoon, sweet-milk fresh in my memory, she stopped at the Store to buy provisions. Another Negro woman of her health and age would have been expected to carry the paper sacks home in one hand, but Momma said, "Sister Flowers, I'll send Bailey up to your house with these things."

15 She smiled that slow dragging smile, "Thank you, Mrs. Henderson. I'd prefer Marguerite, though." My name was beautiful when she said it. "I've been meaning to talk to her, anyway." They gave each other age-group looks.

16 Momma said, "Well, that's all right then. Sister, go and change your dress. You going to Sister Flowers's."

17 The chifforobe was a maze. What on earth did one put on to go to Mrs. Flowers's house? I knew I shouldn't put on a Sunday dress. It might be sacrilegious. Certainly not a house dress, since I was already wearing a fresh one. I chose a school dress, naturally. It was formal without suggesting that going to Mrs. Flowers's house was equivalent to attending church.

18 I trusted myself back into the Store.

19 "Now, don't you look nice." I had chosen the right thing, for once . . . .

20 There was a little path beside the rocky road, and Mrs. Flowers walked in front swinging her arms and picking her way over the stones.

21 She said, without turning her head, to me, "I hear you're doing very good schoo work, Marguerite, but that it's all written. The teachers report that they have trouble getting you to talk in class." We passed the triangular farm on our left and the path widened to allow us to walk together. I hung back in the separate unasked and unanswerable questions.

22 "Come and walk along with me, Marguerite." I couldn't have refused even if I wanted to. She pronounced my name so nicely. Or more correctly, she spoke each word with such clarity that I was certain a foreigner who didn't understand English could have understood her.

23 "Now no one is going to make you talk—possibly no one can. But bear in mind, language is man's way of communicating with his fellow man and it is language alone which separates him from the lower animals." That was a totally new idea to me, and I would need time to think about it.

24 "Your grandmother says you read a lot. Every chance you get. That's good, but not good enough. Words mean more than what is set down on paper. It takes the human voice to infuse them with the shades of deeper meaning."

25 I memorized the part about the human voice infusing words. It seemed so valid and poetic.

26 She said she was going to give me some books and that I not only must read them, I must read them aloud. She suggested that I try to make a sentence sound in as many different ways as possible.

27 "I'll accept no excuse if you return a book to me that has been badly handled." My imagination boggled at the punishment I would deserve if in fact I did abuse a book of Mrs. Flowers's. Death would be too kind and brief.

28 The odors in the house surprised me. Somehow I had never connected Mrs. Flowers with food or eating or any other common experience of common people. There must have been an outhouse, too, but my mind never recorded it.

29 The sweet scent of vanilla had met us as she opened the door.

30 "I made tea cookies this morning. You see, I had planned to invite you for cookies and lemonade so we could have this little chat. The lemonade is in the icebox."

It followed that Mrs. Flowers would have ice on an ordinary day, when most families in our town bought ice late on Saturdays only a few times during the summer to be used in the wooden ice-cream freezers. 31

She took the bags from me and disappeared through the kitchen door. I looked around the room that I had never in my wildest fantasies imagined I would see. Browned photographs leered or threatened from the walls and the white, freshly done curtains pushed against themselves and against the wind. I wanted to gobble up the room entire and take it to Bailey, who would help me analyze and enjoy it. 32

"Have a seat, Marguerite. Over there by the table." She carried a platter covered with a tea towel. Although she warned that she hadn't tried her hand at baking sweets for some time, I was certain that like everything else about her the cookies would be perfect. 33

They were flat round wafers, slightly browned on the edges and butter-yellow in the center. With the cold lemonade they were sufficient for childhood's lifelong diet. Remembering my manners, I took nice little lady-like bites off the edges. She said she had made them expressly for me and that she had a few in the kitchen that I could take home to my brother. So I jammed one whole cake in my mouth and the rough crumbs scratched the insides of my jaws, and if I hadn't had to swallow, it would have been a dream come true. 34

As I ate she began the first of what we later called "my lessons in living." She said that I must always be intolerant of ignorance but understanding of illiteracy. That some people, unable to go to school, were more educated and even more intelligent than college professors. She encouraged me to listen carefully to what country people called mother wit. That in those homely sayings was couched the collective wisdom of generations. 35

When I finished the cookies she brushed off the table and brought a thick, small book from the bookcase. I had read *A Tale of Two Cities* and found it up to my standards as a romantic novel. She opened the first page and I heard poetry for the first time in my life. 36

"It was the best of times and the worst of times . . . " Her voice slid in and curved down through and over the words. She was nearly singing. I wanted to look at the pages. Were they the same that I had read? Or were there notes, music, lined on the pages, as in a hymn book? Her sounds began cascading gently. I knew from listening to a thousand preachers that she was nearing the end of her reading, and I hadn't really heard, heard to understand, a single word. 37

"How do you like that?" 38

It occurred to me that she expected a response. The sweet vanilla flavor was still on my tongue and her reading was a wonder in my ears. I had to speak. 39

I said, "Yes, ma'am." It was the least I could do, but it was the most also. 40

"There's one more thing. Take this book of poems and memorize one for me. Next time you pay me a visit, I want you to recite." 41

I have tried often to search behind the sophistication of years for the enchantment I so easily found in those gifts. The essence escapes but its aura remains. To be allowed, no, invited, into the private lives of strangers, and to share their joys and fears, was a chance to exchange the Southern bitter wormwood for a cup of mead with Beowulf[1] or a hot cup of tea and milk with Oliver Twist.[2] When I said aloud, "It is a far, far better thing that I do, than I have ever done . . . "[3] tears of love filled my eyes at my selflessness. 42

43 On that first day, I ran down the hill and into the road (few cars ever came along it) and had the good sense to stop running before I reached the Store.

44 I was liked, and what a difference it made. I was respected not as Mrs. Henderson's grandchild or Bailey's sister but for just being Marguerite Johnson.

45 Childhood's logic never asks to be proved (all conclusions are absolute). I didn't question why Mrs. Flowers had singled me out for attention, nor did it occur to me that Momma might have asked her to give me a little talking to. All I cared about was that she had made tea cookies for *me* and read to *me* from her favorite book. It was enough to prove that she liked me.

---

[1]The hero of an Old English epic poem dating from the eighth century (editors' note).

[2]The main character in Charles Dickens's novel *Oliver Twist* (1837) (editors' note).

[3]The last words of Sydney Carton, the selfless hero of Charles Dickens's novel *A Tale of Two Cities* (1859) (editors' note).

Questions for Close Reading

1. What is the selection's thesis (or dominant impression)? Locate the sentence(s) in which Angelou states her main idea. If she doesn't state the thesis explicitly, express it in your own words.

2. Angelou states that Mrs. Flowers "has remained throughout my life the measure of what a human being can be" (5). What does Angelou admire about Mrs. Flowers?

3. Why is young Angelou so ashamed of Momma when Mrs. Flowers is around? How do Momma and Mrs. Flowers behave with each other?

4. What are the "lessons in living" that Angelou receives from Mrs. Flowers during their first visit? How do you think these lessons might have subsequently influenced Angelou?

5. Refer to your dictionary as needed to define the following words used in the selection: *taut* (paragraph 2), *voile* (2), *benign* (4), *unceremonious* (8), *gait* (8), *moors* (11), *incessantly* (11), *scones* (11), *crumpets* (11), *heath* (11), *chifforobe* (17), *sacrilegious* (17), *infuse* (24), *couched* (35), and *aura* (42).

Questions About the Writer's Craft

1. **The pattern.** Reread the essay, focusing on the descriptive passages first of Mrs. Flowers and then of Angelou's visit to Mrs. Flowers's house. To what senses does Angelou appeal in these passages? What method of organization (see page 156) does she use to order these sensory details?

FIGURE 10.2
Essay Structure Diagram: "Sister Flowers" by Maya Angelou

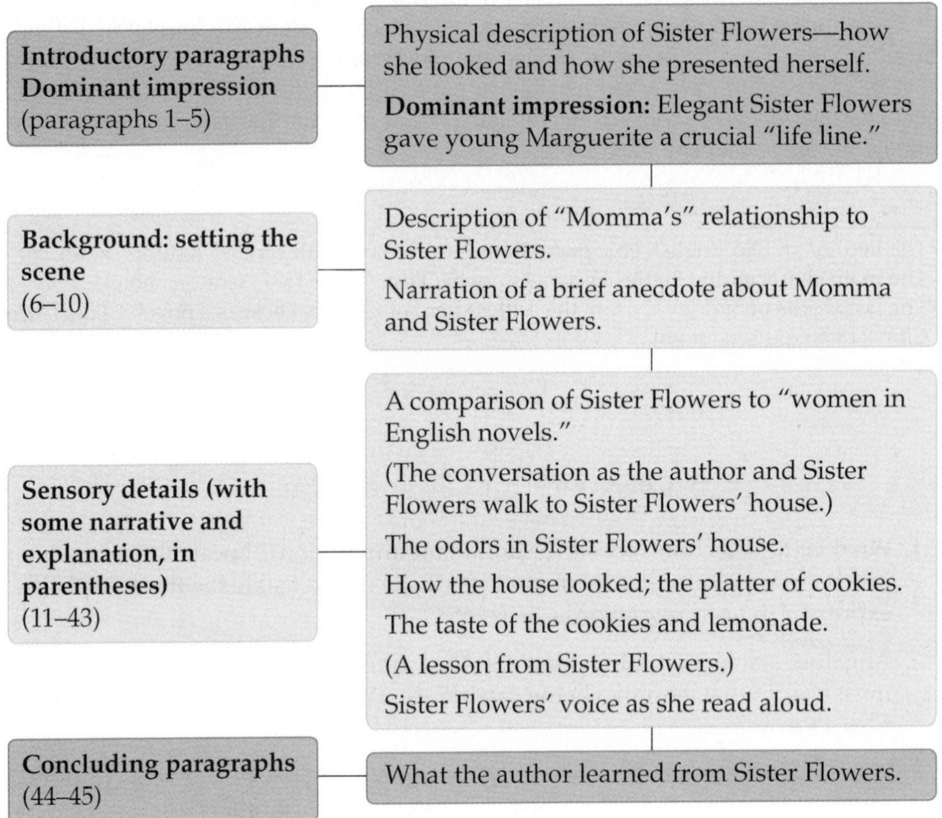

2. To enrich the description of her eventful encounter with Mrs. Flowers, Angelou draws upon figures of speech (see pages 130–131 and 157). Consider, for example, the similes in paragraphs 1 and 11. How do these figures of speech contribute to the essay's dominant impression?

3. Other patterns. Because Angelou's description has a strong *narrative* component, it isn't surprising that there's a considerable amount of dialog in the selection. For example, in paragraphs 7 and 10, Angelou quotes Momma's incorrect grammar. She then provides an imagined conversation in which the young Angelou scolds Momma and corrects her speech. What do these imagined scoldings of Momma reveal about young Angelou? How do they relate to Mrs. Flowers's subsequent "lessons in life"?

4. Although it's not the focus of this selection, the issue of race remains in the background of Angelou's portrait of Mrs. Flowers. Where in the selection does

Angelou imply that race was a fact of life in her town? How does this specter of racism help Angelou underscore the significance of her encounter with Mrs. Flowers?

Writing Assignments Using Description as a Pattern of Development

1. At one time or another, just about all of us have met someone who taught us to see ourselves more clearly and helped us understand what we wanted from life. Write an essay describing such a person. Focus on the individual's personal qualities, as a way of depicting the role he or she played in your life. Be sure not to limit yourself to an objective description. Subjective description, filled with lively language and figures of speech, will serve you well as you provide a portrait of this special person.

2. Thrilled by the spectacle of Mrs. Flowers's interesting home, Angelou says she wanted to "gobble up the room entire" and share it with her brother. Write an essay describing in detail a place that vividly survives in your memory. You may describe a setting that you visited only once or a familiar setting that holds a special place in your heart. Before you write, list the qualities and sensory impressions you associate with this special place; then refine the list so that all details support your dominant impression. You may want to read Gordon Parks's "Flavio's Home" (page 182) to see how another writer evokes the qualities of an unforgettable place.

Writing Assignments Combining Patterns of Development

3. When the young Angelou discovers, thanks to Mrs. Flowers, the thrill of acceptance, she experiences a kind of *epiphany*—a moment of enlightenment. Write an essay about an event in your life that represented a kind of epiphany. You might write about a positive discovery, such as when you realized you had a special talent for something, or about a negative discovery, such as when you realized that a beloved family member had a serious flaw. To make the point that the moment was a turning point in your life, start by *describing* what kind of person you were before the discovery. Then *narrate* the actual incident, using vivid details and dialogue to make the event come alive. End by discussing the importance of this epiphany in your life. For additional accounts of personal epiphanies, read Audre Lorde's "The Fourth of July" (page 208), Charmie Gholson's "Charity Display?" (page 220), and Beth Johnson's "Bombs Bursting in Air" (page 252).

4. Think of an activity that engages you completely, one that provides—as reading does for Angelou—an opportunity for growth and expansion. Possibilities

include reading, writing, playing an instrument, doing crafts, dancing, hiking, playing a sport, cooking, or traveling. Write an essay in which you *argue* the merits of your chosen pastime. Assume that some of your readers are highly skeptical. To win them over, you'll need to provide convincing *examples* that demonstrate the pleasure and benefits you have discovered in the activity.

Writing Assignment Using a Journal Entry as a Starting Point

5. Write an essay about a time when someone threw you a much-needed "life line" at a challenging time. Review your pre-reading journal entry, selecting *one* time when a person's encouragement and support made a great difference in your life. Be sure to describe the challenge you faced before recounting the specific details of the person's help. Dialog and descriptive details will help you re-create the power of the experience.

DAVID HELVARG

David Helvarg is a journalist and environmental activist. Born in 1951, he started his career as a freelance journalist and then became a war correspondent. Today he writes primarily about politics, AIDS, and marine life. Helvarg is also the founder and president of Blue Frontier Campaign, a marine conservation lobbying group that was inspired by his book about the world's oceans, *Blue Frontier*. Helvarg's lobbying on environmental issues grows out of his experiences covering war, political conflict, and marine biology. This article is excerpted from the September/October 2005 issue of *Multinational Monitor,* a magazine that examines multinational corporations and also covers issues relating to the environment and development.

Pre-Reading Journal Entry

Although humans have shaped the environment in many ways, we are still at the mercy of nature at times. Recall a hurricane, tornado, thunderstorm, windstorm, mudslide, earthquake, volcanic eruption, tsunami, drought, flood, or other natural event that affected you and your community. What was the event? What was the experience like? Use your journal to answer these questions.

THE STORM THIS TIME

Urban Floodplain

I arrive in Baton Rouge with a planeload of relief workers, FEMA functionaries and crew cut contractors, all working their cell phones and BlackBerries. After renting a car and making my way through the daily traffic jam (Baton Rouge's population has 1 exploded since the storm) I head south on Interstate 10, tuning into the United Radio Broadcasters of New Orleans, a consortium of local stations playing 24/7 information and call-in reports on Katrina's aftermath.

2 A police spokesperson assures listeners there are still 20 to 30 roadblocks around New Orleans and 11,000 guardsmen in the city. The mayor wants to open the city back up to residents but the approach of Hurricane Rita has forced him to postpone his plan.

3 Around the New Orleans airport in Jefferson Parish, I begin to see box stores, warehouses and motels with their roofs ripped off or caved in, downed trees and broken street signs, house roofs covered in blue tarps and high-rises with glass windows popped out like broken eyes. I hit a traffic jam and follow an SUV across the median strip to an exit where I stop to take a picture of a small office complex with its second story front and roof gone. Rain-soaked cardboard boxes fill the exposed floor above a CPA's office. I talk to a carpet-store owner removing samples. He helps me locate where we are on a map. I get a call from a contact at the New Orleans Aquarium. They lost most of their fish when the pumps failed but managed to evacuate the penguins and sea otters to Monterey. I get on a wide boulevard that leads to a roadblock where a police officer checks my press identification. "This is only for emergency vehicles, but go ahead," she says.

4 I drive into Lakeview, one of the large sections of the city that sat underwater for two weeks and will likely have to be bulldozed. It reminds me of war zones I've been in after heavy street fighting. There are trees and power poles down, electric lines hanging, metal sheets and street signs on mud-caked pavement, smashed cars, boats on sidewalks and torn-open houses, all colored in sepia tones of gray and brown. Unable to drive far in the debris chocked streets, I get out of my car, half expecting the sweet, rotting smell of death. Instead, I'm confronted with an equally noxious odor. It's what I'll come to think of as the smell of a dead city, like dried cow pies and mold with a stinging chemical aftertaste. Fine yellow dust starts rising up from under my boots and infiltrating the car. I retreat. The I-10 exit is barricaded, forcing me north again. I do a U-turn at a major roadblock and get chased down by some angry cops. I explain that I'm just following another cop's helpful directions and soon find myself speeding along a near-empty freeway bridge approaching downtown.

5 The rusted ruined roof of the Superdome inspires me to choose an exit and, after getting turned around at a friendly National Guard checkpoint, I'm soon in the deserted streets of the central business district, checking out the rubble piles and empty highrises. A big wind-damaged 'Doubletree' hotel sign reads D UL EE. The French Quarter is still intact with even a few bars open for soldiers, FBI agents and fire fighters. On Canal Street, it looks like a Woodstock for first responders with Red Cross and media satellite trucks, tents and RVs pulled up on the central streetcar median by the Sheraton. Red-bereted troops from the 82nd Airborne cruise by in open-sided trucks, M-4s at the ready in case the undead should appear at sunset. Uptown, some boats lie in the middle of the street, along with cars crushed by a falling wall and a pharmacy trashed by looters. Further on are the smashed homes and muddied boulevards and still-flooded underpasses and cemeteries, abandoned cars and broken levees of an eerily hollow city.

6 In the coming days, I'll travel across this new urban landscape, tracing the brown floodwater line that marks tens of thousands of homes, schools, offices, banks, churches, grocery stores and other ruined structures, including the main sewage plant. I'll cross paths with animal rescue crews, military patrols, utility crews from New York

New Orleans house showing flood line and searcher's graffiti. The zero indicates that no bodies were found in the house. (© David Helvarg)

and Pennsylvania, and body recovery search teams with K-9 dogs using orange spray paint to mark the doors of still unexamined buildings, writing the date and adding a zero for no bodies or numbers where bodies have been found . . . .

Life After Katrina

I put up with an AP colleague in the less damaged Algiers Point section of the city just across the Mississippi from where the helicopter assault ship Iwo Jima and Carnival Cruise Line ship Ecstasy are being used to house city employees and relief workers. Blackhawk helicopters fly overhead at sunset while a Red Cross truck down the street offers hot food to the handful of residents still here. 7

Back in Lakeview, I encounter Bob Chick. Bob snuck past the checkpoints to see if he can salvage anything from his green Cajun Cottage near where the 17th Street floodwall breached. 8

He hasn't had much luck, "just some tools that might be OK," he says. "I left all my photos on top of a chest of drawers thinking the water wouldn't get that high. They say if you have more than five inches of water in your house for five days it's a loss. We had eight feet for two weeks." He's found one of his cats dead but thinks the other two might have escaped. He invites me to look inside. From the door it's a jumble of furniture, including a sofa, table, twisted carpet, lamps and wooden pieces all covered in black and gray gunk, reeking of mold and rotted cat food. I try not to breathe too deeply. "I had a collection of Jazz Fest T shirts going back to '79 but they're gone." He's wearing a mask, rubber boots and gloves, but still manages to give an expressive shrug of resignation when I take his picture. "I lived in this house 16 years. We'd have been fine if the levee hadn't broke. We'd be moving back right now." . . . 9

A Disappeared Town

I catch a ride along the west bank of the Mississippi in Plaquemines Parish south of New Orleans with deputy Sheriff Ken Harvey. This is where towns of several thousand, like Empire and Buras, got washed away and some oil tank farms ruptured. Where the 10

Bob Chick examines his flood-ruined house in the Lakeview section of New Orleans. (© David Helvarg)

road's cut by water, we drive up on the eroded levee and keep going. There are boats on the land, and houses in the water or washed onto the road or turned into woodpiles. At one point where the levee broke and the water poured through, there's nothing but a field where Diamond, an unincorporated town of about 300 including many trailer-park residents, stood. Those folks never seem to catch a break.

11 I take a picture of an antebellum white mansion in the water along with a floating pickup, a larger truck hanging off a tree, a semi-trailer cab under the bottom of an uplifted house, a speedboat through a picture window, the Buras water tower collapsed next to a wrecked store, shrimp boats on the levee, on the road and in the bushes with military patrols passing by. We stop and stare in awe at a 200-foot barge tossed atop the levee like a bath toy on a tub rim.

12 Approaching the Empire Bridge, I note the white church facing north towards us is still intact and suggest that's a hopeful sign. "It used to face the road," Ken points out. . . .

13 Unfortunately, as I drive east through Mississippi and Alabama I find most of [the] coastal trees and wetlands festooned with plastic like Tibetan prayer flags (as if monks were praying over dead turtles and seabirds). In Biloxi, along with smashed casinos, historic homes and neighborhoods, I find miles of beachfront covered in plastic buckets and insulation, mattresses, furniture, chunks of drywall and Styrofoam pellets that the seabirds are eyeing as potential snack food. I wave down a truck marked "Department of Natural Resources," but the guys inside are from Indiana.

14 I feel like an eco-geek being more concerned about the gulls and wetlands than the lost revenue from the casinos that everyone else seems to be obsessing on. The waterside wing of the new Hard Rock Casino is now a smashed tangle of twisted girders and concrete. I pull over by an 8,000 ton, 600-foot-long casino barge that was pushed half a mile by the storm, landing on Beach Drive. Somewhere underneath its barnacle-encrusted black hull is a historic mansion. Nearby, the Grand Casino barge has taken out much of the stately facade of the six story yellow brick Biloxi Yacht Club before grounding next to it. Another barge landed on the Holiday Inn, where more than 25 people may have been trying to ride out the hurricane. No one's been able to do a body-recovery there yet.

Because Southern Baptist and other religious conservatives objected to 'land-based' gambling in Mississippi, much of Biloxi's wetlands were torn up to make way for these floating casinos. 15

I talk with Phil Sturgeon, a Harrah's security agent hanging out with some cops from Winter Park, Florida. He's in jeans and a gray shirt with a toothbrush and pen sticking out the pocket. He tells me the storm surge crested at about 35 feet, at least five feet higher than Camille in '69. 16

In Waveland, I drive over twisted railroad tracks where the eye of Katrina passed into neighborhoods of jagged wooden debris. A middle-aged couple is trying to clear the drive to the lot where their home once stood. A surfboard leans up against one of the live oaks that seem to have fared better then the houses in between them. 17

"Are you an adjuster?" the woman asks. 18

"No, a reporter." 19

"Good, because we don't like adjusters. Nationwide was not on our side." 20

Apparently they've been offered $1,700 on their $422,000 home. 21

"At least you've got your surfboard," I tell John, her husband, "Oh, that's not my surfboard," he grins, pointing around. "And that's not my boat, and that's not my Corvette (buried to its hood in the rubble), and that's not our roof. We think it might belong to the house at the end of the street." . . . 22

Starting Again

I'm back in New Orleans on Canal Street, where the Salvation Army offers me cold water, a baloney sandwich (I decline) and a fruit cocktail. It's been a long day with the Army Corps of Engineers, who've leased helicopters that are dropping 3,000 and 7,000 pound sandbags on the latest breach in the Industrial Canal which has reflooded the Lower Ninth Ward. I enter the Sheraton after getting cleared by muscular Blackwater Security guys in tan and khaki tee shirts and shorts with Glocks on their hips. Another one sits by the elevators checking room IDs. I wonder if being a professional mercenary is good training for concierge duty. I sit by the Pelican bar in the lobby looking out the big three-story glass window at the media RVs and SUVs on the street—feeling as if I've been in this hotel before in various war zones and Third World capitals like Managua, Tegucigalpa, and Suva. 23

The Gulf region is now very much like a war zone, only with fewer deaths (about 1,200 bodies recovered at the time of my visit) and far more extensive damage. It also offers many of the same ironies and bizarre moments. Unity Radio announces that if you're going to tonight's Louisiana State University football game in Baton Rouge you can return after curfew provided you show your game stubs to the deputies at the roadblocks. 24

Three years ago I made a decision. I'd lost a key person in my life and was trying to decide what to do next. I was considering either going back to war reporting, as George Bush was clearly planning a pre-emptive invasion of Iraq, or turning from journalism to ocean advocacy . . . . Finally, I decided that while we'll probably always have wars, we may not always have living reefs, wild fish or protective coastal wetlands. 25

What we know we are going to have are more environmental disasters like the Hurricane Season of '05 linked to fossil-fuel-fired climate change and bad coastal policies driven by saltwater special interests. 26

Still, destruction on a biblical scale also offers Noah-like opportunities for restoration after the flood. There are practical solutions to the dangers we confront, along 27 with models of how to live safely by the sea. Things can be done right in terms of building wisely along the coasts, and advancing social and environmental equity. But it will take a new wave of citizen activism to avoid repetition of old mistakes, with even more dire consequences.

Questions for Close Reading

1. What is the selection's thesis? Locate the sentence(s) in which Helvarg states his main idea. If he doesn't state his thesis explicitly, express it in your own words.
2. Helvarg uses headings to divide his essay into sections. What is the subject of the section entitled "Urban Floodplain"? How does this section frame the remainder of the essay?
3. Most of the details in Helvarg's essay focus on the destruction caused by the hurricane and the recovery effort. However, he does give a description of an activity that shows life going on as normal. What is it? Why does Helvarg include this description?
4. Some words are so new they are not yet in dictionaries. Helvarg uses such a word when he describes himself as an "eco-geek" in paragraph 14. Given the context, and the meanings of the root *eco* and the word *geek*, how would you define this word?
5. Refer to your dictionary as needed to define the following words used in the selection: *consortium* (paragraph 1), *infiltrating* (4), *Woodstock* (5), *salvage* (8), *ruptured* (10), *antebellum* (11), *festooned* (13), *storm surge* (16), *adjuster* (18), and *mercenary* (23).

Questions About the Writer's Craft

1. **The pattern.** How does Helvarg organize his points in this essay? What transitional words and phrases does he use to keep the reader oriented as his essay progresses?
2. Most of the description in this essay focuses on visual details, but Helvarg also describes some other sensations. Find the passages in which Helvarg describes something other than the sights of the post-Katrina landscape, and evaluate their vividness. What do these passages contribute to the essay?
3. In paragraphs 4 and 24, to what does Helvarg compare the post-Katrina Gulf Coast? How does this analogy help the reader envision the destruction? How does it help express the dominant impression of the essay?
4. Helvarg took the photographs that accompany this essay. Compare the photograph of the marked door on page 176 with the author's description of it in paragraph 6. Does this photograph add to the description in the essay, or is the author's description so vivid that the photograph is unnecessary? Now

compare the photograph of Bob Chick on page 177 with the author's description of him in paragraph 9. Does this photograph add to the description of Bob in the essay, or is the author's description so vivid that the photograph is unnecessary? If you were writing this essay, would you include the photographs? If so, how would they affect the way you wrote the essay?

Writing Assignments Using Description as a Pattern of Development

1. One reason Helvarg's essay has such an impact is that destruction of the normal Gulf Coast environment was sudden as well as devastating. Not all environmental destruction is so dramatic, however. Find something in your own environment—your home, neighborhood, city, or region—that has been damaged or destroyed by gradual overuse or neglect. For example, your home may have a shabby room, or part of your yard may be overgrown. Or your neighborhood may have a rundown playground or park, or roads full of potholes, or an abandoned building. Select a location that has been neglected or overused, and write an essay in which you describe this damaged environment. Gordon Parks's descriptions of Brazilian *favelas* in "Flavio's Home" (page 182) might provide additional inspiration for your own writing.
2. Although severe weather, like Hurricane Katrina, provides good subject matter for description, so does more common, less destructive weather. Think of a day on which the weather was important to you but turned out badly. For example, you might have planned an outdoor event and it rained, or you might have scheduled a trip and it snowed, or you might have worn great new clothes and been too hot or too cold. Write an essay in which you describe this uncooperative weather. Use sensory details and figures of speech to convey your feelings about this day.

Writing Assignments Combining Patterns of Development

3. In "The Storm This Time," the enviromental devastation was caused by a natural event. However, much destruction of the environment is caused by people rather than by weather or other natural disasters. Select a place you know that has changed for the worse through human use. For example, you might choose an industrial site, a polluted river or lake, or a park. *Compare* and *contrast* the place as it once was and as it is now. Provide vivid *descriptions* of how the place has changed.

4. The Gulf Coast has a lot of experience with hurricanes; Katrina was just the most destructive one in recent years. Other areas are prone to other

types of natural disasters. Research the destructive weather and other natural events that your area typically experiences. Good places to start are the websites of the Federal Emergency Management Agency (www.fema.gov) and the National Oceanic and Atmospheric Administration (www.noaa.gov). Then write an essay in which you *classify* the natural disasters that occur in your area and *describe* each type, giving specific *examples* where possible.

Writing Assignment Using a Journal Entry as a Starting Point

5. Review your pre-reading journal entry about the natural disaster or event that you experienced. Write an essay in which you *describe* its aftermath. How did it *affect* you and others in your community? How did the event change your attitude toward nature? How did it *affect* the way you prepare for future natural emergencies? For another account of a life-changing series of events, see Beth Johnson's "Bombs Bursting in Air" (page 252).

GORDON PARKS

The son of deeply religious tenant farmers, Gordon Parks (1912–2006) grew up in Kansas knowing both the comforts of familial love and the torments of poverty and racism. A series of odd jobs when he was a teenager gave Parks the means to buy his first camera. So evocative were his photographic studies that both *Life* and *Vogue* brought him on staff, the first black photographer to be hired by the two magazines. Parks's prodigious creativity found expression in filmmaking (*Shaft* in 1971), musical composition (both classical and jazz), fiction, nonfiction, and poetry (titles include *The Learning Tree*, *A Choice of Weapons*, *To Smile in Autumn*, *Arias in Silence*, *Glimpses Toward Infinity*, *A Star for Noon*, and *The Sun Stalker*, published, respectively, in 1986, 1987, 1988, 1994, 1996, 2000, and 2003). In the following essay, taken from his 1990 autobiography, *Voices in the Mirror*, Parks tells the story behind one of his most memorable photographic works—that of a twelve-year-old boy and his family, living in the slums of Rio de Janeiro.

Pre-Reading Journal Entry

The problem of poverty has provoked a wide array of proposed solutions. One controversial proposal argues that the government should pay poor women financial incentives to use birth control. What do you think of this proposal? Why is such a policy controversial? Use your journal to explore your thinking on this issue.

FLAVIO'S HOME

I've never lost my fierce grudge against poverty. It is the most savage of all human afflictions, claiming victims who can't mobilize their efforts against it, who often lack strength to digest what little food they scrounge up to survive. It keeps growing, multiplying, spreading like a cancer. In my wanderings I attack it wherever I can—in barrios, slums and favelas. 1

Catacumba was the name of the favela[1] where I found Flavio da Silva. It was wickedly hot. The noon sun baked the mud-rot of the wet mountainside. Garbage and human excrement clogged the open sewers snaking down the slopes. José Gallo, a *Life* reporter, and I rested in the shade of a jacaranda tree halfway up Rio de Janeiro's most infamous deathtrap. Below and above us were a maze of shacks, but in the distance alongside the beach stood the gleaming white homes of the rich. 2

Breathing hard, balancing a tin of water on his head, a small boy climbed toward us. He was miserably thin, naked but for filthy denim shorts. His legs resembled sticks covered with skin and screwed into his feet. Death was all over him, in his sunken eyes, cheeks and jaundiced coloring. He stopped for breath, coughing, his chest heaving as water slopped over his bony shoulders. Then jerking sideways like a mechanical toy, he smiled a smile I will never forget. Turning, he went on up the mountainside. 3

The detailed *Life* assignment in my back pocket was to find an impoverished father with a family, to examine his earnings, political leanings, religion, friends, dreams and frustrations. I had been sent to do an essay on poverty. This frail boy bent under his load said more to me about poverty than a dozen poor fathers. I touched Gallo, and we got up and followed the boy to where he entered a shack near the top of the mountainside. It was a leaning crumpled place of old plankings with a rusted tin roof. From inside we heard the babblings of several children. José knocked. The door opened and the boy stood smiling with a bawling naked baby in his arms. 4

Still smiling, he whacked the baby's rump, invited us in and offered us a box to sit on. The only other recognizable furniture was a sagging bed and a broken baby's crib. Flavio was twelve, and with Gallo acting as interpreter, he introduced his younger brothers and sisters: "Mario, the bad one; Baptista, the good one; Albia, Isabel and the baby Zacarias." Two other girls burst into the shack, screaming and pounding on one another. Flavio jumped in and parted them. "Shut up, you two." He pointed at the older girl. "That's Maria, the nasty one." She spit in his face. He smacked her and pointed to the smaller sister. "That's Luzia. She thinks she's pretty." 5

Having finished the introductions, he went to build a fire under the stove—a rusted, bent top of an old gas range resting on several bricks. Beneath it was a piece of tin that caught the hot coals. The shack was about six by ten feet. Its grimy walls were a patchwork of misshapen boards with large gaps between them, revealing other shacks below stilted against the slopes. The floor, rotting under layers of grease and dirt, caught shafts of light slanting down through spaces in the roof. A large hole in the far corner served as a toilet. Beneath that hole was the sloping mountainside. Pockets of poverty in New York's Harlem, on Chicago's south side, in Puerto Rico's infamous El Fungito seemed pale by comparison. None of them had prepared me for this one in the favela of Catacumba. 6

[1]Slums on the outskirts of Rio de Janeiro, Brazil, inhabited by seven hundred thousand people (editors' note).

7 Flavio washed rice in a large dishpan, then washed Zacarias's feet in the same water. But even that dirty water wasn't to be wasted. He tossed in a chunk of lye soap and ordered each child to wash up. When they were finished he splashed the water over the dirty floor, and, dropping to his knees, he scrubbed the planks until the black suds sank in. Just before sundown he put beans on the stove to warm, then left, saying he would be back shortly. "Don't let them burn," he cautioned Maria. "If they do and Poppa beats me, you'll get it later." Maria, happy to get at the licking spoon, switched over and began to stir the beans. Then slyly she dipped out a spoonful and swallowed them. Luzia eyed her. "I see you. I'm going to tell on you for stealing our supper."

8 Maria's eyes flashed anger. "You do and I'll beat you, you little bitch." Luzia threw a stick at Maria and fled out the door. Zacarias dropped off to sleep. Mario, the bad one, slouched in a corner and sucked his thumb. Isabel and Albia sat on the floor clinging to each other with a strange tenderness. Isabel held onto Albia's hair and Albia clutched at Isabel's neck. They appeared frozen in an act of quiet violence.

9 Flavio returned with wood, dumped it beside the stove and sat down to rest for a few minutes, then went down the mountain for more water. It was dark when he finally came back, his body sagging from exhaustion. No longer smiling, he suddenly had the look of an old man and by now we could see that he kept the family going. In the closed torment of that pitiful shack, he was waging a hopeless battle against starvation. The da Silva children were living in a coffin.

10 When at last the parents came in, Gallo and I seemed to be part of the family. Flavio had already told them we were there. "Gordunn Americano!" Luzia said, pointing at me. José, the father, viewed us with skepticism. Nair, his pregnant wife, seemed tired beyond speaking. Hardly acknowledging our presence, she picked up Zacarias, placed him on her shoulder and gently patted his behind. Flavio scurried about like a frightened rat, his silence plainly expressing the fear he held of his father. Impatiently, José da Silva waited for Flavio to serve dinner. He sat in the center of the bed with his legs crossed beneath him, frowning, waiting. There were only three tin plates. Flavio filled them with black beans and rice, then placed them before his father. José da Silva tasted them, chewed for several moments, then nodded his approval for the others to start. Only he and Nair had spoons; the children ate with their fingers. Flavio ate off the top of a coffee can. Afraid to offer us food, he edged his rice and beans toward us, gesturing for us to take some. We refused. He smiled, knowing we understood.

11 Later, when we got down to the difficult business of obtaining permission from José da Silva to photograph his family, he hemmed and hawed, wallowing in the pleasant authority of the decision maker. He finally gave in, but his manner told us that he expected something in return. As we were saying good night Flavio began to cough violently. For a few moments his lungs seemed to be tearing apart. I wanted to get away as quickly as possible. It was cowardly of me, but the bluish cast of his skin beneath the sweat, the choking and spitting were suddenly unbearable.

12 Gallo and I moved cautiously down through the darkness trying not to appear as strangers. The Catacumba was no place for strangers after sundown. Desperate criminals hid out there. To hunt them out, the police came in packs, but only in daylight. Gallo cautioned me. "If you get caught up here after dark it's best to stay at the da Silvas' until morning." As we drove toward the city the large white buildings of the rich loomed up. The world behind us seemed like a bad dream. I had already decided to get the boy Flavio to a doctor, and as quickly as possible.

13 The plush lobby of my hotel on the Copacabana waterfront was crammed with people in formal attire. With the stink of the favela in my clothes, I hurried to the

elevator hoping no passengers would be aboard. But as the door was closing a beautiful girl in a white lace gown stepped in. I moved as far away as possible. Her escort entered behind her, swept her into his arms and they indulged in a kiss that lasted until they exited on the next floor. Neither of them seemed to realize that I was there. The room I returned to seemed to be oversized; the da Silva shack would have fitted into one corner of it. The steak dinner I had would have fed the da Silvas for three days.

Billowing clouds blanketed Mount Corcovado as we approached the favela the following morning. Suddenly the sun burst through, silhouetting Cristo Redentor, the towering sculpture of Christ with arms extended, its back turned against the slopes of Catacumba. The square at the entrance to the favela bustled with hundreds of favelados. Long lines waited at the sole water spigot. Others waited at the only toilet on the entire mountainside. Women, unable to pay for soap, beat dirt from their wash at laundry tubs. Men, burdened with lumber, picks and shovels and tools important to their existence threaded their way through the noisy throngs. Dogs snarled, barked and fought. Woodsmoke mixed with the stench of rotting things. In the mist curling over the higher paths, columns of favelados climbed like ants with wood and water cans on their heads. 14

We came upon Nair bent over her tub of wash. She wiped away sweat with her apron and managed a smile. We asked for her husband and she pointed to a tiny shack off to her right. This was José's store, where he sold kerosene and bleach. He was sitting on a box, dozing. Sensing our presence, he awoke and commenced complaining about his back. "It kills me. The doctors don't help because I have no money. Always talk and a little pink pill that does no good. Ah, what is to become of me?" A woman came to buy bleach. He filled her bottle. She dropped a few coins and as she walked away his eyes stayed on her backside until she was out of sight. Then he was complaining about his back again. 15

"How much do you earn a day?" Gallo asked. 16

"Seventy-five cents. On a good day maybe a dollar." 17

"Why aren't the kids in school?" 18

"I don't have money for the clothes they need to go to school." 19

"Has Flavio seen a doctor?" 20

He pointed to a one-story wooden building. "That's the clinic right there. They're mad because I built my store in front of their place. I won't tear it down so they won't help my kids. Talk, talk, talk and pink pills." We bid him good-bye and started climbing, following mud trails, jutting rock, slime-filled holes and shack after shack propped against the slopes on shaky pilings. We sidestepped a dead cat covered with maggots. I held my breath for an instant, only to inhale the stench of human excrement and garbage. Bare feet and legs with open sores climbed above us—evils of the terrible soil they trod every day, and there were seven hundred thousand or more afflicted people in favelas around Rio alone. Touching me, Gallo pointed to Flavio climbing ahead of us carrying firewood. He stopped to glance at a man descending with a small coffin on his shoulder. A woman and a small child followed him. When I lifted my camera, grumbling erupted from a group of men sharing beer beneath a tree. 21

"They're threatening," Gallo said. "Keep moving. They fear cameras. Think they're evil eyes bringing bad luck." Turning to watch the funeral procession, Flavio caught sight of us and waited. When we took the wood from him he protested, saying he was used to carrying it. He gave in when I hung my camera around his neck. Then, beaming, he climbed on ahead of us. 22

The fog had lifted and in the crisp morning light the shack looked more squalid. Inside the kids seemed even noisier. Flavio smiled and spoke above their racket. "Someday I want 23 to live in a real house on a real street with good pots and pans and a bed with sheets." He lit the fire to warm leftovers from the night before. Stale rice and beans—for breakfast and supper. No lunch; midday eating was out of the question. Smoke rose and curled up through the ceiling's cracks. An air current forced it back, filling the place and Flavio's lungs with fumes. A coughing spasm doubled him up, turned his skin blue under viscous sweat. I handed him a cup of water, but he waved it away. His stomach tightened as he dropped to his knees. His veins throbbed as if they would burst. Frustrated, we could only watch; there was nothing we could do to help. Strangely, none of his brothers or sisters appeared to notice. None of them stopped doing whatever they were doing. Perhaps they had seen it too often. After five interminable minutes it was over, and he got to his feet, smiling as though it had all been a joke. "Maria, it's time for Zacarias to be washed!"

24 "But there's rice in the pan!"

25 "Dump it in another pan—and don't spill water!"

26 Maria picked up Zacarias, who screamed, not wanting to be washed. Irritated, Maria gave him a solid smack on his bare bottom. Flavio stepped over and gave her the same, then a free-for-all started with Flavio, Maria and Mario slinging fists at one another. Mario got one in the eye and fled the shack calling Flavio a dirty son-of-a-bitch. Zacarias wound up on the floor sucking his thumb and escaping his washing. The black bean and rice breakfast helped to get things back to normal. Now it was time to get Flavio to the doctor.

27 The clinic was crowded with patients—mothers and children covered with open sores, a paralytic teenager, a man with an ear in a state of decay, an aged blind couple holding hands in doubled darkness. Throughout the place came wailings of hunger and hurt. Flavio sat nervously between Gallo and me. "What will the doctor do to me?" he kept asking.

28 "We'll see. We'll wait and see."

29 In all, there were over fifty people. Finally, after two hours, it was Flavio's turn and he broke out in a sweat, though he smiled at the nurse as he passed through the door to the doctor's office. The nurse ignored it; in this place of misery, smiles were unexpected.

30 The doctor, a large, beady-eyed man with a crew cut, had an air of impatience. Hardly acknowledging our presence, he began to examine the frightened Flavio. "Open your mouth. Say 'Ah.' Jump up and down. Breathe out. Take off those pants. Bend over. Stand up. Cough. Cough louder. Louder." He did it all with such cold efficiency. Then he spoke to us in English so Flavio wouldn't understand. "This little chap has just about had it." My heart sank. Flavio was smiling, happy to be over with the examination. He was handed a bottle of cough medicine and a small box of pink pills, then asked to step outside and wait.

31 "This the da Silva kid?"

32 "Yes."

33 "What's your interest in him?"

34 "We want to help in some way."

35 "I'm afraid you're too late. He's wasted with bronchial asthma, malnutrition and, I suspect, tuberculosis. His heart, lungs and teeth are all bad." He paused and wearily rubbed his forehead. "All that at the ripe old age of twelve. And these hills are packed with other kids just as bad off. Last year ten thousand died from dysentery alone. But what can we do? You saw what's waiting outside. It's like this every day. There's hardly enough money to buy aspirin. A few wealthy people who care help keep us going." He was quiet for a moment. "Maybe the right climate, the right diet, and constant medical care might . . . " He stopped and shook his head. "Naw. That poor lad's finished. He might last another year—maybe not." We thanked him and left.

36 "What did he say?" Flavio asked as we scaled the hill.

37 "Everything's going to be all right, Flav. There's nothing to worry about."

38 It had clouded over again by the time we reached the top. The rain swept in, clearing the mountain of Corcovado. The huge Christ figure loomed up again with clouds swirling around it. And to it I said a quick prayer for the boy walking beside us. He smiled as if he had read my thoughts. "Papa says 'El Cristo' has turned his back on the favela."

39 "You're going to be all right, Flavio."

40 "I'm not scared of death. It's my brothers and sisters I worry about. What would they do?"

41 "You'll be all right, Flavio."[2]

---

[2]Parks's photo-essay on Flavio generated an unprecedented response from *Life* readers. Indeed, they sent so much money to the da Silvas that the family was able to leave the *favela* for better living conditions. Parks brought Flavio to the United States for medical treatment, and the boy's health was restored. However, Flavio's story didn't have an unqualified happy ending. Although he overcame his illness and later married and had a family, Flavio continuously fantasized about returning to the United States, convinced that only by returning to America could he improve his life. His obsession eventually eroded the promise of his life in Brazil (editors' note).

Questions for Close Reading

1. What is the selection's thesis (or dominant impression)? Locate the sentence(s) in which Parks states his main idea. If he doesn't state the thesis explicitly, express it in your own words.
2. What is Flavio's family like? Why does Flavio have so much responsibility in the household?
3. What are some of the distinctive characteristics of Flavio's neighborhood and home?
4. What seems to be the basis of Flavio's fear of giving food to Parks and Gallo? What did Parks and Gallo understand that led them to refuse?
5. Refer to your dictionary as needed to define the following words used in the selection: *barrios* (paragraph 1), *jacaranda* (2), *jaundiced* (3), and *spigot* (14).

Questions About the Writer's Craft

1. **The pattern.** Without stating it explicitly, Parks conveys a dominant impression about Flavio. What is that impression? What details create it?
2. **Other patterns.** When relating how Flavio performs numerous household tasks, Parks describes several *processes*. How do these step-by-step explanations reinforce Parks's dominant impression of Flavio?
3. Parks provides numerous sensory specifics to depict Flavio's home. Look closely, for example, at the description in paragraph 6. Which words and

phrases convey strong sensory images? How does Parks use transitions to help the reader move from one sensory image to another?

4. Paragraph 13 includes a scene that occurs in Parks's hotel. What's the effect of this scene? What does it contribute to the essay that the most detailed description of the *favela* could not?

Writing Assignments Using Description as a Pattern of Development

1. Parks paints a wrenching portrait of a person who remains vibrant and hopeful even though he is suffering greatly—from physical illness, poverty, overwork, and worry. Write a description about someone you know who has shown courage or other positive qualities during a time of personal trouble. Include, as Parks does, plentiful details about the person's appearance and behavior so that you don't have to state directly what you admire about the person. Maya Angelou's "Sister Flowers" (page 167) shows how one writer conveys the special quality of an admirable individual.

2. Parks presents an unforgettable description of the *favela* and the living conditions there. Write an essay about a region, city, neighborhood, or building that also projects an overwhelming negative feeling. Include only those details that convey your dominant impression, and provide—as Parks does—vivid sensory language to convey your attitude toward your subject.

Writing Assignments Combining Patterns of Development

3. The doctor reports that a few wealthy people contribute to the clinic, but the reader can tell from the scene in Parks's hotel that most people are insensitive to those less fortunate. Write an essay *describing* a specific situation that you feel reflects people's tendency to ignore the difficulties of others. Analyze why people distance themselves from the problem; then present specific *steps* that could be taken to sensitize them to the situation. Charmie Gholson's "Charity Display?" (page 220) and Diane Cole's "Don't Just Stand There" (page 333) will provide some perspective on the way people deal with the pain of others.

4. Although Parks celebrates Flavio's generosity of spirit, the writer also *illustrates* the brutalizing effect of an impoverished environment. Prepare an essay in which you also show that setting, architecture, even furnishings can influence mood and behavior. You may, as Parks does, focus on the corrosive effect of a negative environment, or you may write about the nurturing effect of a positive environment. Either way, provide vivid *descriptive* details of the

environment you're considering. Possible subjects include a park in the middle of a city, a bus terminal, and a college library.

Writing Assignment Using a Journal Entry as a Starting Point

5. Write an essay explaining why you think impoverished women should—or should not—be paid financial incentives to practice birth control. To help define your position, review your pre-reading journal entry, and interview classmates, friends, and family members to get their opinions. Consider supplementing this informal research with material gathered in the library and/or on the Internet. Weigh all the evidence carefully before formulating your position.

ADDITIONAL WRITING TOPICS: DESCRIPTION

General Assignments

Write an essay using description to develop one of the following topics. Remember that an effective description focuses on a dominant impression and arranges details in a way that best supports that impression. Your details—vivid and appealing to the senses—should be carefully chosen so that the essay isn't overburdened with material of secondary importance. When writing, keep in mind that varied sentence structure and imaginative figures of speech are ways to make a descriptive piece compelling.

1. A favorite item of clothing
2. A school as a young child might see it
3. A hospital room you have visited or stayed in
4. An individualist's appearance
5. A coffee shop, bus shelter, newsstand, or some other small place
6. A parade or victory celebration
7. A banana, squash, or other fruit or vegetable
8. A particular drawer in a desk or bureau
9. A houseplant
10. A "media event"
11. A dorm room

12. An elderly person
13. An attractive man or woman
14. A prosthetic device or wheelchair
15. A TV, film, or music celebrity
16. A student lounge
17. A once-in-a-lifetime event
18. The inside of something, such as a cave, boat, car, shed, or machine
19. A friend, roommate, or other person you know well
20. An essential gadget or a useless gadget

Assignments with a Specific Purpose, Audience, and Point of View

On Campus

1. For an audience of incoming first-year students, prepare a speech describing registration day at your college. Use specific details to help prepare students for the actual event. Choose an adjective that represents your dominant impression of the experience, and keep that word in mind as you write.

2. Your college has decided to replace an old campus structure (for example, a dorm or dining hall) with a new version. Write a letter of protest to the administration, describing the place so vividly and appealingly that its value and need for preservation are unquestionable.

3. As a staff member of the campus newspaper, you have been asked to write a weekly column of social news and gossip. For your first column, you plan to describe a recent campus event—a dance, party, concert, or other social activity. With a straightforward or tongue-in-cheek tone, describe where the event was held, the appearance of the people who attended, and so on.

At Home or in the Community

4. As a subscriber to a community-wide dating service, you've been asked to submit a description of the kind of person you'd like to meet. Describe your ideal date. Focus on specifics about physical appearance, personal habits, character traits, and interests.

5. As a resident of a particular town, you're angered by the appearance of a certain spot and by the activities that take place there. Write a letter to the town council, describing in detail the undesirable nature of this place (an adult bookstore, a bar, a bus station, a neglected park or beach). End with some suggestions about ways to improve the situation.

On the Job

6. You've noticed a recurring problem in your workplace and want to bring it to the attention of your boss, who typically is inattentive. Write a letter to your boss describing the problem. Your goal is not to provide solutions, but rather, to provide vivid description—complete with sensory details—so that your boss can no longer deny the problem.

For additional writing, reading, and research resources, go to **www.mycomplab.com** and choose **Nadell/Langan/Comodromos'** ***The Longman Writer, 7/e***.

Narration

11

Bill Pugliano/Getty Images

WHAT IS NARRATION?

Human beings are instinctively storytellers. In prehistoric times, our ancestors huddled around campfires to hear tales of hunting and magic. In ancient times, warriors gathered in halls to listen to bards praise in song the exploits of epic heroes. Things are no different today. Boisterous children invariably settle down to listen when their parents read to them; millions of people tune in day after day to the ongoing drama of their favorite soap operas; vacationers sit motionless on the beach, caught up in the latest best-sellers; and all of us enjoy saying, "Just listen to what happened to me today." Our hunger for storytelling is basic.

Narration means telling a single story or several related stories. The story can be a means to an end, a way to support a main idea or thesis. To demonstrate that television has become the constant companion of many children, you might narrate a typical child's day in front of the television—starting with cartoons in the morning and ending with situation comedies at night. Or to support the point that the college registration process should be reformed, you could tell the tale of a chaotic morning spent trying to enroll in classes.

Narration is powerful. Every public speaker, from politician to classroom teacher, knows that stories capture the attention of listeners as nothing else can. We want to know what happened to others, not simply because we're curious, but also because their experiences shed light on our own lives. Narration lends force to opinion, triggers the flow of memory, and evokes places, times, and people in ways that are compelling and affecting.

HOW NARRATION FITS YOUR PURPOSE AND AUDIENCE

Since narratives tell a story, you may think they're found only in novels or short stories. But narration can also appear in essays, sometimes as a supplemental pattern of development. For example, if your purpose in a paper is to *persuade* apathetic readers that airport security regulations must be followed strictly, you might lead off with a brief account of armed terrorists who easily boarded planes on September 11. In a paper *defining* good teaching, you might keep readers engaged by including satirical anecdotes about one hapless instructor, the antithesis of an effective teacher. An essay on the *effects* of an overburdened judicial system might provide—in an attempt to involve readers—a dramatic account of the way one clearly guilty murderer plea-bargained his way to freedom.

In addition to providing effective support in one section of your paper, narration can also serve as an essay's dominant pattern of development. In fact, most of this chapter shows you how to use a single narrative to convey a central point and share with readers your view of what happened. You might choose to narrate the events of an afternoon spent with your three-year-old nephew as a way of revealing how you rediscovered the importance of family life. Or you might relate the story of your roommate's mugging, evoking the powerlessness and terror of being a victim.

Although some narratives relate unusual experiences, most tread familiar ground, telling tales of joy, love, loss, frustration, fear—all common emotions experienced during life. Narratives can take the ordinary and transmute it into something significant, even extraordinary. As Willa Cather, the American novelist, wrote: "There are only two or three human stories and they go on repeating themselves as fiercely as if they had never happened before." The challenge lies in applying your own vision to a tale, thereby making it unique.

At this point, you have a good sense of the way writers use narration to achieve their purpose and to connect with their readers. Now take a moment to look closely at the photograph at the beginning of this chapter. Imagine you're writing a "Recent Events" update, accompanied by the photo, for the website of an organization that supports (*or* opposes) the war in Iraq. Your purpose is to recount what happened at the protest in such a way that your account supports the website's position on the conflict. Jot down some phrases you might use when *narrating* the events of the day.

Prewriting Strategies

The following checklist shows how you can apply to narration some of the prewriting strategies discussed in Chapter 2.

NARRATION: A PREWRITING CHECKLIST

Select Your Narrative Event(s)

- ☐ What event evokes strong emotion in you and is likely to have a powerful effect on your readers?
- ☐ Does your journal suggest any promising subjects—for example, an entry about a bully's surprisingly respectful behavior toward a disabled student or a painful encounter with racial prejudice?
- ☐ Does a scrapbook souvenir, snapshot, old letter, or prized object (an athletic trophy, a political button) point to an event worth writing about?
- ☐ Will you focus on a personal experience (your high school graduation ceremony), an incident in someone else's life (a friend's battle with chronic illness), or a public event (a community effort to save a beached whale)?
- ☐ Can you recount your story effectively, given the length of a typical college essay? If not, will relating one key incident from the fuller, more complete event enable you to convey the point and feeling of the entire experience?
- ☐ If you write about an event in someone else's life, will you have time to interview the person? ("Why did you cross the picket line?" "What did you do when your boss told you to lie?")

Focus on the Conflict in the Event

- ☐ What is the source of tension in the event: one person's internal dilemma, a conflict between characters, or a struggle between a character and a social institution or natural phenomenon?
- ☐ Will the conflict create enough tension to "hook" readers and keep them interested?
- ☐ What point does the conflict and its resolution convey to readers?
- ☐ What tone is appropriate for recounting the conflict?

Use Prewriting to Generate Specifics About the Conflict

- ☐ Would the questioning technique ("Why did the argument occur?"), brainstorming, freewriting, mapping, or interviewing help you generate details about the conflict? Does your journal suggest ways to explore aspects of the conflict? ("When my friends participated in the violence at the rock concert, why didn't I try to stop them?")

STRATEGIES FOR USING NARRATION IN AN ESSAY

After prewriting, you're ready to draft your essay. Figure 11.1 and the suggestions that follow will be helpful whether you use narration as a dominant or supportive pattern of development.

FIGURE 11.1
Development Diagram: Writing a Narration Essay

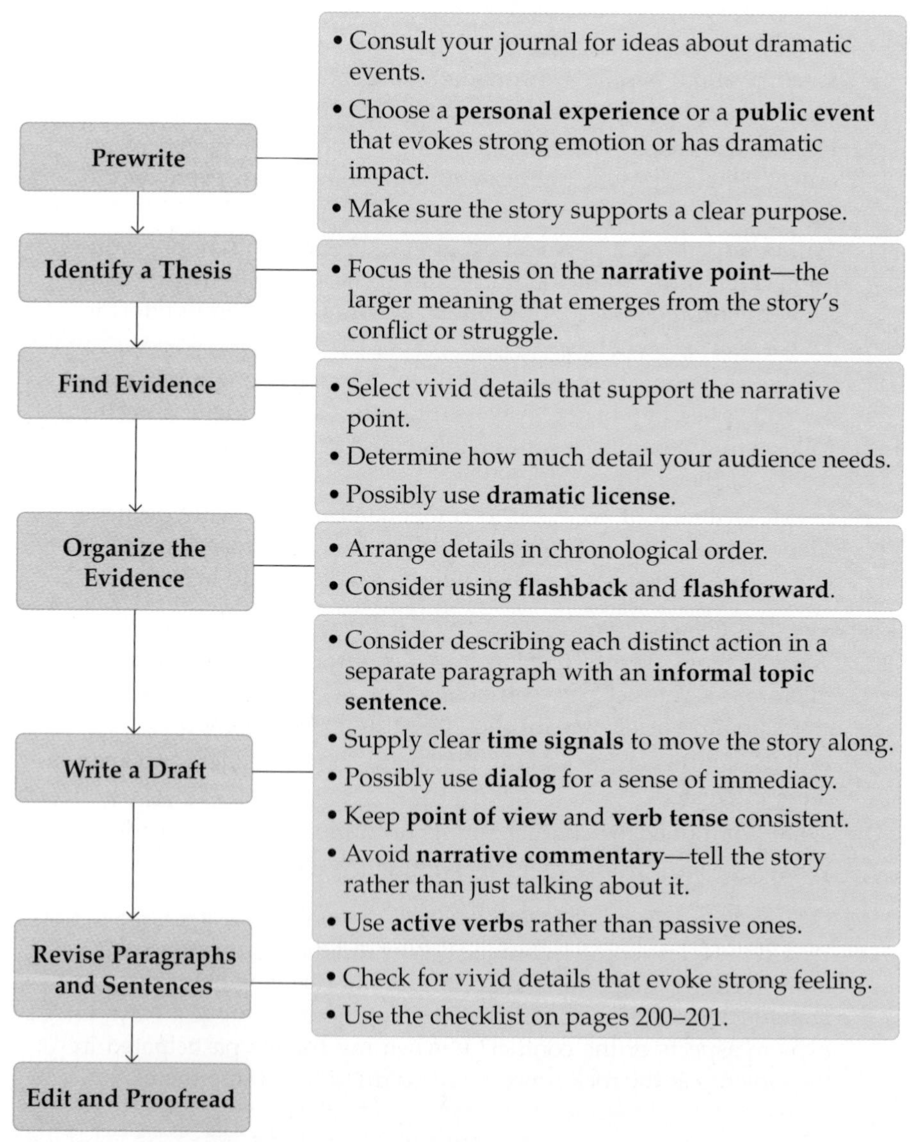

1. **Identify the point of the narrative conflict.** As you know, most narratives center around a conflict (see the checklist on page 193). When you relate a story, it's up to you to convey the *significance* or *meaning* of the event's conflict. In *The Adventures of Huckleberry Finn,* Mark Twain warned: "Persons attempting to find a motive in this narrative will be prosecuted; persons attempting to find a moral in it will be banished. . . . " Twain was, of course, being ironic; his novel's richness lies in its "motives" and "morals." Similarly, when recounting your narrative, be sure to begin with a clear sense of your *narrative point,* or *thesis.* Then either state that point directly or select details and a tone that imply the point you want readers to take away from your story.

   For example, suppose you decide to write about the time you got locked in a mall late at night. Your narrative might focus on the way the mall looked after hours and the way you struggled with mounting terror. But you would also use the narrative to make a point. Perhaps you want to emphasize that fear can be instructive. Or your point might be that malls have a disturbing, surreal underside. You could state this thesis explicitly. ("After hours, the mall shed its cheerful daytime demeanor and took on a more sinister quality.") Or you could refrain from stating the thesis directly, relying on your details and language to convey the point of the narrative: "The mannequins stared at me with glazed eyes and frozen smiles," and "The steel grates pulled over each store entrance glinted in the cold light, making each shop look like a prison cell."

2. **Develop only those details that advance the narrative point.** Nothing is more boring than a storyteller who gets sidetracked and drags out a story with nonessential details. When telling a story, you maintain an effective narrative pace by focusing on your point and eliminating any details that don't support it. A good narrative depends not only on what is included, but also on what has been left out.

   How do you determine which specifics to omit, which to treat briefly, and which to emphasize? Having a clear sense of your narrative point and knowing your audience are crucial. Assume you're writing a narrative about a disastrous get-acquainted dance sponsored by your college the first week of the academic year. In addition to telling what happened, you also want to make a point; perhaps you want to emphasize that, despite the college's good intentions, such "official" events actually make it difficult to meet people. With this purpose in mind, you might write about how stiff and unnatural students seemed, all dressed up in their best clothes; you might narrate portions of strained conversation you overheard; you might describe the way males gathered on one side of the room, females on the other—reverting to behaviors supposedly abandoned in fifth grade. All these details would support your narrative point.

   Because you don't want to lead away from that point, you would leave out details about the top-notch band and the appetizing refreshments at the dance. The music and food may have been surprisingly good, but since these details don't advance the point you want to make, they should not be included in your narrative.

   You also need to keep your audience in mind when selecting narrative details. If the audience consists of your instructor and other students—all of them familiar with the new student center where the dance was held—specific details about the center probably wouldn't have to be provided. But imagine that the essay is going to appear in the quarterly magazine published by the college's community relations office. Many of the magazine's readers are former graduates who haven't been on campus for several years. They may need additional specifics about the student center: its location, how many people it holds, how it is furnished.

As you write, keep asking yourself, "Is this detail or character or snippet of conversation essential? Does my audience need this detail to understand the conflict in the situation? Does this detail advance or intensify the narrative action?" Summarize details that have some importance but do not deserve lengthy treatment ("Two hours went by . . . "). And try to limit *narrative commentary*—statements that tell rather than show what happened—since such remarks interrupt the narrative flow. Focus instead on the specifics that propel action forward in a vigorous way.

Sometimes, especially if the narrative re-creates an event from the past, you won't be able to remember what happened detail for detail. In such a case, you should take advantage of what is called **dramatic license.** Using your current perspective as a guide, feel free to add or reshape details to suit your narrative point.

3. **Organize the narrative sequence.** All of us know the traditional beginning of fairy tales: "Once upon a time . . . " Every narrative begins somewhere, presents a span of time, and ends at a certain point. Frequently, you will want to use a straightforward time order, following the event *chronologically* from beginning to end: first this happened, next this happened, finally this happened.

   But sometimes a strict chronological recounting may not be effective—especially if the high point of the narrative gets lost somewhere in the middle of the time sequence. To avoid that possibility, you may want to disrupt chronology, plunge the reader into the middle of the story, and then return in a **flashback** to the tale's beginning. You are probably familiar with the way flashback is used on television and in film. You see someone appealing to the main characters for financial help, then return in a flashback to an earlier time when both were students in the same class. Narratives can also use **flashforward**—you give readers a glimpse of the future (the main character being jailed) before the story continues in the present (the events leading to the arrest). These techniques shift the story onto several planes and keep it from becoming a step-by-step, predictable account. Reserve flashforwards and flashbacks, however, for crucial incidents only, since breaking out of chronological order acts as emphasis. Here are examples of how flashback and flashforward can be used in narrative writing:

Flashback

Standing behind the wooden counter, Greg wielded his knife expertly as he shucked clams—one every ten seconds—with practiced ease. The scene contrasted sharply with his first day on the job, when his hands broke out in blisters and when splitting each shell was like prying open a safe.

Flashforward

Rushing to move my car from the no-parking zone, I waved a quick good-bye to Karen as she climbed the steps to the bus. I didn't know then that by the time I picked her up at the bus station later that day, she had made a decision that would affect both our lives.

Whether or not you choose to include flashbacks or flashforwards in an essay, remember to limit the time span covered by the narrative. Otherwise, you'll have trouble generating the details needed to give the story depth and meaning. Also, regardless of the time sequence you select, organize the tale so it drives toward a strong finish. Be careful that your story doesn't trail off into minor, anticlimactic details.

4. **Make the narrative easy to follow.** Describing each distinct action in a separate paragraph helps readers grasp the flow of events. Although narrative essays don't always have conventional topic sentences, each narrative paragraph should have a clear focus. Often this focus is indicated by a sentence early in the paragraph that directs attention to the action taking place. Such a sentence functions as a kind of *informal topic sentence;* the rest of the paragraph then develops that topic sentence. You should also be sure to use time signals when narrating a story. Words like *now, then, next, after,* and *later* ensure that your reader won't get lost as the story progresses.

5. **Make the narrative vigorous and immediate.** A compelling narrative provides an abundance of specific details, making readers feel as if they're experiencing the story being told. Readers must be able to see, hear, touch, smell, and taste the event you're narrating. *Vivid sensory description* is, therefore, an essential part of an effective narrative. (See pages 72–73 in Chapter 6 and pages 127–128 in Chapter 8 for more on concrete, sensory language.) Not only do specific sensory details make writing a pleasure to read—we all enjoy learning the particulars about people, places, and things—but they also give the narrative the stamp of reality. The specifics convince the reader that the event being described actually did, or could, occur.

   Compare the following excerpts from a narrative essay. The first version is lifeless and dull; the revised version, packed with sensory images, grabs readers with its sense of foreboding:

Original Version

That eventful day started out like every other summer day. My sister Tricia and I made several elaborate mud pies that we decorated with care. A little later on, as we were spraying each other with the garden hose, we heard my father walk up the path.

Revised

That sad summer day started out uneventfully enough. My sister Tricia and I spent a few hours mixing and decorating mud pies. Our hands caked with dry mud, we sprinkled each lopsided pie with alternating rows of dandelion and clover petals. Later, when the sun got hotter, we tossed our white T-shirts over the red picket fence—forgetting my grandmother's frequent warnings to be more ladylike. Our sweaty backs bared to the sun, we doused each other with icy sprays from the garden hose. Caught up in the primitive pleasure of it all, we barely heard my father as he walked up the garden path, the gravel crunching under his heavy work boots.

A caution: Sensory language enlivens narration, but it also slows the pace. Be sure that the slower pace suits your purpose. For example, a lengthy description fits an account of a leisurely summer vacation but is inappropriate in a tale about a frantic search for a misplaced wallet.

Another way to create an aura of narrative immediacy is to use **dialog** while telling a story. Our sense of other people comes, in part, from what they say and the way they sound. Conversational exchanges allow the reader to experience characters directly. Compare the following fragments of a narrative, one with dialog and one without, noting how much more energetic the second version is.

Original

As soon as I found my way back to the campsite, the trail guide commented on my disheveled appearance. I explained that I had heard some gunshots and had run back to camp as soon as I could.

Revised

As soon as I found my way back to the campsite, the trail guide took one look at me and drawled, "What on earth happened to you, Daniel Boone? You look as though you've been dragged through a haystack backwards."

"I'd look a lot worse if I hadn't run back here. When a bullet whizzes by me, I don't stick around to see who's doing the shooting."

Note that, when using dialog, you generally begin a new paragraph to indicate a shift from one person's speech to another's (as in the second example). Dialog can also be used to convey a person's inner thoughts. Like conversation between people, such interior dialog is enclosed in quotation marks.

The challenge in writing dialog, both exterior and interior, is to make each character's speech distinctive and convincing. Reading the dialog aloud—even asking friends or family members to speak the lines—will help you develop an ear for authentic speech. What sounds most natural is often a compressed and reshaped version of what was actually said. As with other narrative details, include only those portions of dialog that serve your purpose, fit the mood you want to create, and reveal character.

Another way to enliven narratives is to use *varied sentence structure.* Sentences that plod along with the same predictable pattern put readers to sleep. Experiment with your sentences by varying their length and type; mix long and short sentences, simple and complex. (For more on sentence structure, see pages 115–120 in Chapter 8.) Compare the following original and revised versions to get an idea of how effective varied sentence structure can be in narrative writing:

Original

The store manager went to the walk-in refrigerator every day. The heavy metal door clanged shut behind her. I had visions of her freezing to death among the hanging carcasses. The shiny door finally swung open. She waddled out.

Revised

Each time the store manager went to the walk-in refrigerator, the heavy metal door clanged shut behind her. Visions of her freezing to death among the hanging carcasses crept into my mind until, finally, the shiny door swung open and out she waddled.

Original

The yellow-and-blue striped fish struggled on the line. Its scales shimmered in the sunlight. Its tail waved frantically. I saw its desire to live. I decided to let it go.

Revised

Scales shimmering in the sunlight, tail waving frantically, the yellow-and-blue striped fish struggled on the line. Seeing its desire to live, I let it go.

Finally, *vigorous verbs* lend energy to narratives. Use active verb forms ("The boss *yelled* at him") rather than passive ones ("He *was yelled at* by the boss"), and try to replace anemic *to be* verbs ("She *was* a good basketball player") with more dynamic constructions ("She *played* basketball well"). (For more on strong verbs, see pages 128–130 in Chapter 8.)

6. **Keep your point of view and verb tense consistent.** All stories have a *narrator,* the person who tells the story. If you, as narrator, tell a story as you experienced it, the story is written in the *first-person point of view* ("I saw the dog pull loose"). But if you observed the event (or heard about it from others) and want to tell how someone else experienced the incident, you would use the *third-person point of view* ("Anne saw the dog pull loose"). Each point of view has advantages and limitations. First person allows you to express ordinarily private thoughts and to re-create an event as you actually experienced it. This point of view is limited, though, in its ability to depict the inner thoughts of other people involved in the event. By way of contrast, third person makes it easier to provide insight into the thoughts of all the participants. However, its objective, broad perspective may undercut some of the subjective immediacy typical of the "I was there" point of view. No matter which point of view you select, stay with that vantage point throughout the entire narrative. (For more on point of view, see pages 22–23 in Chapter 2.)

   Knowing whether to use the ***past*** or ***present tense*** ("I *strolled* into the room" as opposed to "I *stroll* into the room") is important. In most narrations, the past tense predominates, enabling the writer to span a considerable period of time. Although more rarely used, the present tense can be powerful for events of short durations—a wrestling match or a medical emergency, for instance. A narrative in the present tense prolongs each moment, intensifying the reader's sense of participation. Be careful, though; unless the event is intense and fast-paced, the present tense can seem contrived. Whichever tense you choose, avoid shifting midstream—starting, let's say, in the past tense ("she skated") and switching to the present tense ("she runs").

REVISION STRATEGIES

Once you have a draft of the essay, you're ready to revise. The following checklist will help you and those giving you feedback apply to narration some of the revision techniques discussed in Chapters 7 and 8.

NARRATION: A REVISION/PEER REVIEW CHECKLIST

Revise Overall Meaning and Structure

- ☐ What is the essay's main point? Is it stated explicitly or is it implied? Could the point be conveyed more clearly? How?
- ☐ What is the narrative's conflict? Is it stated explicitly or is it implied? Could the conflict be made more dramatic? How?

- ☐ From which point of view is the narrative told? Is it the most effective point of view for this essay? Why or why not?

Revise Paragraph Development

- ☐ Which paragraphs (or passages) fail to advance the action, reveal character, or contribute to the story's mood? Should these sections be condensed or eliminated?
- ☐ Where should the narrative pace be slowed down or quickened?
- ☐ Where is it difficult to follow the chronology of events? Should the order of paragraphs be changed? How? Where would additional time signals help?
- ☐ How could flashback or flashforward paragraphs be used to highlight key events?
- ☐ What can be done to make the essay's opening paragraph more compelling? Would dramatic dialog or mood-setting description help?
- ☐ What could be done to make the essay's closing paragraph more effective? Should the essay end earlier? Should it close by echoing an idea or image from the opening?

Revise Sentences and Words

- ☐ Where is sentence structure monotonous? Where would combining sentences, mixing sentence type, and alternating sentence length help?
- ☐ Where could dialog replace commentary to convey character and propel the story forward?
- ☐ Which sentences and words are inconsistent with the essay's tone?
- ☐ Which sentences would benefit from sensory details that heighten the narrative mood?
- ☐ Where do vigorous verbs convey action? Where could active verbs ("Many of us made the same error") replace passive ones ("The same error was made by many of us")? Where could dull *to be* verbs ("The room was dark") be converted to more dynamic forms ("The room darkened")?
- ☐ Where are there inappropriate shifts in point of view or verb tense?

STUDENT ESSAY: FROM PREWRITING THROUGH REVISION

The student essay that follows was written by Paul Monahan in response to this assignment:

> In "Shooting an Elephant," George Orwell tells about an incident that forced him to act in a manner contrary to his better instincts. Write a narrative about a time you faced a disturbing conflict and ended up doing something you later regretted.

After deciding to write about an encounter he had with an elderly woman in the store where he worked, Paul did some *freewriting* on his computer to gather material on his subject. When he later reviewed this freewriting, he crossed out unnecessary commentary, wrote notes signaling where dialog and descriptive details were needed, and indicated where paragraph breaks might occur. After annotating his freewriting in this manner, Paul felt comfortable launching into his first draft, without further shaping his freewriting or preparing an outline. As he wrote, though, he frequently referred to his warm-up material to organize his narrative and retrieve details. Paul's original freewriting is shown here; the handwritten marks indicate Paul's later efforts to shape and develop this material:

Freewriting

Set up contrast

Give details about her appearance

Add dialog

An old woman entered the store. She pushed the door, hobbled in, coughed, and seemed to be in pain. She wore a faded dress and a sweater that was much too small for her. The night was cold, but she didn't wear any stockings. You could see her veins. She strolled around the store, sneezing and hacking. She picked up a can of corn and stared at it. ~~She made me nervous~~. I walked over to see what was going on. Asked if she needed help.

Background information—move to first paragraph

I was the one to do this because I was on duty. Had worked at 7-11 for two years. Felt confident. Always tried to be friendly and polite. Hadn't had any trouble. ~~But the old woman worried me~~.

Add dialog

More specifics

Good title?

"I need food," she said. I told her how much the corn cost and also that the bologna was on sale (what a stupid, insensitive thing to do!). She said she couldn't pay. I almost told her to take the can of corn, but all the rules stopped me. Be polite, stay in control. I told her I couldn't give anything away.¶ Her face looked even more saggy. She kind of shook and put the can back. She left, I rushed out after her. Too late. Felt ashamed about acting like a robot. Mad at myself. If only I'd acted differently.

Now read Paul's paper, "If Only," noting the similarities and differences between his prewriting and final essay. You'll notice, for example, that Paul decided to move background information to the essay's opening, and that he ended up using as his title a shortened version of the final sentence in his prewriting. Finally, consider how well the essay applies the principles of narration discussed in this chapter. (The commentary that follows the paper will help you look at Paul's essay more closely and will give you some sense of how he went about revising his first draft.)

If Only

by Paul Monahan

1 Having worked at a 7-Eleven store for two years, I thought I had become successful at what our manager calls "customer relations." I firmly believed that a friendly smile and an automatic "sir," "ma'am," and "thank you" would see me through any situation that might arise, from soothing impatient or unpleasant people to apologizing for giving out the wrong change. But the other night an old woman shattered my belief that a glib response could smooth over the rough spots of dealing with other human beings.

Introduction

Narrative point (thesis)

2 The moment she entered, the woman presented a sharp contrast to our shiny store with its bright lighting and neatly arranged shelves. Walking as if each step were painful, she slowly pushed open the glass door and hobbled down the nearest aisle. She coughed dryly, wheezing with each breath. On a forty-degree night, she was wearing only a faded print dress, a thin, light-beige sweater too small to button, and black vinyl slippers with the backs cut out to expose calloused heels. There were no stockings or socks on her splotchy, blue-veined legs.

Informal topic sentence

Sensory details

3 After strolling around the store for several minutes, the old woman stopped in front of the rows of canned vegetables. She picked up some corn niblets and stared with a strange intensity at the label. At that point, I decided to be a good, courteous employee and asked her if she needed help. As I stood close to her, my smile became harder to maintain; her red-rimmed eyes were partially closed by yellowish crusts; her hands were covered with layer upon layer of grime, and the stale smell of sweat rose in a thick vaporous cloud from her clothes.

Informal topic sentence

Sensory details

4 "I need some food," she muttered in reply to my bright "Can I help you?"

Start of dialog

5 "Are you looking for corn, ma'am?"

6 "I need some food," she repeated. "Any kind."

7 "Well, the corn is ninety-five cents," I said in my most helpful voice. "Or, if you like, we have a special on bologna today."

8 "I can't pay," she said.

9 For a second, I was tempted to say, "Take the corn." But the employee rules flooded into my mind: Remain polite, but do not

Conflict established

let customers get the best of you. Let them know that you are in control. For a moment, I even entertained the idea that this was some sort of test, and that this woman was someone from the head office, testing my loyalty. I responded dutifully, "I'm sorry, ma'am, but I can't give away anything for free."

Informal topic sentence → The old woman's face collapsed a bit more, if that were 10
possible, and her hands trembled as she put the can back on the shelf. She shuffled past me toward the door, her torn and dirty clothing barely covering her bent back.

Conclusion

Moments after she left, I rushed out the door with the can 11
of corn, but she was nowhere in sight. For the rest of my shift, the image of the woman haunted me. I had been young, healthy, and smug. She had been old, sick, and desperate. Wishing with all my heart that I had acted like a human being rather than a robot, I was saddened to realize how fragile a hold we have on our better instincts.

Echoing of narrative point in the introduction

Commentary

Point of View, Tense, and Conflict

Paul chose to write "If Only" from the *first-person point of view,* a logical choice because he appears as a main character in his own story. Using the *past tense,* Paul recounts an incident filled with *conflict*—between him and the woman and between his fear of breaking the rules and his human instinct to help someone in need.

Narrative Point

It isn't always necessary to state the *narrative point* of an essay; it can be implied. But Paul decided to express the controlling idea of his narrative in two places—in the introduction ("But the other night an old woman shattered my belief that a glib response could smooth over the rough spots of dealing with other human beings") and again in the conclusion, where he expands his idea about rote responses overriding impulses of independent judgment and compassion. All of the essay's *narrative details* contribute to the point of the piece; Paul does not include any extraneous information that would detract from the central idea he wants to convey.

Organization

The narrative is *organized chronologically,* from the moment the woman enters the store to Paul's reaction after she leaves. Paul limits the narrative's time span. The entire incident probably occurs in under ten minutes, yet the introduction serves as a kind of *flashback* by providing some necessary background about Paul's past experiences. To help the reader follow the course of the narrative, Paul uses *time signals: "The moment* she entered, the woman presented a sharp contrast" (paragraph 2); *"At that point,* I decided to be a good, courteous employee" (3); *"For the rest of my shift,* the image of the woman haunted me" (11).

The paragraphs (except for those consisting solely of dialog) also contain *informal topic sentences* that direct attention to the specific stage of action being narrated. Indeed, each paragraph focuses on a distinct event: the elderly woman's actions when she first enters the store, the encounter between Paul and the woman, Paul's resulting inner conflict, the woman's subsequent response, and Paul's delayed reaction.

Combining Patterns of Development

This chronological chain of events, with one action leading to another, illustrates that the *cause-effect* pattern underlies the basic structure of Paul's essay. And by means of another pattern—*description*—Paul gives dramatic immediacy to the events being recounted. Throughout, he provides rich sensory details to engage the reader's interest. For instance, the sentence "her red-rimmed eyes were partially closed by yellowish crusts" (3) vividly re-creates the woman's appearance while also suggesting Paul's inner reaction to the woman.

Dialog and Sentence Structure

Paul uses other techniques to add energy and interest to his narrative. For one thing, he dramatizes his conflict with the woman through *dialog* that crackles with tension. And he achieves a vigorous narrative pace by *varying the length and structure of his sentences.* In the second paragraph, a short sentence ("There were no stockings or socks on her splotchy, blue-veined legs") alternates with a longer one ("On a forty-degree night, she was wearing only a faded print dress, a thin, light-beige sweater too small to button, and black vinyl slippers with the backs cut out to expose calloused heels"). Some sentences in the essay open with a subject and verb ("She coughed dryly"), while others start with dependent clauses or participial phrases ("As I stood close to her, my smile became harder to maintain"; "Walking as if each step were painful, she slowly pushed open the glass door") or with a prepositional phrase ("For a second, I was tempted").

Revising the First Draft

To get a sense of how Paul went about revising his essay, take a moment to look at the original version of his third paragraph shown here. The handwritten annotations, numbered in order of importance, represent Paul's ideas for revision. Compare this preliminary version with the final version in the full essay:

Original Version of Third Paragraph

After sneezing and hacking her way around the store, the old woman stopped in front of the vegetable shelves. She picked up a can of corn and stared at the label. She stayed like this for several minutes. Then I walked over to her and asked if I could be of help.

③ Inappropriate words—sound humorous

① Boring—not enough details

② Choppy sentences

As you can see, Paul realized the paragraph lacked power, so he decided to add compelling descriptive details about the woman ("the stale smell of sweat," for example). When revising, he also worked to reduce the paragraph's choppiness. By expanding and combining sentences, he gave the paragraph an easier, more graceful rhythm. Much of the time, revision involves paring down excess material. In this case, though, Paul made the right decision to elaborate his sentences. Furthermore, he added the following comment to the third paragraph: "I decided to be a good, courteous employee." These few words introduce an appropriate note of irony and serve to echo the essay's controlling idea.

Finally, Paul decided to omit the words "sneezing and hacking" because he realized they were too comic or light for his subject. Still, the first sentence in the revised paragraph is somewhat jarring. The word *strolling* isn't quite appropriate since it implies a leisurely grace inconsistent with the impression he wants to convey. Replacing *strolling* with, say, *shuffling* would bring the image more into line with the essay's overall mood.

Despite this slight problem, Paul's revisions are right on the mark. The changes he made strengthened his essay, turning it into a more evocative, more polished piece of narrative writing.

ACTIVITIES: NARRATION

Prewriting Activities

1. Imagine you're writing two essays: One analyzes the effect of insensitive teachers on young children; the other argues the importance of family traditions. With the help of your journal or freewriting, identify different narratives you could use to open each essay.

2. Use brainstorming or any other prewriting technique to generate narrative details about *one* of the following events. After examining your raw material, identify two or three narrative points (thesis statements) that might focus an essay. Then edit the prewriting material for each narrative point, noting which items would be appropriate, which would be inappropriate, and which would have to be developed more fully.

   a. An injury you received
   b. The loss of an important object
   c. An event that made you wish you had a certain skill

3. For each of the following situations, identify two different conflicts that would make a story worth relating:

   a. Going to the supermarket with a friend
   b. Telling your parents which college you've decided to attend

c. Participating in a demonstration
d. Preparing for an exam in a difficult course

4. Prepare six to ten lines of vivid and natural-sounding dialog to convey the conflict in *two* of the following situations:

a. One member of a couple trying to break up with the other
b. A ten-year-old brother and a teenage sister shopping for a parent's birthday present
c. A teacher talking to a student who plagiarized a paper
d. A young person talking to his or her parents about dropping out of college for a semester

Revising Activities

5. Revise each of the following narrative sentence groups twice: once with words that carry negative connotations, and again with words that carry positive connotations. Use varied sentence structure, sensory details, and vigorous verbs to convey mood.

a. The bell rang. It rang loudly. Students knew the last day of class was over.
b. Last weekend, our neighbors burned leaves in their yard. We went over to speak with them.
c. The sun shone in through my bedroom window. It made me sit up in bed. Daylight was finally here, I told myself.

6. The following paragraph is the introduction from the first draft of an essay proposing harsher penalties for drunk drivers. Revise this narrative paragraph to make it more effective. How can you make sentence structure less predictable? Which details should you delete? As you revise, provide language that conveys the event's sights, smells, and sounds. Also, clarify the chronological sequence.

As I drove down the street in my bright blue sports car, I saw a car coming rapidly around the curve. The car didn't slow down as it headed toward the traffic light. The light turned yellow and then red. A young couple, dressed like models, started crossing the street. When the woman saw the car, she called out to her husband. He jumped onto the shoulder. The man wasn't hurt but, seconds later, it was clear the woman was. I ran to a nearby emergency phone and called the police. The ambulance arrived, but the woman was already dead. The driver, who looked terrible, failed the sobriety test, and the police found out that he had two previous offenses. It's apparent that better ways have to be found for getting drunk drivers off the road.

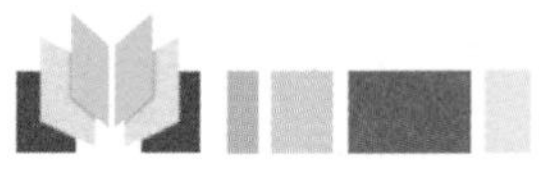

PROFESSIONAL SELECTIONS: NARRATION

AUDRE LORDE

Named poet laureate of the state of New York in 1991, Audre Lorde (1934–92) was a New Yorker born of African-Caribbean parents. Lorde taught at Hunter College for many years and published numerous poems and nonfiction pieces in a variety of magazines and literary journals. Her books include *A Burst of Light* (1988), *Sister Outsider: Essays and Speeches* (1984), and *The Black Unicorn: Poems* (1978). "The Fourth of July" is an excerpt from her autobiography, *Zami: A New Spelling of My Name* (1982).

Please note the essay structure diagram that appears following this selection (Figure 11.2 on page 211).

Pre-Reading Journal Entry

When you were a child, what beliefs about the United States did you have? List these beliefs. For each, indicate whether subsequent experience maintained or shattered your childhood understanding of these beliefs. Take a little time to explore these issues in your journal.

THE FOURTH OF JULY

The first time I went to Washington, D.C., was on the edge of the summer when I was supposed to stop being a child. At least that's what they said to us all at graduation from the eighth grade. My sister Phyllis graduated at the same time from high school. I don't know what she was supposed to stop being. But as graduation presents for us both, the whole family took a Fourth of July trip to Washington, D.C., the fabled and famous capital of our country. 1

It was the first time I'd ever been on a railroad train during the day. When I was little, and we used to go to the Connecticut shore, we always went at night on the milk train, because it was cheaper. 2

Preparations were in the air around our house before school was even over. We packed for a week. There were two very large suitcases that my father carried, and a box filled with food. In fact, my first trip to Washington was a mobile feast; I started eating as soon as we were comfortably ensconced in our seats, and did not stop until somewhere after Philadelphia. I remember it was Philadelphia because I was disappointed not to have passed by the Liberty Bell. 3

My mother had roasted two chickens and cut them up into dainty bite-size pieces. She packed slices of brown bread and butter and green pepper and carrot sticks. There were little violently yellow iced cakes with scalloped edges called "marigolds," that came from Cushman's Bakery. There was a spice bun and rock-cakes from Newton's, the West Indian bakery across Lenox Avenue from St. Mark's School, and iced tea in a wrapped mayonnaise jar. There were sweet pickles for us and dill pickles for my father, and peaches with the 4 fuzz still on them, individually wrapped to keep them from bruising. And, for neatness, there were piles of napkins and a little tin box with a washcloth dampened with rosewater and glycerine for wiping sticky mouths.

5 I wanted to eat in the dining car because I had read all about them, but my mother reminded me for the umpteenth time that dining car food always cost too much money and besides, you never could tell whose hands had been playing all over that food, nor where those same hands had been just before. My mother never mentioned that Black people were not allowed into railroad dining cars headed south in 1947. As usual, whatever my mother did not like and could not change, she ignored. Perhaps it would go away, deprived of her attention.

6 I learned later that Phyllis's high school senior class trip had been to Washington, but the nuns had given her back her deposit in private, explaining to her that the class, all of whom were white, except Phyllis, would be staying in a hotel where Phyllis "would not be happy," meaning, Daddy explained to her, also in private, that they did not rent rooms to Negroes. "We will take you to Washington, ourselves," my father had avowed, "and not just for an overnight in some measly fleabag hotel."

7 American racism was a new and crushing reality that my parents had to deal with every day of their lives once they came to this country. They handled it as a private woe. My mother and father believed that they could best protect their children from the realities of race in america and the fact of american racism by never giving them name, much less discussing their nature. We were told we must never trust white people, but *why* was never explained, nor the nature of their ill will. Like so many other vital pieces of information in my childhood, I was supposed to know without being told. It always seemed like a very strange injunction coming from my mother, who looked so much like one of those people we were never supposed to trust. But something always warned me not to ask my mother why she wasn't white, and why Auntie Lillah and Auntie Etta weren't, even though they were all that same problematic color so different from my father and me, even from my sisters, who were somewhere in-between.

8 In Washington, D.C., we had one large room with two double beds and an extra cot for me. It was a back-street hotel that belonged to a friend of my father's who was in real estate, and I spent the whole next day after Mass squinting up at the Lincoln Memorial where Marian Anderson[1] had sung after the D.A.R.[2] refused to allow her to sing in their auditorium because she was Black. Or because she was "Colored," my father said as he told us the story. Except that what he probably said was "Negro," because for his time, my father was quite progressive.

9 I was squinting because I was in that silent agony that characterized all of my childhood summers, from the time school let out in June to the end of July, brought about by my dilated and vulnerable eyes exposed to the summer brightness.

10 I viewed Julys through an agonizing corolla of dazzling whiteness and I always hated the Fourth of July, even before I came to realize the travesty such a celebration was for Black people in this country.

---

[1]An acclaimed African-American opera singer (1902–93), famed for her renderings of Black spirituals.

[2]Daughters of the American Revolution. A society, founded in 1890, for women who can prove direct lineage to soldiers or others who aided in winning American independence from Great Britain during the Revolutionary War (1775–83).

My parents did not approve of sunglasses, nor of their expense. 11

I spent the afternoon squinting up at monuments to freedom and past presidencies and democracy, and wondering why the light and heat were both so much stronger in Washington, D.C., than back home in New York City. Even the pavement on the streets was a shade lighter in color than back home. 12

Late that Washington afternoon my family and I walked back down Pennsylvania Avenue. We were a proper caravan, mother bright and father brown, the three of us girls step-standards in-between. Moved by our historical surroundings and the heat of the early evening, my father decreed yet another treat. He had a great sense of history, a flair for the quietly dramatic and the sense of specialness of an occasion and a trip. 13

"Shall we stop and have a little something to cool off, Lin?" 14

Two blocks away from our hotel, the family stopped for a dish of vanilla ice cream at a Breyer's ice cream and soda fountain. Indoors, the soda fountain was dim and fan-cooled, deliciously relieving to my scorched eyes. 15

Corded and crisp and pinafored, the five of us seated ourselves one by one at the counter. There was I between my mother and father, and my two sisters on the other side of my mother. We settled ourselves along the white mottled marble counter, and when the waitress spoke at first no one understood what she was saying, and so the five of us just sat there. 16

The waitress moved along the line of us closer to my father and spoke again. "I said I kin give you to take out, but you can't eat here. Sorry." Then she dropped her eyes looking very embarrassed, and suddenly we heard what it was she was saying all at the same time, loud and clear. 17

Straight-backed and indignant, one by one, my family and I got down from the counter stools and turned around and marched out of the store, quiet and outraged, as if we had never been Black before. No one would answer my emphatic questions with anything other than a guilty silence. "But we hadn't done anything!" This wasn't right or fair! Hadn't I written poems about Bataan and freedom and democracy for all? 18

My parents wouldn't speak of this injustice, not because they had contributed to it, but because they felt they should have anticipated it and avoided it. This made me even angrier. My fury was not going to be acknowledged by a like fury. Even my two sisters copied my parents' pretense that nothing unusual and anti-american had occurred. I was left to write my angry letter to the president of the united states all by myself, although my father did promise I could type it out on the office typewriter next week, after I showed it to him in my copybook diary. 19

The waitress was white, and the counter was white, and the ice cream I never ate in Washington, D.C., that summer I left childhood was white, and the white heat and the white pavement and the white stone monuments of my first Washington summer made me sick to my stomach for the whole rest of that trip and it wasn't much of a graduation present after all. 20

Questions for Close Reading

1. What is the selection's thesis (or narrative point)? Locate the sentence(s) in which Lorde states her main idea. If she doesn't state the thesis explicitly, express it in your own words.

FIGURE 11.2
Essay Structure Diagram: "The Fourth of July" by Audre Lorde

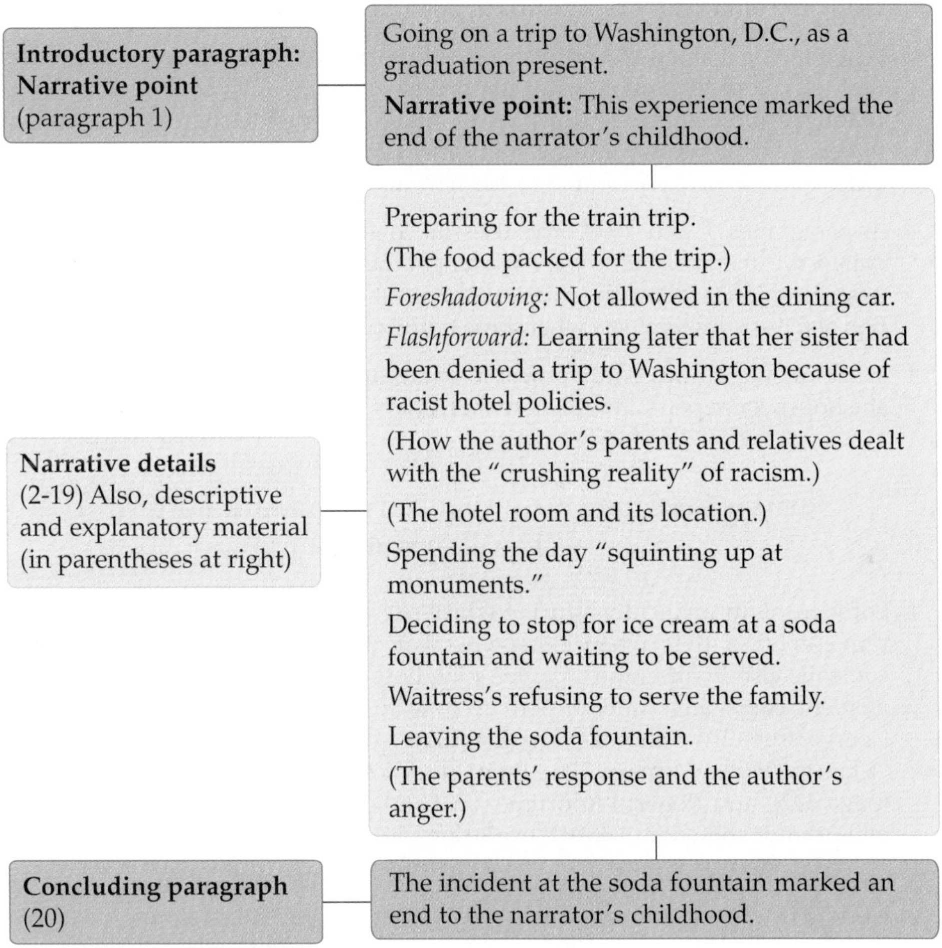

Introductory paragraph: Narrative point (paragraph 1)

Going on a trip to Washington, D.C., as a graduation present.

Narrative point: This experience marked the end of the narrator's childhood.

Narrative details (2-19) Also, descriptive and explanatory material (in parentheses at right)

Preparing for the train trip.

(The food packed for the trip.)

Foreshadowing: Not allowed in the dining car.

Flashforward: Learning later that her sister had been denied a trip to Washington because of racist hotel policies.

(How the author's parents and relatives dealt with the "crushing reality" of racism.)

(The hotel room and its location.)

Spending the day "squinting up at monuments."

Deciding to stop for ice cream at a soda fountain and waiting to be served.

Waitress's refusing to serve the family.

Leaving the soda fountain.

(The parents' response and the author's anger.)

Concluding paragraph (20)

The incident at the soda fountain marked an end to the narrator's childhood.

2. In paragraph 4, Lorde describes the elaborate picnic her mother prepared for the trip to Washington, D.C. Why did Lorde's mother make such elaborate preparations? What do these preparations tell us about Lorde's mother?
3. Why does Lorde have trouble understanding her parents' dictate that she "never trust white people" (paragraph 7)?
4. In general, how do Lorde's parents handle racism? How does the family as a whole deal with the racism they encounter in the ice cream parlor? How does the family's reaction to the ice cream parlor incident make Lorde feel?
5. Refer to your dictionary as needed to define the following words used in the selection: *fabled* (paragraph 1), *injunction* (7), *progressive* (8), *dilated* (9), *vulnerable* (9), *travesty* (10), *decreed* (13), *pretense* (19).

Questions About the Writer's Craft

1. **The pattern.** What techniques does Lorde use to help readers follow the unfolding of the story as it occurs in both time and space?
2. When telling a story, skilled writers limit narrative commentary—statements that tell rather than show what happened—because such commentary tends to interrupt the narrative flow. Lorde, however, provides narrative commentary in several spots. Find these instances. How is the information she provides in these places essential to her narrative?
3. In paragraphs 7 and 19, Lorde uses all lowercase letters when referring to America/American and to the President of the United States. Why do you suppose she doesn't follow the rules of capitalization? In what ways does her rejection of these rules reinforce what she is trying to convey through the essay's title?
4. What key word does Lorde repeat in paragraph 20? What effect do you think she hopes the repetition will have on readers?

Writing Assignments Using Narration as a Pattern of Development

1. Lorde recounts an incident during which she was treated unfairly. Write a narrative about a time when either you were treated unjustly or you treated someone else in an unfair manner. Like Lorde, use vivid details to make the incident come alive and to convey how it affected you. Essays including George Orwell's "Shooting an Elephant" (page 214), Charmie Gholson's "Charity Display?" (page 220), Brent Staples's "Black Men and Public Space" (page 412), and Roberto Rodriguez's "The Border on Our Backs" (page 517) will prompt some ideas worth exploring.

2. Write a narrative about an experience that dramatically changed your view of the world. The experience might have been jarring and painful, or it may have been positive and uplifting. In either case, recount the incident with compelling narrative details. To illustrate the shift in your perspective, begin with a brief statement of the way you viewed the world before the experience. The following essays provide insight into the way a single experience can alter one's understanding of the world: Maya Angelou's "Sister Flowers" (page 167), David Helvarg's "The Storm This Time" (page 175), Charmie Gholson's "Charity Display?" (page 220), and Diane Cole's "Don't Just Stand There" (page 333).

Writing Assignments Combining Patterns of Development

3. Lorde suggests that her parents use the coping mechanism of denial to deal with life's harsh realities. For example, she writes that whatever her mother

"did not like and could not change, she ignored." Refer to a psychology textbook to learn more about denial as a coping mechanism. When is it productive? When is it counterproductive? Drawing upon your own experiences as well as those of friends, family, and classmates, write an essay *contrasting* effective and ineffective uses of denial. Near the end of the paper, present brief *guidelines* that will help readers identify when denial may be detrimental.

4. In her essay, Lorde decries and by implication takes a strong stance against racial discrimination. Brainstorm with friends, family members, and classmates to identify other injustices in American society. To prompt discussion, you might begin by considering attitudes toward the elderly, the overweight, the physically disabled; the funding of schools in poor and affluent neighborhoods; the portrayal of a specific ethnic group on television; and so on. Focusing on *one* such injustice, write an essay *arguing* that such an injustice indeed exists. To document the nature and extent of the injustice, use library and/or Internet research. You should also consider *recounting* your own and other people's experiences. Acknowledge and, when you can, dismantle the views of those who think there isn't a problem.

Writing Assignment Using a Journal Entry as a Starting Point

5. Write an essay comparing and/or contrasting the beliefs you had about the United States as a child with those you have as an adult. Review your pre-reading journal entry, and select *one* American belief to focus on. Provide strong, dramatic examples that show why your childhood belief in this concept has been strengthened or weakened. Before writing, you should consider reading one or more of the following powerful accounts of personal confrontation with American ideals: Stanley Fish's "Free Speech Follies" (page 495), Robert Rodriguez's "The Border on Our Backs" (page 517) and Star Parker's "*Se Habla* Entitlement" (page 333).

GEORGE ORWELL

Born Eric Blair in the British colony of India, George Orwell (1903–50) is best known for his two novels *Animal Farm* (1946) and *1984* (1949)—both searing depictions of totalitarian societies. A fierce critic of political and economic injustice, Orwell also wrote a number of essays about the desperate lives of English factory workers and miners. Orwell's position with the Indian Imperial Police provided the basis for the following essay, which is taken from the collection *"Shooting an Elephant" and Other Essays* (1950).

Pre-Reading Journal Entry

Think of times when you were keenly aware of institutional injustice—an action, law, or regulation that is legally in the right but that you felt was wrong.

In your journal, record several such examples. Why do you consider them wrong? Have you always felt that way? If not, what changed your opinion?

SHOOTING AN ELEPHANT

In Moulmein, in Lower Burma, I was hated by large numbers of people—the only time in my life that I have been important enough for this to happen to me. I was subdivisional police officer of the town, and in an aimless, petty kind of way anti-European feeling was very bitter. No one had the guts to raise a riot, but if a European woman went through the bazaars alone somebody would probably spit betel juice over her dress. As a police officer I was an obvious target and was baited whenever it seemed safe to do so. When a nimble Burman tripped me up on the football field and the referee (another Burman) looked the other way, the crowd yelled with hideous laughter. This happened more than once. In the end the sneering yellow faces of young men that met me everywhere, the insults hooted after me when I was at a safe distance, got badly on my nerves. The young Buddhist priests were the worst of all. There were several thousand of them in the town and none of them seemed to have anything to do except stand on street corners and jeer at Europeans. 1

All this was perplexing and upsetting. For at that time I had already made up my mind that imperialism was an evil thing and the sooner I chucked up my job and got out of it the better. Theoretically—and secretly, of course—I was all for the Burmese and all against their oppressors, the British. As for the job I was doing, I hated it more bitterly than I can perhaps make clear. In a job like that you see the dirty work of Empire at close quarters. The wretched prisoners huddling in the stinking cages of the lock-ups, the grey, cowed faces of the long-term convicts, the scarred buttocks of the men who had been flogged with bamboos—all these oppressed me with an intolerable sense of guilt. But I could get nothing into perspective. I was young and ill-educated and I had to think out my problems in the utter silence that is imposed on every Englishman in the East. I did not even know that the British Empire is dying, still less did I know that it is a great deal better than the younger empires that are going to supplant it. All I knew was that I was stuck between my hatred of the empire I served and my rage against the evil-spirited little beasts who tried to make my job impossible. With one part of my mind I thought of the British Raj as an unbreakable tyranny, as something clamped down, *in saecula saeculorum*,[1] upon the will of prostrate peoples; with another part I thought that the greatest joy in the world would be to drive a bayonet into a Buddhist priest's guts. Feelings like these are the normal by-products of imperialism; ask any Anglo-Indian official, if you can catch him off duty. 2

One day something happened which in a roundabout way was enlightening. It was a tiny incident in itself, but it gave me a better glimpse than I had had before of the real nature of imperialism—the real motives for which despotic governments act. Early one morning the sub-inspector at a police station the other end of the town rang me up on the 'phone and said that an elephant was ravaging the bazaar. Would I please come and do something about it? I did not know what I could do, but I wanted to see what was happening and I got onto a pony and started out. I took my rifle, an 3

[1]Latin phrase meaning "for ever and ever" (editors' note).

old .44 Winchester and much too small to kill an elephant, but I thought the noise might be useful *in terrorem*.[2] Various Burmans stopped me on the way and told me about the elephant's doings. It was not, of course, a wild elephant, but a tame one which had gone "must." It had been chained up, as tame elephants always are when their attack of "must" is due, but on the previous night it had broken its chain and escaped. Its mahout, the only person who could manage it when it was in that state, had set out in pursuit, but had taken the wrong direction and was now twelve hours' journey away, and in the morning the elephant had suddenly reappeared in the town. The Burmese population had no weapons and were quite helpless against it. It had already destroyed somebody's bamboo hut, killed a cow and raided some fruit-stalls and devoured the stock; also it had met the municipal rubbish van and, when the driver jumped out and took to his heels, had turned the van over and inflicted violences upon it.

4 The Burmese sub-inspector and some Indian constables were waiting for me in the quarter where the elephant had been seen. It was a very poor quarter, a labyrinth of squalid bamboo huts, thatched with palm-leaf, winding all over a steep hillside. I remember that it was a cloudy, stuffy morning at the beginning of the rains. We began questioning the people as to where the elephant had gone and, as usual, failed to get any definite information. That is invariably the case in the East; a story always sounds clear enough at a distance, but the nearer you get to the scene of events the vaguer it becomes. Some of the people said that the elephant had gone in one direction, some said that he had gone in another, some professed not even to have heard of any elephant. I had almost made up my mind that the whole story was a pack of lies, when we heard yells a little distance away. There was a loud, scandalized cry of 'Go away, child! Go away this instant!' and an old woman with a switch in her hand came round the corner of a hut, violently shooing away a crowd of naked children. Some more women followed, clicking their tongues and exclaiming; evidently there was something that the children ought not to have seen. I rounded the hut and saw a man's dead body sprawling in the mud. He was an Indian, a black Dravidian coolie, almost naked, and he could not have been dead many minutes. The people said that the elephant had come suddenly upon him round the corner of the hut, caught him with its trunk, put its foot on his back and ground him into the earth. This was the rainy season and the ground was soft, and his face had scored a trench a foot deep and a couple of yards long. He was lying on his belly with arms crucified and head sharply twisted to one side. His face was coated with mud, the eyes wide open, the teeth bared and grinning with an expression of unendurable agony. (Never tell me, by the way, that the dead look peaceful. Most of the corpses I have seen looked devilish.) The friction of the great beast's foot had stripped the skin from his back as neatly as one skins a rabbit. As soon as I saw the dead man I sent an orderly to a friend's house nearby to borrow an elephant rifle. I had already sent back the pony, not wanting it to go mad with fright and throw me if it smelt the elephant.

5 The orderly came back in a few minutes with a rifle and five cartridges, and meanwhile some Burmans had arrived and told us that the elephant was in the paddy fields below, only a few hundred yards away. As I started forward practically the whole population of the quarter flocked out of the houses and followed me. They had seen the rifle and were all shouting excitedly that I was going to shoot the elephant. They had not

---

[2]Latin phrase meaning "as a warning" (editors' note).

shown much interest in the elephant when he was merely ravaging their homes, but it was different now that he was going to be shot. It was a bit of fun to them, as it would be to an English crowd; besides they wanted the meat. It made me vaguely uneasy. I had no intention of shooting the elephant—I had merely sent for the rifle to defend myself if necessary—and it is always unnerving to have a crowd following you. I marched down the hill looking and feeling a fool, with the rifle over my shoulder and an ever-growing army of people jostling at my heels. At the bottom, when you got away from the huts, there was a metalled road and beyond that a miry waste of paddy fields a thousand yards across, not yet ploughed but soggy from the first rains and dotted with coarse grass. The elephant was standing eight yards from the road, his left side towards us. He took not the slightest notice of the crowd's approach. He was tearing up bunches of grass, beating them against his knees to clean them and stuffing them into his mouth.

I had halted on the road. As soon as I saw the elephant I knew with perfect certainty that I ought not to shoot him. It is a serious matter to shoot a working elephant—it is comparable to destroying a huge and costly piece of machinery—and obviously one ought not to do it if it can possibly be avoided. And at that distance, peacefully eating, the elephant looked no more dangerous than a cow. I thought then and I think now that his attack of "must" was already passing off; in which case he would merely wander harmlessly about until the mahout came back and caught him. Moreover, I did not in the least want to shoot him. I decided that I would watch him for a little while to make sure that he did not turn savage again, and then go home. 6

But at that moment I glanced round at the crowd that had followed me. It was an immense crowd, two thousand at the least and growing every minute. It blocked the road for a long distance on either side. I looked at the sea of yellow faces above the garish clothes—faces all happy and excited over this bit of fun, all certain that the elephant was going to be shot. They were watching me as they would watch a conjurer about to perform a trick. They did not like me, but with the magical rifle in my hands I was momentarily worth watching. And suddenly I realized that I should have to shoot the elephant after all. The people expected it of me and I had got to do it; I could feel their two thousand wills pressing me forward, irresistibly. And it was at this moment, as I stood there with the rifle in my hands, that I first grasped the hollowness, the futility of the white man's dominion in the East. Here was I, the white man with his gun, standing in front of the unarmed native crowd—seemingly the leading actor of the piece; but in reality I was only an absurd puppet pushed to and fro by the will of those yellow faces behind. I perceived in this moment that when the white man turns tyrant it is his own freedom that he destroys. He becomes a sort of hollow, posing dummy, the conventionalized figure of a sahib. For it is the condition of his rule that he shall spend his life in trying to impress the "natives," and so in every crisis he has got to do what the "natives" expect of him. He wears a mask, and his face grows to fit it. I had got to shoot the elephant. I had committed myself to doing it when I sent for the rifle. A sahib has got to act like a sahib; he has got to appear resolute, to know his own mind and do definite things. To come all that way, rifle in hand, with two thousand people marching at my heels, and then to trail feebly away, having done nothing—no, that was impossible. The crowd would laugh at me. And my whole life, every white man's life in the East, was one long struggle not to be laughed at. 7

But I did not want to shoot the elephant. I watched him beating his bunch of grass against his knees, with that preoccupied grandmotherly air that elephants have. It 8 seemed to me that it would be murder to shoot him. At that age I was not squeamish about killing animals, but I had never shot an elephant and never wanted to. (Somehow it always seems worse to kill a *large* animal.) Besides, there was the beast's owner to be considered. Alive, the elephant was worth at least a hundred pounds; dead, he would only be worth the value of his tusks, five pounds, possibly. But I had got to act quickly. I turned to some experienced-looking Burmans who had been there when we arrived, and asked them how the elephant had been behaving. They all said the same thing: he took no notice of you if you left him alone, but he might charge if you went too close to him.

9 It was perfectly clear to me what I ought to do. I ought to walk up to within, say, twenty-five yards of the elephant and test his behavior. If he charged, I could shoot; if he took no notice of me, it would be safe to leave him until the mahout came back. But also I knew that I was going to do no such thing. I was a poor shot with a rifle and the ground was soft mud into which one would sink at every step. If the elephant charged and I missed him, I should have about as much chance as a toad under a steam-roller. But even then I was not thinking particularly of my own skin, only of the watchful yellow faces behind. For at that moment, with the crowd watching me, I was not afraid in the ordinary sense, as I would have been if I had been alone. A white man mustn't be frightened in front of "natives"; and so, in general he isn't frightened. The sole thought in my mind was that if anything went wrong those two thousand Burmans would see me pursued, caught, trampled on and reduced to a grinning corpse like that Indian up the hill. And if that happened it was quite probable that some of them would laugh. That would never do. There was only one alternative. I shoved the cartridges into the magazine and lay down on the road to get a better aim.

10 The crowd grew very still, and a deep, low, happy sigh, as of people who see the theatre curtain go up at last, breathed from innumerable throats. They were going to have their bit of fun after all. The rifle was a beautiful German thing with cross-hair sights. I did not then know that in shooting an elephant one would shoot to cut an imaginary bar running from ear-hole to ear-hole. I ought, therefore, as the elephant was sideway on, to have aimed straight at his ear-hole; actually I aimed several inches in front of this, thinking the brain would be further forward.

11 When I pulled the trigger I did not hear the bang or feel the kick—one never does when a shot goes home—but I heard the devilish roar of glee that went up from the crowd. In that instant, in too short a time, one would have thought, even for the bullet to get there, a mysterious, terrible change had come over the elephant. He neither stirred nor fell, but every line of his body had altered. He looked suddenly stricken, shrunken, immensely old, as though the frightful impact of the bullet had paralyzed him without knocking him down. At last, after what seemed a long time—it might have been five seconds, I dare say—he sagged flabbily to his knees. His mouth slobbered. An enormous senility seemed to have settled upon him. One could have imagined him thousands of years old. I fired again into the same spot. At the second shot he did not collapse but climbed with desperate slowness to his feet and stood weakly upright, with legs sagging and head drooping. I fired a third time. That was the shot that did for him. You could see the agony of it jolt his whole body and knock the last remnant of strength from his legs. But in falling he seemed for a moment to rise, for as his hind legs collapsed beneath him he seemed to tower upward like a huge rock toppling, his trunk reaching skywards like a tree. He

trumpeted, for the first and only time. And then down he came, his belly towards me, with a crash that seemed to shake the ground even where I lay.

I got up. The Burmans were already racing past me across the mud. It was obvious that the elephant would never rise again, but he was not dead. He was breathing very rhythmically with long rattling gasps, his great mound of a side painfully rising and falling. His mouth was wide open—I could see far down into caverns of pale pink throat. I waited a long time for him to die, but his breathing did not weaken. Finally I fired my two remaining shots into the spot where I thought his heart must be. The thick blood welled out of him like red velvet, but still he did not die. His body did not even jerk when the shots hit him, the tortured breathing continued without a pause. He was dying, very slowly and in great agony, but in some world remote from me where not even a bullet could damage him further. I felt that I had got to put an end to that dreadful noise. It seemed dreadful to see the great beast lying there, powerless to move and yet powerless to die, and not even to be able to finish him. I sent back for my small rifle and poured shot after shot into his heart and down his throat. They seemed to make no impression. The tortured gasps continued as steadily as the ticking of a clock. 12

In the end I could not stand it any longer and went away. I heard later that it took him half an hour to die. Burmans were bringing dahs and baskets even before I left, and I was told they had stripped the body almost to the bones by the afternoon. 13

Afterwards, of course, there were endless discussions about the shooting of the elephant. The owner was furious, but he was only an Indian and could do nothing. Besides, legally I had done the right thing, for a mad elephant has to be killed, like a mad dog, if its owner fails to control it. Among the Europeans opinion was divided. The older men said I was right, the younger men said it was a damn shame to shoot an elephant for killing a coolie, because an elephant was worth more than any damn Coringhee coolie. And afterwards I was very glad that the coolie had been killed; it put me legally in the right and it gave me a sufficient pretext for shooting the elephant. I often wondered whether any of the others grasped that I had done it solely to avoid looking a fool. 14

Questions for Close Reading

1. What is the selection's thesis (or narrative point)? Locate the sentence(s) in which Orwell states his main idea. If he doesn't state the thesis explicitly, express it in your own words.

2. How does Orwell feel about the Burmans? What words does he use to describe them?

3. What reasons does Orwell give for shooting the elephant?

4. In paragraph 3, Orwell says that the elephant incident gave him a better understanding of "the real motives for which despotic governments act." What do you think he means? Before you answer, reread paragraph 7 carefully.

5. Refer to your dictionary as needed to define the following words used in the selection: *imperialism* (paragraph 2), *prostrate* (2), *despotic* (3), *mahout* (3), *miry* (5), *conjurer* (7), *futility* (7), and *sahib* (7).

Questions About the Writer's Craft

1. **The pattern.** Most effective narratives encompass a restricted time span. How much time elapses from the moment Orwell gets his gun to the death of the elephant? What time signals does Orwell provide to help the reader follow the sequence of events in this limited time span?

2. Orwell doesn't actually begin his narrative until the third paragraph. What purposes do the first two paragraphs serve?

3. In paragraph 6, Orwell says that shooting a working elephant "is comparable to destroying a huge and costly piece of machinery." This kind of comparison is called an *analogy*—describing something unfamiliar, often abstract, in terms of something more familiar and concrete. Find at least three additional analogies in Orwell's essay. What effect do they have?

4. **Other patterns.** Much of the power of Orwell's narrative comes from his ability to convey sensory impressions—what he saw, heard, smelled. Orwell's *description* becomes most vivid when he writes about the elephant's death in paragraphs 11 and 12. Find some evocative words and phrases that give the description its power.

Writing Assignments Using Narration as a Pattern of Development

1. Orwell recounts a time he acted under great pressure. Write a narrative about an action you once took simply because you felt pressured. Perhaps you were attempting to avoid ridicule or to fulfill someone else's expectations. Like Orwell, use vivid details to bring the incident to life and to convey its effect on you. Reading Kay S. Hymowitz's "Tweens: Ten Going on Sixteen" (page 245) will help you see the sometimes disastrous consequence of the pressure to conform.

2. Write a narrative essay about an experience that gave you, like Orwell, a deeper insight into your own nature. You may have discovered, for instance, that you can be surprisingly naive, compassionate, petty, brave, rebellious, or good at something. Your essay may be serious or light in tone. Consider first reading Diane Cole's "Don't Just Stand There" (page 333), an essay showing how the author's response to a challenge revealed much about her character.

Writing Assignments Combining Patterns of Development

3. Was Orwell justified in shooting the elephant? Write an essay *arguing* either that Orwell was justified *or* that he was not. To develop your thesis, cite several specific reasons, each supported by *examples* drawn from the essay. Here are some points you might consider: the legality of Orwell's act, the elephant's temperament, the crowd's presence, the aftermath of the elephant's death, the death itself.

4. Orwell's essay concerns, in part, the tendency to conceal indecision and confusion behind a facade of authority. Focusing on one or two groups of people (parents, teachers, doctors, politicians, and so on), write an essay *arguing* that people in authority sometimes *pretend* to know what they are doing so that subordinates won't suspect their insecurity or incompetence. Part of your essay should focus on the *consequences* of such behaviors.

Writing Assignment Using a Journal Entry as a Starting Point

5. Review your pre-reading journal entry, and select *one* action, law, or regulation that you consider indefensible. Interview friends, family, and classmates in an effort to gather views on all sides of the issue. Also consider supplementing this informal research with information gathered in the library and/or on the Internet. After weighing all your material, formulate a thesis; then write an essay convincing readers of the validity of your position.

CHARMIE GHOLSON

Born in 1962, Charmie Gholson has had a varied career. She has been a waitress, a birthing coach, a radio producer, and a nutrition counselor. Today she writes features and reviews for the *Ann Arbor Observer* and a cooking column for *Current Magazine*. She also hosts a local public affairs radio show called *Renegade Solutions*. The mother of three sons, Gholson lives in Ann Arbor, Michigan. This article was published in *The New York Times Magazine* on January 2, 2005.

Pre-Reading Journal Entry

Americans usually respond generously to others in times of need, either by volunteering their time and labor in community service or by donating money. Reflect on an occasion in which you made a donation to a charitable cause. What caused you to give? Did you give time, money, or both? What effect, if any, did your actions have? How did volunteering or donating make you feel? Use your journal to respond to these questions.

CHARITY DISPLAY?

I didn't recognize the cellphone on caller ID but answered anyway. A man started talking about a local charity. "Look," I interrupted, "I don't have any money to give you. My husband left me. I've got two little kids, and I'm behind on the rent." 1

He quickly clarified that he wasn't calling for a donation but to help. He said he was a doctor and a volunteer for an organization called Warm the Children, and I had signed 2 up for help at my son's school. He offered to give me $80 for each of my children to buy clothes. All I had to do was meet him at Meijer—a local, family-owned superstore—to do the shopping. I was shoving pants onto my son Gabriel, who never wants to get dressed, so it took a minute to comprehend: Could it be true?

3 The doctor mentioned filling out forms. While I imagined letting a stranger pay for our clothes, Gabriel took off his pants and ran away. Did I really want a handout? Should I endure a bit of humiliation to provide some essentials for my kids? I felt as if I had no choice. Sammy, my 7-year-old, had outgrown his shoes.

4 The night before we were to meet, the kids were with their dad, so I went to the store to shop, making sure to stay within the allotted amount. Then, I found a manager. We put a note on the clothes and left it behind the customer-service counter. I was hoping this would expedite the process and minimize my contact with the doctor: here we go, hey, thanks, goodbye.

5 In the morning I dressed the kids in clean clothes. (There, I thought, we don't look poor.) On the way to Meijer, the boys jumped in puddles, soaking themselves to the waist. With mud.

6 The lady behind the service counter couldn't find my basket but had a good idea where it went. "There's an Asian woman who doesn't speak English," she said. "I bet she put it all back." I ran around the store grabbing snow boots, dress shirts and socks I chose the night before.

7 While we waited by the entrance, my littlest guy climbed out of the cart and started hopping up and down while watching himself on a security monitor. I knew this dance; it meant I had about 10 minutes before he had a meltdown. I thought about leaving; maybe my father would give me more money. But then I saw Sammy, who never complains, just sitting bleary-eyed in the cart, tolerating his boredom.

8 When the doctor arrived, he looked as kind and reassuring as he sounded on the phone. He greeted me and introduced a lanky teenager: "This is my son, Jack." He didn't tell Jack my name or introduce my kids. I shook Jack's hand before he retreated a safe distance behind his father, eyeballing my kids and me. I could not imagine why the doctor brought him along.

9 Once we were in line, I tried to keep the kids quiet; the doctor smiled and blinked at me. I talked nonstop, peppering Jack with polite questions: "What school do you go to? Do you play sports?" He gazed at the ground in my general direction. Occasionally he spat out a one-word answer. This stage of growing up is so awkward. I wondered who had it worse that morning, Jack or I.

10 The doctor showed me the forms we had to fill out. By mistake, he also handed me a set of instructions for how to facilitate this "encounter." At the top, it said: "DO NOT OFFER TRANSPORTATION TO THE CLIENTS." I looked at him in disbelief and repeated it aloud. *Do not offer transportation to the clients?* The doctor just shrugged. I couldn't tell if he was as embarrassed as I was, or if he had any idea how hard it was to accept charity.

11 Our cashier didn't know how to process my forms. After the manager showed her how, I realized I'd overshot my limit, so the cashier called the manager back for an override. The line behind us had grown long with frustrated shoppers, all of whom I assumed intended to pay for their purchases. Everyone stood in an uncomfortable silence—except my boys, who pestered me for some water and got way too close to the doctor. I fantasized about adopting a hillbilly accent and shouting, "Now you kids shut

up er Santa ain't coming!" Finally we were done. Gabriel was clinging to me and chanting, "I want a drink." The doctor and his son said goodbye and hightailed it out of there.

Back at home, a friend called. I couldn't shake the feeling that the doctor used me as an example. "For what?" she asked when I told her. "I'm not even sure," I said. To make his son grateful? To put a face on poverty? Realistically, the doctor could have just been on his way to drop his son somewhere, but now I was angry. At my soon-to-be ex-husband. At the polarized society we live in where the working poor voted themselves into deeper poverty while the rich still coast. Despite the doctor's best intentions, I felt scrutinized—especially with his son there to witness my inability to buy my own kids their damn socks. 12

"You are under an incredible amount of stress," my friend insisted. "I hardly remember most of my divorce." 13

With luck, niether will I. 14

Questions for Close Reading

1. What is the selection's thesis? Locate the sentence(s) in which Gholson states her main idea. If she doesn't state her thesis explicity, express it in your own words.
2. What is the internal conflict that Gholson experiences in her encounters with the doctor?
3. In paragraph 10, the author sees one of the instructions the doctor has been given: "Do not offer transportation to the clients." Why does she react to this warning "in disbelief"?
4. What does the title of the essay mean? Why does Gholson use a question mark?
5. Refer to your dictionary as needed to define the following words used in the selection: *humiliation* (paragraph 3), *expedite* (4), *lanky* (8), *facilitate* (10), *polarized* (12), and *scrutinized* (12).

Questions About the Writer's Craft

1. **The pattern.** How does Gholson organize the events in this essay? What transitional words and phrases does she use to keep the reader oriented as her story progresses?
2. **Other patterns.** In some passages, Gholson *describes* the behavior of her sons. What do these descriptions contribute to the narrative?
3. In paragraphs 3, 4, 5, and elsewhere, Gholson tells us her thoughts. What effect do these sections have on the pace of the narrative? How do they affect our understanding of what is happening?
4. There are several places in this essay in which Gholson uses dialogue. Find one of these places, and explain why the use of dialogue is (or is not) effective. What function does the dialogue have?

Writing Assignments Using Narration as a Pattern of Development

1. All of us have experienced humiliation at some point, and for Gholson, being the object of charity was such an experience. Think of an experience from your own life that made you feel humiliated. It might have been an important experience, like completely flubbing a performance in front of a hundred people, or a minor experience, like having an assignment criticized by an instructor. Write a narrative of this experience. Be sure to discuss your thoughts and feelings as well as the actions involved in the story. Before writing, consider reading Audre Lorde's "The Fourth of July" (page 208), another account of a painful realization.

2. Write a narrative about a time in your life in which you needed help from others, and explain how this made you feel. The experience might have been painful, like Gholson's, or empowering, or somewhere in between. Use either flashback or flashforward to emphasize an event in your narrative.

Writing Assignments Combining Patterns of Development

3. In paragraph 9, Gholson describes how she tried to keep up a conversation with Jack as they waited in line to pay for her purchases. The conversation lacked any real content or exchange of information, but for Gholson it had other functions. Write an essay in which you describe the *causes* and *effects* of Gholson's effort to carry on a polite conversation. Why did Gholson try to engage Jack even though he was uncommunicative? What were the *results* of her attempts at conversation? *Compare* and *contrast* Gholson's approach to this interaction with Jack's. Are the differences between them related to gender? To age? To the social situation? To gain another perspective on obstacles to communication, read "Euromail and Amerimail" by Eric Weiner (page 375).

4. Warm the Children, the charitable group helping Gholson's sons, is an organization dedicated to providing clothes to needy children. Research this organization or another charitable organization on the Internet, and write an essay analyzing the *process* involved in participating in it and *persuading* others to join it.

Writing Assignment Using a Journal Entry as a Starting Point

5. Review your pre-reading journal entry, in which you *recounted* a time that you either volunteered your time or donated money to a cause. *Compare* your story

to that of the doctor in Gholson's essay. How did your experience differ from his? How was it similar? If you were to give time or money again, would you do so the same way, or would you do it differently? Why?

ADDITIONAL WRITING TOPICS: NARRATION

General Assignments

Write an essay on any of the following topics, using narration as the paper's dominant method of development. Be sure to select details that advance the essay's narrative purpose; you may even want to experiment with flashback or flashforward. In any case, keep the sequence of events clear by using transitional cues. Within the limited time span covered, use vigorous details and varied sentence structure to enliven the narrative. Tell the story from a consistent point of view.

1. An emergency that brought out the best or worst in you
2. The hazards of taking children out to eat
3. An incident that made you believe in fate
4. Your best or worst day at school or work
5. A major decision
6. An encounter with a machine
7. An important learning experience
8. A narrow escape
9. Your first date, first day on the job, or first anything
10. A memorable childhood experience
11. A fairy tale the way you would like to hear it told
12. A painful moment
13. An incredible but true story
14. A significant family event
15. An experience in which a certain emotion (pride, anger, regret, or some other) was dominant
16. A surprising coincidence
17. An act of heroism
18. An unpleasant confrontation
19. A cherished family story
20. An imagined meeting with an admired celebrity or historical figure

Assignments with a Specific Purpose, Audience, and Point of View

On Campus

1. Write an article for your old high school newspaper. The article will be read primarily by seniors who are planning to go away to college next year. In the article, narrate a story that points to some truth about the "breaking away" stage of life.

2. A friend of yours has seen someone cheat on a test, plagiarize an entire paper, or seriously violate some other academic policy. In a letter, convince this friend to inform the instructor or a campus administrator by narrating an incident in which a witness did (or did not) speak up in such a situation. Tell what happened as a result.

At Home or in the Community

3. You have had a disturbing encounter with one of the people who seems to have "fallen through the cracks" of society—a street person, an unwanted child, or anyone else who is alone and abandoned. Write a letter to the local newspaper describing this encounter. Your purpose is to arouse people's indignation and compassion and to get help for such unfortunates.

4. Your younger brother, sister, relative, or neighborhood friend can't wait to be your age. Write a letter in which you narrate a dramatic story that shows the young person that your age isn't as wonderful as he or she thinks. Be sure to select a story that the person can understand and appreciate.

On the Job

5. As fund-raiser for a particular organization (for example, Red Cross, SPCA, Big Brothers/Big Sisters), you're sending a newsletter to contributors. Support your cause by telling the story of a time when your organization made all the difference—the blood donation that saved a life, the animal that was rescued from abuse, and so on.

6. A customer has written a letter to you (or your boss) telling about a bad experience that he or she had with someone in your workplace. On the basis of that single experience, the customer now regards your company and its employees with great suspicion. It's your responsibility to respond to this complaint. Write a letter to the customer balancing his or her negative picture by narrating a story that shows the "flip side" of your company and its employees.

Illustration

12

Bill Arnon/Photoedit, Inc.

WHAT IS ILLUSTRATION?

If someone asked you, "Have you been to any good restaurants lately?" you probably wouldn't answer "Yes" and then immediately change the subject. Most likely, you would go on to **illustrate** with examples. Perhaps you'd give the names of restaurants you've enjoyed and talk briefly about the specific things you liked: the attractive prices, the tasty main courses, the pleasant service, the tempting desserts. Such examples and details are needed to convince others that your opinion—in this or any matter—is valid. Similarly, when you talk about larger and more important issues, people won't pay much attention to your opinion if all you do is string together vague generalizations: "We have to do something about acid rain. It's had disastrous consequences for the environment. Its negative effects increase every year. Action must be taken to control the problem." To be taken seriously and convince others that your point is well founded, you must provide specific supporting examples: "The forests in the Adirondacks are dying"; "Yesterday's rainfall was fifty times more acidic than normal"; "Pine Lake, in the northern part of the state, was once a great fishing spot but now has no fish population."

Examples are equally important when you write an essay. It's not vague generalities and highfalutin abstractions that make writing impressive. Just the opposite is true. Facts, details, anecdotes, statistics, expert opinion, and personal observations are at the heart of effective writing, giving your work substance and solidity.

HOW ILLUSTRATION FITS YOUR PURPOSE AND AUDIENCE

The wording of assignments and essay exam questions may signal the need for illustration:

> Soap operas, whether shown during the day or in the evening, are among the most popular television programs. Why do you think this is so? Provide specific examples to support your position.
>
> Some observers claim that college students are less interested in learning than in getting ahead in their careers. Cite evidence to support or refute this claim.
>
> A growing number of people feel that parents should not allow young children to participate in highly competitive team sports. Basing your conclusion on your own experiences and observations, indicate whether you think this point of view is reasonable.

Such phrases as "Provide specific examples," "Cite evidence," and "Basing your conclusion on your own experiences and observations" signal that each essay would be developed through illustration.

Usually, though, you won't be told so explicitly to provide examples. Instead, as you think about the best way to achieve your essay's purpose, you'll see the need for illustrative details—no matter which patterns of development you use. For instance, to *persuade* skeptical readers that the country needs a national health system, you might mention specific cases to dramatize the inadequacy of our current health-care system: a family bankrupted by medical bills; an uninsured accident victim turned away by a hospital; a chronically ill person rapidly deteriorating because he didn't have enough money to visit a doctor. Or imagine a lightly satiric piece that pokes fun at cat lovers. Insisting that "cat people" are pretty strange creatures, you might make your point—and make readers chuckle—with a series of examples *contrasting* cat lovers and dog lovers: the qualities admired by each group (loyalty in dogs versus independence in cats) and the different expectations each group has for its pets (dog lovers want Fido to be obedient and lovable, whereas cat lovers are satisfied with Felix's occasional spurts of docility and affection). Similarly, you would supply examples in a *causal analysis* speculating on the likely impact of a proposed tuition hike at your college. To convince the college administration of the probable negative effects of such a hike, you might cite the following examples: articles reporting a nationwide upswing in student transfers to less expensive schools; statistics indicating a significant drop in grades among already employed students forced to work more hours to pay increased tuition costs; interviews with students too financially strapped to continue their college education.

Whether you use illustration as a primary or supplemental method of development, it serves a number of important purposes. For one thing, illustrations make writing *interesting*. Assume you're writing an essay showing that television commercials are biased against women. Your essay would be lifeless and boring if all it did was repeat, in a general way, that commercials present stereotyped views of women:

Original

An anti-female bias is rampant in television commercials. It is very much alive, yet most viewers seem to take it all in stride. Few people protest the obviously sexist characters and statements on such commercials. Surely, these commercials misrepresent the way most of us live.

Without interesting particulars, readers may respond, "Who cares?" But if you provide specific examples, you'll attract your readers' attention:

Revised

An anti-female bias is rampant in television commercials. Although millions of women hold responsible jobs outside the home, commercials continue to portray women as simple creatures who spend much of their time thinking about wax buildup, cottony-soft bathroom tissue, and static-free clothes. Men, apparently, have better things to do than fret over such mundane household matters. How many commercials can you recall that depict men proclaiming the virtues of squeaky-clean dishes or sparkling bathrooms? Not many.

Illustrations also make writing *persuasive.* Most writing conveys a point, but many readers are reluctant to accept someone else's point of view unless evidence demonstrates its validity. Imagine you're writing an essay showing that latchkey children are more self-sufficient and emotionally secure than children who return from school to a home where a parent awaits them. Your thesis is obviously controversial. Without specific examples—from your own experience, personal observations, or research studies—your readers would undoubtedly question your position's validity.

Further, illustrations help *explain* difficult, abstract, or unusual ideas. Suppose you're assigned an essay on a complex subject such as inflation, zero population growth, or radiation exposure. As a writer, you have a responsibility to your readers to make these difficult concepts concrete and understandable. If writing an essay on radiation exposure in everyday life, you might start by providing specific examples of home appliances that emit radiation—color televisions, computers, and microwave ovens—and tell exactly how much radiation we absorb in a typical day from such equipment. To illustrate further the extent of our radiation exposure, you could also provide specifics about unavoidable sources of natural radiation (the sun, for instance) and details about the widespread use of radiation in medicine (X rays, radiation therapy).

These examples would ground your discussion, making it immediate and concrete, preventing it from flying off into the vague and theoretical.

Finally, examples help *prevent unintended ambiguity.* All of us have experienced the frustration of having someone misinterpret what we say. In face-to-face communication, we can provide on-the-spot clarification. In writing, however, instantaneous feedback isn't available, so it's crucial that meaning be as unambiguous as possible. Illustrations will help. Assume you're writing an essay asserting that ineffective teaching is on the rise in today's high schools. To clarify what you mean by "ineffective," you provide illustrations: the instructor who spends so much time disciplining unruly students that he never gets around to teaching; the moonlighting teacher who is so tired in class that she regularly takes naps during tests; the teacher who accepts obviously plagiarized reports because he's grateful that students hand in something. Without such concrete examples, your readers will supply their own ideas—and these may not be what you had in mind. Readers might imagine "ineffective" to mean harsh and punitive, whereas concrete examples would show that you intend it to mean out of control and irresponsible.

At this point, you have a good sense of the way writers use illustration to achieve their purposes and to connect with their readers. Now take a moment to look closely at the advertisement at the beginning of this chapter. Imagine you're taking part in a "focus group" assembled by the advertiser of this product. Your task is to rate the ad on a scale of 1 (negative) to 10 (positive) on the basis of the images it promotes. To support your rating, jot down some phrases that express the values that you believe are *illustrated* by the ad.

PREWRITING STRATEGIES

The following checklist shows how you can apply to illustration some of the prewriting techniques discussed in Chapter 2.

ILLUSTRATION: A PREWRITING CHECKLIST

Choose a Subject to Illustrate

- ☐ What general situation or phenomenon (for example, campus apathy, organic farming) can you depict through illustration?
- ☐ What difficult or misunderstood concept (nuclear winter, passive aggression) would examples help to explain and make concrete?

Determine Your Purpose, Audience, Tone, and Point of View

- ☐ What is your purpose in writing?
- ☐ What audience do you have in mind?
- ☐ What tone and point of view will best serve your purpose and lead readers to adopt the desired attitude toward the subject being illustrated?

Use Prewriting to Generate Examples

- ☐ How can brainstorming, freewriting, journal entries, or mapping help you generate relevant examples (events, facts, anecdotes, quotations) from your own or others' experiences?
- ☐ How could library research help you gather pertinent examples (expert opinion, case studies, statistics)?

STRATEGIES FOR USING ILLUSTRATION IN AN ESSAY

After prewriting, you're ready to draft your essay. The following suggestions and Figure 12.1 will be helpful whether you use illustration as a dominant or supportive pattern of development.

1. **Select the examples to include.** Examples can take several forms, including specific names (of people, places, products, and so on), anecdotes, personal observations, expert opinion, as well as facts, statistics, and case studies gathered through research. Once you've used prewriting to generate as many examples as possible, you're ready to limit your examples to the strongest. Keeping your thesis, audience, tone, and point of view in mind, ask yourself several key questions: "Which examples support my thesis? Which do not? Which are most convincing? Which are most likely to interest readers and clarify meaning?"

   You may include several brief examples within a single sentence:

   > The French people's fascination with some American literary figures, such as Poe and Hawthorne, is understandable, but their great respect for "artists" like comedian Jerry Lewis is a mystery.

   Or you may develop a paragraph with a number of "for instances":

   > A uniquely American style of movie-acting reached its peak in the 1950s. Certain charismatic actors completely abandoned the stage techniques and tradition that had been the foundation of acting up to that time. Instead of articulating their lines clearly, the actors mumbled; instead of making firm eye contact with their colleagues, they hung their heads, shifted their eyes, even talked with their eyes closed. Marlon Brando, Montgomery Clift, and James Dean were three actors who exemplified this new trend.

FIGURE 12.1
Development Diagram: Writing an Illustration Essay

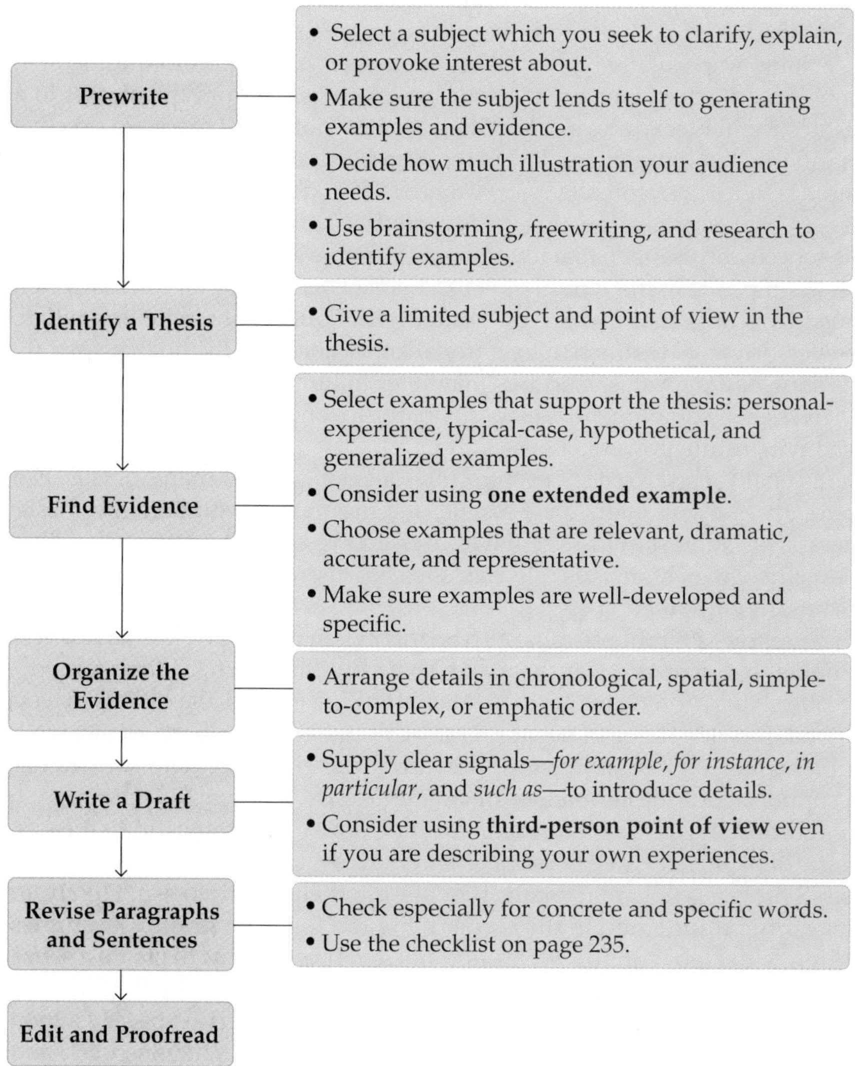

As the preceding paragraph shows, *several examples* are usually needed to achieve your purpose. An essay with the thesis, "Video games are dangerously violent" wouldn't be convincing if you gave only one example of a violent video game. Several strong examples would be needed for readers to feel you had illustrated your point sufficiently.

As a general rule, you should strive for variety in the kinds of examples you include. For instance, you might choose a *personal-experience example* drawn from your own life or from the life of someone you know. Such examples pack the wallop of personal authority and lend drama to writing. Or you might include a *typical-case example,* an actual event or situation that did occur—but not to you or to anyone you know. (Perhaps you learned about the event through a magazine article, newspaper account, or television report.) The objective nature of such cases makes them especially convincing. You might also include a speculative or *hypothetical example* ("Imagine how difficult it must be for an elderly person to carry bags of groceries from the market to a bus stop several blocks away"). You'll find that hypothetical cases are effective for clarifying and dramatizing key points, but be sure to acknowledge that the example is indeed invented ("*Suppose* that . . . " or "Let's for a moment *assume* that . . . "). Make certain, too, that the invented situation is easily imagined and could conceivably happen. Finally, you might create a *generalized example*—one that is a composite of the typical or usual. Such generalized examples are often signaled by words that involve the reader ("*All of us,* at one time or another, have been driven to distraction by a trivial annoyance like the buzzing of a fly or the sting of a papercut"), or they may refer to humanity in general ("When *most people* get a compliment, they perk up, preen, and think the praise-giver is blessed with astute powers of observation").

Occasionally, *one extended example,* fully developed with many details, can support an essay. It might be possible, for instance, to support the thesis, "Federal legislation should raise the legal drinking age to twenty-one" with a single compelling, highly detailed example of the effects of one teenager's drunken-driving spree.

The examples you choose must also be *relevant;* that is, they must have direct bearing on the point you want to make. You would have a hard time convincing readers that Americans have callous attitudes toward the elderly if you described the wide range of new programs, all staffed by volunteers, at a well-financed center for senior citizens. Because these examples *contradict,* rather than support, your thesis, readers are apt to dismiss what you have to say.

In addition, try to select *dramatic* examples. Say you're writing an essay to show that society needs to take more steps to protect children from abuse. Simply stating that many parents hit their children isn't likely to form a strong impression in the reader's mind. However, graphic examples (children with stab wounds, welts, and burn marks) are apt to create a sense of urgency in the reader.

Make certain, too, that your examples are *accurate.* Exercise special caution when using statistics. An old saying warns that there are lies, damned lies, and statistics—meaning that statistics can be misleading. A commercial may claim, "In a taste test, eighty percent of those questioned indicated that they preferred Fizzy Cola." Impressed? Don't be—at least, not until you find out how the test was conducted. Perhaps the participants had to choose between Fizzy Cola and battery acid, or perhaps there were only five participants, all Fizzy Cola vice presidents.

Finally, select *representative* examples. Picking the oddball, one-in-a-million example to support a point—and passing it off as typical—is dishonest. Consider an essay with the thesis, "Part-time jobs contribute to academic success." Citing only one example of a student who works at a job twenty-five hours a week while earning straight *A*'s isn't playing fair. Why not? You've made a *hasty generalization* based on only one case. To be convincing, you need to show how holding down a job affects *most* students' academic performance. (For more on hasty generalizations, see page 470.)

2. **Develop your examples sufficiently.** To ensure that you get your ideas across, your examples must be *specific.* An essay on the types of heroes in American movies wouldn't succeed if you simply strung together a series of undeveloped examples in paragraphs like this one:

Original

Heroes in American movies usually fall into types. One kind of hero is the tight-lipped loner, men like Clint Eastwood and Humphrey Bogart. Another movie hero is the quiet, shy, or fumbling type who has appeared in movies since the beginning. The main characteristic of this hero is lovableness, as seen in actors like Jimmy Stewart. Perhaps the most one-dimensional and predictable hero is the superman who battles tough odds. This kind of hero is best illustrated by Sylvester Stallone as Rocky and Rambo.

If you developed the essay in this way—moving from one undeveloped example to another—you would be doing little more than making a list. To be effective, key examples must be expanded in sufficient detail. The examples in the preceding paragraph could be developed in paragraphs of their own. You could, for instance, develop the first example this way:

Revised

Heroes can be tight-lipped loners who appear out of nowhere, form no permanent attachments, and walk, drive, or ride off into the sunset. In most of his Westerns, from the low-budget "spaghetti Westerns" of the 1960s to *Unforgiven* in 1992, Clint Eastwood personifies this kind of hero. He is remote, mysterious, and untalkative. Yet he guns down an evil sheriff, runs other villains out of town, and helps a handicapped girl—acts that cement his heroic status. The loner might also be Sam Spade as played by Humphrey Bogart. Spade solves the crime and sends the guilty off to jail, yet he holds his emotions in check and has no permanent ties beyond his faithful secretary and shabby office. One gets the feeling that he could walk away from these, too, if necessary.

Even in *The Right Stuff*, an account of America's early astronauts, the scriptwriters mold Chuck Yeager, the man who broke the sound barrier, into a classic loner. Yeager, portrayed by the aloof Sam Shepherd, has a wife, but he is nevertheless insular. Taking mute pride in his ability to distance himself from politicians, bureaucrats, even colleagues, he soars into space, dignified and detached.

(For hints on making evidence specific, see pages 71–74 in Chapter 6.)

3. **Organize the examples.** If, as is usually the case, several examples support your point, be sure to present the examples in an *organized* manner. Often you'll find that other *patterns of development* (cause-effect, comparison-contrast, definition, and so on) suggest ways to sequence examples. Let's say you're writing an essay showing that stay-at-home vacations offer numerous opportunities to relax. You might begin the essay with examples that *contrast* stay-at-home and get-away vacations. Then you might move to a *process analysis* that illustrates different techniques for unwinding at home. The essay might end with examples showing the *effect* of such leisurely at-home breaks.

   Finally, you need to select an *organizational approach consistent* with your *purpose* and *thesis.* Imagine you're writing an essay about students' adjustment during the first months of college. The supporting examples could be arranged *chronologically.* You might start by illustrating the ambivalence many students feel the first day of college when their parents leave for home; you might then offer an anecdote or two about students' frequent calls to Mom and Dad during the opening weeks of the semester; the essay might close with an account of students' reluctance to leave campus at the midyear break.

   Similarly, an essay demonstrating that a room often reflects the character of its occupant might be organized *spatially:* from the empty soda cans on the floor to the spitballs on the ceiling. In an essay illustrating the kinds of skills taught in a composition course, you might move from *simple* to *complex* examples: starting with relatively matter-of-fact skills like spelling and punctuation and ending with more conceptually difficult skills like formulating a thesis and organizing an essay. Last, the *emphatic sequence*—in which you lead from your first example to your final, most significant one—is another effective way to organize an essay with many examples. A paper about Americans' characteristic impatience might progress from minor examples (dependence on fast food, obsession with ever-faster mail delivery) to more disturbing manifestations of impatience (using drugs as quick solutions to problems, advocating simple answers to complex international problems: "Bomb them!").

4. **Choose a point of view.** Many essays developed by illustration place the subject in the foreground and the writer in the background. Such an approach

calls for the *third-person point of view.* For example, even if you draw examples from your own personal experience, you can present them without using the *first-person "I."* You might convert such personal material into generalized examples (see pages 231–232), or you might describe the personal experience as if it happened to someone else. Of course, you may use the first person if the use of "I" will make the example more believable and dramatic. But remember: Just because an event happened to you personally doesn't mean you have to use the first-person point of view.

REVISION STRATEGIES

Once you have a draft of the essay, you're ready to revise. The following checklist will help you and those giving you feedback apply to illustration some of the revision techniques discussed in Chapters 7 and 8.

ILLUSTRATION: A REVISION/PEER REVIEW CHECKLIST

Revise Overall Meaning and Structure

- ☐ What thesis is being advanced? Which examples don't support the thesis? Should these examples be deleted, or should the thesis be reshaped to fit the examples? Why?
- ☐ Which patterns of development and methods of organization (chronological, spatial, simple-to-complex, emphatic) provide the essay's framework? Would other ordering principles be more effective? If so, which ones?

Revise Paragraph Development

- ☐ Which paragraphs contain too many or too few examples? Which contain examples that are too brief or too extended? Which include insufficiently or overly detailed examples?
- ☐ Which paragraphs rely on predictable examples? How could the examples be made more compelling?
- ☐ Which paragraphs include examples that are atypical or inaccurate?

Revise Sentences and Words

- ☐ What signal devices (*for example, for instance, in particular, such as*) introduce examples and clarify the line of thought? Where are there too many or too few of these devices?
- ☐ Where would more varied sentence structure heighten the effect of the essay's illustrations?
- ☐ Where would more concrete and specific words make the examples more effective?

STUDENT ESSAY: FROM PREWRITING THROUGH REVISION

The student essay that follows was written by Michael Pagano in response to this assignment:

> One implication in Beth Johnson's "Bombs Bursting in Air" is that, given life's unanticipated tragedies, people need to focus on what's really important rather than on trivial complications and distractions. Observe closely the way you and others conduct your daily lives. Use your observations for an essay that supports or refutes Johnson's point of view.

After deciding to write an essay on the way possessions complicate life, Michael sat down at his computer and did some *freewriting* to generate material on the topic. His original freewriting follows; the handwritten comments indicate Michael's later efforts to develop and shape this material. Note that Michael deleted some points, added others, and made several items more specific; he also labeled and sequenced key ideas. These annotations paved the way for a sentence outline, which is presented after the freewriting.

Freewriting

① Buying

I shop too much. So do my parents—practically every weekend ~~and nearly every holiday except Christmas and Easter. All those Washington's Birthday sales~~. Then they yell at us kids for watching so much TV, although they're not around to do much with us.

④ Discarding items

In fact, Mom and Dad were the ones who thought our [19-inch] old TV wasn't good enough anymore so they replaced it with a [35-inch] huge flat-screen set. I remember all those annoying phone calls when they put the [classified section] ad in the paper to sell the old set. People coming and going. Then Mom and Dad only got $25 for it anyway. It wasn't worth paying for the ad. ~~They never seem to come out ahead~~.

⑤ Running into debt

No wonder Mom works part-time at the library and Dad [2nd job-] stays so late at the office. I'm getting [overtime] into the same situation. Already up to my ears in debt, [time payments] paying off the car. I spend hours washing it and [③ vacuuming car—maintenance] waxing it, and it doesn't even fit into the garage,

② Running out of room

which is loaded with discarded junk. The whole house is cluttered. Maybe that's why people move so much—to escape the clutter. There was hardly room for my new computer in my room. I also have to shove my new clothes into the closets and drawers. My snazzy new pants get all wrinkled. They shrank when I washed them. Now they're too tight. I should have sent them to the dry cleaners. But I'd already paid enough for them. ~~Well, everything's shoddy nowadays~~. My computer's giving me trouble Possessions don't hold up. So what lasts? Basic values—love, family, friends. conclusion?

③ Having maintenance problems

Outline

Thesis: We clutter our lives with material goods.

I. We waste a lot of time deciding what to buy.
   A. We window-shop for good-looking footwear.
   B. We look through magazines for stereos and exercise equipment.
   C. Family life suffers when everyone is out shopping.

II. Once we take our new purchases home, we find we don't have enough room for them.
   A. We stack things in crowded closets, garages, and basements.
   B. When things get too cluttered, we simply move.

III. Our possessions require continual maintenance.
   A. Cars have to be washed and waxed.
   B. New pants have to go to the cleaners.
   C. Computers and other items break down and have to be replaced.

IV. Before we replace broken items, we try to get rid of them by placing ads in the classified section.
   A. We have to deal with annoying phone calls.
   B. We have to deal with people coming to the house to see the items.

V. Our mania for possessions puts us in debt.
   A. We accumulate enormous credit-card balances.
   B. We take second jobs or work overtime to make time payments.

Now read Michael's paper, "Pursuit of Possessions," noting the similarities and differences among his freewriting, outline, and final essay. You'll see, for example, that Michael changed the "I" of his freewriting to the more general "We" in the outline and essay. He made this change because he wanted readers to see themselves in the situations being illustrated. In addition, Michael's outline, while more detailed than his freewriting, doesn't include highly concrete examples, but the essay does. In the outline, for instance, he simply states, "Computers and other items break down . . . " In the essay, though, he spins out this point with vivid details: "The home computer starts to lose data, the microwave has to have its temperature controls adjusted, and the DVD player has to be serviced when a disc becomes jammed."

As you read Michael's essay, also consider how well it applies the principles of illustration. (The commentary that follows the paper will help you look at the essay more closely and will give you some sense of how Michael went about revising his first draft.)

Pursuit of Possessions

By Michael Pagano

Introduction

In the essay "Bombs Bursting in Air," Beth Johnson develops the extended metaphor of bombs exploding unexpectedly to represent the tragedies that occur without warning in our daily lives. Herself a survivor of innumerable life bombs, Johnson suggests that in light of life's fragility, we need to remember and appreciate what's really important to us. But very often, we lose sight of what really matters in our lives, instead occupying ourselves with trivial distractions. In particular, many of us choose to spend our lives in pursuit of material possessions. Much of our time goes into buying new things, dealing with the complications they create, and working madly to buy more things or pay for the things we already have. 1

Thesis

Plan of development

Topic sentence

The first of three paragraphs in a chronological sequence

We devote a great deal of our lives to acquiring the material goods we imagine are essential to our well-being. Hours are spent planning and thinking about our future purchases. We window-shop for designer running shoes; we leaf through magazines looking at ads for elaborate sound equipment; we research back issues of *Consumer Reports* to find out about recent developments in exercise equipment. Moreover, once we find what we are looking for, more time is taken up when we decide to actually buy the items. How do we find this time? That's easy. We turn evenings, weekends, and holidays—times that used to be set aside for family and friends—into shopping expeditions. No wonder family life is deteriorating and children spend so much time in front of television sets. Their parents are seldom around. 2

Topic sentence

The second paragraph in the chronological sequence

As soon as we take our new purchases home, they begin to complicate our lives. A sleek new sports car has to be washed, waxed, and vacuumed. A fashionable pair of overpriced dress pants can't be thrown in the washing machine but has to be taken to the dry cleaner. New sound equipment has to be connected with a tangled network of cables to the TV, computer, and speakers. 3

Eventually, of course, the inevitable happens. Our indispensable possessions break down and need to be repaired. The home computer starts to lose data, the microwave has to have its temperature controls adjusted, and the DVD player has to be serviced when a disc becomes jammed in the machine.

A paragraph with many specific examples

Topic sentence

The third paragraph in the chronological sequence

4 After more time has gone by, we sometimes discover that our purchases don't suit us anymore, and so we decide to replace them. Before making our replacement purchases, though, we have to find ways to get rid of the old items. If we want to replace our 19-inch television set with a 35-inch flat-screen, we have to find time to put an ad in the classified section of the paper. Then we have to handle phone calls and set up times people can come to look at the old TV. We could store the set in the basement—if we are lucky enough to find a spot that isn't already filled with other discarded purchases.

Topic sentence with emphasis signal

5 Worst of all, this mania for possessions often influences our approach to work. It is not unusual for people to take a second or even a third job to pay off the debt they fall into because they have overbought. After paying for food, clothing, and shelter, many people see the rest of their paycheck go to Visa, MasterCard, department store charge accounts, and time payments. Panic sets in when they realize there simply is not enough money to cover all their expenses. Just to stay afloat, people may have to work overtime or take on additional jobs.

Conclusion

6 It is clear that many of us have allowed the pursuit of possessions to dominate our lives. We are so busy buying, maintaining, and paying for our worldly goods that we do not have much time to think about what is really important. We should try to step back from our compulsive need for more of everything and get in touch with the basic values that are the real point of our lives.

Commentary

Thesis, Combining Patterns of Development, and Plan of Development

In "Pursuit of Possessions," Michael analyzes the mania for acquiring material goods that permeates our society. He begins by addressing an implication conveyed in Beth Johnson's "Bombs Bursting in Air"—that life's fragility dictates that we need to focus on what really matters in our lives. This reference to Johnson gives Michael a chance to contrast the reflective way she suggests we should live with the acquisitive and frenzied way many people lead their lives. This contrast leads to the essay's thesis: "[M]any of us choose to spend our lives in pursuit of material possessions."

Besides introducing the basic contrast at the heart of the essay, Michael's opening paragraph helps readers see that the essay contains an element of *causal analysis.* The final sentence of the introductory paragraph lays out the effects of our possession obsession. This sentence also serves as the essay's *plan of development* and reveals that Michael feels the pursuit of possessions negatively affects our lives in three key ways.

Essays of this length often don't need a plan of development. But since Michael's paper is filled with many *examples,* the plan of development helps readers see how all the details relate to the essay's central point.

Evidence

Support for the thesis consists of numerous examples presented in the *first-person plural point of view* ("*We* lose sight . . . ," "*We* devote a great deal of our lives . . . ," and so on). Many of these examples seem drawn from Michael's, his friends', or his family's experiences; however, to emphasize the events' universality, Michael converts these essentially personal examples into generalized ones that "we" all experience.

These examples, in turn, are organized around the three major points signaled by the plan of development. Michael uses one paragraph to develop his first and third points and two paragraphs to develop his second point. Each of the four supporting paragraphs is focused by a *topic sentence* that appears at the beginning of the paragraph. The transitional phrase, "Worst of all" (paragraph 5) signals that Michael has sequenced his major points *emphatically,* saving for last the issue he considers most significant: how the "mania for possessions . . . influences our approach to work."

Organizational Strategies

Emphatic order isn't Michael's only organizational technique. When reading the paper, you probably felt that there was an easy flow from one supporting paragraph to the next. How does Michael achieve such *coherence between paragraphs?* For one thing, he sequences paragraphs 2–4 *chronologically:* what happens before a purchase is made; what happens afterward. Secondly, topic sentences in paragraphs 3 and 4 include *signal devices* that indicate this passage of time. The topic sentences also strengthen coherence by *linking back* to the preceding paragraph: "*As soon as we take our new purchases home, they* . . . complicate our lives" and "*After more time has gone by,* we . . . discover that our purchases don't suit us anymore."

The same organizing strategies are used *within paragraphs* to make the essay coherent. Details in paragraphs 2–4 are sequenced *chronologically,* and to help readers follow the chronology, Michael uses *signal devices:* "*Moreover, once* we find what we are looking for, more time is taken up . . . " (2); "*Eventually,* of course, the inevitable happens" (3); "*Then* we have to handle phone calls . . . " (4).

Problems with Paragraph Development

You probably recall that an essay developed primarily through illustration must include examples that are *relevant, interesting, convincing, representative, accurate,* and *specific.* On the whole, Michael's examples meet these requirements. The third and fourth paragraphs, especially, include vigorous details that show how our mania for buying things can govern our lives. We may even laugh with self-recognition when reading about "overpriced dress pants that can't be thrown in the washing machine" or a basement "filled . . . with discarded purchases."

The fifth paragraph, however, is underdeveloped. We know that this paragraph presents what Michael considers his most significant point, but the paragraph's examples are rather *flat* and *unconvincing.* To make this final section more compelling, Michael could mention specific people who overspend, revealing how much they are in debt and how much they have to work to become solvent again. Or he could cite a television documentary or magazine article dealing with the issue of consumer debt. Such specifics would give the paragraph the solidity it now lacks.

Shift in Tone

The fifth paragraph has a second, more subtle problem: a *shift in tone.* Although Michael has, up to this point, been critical of our possession-mad culture, he has poked fun at our obsession and kept his tone conversational and gently satiric. In this paragraph, though, he adopts a serious tone, and, in the next paragraph, his tone becomes even weightier, almost preachy. It is, of course, legitimate to have a serious message in a lightly satiric piece. In fact, most satiric writing has such an additional layer of meaning. But because Michael has trouble blending these two moods, there's a jarring shift in the essay.

Shift in Focus

The second paragraph shows another kind of shift—in *focus.* The paragraph's controlling idea is that too much time is spent acquiring possessions. However, starting with "No wonder family life is deteriorating," Michael includes two sentences that introduce a complex issue beyond the scope of the essay. Since the sentences disrupt the paragraph's unity, they should be deleted.

Revising the First Draft

Although the final version of the essay needs work in spots, it's much stronger than Michael's first draft. To see how Michael went about revising the draft, compare his paper's second and third supporting paragraphs with his draft version reprinted here. The annotations, numbered in order of importance, show the ideas Michael hit upon when he returned to his first draft and reworked this section.

Original Version of the Second Paragraph

② Awkward first sentence

Our lives are spent not only buying things but in dealing with the inevitable complications that are created by our newly acquired possessions. First, we have to find places to put all the objects we bring home.

① Paragraph goes in too many directions. Cut idea about moving since not enough space.

③ Make problem with pants more specific

④ Develop more fully

```
More clothes demand more closets; a second car demands more garage
space; a home-entertainment center requires elaborate shelving. We
shouldn't be surprised that the average American family moves once
every three years. A good many families move simply because they
need more space to store all the things they buy. In addition, our
possessions demand maintenance time. A person who gets a new car
will spend hours washing it, waxing it, and vacuuming it. A new
pair of pants has to go to the dry cleaners. New sound systems have
to be connected to already existing equipment. Eventually, of
course, the inevitable happens. Our new items need to be repaired.
Or we get sick of them and decide to replace them. Before making
our replacement purchases, though, we have to get rid of the old
items. That can be a real inconvenience.
```

Referring to the revision checklist on page 235 helped Michael see that the paragraph rambled and lacked energy. He started to revise by tightening the first sentence, making it more focused and less awkward. Certainly, the revised sentence ("As soon as we take our new purchases home, they begin to complicate our lives") is crisper than the original. Next, he decided to omit the discussion about finding places to put new possessions; these sentences about inadequate closet, garage, and shelf space were so exaggerated that they undercut the valid point he wanted to make. He also chose to eliminate the sentences about the mobility of American families. This was, he felt, an interesting point, but it introduced an issue too complex to be included in the paragraph.

Michael strengthened the rest of the paragraph by making his examples more specific. A "new car" became a "sleek new sports car," and a "pair of pants" became a "fashionable pair of overpriced dress pants." Michael also realized he had to do more than merely write, "Eventually, . . . our new items need to be repaired." This point had to be dramatized by sharp, convincing details. Therefore, Michael added lively examples to describe how high-tech possessions—microwaves, home computers, DVD players—break down. Similarly, Michael realized it wasn't enough simply to say, as he had in the original, that we run into problems when we try to replace out-of-favor purchases. Vigorous details were again needed to illustrate the point. Michael thus used a typical "replaceable" (an old TV) as his key example and showed the annoyance involved in handling phone calls and setting up appointments so that people could see the TV.

After adding these specifics, Michael realized that he had enough material to devote a separate paragraph to the problems associated with replacing old purchases. By dividing his original paragraph, Michael ended up with two well-focused paragraphs, rather than a single rambling one.

In short, Michael strengthened his essay through substantial revision. Another round of rewriting would have made the essay stronger still. Even without this additional work, Michael's essay provides an interesting perspective on a current social preoccupation.

ACTIVITIES: ILLUSTRATION

Prewriting Activities

1. Imagine you're writing two essays: One is a serious paper analyzing why large numbers of public school teachers leave the profession each year; the other is a light essay defining *preppie, thug,* or some other slang term used to describe a kind of person. Jot down ways you might use examples in each essay.

2. Use mapping or another prewriting technique to gather examples illustrating the truth of *one* of the following familiar sayings. Then, using the same or a different prewriting technique, accumulate examples that counter the saying. Weigh both sets of examples to determine the saying's validity. After developing an appropriate thesis, decide which examples you would elaborate in an essay.

   a. Haste makes waste.
   b. There's no use crying over spilled milk.
   c. A bird in the hand is worth two in the bush.

3. Turn back to activity 4 and activity 5 in Chapter 4, and select *one* thesis statement for which you didn't develop supporting evidence earlier. Identify a purpose, audience, tone, and point of view for an essay with this thesis. Then meet with at least one other person to generate as many examples as possible to support the thesis. Next, evaluate the material to determine which examples should be eliminated. Finally, from the remaining examples, take the strongest one and develop it as fully as you can.

4. Freewrite or use your journal to generate examples illustrating how widespread a recent fad or trend has become. After reviewing your prewriting to determine a possible thesis, narrow the examples to those you would retain for an essay. How might the patterns of development or a chronological, emphatic, spatial, or simple-to-complex approach help you sequence the examples?

Revising Activities

5. The following paragraph is from the first draft of an essay about the decline of small-town shopping districts. The paragraph is meant to show what small towns can do to revitalize business. Revise the paragraph, strengthening it with specific and convincing examples.

   A small town can compete with a large new mall for shoppers. But merchants must work together, modernizing the stores and making the town's main street pleasant, even fun to walk. They should also copy the malls' example by including attention-getting events as often as possible.

6. The paragraph that follows is from the first draft of an essay showing how knowledge of psychology can help us understand behavior that might otherwise seem baffling. The paragraph is intended to illustrate the meaning of the psychological term *superego.* Revise the paragraph, replacing its vague, unconvincing examples with one extended example that conveys the meaning of *superego* clearly and dramatically.

    The superego is the part of us that makes us feel guilty when we do something that we know is wrong. When we act foolishly or wildly, we usually feel qualms about our actions later on. If we imagine ourselves getting revenge, we most likely discover that the thoughts make us feel bad. All of these are examples of the superego at work.

7. Reprinted here is a paragraph from the first draft of a light-spirited essay showing that Americans' pursuit of change for change's sake has drawbacks. The paragraph is meant to illustrate that infatuation with newness costs consumers money yet leads to no improvement in product quality. How effective is the paragraph? Which examples are specific and convincing? Which are not? Do any seem nonrepresentative, offensive, or sexist? How could the paragraph's organization be improved? Consider these questions as you rewrite the paragraph. Add specific examples where needed. Depending on the way you revise, you may want to break this one paragraph into several.

    We end up paying for our passion for the new and improved. Trendy clothing styles convince us that last year's outfits are outdated, even though our old clothes are fine. Women are especially vulnerable in this regard. What, though, about items that have to be replaced periodically, like shampoo? Even slight changes lead to new formulations requiring retooling of the production process. That means increased manufacturing costs per item—all of which get passed on to us, the consumer. Then there are those items that tout new, trend-setting features that make earlier versions supposedly obsolete. Some manufacturers, for example, boast that their stereo sound systems transmit an expanded-frequency range. The problem is that humans can't even hear such frequencies, But the high-tech feature dazzles men who are too naive to realize they're being hoodwinked.

PROFESSIONAL SELECTIONS: ILLUSTRATION

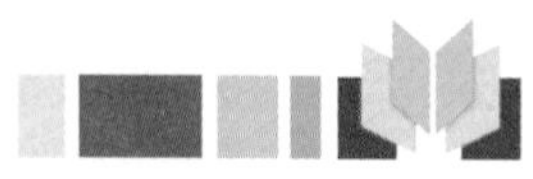

KAY S. HYMOWITZ

A senior fellow at the Manhattan Institute and a contributing editor of the urban-policy magazine *City Journal*, Kay S. Hymowitz (1948–) writes on education and childhood in America. A native of Philadelphia, Hymowitz received an undergraduate English degree from Brandeis University and graduate degrees from Tufts University and Columbia University. She has taught English literature and composition at Brooklyn College and at Parsons School of Design. Hymowitz is the author of *Liberation's Children: Parents and Kids in a Postmodern Age* (2003) and *Ready or Not: Why Treating Our Children as Small Adults Endangers Their Future and Ours* (1999) and is a principal contributor to *Modern Sex: Liberation and Its Discontents* (2001). In 2006, she published *Marriage and Caste in America: Separate and Unequal Families in a Post-Marital Age,* a collection of her *City Journal* essays. Her work has appeared in publications including *The New York Times*, *The Washington Post*, and *The New Republic*. Hymowitz lives in Brooklyn with her husband and three children. The following essay appeared in the Autumn 1998 issue of *City Journal*.

Please note the essay structure diagram that appears following this selection (Figure 12.2 on page 250).

Pre-Reading Journal Entry

Think back on your childhood. What were some possessions and activities that you cherished and enjoyed? Freewrite for a few moments in your pre-reading journal about these beloved objects and/or pastimes. What exactly were they? Why did you enjoy them so much? Did your feelings about them change as you matured into adolescence?

TWEENS: TEN GOING ON SIXTEEN

1 During the past year my youngest morphed from child to teenager. Down came the posters of adorable puppies and the drawings from art class; up went the airbrushed faces of Leonardo di Caprio and Kate Winslet. CDs of Le Ann Rimes and Paula Cole appeared mysteriously, along with teen fan magazines featuring glowering movie and rock-and-roll hunks. . . . She started reading the newspaper—or at least the movie ads—with all the intensity of a Talmudic scholar, scanning for glimpses of her beloved Leo or, failing that, Matt Damon. As spring approached and younger children skipped past our house on their way to the park, she swigged from a designer water bottle, wearing the obligatory tank top and denim shorts as she whispered on the phone to friends about games of Truth or Dare. The last rites for her childhood came when, embarrassed at reminders of her foolish past, she pulled a sheet over her years-in-the-making American Girl doll collection, now dead to the world.

So what's new in this dog-bites-man story? Well, as all this was going on, my daughter was ten years old and in the fourth grade. 2

Those who remember their own teenybopper infatuation with Elvis or the Beatles might be inclined to shrug their shoulders as if to say, "It was ever thus." But this is different. Across class lines and throughout the country, elementary and middle-school principals and teachers, child psychologists and psychiatrists, marketing and demographic researchers all confirm the pronouncement of Henry Trevor, middle-school director of the Berkeley Carroll School in Brooklyn, New York: "There is no such thing as preadolescence anymore. Kids are teenagers at ten." 3

Marketers have a term for this new social animal, kids between eight and 12: they call them "tweens." The name captures the ambiguous reality: though chronologically midway between early childhood and adolescence, this group is leaning more and more toward teen styles, teen attitudes, and, sadly, teen behavior at its most troubling. 4

The tween phenomenon grows out of a complicated mixture of biology, demography, and the predictable assortment of Bad Ideas. But putting aside its causes for a moment, the emergence of tweendom carries risks for both young people and society. Eight- to 12-year-olds have an even more wobbly sense of themselves than adolescents; they rely more heavily on others to tell them how to understand the world and how to place themselves in it. Now, for both pragmatic and ideological reasons, they are being increasingly "empowered" to do this on their own, which leaves them highly vulnerable both to a vulgar and sensation-driven marketplace and to the crass authority of their immature peers. In tweens, we can see the future of our society taking shape, and it's not at all clear how it's going to work. 5

Perhaps the most striking evidence for the tweening of children comes from market researchers. "There's no question there's a deep trend, not a passing fad, toward kids getting older younger," says research psychologist Michael Cohen of Arc Consulting, a public policy, education, and marketing research firm in New York. "This is not just on the coasts. There are no real differences geographically." It seems my daughter's last rites for her American Girl dolls were a perfect symbol not just for her own childhood but for childhood, period. The Toy Manufacturers of America Factbook states that, where once the industry could count on kids between birth and 14 as their target market, today it is only birth to ten. "In the last ten years we've seen a rapid development of upper-age children," says Bruce Friend, vice president of worldwide research and planning for Nickelodeon, a cable channel aimed at kids. "The 12- to 14-year-olds of yesterday are the ten to 12s of today." The rise of the preteen teen is "the biggest trend we've seen." 6

Scorning any symbols of their immaturity, tweens now cultivate a self-image that emphasizes sophistication. The Nickelodeon-Yankelovich Youth Monitor found that by the time they are 12, children describe themselves as "flirtatious, sexy, trendy, athletic, cool." Nickelodeon's Bruce Friend reports that by 11, children in focus groups say they no longer even think of themselves as children. 7

They're very concerned with their "look," Friend says, even more so than older teens. Sprouting up everywhere are clothing stores like the chain Limited Too and the catalog company Delia, geared toward tween girls who scorn old-fashioned, little-girl flowers, ruffles, white socks, and Mary Janes[1] in favor of the cool—black mini-dresses 8

[1]Trademark name of patent-leather shoes for girls, usually having a low heel and a strap that fastens at the side (editors' note).

and platform shoes. . . . Teachers complain of ten- or 11-year-old girls arriving at school looking like madams, in full cosmetic regalia, with streaked hair, platform shoes, and midriff-revealing shirts. Barbara Kapetanakes, a psychologist at a conservative Jewish day school in New York, describes her students' skirts as being about "the size of a belt." Kapetanakes says she was told to dress respectfully on Fridays, the eve of the Jewish Sabbath, which she did by donning a long skirt and a modest blouse. Her students, on the other hand, showed their respect by looking "like they should be hanging around the West Side Highway," where prostitutes ply their trade.

9 Lottie Sims, a computer teacher in a Miami middle school, says that the hooker look for tweens is fanning strong support for uniforms in her district. But uniforms and tank-top bans won't solve the problem of painted young ladies. "You can count on one hand the girls not wearing makeup," Sims says. "Their parents don't even know. They arrive at school with huge bags of lipstick and hair spray, and head straight to the girls' room."

10 Though the tweening of youth affects girls more visibly than boys, especially since boys mature more slowly, boys are by no means immune to these obsessions. Once upon a time, about ten years ago, fifth- and sixth-grade boys were about as fashion-conscious as their pet hamsters. But a growing minority have begun trading in their baseball cards for hair mousse and baggy jeans. In some places, $200 jackets, emblazoned with sports logos like the warm-up gear of professional athletes, are *de rigueur*; in others, the preppy look is popular among the majority, while the more daring go for the hipper style of pierced ears, fade haircuts, or ponytails. Often these tween peacocks strut through their middle-school hallways taunting those who have yet to catch on to the cool look. . . .

11 Those who seek comfort in the idea that the tweening of childhood is merely a matter of fashion—who maybe even find their lip-synching, hip-swaying little boy or girl kind of cute—might want to think twice. There are disturbing signs that tweens are not only eschewing the goody-goody childhood image but its substance as well. . . .

12 The clearest evidence of tweendom's darker side concerns crime. Although children under 15 still represent a minority of juvenile arrests, their numbers grew disproportionately in the past 20 years. According to a report by the Office of Juvenile Justice and Delinquency Prevention, "offenders under age 15 represent the leading edge of the juvenile crime problem, and their numbers are growing." Moreover, the crimes committed by younger teens and preteens are growing in severity. "Person offenses,[2] which once constituted 16 percent of the total court cases for this age group," continues the report, "now constitute 25 percent." Headline grabbers—like Nathaniel Abraham of Pontiac, Michigan, an 11-year-old who stole a rifle from a neighbor's garage and went on a shooting spree in October 1997, randomly killing a teenager coming out of a store; and 11-year-old Andrew Golden, who, with his 13-year-old partner, killed four children and one teacher at his middle school in Jonesboro, Arkansas—are extreme, exceptional cases, but alas, they are part of a growing trend toward preteen violent crime. . . .

13 The evidence on tween sex presents a troubling picture, too. Despite a decrease among older teens for the first time since records have been kept, sexual activity among tweens increased during that period. It seems that kids who are having sex are doing so at earlier ages. Between 1988 and 1995, the proportion of girls saying they

---

[2]Crimes against a person. They include assault, robbery, rape, and homicide (editors' note).

began sex before 15 rose from 11 percent to 19 percent. (For boys, the number remained stable, at 21 percent.) This means that approximately one in five middle-school kids is sexually active. Christie Hogan, a middle-school counselor for 20 years in Louisville, Kentucky, says: "We're beginning to see a few pregnant sixth-graders." Many of the principals and counselors I spoke with reported a small but striking minority of sexually active seventh-graders. . . .

Certainly the days of the tentative and giggly preadolescent seem to be passing. Middle-school principals report having to deal with miniskirted 12-year-olds "draping themselves over boys" or patting their behinds in the hallways, while 11-year-old boys taunt girls about their breasts and rumors about their own and even their parents' sexual proclivities. Tweens have even given new connotations to the word "playground": one fifth-grade teacher from southwestern Ohio told me of two youngsters discovered in the bushes during recess. 14

Drugs and alcohol are also seeping into tween culture. The past six years have seen more than a doubling of the number of eighth-graders who smoke marijuana (10 percent today) and those who no longer see it as dangerous. "The stigma isn't there the way it was ten years ago," says Dan Kindlon, assistant professor of psychiatry at Harvard Medical School and co-author with Michael Thompson of *Raising Cain*. "Then it was the fringe group smoking pot. You were looked at strangely. Now the fringe group is using LSD." 15

Aside from sex, drugs, and rock and roll, another teen problem—eating disorders—is also beginning to affect younger kids. This behavior grows out of premature fashion-consciousness, which has an even more pernicious effect on tweens than on teens, because, by definition, younger kids have a more vulnerable and insecure self-image. Therapists say they are seeing a growing number of anorexics and obsessive dieters even among late-elementary-school girls. "You go on Internet chat rooms and find ten-and 11-year-olds who know every [fashion] model and every statistic about them," says Nancy Kolodny, a Connecticut-based therapist and author of *When Food's a Foe: How You Can Confront and Conquer Your Eating Disorder*. "Kate Moss is their god. They can tell if she's lost a few pounds or gained a few. If a powerful kid is talking about this stuff at school, it has a big effect." 16

What change in our social ecology has led to the emergence of tweens? Many note that kids are reaching puberty at earlier ages, but while earlier physical maturation may play a small role in defining adolescence down, its importance tends to be overstated. True, the average age at which girls begin to menstruate has fallen from 13 to between 11 and 12½ today, but the very gradualness of this change means that 12-year-olds have been living inside near-adult bodies for many decades without feeling impelled to build up a cosmetics arsenal or head for the bushes at recess. In fact, some experts believe that the very years that have witnessed the rise of the tween have also seen the age of first menstruation stabilize. Further, teachers and principals on the front lines see no clear correlation between physical and social maturation. Plenty of budding girls and bulking boys have not put away childish things, while an abundance of girls with flat chests and boys with squeaky voices ape the body language and fashions of their older siblings. . . . 17

Of course, the causes are complex, and most people working with tweens know it. In my conversations with educators and child psychologists who work primarily with middle-class kids nationwide, two major and fairly predictable themes emerged: a sexualized and glitzy media-driven marketplace and absentee parents. What has 18 been less commonly recognized is that at this age, the two causes combine to augment the authority of the peer group, which in turn both weakens the influence of parents and reinforces the power of the media. Taken together, parental absence, the market, and the peer group form a vicious circle that works to distort the development of youngsters. . . .

Questions for Close Reading

1. What is the selection's thesis? Locate the sentence(s) in which Hymowitz states her main idea. If she doesn't state the thesis explicitly, express it in your own words.
2. According to Hymowitz, what self-image do tweens cultivate? How do they project this image to others?
3. What physically dangerous behavioral trends does Hymowitz link to the tween phenomenon?
4. According to Hymowitz, what are the primary causes of the tween phenomenon?
5. Refer to your dictionary as needed to define the following words used in the selection: *glowering* (1), *Talmudic* (1), *rites* (1), *demographic* (3), *pragmatic* (5), *ideological* (5), *regalia* (8), *donning* (8), *ply* (8), *emblazoned* (10), *de rigueur* (10), *eschewing* (11), *tentative* (14), *proclivities* (14), *connotations* (14), *stigma* (15), *pernicious* (16), *correlation* (17), and *augment* (18).

Questions About the Writer's Craft

1. **The pattern.** Hymowitz opens her essay with an anecdotal example of tweenhood—her daughter's. What does this example add to her essay?
2. **The pattern.** What types of examples does Hymowitz provide in her essay? (See pages 230–235 for a discussion of the various forms that examples can take.) Cite at least one example of each type. How does each type of example contribute to her thesis?
3. How would you characterize Hymowitz's tone in the selection? Cite vocabulary that conveys this tone.
4. **Other patterns.** In paragraph 8, Hymowitz uses clothing as a means of presenting an important *contrast*. What does she contrast in these paragraphs? How does this contribute to her thesis?

Writing Assignments Using Illustration as a Pattern of Development

1. Hymowitz is troubled and perplexed by her daughter's behavior. Think about an older person, such as a parent or another relative, who finds *your* behavior

FIGURE 12.2
Essay Structure Diagram: "Tweens: Ten Going on Sixteen" by Kay S. Hymowitz

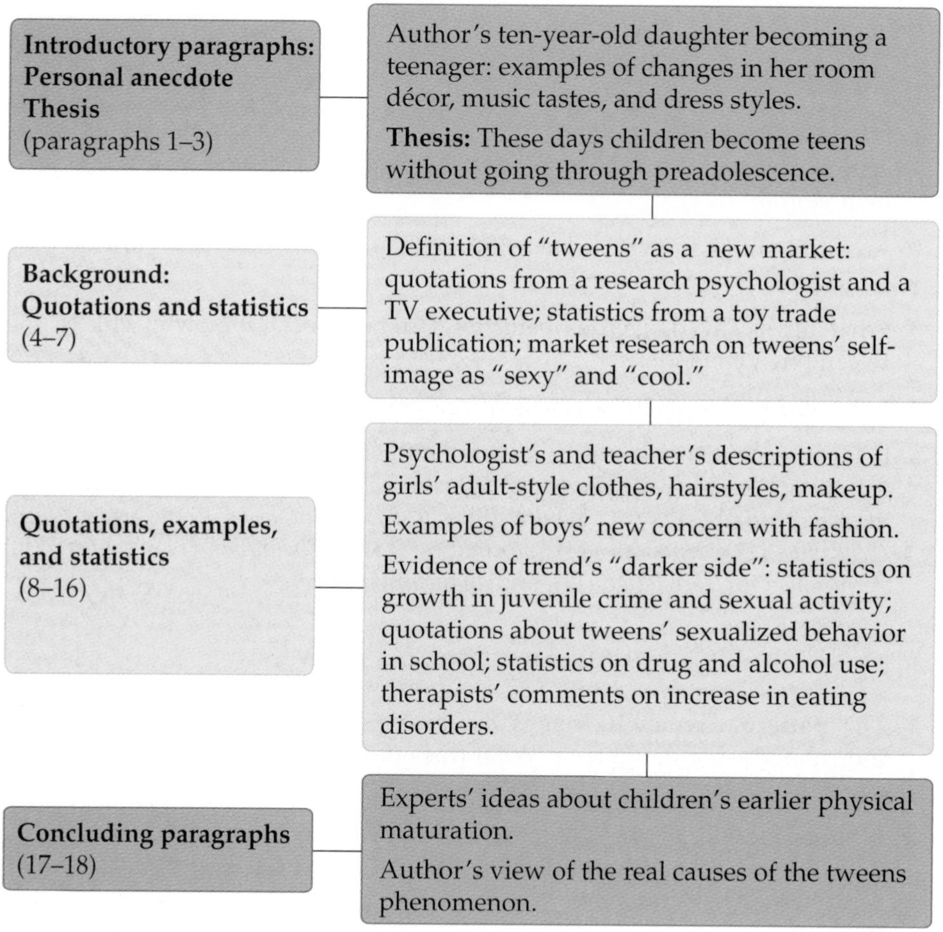

Introductory paragraphs: Personal anecdote Thesis (paragraphs 1–3)	Author's ten-year-old daughter becoming a teenager: examples of changes in her room décor, music tastes, and dress styles. **Thesis:** These days children become teens without going through preadolescence.
Background: Quotations and statistics (4–7)	Definition of "tweens" as a new market: quotations from a research psychologist and a TV executive; statistics from a toy trade publication; market research on tweens' self-image as "sexy" and "cool."
Quotations, examples, and statistics (8–16)	Psychologist's and teacher's descriptions of girls' adult-style clothes, hairstyles, makeup. Examples of boys' new concern with fashion. Evidence of trend's "darker side": statistics on growth in juvenile crime and sexual activity; quotations about tweens' sexualized behavior in school; statistics on drug and alcohol use; therapists' comments on increase in eating disorders.
Concluding paragraphs (17–18)	Experts' ideas about children's earlier physical maturation. Author's view of the real causes of the tweens phenomenon.

troubling and perplexing. Write an essay in which you illustrate why your behavior distresses this person. (Or, conversely, think of an elder whose behavior *you* find problematic, and write an essay illustrating why that person evokes this response in you.) You might structure your essay by picking the two or three most irksome characteristics or habits and developing supporting paragraphs around each of them. However you choose to organize your essay, be sure to provide abundant examples throughout.

2. The cultivation of a sophisticated self-image is, according to Hymowitz, a hallmark of tweenhood. Think back to when you were around that age. What

was your self-image at that time? Did you think of yourself as worldly or inexperienced? Cool or awkward? Attractive or unappealing? In your journal, freewrite about the traits that you would have identified in yourself as either a tween or an adolescent. Write an essay in which you illustrate your self-image at that age, focusing on two to three dominant characteristics you associated with yourself. It's important that you illustrate each trait with examples of when and how you displayed it. For example, if you saw yourself as "dorky," you might recall an embarrassing time when you tripped and fell in the middle of your school lunchroom. Conclude your essay by reflecting on whether the way you saw yourself at the time was accurate, and whether your feelings about yourself have changed since then. You'd also benefit from reading any of the following authors' musings on their childhood self-perceptions: Maya Angelou's "Sister Flowers" (page 167), Audre Lorde's "The Fourth of July" (page 208), and Beth Johnson's "Bombs Bursting in Air" (page 252).

Writing Assignments Combining Patterns of Development

3. Hymowitz advances a powerful argument about the alarming contemporary trend of tweenhood. But many would disagree with her entirely pessimistic analysis. Write an essay in which you *argue,* contrary to Hymowitz, that tweens today actually exhibit several *positive* characteristics. You might say, for example, that tweens today are more independent or more socially conscious than kids in the past. In order to develop your argument, you'll need to show how each characteristic you're discussing *contrasts* favorably with that characteristic in a previous generation of kids. Be sure, too, to acknowledge opposing arguments as you proceed. Research conducted in the library and/or on the Internet might help you develop your pro-tween argument.

4. Though she doesn't use the term explicitly, Hymowitz points to peer pressure as a significant factor in tweens' premature maturity. In your journal, take a few moments to reflect on your own experiences with peer pressure, whether as a pre-teen or teen, or even into adulthood. What are some incidents that stand out in your memory? Write an essay *narrating* a particularly memorable incident of peer pressure in which you were involved. You may have been the object of the pressure, or even perhaps the source. What were the circumstances? Who was involved? How did you respond at the time? How did the episode *affect* you? In retrospect, how do you feel about the incident today? Be sure to use dialogue as well as *descriptive* language in order to make the episode come alive. For another account of some alarming pressures on young people—specifically, young athletes—read Buzz Bissinger's "Innocents Afield" (page 407).

Writing Assignment Using a Journal Entry as a Starting Point

5. As a way of illustrating her daughter's evolving tween tastes, Hymowitz cites the "years-in-the-making American Girl doll collection" over which her disaffected daughter has now drawn a sheet. Reviewing what you wrote in your pre-reading journal entry, identify some once-loved childhood items or activities that you distanced yourself from as you got older. Write an essay in which you exemplify your growth into adolescence by identifying two or three childhood possessions or activities that you cast off. You might, for example, discuss building up a beloved rock collection or playing with action figures. As you introduce these items, be sure to describe them and to explain the significance they once held for you, as well as your reasons for leaving them behind. Conclude your essay by offering some reflections on whether you currently regard the childhood items with the same distaste or disinterest you felt as a teen.

BETH JOHNSON

Beth Johnson (1956–) is a writer, occasional college teacher, and freelance editor. A graduate of Goshen College and Syracuse University, Johnson is the author of numerous inspirational real-life accounts, including *Facing Addiction* (2006) and *Surviving Abuse* (2006) as well as several college texts, including *Everyday Heroes* (1996) and *Reading Changed My Life* (2003); she also coauthored *Voices and Values* (2002) and *English Essentials* (2004). Containing profiles of men and women who have triumphed over obstacles to achieve personal and academic success, the books have provided a motivational boost to college students nationwide. She lives with her husband and three children in Lederach, Pennsylvania. The following piece is one of several that Johnson has written about the complexities and wonders of life.

Pre-Reading Journal Entry

When you were young, did adults acknowledge the existence of life's tragedies, or did they deny such harsh truths? In your journal, list several difficult events that you observed or experienced firsthand as a child. How did the adults in your life explain these hardships? In each case, do you think the adults acted appropriately? If not, how should they have responded?

BOMBS BURSTING IN AIR

It's Friday night and we're at the Olympics, the Junior Olympics, that is. My son is on a relay-race team competing against fourth-graders from all over the school district. His little sister and I sit high in the stands, trying to pick Isaac out from the crowd of figures milling around on the field during these moments of pre-game 1 confusion. The public address system sputters to life and summons our attention. "And now," the tinny voice rings out, "please join together in the singing of our national anthem."

2 "Oh saaay can you seeeeee," we begin. My arm rests around Maddie's shoulders. I am touching her a lot today, and she notices. "Mom, you're *squishing* me," she chides, wriggling from my grip. I content myself with stroking her hair. News that reached me today makes me need to feel her near. We pipe along, squeaking out the impossibly high note of "land of the freeeeeeeee." Maddie clowns, half-singing, half-shouting the lyrics, hitting the "b's" explosively on "bombs bursting in air."

3 Bombs indeed, I think, replaying the sound of my friend's voice over the phone that afternoon: "Bumped her head sledding. Took her in for an x-ray, just to make sure. There was something strange, so they did more tests . . . a brain tumor . . . Children's Hospital in Boston Tuesday . . . surgery, yes, right away. . . . " Maddie's playmate Shannon, only five years old. We'd last seen her at Halloween, dressed in her blue princess costume, and we'd talked of Furby and Scooby-Doo and Tootsie Rolls. Now her parents were hurriedly learning a new vocabulary—CAT scans, glioma, pediatric neurosurgery, and frontal lobe.[1] A bomb had exploded in their midst, and, like troops under attack, they were rallying in response.

4 The games over, the children and I edge our way out of the school parking lot, bumper to bumper with other parents ferrying their families home. I tell the kids as casually as I can about Shannon. "She'll have to have an operation. It's lucky, really, that they found it by accident this way while it's small."

5 "I want to send her a present," Maddie announces. "That'd be nice," I say, glad to keep the conversation on a positive note.

6 But my older son is with us now. Sam, who is thirteen, says, "She'll be OK, though, right?" It's not a question, really; it's a statement that I must either agree with or contradict. I want to say yes. I want to say of course she'll be all right. I want them to inhabit a world where five-year-olds do not develop silent, mysterious growths in their brains, where "malignancy" and "seizure" are words for *New York Times* crossword puzzles, not for little girls. They would accept my assurance; they would believe me and sleep well tonight. But I can't; the bomb that exploded in Shannon's home has sent splinters of shrapnel into ours as well, and they cannot be ignored or lied away. "We hope she'll be just fine," I finally say. "She has very good doctors. She has wonderful parents who are doing everything they can. The tumor is small. Shannon's strong and healthy."

7 "*She'll* be OK," says Maddie matter-of-factly. "In school we read about a little boy who had something wrong with his leg and he had an operation and got better. Can we go to Dairy Queen?"

8 Bombs on the horizon don't faze Maddie. Not yet. I can just barely remember from my own childhood the sense that still surrounds her, that feeling of being cocooned within reassuring walls of security and order. Back then, Monday meant gym, Tuesday was pizza in the cafeteria, Wednesday brought clarinet lessons. Teachers stood in

---

[1]A CAT scan is a computerized cross-sectional image of an internal body structure; a glioma is a tumor in the brain or spinal cord; pediatric neurosurgery is surgery performed on the nerves, brain, or spinal cord of a child; the frontal lobe is the largest section of the brain (editors' note).

their familiar spots in the classrooms, telling us with reassuring simplicity that World War II happened because Hitler, a very bad man, invaded Poland. Midterms and report cards, summer vacations and new notebooks in September gave a steady rhythm to the world. It wasn't all necessarily happy—through the years there were poor grades, grouchy teachers, exclusion from the desired social group, dateless weekends when it seemed the rest of the world was paired off—but it was familiar territory where we felt walled off from the really bad things that happened to other people.

There were hints of them, though, even then. Looking back, I recall the tiny shock 9
waves, the tremors from far-off explosions that occasionally rattled our shelter. There was the little girl who was absent for a week and when she returned wasn't living with her mother and stepfather anymore. There was a big girl who threw up in the bathroom every morning and then disappeared from school. A playful, friendly custodian was suddenly fired, and it had something to do with an angry parent. A teacher's husband had a heart attack and died. These were interesting tidbits to report to our families over dinner, mostly out of morbid interest in seeing our parents bite their lips and exchange glances.

As we got older, the bombs dropped closer. A friend's sister was arrested for sell- 10
ing drugs; we saw her mother in tears at church that Sunday. A boy I thought I knew, a school clown with a sweet crooked grin, shot himself in the woods behind his house. A car full of senior boys, going home from a dance where I'd been sent into ecstasy when the cutest of them all greeted me by name, rounded a curve too fast and crashed, killing them. We wept and hugged each other in the halls. Our teachers listened to us grieve and tried to comfort us, but their words came out impatient and almost angry. I realize now that what sounded like anger was a helplessness to teach us lessons we were still too young or too ignorant to learn. For although our sorrow was real, we still had some sense of a protective curtain between us and the bombs. If only, we said. If only she hadn't used drugs. If only he'd told someone how depressed he was. If only they'd been more careful. *We* weren't like them; we were careful. Like magical incantations, we recited the things that we would or wouldn't do in order to protect ourselves from such sad, unnecessary fates.

And then my best friend, a beautiful girl of sixteen, went to sleep one January night 11
and never woke up. I found myself shaken to the core of my being. My grief at the loss of my vibrant, laughing friend was great. But what really tilted my universe was the nakedness of my realization that there was no "if only." There were no drugs, no careless action, no crime, no accident, nothing I could focus on to explain away what had happened. She had simply died. Which could only mean that there was no magic barrier separating me and my loved ones from the bombs. We were as vulnerable as everyone else. For months the shock stayed with me. I sat in class watching my teachers draw diagrams of Saturn, talk about Watergate,[2] multiply fractions, and wondered at their apparent cheer and normalcy. Didn't they *know* we were all doomed? Didn't they

[2]In June 1972, supporters of Republican President Richard Nixon were caught breaking into the Democratic campaign headquarters in the Watergate office complex in Washington, D.C. The resulting investigation of the White House connection to the break-in led to President Nixon's eventual resignation in August 1974 (editors' note).

know it was only a matter of time until one of us took a direct hit? What was the point of anything?

12 But time moved on, and I moved with it. College came and went, graduate school, adulthood, middle age. My heightened sense of vulnerability began to subside, though I could never again slip fully into the soothing security of my younger days. I became more aware of the intertwining threads of joy, pain, and occasional tragedy that weave through all our lives. College was stimulating, exciting, full of friendship and challenge. I fell in love for the first time, reveled in its sweetness, then learned the painful lesson that love comes with no guarantee. A beloved professor lost two children to leukemia, but continued with skill and passion to introduce students to the riches of literature. My father grew ill, but the last day of his life, when I sat by his bed holding his hand, remains one of my sweetest memories. The marriage I'd entered into with optimism ended in bitter divorce, but produced three children whose existence is my daily delight. At every step along the way, I've seen that the most rewarding chapters of my life have contained parts that I not only would not have chosen, but would have given much to avoid. But selecting just the good parts is not an option we are given.

13 The price of allowing ourselves to truly live, to love and be loved, is (and it's the ultimate irony) the knowledge that the greater our investment in life, the larger the target we create. Of course, it is within our power to refuse friendship, shrink from love, live in isolation, and thus create for ourselves a nearly impenetrable bomb shelter. There are those among us who choose such an existence, the price of intimacy being too high. Looking about me, however, I see few such examples. Instead, I am moved by the courage with which most of us, ordinary folks, continue soldiering on. We fall in love, we bring our children into the world, we forge our friendships, we give our hearts, knowing with increasing certainty that we do so at our own risk. Still we move ahead with open arms, saying yes, yes to life.

14 Shannon's surgery is behind her; the prognosis is good. Her mother reports that the family is returning to its normal routines, laughing again and talking of ordinary things, even while they step more gently, speak more quietly, are more aware of the precious fragility of life and of the blessing of every day that passes without explosion.

15 Bombs bursting in air. They can blind us, like fireworks at the moment of explosion. If we close our eyes and turn away, all we see is their fiery image. But if we have the courage to keep our eyes open and welcoming, even bombs finally fade against the vastness of the starry sky.

Questions for Close Reading

1. What is the selection's thesis? Locate the sentence(s) in which Johnson states her main idea. If she doesn't state the thesis explicitly, express it in your own words.

2. In paragraph 2, Johnson describes her "need to feel her [daughter] near." What compels her to want to be physically close to her daughter? Why do you think Johnson responds this way?

3. In describing her family's responses to Shannon's illness, Johnson presents three reactions: Maddie's, Sam's, and her own. How do these responses

differ? In what ways do Maddie's, Sam's, and Johnson's reactions typify the age groups to which they belong?

4. In paragraph 13, Johnson describes two basic ways people respond to life's inevitable "bombs." What are these ways? Which response does Johnson endorse?

5. Refer to your dictionary as needed to define the following words used in the selection: *ferrying* (paragraph 4), *shrapnel* (6), *faze* (8), *cocooned* (8), *tremors* (9), *incantations* (10), *vulnerable* (11), *intertwining* (12), *impenetrable* (13), *soldiering on* (13), *prognosis* (14), and *fragility* (14).

Questions About the Writer's Craft

1. **The pattern.** Although Johnson provides many examples of life's "bombs," she gives more weight to some examples than to others. Which examples does she emphasize? Which ones receive less attention? Why?

2. **Other patterns.** What important *contrast* does Johnson develop in paragraph 6? How does this contrast reinforce the essay's main idea?

3. Writers generally vary sentence structure in an effort to add interest to their work. But in paragraphs 9 and 10, Johnson employs a repetitive sentence structure. Where is the repetition in these two paragraphs? Why do you think she uses this technique?

4. Johnson develops her essay by means of an extended metaphor (see page 167), using bombs as her central image. Identify all the places where Johnson draws upon language and imagery related to bombs and battles. What do you think Johnson hopes to achieve with this sustained metaphor?

Writing Assignments Using Illustration as a Pattern of Development

1. In paragraphs 9 and 10, Johnson catalogues a number of events that made her increasingly aware of life's bombs. Write an essay of your own, illustrating how you came to recognize the inevitability of painful life events. Start by listing the difficult events you've encountered. Select the three most compelling occurrences, and do some freewriting to generate details about each. Before writing, decide whether you will order your examples chronologically or emphatically; use whichever illustrates more effectively your dawning realization of life's complexity. End with some conclusions about your ability to cope with difficult times.

2. Johnson describes her evolving understanding of life. In an essay of your own, show the way several events combined to change your understanding of a specific aspect of your life. Perhaps a number of incidents prompted you to reconsider career choices, end a relationship, or appreciate the importance of family. Cite only those events that illustrate your emerging understanding.

Your decision to use either chronological or emphatic sequence depends on which illustrates more dramatically the change in your perception. To see how other writers describe their journeys of self-discovery, read Maya Angelou's "Sister Flowers" (page 167), Charmie Gholson's "Charity Display?" (page 220), and Brent Staples's "Black Men and Public Space" (page 412).

Writing Assignments Combining Patterns of Development

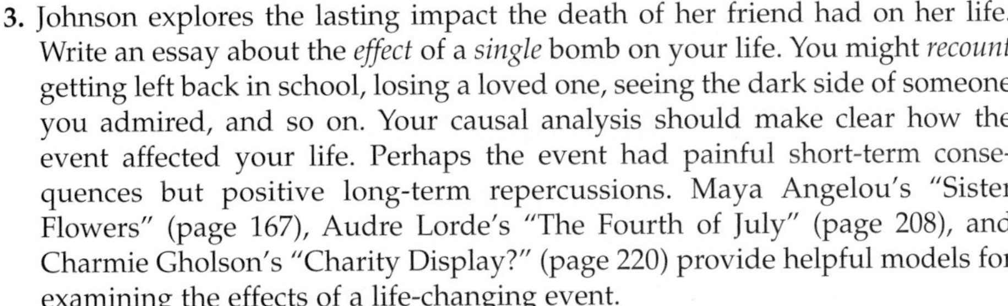

3. Johnson explores the lasting impact the death of her friend had on her life. Write an essay about the *effect* of a *single* bomb on your life. You might *recount* getting left back in school, losing a loved one, seeing the dark side of someone you admired, and so on. Your causal analysis should make clear how the event affected your life. Perhaps the event had painful short-term consequences but positive long-term repercussions. Maya Angelou's "Sister Flowers" (page 167), Audre Lorde's "The Fourth of July" (page 208), and Charmie Gholson's "Charity Display?" (page 220) provide helpful models for examining the effects of a life-changing event.

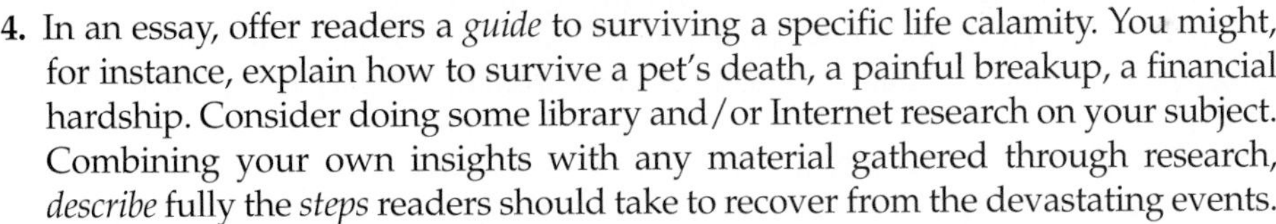

4. In an essay, offer readers a *guide* to surviving a specific life calamity. You might, for instance, explain how to survive a pet's death, a painful breakup, a financial hardship. Consider doing some library and/or Internet research on your subject. Combining your own insights with any material gathered through research, *describe* fully the *steps* readers should take to recover from the devastating events.

Writing Assignment Using a Journal Entry as a Starting Point

5. Johnson asserts that painful truths shouldn't "be ignored or lied away" by adults. Do you agree? Write an essay explaining why you think adults should protect children from harsh realities—or why they should present the whole truth, even when it's painful. Review your pre-reading journal entry, searching for strong examples to support your position. Discussing this topic with others will also help you shape your point of view, as will reading Audre Lorde's "The Fourth of July" (page 208) and Toni Morrison's "A Slow Walk of Trees" (page 364).

LESLIE SAVAN

Leslie Savan is a critic and writer whose work has appeared in *The Village Voice*, *Time*, *The New Yorker*, *The New York Times*, and *Salon*. Born in 1951, she has been a finalist for the Pulitzer Prize and a commentator on National Public Radio. In 1994, she published her first book, *The Sponsored Life: Ads, TV, and American Culture*. For several years, Savan wrote a column on advertising for *The Village Voice*, and she began to notice that certain popular words and phrases kept reoccurring in ads.

She paid attention to the "pop" language of advertising and other media and eventually wrote a book about it. This essay is excerpted from *Slam Dunks and No-Brainers: Language in Your Life, the Media, Business, Politics, and Like, Whatever*, which was published in 2005.

Pre-Reading Journal Entry

Different groups of people have special words and phrases—often slang—that they frequently use among themselves. Think about the slang words and phrases that are in common use among your friends. In your journal, list some of these words and phrases. What do they mean?

BLACK TALK AND POP CULTURE

African-American vernacular, black English, black talk, Ebonics, hip-hop slang—whatever you want to call it, black-inspired language is all over mainstream pop talk like white on rice. 1

The talk may be everywhere, but, oddly enough, even during the rabid debate over Ebonics in the late 1990s rarely was there any mention of black English's deep imprint on American English. Yet linguists and other language experts know that America's language wouldn't be what it is—and certainly wouldn't pop as much—without black English. 2

"In the past, White society has resisted the idea," wrote Robert McCrum, William Cran, and Robert MacNeil in *The Story of English*, "but there is now no escaping the fact that [Blacks' influence] has been one of the most profound contributions to the English language." 3

"First, one cannot help but be struck by the powerful influence of African-American vernacular on the slang of all 20th-century American youth," Tom Dalzell wrote in *Flappers 2 Rappers*. "There were other influences, to be sure, on the slang of America's young, but none as powerful as that of the streets of Harlem and Chicago." 4

The linguist Connie Eble, author of *Slang and Sociability* and a college and youth slang expert at the University of North Carolina, Chapel Hill, calls the black influence on the American language "overwhelming." 5

White people (and not just the young) draw from a black lexicon every day, sometimes unaware of the words' origins, sometimes using them because of their origins. Here are just some of the words and phrases—born in different decades and now residing at various levels of popdom—that African Americans either coined or popularized, and, in either case, that they created the catchiest meaning of: *all that, back in the day, bling bling, blues, bogus, boogie, bootie, bro, chick, chill, come again, cook, cool, dawg, dig, dis, do your own thing, don't go there, freak, funky, get-go, get it on, get over, gig, give it up, groovy, heavy, hip, homeboy, hot, in your face, kick back, lame, living large, man, my bad, Micky D's, old school, nitty gritty, player, riff, righteous, rip off, rock 'n' roll, soul, tell it like it is, 24/7, uptight, wannabe, whack, Whassup?/sup?, Whassup with that?, when the shit hits the fan, you know what I'm saying?* 6

7 You know what I'm saying. Most of us talk, and all of us hear in the media, some of that talk every day. Some phrases are said with an implicit nod to their source (*street cred, chill, You the man*, as well as a fist pound or high five), while others have been so widely adopted that they're beginning to feel sourceless (*24/7, lame, in your face*). *It's a black thang* has become everybody's thing, from *It's a dick thing* to (most offensively, considering who pushed it) "Virginia Slims: It's a Woman Thing."

8 But black vernacular didn't just add more lively, "colorful" words to the pop vocabulary. Much as marketing has influenced pop language, so black English has changed the American language in more fundamental ways. And that's what we're talking here—not about black talk per se, but about what happens when black talk meets, and transforms, the wider, whiter pop.

9 First and foremost, this language of outsiders has given us *cool*: the word itself—the preeminent pop word of all time—and quite a sizable chunk of the cool stance that underlies pop culture itself. Pop culture's desire for cool is second only to its desire for money—the two, in fact, are inextricably linked. (Cool may be first and foremost, but more on why it rules later.)

10 A second way African-American vernacular has affected the broader pop is that black talk has operated as a template for what it means to talk pop in the first place. As an often playful, ironic alternative to the official tongue, black slang has prefigured pop language in much the same way that black music has prefigured, and has often become, pop music. While there are important differences, some of the dynamics underlying black talk and pop talk are similar: Like black English pop language sparks with wordplays and code games; it assumes that certain, often previously unacknowledged experiences deserve their own verbal expression; and it broadcasts the sense that only those who share the experiences can really get the words. For instance, black talk's running commentary on social exclusion is a model for pop talk's running commentary on media experiences.

11 Why do I say that pop is modeled on black and not the other way around? It's not just because black talk did these things earlier and still does them more intensely than pop, but as the original flipside to the voice of the Man, as the official unofficial speech of America, black talk is the object of pop talk's crush on everything "alternative" and "outsider."

12 There's an attitude in pop language that it is somehow undermining the stale old ways and sending a wake-up call to anyone who just doesn't get it. You can feel the attitude in everything from advertising's furious but phony rebelliousness to the faintly up-yours, tough-talking phrases like *Get a life* and *Don't even* think *about it*. It's not that these particular phrases are black or black-inspired, or that white people aren't perfectly capable of rebelliousness, anger at authority, and clever put-downs on their own. But the black experience, publicized more widely than ever now through hip-hop and its celebrities, has encouraged everyone else to more vigorously adopt the style of fighting the power—at least with the occasional catchphrase.

13 It may seem twisted, given American history, that general pop language draws from the experience of black exclusion at all. But white attempts to *yo* here and *dis* there are an important piece of identity-and-image building for individuals and corporations alike. Today, the language of an excluded people is repeated by the nonexcluded in order to make themselves sound more included. As the mainstream plays the titillating notes of marginalization, we are collectively creating that ideal mass personality mentioned earlier: We can be part black (the part presumed to be cool and soulful, real

and down, jazzy or hip-hop, choose your sound) and be part white (the privileged part, the part that has the luxury to easily reference other parts).

Related to all this imitation and referencing is the most noticeable way that pop talk is affected by black talk: Black talk has openly joined the sales force. At white society's major intersection with black language—that is, in entertainment—white society has gone from mocking black talk, as in minstrel shows, to marketing it, as in hip-hop. In the more than a hundred years between these two forms of entertainment, black language has by and large entered white usage as if it were a sourceless slang or perhaps the latest lingo of some particularly hep white cats, like the fast-talking disc jockeys of the 1950s and 1960s who purveyed black jive to white teenagers. Black language may have been the single most important factor in shaping generations of American slang, primarily through blues, jazz, and rock 'n' roll. But only relatively recently has black talk been used openly, knowingly, and not mockingly to sell products. 14

This would have been unthinkable once. Even fifteen or twenty years ago, car makers were loath to show black people in commercials for fear that their product would be tainted as inferior or, worse, as "a black car." Although many car companies are still skittish, by 2001 Buick was actually ending its commercials with the rap-popularized phrase "It's all good." (And by 2004, a BMW ad was featuring an interracial couple.) The phrase went from M. C. Hammer's 1994 song "It's All Good" to replacing "I love this game" as the official slogan of the National Basketball Association in 2001. Both Buick and the NBA have since dropped *It's all good*, but with their help the phrase massified, at least for a while. "It's huge" among white "sorority sisters and stoners alike," a twenty-seven-year-old white friend in Chicago told me in 2003. 15

So it's not all bad, this commercialization of black talk, especially if it can get the auto industry to move from shunning to quoting African Americans. But it comes laden with price tags. To read them, look at MTV, which has to be *the* major force in the sea change from whites-only to black's-da-bomb. 16

It may be difficult to believe now, but for years MTV wouldn't touch black music videos. The channel relented only under pressure, with videos by Prince and Michael Jackson. Black just wouldn't appeal to its white suburban teen audience, MTV explained. In 1989 with the appearance of the successful *Yo! MTV Raps*, that rationale was turned inside out, and—ka-ching!—black videos began to appear regularly. Since so much of MTV is advertising posing as entertainment (the videos are record company promotions, the parties and other bashes that appear are often visibly sponsored events), MTV has contributed significantly to two marketing trends: To the young, advertising has become an acceptable—nay, desirable—part of the cool life they aspire to; and a black, hip-hop-ish vernacular has become a crucial cog in the youth market machinery. 17

The outsider style is not solely black or hip-hop, but, at least in the marketing mind, a black package can be the most efficient buy to achieve that style. For corporate purposes, hip-hop in particular is a lucrative formula. Not only does the hip-hop black man represent the ultimate outsider who simultaneously stands at the nexus of cool, but much of hip-hop, created by the kind of people gated communities were meant to exclude, sings the praises of acquiring capitalism's toys. These paradoxes of racism are commercial-ready. . . . 18

When Sprite realized that teenagers no longer believed its TV commercials telling them that "Image Is Nothing" and that they shouldn't trust commercials or celebrity endorsements (said only half tongue-in-cheek by celebrities like NBA star Grant Hill), 19 the soft drink's marketing department decided to up the ante. So, when you need outsider verisimilitude, who ya gonna call? Why, black rappers, of course, preferably on the hardcore side. Get *them* to testify to the soft drink's beyond-the-bounds, can't-be-bought spirit at Sprite.com launch parties (to be run later on MTV). Or get real kids, looking and sounding ghetto, to rap their own lyrics in TV spots about, say, "a situation that is not too sweet, which is an attribute of Sprite," as a Sprite publicist said. How else to get kids, usually white kids, to understand that you understand that they're sick of commercials telling them what's cool?

20 And so, while Sprite had long used rappers in its overall "Obey Your Thirst" campaign, now it pumped up the volume. Only by obeying the first commandment that image is everything can you become, as Sprite did by the late nineties, the fastest-growing soft-drink brand in the world. . . .

21 When whites talk black—or, just as commonly, when major corporations do it for them—it makes you wanna shout, *Whassup with that?!*

Terms and Props

22 Before I address wannabe black talk and other points where black language crosses over into pop, a few words about what "black language" and "black words" are.

23 I've been using the terms "black English," "black slang," "black talk," and "African-American vernacular" rather interchangeably, which, in plain English, seems OK. Yet, at the same time, each term is a bit off the mark.

24 No one phrase is the perfect vehicle to explain how a people speak, because "a people" don't all speak (or do anything) one way. That's one of the problems with the terms "black English" and "black dialect." "Black English" was more or less booted out of formal linguistic circles, because, as linguist Peter Trudgill wrote in the 1995 revised edition of his book *Sociolinguistics*, "it suggested that all Blacks speak this one variety of English—which is not the case." The newer scholarly term, African American Vernacular English (AAVE), has pros and cons: It "distinguishes those Blacks who do not speak standard American English from those who do," wrote Trudgill, "although it still suggests that only one nonstandard variety, homogeneous through the whole of the USA, is involved, which is hardly likely." The word *Ebonics* was created in 1973 by African-American scholars to "define black language from a black perspective," writes Geneva Smitherman, director of the African American Language and Literacy Program at Michigan State University. But the 1997 Ebonics controversy loaded the word with so much baggage . . . that, outside of some hip-hop use, it has become nearly immobile.

25 "Black slang" can't describe black language, because clearly most black language is composed of standard English. However, when referring to actual slang that blacks created (*my bad, dis*), "black slang" is the right term. Personally, I like "black talk" (which is also the title of one of Smitherman's books). Although, like any phrase starting with the adjective "black," it might suggest that all black people talk this way all the time, "black talk" (like "pop talk") is colloquial and flexible, encompassing vocabulary and then some. . . .

26 Origins tend to get lost in the roaring mainstream. Some words that seem white are black, and vice versa. For instance, until I looked into *24/7*, I would have guessed its roots were cyber or maybe something out of the convenience-store industry. But

24/7 arose from a hip-hop fondness for number phrases. Rapdict.org lists some sixty number phrases, many of which are too obscure or gangsta to cross over; *411* is one of the few others that has gone pop. (A recent Mercedes-Benz magazine ad advised, "Get the 411.")

Bogus, which sounds so surfer, dude, dates back at least as far as 1798, when a glossary defined it as a "spurious coin," write David Barnhart and Allan Metcalf in *America in So Many Words*. "Its origins are obscure, but one guess that is as good as any is that it is from *boko*, meaning 'deceit' or 'fake' in the Hausa language of west central Africa. The word then would have been brought over by Africans sold into slavery here." In addition, some nuances that no one doubts are African American may run deeper in black history than most people, black or white, imagine. When *bad* is used to mean good, the meaning (though obviously not the word itself) is derived, Smitherman writes,[1] from a phrase in the Mandinka language in West Africa, "*a ka nyi ko-jugu*, which means, literally, 'it is good badly,' that is, it is very good, or it is so good that it's bad!" 27

Meanwhile, some words that most people would identify as black, and that black people did indeed popularize, originated among others. Southern phrases in particular jumped races, "from black to white in the case of *bubba* and *big daddy*, from white to black in the case of *grits* and *chitlins*," write the Rickfords.[2] *Cat*, meaning a hip guy, is a dated piece of slang (though often on the verge of a comeback) that most people attribute to black jazz musicians; Ken Burns's television series *Jazz* states that Louis Armstrong was the first person to have said it. But, as Tom Dalzell writes, in "the late 19th century and early 20th century, *cat* in the slang and jargon of hobos meant an itinerant worker . . . possibly because the migratory worker slunk about like a 'homeless cat.'" However, it did take Armstrong, and then other jazz musicians in the 1920s, to introduce the word into broader usage. That old rap word *fly* (stylish, good-looking, smooth) was flying long before rap. "The most well-established slang meaning of *fly* was in the argot of thieves, where *fly* meant sly, cunning, wide-awake, knowing, or smart," writes Dalzell, who notes those uses of *fly* as early as 1724 and in *Bleak House* by Dickens in 1853. But again, *fly* didn't really buzz until black musicians picked up on it, beginning around 1900, well before *Superfly* in the 1970s and rap in the 1980s. 28

Wannabe Nation

Whether black-born or black-raised, black words are the ones that many white people are wearing like backwards baseball caps. That brings us to a particularly telling term that went from black to pop. *Wannabe* originally referred to people who wanted to be something they weren't; it was often said of a black person who wanted to be white. In Spike Lee's 1988 film *School Daze*, the conflict was between the dark-skinned, activist "Jigaboos" and the light-skinned sorority sister "Wannabes." Beginning around the time of that movie, *wannabe* was used by just about everybody 29

[1]In her book, *Black Talk: Words and Phrases from the Hood to the Amen Corner* (editors' note).

[2]In *Spoken Soul: The Story of Black English*, by John R. Rickford and Russell J. Rickford (editors' note).

to mean anybody who wanted to be somebody he or she wasn't—there have been surfer wannabes, Madonna wannabes, and dot.com start-up wannabes. But *wannabe* is not just a blast from decades past. More recently, "podcaster wannabes" have developed, and in just one week on TV and radio in late 2004, I heard of "artist wannabes," "geek wannabes," and "wannabe homeland security chief" Bernard Kerik.

30 Racially speaking, *wannabe* has reversed field. Since at least the early nineties, with hip-hop an entrenched, virtually mainstream hit, *wannabe* has been far more likely to refer to whites, especially teenagers, who want to be black or do the style. Sometimes called *wiggers* or *wiggas* (*white* plus *nigger/nigga*), black wannabes try to dance the dance and talk the talk. Even whites who would hate to be black will maintain the right to add the occasional black flourish. Some whites flash a black word or gesture like an honorary badge of cool, to show they're down with black people on certain occasions, usually involving sports or entertainment. Or maybe they do it because some of their best friends and some of the best commercials are flashing it, too. Or maybe they just need to know that black people like them. Take "Johnny and Sally," the fictitious white couple on the very funny Web site BlackPeople LoveUs.com, which is full of "testimonials" to their racial bigheartedness. As one unnamed black man attested, "Johnny always alters his given name and refers to himself in the third person—for example, 'J-Dog don't play that' or 'J-Dog wants to know wusssaappp.' It comforts me to know that my parlance has such broad appeal."

31 African Americans aren't the only people whose parlance has broad appeal. Non-Latino blacks dabble in Spanish, Catholics in Yiddish, adults in teenage talk. Cultural skin is always permeable, absorbing any word that has reached a critical mass of usefulness or fun. The human species can't help but borrow—after all, that's how languages develop.

32 But whether we call it wannabe talk or the less derogatory crossover talk, something about white society's sampling of black speech is more loaded than the usual borrowing. Black vernacular's contributions to English are larger in number and run deeper linguistically and psychologically than do any other ethnic group's. And black English, born in slavery, resounds with our society's senses of guilt, fear, identity, and style.

33 Black-to-white crossover talk, which also began during slavery, is hardly new. But, like most pop talk today, it radiates a new gloss, a veneer in which you can catch the reflection of its increased market value. Black talk comes from something real—"serious as a heart attack," Smitherman says—but, whoop, there it is, sparking out of TV commercials, out of white politicians, out of anyone who has something to promote, spin, or get over.

Questions for Close Reading

1. What is the selection's thesis? Locate the sentence(s) in which Savan states her main idea. If she doesn't state her thesis explicitly, express it in your own words.

2. What does Savan mean by "pop language" and "pop talk"? What are some examples of these?

3. Why does Savan characterize the word *cool* as the most important pop word of all time?

4. In the section "Wannabe Nation," Savan describes the appeal of being Black to white Americans. According to Savan, what is troubling about the white mainstream culture's appropriation of Black words and phrases?

5. Refer to your dictionary as needed to define the following words used in the selection: *vernacular* (paragraph 1), *lexicon* (6), *per se* (8), *preeminent* (9), *template* (10), *catchphrase* (12), *minstrel shows* (14), *loath* (15), *lucrative* (18), *nexus* (18), *verisimilitude* (19), *colloquial* (25), *spurious* (27), and *argot* (28).

Questions About the Writer's Craft

1. **The pattern.** Why does Savan use so many examples of Black talk to illustrate its role in modern American English? Why does she use several lengthy examples as well? What are some of these extended examples?

2. **The pattern.** In paragraphs 16 through 21, Savan discusses the use of Black talk in marketing products. How does she organize the examples in this section of the essay? What is the purpose of this organization?

3. **Other patterns.** In the section entitled "Terms and Props," Savan discusses the *definitions* of the terms she has been using for Black talk. Why does she stop the flow of the essay to delve deeper into these terms? Why does she prefer the term "black talk" over the terms "black English," "black dialect," and "African American Vernacular English"? How effective is this section of the essay?

4. To support her thesis, Savan uses evidence from advertising, MTV, and the Internet. Find one example of a use of Black talk in each of these media. Why do you think Savan chose each example? How does each example support the essay's thesis? Would the essay have been as effective without these examples?

Writing Assignments Using Illustration as a Pattern of Development

1. Savan discusses the role hip-hop artists play in modern marketing. Select a current hip-hop artist who markets products and do research on him or her. Write an essay about the role of marketing and advertising in this artist's career, providing *examples* to support your thesis.

2. Savan's essay focuses on Black talk, but there are many other subgroups of American English. For example, there is "Spanglish," a blend of Spanish and English occasionally spoken by Hispanic Americans; jargon, which includes words such as *debug* associated with a specific field like computer science; place names that have their origin in Native American languages; and regional dialects that have their own special words and phrases. Select one

type of specialized American English words with which you are familiar and write an essay that *illustrates* it. Include specific examples of words and phrases and their use to make your essay interesting.

Writing Assignments Combining Patterns of Development

3. Savan discusses how marketers use Black language and culture to sell products. Select two TV commercials or print ads for the same type of product and *describe* them using vivid, sensory language. Then analyze each commercial or ad, *dividing* your analysis into the various techniques it uses to persuade you, the consumer, to buy the product. *Compare* and *contrast* the effectiveness of the two ads. For another perspective on language and manipulations, you may want to read William Lutz's "Doublespeak" (page 288).

4. Most of the examples in Savan's essay are of the use of Black talk in spoken popular language. In contrast, written language is usually more formal. Write an essay in which you *compare* and *contrast* the language you use when speaking with the language you use when writing. Give examples of both spoken and written language to support your thesis. For additional perspectives on contrasting uses of language, consider reading William Lutz's "Doublespeak" (page 288) and Eric Weiner's "Euromail and Amerimail" (page 375).

Writing Assignment Using a Journal Entry as a Starting Point

5. Review your pre-reading journal entry, and select two or three of the words and phrases that you as your friends use among yourselves. Then write an essay giving examples of situations in which these words are used. Explain why you choose to use them rather than using conventional phrases from standard English. What function do these words and phrases have in the psychology of the group?

ADDITIONAL WRITING TOPICS: ILLUSTRATION

General Assignments

Use illustration to develop one of the following topics into a well-organized essay. When writing the paper, choose enough relevant examples to support your thesis.

Organize the material into a sequence that most effectively illustrates the thesis, keeping in mind that emphatic order is often the most compelling way to present specifics.

1. Many of today's drivers have dangerous habits.
2. Drug and alcohol abuse is (or is not) a serious problem among many young people.
3. One rule of restaurant dining is "Management often seems oblivious to problems that are perfectly obvious to customers."
4. Children today are not encouraged to use their imaginations.
5. The worst kind of hypocrite is a religious hypocrite.
6. The best things in life are definitely not free.
7. A part-time job is an important experience that every college student should have.
8. The Internet has resulted in a generation of lazy young people.
9. ________ (name someone you know well) is a ________ (use a quality: open-minded, dishonest, compulsive, reliable, gentle, and so on) person.
10. Television commercials stereotype the elderly (or another minority group).
11. Today, salespeople act as if they're doing you a favor by taking your money.
12. Most people behave decently in their daily interactions with each other.
13. Pettiness, jealousy, and selfishness abound in our daily interactions with each other.
14. You can tell a lot about people by observing what they wear and eat.
15. Too many Americans are overly concerned/completely unconcerned with being physically fit.
16. There are several study techniques that will help a student learn more efficiently.
17. Some teachers seem to enjoy turning tests into ordeals.
18. "How to avoid bad eating habits" is one course all college students should take.
19. More needs to be done to eliminate obstacles faced by the physically handicapped.
20. Some of the best presents are those that cost the least.

Assignments with a Specific Purpose, Audience, and Point of View

On Campus

1. Lately, many people at your college have been experiencing stress. As a member of the Student Life Committee, you've been asked to prepare a pamphlet

illustrating strategies for reducing different kinds of stress. Decide which stresses to discuss and explain coping strategies for each, providing helpful examples as you go.

2. A friend of yours will be going away to college in an unfamiliar environment—in a bustling urban setting or in a quiet rural one. To help your friend prepare for this new environment, write a letter giving examples of what life on an urban or a rural campus is like. You might focus on the benefits and dangers with which your friend is unlikely to be familiar.

At Home or in the Community

3. Shopping for a new car, you become annoyed at how many safety features are available only as expensive options. Write a letter of complaint to the auto manufacturer, citing at least three examples of such options. Avoid sounding hostile.

4. A pet food company is having an annual contest to choose a new animal to feature in its advertising. To win the contest, you must convince the company that your pet is personable, playful, and unique. Write an essay giving examples of your pet's special qualities.

On the Job

5. Assume that you're an elementary school principal planning to give a speech in which you'll try to convince parents that television distorts children's perceptions of reality. Write the speech, illustrating your point with vivid examples.

6. The online publication you work for has asked you to write an article on what you consider to be the "three best consumer products of the past twenty-five years." Support your opinion with lively, engaging specifics that are consistent with the website's offbeat and slightly ironic tone.

For additional writing, reading, and research resources, go to **www.mycomplab.com** and choose **Nadell/Langan/Comodromos'** ***The Longman Writer,*** **7/e**.

Division-Classification

13

LWA-Dann Tardif/CORBIS

WHAT IS DIVISION-CLASSIFICATION?

Imagine what life would be like if this were how an average day unfolded:

> You plan to stop at the supermarket for only a few items, but your marketing takes over an hour because all the items in the store are jumbled together. Clerks put new shipments anywhere they please; milk is with vegetables on Monday but with laundry detergent on Thursday. Next, you go to the drugstore to pick up some photos you left to be developed. You don't have time, though, to wait while the cashier roots through the large carton into which all the pick-up envelopes have been thrown. You return to your car and decide to stop at the town hall to pay a parking ticket. But the town hall baffles you. The offices are unmarked, and there isn't even a directory to tell you on which floor the Violations Bureau can be found. Annoyed, you get back into your car and, minutes later, end up colliding with another car that was driving toward you in your lane. When you wake up in the hospital, you find there are three other patients in your room: a middle-aged man with a heart problem, a young boy ready to have his tonsils removed, and a woman about to go into labor.

Such a muddled world, lacking the most basic forms of organization, would make daily life chaotic. All of us instinctively look for ways to order our environment. Without systems, categories, or sorting mechanisms, we would be overwhelmed by life's complexity. An organization like a college or university, for example, is made manageable by being divided into various schools (Liberal Arts, Performing Arts, Engineering, and so on). The schools are then separated into departments (English, History, Political Science), and each department's offerings are grouped into distinct categories—English, for instance, into Literature and Composition—before being further divided into specific courses.

The kind of ordering system we've been discussing is called **division-classification,** a way of thinking that allows us to make sense of a complex world. Division and classification, though separate processes, often complement each other. **Division** involves taking a single unit or concept, breaking it down into parts, and then analyzing the connection among the parts and between the parts and the whole. For instance, if we wanted to organize the chaotic hospital described at the beginning of the chapter, we might think about how the single concept **hospital** could be broken down into its components. We might come up with the following breakdown: pediatric wing, cardiac wing, maternity wing, and so on. What we have just done involves division: We've taken a single entity (a hospital) and divided it into some of its component parts (wings), each with its own facilities and patients.

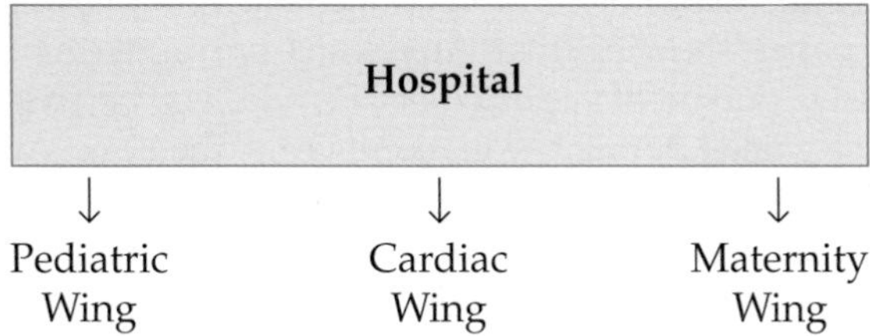

In contrast, **classification** brings two or more related items together and categorizes them according to type or kind. If the disorganized supermarket described earlier were to be restructured, the clerks would have to classify the separate items arriving at the store. Cartons of lettuce, tomatoes, cucumbers, butter, yogurt, milk, shampoo, conditioner, and hair gel would be assigned to the appropriate categories:

How division-classification fits your purpose and audience

The reorganized hospital and supermarket show the way division and classification work in everyday life. But division and classification also come into play during the writing process. Because division involves breaking a subject into parts, it can be a helpful strategy during prewriting, especially if you're analyzing a broad, complex subject: the structure of a film; the motivation of a character in a novel; the problem your community has with vandalism; the controversy surrounding school prayer. An editorial examining a recent hostage crisis, for example, might divide the crisis into three areas: how the hostages were treated by (1) their captors, (2) the governments negotiating their release, and (3) the media. The purpose of the editorial might be to show readers that the governments' treatment of the hostages was particularly exploitative.

Classification can be useful for imposing order on the hodgepodge of ideas generated during prewriting. You examine that material to see which of your rough ideas are alike and which are dissimilar, so that you can cluster related items in the same category. Classification would, then, be a helpful strategy when analyzing topics like these: techniques for impressing teachers; comic styles of talk-show hosts; views on abortion; reasons for the current rise in volunteerism. You might, for instance, use classification in a paper showing that Americans are undermining their health through their obsessive pursuit of various diets. Perhaps you begin by brainstorming all the diets that have gained popularity in recent years (the Zone, Atkins, whatever). Then you categorize the diets according to type: high fiber, low protein, high carbohydrate, and so on. Once the diets are grouped, you can discuss the problems within each category, demonstrating to readers that none of the diets is safe or effective.

Division-classification can be crucial when responding to college assignments like the following:

> Based on your observations, what kinds of appeals do television advertisers use when selling automobiles? In your view, are any of these appeals morally irresponsible?
>
> Analyze the components that go into being an effective parent. Indicate those you consider most vital for raising confident, well-adjusted children.
>
> Describe the hierarchy of the typical high school clique, identifying the various parts of the hierarchy. Use your analysis to support or refute the view that adolescence is a period of rigid conformity.
>
> Many social commentators have observed that discourtesy is on the rise. Indicate whether you think this is a valid observation by characterizing the types of everyday encounters you have with people.

These assignments suggest division-classification through the use of such words as *kinds, components, parts,* and *types.* Generally, though, you won't receive such clear signals to use division-classification. Instead, the broad purpose of the essay—and the point you want to make—will lead you to the analytical thinking characteristic of division-classification.

Sometimes division-classification will be the dominant technique for structuring an essay; other times it will be used as a supplemental pattern in an essay organized primarily according to another pattern of development. Let's look at some examples. Say you want to write a paper *explaining a process* (surviving divorce; creating a hit recording; shepherding a bill through Congress; using the Heimlich maneuver on people who are choking). You could *divide* the process into parts or stages, showing, for instance, that the Heimlich maneuver is an easily mastered skill that readers should acquire. Or imagine you plan to write a light-spirited essay analyzing the *effect* that increased awareness of sexual stereotypes has had on college students' social lives. In such a case, you might use *classification.* To show readers that shifting gender roles make young men and women comically self-conscious, you could categorize the places where students scope out each other in class, at the library, at parties, in dorms. You could then show how students—not wanting to be macho or coyly feminine—approach each other with laughable tentativeness in these four environments.

Now imagine that you're writing an *argumentation-persuasion* essay urging that the federal government prohibit the use of growth-inducing antibiotics in livestock feed. The paper could begin by *dividing* the antibiotics cycle into stages: the effects of antibiotics on livestock; the short-term effects on humans who consume the animals; the possible long-term effects of consuming antibiotic-tainted meat. To increase readers' understanding of the problem, you might also discuss the antibiotics controversy in terms of an even larger issue: the dangerous ways food is treated before being consumed. In this case, you would consider the various procedures (use of additives, preservatives, artificial colors, and so on), *classifying* these treatments into several types—from least harmful (some additives or artificial colors, perhaps) to most harmful (you might slot the antibiotics here). Such an essay would be developed using both division *and* classification: first, the division of the antibiotics cycle and then the classification of the various food treatments. Frequently, this interdependence will be reversed, and classification will precede rather than follow division.

At this point, you have a good sense of the way writers use division-classification to achieve their purpose and to connect with their readers. Now take a moment to look closely at the photograph at the beginning of this chapter. Imagine you're writing an article, accompanied by the photo, for a parenting magazine. Your purpose is twofold: to alert parents to the danger of pushing young children to achieve, and to help parents foster in children healthy attitudes toward achievement. Jot down some ideas you might include when *dividing* and/or *classifying* things parents should and shouldn't do to foster a balanced view of accomplishment and success in youngsters.

PREWRITING STRATEGIES

The following checklist shows how you can apply to division-classification some of the prewriting techniques discussed in Chapter 2.

☑ DIVISION-CLASSIFICATION: A PREWRITING CHECKLIST

Choose a Subject to Analyze

- ☐ What fairly complex subject (sibling rivalry, religious cults) can be made more understandable through division-classification?
- ☐ Will you divide a single entity or concept (domestic violence) into parts (toward spouse, parent, or child)? Will you classify a number of similar things (college courses) into categories (easy, of average difficulty, tough)? Or will you use both division and classification?

Determine Your Purpose, Audience, Tone, and Point of View

- ☐ What is the purpose of your analysis?
- ☐ Toward what audience will you direct your explanations?
- ☐ What tone and point of view will make readers receptive to your explanation?

Use Prewriting to Generate Material on Parts or Types

- ☐ How can brainstorming, mapping, or any other prewriting technique help you divide your subject into parts? What differences or similarities among parts will you emphasize?
- ☐ How can brainstorming, mapping, or any other prewriting technique help you categorize your subjects? What differences or similarities among categories will you emphasize?

- ☐ How can the patterns of development help you generate material about your subjects' parts or categories? How can you describe the parts or categories? What can you narrate about them? What examples illustrate them? What process do they help explain? How can they be compared or contrasted? What causes them? What are their effects? How can they be defined? What arguments do they support?

STRATEGIES FOR USING DIVISION-CLASSIFICATION IN AN ESSAY

After prewriting, you're ready to draft your essay. Figure 13.1 and the suggestions that follow will be helpful whether you use division-classification as a dominant or supportive pattern of development.

FIGURE 13.1
Development Diagram: Writing a Division-Classification Essay

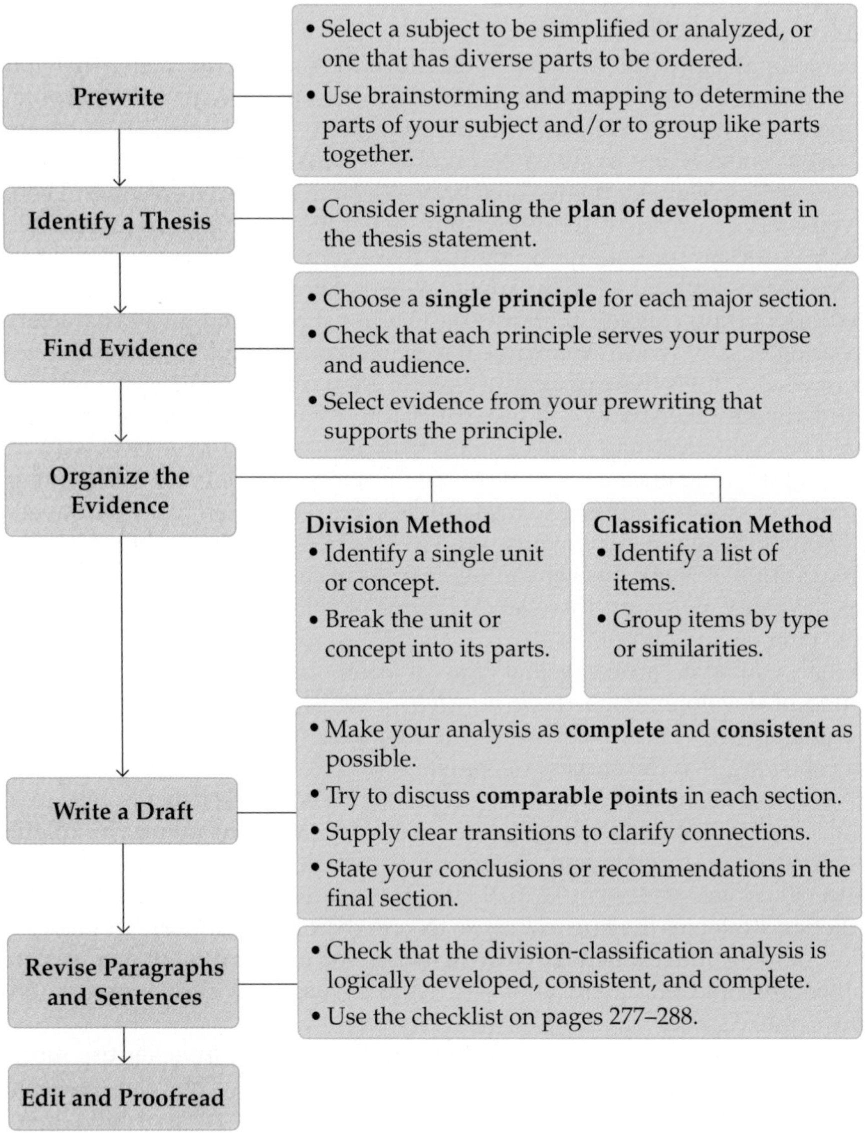

Prewrite
- Select a subject to be simplified or analyzed, or one that has diverse parts to be ordered.
- Use brainstorming and mapping to determine the parts of your subject and/or to group like parts together.

↓

Identify a Thesis
- Consider signaling the **plan of development** in the thesis statement.

↓

Find Evidence
- Choose a **single principle** for each major section.
- Check that each principle serves your purpose and audience.
- Select evidence from your prewriting that supports the principle.

↓

Organize the Evidence

Division Method	**Classification Method**
• Identify a single unit or concept. • Break the unit or concept into its parts.	• Identify a list of items. • Group items by type or similarities.

↓

Write a Draft
- Make your analysis as **complete** and **consistent** as possible.
- Try to discuss **comparable points** in each section.
- Supply clear transitions to clarify connections.
- State your conclusions or recommendations in the final section.

↓

Revise Paragraphs and Sentences
- Check that the division-classification analysis is logically developed, consistent, and complete.
- Use the checklist on pages 277–288.

↓

Edit and Proofread

1. **Select a principle of division-classification consistent with your purpose.** Most subjects can be divided or classified according to *several different principles.* For example, when writing about an ideal vacation, you could divide your subject according to any of these principles: location, cost, recreation available. Similarly, when analyzing students at your college, you could base

your classification on a variety of principles: students' majors, their racial or ethnic background, whether they belong to a fraternity or sorority. In all cases, though, the principle of division-classification you select must meet one stringent requirement: It must help you meet your overall purpose and reinforce your central point.

Sometimes a principle of division-classification seems so attractive that you latch on to it without examining whether it's consistent with your purpose. Suppose you want to write a paper asserting that several episodes of a new television comedy are destined to become classics. Here's how you might go wrong. You begin by doing some brainstorming about the episodes. Then, as you start to organize the prewriting material, you hit upon a possible principle of classification: grouping the characters in the show according to the frequency with which they appear (main characters appearing in every show, supporting characters appearing in most shows, and guest characters appearing once or twice). You name the characters and explain which characters fit where. But is this principle of classification significant? Has it anything to do with why the shows will become classics? No, it hasn't. Such an essay would be little more than a meaningless exercise.

In contrast, a significant principle of classification might involve categorizing a number of shows according to the easily recognized human types portrayed: the Pompous Know-It-All, the Boss Who's Out of Control, the Lovable Grouch, the Surprisingly Savvy Innocent. You might illustrate the way certain episodes offer delightful twists on these stock figures, making such shows models of comic plotting and humor.

When you write an essay that uses division-classification as its primary method of development, a *single principle* of division-classification provides the foundation for each major section of the paper. Imagine you're writing an essay showing that the success of contemporary music groups has less to do with musical talent than with the group's ability to market themselves to a distinct segment of the listening audience. To develop your point, you might categorize several performers according to the age ranges they appeal to (preteens, adolescents, people in their late twenties) and then analyze the marketing strategies the musicians use to gain their fans' support. The essay's logic would be undermined if you switched, in the middle of your analysis, to another principle of classification—say, the influence of earlier groups on today's music scene.

Don't, however, take this caution to mean that essays can never use more than one principle of division-classification as they unfold. They can—as long as the *shift from one principle to another* occurs in *different parts* of the paper. Imagine you want to write about widespread disillusionment with student government leaders at your college. You could develop this point by breaking down the dissatisfaction into the following: disappointment with the students' qualifications for office; disenchantment with their campaign tactics; frustration with their performance once elected. That section of the essay completed, you might move to a second principle of division—how students can get involved in campus government. Perhaps you break the proposed involvement into the following possibilities: serving on nominating committees; helping to run candidates' campaigns; attending open sessions of the student government.

2. **Apply the principle of division-classification logically.** In an essay using division-classification, you need to demonstrate to readers that your analysis is the result of careful thought. First of all, your division-classification should be as *complete* as possible. Your analysis should include—within reason—all the parts into which you can divide your subject, or all the types into which you can categorize your subjects. Let's say you're writing an essay showing that where college students live is an important factor in determining how satisfied they are with college life. Keeping your purpose in mind, you classify students according to where they live: with parents, in dorms, in fraternity and sorority houses. But what about all the students who live in rented apartments, houses, or rooms off campus? If these places of residence are ignored, your classification won't be complete; you will lose credibility with your readers because they'll probably realize that you have overlooked several important considerations.

   Your division-classification should also be *consistent:* the parts into which you break your subject or the groups into which you place your subjects should be as mutually exclusive as possible. The parts or categories should not be mixed, nor should they overlap. Assume you're writing an essay describing the animals at the zoo in a nearby city. You decide to describe the zoo's mammals, reptiles, birds, and endangered species. But such a classification is inconsistent. You begin by categorizing the animals according to scientific class (mammals, birds, reptiles), then switch to another principle when you classify some animals according to whether they are endangered. Because you drift over to a different principle of classification, your categories are no longer mutually exclusive: endangered species could overlap with any of the other categories. In which section of the paper, for instance, would you describe an exotic parrot that is obviously a bird but is also nearly extinct? And how would you categorize the zoo's rare mountain gorilla? This impressive creature is a mammal, but it is also an endangered species. Such overlapping categories undercut the logic that gives an essay its integrity.

3. **Prepare an effective thesis.** If your essay uses division-classification as its dominant method of development, it might be helpful to prepare a thesis that does more than signal the paper's subject and suggest your attitude toward that subject. You might also want the thesis to state the principle of division-classification at the heart of the essay. Furthermore, you might want the thesis to reveal which part or category you regard as most important.

   Consider the two thesis statements that follow:

   Thesis 1

   As the observant beachcomber moves from the tidal area to the upper beach to the sandy dunes, rich variations in marine life become apparent.

Thesis 2

```
Although most people focus on the dangers associated with the
disposal of toxic waste in the land and ocean, the
incineration of toxic matter may pose an even more serious
threat to human life.
```

The first thesis statement makes clear that the writer will organize the paper by classifying forms of marine life according to location. Since the purpose of the essay is to inform as objectively as possible, the thesis doesn't suggest the writer's opinion about which category is most significant.

The second thesis signals that the essay will evolve by dividing the issue of toxic waste according to methods of disposal. Moreover, because the paper takes a stance on a controversial subject, the thesis is worded to reveal which aspect of the topic the writer considers most important. Such a clear statement of the writer's position is an effective strategy in an essay of this kind.

You may have noted that each thesis statement also signals the paper's plan of development. The first essay, for example, will use specific facts, examples, and details to describe the kinds of marine life found in the tidal area, upper beach, and dunes. However, thesis statements in papers developed primarily through division-classification don't have to be so structured. If a paper is well written, your principle of division-classification, your opinion about which part or category is most important, and the essay's plan of development will become apparent as the essay unfolds.

4. **Organize the paper logically.** Whether your paper is developed wholly or in part by division-classification, it should have a logical structure. As much as possible, you should try to discuss *comparable points* in each section of the paper. In the essay on seashore life, for example, you might describe life in the tidal area by discussing the mollusks, crustaceans, birds, and amphibians that live or feed there. You would then follow through, as much as possible, with this arrangement in the paper's other sections (upper beach and dunes). Forgetting to describe the birdlife thriving in the dunes, especially when you had discussed birdlife in the tidal and upper-beach areas, would compromise the paper's structure. Of course, perfect parallelism is not always possible—there are no mollusks in the dunes, for instance. You should also use *signal devices* to connect various parts of the paper: "*Another* characteristic of marine life battered by the tides"; "A *final* important trait of both tidal and upper-beach crustaceans"; "*Unlike* the creatures of the tidal area and the upper beach." Such signals clarify the connections among the essay's ideas.

5. **State any conclusions or recommendations in the paper's final section.** The analytic thinking that occurs during division-classification often leads to surprising insights. Such insights may be introduced early on, or they may be reserved for the end, where they are stated as conclusions or recommendations. A paper might categorize different kinds of coaches—from inspiring to

incompetent—and make the point that athletes learn a great deal about human relations simply by having to get along with their coaches, regardless of the coaches' skills. Such a paper might conclude that participation in a team sport teaches more about human nature than several courses in psychology. Or the essay might end with a proposal: Rookies and seasoned team members should be paired, so that novice players can get advice on dealing with coaching eccentricities.

REVISION STRATEGIES

Once you have a draft of the essay, you're ready to revise. The following checklist will help you and those giving you feedback apply to division-classification some of the revision techniques discussed in Chapters 7 and 8.

DIVISION-CLASSIFICATION: A REVISION/PEER REVIEW CHECKLIST

Revise Overall Meaning and Structure

- ☐ What is the principle of division-classification at the heart of the essay? How does this principle contribute to the essay's overall purpose and thesis?
- ☐ Does the thesis state the essay's principle of division-classification? Should it? Does the thesis signal which part or category is most important? Should it? Does the thesis reveal the essay's plan of development? Should it?
- ☐ Is the essay organized primarily through division, classification, or a blend of both?
- ☐ If the essay is organized mainly through division, is the subject sufficiently broad and complex to be broken down into parts? What are the parts?
- ☐ If the essay is organized mainly through classification, what are the categories? How does this categorizing reveal similarities and/or differences that would otherwise not be apparent?

Revise Paragraph Development

- ☐ Are comparable points discussed in each of the paper's sections? What are these points?
- ☐ In which paragraphs does the division-classification seem illogical, incomplete, or inconsistent? In which paragraphs are parts or categories not clearly explained?
- ☐ Are the subject's different parts or categories discussed in separate paragraphs? Should they be?

Revise Sentences and Words

- □ What signal devices ("Another characteristic"; "A third type"; "The most important trait") help integrate the paper? Are there enough signals? Too many?
- □ Where should sentences and words be made more specific in order to clarify the parts and categories being discussed?

Student Essay: From Prewriting Through Revision

The student essay that follows was written by Gail Oremland in response to this assignment:

> In "Euromail and Amerimail," Eric Weiner describes the conflicting ways in which Europeans and Americans communicate. Choose a specific group of people whose job it is to communicate—for example, parents, bosses, teachers. Then, in an essay of your own, divide the group into types according to the flaws they reveal when communicating.

Gail wanted to prepare a light-spirited paper about college professors' foibles. Right from the start, she decided to focus on three kinds of professors: the "Knowledgeable One," the "Leader of Intellectual Discussion," and the "Buddy." She used the *patterns of development* to generate prewriting material about each kind, typing whatever ideas came to mind as she focused on one pattern at a time. Reprinted here is Gail's prewriting for the Knowledgeable One. Note that not every pattern sparked ideas. When Gail later reviewed her prewriting, she added some details and deleted others. The handwritten marks on the prewriting indicate Gail's later efforts to refine her rough material.

After annotating her prewriting for all the categories, Gail prepared her first draft, without shaping her prewriting further or making an outline. As she wrote, though, she frequently referred to her warm-up material to retrieve specifics about each professorial type.

Prewriting Using the Patterns of Development

Knowledgeable One

Even in a blizzard or hurricane

Narration: Enters, walks to podium, puts notes on stand, begins lecture exactly on schedule. Talks on and on, stating facts. ~~Even when she had a cold, she kept on lecturing, although we could hardly hear her and her voice kept cracking~~. Always ends lecture exactly on time. Packs her notes. Hurries away. Shoots out the back door. Back to the privacy of her office, away from students.

Description: Self-important air, yellowed notes, all weather, drones, students' glazed eyes, yawns

Cause-Effect: Thinks she's an expert and that students are ignorant, so students are intimidated. States one dry fact after another, so students get bored. Addresses students as "Mr." or "Miss," so she establishes distance.

Doesn't stop, so students feel they can't interrupt

Definition: A fact person

Illustration: History prof who knows death toll of every battle; biology prof who knows all the molecules; accounting prof who knows every clause of tax form

Comparison-Contrast: Interest in specialized academic area vs. no interest in students

Now read Gail's paper, "The Truth About College Teachers," noting the similarities and differences between her prewriting and final essay. As you may imagine, the patterns of development that yielded the most details during prewriting became especially prominent in the final essay. Note, too, that Gail's prewriting consisted of unconnected details within each pattern, whereas the essay flows easily. To achieve such coherence, Gail used commentary and transitional phrases to connect the prewriting details. As you read the essay, also consider how well it applies the principles of division-classification discussed in this chapter. (The commentary that follows the paper will help you look at the essay more closely and will give you some sense of how Gail went about revising her first draft.)

The Truth About College Teachers
by Gail Oremland

1 A recent TV news story told about a group of college professors from a nearby university who were hired by a local school system to help upgrade the teaching in the community's public schools. The professors were to visit classrooms, analyze teachers' skills, and then conduct workshops to help the teachers become more effective at their jobs. But after the first round of workshops, the superintendent of schools decided to cancel the whole project. He fired the learned professors and sent them back to their ivory tower. Why did the project fall apart? There was a simple reason. The college professors, who were supposedly going to show the public school teachers how to be more effective, were themselves poor teachers. Many college students could have predicted such a disastrous outcome. They know, firsthand, that

Introduction

Thesis

college teachers are strange. They know that professors often exhibit bizarre behaviors, relating to students in ways that make it difficult for students to stay awake, or—if awake—to learn.

Topic sentence

The first of three paragraphs on the first category of teacher

The first paragraph in a three-part chronological sequence: What happens *before* class

One type of professor assumes, legitimately enough, that her function is to pass on to students the vast store of knowledge she has acquired. But because the "Knowledgeable One" regards herself as an expert and her students as the ignorant masses, she adopts an elitist approach that sabotages learning. The Knowledgeable One enters a lecture hall with a self-important air, walks to the podium, places her yellowed-with-age notes on the stand, and begins her lecture at the exact second the class is officially scheduled to begin. There can be a blizzard or hurricane raging outside the lecture hall; students can be running through freezing sleet and howling winds to get to class on time. Will the Knowledgeable One wait for them to arrive before beginning her lecture? Probably not. The Knowledgeable One's time is precious. She's there, set to begin, and that's what matters. 2

Topic sentence

The second paragraph on the first category of teacher

The second paragraph in the chronological sequence: What happens *during* class

Once the monologue begins, the Knowledgeable One drones on and on. The Knowledgeable One is a fact person. She may be the history prof who knows the death toll of every Civil War battle, the biology prof who can diagram all the common biological molecules, the accounting prof who enumerates every clause of the federal tax form. Oblivious to students' glazed eyes and stifled yawns, the Knowledgeable One delivers her monologue, dispensing one dry fact after another. The only advantage to being on the receiving end of this boring monologue is that students do not have to worry about being called on to question a point or provide an opinion; the Knowledgeable One is not willing to relinquish one minute of her time by giving students a voice. Assume for one improbable moment that a student actually manages to stay awake during the monologue and is brave enough to ask a question. In such a case, the Knowledgeable One will address the questioning student as "Mr." or "Miss." This formality does not, as some students mistakenly suppose, indicate respect for the student as a fledgling member of the academic community. Not at all. This impersonality represents the Knowledgeable One's desire to keep as wide a distance as possible between her and her students. 3

4 The Knowledgeable One's monologue always comes to a close at the precise second the class is scheduled to end. No sooner has she delivered her last forgettable word than the Knowledgeable One packs up her notes and shoots out the door, heading back to the privacy of her office, where she can pursue her specialized academic interests—free of any possible interruption from students. The Knowledgeable One's hasty departure from the lecture hall makes it clear she has no desire to talk with students. In her eyes, she has met her obligations; she has taken time away from her research to transmit to students what she knows. Any closer contact might mean she would risk contagion from students, that great unwashed mass. Such a danger is to be avoided at all costs.

Topic sentence

The third paragraph on the first category of teacher

The final paragraph in the chronological sequence: What happens *after* class

5 Unlike the Knowledgeable One, the "Leader of Intellectual Discussion" seems to respect students. Emphasizing class discussion, the Leader encourages students to confront ideas ("What is Twain's view of morality?" "Was our intervention in Iraq justified?" "Should big business be given tax breaks?") and discover their own truths. Then, about three weeks into the semester, it becomes clear that the Leader wants students to discover *his* version of the truth. Behind the Leader's democratic guise lurks a dictator. When a student voices an opinion that the Leader accepts, the student is rewarded by hearty nods of approval and "Good point, good point." But if a student is rash enough to advance a conflicting viewpoint, the Leader responds with killing politeness: "Well, yes, that's an interesting perspective. But don't you think that . . . ?" Grade-conscious students soon learn not to chime in with their viewpoint. They know that when the Leader, with seeming honesty, says, "I'd be interested in hearing what you think. Let's open this up for discussion," they had better figure out what the Leader wants to hear before advancing their own theories. "Me-tooism" rather than independent thinking, they discover, guarantees good grades in the Leader's class.

Topic sentence

Paragraph on the second category of teacher

6 Then there is the professor who comes across as the students' "Buddy." This kind of professor does not see himself as an imparter of knowledge or a leader of discussion but as a pal, just one in a community of equals. The Buddy may start his course this way: "All of us know that this college stuff—grades,

Topic sentence

Paragraph on the third category of teacher

degrees, exams, required reading—is a game. So let's not play it, okay?" Dressed in jeans, sweatshirt, and scuffed sneakers, the Buddy projects a relaxed, casual attitude. He arranges the class seats in a circle (he would never take a position in front of the room) and insists that students call him by his first name. He uses no syllabus and gives few tests, believing that such constraints keep students from directing their own learning. A free spirit, the Buddy often teaches courses like "The Psychology of Interpersonal Relations" or "The Social Dynamics of the Family." If students choose to use class time to discuss the course material, that's fine. If they want to discuss something else, that's fine, too. It's the self-expression, the honest dialog, that counts. In fact, the Buddy seems especially fond of digressions from academic subjects. By talking about his political views, his marital problems, his tendency to drink one too many beers, the Buddy lets students see that he is a regular guy—just like them. At first, students look forward to classes with the Buddy. They enjoy the informality, the chitchat, the lack of pressure. But after a while, they wonder why they are paying for a course where they learn nothing. They might as well stay home and watch talk shows.

Conclusion

Echoes opening anecdote

Obviously, some college professors are excellent. They are 7 learned, hardworking, and imaginative; they enjoy their work and like being with students. On the whole, though, college professors are a strange lot. Despite their advanced degrees and their own exposure to many different kinds of teachers, they do not seem to understand how to relate to students. Rather than being hired as consultants to help others upgrade their teaching skills, college professors should themselves hire consultants to tell them what they are doing wrong and how they can improve. Who should these consultants be? That's easy: the people who know them best—their students.

Commentary

Introduction and Thesis

After years of being graded by teachers, Gail took special pleasure in writing an essay that gave her a chance to evaluate her teachers—in this case, her college professors. Even the essay's title, "The Truth About College Teachers," implies that Gail is going to have fun knocking profs down from their ivory towers. To introduce her subject, she uses a timely news story. This brief anecdote leads directly to the essay's *thesis:* "Professors often exhibit bizarre behaviors, relating to students in ways that make it difficult for students to stay awake, or—if awake—to learn." Note that Gail's thesis isn't highly structured; it doesn't, for example, name the specific categories to be discussed. Still, her thesis suggests that the essay is going to *categorize* a range of teaching behaviors, using as a *principle of classification* the strange ways that college profs relate to students.

Purpose

As with all good papers developed through division-classification, Gail's essay doesn't use classification as an end in itself. Gail uses classification because it helps her achieve a broader *purpose.* She wants to *convince* readers—without moralizing or abandoning her humorous tone—that such teaching styles inhibit learning. In other words, there's a serious undertone to her essay. This additional layer of meaning is characteristic of satiric writing.

Categories and Topic Sentences

The essay's body, consisting of five paragraphs, presents the three categories that make up Gail's analysis. According to Gail, college teachers can be categorized as the Knowledgeable One (paragraphs 2–4), the Leader of Intellectual Discussion (5), or the Buddy (6). Obviously, there are other ways professors might be classified. But given Gail's purpose, audience, tone, and point of view, her categories are appropriate; they are reasonably *complete, consistent,* and *mutually exclusive.* Note, too, that Gail uses *topic sentences* near the beginning of each category to help readers see which professorial type she's discussing.

Overall Organization and Paragraph Structure

Gail is able to shift smoothly and easily from one category to the next. How does she achieve such graceful transitions? Take a moment to reread the sentences that introduce her second and third categories (paragraphs 5 and 6). Look at the way each sentence's beginning (in italics here) links back to the preceding category or categories: "*Unlike the Knowledgeable One,* the 'Leader of Intellectual Discussion' seems to respect students"; and the "Buddy . . . *does not see himself as an imparter of knowledge or a leader of discussion* but as a pal. . . . "

Gail is equally careful about providing an easy-to-follow structure within each section. She uses a *chronological sequence* to organize her three-paragraph discussion of the Knowledgeable One. The first paragraph deals with the beginning of the Knowledgeable One's lecture; the second, with the lecture itself; the third, with the end of the lecture. And the paragraphs' *topic sentences* clearly indicate this passage of time. Similarly, *transitions* are used in the paragraphs on the Leader of Intellectual Discussion and the Buddy to ensure a logical progression of points: "*Then,* about three weeks into the semester, it becomes clear that the Leader wants students to discover *his* version of the truth" (5), and "*At first,* students look forward to classes with the Buddy. . . . But *after a while,* they wonder why they are paying for a course where they learn nothing" (6).

Tone

The essay's unity can also be traced to Gail's skill in sustaining her satiric tone. Throughout the essay, Gail selects details that fit her gently mocking attitude. She depicts the Knowledgeable One lecturing from "yellowed-with-age notes . . . , oblivious to students' glazed eyes and stifled yawns," unwilling to wait for students who "run . . . through freezing sleet and howling winds to get to class on time." Then she presents another tongue-in-cheek description, this one focusing on the way the Leader of Intellectual Discussion conducts class: "Good point, good point . . . Well, yes, that's an interesting perspective. But don't you think that . . . ?" Finally, with similar killing accuracy, Gail portrays the Buddy, democratically garbed in "jeans, sweatshirt, and scuffed sneakers."

Combining Patterns of Development

Gail's satiric depiction of her three professorial types employs a number of techniques associated with *narrative* and *descriptive writing:* vigorous images, highly connotative language, and dialog. *Definition, illustration, causal analysis,* and *comparison-contrast* also come into play. Gail defines the characteristics of each type of professor; she provides numerous examples to support her categories; she explains the effects of the different teaching styles on students; and, in her description of the Leader of Intellectual Discussion, she contrasts the appearance of democracy with the dictatorial reality.

Unequal Development of Categories

Although Gail's essay is unified, organized, and well developed, you may have felt that the first category outweighs the other two. There is, of course, no need to balance the categories exactly. But Gail's extended treatment of the first category sets up an expectation that the others will be treated as fully. One way to remedy this problem would be to delete some material from the discussion of the Knowledgeable One. Gail might, for instance, omit the first five sentences in the third paragraph (about the professor's habit of addressing students as Mr. or Miss). Such a change could be made without taking the bite out of her portrayal. Even better, Gail could simply switch the order of her sections, putting the portrait of the Knowledgeable One at the essay's end. Here, the extended discussion wouldn't seem out of proportion. Instead, the sections would appear in *emphatic order,* with the most detailed category saved for last.

Revising the First Draft

It's apparent that an essay as engaging as Gail's must have undergone a good deal of revising. Along the way, Gail made many changes in her draft, but it's particularly interesting to see how she changed her original introduction (reprinted here). The annotation represents her peer reviewers' impressions of the paragraph's problems.

Original Version of the Introduction

Despite their high IQs, advanced degrees, and published papers, some college professors just don't know how to teach. Found almost in any department, in tenured and untenured positions, they prompt student apathy. They fail to convey ideas effectively and to challenge or inspire students. Students thus finish their courses having learned very little. Contrary to popular opinion, these professors' ineptitude is not simply a matter of delivering boring lectures or not caring about students. Many of them care a great deal. Their failure actually stems from their unrealistic perceptions of what a teacher should be. Specifically, they adopt teaching styles or roles that alienate students and undermine learning. Three of the most common ones are "The Knowledgeable One," "The Leader of Intellectual Discussion," and "The Buddy."

Too serious. Doesn't fit rest of essay.

When Gail showed the first draft of the essay to her composition instructor, he laughed—and occasionally squirmed—as he read what she had prepared. He was enthusiastic about the paper but felt there was a problem with the introduction's tone; it was too serious when compared to the playful, lightly satiric mood of the rest of the essay. When Gail reread the paragraph, she agreed, but she was uncertain about the best way to remedy the problem. After revising other sections of the essay, she decided to let the paper sit for a while before going back to rewrite the introduction.

In the meantime, Gail switched on the TV. The timing couldn't have been better; she tuned into a news story about several supposedly learned professors who had been fired from a consulting job because they had turned out to know so little about teaching. This was exactly the kind of item Gail needed to start her essay. Now she was able to prepare a completely new introduction, making it consistent in spirit with the rest of the paper.

With this stronger introduction and the rest of the essay well in hand, Gail was ready to write a conclusion. Now, as she worked on the concluding paragraph, she deliberately shaped it to recall the story about the fired consultants. By echoing the opening anecdote in her conclusion, Gail was able to end the paper with another poke at professors—a perfect way to close her clever and insightful essay.

ACTIVITIES: DIVISION-CLASSIFICATION

Prewriting Activities

1. Imagine you're writing two essays: One is a humorous paper showing how to impress college instructors; the other is a serious essay explaining why volunteerism is on the rise. What about the topics might you divide and/or classify?

2. Use group brainstorming to identify at least three possible principles of division for *one* of the following topics. For each principle, determine what your thesis might be if you were writing an essay.

   a. Prejudice
   b. Pop music
   c. A shopping mall
   d. A good horror movie

3. Through group brainstorming, identify three different principles of classification that might provide the structure for an essay about the possible effects of a controversial decision to expand your college's enrollment. Focusing on one of the principles, decide what your thesis might be. How would you sequence the categories?

Revising Activities

4. Following is a scratch outline for an essay developed through division-classification. On what principle of division-classification is the essay based? What problem do you see in the way the principle is applied? How could the problem be remedied?

   Thesis: The same experience often teaches opposite things to different people.

   - What working as a fast-food cook teaches: Some learn responsibility; others learn to take a "quick and dirty" approach.
   - What a negative experience teaches optimists: Some learn from their mistakes; others continue to maintain a positive outlook.
   - What a difficult course teaches: Some learn to study hard; others learn to avoid demanding courses.
   - What the breakup of a close relationship teaches: Some learn how to negotiate differences; others learn to avoid intimacy.

5. Following is a paragraph from the first draft of an essay urging that day-care centers adopt play programs tailored to children's developmental needs. What principle of division-classification focuses the paragraph? Is the principle applied consistently and logically? Are parts/categories developed sufficiently? Revise the paragraph, eliminating any problems you discover and adding specific details where needed.

   Within a few years, preschool children move from self-absorbed to interactive play. Babies and toddlers engage in solitary play. Although they sometimes prefer being near other children, they focus primarily on their own actions. This is very different from the highly interactive play of the elementary school years. Sometime in children's second year, solitary play is replaced by parallel play, during which children engage in similar activities near one another. However, they interact only occasionally. By age three, most children show at least some cooperative play, a form that involves interaction and cooperative role-taking. Such role-taking can be found in the "pretend" games that children play to explore adult relationships (games of "Mommy and Daddy") and anatomy (games of "Doctor"). Additional signs of youngsters' growing awareness of peers can be seen at about age four. At this age, many children begin showing a special devotion to one other child and may want to play only with that child. During this time, children also begin to take special delight in physical activities such as running and jumping, often going off by themselves to expend their abundant physical energy.

PROFESSIONAL SELECTIONS: DIVISION-CLASSIFICATION

WILLIAM LUTZ

With a dash of humor, William Lutz (1941–), professor of English at Rutgers University, writes about a subject he takes very seriously: doublespeak—the use of language to evade, deceive, and mislead. An expert on language, Lutz has appeared on many national television programs, among them the *Today* show, the *Larry King Live Show*, and the *MacNeil-Lehrer News Hour*. Lutz has written over two dozen articles and is the author or coauthor of fourteen books, including the best-selling *Doublespeak: From Revenue Enhancement to Terminal Living* (1989) as well as its sequels, *The New Doublespeak: Why No One Knows What Anyone's Saying Anymore* (1996) and *Doublespeak Defined: Cut Through the Bull**** and Get to the Point* (1999). He is also the coauthor of *Firestorm at Peshtigo* (2002) about the devastating 1871 fire in a Wisconsin mining town. The following piece is from *Doublespeak*.

Please note the essay structure diagram that appears following this selection (Figure 13.2 on page 292).

Pre-Reading Journal Entry

At one time or another, everyone twists language in order to avoid telling the full truth. In your journal, list several instances that demonstrate that indirect, partially true language ("doublespeak") is sometimes desirable, even necessary. In each case, why was this evasive language used?

DOUBLESPEAK

There are no potholes in the streets of Tucson, Arizona, just "pavement deficiencies." 1
The Reagan Administration didn't propose any new taxes, just "revenue enhancement" through new "user's fees." Those aren't bums on the street, just "nongoal oriented members of society." There are no more poor people, just "fiscal underachievers." There was no robbery of an automatic teller machine, just an "unauthorized withdrawal." The patient didn't die because of medical malpractice, it was just a "diagnostic misadventure of a high magnitude." The U.S. Army doesn't kill the enemy anymore, it just "services the target." And the doublespeak goes on.

Doublespeak is language that pretends to communicate but really doesn't. It is lan- 2
guage that makes the bad seem good, the negative appear positive, the unpleasant appear attractive or at least tolerable. Doublespeak is language that avoids or shifts responsibility, language that is at variance with its real or purported meaning. It is language that conceals or prevents thought; rather than extending thought, doublespeak limits it. . . .

How to Spot Doublespeak

How can you spot doublespeak? Most of the time you will recognize doublespeak when 3
you see or hear it. But, if you have any doubts, you can identify doublespeak just by answering these questions: Who is saying what to whom, under what conditions and circumstances, with what intent, and with what results? Answering these questions will usually help you identify as doublespeak language that appears to be legitimate or that at first glance doesn't even appear to be doublespeak.

First Kind of Doublespeak

There are at least four kinds of doublespeak. The first is the euphemism, an inoffen- 4
sive or positive word or phrase used to avoid a harsh, unpleasant, or distasteful reality. But a euphemism can also be a tactful word or phrase which avoids directly mentioning a painful reality, or it can be an expression used out of concern for the feelings of someone else, or to avoid directly discussing a topic subject to a social or cultural taboo.

When you use a euphemism because of your sensitivity for someone's feelings or out 5
of concern for a recognized social or cultural taboo, it is not doublespeak. For example, you express your condolences that someone has "passed away" because you do not want to say to a grieving person, "I'm sorry your father is dead." When you use the euphemism "passed away," no one is misled. Moreover, the euphemism functions here not just to protect the feelings of another person, but to communicate also your concern for that person's feelings during a period of mourning. When you excuse yourself to go to the "restroom," or you mention that someone is "sleeping with" or "involved with" someone else, you do not mislead anyone about your meaning, but you do respect the social taboos about discussing bodily functions and sex in direct terms. You also indicate your sensitivity to the feelings of your audience, which is usually considered a mark of courtesy and good manners.

6 However, when a euphemism is used to mislead or deceive, it becomes doublespeak. For example, in 1984 the U.S. State Department announced that it would no longer use the word "killing" in its annual report on the status of human rights in countries around the world. Instead, it would use the phrase "unlawful or arbitrary deprivation of life," which the department claimed was more accurate. Its real purpose for using this phrase was simply to avoid discussing the embarrassing situation of government-sanctioned killings in countries that are supported by the United States and have been certified by the United States as respecting the human rights of their citizens. This use of a euphemism constitutes doublespeak, since it is designed to mislead, to cover up the unpleasant. Its real intent is at variance with its apparent intent. It is language designed to alter our perception of reality.

7 The Pentagon, too, avoids discussing unpleasant realities when it refers to bombs and artillery shells that fall on civilian targets as "incontinent ordnance." And in 1977 the Pentagon tried to slip funding for the neutron bomb unnoticed into an appropriations bill by calling it a "radiation enhancement device."

Second Kind of Doublespeak

8 A second kind of doublespeak is jargon, the specialized language of a trade, profession, or similar group, such as that used by doctors, lawyers, engineers, educators, or car mechanics. Jargon can serve an important and useful function. Within a group, jargon functions as a kind of verbal shorthand that allows members of the group to communicate with each other clearly, efficiently, and quickly. Indeed, it is a mark of membership in the group to be able to use and understand the group's jargon.

9 But jargon, like the euphemism, can also be doublespeak. It can be—and often is—pretentious, obscure, and esoteric terminology used to give an air of profundity, authority, and prestige to speakers and their subject matter. Jargon as doublespeak often makes the simple appear complex, the ordinary profound, the obvious insightful. In this sense it is used not to express but impress. With such doublespeak, the act of smelling something becomes "organoleptic analysis," glass becomes "fused silicate," a crack in a metal support beam becomes a "discontinuity," conservative economic policies become "distributionally conservative notions."

10 Lawyers, for example, speak of an "involuntary conversion" of property when discussing the loss or destruction of property through theft, accident, or condemnation. If your house burns down or if your car is stolen, you have suffered an involuntary conversion of your property. When used by lawyers in a legal situation, such jargon is a legitimate use of language, since lawyers can be expected to understand the term.

11 However, when a member of a specialized group uses its jargon to communicate with a person outside the group, and uses it knowing that the nonmember does not understand such language, then there is doublespeak. For example, on May 9, 1978, a National Airlines 727 airplane crashed while attempting to land at the Pensacola, Florida airport. Three of the fifty-two passengers aboard the airplane were killed. As a result of the crash, National made an after-tax insurance benefit of $1.7 million, or an extra 18¢ a share dividend for its stockholders. Now National Airlines had two problems: It did not want to talk about one of its airplanes crashing, and it had to account

for the $1.7 million when it issued its annual report to its stockholders. National solved the problem by inserting a footnote in its annual report which explained that the $1.7 million income was due to "the involuntary conversion of a 727." National thus acknowledged the crash of its airplane and the subsequent profit it made from the crash, without once mentioning the accident or the deaths. However, because airline officials knew that most stockholders in the company, and indeed most of the general public, were not familiar with legal jargon, the use of such jargon constituted doublespeak.

Third Kind of Doublespeak

A third kind of doublespeak is gobbledygook or bureaucratese. Basically, such doublespeak is simply a matter of piling on words, of overwhelming the audience with words, the bigger the words and the longer the sentences the better. Alan Greenspan, then chair of President Nixon's Council of Economic Advisors, was quoted in *The Philadelphia Inquirer* in 1974 as having testified before a Senate committee that "It is a tricky problem to find the particular calibration in timing that would be appropriate to stem the acceleration in risk premiums created by falling incomes without prematurely aborting the decline in the inflation-generated risk premiums." 12

Nor has Mr. Greenspan's language changed since then. Speaking to the meeting of the Economic Club of New York in 1988, Mr. Greenspan, now Federal Reserve chair,[1] said, "I guess I should warn you, if I turn out to be particularly clear, you've probably misunderstood what I've said." Mr. Greenspan's doublespeak doesn't seem to have held back his career. 13

Sometimes gobbledygook may sound impressive, but when the quote is later examined in print it doesn't even make sense. During the 1988 presidential campaign, vice-presidential candidate Senator Dan Quayle explained the need for a strategic-defense initiative by saying, "Why wouldn't an enhanced deterrent, a more stable peace, a better prospect to denying the ones who enter conflict in the first place to have a reduction of offensive systems and an introduction to defense capability? I believe this is the route the country will eventually go." 14

The investigation into the *Challenger* disaster in 1986 revealed the doublespeak of gobbledygook and bureaucratese used by too many involved in the shuttle program. When Jesse Moore, NASA's associate administrator, was asked if the performance of the shuttle program had improved with each launch or if it had remained the same, he answered, "I think our performance in terms of the liftoff performance and in terms of the orbital performance, we knew more about the envelope we were operating under, and we have been pretty accurately staying in that. And so I would say the performance has not by design drastically improved. I think we have been able to characterize the performance more as a function of our launch experience as opposed to it improving as a function of time." While this language may appear to be jargon, a close look will reveal that it is really just gobbledygook laced with jargon. But you really have to wonder if Mr. Moore had any idea what he was saying. 15

---

[1]Alan Greenspan stepped down from his position as Federal Reserve chair in 2006 (editors' note).

Fourth Kind of Doublespeak

16 The fourth kind of doublespeak is inflated language that is designed to make the ordinary seem extraordinary; to make everyday things seem impressive; to give an air of importance to people, situations, or things that would not normally be considered important; to make the simple seem complex. Often this kind of doublespeak isn't hard to spot, and it is usually pretty funny. While car mechanics may be called "automotive internists," elevator operators members of the "vertical transportation corps," used cars "pre-owned" or "experienced cars," and black-and-white television sets described as having "non-multicolor capability," you really aren't misled all that much by such language.

17 However, you may have trouble figuring out that, when Chrysler "initiates a career alternative enhancement program," it is really laying off five thousand workers; or that "negative patient care outcome" means the patient died; or that "rapid oxidation" means a fire in a nuclear power plant.

18 The doublespeak of inflated language can have serious consequences. In Pentagon doublespeak, "pre-emptive counterattack" means that American forces attacked first; "engaged the enemy on all sides" means American troops were ambushed; "backloading of augmentation personnel" means a retreat by American troops. In the doublespeak of the military, the 1983 invasion of Grenada was conducted not by the U.S. Army, Navy, Air Force, and Marines, but by the "Caribbean Peace Keeping Forces." But then, according to the Pentagon, it wasn't an invasion, it was a "predawn vertical insertion." . . .

The Dangers of Doublespeak

19 These . . . examples of doublespeak should make it clear that doublespeak is not the product of carelessness or sloppy thinking. Indeed, most doublespeak is the product of clear thinking and is carefully designed and constructed to appear to communicate when in fact it doesn't. It is language designed not to lead but mislead. It is language designed to distort reality and corrupt thought. . . . When a fire in a nuclear reactor building is called "rapid oxidation," an explosion in a nuclear power plant is called an "energetic disassembly," the illegal overthrow of a legitimate government is termed "destabilizing a government," and lies are seen as "inoperative statements," we are hearing doublespeak that attempts to avoid responsibility and make the bad seem good, the negative appear positive, something unpleasant appear attractive; and which seems to communicate but doesn't. It is language designed to alter our perception of reality and corrupt our thinking. Such language does not provide us with the tools we need to develop, advance, and preserve our culture and our civilization. Such language breeds suspicion, cynicism, distrust, and, ultimately, hostility.

Questions for Close Reading

1. What is the selection's thesis? Locate the sentence(s) in which Lutz states his main idea. If he doesn't state the thesis explicitly, express it in your own words.

FIGURE 13.2
Essay Structure Diagram: "Doublespeak" by William Lutz

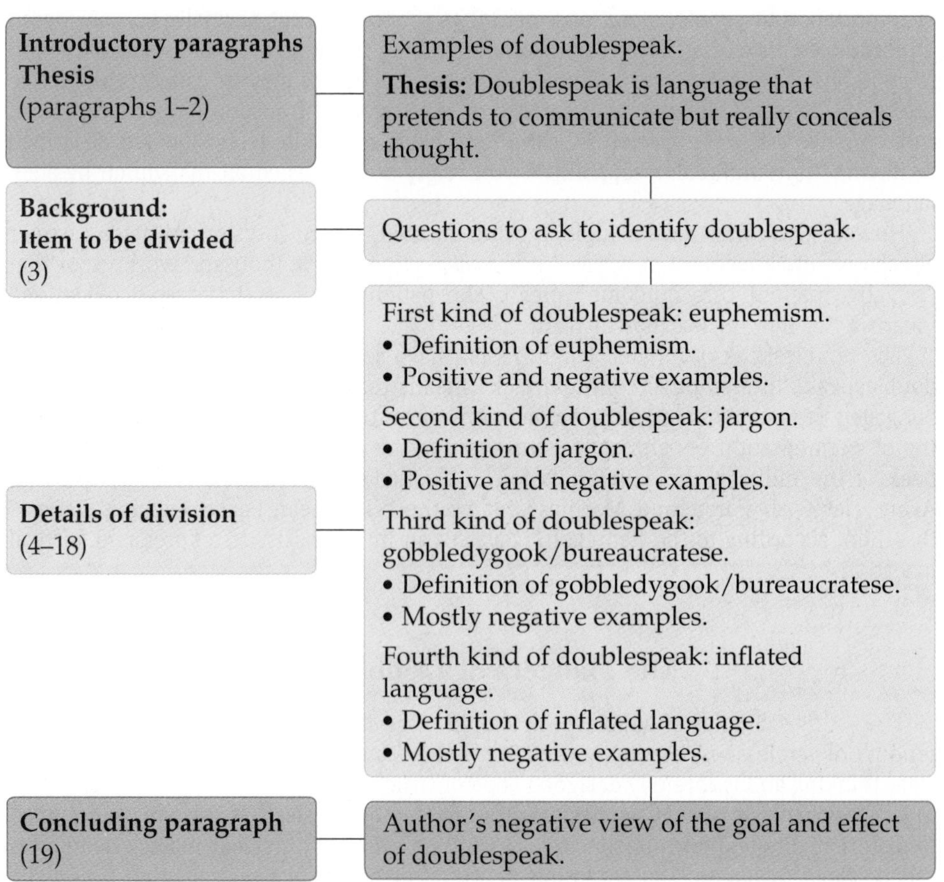

2. According to Lutz, four questions help people "spot" doublespeak. What are the questions? How do they help people distinguish between legitimate language and doublespeak?

3. Lutz's headings indicate simply "First Kind of Doublespeak," "Second Kind of Doublespeak," and so on. What terms does Lutz use to identify the four kinds of doublespeak? Cite one example of each kind.

4. What, according to Lutz, are the dangers of doublespeak?

5. Refer to your dictionary as needed to define the following words used in the selection: *variance* (paragraph 6), *esoteric* (9), *profundity* (9), *dividend* (11), and *initiative* (14).

Questions About the Writer's Craft

1. **The pattern.** Does Lutz make his four categories of doublespeak mutually exclusive, or does he let them overlap? Cite specific examples to support your answer. Why do you think Lutz took the approach he did?
2. **Other patterns.** What other patterns, besides division-classification, does Lutz use in this selection? Cite examples of at least two other patterns. Explain how each pattern reinforces Lutz's thesis.
3. Lutz quotes Alan Greenspan twice: first in paragraph 12 and again in paragraph 13. What is surprising about Greenspan's second comment (paragraph 13)? Why might Lutz have included this second quotation?
4. How would you characterize Lutz's tone in the essay? What key words indicate his attitude toward the material he discusses? Why do you suppose he chose this particular tone?

Writing Assignments Using Division-Classification as a Pattern of Development

1. According to Lutz, doublespeak "is language designed to alter our perception of reality." Using two of Lutz's categories (or any others you devise), analyze an advertisement or commercial that you think deliberately uses doublespeak to mislead consumers. Before writing your paper, read Kay S. Hymowitz's "Tweens: Ten Going on Sixteen" (page 245) and Leslie Savan's "Black Talk and Pop Culture" (page 258) for two perspectives on commercial doublespeak.
2. Select *one* area of life that you know well. Possibilities include life in a college dormitory, the parent-child relationship, the dating scene, and sibling conflicts. Focus on a specific type of speech (for example, gossip, reprimands, flirtation, or criticism) that occurs in this area. Then identify the component parts of that type of speech. You might, for example, analyze dormitory gossip about individual students, couples, and professors. Reach some conclusions about the kinds of speech you discuss. Do you consider them funny, pathetic, or troubling? Your tone should be consistent with the conclusions you reach.

Writing Assignments Combining Patterns of Development

3. Find a spoken or written *example* of doublespeak that disturbs you. Possibilities include a political advertisement, television commercial, newspaper article, or

legal document. Write a letter of complaint to the appropriate person or office, using convincing examples to point out what is misleading about the communication. Pointing out negative impressions or *consequences resulting* from the doublespeak will enhance your position.

4. In his essay, Lutz examines the relationship between language and perception. Identify two closely related terms, and *contrast* the different perceptions of reality represented by each term. For example, you might contrast "African-American" and "Negro," "Ms." and "Miss," "gay" and "homosexual," "dolls" and "action figures," or "pro-life" and "anti-abortion." Interviewing family, friends, and classmates will help you identify ideas and *examples* to explore in the essay. For a discussion of the connection between language and perception, read Maya Angelou's "Sister Flowers" (page 167), Leslie Savan's "Black Talk and Pop Culture" (page 258), David Shipley's "Talk About Editing" (page 340), Eric Weiner's "Euromail and Amerimail" (page 375), and Mary Sherry's "In Praise of the 'F' Word" (page 502).

Writing Assignment Using a Journal Entry as a Starting Point

5. Select from your pre-reading journal entry two or three compelling instances of *beneficial* doublespeak. Use these examples in an essay arguing that doublespeak isn't always harmful. For each example cited, contrast the positive effects of doublespeak with the potentially negative consequences of *not* using it. Brainstorming with others will help you generate convincing examples. Before you begin writing, consider reading the following essays, which illustrate varying instances of doublespeak: Audre Lorde's "The Fourth of July" (page 208) and Beth Johnson's "Bombs Bursting in Air" (page 252).

SCOTT RUSSELL SANDERS

Scott Russell Sanders was born in 1945 to a farming family in Tennessee. After graduating from Brown University, where he studied physics and English, he began a writing career that has grown to include more than a dozen books. His work has been diverse, encompassing historical novels, children's stories, essays, and fiction. Two of Sander's best-known works are the fictional *Fetching the Dead* (1984) and *The Engineer of Beasts* (1988), a science-fiction novel for young adults. His more recent books include the novel *Bad Man Ballad* (2004), the environmental narrative *Crawdad Creek* (2002), the children's book *A Place Called Freedom* (1997), and the memoir A *Private History of Awe* (2007). The following essay is taken from *The Paradise of Bombs* (1987), an essay collection for which Sanders won the Associated Writing Programs Award for Creative Nonfiction.

Pre-Reading Journal Entry

Though one might argue that gender roles haven't evolved quickly or dramatically enough, they have changed considerably in recent decades. In your own lifetime, what are some changes that you've witnessed in the roles men and women play? Using your journal, brainstorm your ideas about gender transformations in areas such as education, athletics, employment, dating, marriage, and parenting. Then, for each category, go back and indicate whether the changes have been for the better. As you explore this issue, you might also benefit from discussing it with your friends and family, especially individuals from an older generation.

THE MEN WE CARRY IN OUR MINDS

1 The first men, besides my father, I remember seeing were black convicts and white guards, in the cotton field across the road from our farm on the outskirts of Memphis. I must have been three or four. The prisoners wore dingy gray-and-black zebra suits, heavy as canvas, sodden with sweat. Hatless, stooped, they chopped weeds in the fierce heat, row after row, breathing the acrid dust of boll-weevil poison. The overseers wore dazzling white shirts and broad shadowy hats. The oiled barrels of their shotguns flashed in the sunlight. Their faces in memory are utterly blank. Of course those men, white and black, have become for me an emblem of racial hatred. But they have also come to stand for the twin poles of my early vision of manhood—the brute toiling animal and the boss.

2 When I was a boy, the men I knew labored with their bodies. They were marginal farmers, just scraping by, or welders, steelworkers, carpenters; they swept floors, dug ditches, mined coal, or drove trucks, their forearms ropy with muscle; they trained horses, stoked furnaces, built fires, stood on assembly lines wrestling parts onto cars and refrigerators. They got up before light, worked all day long whatever the weather, and when they came home at night they looked as though somebody had been whipping them. In the evenings and on weekends they worked on their own places, tilling gardens that were lumpy with clay, fixing broken-down cars, hammering on houses that were always too drafty, too leaky, too small.

3 The bodies of the men I knew were twisted and maimed in ways visible and invisible. The nails of their hands were black and split, the hands tattooed with scars. Some had lost fingers. Heavy lifting had given many of them finicky backs and guts weak from hernias. Racing against conveyor belts had given them ulcers. Their ankles and knees ached from years of standing on concrete. Anyone who had worked for long around machines was hard of hearing. They squinted, and the skin of their faces was creased like the leather of old work gloves. There were times, studying them, when I dreaded growing up. Most of them coughed, from dust or cigarettes, and most of them drank cheap wine or whisky, so their eyes looked bloodshot and bruised. The fathers of my friends always seemed older than the mothers. Men wore out sooner. Only women lived into old age.

As a boy I also knew another sort of men, who did not sweat and break down like mules. They were soldiers, and so far as I could tell they scarcely worked at all. During my early school years we lived on a military base, an arsenal in Ohio, and every day I saw GIs in the guard shacks, on the stoops of barracks, at the wheels of olive drab Chevrolets. The chief fact of their lives was boredom. Long after I left the Arsenal I came to recognize the sour smell the soldiers gave off as that of souls in limbo. They were all waiting—for wars, for transfers, for leaves, for promotions, for the end of their hitch—like so many braves waiting for the hunt to begin. Unlike the warriors of older tribes, however, they would have no say about when the battle would start or how it would be waged. Their waiting was broken only when they practiced for war. They fired guns at targets, drove tanks across the churned-up fields of the military reservation, set off bombs in the wrecks of old fighter planes. I knew this was all play. But I also felt certain that when the hour for killing arrived, they would kill. When the real shooting started, many of them would die. This was what soldiers were *for*, just as a hammer was for driving nails. 4

Warriors and toilers: those seemed, in my boyhood vision, to be the chief destinies for men. They weren't the only destinies, as I learned from having a few male teachers, from reading books, and from watching television. But the men on television—the politicians, the astronauts, the generals, the savvy lawyers, the philosophical doctors, the bosses who gave orders to both soldiers and laborers—seemed as removed and unreal to me as the figures in tapestries. I could no more imagine growing up to become one of these cool, potent creatures than I could imagine becoming a prince. 5

A nearer and more hopeful example was that of my father, who had escaped from a red-dirt farm to a tire factory, and from the assembly line to the front office. Eventually he dressed in a white shirt and tie. He carried himself as if he had been born to work with this mind. But his body, remembering the earlier years of slogging work, began to give out on him in his fifties, and it quit on him entirely before he turned sixty-five. Even such a partial escape from man's fate as he had accomplished did not seem possible for most of the boys I knew. They joined the Army, stood in line for jobs in the smoky plants, helped build highways. They were bound to work as their fathers had worked, killing themselves or preparing to kill others. 6

A scholarship enabled me not only to attend college, a rare enough feat in my circle, but even to study in a university meant for the children of the rich. Here I met for the first time young men who had assumed from birth that they would lead lives of comfort and power. And for the first time I met women who told me that men were guilty of having kept all the joys and privileges of the earth for themselves. I was baffled. What privileges? What joys? I thought about the maimed, dismal lives of most of the men back home. What had they stolen from their wives and daughters? The right to go five days a week, twelve months a year, for thirty or forty years to a steel mill or a coal mine? The right to drop bombs and die in war? The right to feel every leak in the roof, every gap in the fence, every cough in the engine, as a wound they must mend? The right to feel, when the lay-off comes or the plant shuts down, not only afraid but ashamed? 7

8 I was slow to understand the deep grievances of women. This was because, as a boy, I had envied them. Before college, the only people I had ever known who were interested in art or music or literature, the only ones who read books, the only ones who ever seemed to enjoy a sense of ease and grace were the mothers and daughters. Like the menfolk, they fretted about money, they scrimped and made do. But, when the pay stopped coming in, they were not the ones who had failed. Nor did they have to go to war, and that seemed to me a blessed fact. By comparison with the narrow, ironclad days of fathers, there was an expansiveness, I thought, in the days of mothers. They went to see neighbors, to shop in town, to run errands at school, at the library, at church. No doubt, had I looked harder at their lives, I would have envied them less. It was not my fate to become a woman, so it was easier for me to see the graces. Few of them held jobs outside the home, and those who did filled thankless roles as clerks and waitresses. I didn't see, then, what a prison a house could be, since houses seemed to me brighter, handsomer places than any factory. I did not realize—because such things were never spoken of—how often women suffered from men's bullying. I did learn about the wretchedness of abandoned wives, single mothers, widows; but I also learned about the wretchedness of lone men. Even then I could see how exhausting it was for a mother to cater all day to the needs of young children. But if I had been asked, as a boy, to choose between tending a baby and tending a machine, I think I would have chosen the baby. (Having now tended both, I know I would choose the baby.)

9 So I was baffled when the women at college accused me and my sex of having cornered the world's pleasures. I think something like my bafflement has been felt by other boys (and girls as well) who grew up in dirt-poor farm country, in mining country, in black ghettos, in Hispanic barrios, in the shadows of factories, in Third World nations—any place where the fate of men is as grim and bleak as the fate of women. Toilers and warriors. I realize now how ancient these identities are, how deep the tug they exert on men, the undertow of a thousand generations. The miseries I saw, as a boy, in the lives of nearly all men I continue to see in the lives of many—the body-breaking toil, the tedium, the call to be tough, the humiliating powerlessness, the battle for a living and for territory.

10 When the women I met at college thought about the joys and privileges of men, they did not carry in their minds the sort of men I had known in my childhood. They thought of their fathers, who were bankers, physicians, architects, stockbrokers, the big wheels of the big cities. These fathers rode the train to work or drove cars that cost more than any of my childhood houses. They were attended from morning to night by female helpers, wives and nurses and secretaries. They were never laid off, never short of cash at month's end, never lined up for welfare. These fathers made decisions that mattered. They ran the world.

11 The daughters of such men wanted to share in this power, this glory. So did I. They yearned for a say over their future, for jobs worthy of their abilities, for the right to live at peace, unmolested, whole. Yes, I thought, yes yes. The difference between me and these daughters was that they saw me, because of my sex, as destined from birth to become like their fathers, and therefore as an enemy to their desires. I was an ally. If I had known, then, how to tell them so, would they have believed me? Would they now?

Questions for Close Reading

1. What is the selection's thesis? Locate the sentence(s) in which Sanders states his main idea. If he doesn't state the thesis explicitly, express it in your own words.
2. Who were the men Sanders knew most about in his childhood? What does Sanders mean when he says that these men were damaged "in ways both visible and invisible" (paragraph 3)?
3. How did Sanders learn that some men don't toil with their bodies? How did he feel about such men?
4. Why, according to Sanders, was he "slow to understand the deep grievances of women" (8)? Why did the women Sanders met at college consider men to be privileged? Why does Sanders feel he is "an ally" rather than "an enemy" of these women? What prevented the women from understanding how he felt?
5. Refer to your dictionary as needed to define the following words used in the selection: *sodden* (paragraph 1), *acrid* (1), *marginal* (2), *tapestries* (5), *potent* (5), *grievances* (8), *expansiveness* (8) and *tedium* (9).

Questions About the Writer's Craft

1. **The pattern.** Sanders categorizes men into three types; toiling animals, warriors, and bosses. Of the three categories, which two does he describe most vividly? Why might he have chosen to describe these two in such detail?
2. In paragraphs 2 and 3, Sanders offers a vivid portrait of workingmen's lives. How does his word choice, as well as his use of parallel structure and repetition, lend power to this portrait?
3. **Other patterns.** In the second half of the essay, Sanders *contrasts* the lives of workingmen with those of women (paragraphs 7–8) and with those of professional men (10). What is the value of these contrasts?
4. From the middle of paragraph 7 to its end, Sanders frames his sentences as questions. Why might he have decided to pose all these questions? How do they help him achieve his purpose?

Writing Assignments Using Division-Classification as a Pattern of Development

1. "Warriors and toilers," Sanders writes, "those seemed, in my boyhood vision, to be the chief destinies for men." Identify several men *or* women who helped create your "vision" of what it means to be male *or* female. (You may focus on

your view of your own sex or your view of the opposite sex.) Group these individuals into types. Then write an essay describing these types and the people representing each type; your goal is to show whether these people enlarged or restricted your understanding of what it means to be male or female. Before writing your paper, you may want to read one or several of the essays in this book that deal with gender expectations: Kay S. Hymowitz's "Tweens: Ten Going on Sixteen" (page 245), Patricia Cohen's "Reality TV: Surprising Throwback to the Past?" (page 370), Camille Paglia's "Rape: A Bigger Danger Than Feminists Know" (page 506), and Susan Jacoby's "Common Decency" (page 512).

2. Sanders admits he was "slow to understand the deep grievances of women" against men. Consider another group that has grievances—for example, smokers and their disagreements with nonsmokers, parents and their complaints about teenagers, or vegetarians and their objections to meat eaters. Start by brainstorming with others to generate examples of the group's grievances; then write an essay in which you categorize the grievances by type, illustrating each with vivid examples. At the end, reach some conclusions about the validity of the group's complaints. For additional perspectives from aggrieved groups, read Audre Lorde's "The Fourth of July" (page 208), Charmie Gholson's "Charity Display?" (page 220), Toni Morrison's "A Slow Walk of Trees' (page 364), Brent Staples' "Black Men and Public Space" (page 412), and the paired immigration essays (pages 517 and 521).

Writing Assignments Combining Patterns of Development

3. Sanders's father transformed his life when he "escaped from a red-dirt farm . . . to the front office." Think about someone else who also made a positive life change. Perhaps you (or someone you know) stopped hanging out with a destructive crowd and became an academic star, or went back to school at age forty-something to prepare for a different career, or found the courage to end a painful marriage. Write an essay in which you *describe* the change that was made and explain the *steps* that the person took to make effective and lasting alterations in his or her life. To highlight the change the person made, start by showing what the person's life was like before it was turned around.

4. Sanders shows how he broke through the "warrior or toiler" legacy by making it to college. What is one undesirable legacy that you've moved beyond in your own life? Write an essay that explores the *causes* for your breaking through such a significant barrier. You might discuss an overt departure, such as being the first in your family to attend college, pursue a different career path, and so on. Or you might prefer to discuss a less tangible parting of ways, such as adopting less racist or sexist attitudes than members of your family or community. Either way, be sure to explain the context for your breakthrough and the reasons why you sought to do so. Along the way, be sure to provide *examples* illustrating the attitudes or expectations from which you diverged.

Writing Assignments Using a Journal Entry as a Starting Point

5. Since the time Sanders was in college, gender roles have become somewhat less rigid. For example, no one is surprised to see a man pushing a stroller or a woman delivering the mail. What gender-role changes do you observe as having occurred in your lifetime? Do you think the changes have been for the better? Review your pre-reading journal entry and select one area that you explored. Then write an essay showing that increased flexibility in gender roles has affected men's or women's (or boys' or girls') lives in either a positive or a negative way. Provide clear examples that illustrate your attitude toward these changes. You might also consider supplementing your observations with research on the subject conducted in the library or online.

DAVID BROOKS

David Brooks is a syndicated columnist whose work appears in newspapers throughout the nation. He was born in 1961 and graduated from the University of Chicago with a degree in history in 1983. Brooks began his journalism career as a police reporter for the City News Bureau in Chicago and then spent nine years at *The Wall Street Journal* as a critic, foreign correspondent, and op-ed page editor. In 1995, he joined *The Weekly Standard* at its inception, and in 2003 he began to write a regular column for *The New York Times*. Brooks is interested in cultural as well as political issues, and he often is on National Public Radio, including *The Diane Rehm Show*, as an analyst. He has written two books, *Bobos in Paradise: The New Upper Class and How They Got There (2000)* and *On Paradise Drive: How We Live Now (and Always Have) in the Future Tense (2004)*. He is editor of the anthology *Backward and Upward: The New Conservative Writing.* This column was published in *The New York Times* on November 13, 2005.

Pre-Reading Journal Entry

When you are a student, it's natural to think of success and failure simply in terms of grades. However, academic accomplishment is not the only measure of success in one's life. What are your own strengths and successes in life, beyond what you may have achieved in school? Who or what has inspired you to undertake each of these pursuits? Take a few minutes to respond to these questions in your journal.

PSST! "HUMAN CAPITAL"

1 Help! I'm turning into the "plastics" guy from *The Graduate*.[1] I'm pulling people aside at parties and whispering that if they want to understand the future, it's just two words: "Human Capital."

2 If we want to keep up with the Chinese and the Indians, we've got to develop our Human Capital. If we want to remain a just, fluid society: Human Capital. If we want to head off underclass riots: Human Capital.

3 As people drift away from me at these parties by pretending to recognize long-lost friends across the room, I'm convinced that they don't really understand what human capital is.

4 Most people think of human capital the way economists and policy makers do—as the skills and knowledge people need to get jobs and thrive in a modern economy. When President [George W.] Bush proposed his big education reform, he insisted on tests to measure skills and knowledge. When commissions issue reports, they call for longer school years, revamped curriculums and more funds so teachers can transmit skills and knowledge.

5 But skills and knowledge—the stuff you can measure with tests—is only the most superficial component of human capital. U.S. education reforms have generally failed because they try to improve the skills of students without addressing the underlying components of human capital.

6 These underlying components are hard to measure and uncomfortable to talk about, but they are the foundation of everything that follows.

7 There's cultural capital: the habits, assumptions, emotional dispositions and linguistic capacities we unconsciously pick up from families, neighbors and ethnic groups—usually by age 3. In a classic study, James S. Coleman found that what happens in the family shapes a child's educational achievement more than what happens in school. In more recent research, James Heckman and Pedro Carneiro found that "most of the gaps in college attendance and delay are determined by early family factors."

8 There's social capital: the knowledge of how to behave in groups and within institutions. This can mean, for example, knowing what to do if your community college loses your transcript. Or it can mean knowing the basic rules of politeness. The University of North Carolina now offers seminars to poorer students so they'll know how to behave in restaurants.

9 There's moral capital: the ability to be trustworthy. Students who drop out of high school, but take the G.E.D. exam, tend to be smarter than high school dropouts. But their lifetime wages tend to be no higher than they are for those with

---

[1]Refers to an oft-cited scene in the 1967 film, *The Graduate*. The main character, Benjamin Braddock, has just graduated college and feels adrift about the future. At a family party, the character of Mr. McGuire cryptically "tips off" Benjamin about the plastics industry. He says, "There's great future in plastics. Think about it. Will you think about it? . . . Shh! Enough said." (editors' note).

no high school diplomas. That's because many people who pass the G.E.D. are less organized and less dependable than their less educated peers—as employers soon discover. Brains and skills don't matter if you don't show up on time.

10 There's cognitive capital. This can mean pure, inherited brainpower. But important cognitive skills are not measured by IQ tests and are not fixed. Some people know how to evaluate themselves and their abilities, while others with higher IQ's are clueless. Some low-IQ people can sense what others are feeling, while brainier peers cannot. Such skills can be improved over a lifetime.

11 Then there's aspirational capital: the fire-in-the-belly ambition to achieve. In his book *The Millionaire Mind*, Thomas J. Stanley reports that the average millionaire had a B-minus collegiate G.P.A.—not very good. But millionaires often had this experience: People told them they were too stupid to achieve something, so they set out to prove the naysayers wrong.

12 Over the past quarter-century, researchers have done a lot of work trying to understand the different parts of human capital. Their work has been almost completely ignored by policy makers, who continue to treat human capital as just skills and knowledge. The result? A series of expensive policy failures.

13 We now spend more per capita on education than just about any other country on earth, and the results are mediocre. No Child Left Behind treats students as skill-acquiring cogs in an economic wheel, and the results have been disappointing. We pour money into Title 1 and Head Start, but the long-term gains are insignificant.

14 These programs are not designed for the way people really are. The only things that work are local, human-to-human immersions that transform the students down to their very beings. Extraordinary schools, which create intense cultures of achievement, work. Extraordinary teachers, who inspire students to transform their lives, work. The programs that work touch all the components of human capital.

15 There's a great future in Human Capital, buddy. Enough said.

Questions for Close Reading

1. What is the selection's thesis? Locate the sentence(s) in which Brooks states his main idea. If he doesn't state his thesis explicity, express it in your own words.

2. According to Brooks, why do policies that focus on teaching children skills and knowledge ultimately fail to develop human capital? What policies does he use as examples of such failure?

3. In Brooks's view, what role does the family play in the development of human capital?

4. What type of human capital do many millionaires possess, and how did they acquire it?

5. Refer to your dictionary as needed to define the following words used in the selection: *capital* (paragraph 1), *revamped* (4), *cognitive* (10), *aspirational* (11), *naysayers* (11), *per capita* (13), and *immersions* (14).

Questions About the Writer's Craft

1. Brooks opens this essay by comparing himself to a character in the 1967 movie *The Graduate*. What are the benefits and risks of using such a reference to frame the contents of an essay? In your opinion, is this a successful opening? Why or why not?
2. **The pattern.** How does Brooks organize his explanation of what human capital really consists of? What cues guide the reader in following Brooks's discussion?
3. **Other patterns.** In paragraphs 7 through 11, Brooks develops his ideas about the components of human capital. What patterns does he use in each of these paragraphs?
4. This essay was published as a newspaper op-ed column, a type of writing that is relatively short—about 750 words. How does the limited length of the piece affect the development of Brooks's ideas and evidence? If the piece were longer, how could Brooks strengthen its argument?

Writing Assignments Using Division-Classification as a Pattern of Development

1. Choose one of the elements of human capital that Brooks describes, and write an essay in which you *divide* it further into its component parts. For example, if you choose cognitive capital, you can write about specific cognitive skills such as memorizing, learning, problem solving, and creativity.
2. According to economists, capital is any human-made resource used to produce goods and services. For example, capital includes buildings, factories, machinery, equipment, parts, tools, roads, and railroads. Do some research on the concept of capital as used by economists, and write an essay *explaining* how economists categorize various types of capital, including the human capital Brooks discusses in his essay.

Writing Assignments Combining Patterns of Development

3. Brooks indicates that the results of the government programs No Child Left Behind, Title I, and Head Start fail to improve human capital. Select one of these programs, and do some research on it at the library or on the Internet. Write an essay that *explains* how aspects of the program are designed to solve specific problems. *Compare* and *contrast* the goals of the program with its actual *effects*.
4. Brooks's concept of moral capital is closely tied to the moral values that society holds important and that children learn from their families and others

with whom they interact. Write an essay in which you *narrate* the story of a moral issue you have faced, *comparing* and *contrasting* the choices you had. Explain the *process* you went through to resolve the problem.

Writing Assignment Using a Journal Entry as a Starting Point

5. Review your pre-reading journal entry about your successes and strengths beyond what you may have achieved in school. Select the two or three most significant ones, and write an essay in which you divide and classify these achievements. Are these achievements athletic, artistic, or service- or family-oriented—or do they belong to some other category? As you write about each achievement, consider who or what has *caused* or inspired you to strive for that accomplishment. To see how other writers address the issue of how children's character can be influenced, read Ellen Goodman's "Family Counterculture" (page 6), Gordon Parks's "Flavio's Home" (page 182), and Buzz Bissinger's "Innocents Afield" (page 407).

ADDITIONAL WRITING TOPICS: DIVISION-CLASSIFICATION

General Assignments

Choose one of the following subjects and write an essay developed wholly or in part through division-classification. Start by determining the purpose of the essay. Do you want to inform, compare and contrast, or persuade? Apply a single, significant principle of division or classification to your subject. Don't switch the principle midway through your analysis. Also, be sure that the types or categories you create are as complete and mutually exclusive as possible.

Division

1. A shopping mall
2. A video and/or stereo system
3. A particular kind of team
4. A school library
5. A playground, gym, or other recreational area
6. A significant event
7. A college campus
8. A meeting

9. A basement or attic
10. A television show or movie

Classification

1. People in a waiting room
2. Parents
3. Holidays
4. Roommates
5. Students in a class
6. Summer movies
7. College courses
8. Television watchers
9. Commercials
10. Computer or Internet users

Assignments with a Specific Purpose, Audience, and Point of View

On Campus

1. You're a dorm counselor. During orientation week, you'll be talking to students on your floor about the different kinds of problems they may have with roommates. Write your talk, describing each kind of problem and explaining how to cope.

2. As your college newspaper's TV critic, you plan to write a review of the fall shows, most of which—in your opinion—lack originality. To show how stereotypical the programs are, select one type (for example, situation comedies or crime dramas). Then use a specific division-classification principle to illustrate that the same stale formulas are trotted out from show to show.

3. Asked to write an editorial for the campus paper, you decide to do a half-serious piece on taking "mental health" days off from classes. Structure your essay around three kinds of occasions when "playing hooky" is essential for maintaining sanity.

At Home or in the Community

4. Your favorite magazine runs an editorial asking readers to send in what they think are the main challenges facing their particular gender group. Write a letter to the editor in which you identify at least three categories of problems that

your sex faces. Be sure to provide lively, specific examples to illustrate each category. In your letter, you may adopt a serious or lighthearted tone, depending on your overall subject matter.

On the Job

5. As a driving instructor, you decide to prepare a lecture on the types of drivers that your students are likely to encounter on the road. In your lecture, categorize drivers according to a specific principle and show the behaviors of each type.

6. A seasoned camp counselor, you've been asked to prepare, for new counselors, an informational sheet on children's emotional needs. Categorizing those needs into types, explain what counselors can do to nurture youngsters emotionally.

For additional writing, reading, and research resources, go to **www.mycomplab.com** and choose **Nadell/Langan/Comodromos'** ***The Longman Writer,*** **7/e**.

Process Analysis

14

What Is Process Analysis?

Angelo Cavalli/The Image Bank/Getty Images

Perhaps you've noticed the dogged determination of small children when they're learning how to do something new. Whether trying to tie their shoelaces or tell time, little children struggle along, creating knotted tangles, confusing the hour with the minute hand. But they don't give up. Mastering such basic skills makes them feel less dependent on the adults of the world—all of whom seem to know how to do everything. Actually, none of us is born knowing how to do very much. We spend a good deal of our lives learning—everything from speaking our first word to balancing our first bank statement. Indeed, the milestones in our lives are often linked to the processes we have mastered: how to cross the street alone; how to drive a car; how to make a speech without being paralyzed by fear.

Process analysis, a technique that explains the steps or sequence involved in doing something, satisfies our need to learn as well as our curiosity about how the world works. All the self-help books flooding the market today (*Managing Stress, How to Make a Million in Real Estate, Ten Days to a Perfect Body*) are examples of process analysis. The instructions on the federal tax form and the recipes in a cookbook are also process analyses. Several television classics, now seen in reruns, capitalize on our desire to learn how things happen: *The Wild Kingdom* shows how animals survive in faraway lands, and *Mission: Impossible* has great fun detailing elaborate plans for preventing the triumph of evil. Process analysis can be more than merely interesting or entertaining, though; it can be of critical importance. Consider a waiter hurriedly skimming the "Choking Aid" instructions posted on a restaurant wall or an air-traffic controller following emergency procedures in an effort to prevent a midair collision. In these last examples, the consequences could be fatal if the process analyses are slipshod, inaccurate, or confusing.

Undoubtedly, all of us have experienced less dramatic effects of poorly written process analyses. Perhaps you've tried to assemble a bicycle and spent hours sorting through a stack of parts, only to end up with one or two extra pieces never mentioned in the instructions. Or maybe you were baffled when putting up a set of wall shelves because the instructions used unfamiliar terms like *mitered cleat, wing nut,* and *dowel pin.* No wonder many people stay clear of anything that actually admits "assembly required."

HOW PROCESS ANALYSIS FITS YOUR PURPOSE AND AUDIENCE

You will use process analysis in two types of writing situations: (1) when you want to give step-by-step instructions to readers showing how they can do something, or (2) when you want readers to understand how something happens even though they won't actually follow the steps outlined. The first kind of process analysis is **directional;** the second is **informational.**

When you look at the cooking instructions on a package of frozen vegetables or follow guidelines for completing a job application, you're reading directional process analysis. A serious essay explaining how to select a college and a humorous essay telling readers how to get on the good side of a professor are also examples of directional process analysis. Using a variety of tones, informational process analyses can range over equally diverse subjects; they can describe mechanical, scientific, historical, sociological, artistic, or psychological processes: for example, how the core of a nuclear power plant melts down; how television became so important in political campaigns; how abstract painters use color; how to survive a blind date.

Process analysis, both directional and informational, is often appropriate in *problem-solving situations.* In such cases, you say, "Here's the problem and here's what should be done to solve the problem." Indeed, college assignments frequently take the form of problem-solving process analyses. Consider these examples:

> Because many colleges and universities have changed the eligibility requirements for financial aid, fewer students can depend on loans or scholarships. How can students cope with the increasing costs of obtaining a higher education?

> Over the years, there have been many reports citing the abuse of small children in day-care centers. What can parents do to guard against the mistreatment of their children?
>
> Community officials have been accused of mismanaging recent unrest over the public housing ordinance. Describe the steps the officials took, indicating why you think their strategy was unwise. Then explain how you think the situation should have been handled.

Note that the last assignment asks students to explain what's wrong with the current approach before they present their own step-by-step solution. Problem-solving process analyses are often organized in this way. You may also have noticed that none of the assignments explicitly requires an essay response using process analysis. However, the wording of the assignments—"*Describe the steps,*" "*What* can parents *do,*" "*How* can students *cope*"—indicates that process analysis would be an appropriate strategy for developing the responses.

Assignments don't always signal the use of process analysis so clearly. But during the prewriting stage, as you generate material to support your thesis, you'll often realize that you can best achieve your purpose by developing the essay—or part of it—using process analysis.

Sometimes process analysis will be the primary strategy for organizing an essay; other times it will be used to help make a point in an essay organized around another pattern of development. Let's take a look at process analysis as a supporting strategy.

Assume that you're writing a *causal analysis* examining the impact of television commercials on people's buying behavior. To help readers see that commercials create a need where none existed before, you might describe the various stages in an advertising campaign to pitch a new, completely frivolous product. In an essay *defining* a good boss, you could convey the point that effective managers must be skilled at settling disputes by explaining the steps your boss took to resolve a heated disagreement between two employees. If you write an *argumentation-persuasion* paper urging the funding of programs to ease the plight of the homeless, you would have to dramatize for readers the tragedy of these people's lives. To achieve your purpose, you could devote part of the paper to an explanation of how the typical street person goes about finding a place to sleep and getting food to eat.

At this point, you have a good sense of the way writers use process analysis to achieve their purpose and to connect with their readers. Now take a moment to look closely at the photograph of the brand-new mall at the beginning of this chapter. Imagine you're writing an article, accompanied by the photo, for a local newspaper. Your purpose is to suggest to local store owners, who are losing business to the new mall, ways they might attract more customers to the area's downtown shopping district. Jot down some ideas you might include in a *process analysis* explaining the steps the business owners should take.

Prewriting Strategies

The following checklist shows how you can apply to process analysis some of the prewriting strategies discussed in Chapter 2.

☑ PROCESS ANALYSIS: A PREWRITING CHECKLIST

Choose a Process to Analyze

- ☐ What processes do you know well and feel you can explain clearly (for example, how to jog without injury, how lobbyists influence legislators)?
- ☐ What processes have you wondered about (how to meditate; how the greenhouse effect works)?
- ☐ What process needs changing if a current problem is to be solved?

Determine Your Purpose, Audience, Tone, and Point of View

- ☐ What is the central purpose of your process analysis? Do you want to inform readers so that they will acquire a new skill (how to buy a used car)? Do you want readers to gain a better understanding of a complex process (how young children develop a conscience)? Do you want to persuade readers to accept your point of view about a process, perhaps even urge them to adopt a particular course of action ("If you disagree with the proposed plan for reorganizing academic advisement, you should take the following steps to register your protest with college officials")?
- ☐ What audience are you writing for? What will they need to know to understand the process? What will they not need to know?
- ☐ What point of view will you adopt when addressing the audience?
- ☐ What tone do you want to project? Do you want to come across as serious, humorous, sarcastic, ironic, objective, impassioned?

Use Prewriting to Generate the Stages of the Process

- ☐ How could brainstorming or mapping help you identify primary and secondary steps in the process?
- ☐ How could brainstorming or mapping help you identify the ingredients or materials that the reader will need?

Strategies for Using Process Analysis in an Essay

After prewriting, you're ready to draft your essay. Figure 14.1 and the suggestions that follow will be helpful whether you use process analysis as a dominant or supportive pattern of development.

FIGURE 14.1
Development Diagram: Writing a Process Analysis Essay

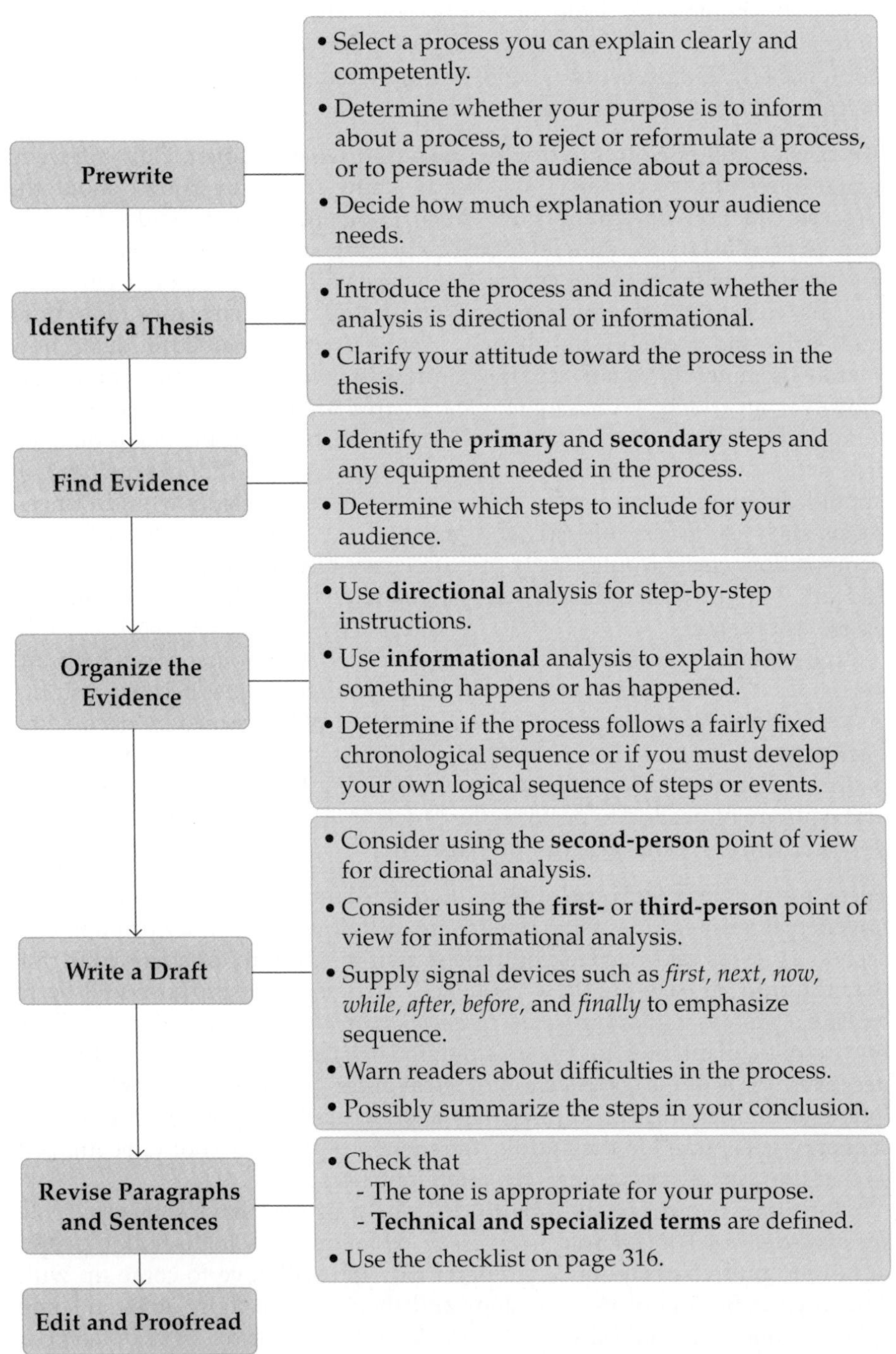

1. **Formulate a thesis that clarifies your attitude toward the process.** Like the thesis in any other paper, the thesis in a process analysis should do more than announce your subject ("Here's how the college's work-study program operates"). It should also state or imply your attitude toward the process: "Enrolling in the college's work-study program has become unnecessarily complicated. The procedure could be simplified if the college adopted the helpful guidelines prepared by the Student Senate."

2. **Keep your audience in mind when deciding what to cover.** Only after you gauge how much your readers already know (or don't know) about the process can you determine how much explanation to provide. Suppose you've been asked to write an article informing students of the best way to use the university computer center. The article will be published in a newsletter for computer science majors. You would seriously misjudge your audience—and probably put them to sleep—if you explained in detail how to transfer material from disk to disk or how to delete information from a file. However, an article on the same topic prepared for a general audience—your composition class, for instance—would probably require such detailed instructions. The audience's level of knowledge also determines whether you should define technical terms. The computer science majors wouldn't need terms such as *modem, interface,* and *byte* defined, whereas students in your composition class would likely require easy-to-understand explanations. Indeed, with any general audience, you should use as little specialized language as possible.

   To determine how much explanation is needed, put yourself in your readers' shoes. Don't assume readers will know something just because you do. Ask questions like these about your audience: "Will my readers need some background about the process before I describe it in depth?" and "If my essay is directional, should I specify near the beginning the ingredients, materials, and equipment needed to perform the process?" (For more help in analyzing your audience, see the checklist on page 310.)

3. **Focusing on your purpose, thesis, and audience, explain the process—one step at a time.** After using prewriting techniques to identify primary and secondary steps and needed equipment, you're ready to organize your raw material into an easy-to-follow sequence. At times your purpose will be to explain a process with a *fairly fixed chronological sequence:* how to make a pizza, how to pot a plant, how to change a tire. In such cases, you should include all necessary steps in the correct chronological order. However, if a strict chronological ordering of steps means that a particularly important part of the sequence gets buried in the middle, the sequence probably should be juggled so that the crucial step receives the attention it deserves.

   Other times your goal will be to describe a process having *no commonly accepted sequence.* For example, in an essay explaining how to discipline a child or how to pull yourself out of a blue mood, you will have to come up with your own definition of the key steps and then arrange those steps in some logical order. You may also use process analysis to *reject* or *reformulate* a traditional sequence. In this case, you would propose a more logical series of steps: "Our system for electing congressional representatives is inefficient and undemocratic; it should be reformed in the following ways."

Whether the essay describes a generally agreed-on process or one that is not commonly accepted, you must provide all the details needed to explain the process. Your readers should be able to understand, even visualize, the process. There should be no fuzzy patches or confusing cuts from one step to another. Don't, however, go into obsessive detail about minor stages or steps. If you dwell for several hundred words on how to butter the pan, your readers will never stay with you long enough to learn how to make the omelet.

It's not unusual, especially in less defined sequences, for some steps in a process to occur simultaneously and to overlap. When this happens, you should present the steps in the most logical order, being sure to tell your readers that several steps are not perfectly distinct and may merge. For example, in an essay explaining how a species becomes extinct, you would have to indicate that overpopulation of hardy strains and destruction of endangered breeds are often simultaneous events. You would also need to clarify that the depletion of food sources both precedes and follows the demise of a species.

4. **Sort out the directional and informational aspects of the process analysis.** As you may have discovered when prewriting, directional and informational process analyses are not always distinct. In fact, they may be complementary: You may need to provide background information about a process before outlining its steps. For example, in a paper describing a step-by-step approach for losing weight, you might first need to explain how the body burns calories. Or, in a paper on gardening, you could provide some theory about the way organic fertilizers work before detailing a plan for growing vegetables. Although both approaches may be appropriate in a paper, one generally predominates.

   The kind of process analysis chosen has implications for the way you will relate to your reader. When the process analysis is *directional*, the reader is addressed in the *second person:* "You should first rinse the residue from the radiator by . . . " or "Wrap the injured person in a blanket and then . . . " (In the second example, the pronoun *you* is implied.)

   If the process analysis has an *informational* purpose, you won't address the reader directly but will choose from a number of other options. For example, you might use the *first person.* In a humorous essay explaining how not to prepare for finals, you could cite your own disastrous study habits: "Filled with good intentions, I sit on my bed, pick up a pencil, open my notebook, and promptly fall asleep." The *third-person singular or plural* can also be used in informational process essays: "The door-to-door salesperson walks up the front walk, heart pounding, more than a bit nervous, but also challenged by the prospect of striking a deal," or "The new recruits next underwent a series of important balance tests in what was called the 'horror chamber.'" Whether you use the first, second, or third person, avoid shifting point of view midstream.

You might have noticed that in the third-person examples, the present tense ("walks up") is used in one sentence, the past tense ("underwent") in the other. The past tense is appropriate for events already completed, whereas the present tense is used for habitual or ongoing actions. ("A dominant male goose usually flies at the head of the V-wedge during migration.") The present tense is also effective when you want to lend a sense of dramatic immediacy to a process, even if the steps were performed in the past. ("The surgeon gently separates the facial skin and muscle from the underlying bony skull.") As with point of view, be on guard against changing tenses in the middle of your explanation.

5. **Provide readers with the help they need to follow the sequence.** As you move through the steps of a process analysis, don't forget to *warn readers about difficulties* they might encounter. For example, in a paper on the artistry involved in butterflying a shrimp, you might write something like this:

    Next, make a shallow cut with your sharpened knife along the convex curve of the shrimp's intestinal tract. The tract, usually a faint black line along the outside curve of the shrimp, is faintly visible beneath the translucent flesh. But some shrimp have a thick orange, blue, or gray line instead of a thin black one. In all cases, be careful not to slice too deeply, or you will end up with two shrimp halves instead of one butterflied shrimp.

    You have told readers what to look for, citing the exceptions, and have warned them against making too deep a cut. Anticipating spots where communication might break down is a key part of writing an effective process analysis.

    Transitional words and phrases are also critical in helping readers understand the order of the steps being described. Time signals like *first, next, now, while, after, before,* and *finally* provide readers with a clear sense of the sequence. Entire sentences can also be used to link parts of the process, reminding your audience of what has already been discussed and indicating what will now be explained: "Once the panel of experts finishes its evaluation of the exam questions, randomly selected items are field-tested in schools throughout the country."

6. **Select and maintain an appropriate tone.** When writing a process analysis essay, be sure your tone is consistent with your purpose, your attitude toward your subject, and the effect you want to have on readers. When explaining how fraternities and sororities recruit new members, do you want to use an objective, nonjudgmental tone, or do you want to project an angry, even accusatory tone? To decide, take into account readers' attitudes toward your subject. Does your audience have a financial or emotional investment in the process being described? Does your own interest in the process coincide or conflict with that of your audience? Awareness of your readers' stance can be

crucial. Consider another example: Assume you're writing a letter to the director of the student health center proposing a new system to replace the currently chaotic one. You'd do well to be tactful in your criticisms. Offend your reader, and your cause is lost. If, however, the letter is slated for the college newspaper and directed primarily to other students, you could adopt a more pointed, even sarcastic tone. Readers, you would assume, will probably share your view and favor change.

Once you settle on the essay's tone, maintain it throughout. If you're writing a light piece on the way computers are taking over our lives, you wouldn't include a grim, step-by-step analysis of the way confidential computerized medical records may become public.

7. **Open and close the process analysis effectively.** A paper developed primarily through process analysis should have a strong beginning. The introduction should state the process to be described and imply whether the essay has an informational or directional intent.

If you suspect readers are indifferent to your subject, use the introduction to motivate them, telling them how important the subject is:

> Do you enjoy the salad bars found in many restaurants? If you do, you probably have noticed that the vegetables are always crisp and fresh—no matter how many hours they have been exposed to the air. What are the restaurants doing to make the vegetables look so inviting? There's a simple answer. Many restaurants dip and spray the vegetables with potent chemicals to make them look appetizing.

If you think your audience may be intimidated by your subject (perhaps because it's complex or relatively obscure), the introduction is the perfect spot to reassure them that the process being described is not beyond their grasp:

> Studies show that many people prefer to accept a defective product rather than deal with the uncomfortable process of making a complaint. But once a few easy-to-learn basics are mastered, anyone can register a complaint that gets results.

Most process analysis essays don't end as soon as the last step in the sequence is explained. Instead, they usually include some brief final comments that round out the piece and bring it to a satisfying close. This final section of the essay may summarize the main steps in the process—not by repeating the steps verbatim but by rephrasing and condensing them in several concise sentences. The conclusion can also be an effective spot to underscore the significance of the process, recalling what may have been said in the introduction about the subject's importance. Or the essay can end by echoing the note of reassurance that may have been included at the start.

REVISION STRATEGIES

Once you have a draft of the essay, you're ready to revise. The following checklist will help you and those giving you feedback apply to process analysis some of the revision techniques discussed in Chapters 7 and 8.

PROCESS ANALYSIS: A REVISION/PEER REVIEW CHECKLIST

Revise Overall Meaning and Structure

- ☐ What purpose does the process analysis serve—to inform, to persuade, or to do both?
- ☐ Is the process analysis primarily *directional* or *informational*? How can you tell?
- ☐ Where does the process seem confusing? Where have steps been left out? Which steps need simplifying?
- ☐ What is the essay's tone? Is the tone appropriate for the essay's purpose and readers? Where are there distracting shifts in tone?

Revise Paragraph Development

- ☐ Does the introduction specify the process to be described? Does it provide an overview? Should it?
- ☐ Which paragraphs are difficult to follow? Have any steps or materials been omitted or explained in too much or too little detail? Which paragraphs should warn readers about potential trouble spots or overlapping steps?
- ☐ Where are additional time signals (*after, before, next*) needed to clarify the sequence within and between paragraphs? Where does overreliance on time signals make the sequence awkward and mechanical?
- ☐ Which paragraph describes the most crucial step in the sequence? How has the step been highlighted?
- ☐ How could the conclusion be more effective?

Revise Sentences and Words

- ☐ What technical or specialized terms appear in the essay? Have they been sufficiently explained? Where could simpler, less technical language be used?
- ☐ Are there any places where the essay's point of view awkwardly shifts? How could this problem be corrected?
- ☐ Does the essay use correct verb tenses—the past tense for completed events, the present tense for habitual or ongoing actions?
- ☐ Where does the essay use the passive voice ("The hole is dug")? Would the active voice ("You dig the hole") be more effective?

STUDENT ESSAY: FROM PREWRITING THROUGH REVISION

The student essay that follows was written by Robert Barry in response to this assignment:

> In "Black Talk and Pop Culture," Leslie Savan describes how the language of African-Americans has infiltrated, if not dominated, the language of the general population. Think of something that is relatively new in our culture and show, step-by-step, how it has worked its way into everyday life. Your essay, either serious or light in tone, might focus on a form of entertainment, a pastime, an invention, or the like.

Before writing his essay, Robert used the prewriting strategy of *mapping* to generate material for the subject he decided to write on: DVR addiction. Then, with his map as a foundation, he prepared a topic outline that organized and developed his thoughts more fully. Both the map and the outline are reprinted here.

Mapping

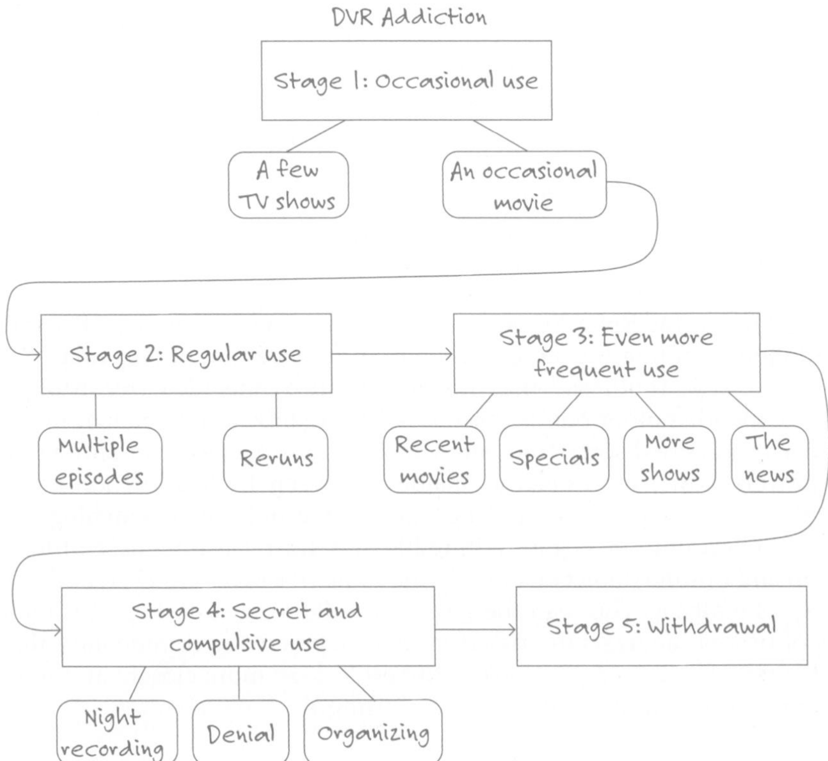

Outline

Thesis: Without realizing it, a person can turn into a compulsive recorder. This movement from innocent hobby to full-blown addiction occurs in several stages.

I. Stage One: Occasional use
   A. TV show reruns
      1. *Seinfeld*
      2. *The Simpsons*
   B. An occasional movie

II. Stage Two: More frequent use
   A. Many episodes of *Seinfeld* and *The Sopranos*
   B. Episodes of *Heroes*, *The Simpsons*, and *Grey's Anatomy*

III. Stage Three: Much more frequent use
   A. Recording of news shows
   B. Recording of recent movies—add examples
   C. Not enough time to watch recorded shows

IV. Stage Four: Secret and compulsive use
   A. Reaction to family's concern
      1. Denial
      2. Sneaking downstairs to record at night
   B. Obsessive organization of recording schedule

V. Stage Five: Withdrawal
   A. Forced withdrawal at college
   B. Success at last

After looking at Robert's map and outline, read his paper, "Becoming a Recordoholic," noting the similarities and differences among his map, outline, and final essay. You'll see that Robert dropped one idea (recording news shows), expanded other points (his obsessive organization by means of a secret calendar), and added some completely new details (his near backsliding during withdrawal). Note, too, that the analogy between DVR addiction and alcoholism doesn't appear in either the map or the outline. The analogy didn't occur to Robert until he began writing his first draft. Despite these differences, the map and outline depict essentially the same five stages in DVR addiction as the essay. Finally, as you read the essay, consider how well it applies the principles of process analysis discussed in this chapter. (The commentary that follows the paper will help you look at Robert's essay more closely and will give you some sense of how he went about revising.)

Becoming a Recordoholic
by Robert Barry

1 As a technological breakthrough, the DVR (Digital Video Recorder) has been an enormous success—almost as popular as television itself. Not only can you watch TV while you record other programs but you can pause and rewind live TV. Better yet, you can program the DVR to record a roster of programs—even entire seasons—with a simple push of a button. No consumer warning labels are attached to this ingenious invention,DVRs but there should be. DVRs can be dangerous. Barely aware of what is happening, a person can turn into a compulsive recorder. The descent from innocent hobby to full-blown addiction takes place in several stages.

Introduction

Start of two-sentence thesis

2 In the first innocent stage, the unsuspecting person buys a DVR for occasional use. I was at this stage when I asked my parents if they would buy me a DVR as a birthday gift. With the DVR, I could record reruns of *Seinfeld* and new episodes of *The Simpsons* while watching *Grey's Anatomy*. The DVR was perfect. I hooked it up to the TV in my bedroom; recorded the antics of Jerry, Elaine, George, and Kramer and the adventures of my favorite cartoon family, while watching the residents of Seattle Grace save lives and make utter fools of themselves. Occasionally,I'd DVR a movie, which my friends and I watched over the weekend. I recorded only a few shows, and once I watched those shows, I'd delete then from the DVR. In these early days, my use of the DVR was the equivalent of light social drinking.

Topic sentence

First stage in process (DVR addiction)

Beginning of analogy to alcoholism

3 In the second phase on the road to recordoholism, an individual uses the DVR more frequently and begins to stockpile recordings rather than watch them. My troubles began in July when my family and I went to the shore for two weeks of vacation. I set my DVR to record all five episodes of *Seinfeld* and *The Sopranos*, and two episodes each of *Heroes*, *The Simpsons*, and *Grey's Anatomy*, while I was at the beach working on my tan. Even I, an avid TV viewer, didn't have time to sit and watch all those shows. The DVR continued to record these programs, but there weren't enough hours in the day to watch everything and do my schoolwork, so the programs piled up in my DVR queue. How did I

Topic sentence

Second stage in process

resolve this problem? Very easily. I set my DVR to record episodes of *Seinfeld* three days a week, rather then five. However, with this notion that I had such control with my DVR, I began to realize that there were probably other shows out there that I could record and watch whereever I desired. I could DVR classics like *Law & Order* and *Buffy the Vampire Slayer*. Very quickly, I accumulated six *Seinfelds*, four *Law & Orders*, and three *Buffy*s. Then a friend—who shall go nameless—told me that only 144 episodes of *Buffy* were ever made. Excited by the thought that I could acquire as impressive a collection of episodes as a Hollywood executive, I continued recording *Buffy*, even recording shows while I watched them. Clearly, my once innocent hobby was getting out of control. I was now using the DVR on a regular basis—the equivalent of several stiff drinks a day.

Continuation of analogy

Topic sentence

Third stage in process

In the third stage of recordoholism, the amount of recording increases significantly, leading to an even more irrational stockpiling of programs in the DVR queue. The catalyst that propelled me into this third stage was my parents' decision to get a premium movie package added to their cable. Selfless guy that I am, I volunteered to move my DVR in to the living room, where the connection was located. Now I could record all the most recent movies and specials. I began to record a couple of other shows every day. I also went movie-crazy and taped *Gangs of New York*, *Barbershop 2*, and *The Godfather I*, *II*, and *III*. I taped an HBO comedy special with Chris Rock and an MTV concert featuring Radiohead. Where did I get time to watch all these shows? I didn't. Using the DVR was more satisfying than watching. Reason and common sense were abandoned. Getting things on the DVR had become an obsession, and I was setting the DVR to record programs all the time. 4

Continuation of analogy

Topic sentence

Fourth stage in process

In the fourth stage, recordoholism creeps into other parts of the addict's life, influencing behavior in strange ways. Secrecy becomes commonplace. One day, my mother came into my room and asked about a recent test I had taken. What she didn't know was that the night before the exam, I had checked my DVR recording list and found that I had run out of storage space. For three hours after everyone went to bed, I watched episodes of *The Sopranos* so I could delete them and record a movie on Showtime. I was so tired the next morning that I wound up getting a bad grade 5 on my Biology exam. "Robert," my mother exclaimed, "isn't this getting a bit out of hand?" I assured her it was just a hobby, but I continued to sneak downstairs in the middle of the night to watch recorded shows, removing any trace of my presence from the living room when I was finished. Also, denial is not unusual during this stage of DVR addiction. At the dinner table, when my younger sister commented, "Robert records all the time," I laughingly told everyone—including myself—that the recording was no big deal. I was getting bored with it and was going to stop any day, I assured my family. Obsessive behavior also characterizes the fourth stage of recordoholism. Each week, I pulled out the TV magazine from the Sunday paper and went through it carefully, circling in red all the shows I wanted to record. Another sign of addiction was the secret calender I kept in my desk drawer. With more diligence than I ever had for any term paper, I would log in each program I recorded and plan for the coming week's recording schedule.

Continuation of analogy

6 In the final stage of an addiction, the individual either succumbs completely to the addiction or is able to break away from the habit. I broke my addiction, and I broke it cold turkey. This total withdrawal occurred when I went off to college. There was no point in taking my DVR to school because TVs were not allowed in the freshman dorms. Even though there were many things to occupy my time during the school week, cold sweats overcame me whenever I thought about everything on TV I was not recording. I even considered calling home and asking members of my family to record things for me, but I knew they would think I was crazy. At the beginning of the semester, I also had to resist the overwhelming desire to travel the three hours home every weekend so I could get my fix. But after a while, the urgent need to record subsided. Now, months later, as I write this, I feel detached and sober.

Topic sentence

Continuation of analogy

Final stage in process

7 I have no illusions, though. I know that once a recordoholic, always a recordoholic. Soon I will return home for the holidays, which, as everyone knows, can be a time for excess eating—and recording. But I will cope with the pressure. I will take each day one at a time. I plan to watch what I'm able to, and no more. And if I feel myself succumbing to the temptations of recording, I will pick up the telephone and dial the recordoholics' hot line: 1-800-DVR-STOP. I will win the battle.

Conclusion

Final references to analogy

Commentary

Purpose, Thesis, and Tone

Robert's essay is an example of *informational process analysis;* his purpose is to describe—rather than teach—the process of becoming a "recordoholic." The title, with its coined term *recordoholic,* tips us off that the essay is going to be entertaining. And the introductory paragraph clearly establishes the essay's playful, mock-serious tone. The tone established, Robert briefly defines the term *recordoholic* as a "compulsive recorder" and then moves to the essay's *thesis:* "Barely aware of what is happening, a person can turn into a compulsive recorder. The descent from innocent hobby to full-blown addiction takes place in several stages."

Throughout the essay, Robert sustains the introduction's humor by mocking his own motivations and poking fun at his quirks: "Selfless guy that I am, I volunteered to move my DVR" (paragraph 4), and "Working more diligently than I ever had for any term paper, I would log in each program I recorded and plan for the coming week's recording Schedule" (5). Robert probably uses a bit of *dramatic license* when reporting some of his obsessive behavior, and we, as readers, understand that he's exaggerating for comic effect. Most likely he didn't break out in a cold sweat at the thought of the TV shows he was unable to record. Nevertheless, this tinkering with the truth is legitimate because it allows Robert to create material that fits the essay's lightly satiric tone.

Organization and Topic Sentences

To meet the requirements of the assignment, Robert needed to provide a *step-by-step* explanation of a process. And because he invented the term *recordoholism,* Robert also needed to invent the stages in the progression of his addiction. During his prewriting, Robert discovered five stages in his recordoholism. Presented *chronologically,* these stages provide the organizing focus for his paper. Specifically, each supporting paragraph is devoted to one stage, with the *topic sentence* for each paragraph indicating the stage's distinctive characteristics.

Transitions

Although Robert's essay is playful, it is nonetheless a process analysis and so must have an easy-to-follow structure. Keeping this in mind, Robert wisely includes *transitions* to signal what happened at each stage of his recordoholism: "*However* with this notion that I had such control" (paragraph 3); "*Now,* I could record all the most recent movies and specials." (4); "*One day,* my mother came into my room" (5); and "*But after a while,* the urgent need to record subsided" (6). In addition to such transitions, Robert uses crisp questions to move from idea to idea within a paragraph: "How did I resolve this problem? Very easily. I set my DVR to record episodes of *Seinfeld* three days a week, rather than five" (3), and "Where did I get time to watch all these shows? I didn't" (4).

Combining Patterns of Development

Even though Robert's essay is a process analysis, it contains elements of other patterns of development. For example, his paper is unified by an *analogy*—a sustained *comparison* between Robert's recording addiction and the obviously more serious addiction to alcohol. Handled incorrectly, the analogy could have been offensive, but Robert makes the comparison work to his advantage. The analogy is stated specifically in several spots: "In these early days, my use of the DVRwas the equivalent of light social drinking" (2); "I was now using the DVR on a regular basis—the equivalent of several stiff drinks a day" (3). Finally, he generates numerous lively details or *examples* to illustrate the different stages in his addiction.

Two Unnecessary Sentences

Perhaps you noticed that Robert runs into a minor problem at the end of the fourth paragraph. Starting with the sentence, "Reason and common sense were abandoned," he begins to ramble and repeat himself. The paragraph's last two sentences fail to add anything substantial. Take a moment to read paragraph 4 aloud, omitting the last two sentences. Note how much sharper the new conclusion is: "Where did I get time to watch all these tapes? I didn't. using the DVR was more satisfying than watching." This new ending says all that needs to be said.

Revising the First Draft

When it was time to revise, Robert—in spite of his apprehension—showed his paper to his roommate and asked him to read it out loud. Robert knew this strategy would provide a more objective point of view on his work. His roommate, at first an unwilling recruit, nonetheless laughed as he read the essay aloud. That was just the response Robert wanted. But when his roommate got to the conclusion, Robert heard that the closing paragraph was flat and anticlimactic. His roommate agreed, so the two of them brainstormed ways to make the conclusion livelier and more in spirit with the rest of the essay.

Reprinted here is Robert's original conclusion. The handwritten notes, numbered in order of importance, represent both Robert's ideas for revision and those of his roommate.

Original Version of the Conclusion

I have no illusions, though, that I am over my recordoholism. Soon I will be returning home for the holidays, which can be a time for excess recording. All I can do is watch what I'm able to and not use the DVR. After that, I will hope for the best.

③ Shorten first sentence.

① Get back to analogy.

② Boring. Add humor.

As you can see, Robert and his roommate decided that the best approach would be to reinforce the playful, mock-serious tone that characterized earlier parts of the essay. Robert thus made three major changes to his conclusion. First, he tightened the first sentence of the paragraph ("I have no illusions, though, that I am over my recordoholism"), making it crisper and more dramatic: "I have no illusions, though." Second, he added a few sentences to sustain the light, self-deprecating tone he had used earlier: "I know that once a recordoholic, always a recordoholic"; "But I will cope with the pressure"; "I will win the battle." Third, and perhaps most important, he returned to the alcoholism analogy: "I will take each day one at a time. . . . And if I feel myself succumbing to the temptations of recording, I will pick up the telephone and dial the recordoholics' hotline . . . "

These weren't the only changes Robert made while reworking his paper, but they help illustrate how sensitive he was to the effect he wanted to achieve. Certainly, the recasting of the conclusion was critical to the overall success of this amusing essay.

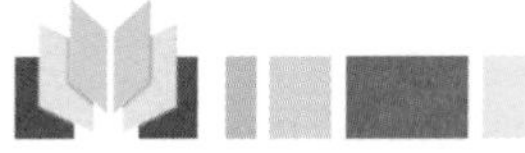

ACTIVITIES: PROCESS ANALYSIS

Prewriting Activities

1. Imagine you're writing two essays: One defines the term *comparison shopping;* the other contrasts two different teaching styles. Jot down ways you might use process analysis in each essay.

2. Look at the essay topics that follow. Assuming that your readers will be students in your composition class, which topics would lend themselves to directional process analysis, informational process analysis, or a blend of both? Explain your responses.

   a. Going on a job interview
   b. Using a computer in the college library
   c. Cleaning up oil spills
   d. Negotiating personal conflicts
   e. Curing a cold
   f. Growing vegetables organically

3. For *one* of the following essay topics, decide—given the audience indicated in parentheses—what your purpose, tone, and point of view might be. Then use brainstorming, questioning, mapping, or another prewriting technique to identify the steps you'd include in a process analysis for that audience. After reviewing the material generated, delete, add, and combine points as needed. Then organize the material in the most logical sequence.

   a. How to write effective essays (*college students*)
   b. How to get along with parents (*high school students*)
   c. How the college administration handled a controversial campus issue (*alumni*)
   d. How to deal with a bully (*elementary school children*)
   e. How a specific ceremony is performed in your religion (*an adult unfamiliar with the practice*)
   f. How malls encourage spending sprees (*general public*)

4. Select *one* of the essay topics that follow and determine what your purpose, tone, and point of view would be for each audience indicated in parentheses. Then use prewriting to identify the points you'd cover for each audience.

Finally, organize the raw material, noting the differences in emphasis and sequence for each group of readers.

a. How to buy a car (*young people who have just gotten a driver's license; established professionals*)
b. How children acquire their values (*first-time parents; elementary school teachers*)
c. How to manage money (*grade-school children; college students*)
d. How loans or scholarships are awarded to incoming students on your campus (*high school graduates applying for financial aid; high school guidance counselors*)
e. How arguments can strengthen relationships (*preteen children; young adults*)
f. How to relax (*college students; parents with young children*)

5. For *one* of the following process topics, identify an appropriate audience, purpose, tone, and point of view. Then use prewriting to generate raw material showing that there's a problem with the way the process is performed. After organizing that material, use prewriting once again—this time to identify how the process *should* be performed. Sequence this new material in a logical order.

a. How students select a college or a major
b. How local television news covers national events
c. How a specific group of people mismanage their finances
d. How your campus or your community is handling a difficult situation

Revising Activities

6. The following paragraph is from an essay making the point that over-the-phone sales can be a challenging career. The paragraph, written as a process analysis, describes the steps involved in making a sales call. Revise the paragraph, deleting any material that undermines the paragraph's unity, organizing the steps in a logical sequence, and supplying transitions where needed. Also be sure to correct any inappropriate shifts in person. Finally, do some brainstorming—individually or in a group—to generate details to bolster underdeveloped steps in the sequence.

Establishing rapport with potential customers is the most challenging part of phone sales. The longer you can keep customers on the phone, the more you can get a sense of their needs. And the more you know about customers, the more successful the salesperson is bound to be. Your opening comments are critical. After setting the right tone, you gently introduce your product. There are a number of ways you can move gracefully from your opening remarks to the actual selling phase of the call. Remember: Don't try to sell the customer at the beginning. Instead, try in a friendly way to keep the prospective customer on the phone. Maintaining such a connection is easier than you think because many people have an almost desperate need to talk. Their lives are isolated and lonely—a sad fact of contemporary life. Once you shift to the distinctly selling phase of the call, you should present the advantages of the product, especially the advantages of price and convenience. Mentioning installment payments is often effective. If the customer says that he or she isn't interested, the salesperson should try to determine—in a genial way—why the person is reluctant to buy. Don't, however, push aggressively for reasons or try to steamroll the person into thinking his or her reservations are invalid. Once the person agrees to buy, try to encourage credit card payment, rather than check or money order. The salesperson can explain that credit card payment means the customer will receive the product sooner. End the call as you began—in an easy, personable way.

7. Reprinted here is a paragraph from the first draft of a humorous essay advising shy college students how to get through a typical day. Written as a process analysis, the paragraph outlines techniques for surviving class. Revise the paragraph, deleting digressions that disrupt the paragraph's unity, eliminating unnecessary repetition, and sequencing the steps in the proper order. Also correct inappropriate shifts in person and add transitions where needed. Feel free to add any telling details.

Simply attending class can be stressful for shy people. Several strategies, though, can lessen the trauma. Shy students should time their arrival to coincide with that of most other class members—about two minutes before the class is scheduled to begin. If you arrive too early, you may be seen sitting alone or, even worse, may actually be forced to talk with another early arrival. If you arrive late, all eyes will be upon you. Before heading to class, the shy student should dress in the least conspicuous manner possible—say, in the blue jeans, sweatshirt, and sneakers that 99.9 percent of your classmates wear. That way you won't stand out from everyone else. Take a seat near the back of the room. Don't, however, sit at the very back since professors often take sadistic pleasure in calling on students back there, assuming they chose those seats because they didn't want to be called on. A friend of mine who is far from shy uses just the opposite ploy. In an attempt to get in good with her professors, she sits in the front row and, incredibly enough, volunteers to participate. However, since shy people don't want to call attention to themselves, they should stifle any urge to sneeze or cough. You run the risk of having people look at you or offer you a tissue or cough drop. And of course, never, ever volunteer to answer. Such a display of intelligence is sure to focus all eyes on you. In other words, make yourself as inconspicuous as possible. How, you might wonder, can you be inconspicuous if you're blessed (or cursed) with great looks? Well, . . . have you ever considered earning your degree through the mail?

PROFESSIONAL SELECTIONS: PROCESS ANALYSIS

CLIFFORD STOLL

An astronomer at the University of California at Berkeley, Clifford Stoll (1950–) is also a lecturer, commentator on MSNBC, and occasional visiting teacher of astronomy in elementary, middle, and high schools. He is the best-selling author of *The Cuckoo's Egg: Tracking a Spy Through the Maze of Computer Espionage* (1990) and *Silicon Snake Oil: Second Thoughts on the Information Superhighway* (1995), both of which address the complications of the computer age. As he reveals in the preface of *High-Tech Heretic: Reflections of a Computer Contrarian* (1999), despite having programmed and used computers since the mid-sixties, Stoll seeks to inject "a few notes of skepticism into the utopian dreams of a digital wonderland." According to his website, he is a "stay-at-home daddy" who lives with his family in the San Francisco Bay Area. The following essay appears as a chapter in *High-Tech Heretic*.

Please note the essay structure diagram that appears following this selection (Figure 14.2 on page 330).

Pre-Reading Journal Entry

Over the past several years, the Internet has become increasingly popular as an educational resource. What do you think are the merits and the drawbacks of including the Internet as part of school assignments? Is your response affected by the age of the students in question? Record in your journal the pros and cons of requiring students—at the elementary, high school, and college levels, respectively—to access the Net as part of their studies.

CYBERSCHOOL

Welcome to the classroom of the future! Complete with electronic links to the world, it'll revolutionize education. Students will interact with information infrastructures and knowledge processors to learn group work and telework, whatever that means. You'll be enriched, empowered, and enabled by the digital classroom; immersed in an optimal learning environment. Yee-ha! 1

Worried that things rarely turn out as promised? Well, let me present a pessimal[1] view of the schoolroom of the future. 2

Suppose you're a harried school board member. Voters complain about high taxes. Teachers' unions strike for higher wages and smaller classes. Parents worry about plummeting scores on standardized tests. Newspapers criticize backward teaching methods, outdated textbooks, and security problems. Unruly students cut classes and rarely pay attention. Instructors teach topics which aren't in the curriculum or, worse, inject their own opinions into subject matter. 3

Sound like a tough call? Naw—it's easy to solve all these problems, placate the taxpayers, and get re-elected. High technology! 4

First, the school district buys a computer for every student. Sure, this'll set back the budget—maybe a few hundred dollars per student. Quantity discounts and corporate support should keep the price down, and classroom savings will more than offset the cost of the equipment. 5

Next buy a pile of CD-ROMs for the students, each preprogrammed with fun edutainment[2] programs. The educational games will exactly cover the curriculum . . . for every paragraph in the syllabus, the game will have an interactive aspect. As students climb to more advanced levels, the game naturally becomes more challenging and rewarding. But always fun. 6

Every student will work at her own pace. The youngest will watch happy cartoon characters and exciting animations. The kid that likes horses will listen to messages from a chatty pony; the child that dreams of fire engines will hear from Fred the Firefighter. High schoolers get multimedia images of film stars and rock and roll celebrities. With access to interactive video sessions, chat rooms, and e-mail, students can collaborate with each other. It's the ultimate in individualized, child-centered instruction. 7

Naturally, the edu-games will be programmed so that students become adept at standardized tests. No reason to teach anything that's not on the ACT, PSAT, or SAT exams. And the students will have fun because all this information will be built into games like Myst, Dungeon, or Doom. They'll master the games, and automatically learn the material. 8

Meanwhile, the computers will keep score, like pinball machines. They'll send e-mail to parents and administrators . . . scores that will become part of each kid's permanent record. No more subjectivity in grading: The principal will know instantly how each child's doing. And if a student gets confused or falls behind, automated help will be just a mouse click away. 9

We'll update crowded classrooms, too. Replace desks with individual cubicles, comfortable chairs, and multimedia monitors. With no outside interruptions, kids' 10

---

[1]The opposite of optimal?

[2]A term, coined by Stoll, combining the words *education* and *entertainment* (editors' note).

attention will be directed into the approved creative learning experiences, built into the software. Well compartmentalized, students will hardly ever see each other . . . neatly ending classroom discipline problems.

11 Naturally, teachers are an unnecessary appendix at this cyberschool. No need for 'em when there's a fun, multimedia system at each student's fingertips. Should students have a question, they can turn to the latest on-line encyclopedia, enter an electronic chat room, or send e-mail to a professional educator. Those laid-off teachers can be retrained as data entry clerks.

12 As librarians and teachers become irrelevant, they'll be replaced by a cadre of instructional specialists, consultants, and professional hall monitors. Any discipline problems could be handled by trained security guards, who'd monitor the cubicles via remote video links.

13 Effect? With no more wasted time on student-teacher interactions or off-topic discussions, education will become more efficient. Since the computers' content would be directed at maximizing test performance, standardized test scores will zoom.

14 Eliminating teachers and luxuries such as art lessons and field trips will save enough to recoup the cost of those fancy computers. With little effort, this electronic education could even become a profit center. Merely sell advertising space in the edutainment programs. Corporate sponsors, eager to market their messages to impressionable minds, would pay school systems to plug their products within the coursework.

15 Concerned that such a system might be dehumanizing? Not to worry. Interactive chat sessions will encourage a sense of community and enhance kids' social skills. Should a student have questions, the Internet will put her in instant touch with a trained support mentor. When necessary, real-time instructors will appear on the distance learning displays, available to interact via two-way video.

16 The Cyberschool will showcase technology and train students for the upcoming electronic workplace. As local employment prospects change, the school board will issue updates to the curriculum over its interactive website. And the school board will monitor what each student learns—without idiosyncratic teachers to raise unpopular topics or challenge accepted beliefs.

17 Advanced students can sign up for on-line extracurricular activities—perhaps joining the Virtual Compassion Corps. There, students will be paired up across racial, gender, and class lines. Our children would offer foreigners advice and even arrange interviews with prospective employers. In this way, students will perform community service and mentor others, while displaying their cultural awareness over the network. All without ever having to shake hands with a real person, travel to a distant country, or (gasp!) face the real problems of another culture.[3] Simple, safe, and sterile.

18 Should parents worry about Johnny's progress, they need only log in over the Internet to see their son's latest test scores. In addition, they'll receive e-mailed reports summarizing their child's work. And at any time, they can click on an icon to see live images of their young scholar, automatically uploaded by a school video camera.

19 Yep, just sign up for the future: the parent-pleasin', tax-savin', teacher-firin', interactive-educatin', child-centerin' Cyberschool. No stuffy classrooms. No more teacher

---

[3]An actual proposal from the director of MIT's Laboratory for Computer Science, Michael Dertouzos.

strikes. No outdated textbooks. No expensive clarinet lessons. No boring homework. No learning. Coming soon to a school district near you.[4]

[4]Idea for a computer game: Cyberschool Superintendent. Players score by saving money. They could eliminate teachers, close libraries, or blow up music studios. Competitors advance by wiring schools, adding computers, and plugging in multimedia systems. Evil monsters might appear in the form of teachers, scholars, and librarians who insist that you read a book. Bonus points, labeled Pilot Project Grants, would be awarded for writing vapid press releases.

FIGURE 14.2
Essay Structure Diagram: "Cyberschool" by Clifford Stoll

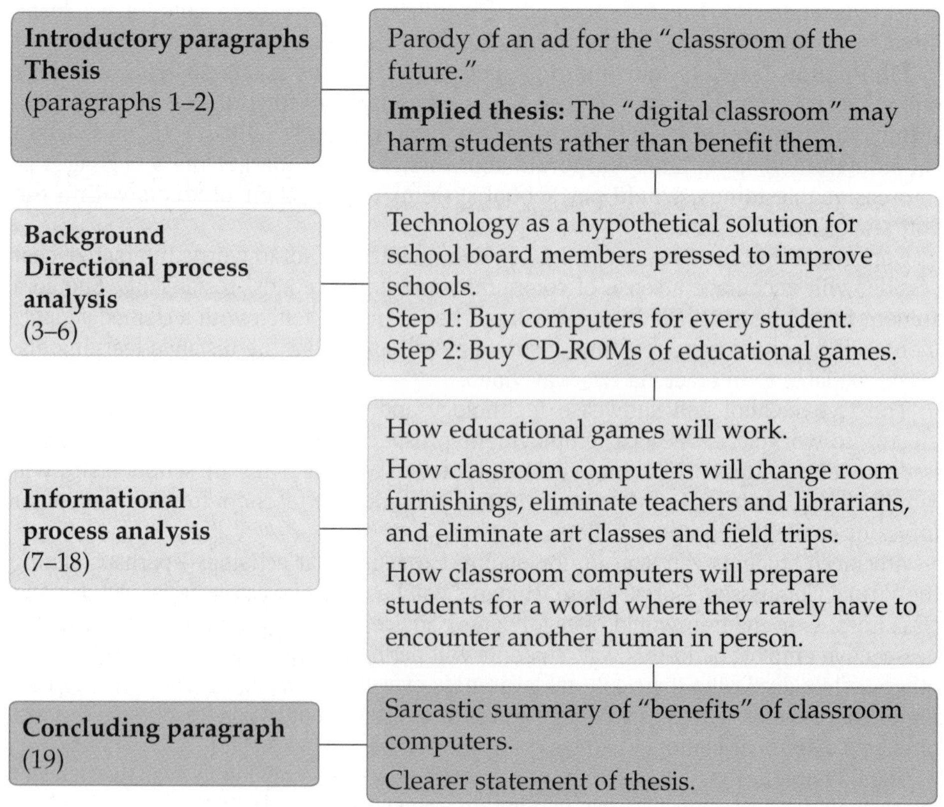

Questions for Close Reading

1. What is the selection's thesis? Locate the sentence(s) in which Stoll states his main idea. If he doesn't state the thesis explicitly, express it in your own words.
2. What process does Stoll describe in the essay? What are the basic steps of this process? What is Stoll's underlying attitude toward these measures?

3. What specific group of people does Stoll imagine as being especially in favor of the "cyberschool"? According to Stoll, how do these individuals justify using computers to teach children?

4. What role does Stoll indicate teachers will play in the "cyberschool"? What attitude does he convey about this role? Explain.

5. Refer to your dictionary as needed to define the following words used in the selection: *infrastructures* (paragraph 1), *optimal* (1), *harried* (3), *placate* (4), *adept* (8), *standardized* (8), *cubicles* (10), *compartmentalized* (10), *cadre* (12), *recoup* (14), and *idiosyncratic* (16).

Questions About the Writer's Craft

1. **The pattern.** Is Stoll's process analysis primarily *directional* or primarily *informational*? Explain. To what extent does Stoll try to persuade readers that the process he describes should be followed?

2. Focusing on his word choices, how would you characterize Stoll's tone in his essay? In your opinion, does his tone enhance or detract from the point he's trying to make? Explain.

3. **Other patterns.** Underlying Stoll's process analysis is an *argument* against a particular form of education. To write an effective argument, writers need to establish their own credibility. Based on what you learned about Stoll in his biography (page 327), what makes him appear qualified to write about his subject?

4. **Other patterns.** In his persona of pro-cyberschool spokesman, Stoll addresses opposition to the idea of the cyberschool in paragraph 15. How does Stoll represent and rebut the *arguments* against the cyberschool? Are his arguments effective, in your opinion?

Writing Assignments Using Process-Analysis as a Pattern of Development

1. In his essay, Stoll offers a cynical recipe for creating an "optimal learning environment." Write an essay in which you present a process analysis of concrete ways the school you currently attend or one you have attended in the past could realistically be improved. You might, for instance, discuss physical improvements such as updating the equipment in the computer lab, or less tangible measures such as cultivating a more interactive classroom environment. Brainstorm on your own or with others to generate specific ideas to include in your process. Reading David Brooks's "Psst! Human Capital" (page 301) may help you zero in on qualities and skills that should be cultivated in students.

2. In his essay, Stoll ironically suggests a course of action that he implies should not be taken in order to improve children's education. Taking a similarly

ironic stance, write an essay *mis*guiding readers on how to "improve" some other significant institution or serious condition. For instance, you might discuss ways to increase the efficiency of a particular government agency, how to even out inequities between classes or races of people, how to protect the environment, and so on—all the while presenting steps that would work to the contrary. Like Stoll, you should ultimately reveal your true position in the concluding paragraph, preferably in a subtle way.

Writing Assignments Combining Patterns of Development

3. According to Stoll, computers serve as a distraction to students rather than a legitimate learning tool. What are other kinds of distractions students face? Write an essay in which you *classify* the different types of distractions that can make learning difficult. You may adopt a serious tone and address categories such as, for example, problems at home and pressure from peers. Or you might adopt a humorous tone and discuss distractions that include interest in the opposite sex and the temptation of computer games. Provide vivid *examples* to illustrate each of the categories you create. For additional viewpoints about the pressures to which students are subject, read Kay S. Hymowitz's "Tweens: Ten Going on Sixteen" (page 245), Buzz Bissinger's "Innocents Afield" (page 407), and Mary Sherry's "In Praise of the 'F' Word" (page 502).

4. With the increasing popularity of the Internet, the future of traditional printed materials—such as books, magazines, and newspapers—has come into question. Write an essay in which you *compare* and *contrast* using printed materials with using the Internet in order to perform research. Be sure to provide at least one extended example or a few briefer examples to *illustrate* the differences and/or similarities you're pointing out. Your best source of information might be a "hands-on" approach: to research a topic using both methods in order to see for yourself what the differences are. By the end of your essay, make clear to your reader which of the two methods you find preferable, and why.

Writing Assignment Using a Journal Entry as a Starting Point

5. In an indirect way, Stoll argues against the wholesale computerization of the classroom. Write an essay in which you argue that the Internet in specific should *or* should not play a significant role in the education of *one* particular age group of students (elementary, high school, or college). In formulating your argument, refer to the material you generated in your pre-reading journal entry. For additional perspectives on this issue, you might consider doing some research on this topic in the library and/or on the Internet. In writing your essay, you should acknowledge and rebut opposing points of view.

DIANE COLE

Diane Cole (1952–), a former contributing editor of *Psychology Today*, has written articles for numerous publications, including *The Wall Street Journal, Newsweek, Ms.*, and *Mademoiselle*. Cole has also written several books, among them *Hunting the Head Hunters: A Woman's Guide* (1988), *After Great Pain: Coping with Loss and Change* (1996), and *After Great Pain: A New Life Emerges 7*(2002). In 1997, she coauthored the book *Is It You or Is It Me?* about problems in romantic relationships. The following selection, which first appeared in *The New York Times* in 1989, was underwritten by the Anti-Defamation League of B'nai B'rith as part of its ongoing campaign against prejudice.

Pre-Reading Journal Entry

Many of us—at some point—have encountered, either in jokes or more serious contexts, offensive language directed at a person or people solely because of their race, ethnicity, gender, sexual preference, or other such characteristic. In your journal, write about one or more such experiences. For each incident, answer the following: Who was involved? What happened? How did the parties, including yourself, respond?

DON'T JUST STAND THERE

1 It was my office farewell party, and colleagues at the job I was about to leave were wishing me well. My mood was one of ebullience tinged with regret, and it was in this spirit that I spoke to the office neighbor to whom I had waved hello every morning for the past two years. He smiled broadly as he launched into a long, rambling story, pausing only after he delivered the punch line. It was a very long pause because, although he laughed, I did not: This joke was unmistakably anti-Semitic.

2 I froze. Everyone in the office knew I was Jewish; what could he have possibly meant? Shaken and hurt, not knowing what else to do, I turned in stunned silence to the next well-wisher. Later, still angry, I wondered, what else should I—could I—have done?

3 Prejudice can make its presence felt in any setting, but hearing its nasty voice in this way can be particularly unnerving. We do not know what to do and often we feel another form of paralysis as well: We think, "Nothing I say or do will change this person's attitude, so why bother?"

4 But left unchecked, racial slurs and offensive ethnic jokes "can poison the atmosphere," says Michael McQuillan, adviser for racial/ethnic affairs for the Brooklyn borough president's office. "Hearing these remarks conditions us to accept them; and if we accept these, we can become accepting of other acts."

5 Speaking up may not magically change a biased attitude, but it can change a person's behavior by putting a strong message across. And the more messages there are, the more likely a person is to change that behavior, says Arnold Kahn, professor of psychology at James Madison University, Harrisonburg, Virginia, who makes this analogy: "You can't keep people from smoking in *their* house, but you can ask them not to smoke in *your* house."

At the same time, "Even if the other party ignores or discounts what you say, people always reflect on how others perceive them. Speaking up always counts," says LeNorman Strong, director of campus life at George Washington University, Washington, D.C. 6

Finally, learning to respond effectively also helps people feel better about themselves, asserts Cherie Brown, executive director of the National Coalition Building Institute, a Boston-based training organization. "We've found that, when people felt they could at least in this small way make a difference, that made them more eager to take on other activities on a larger scale," she says. Although there is no "cookbook approach" to confronting such remarks—every situation is different, experts stress—these are some effective strategies. 7

> When the "joke" turns on who you are—as a member of an ethnic or religious group, a person of color, a woman, a gay or lesbian, an elderly person, or someone with a physical handicap—shocked paralysis is often the first response. Then, wounded and vulnerable, on some level you want to strike back. 8

Lashing out or responding in kind is seldom the most effective response, however. "That can give you momentary satisfaction, but you also feel as if you've lowered yourself to that other person's level," Mr. McQuillan explains. Such a response may further label you in the speaker's mind as thin-skinned, someone not to be taken seriously. Or it may up the ante, making the speaker, and then you, reach for new insults—or physical blows. 9

"If you don't laugh at the joke, or fight, or respond in kind to the slur," says Mr. McQuillan, "that will take the person by surprise, and that can give you more control over the situation." Therefore, in situations like the one in which I found myself—a private conversation in which I knew the person making the remark—he suggests voicing your anger calmly but pointedly: "I don't know if you realize what that sounded like to me. If that's what you meant, it really hurt me." 10

State how *you* feel, rather than making an abstract statement like, "Not everyone who hears that joke might find it funny." Counsels Mr. Strong: "Personalize the sense of 'this is how I feel when you say this.' That makes it very concrete"—and harder to dismiss. 11

Make sure you heard the words and their intent correctly by repeating or rephrasing the statement: "This is what I heard you say. Is that what you meant?" It's important to give the other person the benefit of the doubt because, in fact, he may *not* have realized that the comment was offensive and, if you had not spoken up, would have had no idea of its impact on you. 12

For instance, Professor Kahn relates that he used to include in his exams multiple-choice questions that occasionally contained "incorrect funny answers." After one exam, a student came up to him in private and said, "I don't think you intended this, but I found a number of those jokes offensive to me as a woman." She explained why. "What she said made immediate sense to me," he says. "I apologized at the next class, and I never did it again." 13

But what if the speaker dismisses your objection, saying, "Oh, you're just being sensitive. Can't you take a joke?" In that case, you might say, "I'm not so sure about that, let's talk about that a little more." The key, Mr. Strong says, is to continue the dialogue, hear the other person's concerns, and point out your own. "There are times when you're just going to have to admit defeat and end it," he adds, "but I have to feel that I did the best I could." 14

15 When the offending remark is made in the presence of others—at a staff meeting, for example—it can be even more distressing than an insult made privately.

16 "You have two options," says William Newlin, director of field services for the Community Relations division of the New York City Commission on Human Rights. "You can respond immediately at the meeting, or you can delay your response until afterward in private. But a response has to come."

17 Some remarks or actions may be so outrageous that they cannot go unnoted at the moment, regardless of the speaker or the setting. But in general, psychologists say, shaming a person in public may have the opposite effect of the one you want: The speaker will deny his offense all the more strongly in order to save face. Further, few people enjoy being put on the spot, and if the remark really was not intended to be offensive, publicly embarrassing the person who made it may cause an unnecessary rift or further misunderstanding. Finally, most people just don't react as well or thoughtfully under a public spotlight as they would in private.

18 Keeping that in mind, an excellent alternative is to take the offender aside afterward: "Could we talk for a minute in private?" Then use the strategies suggested above for calmly stating how you feel, giving the speaker the benefit of the doubt, and proceeding from there.

19 At a large meeting or public talk, you might consider passing the speaker a note, says David Wertheimer, executive director of the New York City Gay and Lesbian Anti-Violence Project: You could write, "You may not realize it, but your remarks were offensive because . . . "

20 "Think of your role as that of an educator," suggests James M. Jones, Ph.D., executive director for public interest at the American Psychological Association. "You have to be controlled."

21 Regardless of the setting or situation, speaking up always raises the risk of rocking the boat. If the person who made the offending remark is your boss, there may be an even bigger risk to consider: How will this affect my job? Several things can help minimize the risk, however. First, know what other resources you may have at work, suggests Caryl Stern, director of the A World of Difference–New York City campaign: Does your personnel office handle discrimination complaints? Are other grievance procedures in place?

22 You won't necessarily need to use any of these procedures, Ms. Stern stresses. In fact, she advises, "It's usually better to try a one-on-one approach first." But simply knowing a formal system exists can make you feel secure enough to set up that meeting.

23 You can also raise the issue with other colleagues who heard the remark: Did they feel the same way you did? The more support you have, the less alone you will feel. Your point will also carry more validity and be more difficult to shrug off. Finally, give your boss credit—and the benefit of the doubt: "I know you've worked hard for the company's affirmative action programs, so I'm sure you didn't realize what those remarks sounded like to me as well as the others at the meeting last week. . . . "

27 If, even after this discussion, the problem persists, go back for another meeting, Ms. Stern advises. And if that, too, fails, you'll know what other options are available to you.

28 It's a spirited dinner party, and everyone's having a good time, until one guest starts reciting a racist joke. Everyone at the table is white, including you. The others are still laughing, as you wonder what to say or do.

No one likes being seen as a party-pooper, but before deciding that you'd prefer not to take on this role, you might remember that the person who told the offensive joke has already ruined your good time. 29

If it's a group that you feel comfortable in—a family gathering, for instance—you will feel freer to speak up. Still, shaming the person by shouting "You're wrong!" or "That's not funny!" probably won't get your point across as effectively as other strategies. "If you interrupt people to condemn them, it just makes it harder," says Cherie Brown. She suggests trying instead to get at the resentments that lie beneath the joke by asking open-ended questions: "Grandpa, I know you always treat everyone with such respect. Why do people in our family talk that way about black people?" The key, Ms. Brown says, "is to listen to them first, so they will be more likely to listen to you." 30

If you don't know your fellow guests well, before speaking up you could turn discreetly to your neighbors (or excuse yourself to help the host or hostess in the kitchen) to get a reading on how they felt, and whether or not you'll find support for speaking up. The less alone you feel, the more comfortable you'll be speaking up: "I know you probably didn't mean anything by that joke, Jim, but it really offended me. . . . " It's important to say that *you* were offended—not state how the group that is the butt of the joke would feel. "Otherwise," LeNorman Strong says, "you risk coming off as a goody two-shoes." 24

If you yourself are the host, you can exercise more control; you are, after all, the one who sets the rules and the tone of behavior in your home. Once, when Professor Kahn's party guests began singing offensive, racist songs, for instance, he kicked them all out, saying, "You don't sing songs like that in my house!" And, he adds, "they never did again." 25

> At school one day, a friend comes over and says, "Who do you think you are, hanging out with Joe? If you can be friends with those people, I'm through with you!" 26

Peer pressure can weigh heavily on kids. They feel vulnerable and, because they are kids, they aren't as able to control the urge to fight. "But if you learn to handle these situations as kids, you'll be better able to handle them as an adult," William Newlin points out. 31

Begin by redefining to yourself what a friend is and examining what friendship means, advises Amy Lee, a human relations specialist at Panel of Americans, an intergroup-relations training and educational organization. If that person from a different group fits your requirement for a friend, ask, "Why shouldn't I be friends with Joe? We have a lot in common." Try to get more information about whatever stereotypes or resentments lie beneath your friend's statement. Ms. Lee suggests: "What makes you think they're so different from us? Where did you get that information?" She explains: "People are learning these stereotypes from somewhere, and they cannot be blamed for that. So examine where these ideas came from." Then talk about how your own experience rebuts them. 32

Kids, like adults, should also be aware of other resources to back them up: Does the school offer special programs for fighting prejudice? How supportive will the principal, the teachers, or other students be? If the school atmosphere is volatile, experts warn, make sure that taking a stand at that moment won't put you in physical danger. If that is the case, it's better to look for other alternatives. 33

34 These can include programs or organizations that bring kids from different backgrounds together. "When kids work together across race lines, that is how you break down the barriers and see that the stereotypes are not true," says Laurie Meadoff, president of CityKids Foundation, a nonprofit group whose programs attempt to do just that. Such programs can also provide what Cherie Brown calls a "safe place" to express the anger and pain that slurs and other offenses cause, whether the bigotry is directed against you or others.

35 In learning to speak up, everyone will develop a different style and a slightly different message to get across, experts agree. But it would be hard to do better than these two messages suggested by teenagers at CityKids: "Everyone on the face of the earth has the same intestines," said one. Another added, "Cross over the bridge. There's a lot of love on the streets."

Questions for Close Reading

1. What is the selection's thesis? Locate the sentence(s) in which Cole states her main idea. If she doesn't state the thesis explicitly, express it in your own words.
2. Why does Cole believe it is better to speak up against prejudice rather than to keep silent or ignore it?
3. Although Cole acknowledges that there is no "cookbook approach" for dealing with offensive comments, she nevertheless presents some general steps that can be followed. What are these general steps? Cole also describes more specific steps that can be taken in particular situations. What are the situations and the steps to be taken?
4. According to Cole's sources, what types of comments and responses are *not* useful in dealing with prejudicial jokes and remarks?
5. Refer to your dictionary as needed to define the following words used in the selection: *ebullience* (paragraph 1), *anti-Semitic* (1), *slurs* (4), *discounts* (6), *lashing* (9), *ante* (9), *abstract* (11), *personalize* (11), *rift* (17), *grievance* (21), and *volatile* (33).

Questions About the Writer's Craft

1. **The pattern.** Does Cole's process analysis have a primarily informative or persuasive purpose? How do you know? Where does the author suggest her purpose? How does her use of the second-person "you" reinforce that purpose?
2. **Other patterns.** What *examples* does Cole provide to *illustrate* the process she's explaining? Why do you think she provides so many examples?
3. Cole uses quotations extensively in the essay. Why do you suppose she quotes so many people? What effect do you think Cole hopes the quotations will have on her readers?

4. What purpose do the essay's three sections set off with smaller type serve? Why might Cole have chosen to set off these sections? Which one of the three sections seems to address a different audience than the other two? Taking into account why this essay was written and where it was published (see the biographical note), do you think Cole is justified in shifting her essay's focus in this way? Why or why not? Is the shift effective? Explain.

Writing Assignments Using Process Analysis as a Pattern of Development

1. Cole describes a process for handling offensive *comments,* but there are many times when we wonder whether to protest someone's objectionable *behavior.* Write an essay explaining a process for dealing with one such behavior. You might describe a process for confronting a friend who forgets to repay loans, a teacher who grades unfairly, or a boss who treats employees rudely. Like Cole, tell readers what they should do if a step in the process doesn't yield the hoped-for results. For additional accounts about how to deal with others' problematic behavior, read Brent Staples's "Black Men and Public Space" (page 412) and Susan Jacoby's "Common Decency" (page 512).

2. In paragraph 27, Cole describes a family gathering during which a grandchild confronts a grandfather as one adult to another. However, dealing with older relatives in such a forthright manner can be difficult, especially when the older adults don't perceive the grown-up child as a mature individual. Write an essay describing the process by which a grown child can confront such relatives and request that they treat the "child" like an adult. Use examples from your own family and from friends' families when explaining how to deal—and not deal—with such relatives.

Writing Assignments Combining Patterns of Development

3. Cole writes about one type of behavior that most of us find obnoxious. But, as we all know, there are many types of obnoxious or annoying people. Focusing on a specific setting (a library, a highway, a store, a classroom), write a light-spirited essay in which you *categorize* the kinds of obnoxious people you typically encounter there. Be sure to provide vivid *descriptions* of the behavior that makes these people so unpleasant.

4. When confronted by offensive language and behavior, people should—Cole argues—take a stand. Write an essay constructing your personal *definition* of *assertiveness. Illustrate* your definition by providing specific *examples* of what it is and what it isn't. To gain additional insight into assertiveness, or the lack thereof, read Audre Lorde's "The Fourth of July" (page 208), and Charmie Gholson's "Charity Display?" (page 220).

Writing Assignment Using a Journal Entry as a Starting Point

5. Cole conveys the short-term discomfort and long-term damage that offensive language can inflict on recipients. Write an essay narrating an incident—that you witnessed or participated in—of hurtful speech directed at an individual or group because of race, ethnicity, gender, or sexual preference. Review your pre-reading journal entry, selecting the *one* occasion that is the most compelling and/or thought-provoking. As you narrate the incident, be sure to use dialog and descriptive language to convey what was said and done and how people reacted. End your essay by reflecting on what you now, in retrospect, realize about the incident and whether you think it could have been handled differently by those involved. Also, consider reading Audre Lorde's "The Fourth of July" (page 208), Toni Morrison's "A Slow Walk of Trees" (page 364), Brent Staples's "Black Men and Public Space" (page 412) and Roberto Rodriguez's "The Border on Our Backs" (page 517) for accounts of how painful racial and ethnic misconceptions can be.

DAVID SHIPLEY

David Shipley, a journalist, is the deputy editor of *The New York Times*'s op-ed page, on which opinion pieces by *New York Times* columnists and other journalists, as well as private citizens, are published. He was born in Portland, Oregon, in 1963 and graduated with a degree in English from Williams College in 1985. Shipley won a Thomas J. Watson Fellowship for 1985–1986, which allowed him to spend a year traveling to do independent study. From 1993 to 1995 he was executive editor of *The New Republic*, and from 1995 to 1997 he was a special assistant and senior speechwriter for President Bill Clinton. Shipley joined *The New York Times* in 1998 and was deputy editor of the Sunday *New York Times Magazine*'s millennium issues, senior editor of the magazine, and enterprise editor of the national desk before moving to his present position as op-ed editor. With coauthor Will Schwalbe, Shipley is writing a book about e-mail entitled *Send*. This essay, originally entitled "What We Talk About When We Talk About Editing," appeared in *The New York Times* on July 31, 2005.

Pre-Reading Journal Entry

People often seek advice and help from others to help them do a job or improve their performance. For example, if you were writing your résumé, you might ask a friend to edit and proofread it. Or if you were trying out for a sports team, you might ask a coach for feedback and advice. Think of some occasions in the past when you asked others for help with your work or gave help to someone else when asked. What was the task? What was your goal in helping or being helped? Did the assistance actually improve the end product, or was it useless? Use your journal to answer these questions.

TALK ABOUT EDITING

. . . Not surprisingly, readers have lots of questions about the editing that goes on [on the *New York Times* op-ed page]. What kind of changes do we suggest—and why? What kind of changes do we insist on—and why? When do we stay out of the way? And the hardy perennial: do we edit articles to make them adhere to a particular point of view? I thought I'd try to provide a few answers. 1

Just like *Times* news articles and editorials, Op-Ed essays are edited. Before something appears in our pages, you can bet that questions have been asked, arguments have been clarified, cuts have been suggested—as have additions—and factual, typographical and grammatical errors have been caught. (We hope.) 2

Our most important rule, however, is that nothing is published on the Op-Ed page unless it has been approved by its author. Articles go to press only after the person under whose name the article appears has explicitly O.K.'d the editing. 3

While it's important to know that we edit, it's also important to know how we edit. The best way to explain this is to take a walk through the process. 4

Say you send us an article by regular mail, e-mail, fax or, this summer at least, owl post[1]—and it's accepted. You'll be told that we'll contact you once your article is scheduled for publication. That could be days, weeks or even months away. 5

When your article does move into the on-deck circle, you'll be sent a contract, and one of the several editors here will get to work. 6

Here are the clear-cut things the editor will do: 7

- Correct grammatical and typographical errors. 8
- Make sure that the article conforms to *The New York Times Manual of Style and Usage*. Courtesy titles, for example, will miraculously appear if they weren't there before; expletives will be deleted; some words will be capitalized, others lowercased. 9
- See to it that the article fits our allotted space. With staff columnists, advertisements and illustrations, there's a limit to the number of words we can squeeze onto the page. 10
- Fact-check the article. While it is the author's responsibility to ensure that everything written for us is accurate, we still check facts—names, dates, places, quotations. 11

We also check assertions. If news articles—from *The Times* and other publications—are at odds with a point or an example in an essay, we need to resolve whatever discrepancy exists. 12

For instance, an Op-Ed article critical of newly aggressive police tactics in Town X can't flatly say the police have no reason to change their strategy if there have been news reports that violence in the town is rising. This doesn't mean the writer can't still argue that there are other ways to deal with Town X's crime problem—he just can't say that the force's decision to change came out of the blue. 13

---

[1]In J. K. Rowling's Harry Potter books, mail is delivered each morning to Hogwarts, Harry's school, by owls (editors' note).

14 How would we resolve the Town X issue? Well, we'd discuss it with the writer—generally by telephone or e-mail—and we'd try to find a solution that preserves the writer's argument while also adhering to the facts.

15 Now to some people, this may sound surprising, as if we're putting words in people's mouths. But there's a crucial distinction to be made between changing a writer's argument—and suggesting language that will help a writer make his point more effectively.

16 Besides grammar and accuracy, we're also concerned about readability. Our editors try to approach articles as average readers who know nothing about the subject. They may ask if a point is clear, if a writer needs transitional language to bridge the gap between two seemingly separate points, if a leap of logic has been made without sufficient explanation.

17 To make a piece as clear and accessible as possible, the editor may add a transition, cut a section that goes off point or move a paragraph. If a description is highly technical, the editor may suggest language that lay readers will understand. If it isn't clear what a writer is trying to say, the editor may take a guess, based on what he knows from the author, and suggest more precise language. (There are also times when we do precious little.)

18 The editor will then send the edited version of the article to the writer. The changes will often be highlighted to make it easy for the author to see what's been done. (I tend to mark edits I've made with an //ok?//.) If a proposed revision is significant, the editor will often write a few sentences to describe the reasoning behind the suggestion.

19 Every change is a suggestion, not a demand. If a solution offered by an editor doesn't work for a writer, the two work together to find an answer to the problem. Editing is not bullying.

20 Of course, it's not always warm and cuddly, either. The people who write for Op-Ed have a responsibility to be forthright and specific in their arguments. There's no room on the page for articles that are opaque or written in code.

21 What our editors expressly do not do is change a point of view. If you've written an article on why New York's street fairs should be abolished, we will not ask you to change your mind and endorse them. We're going to help you make the best case you can. If you followed this page carefully in the run-up to the Iraq war, for example, you saw arguments both for and against the invasion—all made with equal force.

22 Editing is a human enterprise. Like writing, it is by nature subjective. Sometimes an editor will think a writer is saying something that she isn't. But our editing process gives writer and editor plenty of time to sort out any misunderstandings before the article goes to press. And if a mistake gets through, we do our best to correct it as quickly as possible.

23 The Op-Ed page is a venue for people with a wide range of perspectives, experiences and talents. Some of the people who appear in this space have written a lot; others haven't. If we published only people who needed no editing, we'd wind up relying on only a very narrow range of professional writers, and the page would be much the worse for it.

24 So what's the agenda? A lively page of clashing opinions, one where as many people as possible have the opportunity to make the best arguments they can.

25 And just so you know, this article has been edited. Changes have been suggested—and gratefully accepted. Well, most of them.

Questions for Close Reading

1. What is the selection's thesis? Locate the sentence(s) in which Shipley states his main idea. If he doesn't state his thesis explicity, express it in your own words.
2. What tasks are involved in editing an op-ed piece for *The New York Times*? Of these, which does Shipley seem to think need the most explanation?
3. In paragraphs 18 through 22, Shipley describes the relationship between the editor and writer of an op-ed piece. What is the nature of this relationship?
4. In paragraph 22, Shipley says that "Editing is a human enterprise." What does he mean by this?
5. Refer to your dictionary as needed to define the following words used in the selection: *hardy* (paragraph 1), *perennial* (1), *on-deck circle* (6), *expletives* (9), *assertions* (12), *adhering* (14), *readability* (16), and *venue* (23).

Questions About the Writer's Craft

1. **The pattern.** Who is the audience for Shipley's essay? Why would this audience be interested in this topic? What type of process analysis does Shipley use?
2. **Other patterns.** Shipley *divides* the editing process into three main types of tasks and covers each type in its own section. Identify the main editing tasks and the paragraph(s) that introduce each type. Why does he break down the process this way rather than deal with the editing process as a whole?
3. In paragraphs 13 and 14, Shipley uses an example to clarify what he means by checking "assertions." Why does he provide an example here? Is the example effective?
4. Shipley concludes this essay with some mild humor. What is the joke? What does this use of humor contribute to the point he has been making in his essay?

Writing Assignments Using Process Analysis as a Pattern of Development

1. Shipley describes the process involved in editing opinion pieces, or arguments, that appear in a newspaper with national circulation. However, many other types of works are edited. For example, news articles, news broadcasts, documentaries, movies, commercials, advertisements, novels, and comic strips are all edited. Select one of these media and do research on the tasks

involved in editing it. Write an essay in which you *analyze* the editing *process* and explain why it is important.

2. Before a piece can be edited, it must be written. Examine the process involved in producing an essay from the writer's rather than the editor's point of view. What process do you use when you write an essay in your English course? Write an essay in which you analyze your own writing process. Your tone might be serious or humorous as you lay out your process. Consider concluding your essay by evaluating how effective your process is and what you might do differently in the future.

Writing Assignments Combining Patterns of Development

3. Op-ed pieces are usually arguments about current issues; in contrast, news articles are more objective, describing or narrating events. From *The New York Times* or your local newspaper, select one op-ed page essay and one news article on a related topic, if possible. *Compare* and *contrast* the two pieces, analyzing their purpose and content. What patterns of development are used in each piece? Give *examples* to support your analysis.

4. A process analysis essay describes a general procedure, such as how to make chili, whereas a narrative presents a specific story, for example, a story about the time you dropped a pot of chili right before your guests arrived for dinner. Write an essay in which you blend a *process analysis* with a *specific narrative.* You can emphasize either the process analysis or the narrative, whichever seems more effective. Your essay can be humorous, serious, fantastical, or ironic.

Writing Assignment Using a Journal Entry as a Starting Point

5. Review your pre-reading journal entry and select one of the occasions on which you helped someone or were helped to perform a task. First, identify the steps in the process and any missteps or problems. Second, decide whether the process lends itself to an informative or a directional process analysis, or some combination of the two. Finally, write an essay in which you describe the process. To add interest to your essay, you might want to use humor, describe interpersonal conflicts, give examples, or focus on problem areas. Be sure—perhaps in your conclusion—to indicate whether the assistance you gave or received was effective in getting the task done. For a tongue-in-cheek "guide" to performing a task—taking schools into the "computer age"—read Clifford Stoll's "Cyberschool" (page 328).

ADDITIONAL WRITING TOPICS: PROCESS ANALYSIS

General Assignments

Develop one of the following topics through process analysis. Explain the process one step at a time, organizing the steps chronologically. If there's no agreed-on sequence, design your own series of steps. Use transitions to ease the audience through the steps in the process. You may use any tone you want, from serious to light.

Directional: How to Do Something

1. How to improve a course you have taken
2. How to drive defensively
3. How to get away with ______________
4. How to improve the place where you work or study
5. How to relax
6. How to show appreciation to others
7. How to get through school despite personal problems
8. How to look fashionable on a limited budget
9. How to be a responsible pet owner
10. How to meet more people

Informational: How Something Happens

1. How a student becomes burned out
2. How a library's card catalog or computerized catalog organizes books
3. How a dead thing decays (or some other natural process)
4. How the college registration process works
5. How *homo sapiens* choose a mate
6. How a VCR (or some other machine) works
7. How a bad habit develops
8. How people fall into debt
9. How someone becomes an Internet addict/junkie
10. How a child develops a love of reading

Assignments with a Specific Purpose, Audience, and Point of View

On Campus

1. As an experienced campus tour guide for prospective students, you've been asked by your school's Admissions Office to write a pamphlet explaining to new tour guides how to conduct a tour of your school's campus. When explaining the process, keep in mind that tour guides need to portray the school in its best light.

2. You write an "advice to the lovelorn" column for the campus newspaper. A correspondent writes saying that he or she wants to break up with a steady girlfriend/boyfriend but doesn't know how to do it without hurting the person. Give the writer guidance on how to end a meaningful relationship with a minimal amount of pain.

At Home or in the Community

3. To help a sixteen-year-old friend learn how to drive, explain a specific driving maneuver one step at a time. You might, for example, describe how to make a three-point turn, parallel park, or handle a skid. Remember, your friend lacks self-confidence and experience.

4. Your best friend plans to move into his or her own apartment but doesn't know the first thing about how to choose one. Explain the process of selecting an apartment—where to look, what to investigate, what questions to ask before signing a lease.

On the Job

5. As a staff writer for a consumer magazine, you've been asked to write an article on how to shop for a certain product. Give specific steps explaining how to save money, buy a quality product, and the like.

6. An author of books for elementary school children, you want to show children how to do something—take care of a pet, get along with siblings, keep a room clean. Explain the process in terms a child would understand yet not find condescending.

For additional writing, reading, and research resources, go to **www.mycomplab.com** and choose **Nadell/Langan/Comodromos'** ***The Longman Writer*, 7/e**.

Comparison-Contrast

15

The Advertising Archive Ltd.

What Is Comparison-Contrast?

We frequently try to make sense of the world by finding similarities and differences in our experiences. Seeing how things are alike (**comparing**) and seeing how they are different (**contrasting**) help us impose meaning on experiences that otherwise might remain fragmented and disconnected. Barely aware of the fact that we're comparing and contrasting, we may think to ourselves, "I woke up in a great mood this morning, but now I feel uneasy and anxious. I wonder why I feel so different." This inner questioning, which often occurs in a flash, is just one example of the way we use comparison and contrast to understand ourselves and our world.

Comparing and contrasting also helps us make choices. We compare and contrast everything—from two brands of soap we might buy to two colleges we might attend. We listen to a favorite radio station, watch a preferred nightly news show, select a particular dessert from a menu—all because we have done some degree of comparing and contrasting. We often weigh these alternatives in an unstudied, casual manner, as when we flip from one radio station to another. But when we have to make important decisions, we tend to think rigorously about how things are alike or different: Should I live in a dorm or rent an apartment? Should I accept the higher-paying job or the lower-paying one that offers more challenges? Such a deliberate approach to comparison-contrast may also provide us with needed insight into complex contemporary issues: Is television's coverage of political candidates more or less objective than it used to be? What are the merits of the various positions on abortion?

HOW COMPARISON-CONTRAST FITS YOUR PURPOSE AND AUDIENCE

When is it appropriate in writing to use the comparison-contrast pattern of development? Comparison-contrast works well if you want to demonstrate any of the following: (1) that one thing is better than another (the first example below); (2) that things that seem different are actually alike (the second example below); (3) that things that seem alike are actually different (the third example below).

> Compare and contrast the way male and female relationships are depicted in *Cosmopolitan, Ms., Playboy,* and *Esquire.* Which publication has the most limited view of men and women? Which has the broadest perspective?
>
> Football, basketball, and baseball differ in the ways they appeal to fans. Describe the unique drawing power of each sport, but also reach some conclusions about the appeals the three sports have in common.
>
> Studies show that both college students and their parents feel that post-secondary education should equip young people to succeed in the marketplace. Yet the same studies report that the two groups have a very different understanding of what it means to succeed. What differences do you think the studies identify?

Other assignments will, in less obvious ways, lend themselves to comparison-contrast. For instance, although words like *compare, contrast, differ,* and *have in common* don't appear in the following assignments, essay responses to the assignments could be organized around the comparison-contrast format:

> The emergence of the two-career family is one of the major phenomena of our culture. Discuss the advantages and disadvantages of having both parents work, showing how you feel about such two-career households.
>
> Some people believe that the 1950s, often called the golden age of television, produced several never-to-be equaled comedy classics. Do you agree that such shows as *I Love Lucy* and *The Honeymooners* are superior to the situation comedies aired on television today?
>
> There has been considerable criticism recently of the news coverage by the city's two leading newspapers, the *Herald* and the *Beacon.* Indicate whether you think the criticism is valid by discussing the similarities and differences in the two papers' news coverage.

Note: The last assignment shows that a comparison-contrast essay may cover similarities *and* differences, not just one or the other.

As you have seen, comparison-contrast can be the key strategy for achieving an essay's purpose. But comparison-contrast can also be a supplemental method used to help make a point in an essay organized chiefly around another pattern of development. A serious, informative essay intended for laypeople might *define* clinical depression by contrasting that state of mind with ordinary run-of-the-mill blues. Writing humorously about the exhausting *effects* of trying to get in shape, you might dramatize your plight for readers by contrasting the leisurely way you

used to spend your day with your current rigidly compulsive exercise regimen. Or, in an urgent *argumentation-persuasion* essay on the need for stricter controls over drug abuse in the workplace, you might provide readers with background by comparing several companies' approaches to the problem.

At this point, you have a good sense of the way writers use comparison-contrast to achieve their purpose and to connect with their readers. Now take a moment to look closely at the photograph at the beginning of this chapter. Imagine you're writing a blog entry linked to a consumer advocacy website. Jot down some phrases you might use when *comparing* and/or *contrasting* the vehicles featured in this picture, with the end of recommending one over the other.

PREWRITING STRATEGIES

The following checklist shows how you can apply to comparison-contrast some of the prewriting strategies discussed in Chapter 2.

☑ COMPARISON-CONTRAST: A PREWRITING CHECKLIST

Choose Subjects to Compare and Contrast

- ☐ What have you recently needed to compare and contrast (subjects to major in, events to attend, ways to resolve a disagreement) in order to make a choice? What would a comparison-contrast analysis disclose about the alternatives, your priorities, and the criteria by which you judge?
- ☐ Can you show a need for change by contrasting one way of doing something (say, the way your college awards athletic scholarships) with a better way (either imagined or actual)?
- ☐ Do any people you know show some striking similarities and differences? What would a comparison-contrast analysis reveal about their characters and the personal qualities you prize?
- ☐ How does your view on an issue (the legal drinking age, birth control, a new policy at your college) differ from that of other people (your parents, a friend, most students at your college)? What would a comparison-contrast analysis of these views indicate about your values?

Determine Your Purpose, Audience, Tone, and Point of View

- ☐ Is your purpose primarily to inform readers of similarities and differences? To evaluate your subjects' relative merits? To persuade readers to choose between alternative courses of action?

☐ What audience are you writing for? To what tone and point of view will they be most receptive?

Use Prewriting to Generate Points of Comparison-Contrast

☐ How could brainstorming, freewriting, mapping, or journal entries help you gather information about your subjects' most significant similarities and differences?

STRATEGIES FOR USING COMPARISON-CONTRAST IN AN ESSAY

After prewriting, you're ready to draft your essay. The following suggestions and Figure 15.1 (on page 350) will be helpful whether you use comparison-contrast as a dominant or supportive pattern of development.

1. **Be sure your subjects are at least somewhat alike.** Unless you plan to develop an *analogy* (see the following numbered suggestion), the subjects you choose to compare or contrast should share some obvious characteristics or qualities. It makes sense to compare different parts of the country, two comedians, or several college teachers. But a reasonable paper wouldn't result from, let's say, a comparison of a television game show with a soap opera. Your subjects must belong to the same general group so that your comparison-contrast stays within logical bounds and doesn't veer off into pointlessness.

2. **Stay focused on your purpose.** When writing, remember that comparison-contrast isn't an end in itself. That is, your objective isn't to turn an essay into a mechanical list of "how *A* differs from *B*" or "how *A* is like *B*." As with the other patterns of development discussed in this book, comparison-contrast is a strategy for making a point or meeting a larger purpose.

   Consider the assignment on page 347 about the two newspapers. Your purpose here might be simply to *inform,* to present information as objectively as possible: "This is what the *Herald*'s news coverage is like. This is what the *Beacon*'s news coverage is like."

   More frequently, though, you'll use comparison-contrast to *evaluate* your subjects' pros and cons, your goal being to reach a conclusion or make a judgment: "Both the *Herald* and the *Beacon* spend too much time reporting local news," or "The *Herald*'s analysis of the recent hostage crisis was more insightful than the *Beacon*'s." Comparison-contrast can also be used to *persuade* readers to take action: "People interested in thorough coverage of international events should read the *Herald* rather than the *Beacon.*" Persuasive essays may also propose a change, contrasting what now exists with a more ideal situation: "For the *Beacon* to compete with the *Herald,* it must assign more reporters to international stories."

FIGURE 15.1
Development Diagram: Writing a Comparison-Contrast Essay

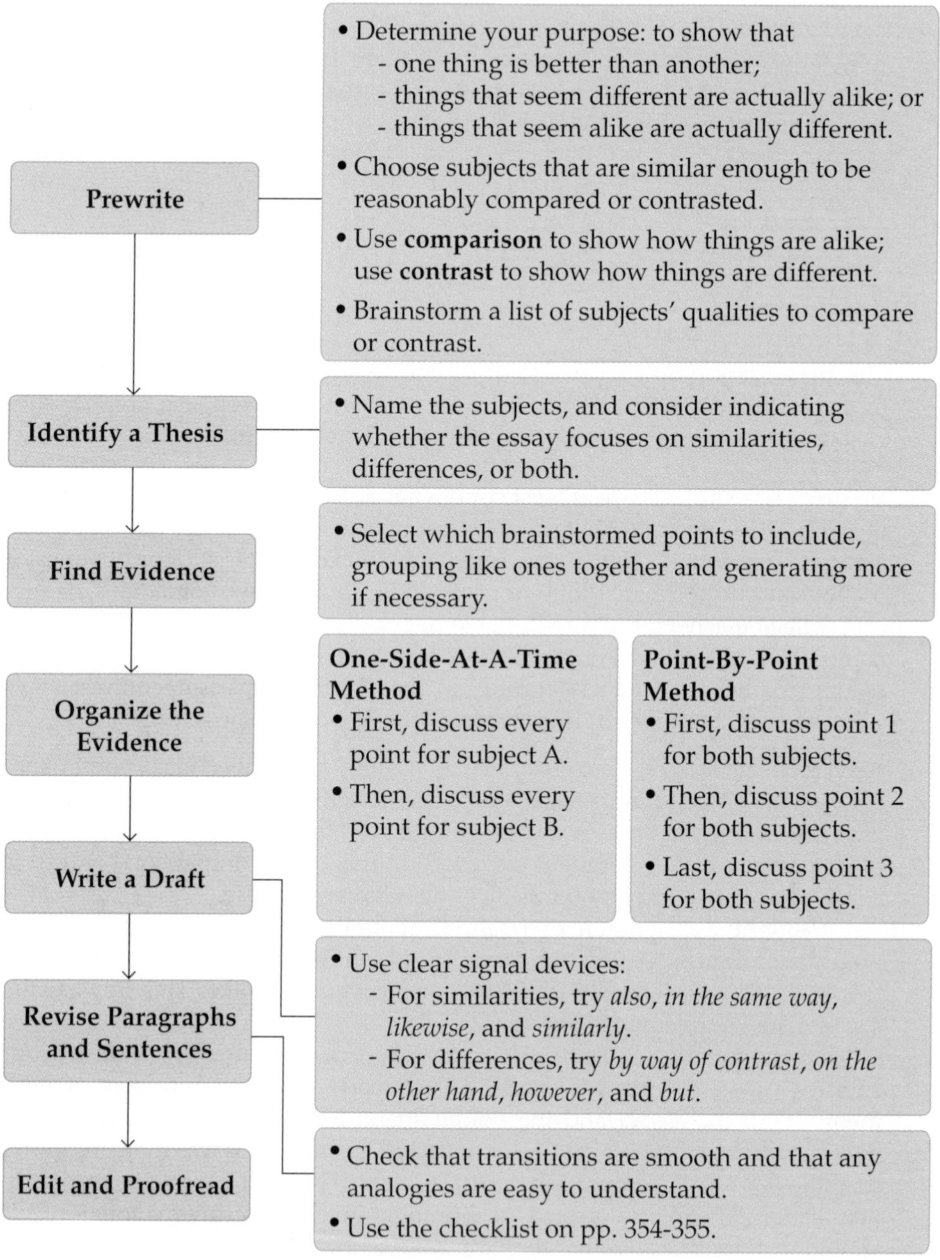

Yet another purpose you might have in writing a comparison-contrast essay is to *clear up misconceptions* by revealing previously hidden similarities or differences. For example, perhaps your town's two newspapers are thought to be sharply different. However, a comparison-contrast analysis might reveal that—although one paper specializes in sensationalized stories while the other adopts a more muted approach—both resort to biased, emotionally charged analyses of local politics. Or the essay might illustrate that the tabloid's treatment of the local arts scene is surprisingly more comprehensive than that of its competitor.

Comparing and contrasting also make it possible to *draw an analogy* between two seemingly unrelated subjects. An analogy is an imaginative comparison that delves beneath the surface differences of subjects in order to expose their significant and often unsuspected similarities or differences. Your purpose may be to show that singles bars and zoos share a number of striking similarities. Or you may want to illustrate that wolves and humans raise their young in much the same way, but that wolves go about the process in a more civilized manner. The analogical approach can make a complex subject easier to understand—as, for example, when the national deficit is compared to a household budget gone awry. Analogies are often dramatic and instructive, challenging you and your audience to consider subjects in a new light. But analogies don't speak for themselves. You must make clear to the reader how the analogy demonstrates your purpose.

3. **Formulate a strong thesis.** An essay that is developed primarily through comparison-contrast should be focused by a solid thesis. Besides revealing your attitude, the thesis will often do the following:

   - Name the subjects being compared and contrasted
   - Indicate whether the essay focuses on the subjects' similarities, differences, or both
   - State the essay's main point of comparison or contrast

   Not all comparison-contrast essays need thesis statements as structured as those that follow. Even so, these examples can serve as models of clarity. Note that the first thesis statement signals similarities, the second differences, and the last both similarities and differences:

   > Middle-aged parents are often in a good position to empathize with adolescent children because the emotional upheavals experienced by the two age groups are much the same.

   > The priorities of most retired people are more conducive to health and happiness than the priorities of most young professionals.

   > College students in their thirties and forties face many of the same pressures as younger students, but they are better equipped to withstand these pressures.

4. **Select the points to be discussed.** Once you have identified the essay's subject, purpose, and thesis, you need to decide which of the many points generated during prewriting you will discuss: You have to identify which

aspects of the subjects to compare or contrast. College professors, for instance, could be compared and contrasted on the basis of their testing methods, ability to motivate students, confidence in front of a classroom, personalities, level of enthusiasm, and so forth.

When selecting points to cover, be sure to consider your audience. Ask yourself: "Will my readers be familiar with this item? Will I need it to get my message across? Will my audience find this item interesting or convincing?" What your readers know, what they don't know, and what you can project about their reactions should influence your choices. And, of course, you need to select points that support your thesis. If your essay explains the differences between healthy, sensible diets and dangerous crash diets, it wouldn't be appropriate to talk about aerobic exercise. Similarly, imagine you want to write an essay making the point that, despite their differences, hard rock of the 1960s and punk rock of the 1970s both reflected young people's disillusionment with society. It wouldn't make much sense to contrast the long, uncombed hairstyles of the 1960s with the short, spiky cuts of the 1970s. But contrasting song lyrics (protest versus nihilistic messages) would help support your thesis and lead to interesting insights.

5. **Organize the points to be discussed.** After deciding which points to include, you should use a systematic, logical plan for presenting those ideas. If the points aren't organized, your essay will be little more than a confusing jumble of ideas. There are two common ways to organize an essay developed wholly or in part by comparison-contrast: the one-side-at-a-time method and the point-by-point method. Although both strategies may be used in a paper, one method usually predominates.

   In the **one-side-at-a-time method** of organization, you discuss everything relevant about one subject before moving to another subject. For example, responding to the earlier assignment that asked you to analyze the news coverage in two local papers, you might first talk about the *Herald*'s coverage of international, national, and local news; then you would discuss the *Beacon*'s coverage of the same categories. Note that the areas discussed should be the same for both newspapers. It wouldn't be logical to review the *Herald*'s coverage of international, national, and local news and then to detail the *Beacon*'s magazine supplements, modern living section, and comics page. Moreover, the areas compared and contrasted should be presented in the same order.

   This is how you would organize the essay using the one-side-at-a-time method:

Everything about subject *A*	*Herald*'s news coverage: • International • National • Local
Everything about subject *B*	*Beacon*'s news coverage: • International • National • Local

In the **point-by-point method** of organization, you alternate from one aspect of the first subject to the same aspect of your other subject(s). For example, to use this method when comparing or contrasting the *Herald* and the *Beacon*, you would first discuss the *Herald*'s international coverage, then the *Beacon*'s international coverage; next, the *Herald*'s national coverage, then the *Beacon*'s; and finally, the *Herald*'s local coverage, then the *Beacon*'s.

An essay using the point-by-point method would be organized like this:

First aspect of subjects *A* and *B*	*Herald:* International coverage *Beacon:* International coverage
Second aspect of subjects *A* and *B*	*Herald:* National coverage *Beacon:* National coverage
Third aspect of subjects *A* and *B*	*Herald:* Local coverage *Beacon:* Local coverage

Deciding which of these two methods of organization to use is largely a personal choice, though there are several factors to consider. The one-side-at-a-time method tends to convey a more unified feeling because it highlights broad similarities and differences. It is, therefore, an effective approach for subjects that are fairly uncomplicated. This strategy also works well when essays are brief; the reader won't find it difficult to remember what has been said about subject *A* when reading about subject *B*.

Because the point-by-point method permits more extensive coverage of similarities and differences, it is often a wise choice when subjects are complex. This pattern is also useful for lengthy essays since readers would probably find it difficult to remember, let's say, ten pages of information about subject *A* while reading the next ten pages about subject *B*. The point-by-point approach, however, may cause readers to lose sight of the broader picture, so remember to keep them focused on your central point.

6. **Supply the reader with clear transitions.** Although a well-organized comparison-contrast format is important, it doesn't guarantee that readers will be able to follow your line of thought easily. *Transitions*—especially those signaling similarities or differences—are needed to show readers where they have been and where they are going. Such cues are essential in all writing, but they're especially crucial in a paper using comparison-contrast. By indicating clearly when subjects are being compared or contrasted, the transitions help weave the discussion into a coherent whole.

   The transitions (in boldface) in the following examples could be used to *signal similarities* in an essay discussing the news coverage in the *Herald* and the *Beacon:*

   - The *Beacon* **also** allots only a small portion of the front page to global news.
   - **In the same way,** the *Herald* tries to include at least three local stories on the first page.

- **Likewise,** the *Beacon* emphasizes the importance of up-to-date reporting of town meetings.
- The *Herald* is **similarly** committed to extensive coverage of high school and college sports.

The transitions (in boldface) in these examples could be used to *signal differences:*

- **By way of contrast,** the *Herald*'s editorial page deals with national matters on the average of three times a week.
- **On the other hand,** the *Beacon* does not share the *Herald*'s enthusiasm for interviews with national figures.
- The *Beacon,* **however,** does not encourage its reporters to tackle national stories the way the *Herald* does.
- **But** the *Herald*'s coverage of the Washington scene is much more comprehensive than its competitor's.

REVISION STRATEGIES

Once you have a draft of the essay, you're ready to revise. The following checklist will help you and those giving you feedback apply to comparison-contrast some of the revision techniques discussed in Chapters 7 and 8.

COMPARISON-CONTRAST: A REVISION/PEER REVIEW CHECKLIST

Revise Overall Meaning and Structure

- ☐ Are the subjects sufficiently alike for the comparison-contrast to be logical and meaningful?
- ☐ What purpose does the essay serve—to inform, to evaluate, to persuade readers to accept a viewpoint, to eliminate misconceptions, or to draw a surprising analogy?
- ☐ What is the essay's thesis? How could the thesis be stated more effectively?
- ☐ Is the overall essay organized primarily by the one-side-at-a-time method or by the point-by-point method? What is the advantage of that strategy for this essay?
- ☐ Are the same features discussed for each subject? Are they discussed in the same order?
- ☐ Which points of comparison and/or contrast need further development? Which points should be deleted? Where do significant points seem to be missing? How has the most important similarity or difference been emphasized?

Revise Paragraph Development

- ☐ If the essay uses the one-side-at-a-time method, which paragraph marks the switch from one subject to another?
- ☐ If the essay uses the point-by-point method, do paragraphs consistently alternate between subjects? If this alternation becomes too elaborate or predictable, what could be done to eliminate the problem?
- ☐ If the essay uses both the one-side-at-a-time and the point-by-point methods, which paragraph marks the switch from one method to the other? If the switch is confusing, how could it be made less so?
- ☐ Where would signal devices (*also, likewise, in contrast*) make it easier to see similarities and differences between the subjects being discussed?

Revise Sentences and Words

- ☐ Where do too many signal devices make sentences awkward and mechanical?
- ☐ Which sentences and words fail to convey the intended tone?

STUDENT ESSAY: FROM PREWRITING THROUGH REVISION

The student essay that follows was written by Carol Siskin in response to this assignment:

> In "Euromail and Amerimail," Eric Weiner contrasts European and American e-mail habits and customs, showing that one is more favorable than the other. In an essay of your own, contrast two personality types, lifestyles, or stages of life, demonstrating that one is superior to the other.

Having recently turned forty, Carol decided to write an essay taking issue with the idea that being young is better than being old. From time to time, Carol had used her *journal* to explore what it means to grow older. Rather than writing a new journal entry on the subject, she decided to look at earlier entries to see if they contained any helpful material for the assignment. One rather free-ranging entry, composed on the evening of her birthday, proved especially valuable. The original entry starts below. The handwritten marks indicate Carol's later efforts to shape and develop this raw material. Note the way Carol added details, circled main ideas, and indicated a possible sequence. These annotations paved the way for her outline, which is presented after the journal entry.

Journal Entry

Forty years old today. At 20 I thought 40 would mean the end of everything, but that's not the case at all. I'm much happier now. Possible conclusion

Mom and Dad made a dinner for the occasion. Talking of happy, they look great. Mom said this is the best part of their lives. They love retirement—and obviously each other. I hope Mitch and I will be that happy when we're in our sixties. And Dave and Elaine seem as good as ever. They look right together. What a pleasure it is to be a couple. I remember how lonely I was before Mitch and how lonely Dave was after his divorce. I sure don't envy young singles.

I (Appearance)

My diets. Hated big waist and legs.

overcoats vs. leather jackets

Dave seems content now. He looks handsome and robust, partly because he feels good about his life, partly because he tries to run pretty regularly. I remember how desperately he used to work out with weights because he worried about his appearance. I'm glad I don't have to be obsessed with my appearance the way I used to be. Mitch loves me the way I am. And I'm not obsessed anymore with being super stylish. Or thin. In fact, tonight, with no qualms whatever, I ate two healthy slices of birthday cake.

II (Decisions)

III (sense of self)

II

Dave says that Nancy (I can't believe she's 22) is thinking of going to graduate school, but she's not sure what to study. I can remember all the confusion I felt about schools and majors. I don't miss those days at all. Dave thinks Nancy is just plain confused about who she is and what she wants. Her goals change from day to day, especially because she's trying to please everyone. One day she feels confident; the next she's frightened. And she blames her parents' unhappy marriage for her confusion. No wonder she can't decide whether to marry and have kids. What chaos!

Tonight, though, was anything but chaos and confusion. It was an evening of quiet contentment. All of us enjoyed each other and got along. Quite different from the way it used to be. How I used to fight with Mom and Dad. I remember slamming the door and yelling, "It's your fault I was born." What unhappy times those were.

Outline

Thesis: Being young is good, but being older is better.

I. Appearance
   A. Dave and I when young
      1. Dave's weight lifting to build himself up
      2. My constant dieting to change my body
      3. Both begging for "right" clothes

- B. Attitudes now
  1. My contentment with my rounded shape
  2. Dave's satisfaction with his thinness
  3. Our clothes fashionable but comfortable

II. Decisions
- A. My major decisions mostly in the past
  1. About education
  2. About marriage and children
- B. Nancy's major decisions mostly in the future
  1. About education
  2. About marriage and children

III. Sense of self
- A. Nancy's uncertainty
  1. Unclear values and goals
  2. Strong need to be liked
  3. Unresolved feelings about parents
- B. Older person's surer self-identity
  1. Have clearer values and goals
  2. Can stand being disliked
  3. Don't blame parents

Now read Carol's paper, "The Virtues of Growing Older," noting the similarities and differences among her journal entry, outline, and final essay. You'll see that the essay is more developed than either the journal entry or outline. In the essay, Carol added numerous specific details—like those about Dave gobbling vitamins and milkshakes when he was a teen. In contrast, she omitted from the essay some journal material because it would have required burdensome explanations. For instance, if she hadn't eliminated the reference to Nancy, it would have been necessary to explain that Nancy is the daughter of Dave's wife by his first marriage. Despite these differences, you'll note that the essay's basic plan is derived largely from the journal entry and outline. As you read the essay, also consider how well it applies the principles of comparison-contrast discussed in this chapter. (The commentary that follows the paper will help you look at Carol's essay more closely and will give you some sense of how she went about revising her first draft.)

The Virtues of Growing Older

by Carol Siskin

1 Our society worships youth. Advertisements convince us to buy Grecian Formula and Oil of Olay so we can hide the gray in our hair and smooth the lines on our face. Television shows feature

The first of a two-paragraph introduction

attractive young stars with firm bodies, perfect complexions, and thick manes of hair. Middle-aged folks work out in gyms and jog down the street, trying to delay the effects of age.

The second introductory paragraph

Thesis

Wouldn't any person over thirty gladly sign with the devil 2
just to be young again? Isn't aging an experience to be dreaded? Perhaps it is un-American to say so, but I believe the answer is "No." Being young is often pleasant, but being older has distinct advantages.

First half of topic sentence for point 1: Appearance

Start of what it's like being young

Second half of topic sentence for point 1

Start of what it's like being older

When young, you are apt to be obsessed with your appearance. 3
When my brother Dave and I were teens, we worked feverishly to perfect the bodies we had. Dave lifted weights, took megadoses of vitamins, and drank a half-dozen milkshakes a day in order to turn his wiry adolescent frame into some muscular ideal. And as a teenager, I dieted constantly. No matter what I weighed, though, I was never satisfied with the way I looked. My legs were too heavy, my shoulders too broad, my waist too big. When Dave and I were young, we begged and pleaded for the "right" clothes. If our parents didn't get them for us, we felt our world would fall apart. How could we go to school wearing loose-fitting overcoats when everyone else would be wearing fitted leather jackets? We could be considered freaks. I often wonder how my parents, and parents in general, manage to tolerate their children during the adolescent years. Now, however, Dave and I are beyond such adolescent agonies. My rounded figure seems fine, and I don't deny myself a slice of pecan pie if I feel in the mood. Dave still works out, but he has actually become fond of his tall, lanky frame. The two of us enjoy wearing fashionable clothes, but we are no longer slaves to style. And women, I'm embarrassed to admit, even more than men, have always seemed to be at the mercy of fashion. Now my clothes—and my brother's—are attractive yet easy to wear. We no longer feel anxious about what others will think. As long as we feel good about how we look, we are happy.

First half of topic sentence for point 2: Life choices

Start of what it's like being older

Second half of topic sentence for point 2

Being older is preferable to being younger in another way. 4
Obviously, I still have important choices to make about my life, but I have already made many of the critical decisions that confront those just starting out. I chose the man I wanted to marry. I decided to have children. I elected to return to college to complete my education. But when you are young, major decisions

await you at every turn. "What college should I attend? What career should I pursue? Should I get married? Should I have children?" These are just a few of the issues facing young people. It's no wonder that, despite their care-free facade, they are often confused, uncertain, and troubled by all the unknowns in their future.

Start of what it's like being younger

5 But the greatest benefit of being forty is knowing who I am. The most unsettling aspect of youth is the uncertainty you feel about your values, goals, and dreams. Being young means wondering what is worth working for. Being young means feeling happy with yourself one day and wishing you were never born the next. It means trying on new selves by taking up with different crowds. It means resenting your parents and their way of life one minute and then feeling you will never be as good or as accomplished as they are. By way of contrast, forty is sanity. I have a surer self-concept now. I don't laugh at jokes I don't think are funny. I can make a speech in front of a town meeting or complain in a store because I am no longer terrified that people will laugh at me; I am no longer anxious that everyone must like me. I no longer blame my parents for my every personality quirk or keep a running score of everything they did wrong raising me. Life has taught me that I, not they, am responsible for who I am. We are all human beings—neither saints nor devils.

Topic sentence for point 3: Self-concept

Start of what it's like being younger

Start of what it's like being older

6 Most Americans blindly accept the idea that newer is automatically better. But a human life contradicts this premise. There is a great deal of happiness to be found as we grow older. My own parents, now in their sixties, recently told me that they are happier now than they have ever been. They would not want to be my age. Did this surprise me? At first, yes. Then it gladdened me. Their contentment holds out great promise for me as I move into the next—perhaps even better—phase of my life.

Conclusion

Commentary

Purpose and Thesis

In her essay, Carol disproves the widespread belief that being young is preferable to being old. The *comparison-contrast* pattern allows her to analyze the drawbacks of one and the merits of the other, thus providing the essay with an *evaluative purpose.* Using the title to indicate her point of view, Carol places the *thesis* at the end of her two-paragraph introduction: "Being young is often pleasant, but being older has distinct advantages." Note that the thesis accomplishes several things. It names the two subjects to be discussed and clarifies Carol's point of view about her subjects. The thesis also implies that the essay will focus on the contrasts between these two periods of life.

Points of Support and Overall Organization

To support her assertion that older is better, Carol supplies examples from her own life and organizes the examples around three main points: attitudes about appearance, decisions about life choices, and questions of self-concept. Using the *point-by-point method* to organize the overall essay, she explores each of these key ideas in a separate paragraph. Each paragraph is further focused by one or two sentences that serve as a topic sentence.

Sequence of Points, Organizational Cues, and Paragraph Development

Let's look more closely at the way Carol presents her three central points in the essay. She obviously considers appearance the least important of a person's worries, life choices more important, and self-concept the most critical. So she uses *emphatic order* to sequence the supporting paragraphs, with the phrase "But the greatest benefit" signaling the special significance of the last issue. Carol is also careful to use *transitions* to help readers follow her line of thinking: "*Now, however,* Dave and I are beyond such adolescent agonies" (3); "*But* when you are young, major decisions await you at every turn" (4); and "*By way of contrast,* forty is sanity" (5).

Although Carol has worked hard to write a well-organized paper—and has on the whole been successful—she doesn't feel compelled to make the paper fit a rigid format. As you've seen, the essay as a whole uses the point-by-point method, but each supporting paragraph uses the *one-side-at-a-time method*—that is, everything about one age group is discussed before there is a shift to the other age group. Notice too that the third and fifth paragraphs start with young people and then move to adults, whereas the fourth paragraph reverses the sequence by starting with older people.

Combining Patterns of Development

Carol uses the comparison-contrast format to organize her ideas, but other patterns of development also come into play. To illustrate her points, she makes extensive use of *illustration,* and her discussion also contains elements typical of *causal analysis.* Throughout the essay, for instance, she traces the effect of being a certain age on her brother, herself, and her parents.

A Problem with Unity

As you read the third paragraph, you might have noted that Carol's essay runs into a problem. Two sentences in the paragraph disrupt the *unity* of Carol's discussion: "I often wonder how my parents, and parents in general, manage to tolerate their children during the adolescent years," and "women, I'm embarrassed to admit . . . have always seemed to be at the mercy of fashion." These sentences should be deleted because they don't develop the idea that adolescents are overly concerned with appearance.

Conclusion

Carol's final paragraph brings the essay to a pleasing and interesting close. The conclusion recalls the point made in the introduction: Americans overvalue youth. Carol also uses the conclusion to broaden the scope of her discussion. Rather than continuing to focus on herself, she briefly mentions her parents and the pleasure they take in life. By bringing her parents into the essay, Carol is able to make a gently philosophical observation about the promise that awaits her as she grows older. The implication is that a similarly positive future awaits us, too.

Revising the First Draft

To help guide her revision, Carol asked her husband to read her first draft aloud. As he did, Carol took notes on what she sensed were the paper's strengths and weaknesses. She then jotted down her observations, as well as her husband's, onto the draft. Because Carol wasn't certain which observations were most valid, she didn't rank them. Carol made a number of changes when revising the essay. You'll get a good sense of how she proceeded if you compare the annotated original introduction reprinted here with the final version in the full essay.

Original Version of the Introduction

America is a land filled with people who worship youth. We admire dynamic young achievers; our middle-aged citizens work out in gyms; all of us wear tight tops and colorful sneakers—clothes that look fine on the young but ridiculous on aging bodies. Television shows revolve around perfect-looking young stars, while commercials entice us with products that will keep us young.

Boring paragraph
First sentence dull
Cut?
Make point about TV more specific

Wouldn't every older person want to be young again? Isn't aging to be avoided? It may be slightly unpatriotic to say so, but I believe the answer is "No." Being young may be pleasant at times, but I would rather be my forty-year-old self. I no longer have to agonize about my physical appearance, I have already made many of my crucial life decisions, and I am much less confused about who I am.

Make questions more vigorous
Maybe cut plan of development

After hearing her original two-paragraph introduction read aloud, Carol was dissatisfied with what she had written. Although she wasn't quite sure how to proceed, she knew that the paragraphs were flat and that they failed to open the essay on a strong note. She decided to start by whittling down the opening sentence, making it crisper and more powerful: "Our society worships youth." That done, she eliminated two bland statements ("We admire dynamic young achievers" and "all of us wear tight tops and colorful sneakers") and made several vague references more concrete and interesting. For example, "commercials entice us with products that will keep us young" became "Grecian Formula and Oil of Olay . . . hide the gray in our hair and smooth the lines on our face"; "perfect-looking young stars" became "attractive young stars with firm bodies, perfect complexions, and thick manes of hair." With the addition of these specifics, the first paragraph became more vigorous and interesting.

Carol next made some subtle changes in the two questions that opened the second paragraph of the original introduction. She replaced "Wouldn't every older person want to be young again?" and "Isn't aging to be avoided?" with two more emphatic questions: "Wouldn't any person over thirty gladly sign with the devil just to be young again?" and "Isn't aging an experience to be dreaded?" Carol also made some changes at the end of the original second paragraph. Because the paper is relatively short and the subject matter easy to understand, she decided to omit her somewhat awkward *plan of development* ("I no longer have to agonize about my physical appearance, I have already made many of my crucial life decisions, and I am much less confused about who I am"). This deletion made it possible to end the introduction with a clear statement of the essay's thesis.

Once these revisions were made, Carol was confident that her essay got off to a stronger start. Feeling reassured, she moved ahead and made changes in other sections of her paper. Such work enabled her to prepare a solid piece of writing that offers food for thought.

ACTIVITIES: COMPARISON-CONTRAST

Prewriting Activities

1. Imagine you're writing two essays: One explores the effects of holding a job while in college; the other explains how to budget money wisely. Jot down ways you might use comparison-contrast in each essay.

2. Suppose you plan to write a series of articles for your college newspaper. What purpose might you have for comparing and/or contrasting each of the following subject pairs?

a. MP3s and CDs
b. Paper or plastic bags at the supermarket
c. Two courses—one taught by an inexperienced newcomer, the other by an old pro
d. Cutting class and not showing up at work

3. Use the patterns of development or another prewriting technique to compare and/or contrast a current situation with the way you would like it to be. After reviewing your prewriting material, decide what your purpose, audience, tone, and point of view might be if you were to write an essay. Finally, write out your thesis and main supporting points.

4. Using your journal or freewriting, jot down the advantages and disadvantages of two ways of doing something (for example, watching movies in the theater versus watching them on a DVD player at home; following trends versus ignoring them; dating one person versus playing the field; and so on). Reread your prewriting and determine what your thesis, purpose, audience, tone, and point of view might be if you were to write an essay. Make a scratch list of the main ideas you would cover. Would a point-by-point or a one-side-at-a-time method of organization work more effectively?

Revising Activities

5. Of the statements that follow, which would *not* make effective thesis statements for comparison-contrast essays? Identify the problem(s) in the faulty statements and revise them accordingly.

   a. Although their classroom duties often overlap, teacher aides are not as equipped as teachers to handle disciplinary problems.
   b. This college provides more assistance to its students than most schools.
   c. During the state's last congressional election, both candidates relied heavily on television to communicate their messages.
   d. There are many differences between American and foreign cars.

6. The following paragraph is from the draft of an essay detailing the qualities of a skillful manager. How effective is this comparison-contrast paragraph? What revisions would help focus the paragraph on the point made in the topic sentence? Where should details be added or deleted? Rewrite the paragraph, providing necessary transitions and details.

   A manager encourages creativity and treats employees courteously, while a boss discourages staff resourcefulness and views it as a threat. At the hardware store where I work, I got my boss's approval to develop a system for organizing excess stock in the storeroom. I shelved items in roughly the same order as they were displayed in the store. The system was helpful to all the salespeople, not just to me, since everyone was stymied by the boss's helter-skelter system. What he did was store overstocked items according to each wholesaler, even though most of us weren't there long enough to know which items came from which wholesaler. His supposed system created chaos. When he saw what I had done, he was furious and insisted that we continue to follow the old slap-dash system. I had assumed he would welcome my ideas the way my manager did last summer when I worked in a drugstore. But he didn't and I had to scrap my work and go back to his eccentric system. He certainly could learn something about employee relations from the drugstore manager.

PROFESSIONAL SELECTIONS: COMPARISON–CONTRAST

TONI MORRISON

One of the most honored contemporary American writers, Nobel Prize–winner Toni Morrison (1931–) also received the National Book Critics Circle Award for Fiction for her novel *Song of Solomon* (1977) and the Pulitzer Prize for her novels *Tar Baby* (1981) and *Beloved* (1986). Her other books include *Dancing Mind* (1967), *Paradise* (1997), and *Love: A Novel* (2003). She has coauthored several works with her son, Slade Morrison, including *The Book of Mean People* (2002) and *Who's Got Game?* (2003–2007), a series of modernized Aesop's fables. In her capacity as an editor for Random House, she worked on autobiographies of boxer Muhammad Ali and civil rights activist Angela Davis, as well as on *To Die for the People* (1995), an account of the Black Panther Party. The essay reprinted here first appeared in *The New York Times Magazine* on July 4, 1976, the date of the American bicentennial.

Please note the essay structure diagram that appears following this selection (Figure 15.2 on page 367).

Pre-Reading Journal Entry

Though the members of a family often share some specific values and beliefs, they are just as likely to differ in their opinions on other subjects. In your journal, list the topics about which you and relatives of an older generation—your parents' or grandparents', for example—hold different, possibly opposite views. Then, for each topic on your list, go back and jot down what these differing beliefs are.

A SLOW WALK OF TREES

His name was John Solomon Willis, and when at age 5 he heard from the old folks that "the Emancipation Proclamation was coming," he crawled under the bed. It was his earliest recollection of what was to be his habitual response to the promise of white people: horror and an instinctive yearning for safety. He was my grandfather, a musician who managed to hold on to his violin but not his land. He lost all 88 acres of his Indian mother's inheritance to legal predators who built their fortunes on the likes of him. He was an unreconstructed black pessimist who, in spite of or because of emancipation, was convinced for 85 years that there was no hope whatever for black 1 people in this country. His rancor was legitimate, for he, John Solomon, was not only an artist but a first-rate carpenter and farmer, reduced to sending home to his family money he had made playing the violin because he was not able to find work. And this during the years when almost half the black male population were skilled craftsmen who lost their jobs to white ex-convicts and immigrant farmers.

2 His wife, however, was of a quite different frame of mind and believed that all things could be improved by faith in Jesus and an effort of the will. So it was she, Ardelia Willis, who sneaked her seven children out of the back window into the darkness, rather than permit the patron of their sharecropper's existence to become their executioner as well, and headed north in 1912, when 99.2 percent of all black people in the U.S. were native-born and only 60 percent of white Americans were. And it was Ardelia who told her husband that they could not stay in the Kentucky town they ended up in because the teacher didn't know long division.

3 They have been dead now for 30 years and more and I still don't know which of them came closer to the truth about the possibilities of life for black people in this country. One of their grandchildren is a tenured professor at Princeton. Another, who suffered from what the Peruvian poet called "anger that breaks a man into children," was picked up just as he entered his teens and emotionally lobotomized by the reformatories and mental institutions specifically designed to serve him. Neither John Solomon nor Ardelia lived long enough to despair over one or swell with pride over the other. But if they were alive today each would have selected and collected enough evidence to support the accuracy of the other's original point of view. And it would be difficult to convince either one that the other was right.

4 Some of the monstrous events that took place in John Solomon's America have been duplicated in alarming detail in my own America. There was the public murder of a President in a theater in 1865 and the public murder of another President on television in 1963. The Civil War of 1861 had its encore as the civil-rights movement of 1960. The torture and mutilation of a black West Point Cadet (Cadet Johnson Whittaker) in 1880 had its rerun with the 1970's murders of students at Jackson State College, Texas Southern and Southern University in Baton Rouge. And in 1976 we watch for what must be the thousandth time a pitched battle between the children of slaves and the children of immigrants—only this time, it is not the New York draft riots of 1863, but the busing turmoil in Paul Revere's home town, Boston.

5 Hopeless, he'd said. Hopeless. For he was certain that white people of every political, religious, geographical and economic background would band together against black people everywhere when they felt the threat of our progress. And a hundred years after he sought safety from the white man's "promise," somebody put a bullet in Martin Luther King's brain. And not long before that some excellent samples of the master race demonstrated their courage and virility by dynamiting some little black girls to death. If he were here now, my grandfather, he would shake his head, close his eyes and pull out his violin—too polite to say, "I told you so." And his wife would pay attention to the music but not to the sadness in her husband's eyes, for she would see what she expected to see—not the occasional historical repetition, but, *like the slow walk of certain species of trees from the flatlands up into the mountains*, she would see the signs of irrevocable and permanent change. She, who pulled her girls out of an inadequate school in the Cumberland Mountains, knew all along that the gentlemen from Alabama who had killed the little girls would be rounded up. And it wouldn't surprise her in the least to know that the number of black college graduates

jumped 12 percent in the last three years: 47 percent in 20 years. That there are 140 black mayors in this country; 14 black judges in the District Circuit, 4 in the Courts of Appeals and one on the Supreme Court. That there are 17 blacks in Congress, one in the Senate; 276 in state legislatures—223 in state houses, 53 in state senates. That there are 112 elected black police chiefs and sheriffs, 1 Pulitzer Prize winner; 1 winner of the Prix de Rome; a dozen or so winners of the Guggenheim; 4 deans of predominantly white colleges . . . Oh, her list would go on and on. But so would John Solomon's sweet sad music.

While my grandparents held opposite views on whether the fortunes of black people 6 were improving, my own parents struck similarly opposed postures, but from another slant. They differed about whether the moral fiber of white people would ever improve. Quite a different argument. The old folks argued about how and if black people could improve themselves, who could be counted on to help us, who would hinder us and so on. My parents took issue over the question of whether it was possible for white people to improve. They assumed that black people were the humans of the globe, but had serious doubts about the quality and existence of white humanity. Thus my father, distrusting every word and every gesture of every white man on earth, assumed that the white man who crept up the stairs one afternoon had come to molest his daughters and threw him down the stairs and then our tricycle after him. (I think my father was wrong, but considering what I have seen since, it may have been very healthy for me to have witnessed that as my first black-white encounter.) My mother, however, *believed* in them—their possibilities. So when the meal we got on relief was bug-ridden, she wrote a long letter to Franklin Delano Roosevelt. And when white bill collectors came to our door, it was she who received them civilly and explained in a sweet voice that we were people of honor and that the debt would be taken care of. Her message to Roosevelt got through—our meal improved. Her message to the bill collectors did not always get through and there was occasional violence when my father (self-exiled to the bedroom for fear he could not hold his temper) would hear that her reasonableness had failed. My mother was always wounded by these scenes, for she thought the bill collector knew that she loved good credit more than life and that being in arrears on a payment horrified her probably more than it did him. So she thought he was rude because he was white. For years she walked to utility companies and department stores to pay bills in person and even now she does not seem convinced that checks are legal tender. My father loved excellence, worked hard (he held three jobs at once for 17 years) and was so outraged by the suggestion of personal slackness that he could explain it to himself only in terms of racism. He was a fastidious worker who was frightened of one thing: unemployment. I can remember now the doomsday-*cum*-graveyard sound of "laid off" and how the minute school was out he asked us, "Where you workin'?" Both my parents believed that all succor and aid came from themselves and their neighborhood, since "they"—white people in charge and those not in charge but in obstructionist positions—were in some way fundamentally, genetically corrupt.

So I grew up in a basically racist household with more than a child's share of con- 7 tempt for white people. And for each white friend I acquired who made a small crack in that contempt, there was another who repaired it. For each one who related to me as a person, there was one who in my presence at least, became actively "white." And like most black people of my generation, I suffer from racial vertigo that can be cured only by taking what one needs from one's ancestors. John Solomon's cynicism and his deployment of his art as both weapon and solace; Ardelia's faith in the magic that can be wrought by sheer effort of the will; my mother's open-mindedness in each new encounter and her habit of trying reasonableness first; my father's temper, his impatience and his efforts to keep "them" (throw them) out of his life. And it is out of these learned and selected attitudes that I look at the quality of life for my people in this country now. These widely disparate and sometimes conflicting views, I suspect, were held not only by me, but by most black people. Some I know are clearer in their positions, have not sullied their anger with optimism or dirtied their hope with despair. But most of us are plagued by a sense of being worn shell-thin by constant repression and hostility as well as the impression of being buoyed by visible testimony of tremendous strides. There *is* repetition of the grotesque in our history. And there *is* the miraculous walk of trees. The question is whether our walk is progress or merely movement. O.J. Simpson leaning on a Hertz car[1] *is* better than the Gold Dust Twins on the back of a soap box. But is *Good Times*[2] better than Stepin Fetchit? Has the first order of business been taken care of? Does the law of the land work for us?

[1]Prior to his arrest and trial for the murder of his ex-wife, O. J. Simpson, a former football superstar, was the spokesperson for Hertz Rent-a-Car (editors' note).

[2]A popular 1970s television show featuring an African American family. Many critics felt that the show perpetuated harmful stereotypes (editors' note).

FIGURE 15.2
Essay Structure Diagram: "A Slow Walk of Trees" by Toni Morrison

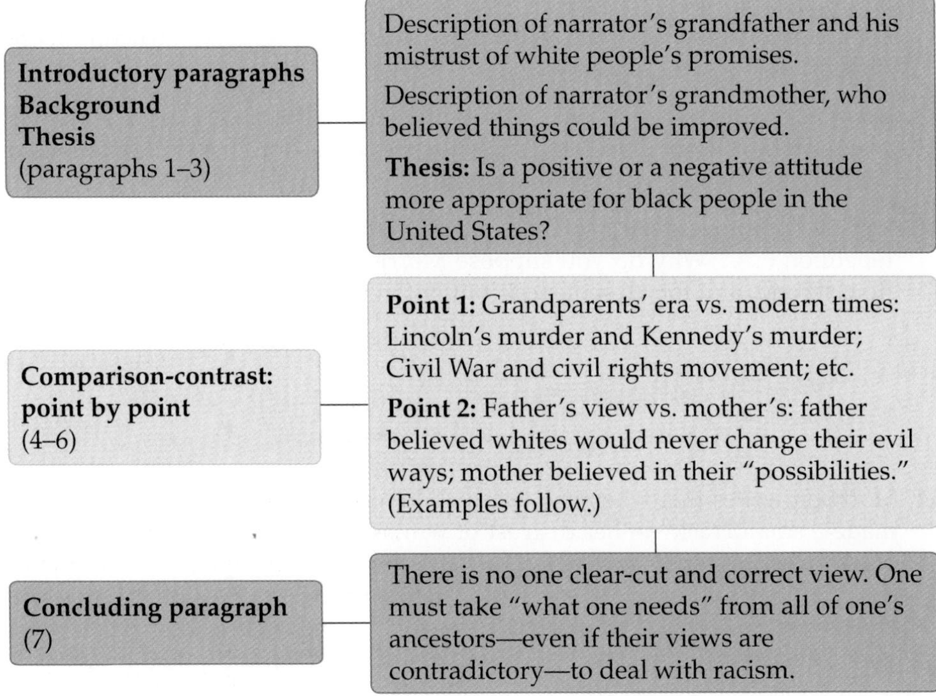

Questions for Close Reading

1. What is the selection's thesis? Locate the sentence(s) in which Morrison states her main idea. If she doesn't state the thesis explicitly, express it in your own words.
2. How did Morrison's grandfather and grandmother feel about opportunities for blacks? Why did they disagree?
3. Why does Morrison say she grew up in a "racist household"? To what extent does Morrison consider herself a racist?
4. What evidence is there, according to Morrison, that life for blacks in the United States has improved? What evidence does she cite to the contrary?
5. Refer to your dictionary as needed to define the following words used in the selection: *unreconstructed* (paragraph 1), *rancor* (1), *sharecropper* (2), *lobotomized* (3), *virility* (5), *irrevocable* (5), *hinder* (6), *arrears* (6), *fastidious* (6), *succor* (6), *vertigo* (7), and *deployment* (7).

Questions About the Writer's Craft

1. **The pattern.** Morrison builds her essay around the comparison-contrast between first, her grandparents, and then her parents. However, numerous other comparisons and contrasts appear in the essay. Identify some of these and explain how Morrison uses them to reinforce her thesis.
2. Look closely at paragraph 5. How does Morrison's sentence structure there underscore her central point?
3. Examine the lengthy analysis of the differences between Morrison's parents (paragraph 6). How does Morrison shift the focus from her grandparents to her parents, then from one parent to the other?
4. Reread the final seven sentences in paragraph 7, starting with "There *is* repetition . . ." Why do you suppose Morrison italicized the word *is* in the first, second, and fourth sentences, but not in the third?

Writing Assignments Using Comparison-Contrast as a Pattern of Development

1. Morrison writes that when she was a child, occasionally "a white friend . . . made a small crack" in her distrust of whites. Who in your life has "made a crack" in your generalizations about an issue, about people, or about yourself? Perhaps an aging but energetic relative changed your opinion that the elderly are to be pitied, or a friend's passion for Bach and Chopin challenged your belief that those who like classical music are boringly highbrow, or a

neighbor showed you that you had real athletic potential. Write an essay contrasting your "before" and "after" beliefs, remembering to provide vivid details to bring the contrast to life. You may want to read Maya Angelou's "Sister Flowers" (page 167) to gain insight into the way one person can alter another individual's entrenched views.

2. Write an essay contrasting the belief systems of two individuals whose views affected the way you think about a particular aspect of life—for example, academic success, tolerance for others, financial well-being. Like Morrison, begin by describing the differences in the individuals' beliefs.

Writing Assignments Combining Patterns of Development

3. Morrison writes that her grandfather's "rancor [toward whites] was legitimate." Write an essay in which you offer your personal *definition* of the phrase "legitimate rancor." Develop your *definition* by *narrating* a single event that shows the circumstances under which you believe rancor would be a valid response. Let the power of your details rather than inflamed language show that anger would be a justified reaction. For narratives about situations that justify anger, read Audre Lorde's "The Fourth of July" (page 208) and Brent Staples's "Black Men and Public Space" (page 412).

4. Despite the racism they encountered, Morrison's grandparents and parents believed in themselves and lived lives of great dignity. Focus on a specific group of individuals who, because of prejudice, often struggle to maintain their self-esteem. Possibilities include immigrants, the elderly, the overweight, the learning disabled, the physically challenged. Write an essay *describing* the specific *steps* that *one* group (for example, parents, schools, communities, or religious organizations) can take to encourage a healthy sense of optimism and possibility in these people.

Writing Assignment Using a Journal Entry as a Starting Point

5. Morrison reveals how members of the same family can hold different beliefs about the same issue. Write an essay in which you contrast your beliefs about *one* subject with the beliefs held by a family member of an older generation. Possible subjects include the status of women or men, the work ethic, racial relations, homosexuality, education, and so on. Before beginning to write, review the material you generated in your pre-reading journal entry, and try to come up with additional details and examples of these contesting viewpoints. At some point in the essay, indicate what you think has caused the shift in thinking between generations.

PATRICIA COHEN

The journalist Patricia Cohen, currently the theater editor at *The New York Times*, previously created and edited the Arts & Ideas section for the same publication. A graduate of Cornell University and the Woodrow Wilson School at Princeton, Cohen also wrote for *The Washington Post*, *Rolling Stone* magazine, and *New York Newsday*. The following essay (originally titled "*Cupid*: Spawn of Austen?") appeared in the Culturebox section of *Slate* online magazine on September 16, 2003.

Pre-Reading Journal Entry

The genre of reality-television shows has flourished in recent years, with the numbers and types of shows multiplying at a head-spinning pace. Consider various types of reality-TV shows: matchmaking and dating, athletic-challenge, housemate, secret-camera, personal makeover, home improvement, and so on. What are your feelings about each type of "real-life" show? Collectively, what is your opinion about the reality-TV genre as a whole? Spend some time recording your thoughts on these questions in your pre-reading journal.

REALITY TV: SURPRISING THROWBACK TO THE PAST?

Will Lisa Shannon find love and fortune? On tonight's finale of *Cupid*, CBS's latest 1 reality dating show, fans will find out which suitor has been chosen to propose to the series's lovely 25-year-old heroine from among the remaining would-be romantics. If Shannon accepts the proposal, the couple will be married right then and there. And if they stay married for a year, they will receive a $1 million check.

To many critics, *Cupid* and other matchmaking shows that mix money and real-life 2 marital machinations represent a cynical and tasteless new genre that is yet another sign of America's moral decline. But there's something familiar about the fortune hunters, the status seekers, the thwarted loves, the meddling friends, the public displays, the comic manners, and the sharp competitiveness—all find their counterparts in Jane Austen and Edith Wharton.[1] Only now, three-minute get-to-know-you tryouts in a TV studio substitute for three-minute waltzes at a ball. Traditional family values, it turns out, are back on television after all.

Lisa Shannon may lack the wit, depth, and cleverness of an Austen heroine, but like 3 many of Austen's women, she has put herself in the hands of others (in this case her friends and the TV audience), trusting that they will choose the right match. Even the idea that Shannon, at 25, feels the need to go to such lengths to find a husband suggests a troubling 19th-century ethos: A woman who is not married by her late 20s is doomed to be an Old Maid.

---

[1]Jane Austen (1775–1817) and Edith Wharton (1862–1937) are renowned for their novels exploring the intricate social workings—particularly as they relate to courtship and marriage—of the upper classes. Austen wrote of England's country elite in the late 1700s and early 1800s, while Wharton most famously examined New York's high society in the late 1800s and early 1900s (editors' note).

4 Undoubtedly, the hundreds of suitors who joined the pursuit are as attracted to the $1 million dowry as to Shannon. But money played a large (and openly discussed) role in the Victorian and Edwardian[2] contract as well. In *Pride and Prejudice*,[3] for example, we learn that "Mr. Darcy soon drew the attention of the room by his fine, tall person, handsome features, noble mien—and the report which was in general circulation within five minutes after his entrance of his having ten thousand a year." And in *Emma*,[4] Mr. Knightly scolds the novel's eponymous heroine for imagining a match between Mr. Elton and her friend Harriet, without understanding he is more interested in money than in love: "I have heard him speak with great animation of a large family of young ladies that his sisters are intimate with, who have all twenty thousand pounds apiece."

5 On *Cupid*, Lisa's friends Laura and Kimberly are there to protect her from such gold diggers. They helped Lisa screen the men who answered a coast-to-coast open call (which produced more candidates than did the California primary). After the three whittled down the list of hopefuls to 10, the final selection was turned over to TV viewers, who called in every week to vote for their favorite.

6 Like the secondary characters in Austen and Wharton, Shannon's companions are clearly there to provide piquant social commentary, deliciously wicked judgments, and intrigue, sabotaging some suitors and championing others. "Freak," "boring," "awful," shrieks Laura, Lisa's confidante, as she ridicules suitors' looks, accents, clothing, schooling, and pronunciation.

7 Of course, nothing but superficial snap judgments can be made in the few minutes that each man is initially given to impress the three women. But the snap judgments aren't necessarily unanimous, and Laura and Kimberly's debating of the various virtues and flaws (is he "an arrogant jerk" or a dependable lawyer?) are a prosaic version of Mr. Knightly's and Emma's spirited sparring over the lovesick Robert Martin:

8 "A respectable, intelligent gentleman-farmer," says Mr. Knightly.

9 "His appearance is so much against him, and his manner so bad," Emma responds.

10 Likewise, the hopeful bachelors on *Cupid* understand what goes into a suitable match. Corey, a rocket scientist with the Air Force, acknowledged up front, "I know you have your friends here because I have to fit in." One contestant, Rob, went so far as to boast, "I come from good stock, too. I have good hair and teeth," as if he were a racehorse, waiting for her to check his gums.

11 Even Richard Kaye, an English professor and the author of *The Flirt's Tragedy: Desire Without End in Victorian and Edwardian Fiction*, confesses to being a "guilty watcher" of the new matchmaking shows, finding the parallels spookily similar. But inevitably, these series—*The Bachelorette*, *Meet My Folks*, *Married by America*, and *For Love or Money* (where a woman can keep the man or the million but not both)—have all been scorned for debasing the sanctity of marriage and for their shallow, indecorous exhibitionism.

[2]The Victorian period refers to the time of Queen Victoria's reign in England (1837–1901), while the Edwardian period refers to the reign of England's King Edward VII (1901–1910) (editors' note).

[3]Novel written by Jane Austen and published in 1813 (editors' note).

[4]Novel written by Austen and published in 1815 (editors' note).

But the shows also betray dissatisfaction with the individualistic, go-it-alone ethic of modern courtship. The Victorians and Edwardians organized balls, dinners, afternoon teas, country walks, and the like to help their younger members find mates. Today, without such formal social arrangements, singles are pretty much left to their own devices to suss out partners. And while the elaborate courtship rituals and codes may now seem curiously antique, they did serve to cushion the brutally competitive marriage market. "I've been looking for Mr. Right and I've just not been able to find him," Lisa confesses. "Based on my track record, I obviously need help." She has discovered what Lily Bart in Wharton's *The House of Mirth*[5] learned after losing a sought-after bachelor. Upon hearing of the wealthy match that Grace Van Osburgh expertly concocted for her daughter, Bart concludes: "The cleverest girl may miscalculate where her own interests are concerned, may yield too much at one moment and withdraw too far at the next." 12

In the end, the American public will choose Lisa's potential spouse in what could be seen simply as a more democratic version of those literary heroes and heroines who gave themselves wholly over to society and allowed their extended family to pick an appropriate mate. And why not? The idea that a good husband is hard to find has become a cultural watchword. Meanwhile, the high divorce rate is evidence that love, American style, hasn't necessarily produced happier unions. Nor should anyone forget that Lisa, too, stands to gain the million only through an advantageous marriage. And if it doesn't work out after a year, she at least has one of the modern conveniences not available to Austen's or Wharton's protagonists: a no-fault divorce.[6] 13

---

[5]Novel published in 1905 (editors' note).

[6]Lisa Shannon and Hank Stapleton, the man selected for her, continued to date in the year following *Cupid's* conclusion, though they rejected the option of marrying during the final episode—along with the possibility of winning one million dollars on their first anniversary (editors' note).

Questions for Close Reading

1. What is the selection's thesis? Locate the sentence(s) in which Cohen states her main idea. If she doesn't state the thesis explicitly, express it in your own words.
2. What does Cohen assert is the common perception of reality-TV dating shows among critics? Does she agree or disagree with this evaluation?
3. What are three similarities between the dating shows and the plots of classic novels?
4. Though her essay is principally a comparison of reality dating shows and classic novels, Cohen also acknowledges some important contrasts between them. What are these differences?
5. Refer to your dictionary as needed to define the following words used in the selection: *suitor* (paragraph 1), *machinations* (2), *cynical* (2), *thwarted* (2),

counterparts (2), *waltzes* (2), *ethos* (3), *dowry* (4), *mien* (4), *eponymous* (4), *animation* (4), *gold diggers* (5), *piquant* (6), *intrigue* (6), *sabotaging* (6), *confidante* (6), *unanimous* (7), *prosaic* (7), *sparring* (7), *debasing* (11), *indecorous* (11), *exhibitionism* (11), *courtship* (12), *suss out* (12), and *protagonists* (13).

Questions About the Writer's Craft

1. **The pattern.** Which comparison-contrast method of organization (point-by-point or one-side-at-a-time) does Cohen use to develop her essay? Why might she have chosen this pattern?
2. What kind of audience do you think Cohen is writing for—one that already agrees with her, disagrees, or is indifferent? How can you tell?
3. Throughout her essay, Cohen uses direct quotes from various sources. What kinds of sources does she quote? Why do you think she chose to quote rather than to paraphrase or summarize them?
4. **Other patterns.** In paragraphs 12 and 13, Cohen presents a *causal analysis* of modern-day dating. How does this examination of *causes* and *effects* help reinforce her thesis?

Writing Assignments Using Comparison-Contrast as a Pattern of Development

1. Cohen draws a surprisingly apt comparison between today's reality dating shows and classic novels of the 1800s and early 1900s. Think of another area, device, or activity in modern life that you think compares to one from a previous time. For example, you might find similarities between sending e-mails and old-fashioned letter writing. Or you might find compelling echoes of stagecoaches of the distant past in today's RV's. Write an essay in which you compare the two things you've selected, presenting two or three ways in which they are similar. Along the way, you should acknowledge obvious differences as a way of accounting for a skeptical audience.

2. One need not look as far back as the classic novels Cohen cites to observe that courtship rituals have changed—even a single generation is enough for such differences to surface. Spend some time interviewing a parent, grandparent, or other member of an older generation. Then write an essay comparing and/or contrasting the dating practices of that generation with those of your own. Either along the way or in your conclusion, offer some analysis of why things have changed so much, and indicate whether you think this change is for the better. Before writing, consider reading Eric Weiner's comparative essay, "Euromail and Amerimail" (page 375).

Writing Assignments Combining Patterns of Development

3. In discussing the role that Lisa's friends play on the dating show, Cohen observes that they "sabotag[e] some suitors and [champion] others." Take a moment to think about an instance when friends were involved, for better or for worse, in a courtship of your own. Write an essay *narrating* a time when your friends either helped or hindered you with a budding romance. Be sure to provide the right amount of background information so that readers can understand the situation, while avoiding getting bogged down in unnecessary detail. Providing dialogue might also help you in recounting events. Along the way or in your conclusion, you should discuss the *effect* your friends had on the romantic relationship as well as whether this episode had an *effect* on your friendship.

4. With the "marriage market" as "brutally competitive" as Cohen asserts, many average people are turning to how-to books for advice on dating and romance. Write your own instructional guide, but one with a twist: a how *not*-to dating guide for today's singles. Adopt whatever tone you'd like, though a humorous one might be especially appropriate. You might address what not to wear (for example, a tattered shirt that smells like mothballs) or what not to eat (an extra garlicky platter of spaghetti) or what not to talk about ("I have this ingrown toenail . . ."). No matter what areas you address, clearly present the *steps* that would ensure romantic failure. Along the way, provide vivid *examples* of what to avoid, indicating the possible *effects* of not following your advice. Before you begin to write, consider reading "Cyberschool" (page 328), in which Clifford Stoll describes a process he'd prefer that his readers not follow.

Writing Assignment Using a Journal Entry as a Starting Point

5. Cohen argues that reality-TV dating shows are not as dreadful—or as original—as some like to argue. What do you think of reality TV as a genre? Review the thoughts you recorded in your pre-reading journal entry as well as your ideas now that you've read the selection. Write an essay in which you argue that reality television is *or* is not a worthwhile form of entertainment. In making your argument, cite two or three categories of reality-TV shows. As you discuss each kind of show, be sure to provide specific *examples* from shows in that category. Before writing, you might benefit from researching in the library and/or on the Internet the subject of reality-TV shows.

ERIC WEINER

Eric Weiner (1963–) is a national correspondent for NPR.org, part of National Public Radio. He began his journalism career by reporting on business issues for

The New York Times and NPR's Washington, D.C., bureau and then spent most of the 1990s reporting on wars and world events from South Asia and the Middle East. A licensed pilot who loves to eat sushi, Weiner occasionally writes lighter pieces drawn on his experience with other cultures. A short version of this piece about e-mail was broadcast on *Day to Day*, a National Public Radio magazine show, on March 24, 2005; the full version, which appears here, was posted on Slate.com the next day.

Pre-Reading Journal Entry

Just one hundred years ago, people communicated only by speaking face to face or by writing a letter—with an occasional brief telegram in emergencies. Today, technology has given us many ways to communicate. Think over all the different ways you communicate with your family, friends, classmates, instructors, co-workers, and others. What methods of communication do you use with each of these groups? Which forms do you prefer, and why? Use your journal to answer these questions.

EUROMAIL AND AMERIMAIL

1 North America and Europe are two continents divided by a common technology: e-mail. Techno-optimists assure us that e-mail—along with the Internet and satellite TV—make the world smaller. That may be true in a technical sense. I can send a message from my home in Miami to a German friend in Berlin and it will arrive almost instantly. But somewhere over the Atlantic, the messages get garbled. In fact, two distinct forms of e-mail have emerged: Euromail and Amerimail.

2 Amerimail is informal and chatty. It's likely to begin with a breezy "Hi" and end with a "Bye." The chances of Amerimail containing a smiley face or an "xoxo" are disturbingly high. We Americans are reluctant to dive into the meat of an e-mail; we feel compelled to first inform hapless recipients about our vacation on the Cape which was really excellent except the jellyfish were biting and the kids caught this nasty bug so we had to skip the whale watching trip but about that investors' meeting in New York . . . Amerimail is a bundle of contradictions: rambling and yet direct; deferential, yet arrogant. In other words, Amerimail *is* America.

3 Euromail is stiff and cold, often beginning with a formal "Dear Mr. X" and ending with a brusque "Sincerely." You won't find any mention of kids or the weather or jellyfish in Euromail. It's all business. It's also slow. Your correspondent might take days, even weeks, to answer a message. Euromail is also less confrontational in tone, rarely filled with the overt nastiness that characterizes American e-mail disagreements. In other words, Euromail is exactly like the Europeans themselves. (I am, of course, generalizing. German e-mail style is not exactly the same as Italian or Greek, but they have more in common with each other than they do with American mail.)

4 These are more than mere stylistic differences. Communication matters. Which model should the rest of the world adopt: Euromail or Amerimail?

5 A California-based e-mail consulting firm called People-onthego sheds some light on the e-mail divide. It recently asked about 100 executives on both sides of the Atlantic

whether they noticed differences in e-mail styles. Most said yes. Here are a few of their observations:

> "Americans tend to write (e-mails) exactly as they speak."
> "Europeans are less obsessive about checking e-mail."
> "In general, Americans are much more responsive to email—they respond faster and provide more information."

One respondent noted that Europeans tend to segregate their e-mail accounts. Rarely do they send personal messages on their business accounts, or vice versa. These differences can't be explained merely by differing comfort levels with technology. Other forms of electronic communication, such as SMS text messaging, are more popular in Europe than in the United States.

The fact is, Europeans and Americans approach e-mail in a fundamentally different way. Here is the key point: For Europeans, e-mail has replaced the business letter. For Americans, it has replaced the telephone. That's why we tend to unleash what e-mail consultant Tim Burress calls a "brain dump": unloading the content of our cerebral cortex onto the screen and hitting the send button. "It makes Europeans go ballistic," he says. 6

Susanne Khawand, a German high-tech executive, has been on the receiving end of American brain dumps, and she says it's not pretty. "I feel like saying, 'Why don't you just call me instead of writing five e-mails back and forth,'" she says. Americans are so overwhelmed by their bulging inboxes that "you can't rely on getting an answer. You don't even know if they read it." In Germany, she says, it might take a few days, or even weeks, for an answer, but one always arrives. 7

Maybe that's because, on average, Europeans receive fewer e-mails and spend less time tending their inboxes. An international survey of business owners in 24 countries (conducted by the accounting firm Grant Thornton) found that people in Greece and Russia spend the least amount of time dealing with e-mail every day: 48 minutes on average. Americans, by comparison, spend two hours per day, among the highest in the world. (Only Filipinos spend more time on e-mail, 2.1 hours.) The survey also found that European executives are skeptical of e-mail's ability to boost their bottom line. 8

It's not clear why European and American e-mail styles have evolved separately, but I suspect the reasons lie within deep cultural differences. Americans tend to be impulsive and crave instant gratification. So we send e-mails rapid-fire and get antsy if we don't receive a reply quickly. Europeans tend to be more methodical and plodding. They send (and reply to) e-mails only after great deliberation. 9

For all their Continental fastidiousness, Europeans can be remarkably lax about e-mail security, says Bill Young, an executive vice president with the Strickland Group. Europeans are more likely to include trade secrets and business strategies in e-mails, he says, much to the frustration of their American colleagues. This is probably because identity theft—and other types of backing—are much less of a problem in Europe than in the United States. Privacy laws are much stricter in Europe. 10

So, which is better: Euromail or Amerimail? Personally, I'm a convert—or a defector, if you prefer—to the former. I realize it's not popular these days to suggest we have anything to learn from Europeans, but I'm fed up with an inbox cluttered with rambling, 11 barely cogent missives from friends and colleagues. If the alternative is a few stiffly written, politely worded bits of Euromail, then I say . . . bring it on.

Questions for Close Reading

1. What is the selection's thesis? Locate the sentence(s) in which Weiner states his main idea. If he doesn't state his thesis explicitly, express it in your own words.
2. According to Weiner, what are the main characteristics of American e-mail? What are the main characteristics of European e-mail?
3. When Americans and Europeans e-mail one another for business reasons, frustration often ensues. Why, according to Weiner, is this so? What are some examples of e-mail differences that cause frustration?
4. Which type of e-mail does Weiner favor? Why?
5. Refer to your dictionary as needed to define the following words used in the selection: *hapless* (paragraph 2), *deferential* (2), *brusque* (3), *confrontational* (3), *overt* (3), *bottom line* (8), *fastidiousness* (10), *lax* (10), *cogent* (11), and *missives* (11).

Questions About the Writer's Craft

1. The opening paragraph of this essay is full of technology-related words: *technology, e-mail, techno-optimists, Internet, Satellite TV, technical sense, Euromail,* and *Amerimail*. What is the effect of using all these "techno-terms"? How does the remainder of the essay contrast with the dominant impression of the first paragraph?
2. **The Pattern.** Make a brief outline of the points Weiner makes about American and European e-mail. What type of organization does he use for the essay? How else could he have organized the points he makes? Which method of organization do you think is more effective for this essay?
3. **The Pattern.** Identify the transitional expressions that Weiner uses to signal similarities and differences. Why do you think there are so few of these expressions? How might the fact that this essay was meant to be read aloud affect Weiner's transitions between Amerimail and Euromail? (You can listen to the short version of the essay at www.npr.org; search using the key term "Euromail.") Do you think the essay would be better if Weiner had used more transitional expressions? Explain.
4. What type of conclusion does Weiner use? (To review strategies for conclusions, see pages 82–84). What is his concluding point? Were you surprised by this conclusion? Why or why not?

Writing Assignments Using Comparison-Contrast as a Pattern of Development

1. Weiner attributes differences between Americans and Europeans in the use of e-mail to underlying cultural differences. Consider the differences in the use of e-mail among specific sub-groups of Americans, for example, among Americans of different generations, different genders, or different ethnic groups. Drawing on your own personal experience and that of people you know, write an essay comparing and contrasting some of the ways these two different groups of Americans use e-mail. For another take on differences in communication—of the racial variety—read Leslie Savan's "Black Talk and Pop Culture" on page 258

2. The etiquette of e-mail correspondence certainly is not the only way in which Americans differ from Europeans. Consider some additional ways that Americans as a whole differ from another specific nationality or ethnic group, European or otherwise. Write an essay in which you *contrast* the way Americans and the other group approach at least three cultural practices. You might look at attitudes toward gender roles, child-rearing, personal fitness, treatment of the ill or the elderly, leisure versus work ratios, the environment, and so on. Before you begin to write, consider what sort of tone might best suit your essay. You might adopt a straightforward tone (like Weiner), or you might find a humorous approach better suits your material.

Writing Assignments Combining Patterns of Development

3. Weiner's essay focuses primarily on the business use of e-mail among Americans and Europeans. Do some research on the Internet about the various uses of e-mail that have developed. Write an essay identifying how e-mail has *affected* our personal lives, our academic lives, and our business lives. Be sure to provide specific examples and data, where possible, to support the claims you make about these areas of change. Consider concluding your essay by summarizing whether e-mail has been beneficial, harmful, or both.

4. Weiner's preference for Euromail indicates that he longs for a more formal approach to communication. Over time, several other types of behaviors have evolved to be less formal than they once were. Select another aspect of behavior that has acquired a more casual mode; examples include dining etiquette, forms of address, dress codes, classroom protocol or student-teacher dynamics, and so on. Write an essay in which you explore at least two to three *causes* for the shift from more formal to more casual expressions of this behavior. As you examine the causes, you'll likely find yourself *contrasting* former and current practices. And your conclusion should *argue* for the superiority of either the casual or the formal approach.

Writing Assignment Using a Journal Entry as a Starting Point

5. Review your pre-reading journal entry about the different communication methods you use. Select three of your favorite methods, and write an essay dividing and classifying each of these methods, analyzing how you use it to communicate, and with whom. What are each method's advantages and disadvantages? Be sure to provide specific examples along the way. For additional perspectives on modern communication, read Leslie Savan's "Black Talk and Pop Culture" (page 258) and David Shipley's "Talk About Editing" (page 340).

ADDITIONAL WRITING TOPICS: COMPARISON-CONTRAST

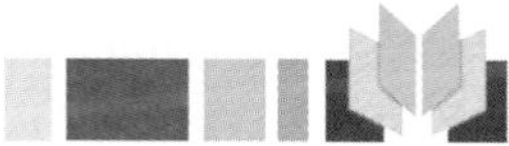

General Assignments

Using comparison-contrast, write an essay on one of the following topics. Your thesis should indicate whether the two subjects are being compared, contrasted, or both. Organize the paper by arranging the details in a one-side-at-a-time or point-by-point pattern. Remember to use organizational cues to help the audience follow your analysis.

1. Living at home versus living in an apartment or dorm
2. Two-career family versus one-career family
3. Two approaches for dealing with problems
4. Children's pastimes today and yesterday
5. Life before the Internet versus after the Internet
6. Neighborhood stores versus shopping malls
7. Two attitudes toward money
8. A sports team then and now
9. Watching a movie on television versus viewing it in a theater
10. Two approaches to parenting
11. Two approaches to studying
12. Marriage versus living together
13. Two views on a controversial issue
14. The coverage of an event on television versus its coverage in a newspaper

15. A typical fan of one type of music versus another
16. The atmosphere in two classes
17. A significant trend versus a passing fad
18. Handwriting a letter versus sending an e-mail message
19. Two candidates for political office
20. Two friends with different lifestyles

Assignments with a Specific Purpose, Audience, and Point of View

On Campus

1. You would like to change your campus living arrangements. Perhaps you want to move from a dormitory to an off-campus apartment or from home to a dorm. Before you do, though, you'll have to convince your parents (who are paying most of your college costs) that the move will be beneficial. Write out what you would say to your parents. Contrast your current situation with your proposed one, explaining why the new arrangement would be better.
2. Write a guide on "Passing Exams" for first-year college students, contrasting the right and wrong ways to prepare for and take exams. Although your purpose is basically serious, write the section on how *not* to approach exams with some humor.

At Home or in the Community

3. As president of your local neighbors' association, you're concerned about the way your local government is dealing with a particular situation (for example, an increase in robberies, muggings, graffiti, and so on). Write a letter to your mayor contrasting the way your local government handles the situation with another city or town's approach. In your conclusion, point out the advantages of adopting the other neighborhood's strategy.
4. Your old high school has invited you back to make a speech before an audience of seniors. The topic will be "how to choose the college that is right for you." Write your speech in the form of a comparison-contrast analysis. Focus on the choices available (two-year versus four-year schools, large versus small, local versus faraway, and so on), showing the advantages and/or disadvantages of each.

On the Job

5. As a store manager, you decide to write a memo to all sales personnel explaining how to keep customers happy. Compare and/or contrast the needs and shopping habits of several different consumer groups (by age, spending ability, or sex), and show how to make each group comfortable in your store.

6. You work as a volunteer for a mental health hot line. Many people call simply because they feel "stressed out." Do some research on the subject of stress management, and prepare a brochure for these people, recommending a "Type B" approach to stressful situations. Focus the brochure on the contrast between "Type A" and "Type B" personalities: the former is nervous, hard-driving, competitive; the latter is relaxed and noncompetitive. Give specific examples of how each "type" tends to act in stressful situations.

For additional writing, reading, and research resources, go to **www.mycomplab.com** and choose **Nadell/Langan/Comodromos'** ***The Longman Writer, 7/e***.

Cause-Effect

16

Ken McGraw/Index Stock Imagery, Inc.

What Is Cause-Effect?

Superstition has it that curiosity killed the cat. Maybe so. Yet our science, technology, storytelling, and fascination with the past and future all spring from our determination to know "Why" and "What if." Seeking explanations, young children barrage adults with endless questions: "Why do trees grow tall?" "What would happen if the sun didn't shine?" But children aren't the only ones who wonder in this way. All of us think in terms of cause and effect, sometimes consciously, sometimes unconsciously: "Why did they give me such an odd look?" we wonder, or "How would I do at another college?" we speculate. This exploration of reasons and results is also at the heart of most professions: "What led to our involvement in Vietnam?" historians question; "What will happen if we administer this experimental drug?" scientists ask.

Cause-effect writing, often called **causal analysis,** is rooted in this elemental need to make connections. Because the drive to understand reasons and results is so fundamental, causal analysis is a common kind of writing. An article analyzing the unexpected outcome of an election, a report linking poor nutrition to low academic achievement, an editorial analyzing the impact of a proposed tax cut—all are examples of cause-effect writing.

Done well, cause-effect pieces uncover the subtle and often surprising connections between events or phenomena. By rooting out causes and projecting effects, causal analysis enables us to make sense of our experiences, revealing a world that is somewhat less arbitrary and chaotic.

HOW CAUSE-EFFECT FITS YOUR PURPOSE AND AUDIENCE

Many assignments and exam questions in college involve writing essays that analyze causes, effects, or both. Sometimes, as in the following examples, you'll be asked to write an essay developed primarily through the cause-effect pattern:

> Although divorces have leveled off in the past few years, the number of marriages ending in divorce is still greater than it was a generation ago. What do you think are the causes of this phenomenon?
>
> Political commentators were surprised that so few people voted in the last election. Discuss the probable causes of this weak voter turnout.
>
> Americans never seem to tire of gossip about the rich and famous. What effect has this fascination with celebrities had on American culture?
>
> The federal government is expected to pass legislation that will significantly reduce the funding of student loans. Analyze the possible effects of such a cutback.

Other assignments and exam questions may not explicitly ask you to address causes and effects, but they may use words that suggest causal analysis would be appropriate. Consider these examples, paying special attention to the italicized words:

Cause

> In contrast to the socially involved youth of the 1960s, many young people today tend to remove themselves from political issues. What do you think are the *sources* of the political apathy found among 18- to 25-year-olds?

Effect

> A number of experts forecast that drug abuse will be the most significant factor affecting American productivity in the coming decade. Evaluate the validity of this observation by discussing the *impact* of drugs on the workplace.

Cause and Effect

> According to school officials, a predictable percentage of entering students drop out of college at some point during their first year. What *motivates* students to drop out? What *happens* to them once they leave?

In addition to serving as the primary strategy for achieving an essay's purpose, causal analysis can also be a supplemental method used to help make a point in an essay developed chiefly through another pattern of development. Assume, for example, that you want to write an essay *defining* the term *the homeless.* To help readers see that unfavorable circumstances can result in nearly anyone becoming homeless, you might discuss some of the unavoidable, everyday factors causing people to live on streets and in subway stations. Similarly, in a *persuasive* proposal urging your college administration to institute an honors program, you would probably spend some time analyzing the positive effects of such a program on students and faculty.

At this point, you have a good sense of the way writers use cause-effect to achieve their purpose and to connect with their readers. Now take a moment to look closely at the photograph at the beginning of this chapter. Imagine you're writing a column, accompanied by the photo, for the website of a local environmental organization. Your purpose is to prevent further development of nearby wilderness areas. Jot down ideas you might include when discussing the *effects* of such development.

PREWRITING STRATEGIES

The following checklist shows how you can apply to cause-effect some of the prewriting techniques discussed in Chapter 2.

CAUSE-EFFECT: A PREWRITING CHECKLIST

Choose a Topic

☐ Do your journal entries reflect an ongoing interest in the causes of and/or effects of something? (What causes friends to drop out of school? What will be the effect of recent legislation regarding abortion?)

☐ Will you analyze a personal phenomenon (for example, your decision to stop smoking), a change at your college (new requirements for graduation), a nationwide trend (the growing popularity of "tabloid television"), or a historical event (the defeat of the Equal Rights Amendment)?

☐ Does your subject intrigue, anger, puzzle you? Is it likely to interest your readers as well?

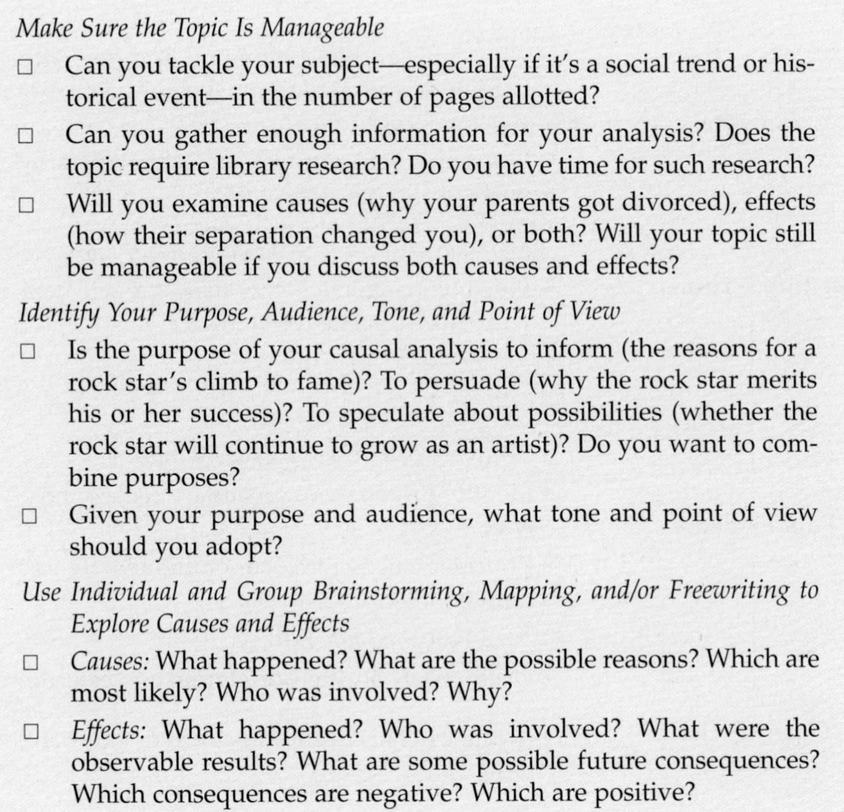

Make Sure the Topic Is Manageable

- ☐ Can you tackle your subject—especially if it's a social trend or historical event—in the number of pages allotted?
- ☐ Can you gather enough information for your analysis? Does the topic require library research? Do you have time for such research?
- ☐ Will you examine causes (why your parents got divorced), effects (how their separation changed you), or both? Will your topic still be manageable if you discuss both causes and effects?

Identify Your Purpose, Audience, Tone, and Point of View

- ☐ Is the purpose of your causal analysis to inform (the reasons for a rock star's climb to fame)? To persuade (why the rock star merits his or her success)? To speculate about possibilities (whether the rock star will continue to grow as an artist)? Do you want to combine purposes?
- ☐ Given your purpose and audience, what tone and point of view should you adopt?

Use Individual and Group Brainstorming, Mapping, and/or Freewriting to Explore Causes and Effects

- ☐ *Causes:* What happened? What are the possible reasons? Which are most likely? Who was involved? Why?
- ☐ *Effects:* What happened? Who was involved? What were the observable results? What are some possible future consequences? Which consequences are negative? Which are positive?

STRATEGIES FOR USING CAUSE-EFFECT IN AN ESSAY

After prewriting, you're ready to draft your essay. The following suggestions and Figure 16.1 (on page 386) will be helpful whether you use causal analysis as a dominant or supportive pattern of development.

1. **Stay focused on the purpose of your analysis.** When writing a causal analysis, don't lose sight of your overall purpose. Consider, for example, an essay on the causes of widespread child abuse. If you're concerned primarily with explaining the problem of child abuse to your readers, you might take a purely *informative* approach:

   > Although parental stress is the immediate cause of child abuse, the more compelling reason for such behavior lies in the way parents were themselves mistreated as children.

FIGURE 16.1
Development Diagram: Writing a Cause-Effect Essay

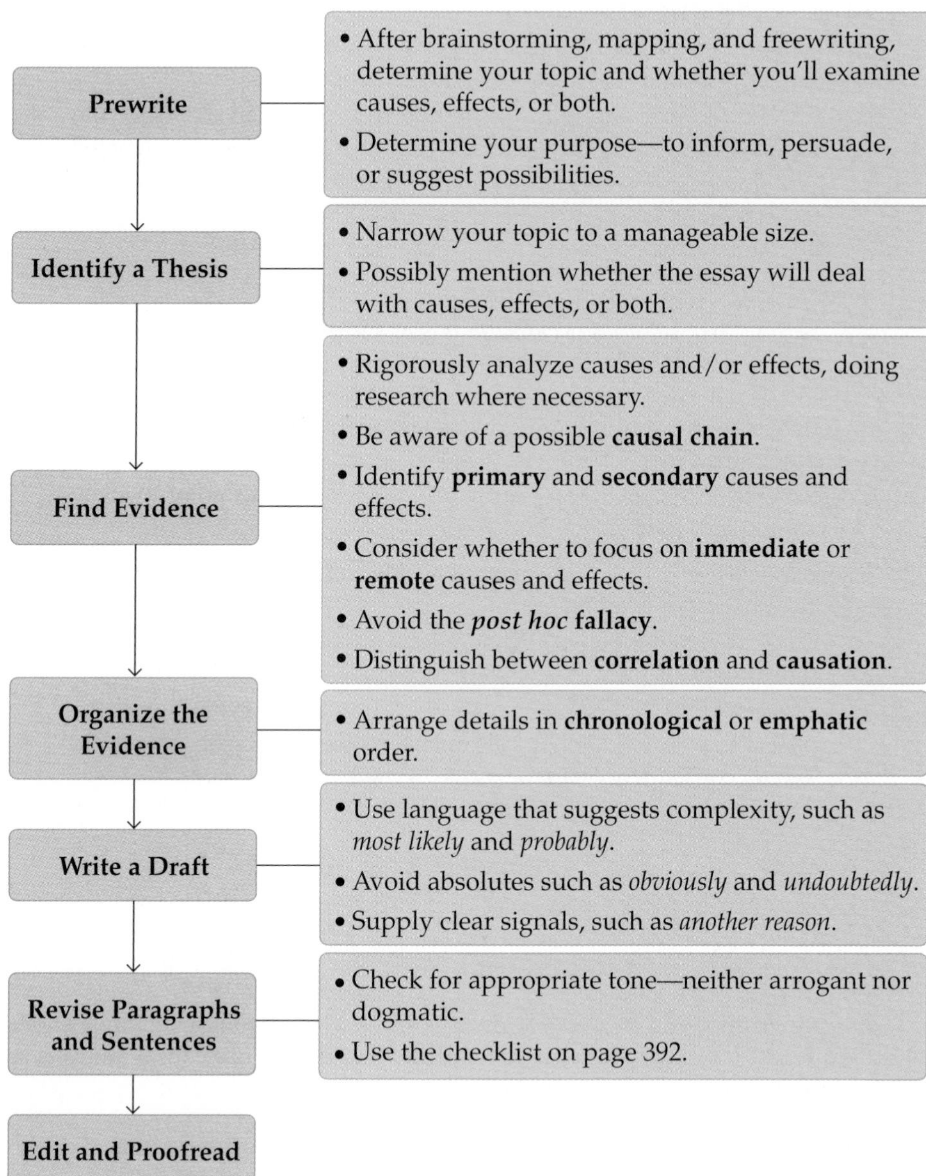

Or you might want to *persuade* your audience about some point or idea concerning child abuse:

```
     The tragic consequences of child abuse provide strong
support for more aggressive handling of such cases by social
workers and judges.
```

Then again, you could choose a *speculative* approach, your main purpose being to suggest possibilities:

```
    Psychologists disagree about the potential effect on
youngsters of all the media attention given to child abuse.
Will children exposed to this media coverage grow up
assertive, self-confident, and able to protect themselves? Or
will they become fearful and distrustful?
```

These examples illustrate that an essay's causal analysis may have more than one purpose. For instance, although the last example points to a paper with a primarily speculative purpose, the essay would probably start by informing readers of experts' conflicting views. The paper would also have a persuasive slant if it ended by urging readers to complain to the media about their sensationalized treatment of the child-abuse issue.

2. **Adapt content and tone to your purpose and readers.** Your purpose and audience determine what supporting material and what tone will be most effective in a cause-effect essay. Assume you want to direct your essay on child abuse to general readers who know little about the subject. To *inform* readers, you might use facts, statistics, and expert opinion to provide an objective discussion of the causes of child abuse. Your analysis might show the following: (1) adults who were themselves mistreated as children tend to abuse their own offspring; (2) marital stress contributes to the mistreatment of children; and (3) certain personality disorders increase the likelihood of child abuse. Sensitive to what your readers would and wouldn't understand, you would stay away from a technical or formal tone. Rather than writing, "Pathological pre-abuse symptomatology predicts adult transference of high aggressivity," you would say, "Psychologists can often predict, on the basis of family histories, who will abuse children."

   Now imagine that your purpose is to *convince* future social workers that the failure of social service agencies to act authoritatively in child-abuse cases often has tragic consequences. Hoping to encourage more responsible behavior in the prospective social workers, you would adopt a more emotional tone in the essay, perhaps citing wrenching case histories that dramatize what happens when child abuse isn't taken seriously.

3. **Think rigorously about causes and effects.** Cause-effect relationships are usually complex. To write a meaningful analysis, you should do some careful thinking about your subject. (The two sets of questions at the end of this chapter's Prewriting Checklist [pages 384–385] will help you think creatively about causes and effects.)

   If you look beyond the obvious, you'll discover that a cause may have many effects. Imagine you're writing a paper on the effects of cigarette smoking. A number of consequences might be discussed, some less obvious but perhaps more interesting than others: increased risk of lung cancer and heart disease, evidence of harm done by secondhand smoke, legal battles regarding the rights of smokers and nonsmokers, lower birth weights in babies of mothers who smoke, and developmental problems experienced by such underweight infants.

In the same way, an effect may have multiple causes. An essay analyzing the reasons for world hunger could discuss many causes, again some less evident but perhaps more thought-provoking than others: overpopulation, climatic changes, inefficient use of land, and poor management of international relief funds.

Your analysis may also uncover a **causal chain** in which one cause (or effect) brings about another, that, in turn, brings about another, and so on. Here's an example of a causal chain: Prohibition went into effect; bootleggers and organized crime stepped in to supply public demand for alcoholic beverages; ordinary citizens began breaking the law by buying illegal alcohol and patronizing speakeasies; disrespect for legal authority became widespread and acceptable. As you can see, a causal chain often leads to interesting points. In this case, the subject of Prohibition leads not just to the obvious (illegal consumption of alcohol) but also to the more complex issue of society's decreasing respect for legal authority.

Don't grapple with so complex a chain, however, that you become hopelessly entangled. If your subject involves multiple causes and effects, limit what you'll discuss. Identify which causes and effects are *primary* and which are *secondary.* How extensively you cover secondary factors will depend on your purpose and audience. In an essay intended to inform a general audience about the harmful effects of pesticides, you would most likely focus on everyday dangers—polluted drinking water, residues in food, and the like. You probably wouldn't include a discussion of more long-range consequences (evolution of resistant insects, disruption of the soil's acid-alkaline balance).

Similarly, decide whether to focus on *immediate,* more obvious causes and effects, or on less obvious, more *remote* ones. Or perhaps you need to focus on both. In an essay about a faculty strike at your college, should you attribute the strike simply to the faculty's failure to receive a salary increase? Or should you also examine other factors: the union's failure to accept a salary package that satisfied most professors; the administration's inability to coordinate its negotiating efforts? It may be more difficult to explore more remote causes and effects, but it can also lead to more original and revealing essays. Thoughtful analyses take these less obvious considerations into account.

When developing a causal analysis, be careful to avoid the ***post hoc* fallacy.** Named after the Latin phrase *post hoc, ergo propter hoc,* meaning "after this, therefore because of this," this kind of faulty thinking occurs when you assume that simply because one event *followed* another, the first event *caused* the second. For example, if the Republicans win a majority of seats in Congress and, several months later, the economy collapses, can you conclude that the Republicans caused the collapse? A quick assumption of "Yes" fails the test of logic, for the timing of events could be coincidental and not indicative of any cause-effect relationship. The collapse may have been triggered by uncontrolled inflation that began well before the congressional elections. (For more on *post hoc* thinking, see page 475 in Chapter 18.)

Also, be careful not to mistake *correlation* for *causation.* Two events correlate when they occur at about the same time. Such co-occurrence, however, doesn't guarantee a cause-effect relationship. For instance, while the number of ice cream cones eaten and the instances of heat prostration both increase during the summer months, this doesn't mean that eating ice cream causes heat prostration! A third factor—in this case, summer heat—is the actual cause. When writing causal analyses, then, use with caution words that imply a causal link (such as *therefore* and *because*). Words that express simply time of occurrence (*following* and *previously*) are safer and more objective.

Finally, keep in mind that a rigorous causal analysis involves more than loose generalizations about causes and effects. Creating plausible connections may require library research, interviewing, or both. Often you'll need to provide facts, statistics, details, personal observations, or other corroborative material if readers are going to accept the reasoning behind your analysis.

4. **Write a thesis that focuses the paper on causes, effects, or both.** The thesis in an essay developed through causal analysis often indicates whether the essay will deal mostly with causes, effects, or both. Here, for example, are three thesis statements for causal analyses dealing with the public school system. You'll see that each thesis signals that essay's particular emphasis:

Causes

Our school system has been weakened by an overemphasis on trendy electives.

Effects

An ineffectual school system has led to crippling teachers' strikes and widespread disrespect for the teaching profession.

Causes and Effects

Bureaucratic inefficiency has created a school system unresponsive to children's emotional, physical, and intellectual needs.

Note that the thesis statement—in addition to signaling whether the paper will discuss causes or effects or both—may also point to the essay's plan of development. Consider the last thesis statement; it makes clear that the paper will discuss children's emotional needs first, their physical needs second, and their intellectual needs last.

The thesis statement in a causal analysis doesn't have to specify whether the essay will discuss causes, effects, or both. Nor does the thesis have to be worded in such a way that the essay's plan of development is apparent. But when first writing cause-effect essays, you may find that a highly focused thesis will help keep your analysis on track.

5. **Choose an organizational pattern.** There are two basic ways to organize the points in a cause-effect essay: you may use a chronological or an emphatic sequence. If you select *chronological order,* you discuss causes and effects in the order in which they occur or will occur. Suppose you're writing an essay on the causes for the popularity of imported cars. These causes might be discussed in chronological sequence: American plant workers became frustrated and dissatisfied on the job; some workers got careless while others deliberately sabotaged the production of sound cars; a growing number of defective cars hit the market; consumers grew dissatisfied with American cars and switched to imports.

   Chronology might also be used to organize a discussion about effects. Imagine you want to write an essay about the need to guard against disrupting delicate balances in the country's wildlife. You might start the essay by discussing what happened when the starling, a non-native bird, was introduced into the American environment. Because the starling had few natural predators, the starling population soared out of control; the starlings took over food sources and habitats of native species; the bluebird, a native species, declined and is now threatened with extinction.

   Although a chronological pattern can be an effective way to organize material, a strict time sequence can present a problem if your primary cause or effect ends up buried in the middle of the sequence. In such a case, you might use *emphatic order,* reserving the most significant cause or effect for the end. For example, time order could be used to present the reasons behind a candidate's unexpected victory: Less than a month after the candidate's earlier defeat, a full-scale fund-raising campaign for the next election was started; the candidate spoke to many crucial power groups early in the campaign; the candidate did exceptionally well in the pre-election debates; good weather and large voter turnout on election day favored the candidate. However, if you believe that the candidate's appearance before influential groups was the key factor in the victory, it would be more effective to emphasize that point by saving it for the end. This is what is meant by emphatic order—saving the most important point for last.

   Emphatic order is an especially effective way to sequence cause-effect points when readers hold what, in your opinion, are mistaken or narrow views about a subject. To encourage readers to look more closely at the issues, you present what you consider the erroneous or obvious views first, show why they are unsound or limited, then present what you feel to be the actual causes and effects. Such a sequence nudges the audience into giving further thought to the causes and effects you have discovered. Here are informal outlines for two causal analyses using this approach:

```
Subject: The causes of the riot at a rock concert

1. Some commentators blame the excessively hot weather.
2. Others cite drug use among the concertgoers.
3. Still others blame the liquor sold at the concessions.
```

```
4. But the real cause of the disaster was poor planning by
   the concert promoters.

Subject: The effects of campus crime

1. Immediate problems

   a. Students feel insecure and fearful.

   b. Many nighttime campus activities have been curtailed.

2. More significant long-term problems

   a. Unfavorable publicity about campus crime will affect
      future student enrollment.

   b. Unfavorable publicity about campus crime will make it
      difficult to recruit top-notch faculty.
```

When using emphatic order, you might want to word the thesis in such a way that it signals which point your essay will stress. Look at the following thesis statements:

```
Although many immigrants arrive in this country without
marketable skills, their most pressing problem is learning how
to make their way in a society whose language they don't know.

The space program has led to dramatic advances in computer
technology and medical science. Even more importantly, though,
the program has helped change many people's attitudes toward
the planet we live on.
```

These thesis statements reflect an awareness of the complex nature of cause-effect relationships. While not dismissing secondary issues, the statements establish which points the writer considers most noteworthy. The second thesis, for instance, indicates that the paper will touch on the technological and medical advances made possible by the space program but will emphasize the way the program has changed people's attitudes toward the earth.

Whether you use a chronological or emphatic pattern to organize your essay, you'll need to provide clear *signals* to identify when you're discussing causes and when you're discussing effects. Expressions such as "Another reason" and "A final outcome" help readers follow your line of thought.

6. **Use language that hints at the complexity of cause-effect relationships.** Because it's difficult—if not impossible—to identify causes and effects with certainty, you should avoid such absolutes as, "It must be obvious" and "There is no doubt." Instead, try phrases such as, "Most likely" or "It is probable." Such language isn't indecisive; it's reasonable and reflects your understanding of the often tangled nature of causes and effects. Don't, however, go to the other extreme and be reluctant to take a stand on the issues.

If you have thought carefully about causes and effects, you have a right to state your analysis with conviction.

REVISION STRATEGIES

Once you have a draft of the essay, you're ready to revise. The following checklist will help you and those giving you feedback apply to cause-effect writing some of the revision techniques discussed in Chapters 7 and 8.

CAUSE-EFFECT: A REVISION/PEER REVIEW CHECKLIST

Revise Overall Meaning and Structure

- ☐ Is the essay's purpose informative, persuasive, speculative, or a combination of these?
- ☐ What is the essay's thesis? Is it stated specifically or implied? Where? Could it be made any clearer? How?
- ☐ Does the essay focus on causes, effects, or both? How do you know?
- ☐ Where has correlation been mistaken for causation? Where is the essay weakened by *post hoc* thinking?
- ☐ Where does the essay distinguish between primary and secondary causes and effects? How do the most critical causes and effects receive special attention?
- ☐ Where does the essay dwell on the obvious?

Revise Paragraph Development

- ☐ Are the essay's paragraphs sequenced chronologically or emphatically? Could they be sequenced more effectively? How?
- ☐ Where would signal devices (such as *afterward, before, then,* and *next*) make it easier to follow the progression of thought within and between paragraphs?
- ☐ Which paragraphs would be strengthened by vivid examples (such as statistics, facts, anecdotes, or personal observations) that support the causal analysis?

Revise Sentences and Words

- ☐ Where do expressions like *as a result, because,* and *therefore* mislead the reader by implying a cause-effect relationship? Would words such as *following* and *previously* eliminate the problem?
- ☐ Do any words or phrases convey an arrogant or dogmatic tone (*there is no question, undoubtedly, always, never*)? What other expressions (*most likely, probably*) would improve credibility?

STUDENT ESSAY: FROM PREWRITING THROUGH REVISION

The student essay that follows was written by Carl Novack in response to this assignment:

> In "Black Men and Public Space," Brent Staples reminds us that, sadly, racist attitudes have not changed much over the years. There are, though, some areas in which people's attitudes *have* changed dramatically. Identify a significant shift in an activity, practice, or institution. Then write an essay in which you discuss the factors that you believe are responsible for the attitudinal change.

Mapping

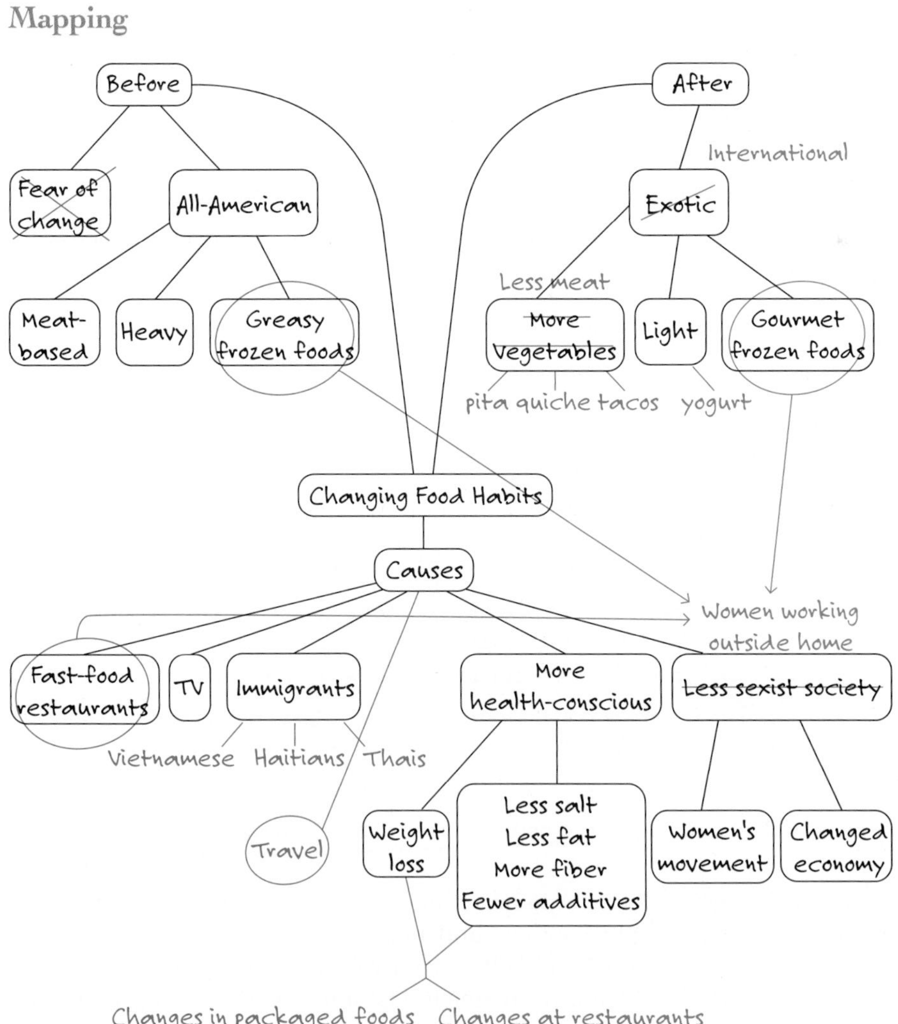

After deciding to write about Americans' changing food habits, Carl used the *mapping technique* to generate material on his subject. His map is shown on the previous page. The marks in color indicate Carl's later efforts to organize and elaborate the original map. Note that he added some branches, eliminated others, drew arrows indicating that some topics should be moved, and changed the wording of some key ideas. These annotations paved the way for Carl's topic outline, which is presented below.

Outline

Thesis: America has changed and so has what we Americans eat and how we eat.

I. We used to eat "All-American" meals.
   A. Heavy
   B. Meat-based
II. Now our tastes are more international.
   A. Lighter—yogurt
   B. Less meat—pita sandwiches, quiches, tacos
III. There are several reasons for our tastes becoming more international.
   A. Television
   B. Travel abroad
   C. Immigrants in this country
IV. Two social trends have also changed how and what we eat.
   A. Health consciousness
      1. Concern about weight
      2. Concern about salt, fat, fiber, additives
         a. Changes in packaged foods (lunch meat, canned vegetables, soups)
         b. Changes in restaurants (salad bars)
   B. More women working outside the home because of the economy and the women's movement
      1. Increase in fast-food restaurants
      2. More frozen foods, some even gourmet

Now read Carl's paper, "Americans and Food," noting the similarities and differences among his map, outline, and final essay. See, for example, how the diagram suggests a "before" and "after" contrast—a contrast the essay develops. Also note Carl's decision to move "frozen foods" and "fast-food restaurants" to the "women working outside home" section of the diagram. This decision is reflected in the outline and in the final essay, where frozen foods and fast-food restaurants are discussed in the same paragraph. As you read the essay, also consider how well it applies the principles of causal analysis discussed in this chapter. (The commentary that follows the paper will help you look at Carl's essay more closely and will give you some sense of how he went about revising his first draft.)

Americans and Food
by Carl Novack

1 An offbeat but timely cartoon recently appeared in the local newspaper. The single panel showed a gravel-pit operation with piles of raw earth and large cranes. Next to one of the cranes stood the owner of the gravel pit—a grizzled, tough-looking character, hammer in hand, pointing proudly to the new sign he had just tacked up. The sign read, "Fred's Fill Dirt and Croissants." The cartoon illustrates an interesting phenomenon: the changing food habits of Americans. Our meals used to consist of something like home-cooked pot roast, mashed potatoes laced with butter and salt, a thick slice of apple pie topped with a healthy scoop of vanilla ice cream—plain, heavy meals, cooked from scratch, and eaten leisurely at home. But America has changed, and because it has, so have what we Americans eat and how we eat it.

Introduction

Thesis

2 We used to have simple, unsophisticated tastes and looked with suspicion at anything more exotic than hamburger. Admittedly, we did adopt some foods from the various immigrant groups who flocked to our shores. We learned to eat Chinese food, pizza, and bagels. But in the last few years, the international character of our diet has grown tremendously. We can walk into any mall in Middle America and buy pita sandwiches, quiches, and tacos. Such foods are often changed on their journey from exotic imports to ordinary "American" meals (no Pakistani, for example, eats frozen-on-a-stick boysenberry-flavored yogurt), but the imports are still a long way from hamburger on a bun.

Topic sentence: Background paragraph

3 Why have we become more worldly in our tastes? For one thing, television blankets the country with information about new food products and trends. Viewers in rural Montana know that the latest craving in Washington, D.C., is Cajun cooking or that something called tofu is now available in the local supermarket. Another reason for the growing international flavor of our food is that many young Americans have traveled abroad and gotten

Topic sentence: Three causes answer the question

First cause

Second cause

hooked on new tastes and flavors. Backpacking students and young professionals vacationing in Europe come home with cravings for authentic French bread or German beer. Finally, continuing waves of immigrants settle in the cities where many of us live, causing significant changes in what we eat. Vietnamese, Haitians, and Thais, for instance, bring their native foods and cooking styles with them and eventually open small markets or restaurants. In time, the new food will become Americanized enough to take its place in our national diet.

Third cause

Topic sentence: Another cause

Our growing concern with health has also affected the way we eat. For the last few years, the media have warned us about the dangers of our traditional diet, high in salt and fat, low in fiber. The media also began to educate us about the dangers of processed foods pumped full of chemical additives. As a result, consumers began to demand healthier foods, and manufacturers started to change some of their products. Many foods, such as lunch meat, canned vegetables, and soups, were made available in low-fat, low-sodium versions. Whole-grain cereals and high-fiber breads also began to appear on the grocery shelves. Moreover, the food industry started to produce all-natural products—everything from potato chips to ice cream—without additives and preservatives. Not surprisingly, the restaurant industry responded to this switch to healthier foods, luring customers with salad bars, broiled fish, and steamed vegetables. 4

Start of a causal chain

Topic sentence: Another cause

Our food habits are being affected, too, by the rapid increase in the number of women working outside the home. Sociologists and other experts believe that two important factors triggered this phenomenon: the women's movement and a changing economic climate. Women were assured that it was acceptable, even rewarding, to work outside the home; many women also discovered that they had to work just to keep up with the cost of living. As the traditional role of homemaker changed, so did the way families ate. With Mom working, there wasn't time for her to prepare the traditional three square meals a day. Instead, families began looking for alternatives to provide quick meals. What was the result? For one thing, there was a boom in fast-food restaurants. The suburban or downtown strip that once contained a lone McDonald's now features Wendy's, Taco Bell, Burger King, and Pizza Hut. Families also began to depend on frozen foods as another 5

Start of a causal chain

time-saving alternative. Once again, though, demand changed the kind of frozen food available. Frozen foods no longer consist of foil trays divided into greasy fried chicken, watery corn niblets, and lumpy mashed potatoes. Supermarkets now stock a range of supposedly gourmet frozen dinners—from fettucini in cream sauce to braised beef en brochette.

6 It may not be possible to pick up a ton of fill dirt and a half-dozen croissants at the same place, but America's food habits are definitely changing. If it is true that "you are what you eat," then America's identity is evolving along with its diet. Conclusion

Commentary

Title and Introduction

Asked to prepare a paper analyzing the reasons behind a change in our lives, Carl decided to write about a shift he had noticed in Americans' eating habits. The title of the essay, "Americans and Food," identifies Carl's subject but could be livelier and more interesting.

Despite his rather uninspired title, Carl starts his *causal analysis* in an engaging way—with the vivid description of a cartoon. He then connects the cartoon to his subject with the following sentence: "The cartoon illustrates an interesting phenomenon: the changing food habits of Americans." To back up his belief that there has been a revolution in our eating habits, Carl uses the first paragraph to summarize the kind of meal that people used to eat. He then moves to his *thesis:* "But America has changed, and because it has, so have what we Americans eat and how we eat it." The thesis implies that Carl's paper will focus on both causes and effects.

Purpose

Carl's purpose was to write an *informative* causal analysis. But before he could present the causes of the change in eating habits, he needed to show that such a change had, in fact, taken place. He therefore uses the second paragraph to document one aspect of this change—the internationalization of our eating habits.

Topic Sentences

At the start of the third paragraph, Carl uses a question—"Why have we become more worldly in our tastes?"—to signal that his discussion of causes is about to begin. This question also serves as the paragraph's *topic sentence,* indicating that the paragraph will focus on reasons for the increasingly international flavor of our food. The next two paragraphs, also focused by topic sentences, identify two other major reasons for the change in eating habits: "Our growing concern with health has also affected the way we eat" (paragraph 4), and "Our food habits are being affected, too, by the rapid increase in the number of women working outside the home" (5).

Combining Patterns of Development

Carl draws on two patterns of development—*comparison-contrast* and *illustration*—to develop his causal analysis. At the heart of the essay is a basic *contrast* between the way we used to eat and the way we eat now. And throughout his essay, Carl provides convincing *examples* to demonstrate the validity of his points. Consider for a moment the third paragraph. Here Carl asserts that one reason for our new eating habits is our growing exposure to international foods. He then presents concrete evidence to show that we have indeed become more familiar with international cuisine: Television exposes rural Montana to Cajun cooking; students traveling abroad take a liking to French bread; urban dwellers enjoy the exotic fare served by numerous immigrant groups. The fourth and fifth paragraphs use similarly specific evidence (for example, "low-fat, low-sodium versions" of "lunch meat, canned vegetables, and soups") to illustrate the soundness of key ideas.

Causal Chains

Let's look more closely at the evidence in the essay. Not satisfied with obvious explanations, Carl thought through his ideas carefully and even brainstormed with friends to arrive at as comprehensive an analysis as possible. Not surprisingly, much of the evidence Carl uncovered took the form of *causal chains.* In the fourth paragraph, Carl writes, "The media also began to educate us about the dangers of processed foods pumped full of chemical additives. As a result, consumers began to demand healthier foods, and manufacturers started to change some of their products." And the next paragraph shows how the changing role of American women caused families to look for alternative ways of eating. This shift, in turn, caused the restaurant and food industries to respond with a wide range of food alternatives.

Making the Paper Easy to Follow

Although Carl's analysis digs beneath the surface and reveals complex cause-effect relationships, he wisely limits his pursuit of causal chains to *primary* causes and effects. He doesn't let the complexities distract him from his main purpose: to show why and how the American diet is changing. Carl is also careful to provide his essay with abundant *connecting devices,* making it easy for readers to see the links between points. Consider the use of *transitions* (signaled by italics) in the following sentences: "*Another* reason for the growing international flavor of our food is that many young Americans have traveled abroad" (paragraph 3); "*As a result,* consumers began to demand healthier foods" (4); and "*As* the traditional role of homemaker changed, so did the way families ate" (5).

A Problem with the Essay's Close

As you read the essay, you probably noticed that Carl's conclusion is a bit weak. Although his reference to the cartoon works well, the rest of the paragraph limps to a tired close. Ending an otherwise vigorous essay with such a slight conclusion undercuts the effectiveness of the whole paper. Carl spent so much energy developing the body of his essay that he ran out of the stamina needed to conclude the piece more forcefully. Careful budgeting of his time would have allowed him to prepare a stronger concluding paragraph.

Revising the First Draft

When Carl was ready to revise, during a peer review session he showed the first draft of his essay to several classmates who used a peer review worksheet customized by their instructor to focus their feedback. Carl jotted down their most helpful comments, numbered in order of importance, on his draft. Comparing Carl's original version of his fourth paragraph (shown below) with his final version in the essay will show you how he went about revising.

Original Version of the Fourth Paragraph

(A growing concern with health has also affected the way we eat, especially because the media has sent us warnings the last few years about the dangers of salt, sugar, food additives, and high-fat and low-fiber diets.) We have started to worry that our traditional meals may have been shortening our lives. As a result, consumers demanded healthier foods and manufacturers started taking some of the salt and sugar out of canned foods. "All-natural" became an effective selling point, leading to many preservative-free products. Restaurants, too, adapted their menus, luring customers with light meals. Because we now know about the link between overweight and a variety of health problems, including heart attacks, we are counting calories. In turn, food companies made fortunes on diet beer and diet cola. Sometimes, though, we seem a bit confused about the health issue; we drink soda that is sugar-free but loaded with chemical sweeteners. Still, we believe we are lengthening our lives through changing our diets.

② First sentence cluttered, too long

③ Add specifics

① Doesn't fit point being made

On the advice of his peer reviewers, Carl decided to omit all references to the way our concern with weight has affected our eating habits. It's true, of course, that calorie-counting has changed how we eat. But as soon as Carl started to discuss this point, he got involved in a causal chain that undercut the paragraph's unity. He ended up describing the paradoxical situation in which we find ourselves: In an attempt to eat healthy, we stay away from sugar and turn to possibly harmful artificial sweeteners. This is an interesting issue, but it detracts from Carl's main point—that our concern with health has affected our eating habits in a *positive* way.

Carl's peer reviewers also pointed out that the fourth paragraph's first sentence contained too much material to be an effective topic sentence. Carl corrected the problem by breaking the overlong sentence into two short ones: "Our growing concern with health has also affected the way we eat. For the last few years, the media have warned us about the dangers of our traditional diet, high in salt and fat, low in fiber." The first of these sentences serves as a crisp topic sentence that focuses the rest of the paragraph.

Finally, when Carl heard the essay read aloud, he realized the fourth paragraph lacked convincing specifics. When revising, he changed "manufacturers started taking some of the salt and sugar out of canned foods" to the more specific "Many foods, such as lunch meat, canned vegetables, and soups, were made available in low-fat, low-sodium versions." Similarly, generalizations about "light meals" and "all-natural" products gained life through the addition of concrete examples: restaurants lured "customers with salad bars, broiled fish, and steamed vegetables," and the food industry produced "everything from potato chips to ice cream—without additives and preservatives."

Carl did an equally good job revising other sections of his paper. With the exception of the weak spots already discussed, he made the changes needed to craft a well-reasoned essay, one that demonstrates his ability to analyze a complex phenomenon.

ACTIVITIES: CAUSE-EFFECT

Prewriting Activities

1. Imagine you're writing two essays: One proposes the need for high school courses in personal finance (how to budget money, balance a checkbook, and the like); the other explains how to show appreciation. Jot down ways you might use cause-effect in each essay.

2. Use mapping, collaborative brainstorming, or another prewriting technique to generate possible causes and/or effects for *one* of the following topics. Then organize your raw material into a brief outline, with related causes and effects grouped in the same section.

   a. Pressure on students to do well
   b. Children's access to pornography on the Internet
   c. Being physically fit
   d. Spiraling costs of a college education

3. For the topic you selected in activity 2, note the two potential audiences indicated below in parentheses. For each audience, devise a thesis and decide whether your essay's purpose would be informative, persuasive, speculative, or some combination of these. Then, with your thesis statements and purposes in mind, review the outline you prepared for the preceding activity. How would you change it to fit each audience? What points should be added? What points would be primary causes and effects for one audience but secondary for the other? Which organizational pattern—chronological, spatial, or emphatic—would be most effective for each audience?

a. Pressure on students to do well (*college students, parents of elementary school children*)
b. Children's access to pornography on the Internet (*legislators, parents of young children*)
c. Being physically fit (*those who show a reasonable degree of concern, those who are obsessed with being fit*)
d. Spiraling costs of a college education (*college officials, high school students planning to attend college*)

Revising Activities

4. Explain how the following statements demonstrate *post hoc* thinking and confuse correlation and cause-effect.

a. Our city now has many immigrants from Latin American countries. The crime rate in our city has increased. Latin American immigrants are the cause of the crime wave.
b. The divorce rate has skyrocketed. More women are working outside the home than ever before. Working outside the home destroys marriages.
c. A high percentage of people in Dixville have developed cancer. The landfill, used by XYZ Industries, has been located in Dixville for twenty years. The XYZ landfill has caused cancer in Dixville residents.

5. The following paragraph is from the first draft of an essay arguing that technological advances can diminish the quality of life. How solid is the paragraph's causal analysis? Which causes and/or effects should be eliminated? Where is the analysis simplistic? Where does the writer make absolute claims even though cause-effect relationships are no more than a possibility? Keeping these questions in mind, revise the paragraph.

How did the banking industry respond to inflation? It simply introduced a new technology—the automated teller machine (ATM). By making money more available to the average person, the ATM gives people the cash to buy inflated goods—whether or not they can afford them. Not surprisingly, automated teller machines have had a number of negative consequences for the average individual. Since people know they can get cash at any time, they use their lunch hours for something other than going to the bank. How do they spend this newfound time? They go shopping, and machine-vended money means more impulse buying, even more than with a credit card. Also, because people don't need their checkbooks to withdraw money, they can't keep track of their accounts and therefore develop a casual attitude toward financial matters. It's no wonder children don't appreciate the value of money. Another problem is that people who would never dream of robbing a bank try to trick the machine into dispensing money "for free." There's no doubt that this kind of fraud contributes to the immoral climate in the country.

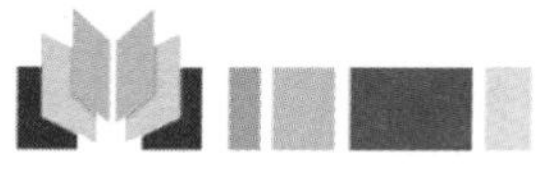

PROFESSIONAL SELECTIONS: CAUSE-EFFECT

STEPHEN KING

Probably the best-known living horror writer, Stephen King (1947–) is the author of more than thirty books. Before earning fame through his vastly popular books, including *Carrie* (1974), *The Shining* (1977), *Cujo* (1981), and *Tommyknockers* (1987), King worked as a high school English teacher and an industrial laundry worker. Much of King's prolific output has been adapted for the screen; movies based on King's work include *Misery* (1990), *Stand by Me* (1986), *The Green Mile* (1999), and *Secret Window* (2004). More recent works include *From a Buick 8* (2002); Volumes V, VI, and VII in the *Dark Tower* series (published in 2003, 2004, and 2004, respectively); and *Faithful: Two Diehard Boston Red Sox Fans Chronicle the Historic 2004 Season* (2004), which he coauthored with Stewart O'Nan. And in *On Writing: A Memoir of the Craft* (2000), King offers insight into the writing process and examines the role that writing has played in his own life—especially following a near-fatal accident in 1999. King lives with his family in Bangor, Maine. The following essay first appeared in *Playboy* in 1982.

Please note the essay structure diagram that appears following this selection (Figure 16.2 on page 405).

Pre-Reading Journal Entry

Several forms of entertainment, besides horror movies, are highly popular despite what many consider a low level of quality. In your journal, list as many "lowbrow" forms of entertainment as you can. Possibilities include professional wrestling, aggressive video games, Internet chat rooms, and so on. Review your list, and respond to the following question in your journal: What is it about each form of entertainment that attracts such popularity—and inspires such criticism?

WHY WE CRAVE HORROR MOVIES

I think that we're all mentally ill: those of us outside the asylums only hide it a little better—and maybe not all that much better, after all. We've all known people who talk to themselves, people who sometimes squinch their faces into horrible grimaces when they believe no one is watching, people who have some hysterical fear—of 1 snakes, the dark, the tight place, the long drop . . . and, of course, those final worms and grubs that are waiting so patiently underground.

2 When we pay our four or five bucks and seat ourselves at tenth-row center in a theater showing a horror movie, we are daring the nightmare.

3 Why? Some of the reasons are simple and obvious. To show that we can, that we are not afraid, that we can ride this roller coaster. Which is not to say that a really good horror movie may not surprise a scream out of us at some point, the way we may scream when the roller coaster twists through a complete 360 or plows through a lake at the bottom of the drop. And horror movies, like roller coasters, have always been the special province of the young; by the time one turns 40 or 50, one's appetite for double twists or 360-degree loops may be considerably depleted.

4 We also go to re-establish our feelings of essential normality; the horror movie is innately conservative, even reactionary. Freda Jackson as the horrible melting woman in *Die, Monster, Die!* confirms for us that no matter how far we may be removed from the beauty of a Robert Redford or a Diana Ross, we are still light-years from true ugliness.

5 And we go to have fun.

6 Ah, but this is where the ground starts to slope away, isn't it? Because this is a very peculiar sort of fun indeed. The fun comes from seeing others menaced—sometimes killed. One critic has suggested that if pro football has become the voyeur's version of combat, then the horror film has become the modern version of the public lynching.

7 It is true that the mythic, "fairytale" horror film intends to take away the shades of gray. . . . It urges us to put away our more civilized and adult penchant for analysis and to become children again, seeing things in pure blacks and whites. It may be that horror movies provide psychic relief on this level because this invitation to lapse into simplicity, irrationality and even outright madness is extended so rarely. We are told we may allow our emotions a free rein . . . or no rein at all.

8 If we are all insane, then sanity becomes a matter of degree. If your insanity leads you to carve up women like Jack the Ripper or the Cleveland Torso Murderer, we clap you away in the funny farm (but neither of those two amateur-night surgeons was ever caught, heh-heh-heh); if, on the other hand your insanity leads you only to talk to yourself when you're under stress or to pick your nose on the morning bus, then you are left alone to go about your business . . . though it is doubtful that you will ever be invited to the best parties.

9 The potential lyncher is in almost all of us (excluding saints, past and present; but then, most saints have been crazy in their own ways), and every now and then, he has to be let loose to scream and roll around in the grass. Our emotions and our fears form their own body, and we recognize that it demands its own exercise to maintain proper muscle tone. Certain of these emotional muscles are accepted—even exalted—in civilized society; they are, of course, the emotions that tend to maintain the status quo of civilization itself. Love, friendship, loyalty, kindness—these are all the emotions that we applaud, emotions that have been immortalized in the couplets of Hallmark cards. . . .

10 When we exhibit these emotions, society showers us with positive reinforcement; we learn this even before we get out of diapers. When, as children, we hug our rotten little puke of a sister and give her a kiss, all the aunts and uncles smile and twit and cry, "Isn't he the sweetest little thing?" Such coveted treats as chocolate-covered graham crackers often follow. But if we deliberately slam the rotten little puke of a sister's fingers in the door, sanctions follow—angry remonstrance from parents, aunts and uncles; instead of a chocolate-covered graham cracker, a spanking.

But anticivilization emotions don't go away, and they demand periodic exercise. We have such "sick" jokes as, "What's the difference between a truckload of bowling balls and a truckload of dead babies?" (You can't unload a truckload of bowling balls with a pitchfork . . . a joke, by the way, that I heard originally from a ten-year-old.) Such a joke may surprise a laugh or a grin out of us even as we recoil, a possibility that confirms the thesis: If we share a brotherhood of man, then we also share an insanity of man. None of which is intended as a defense of either the sick joke or insanity but merely as an explanation of why the best horror films, like the best fairy tales, manage to be reactionary, anarchistic, and revolutionary all at the same time. 11

The mythic horror movie, like the sick joke, has a dirty job to do. It deliberately appeals to all that is worst in us. It is morbidity unchained, our most base instincts let free, our nastiest fantasies realized . . . and it all happens, fittingly enough, in the dark. For those reasons, good liberals often shy away from horror films. For myself, I like to see the most aggressive of them—*Dawn of the Dead*, for instance—as lifting a trap door in the civilized forebrain and throwing a basket of raw meat to the hungry alligators swimming around in that subterranean river beneath. 12

Why bother? Because it keeps them from getting out, man. It keeps them down there and me up here. It was Lennon and McCartney who said that all you need is love, and I would agree with that. 13

As long as you keep the gators fed. 14

Questions for Close Reading

1. What is the selection's thesis? Locate the sentence(s) in which King states his main idea. If he doesn't state the thesis explicitly, express it in your own words.

2. In what ways do King's references to "Jack the Ripper" and the "Cleveland Torso Murderer" (paragraph 8) support his thesis?

3. What does King mean in paragraph 4 when he says that horror movies are "innately conservative, even reactionary"? What does he mean in paragraph 11 when he calls them "anarchistic, and revolutionary"?

4. In paragraphs 12 and 14, King refers to "alligators" and "gators." What does the alligator represent? What does King mean when he says that all the world needs is love—"[a]s long as you keep the gators fed"?

5. Refer to your dictionary as needed to define the following words used in the selection: *hysterical* (paragraph 1), *reactionary* (4), *voyeur's* (6), *lynching* (6), *penchant* (7), *immortalized* (9), *anarchistic* (11), and *morbidity* (12).

Questions About the Writer's Craft

1. **The pattern.** Does King's causal analysis have an essentially informative, speculative, or persuasive (see page 462) purpose? What makes you think so? How might King's profession as a horror writer have influenced his purpose?

FIGURE 16.2
Essay Structure Diagram: "Why We Crave Horror Movies" by Stephen King

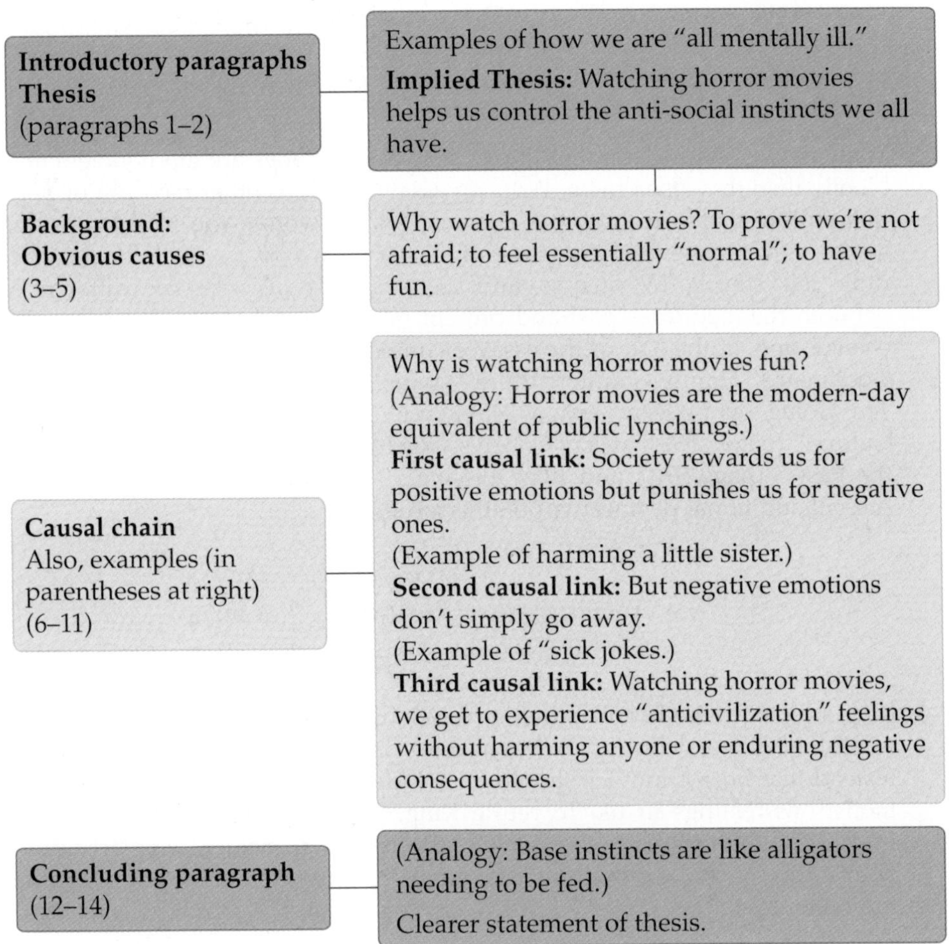

2. **Other patterns.** King *compares* and *contrasts* horror movies to roller coasters (3), public lynchings (6), and sick jokes (11–12). How do these comparisons and contrasts reinforce King's thesis about horror movies?
3. **Other patterns.** Throughout the essay, King uses several *examples* involving children. Identify these instances. How do these examples help King develop his thesis?
4. What is unusual about paragraphs 2, 5, and 14? Why do you think King might have designed these paragraphs in this way?

Writing Assignments Using Cause-Effect as a Pattern of Development

1. King argues that horror movies have "a dirty job to do": they feed the hungry monsters in our psyche. Write an essay in which you put King's thesis to the test. Briefly describe the first horror movie you ever saw; then explain its effect on you. Like King, speculate about the nature of your response—your feelings and fantasies—while watching the movie.

2. Many movie critics claim that horror movies nowadays are more violent and bloody than they used to be. Write an essay about *one* other medium of popular culture that you think has changed for the worse. You might consider action movies, televised coverage of sports, men's or women's magazines, radio talk shows, TV sitcoms, and so on. Briefly describe key differences between the medium's past and present forms. Analyze the reasons for the change, and, at the end of the essay, examine the effects of the change. Ellen Goodman's "Family Counterculture" (page 6), Kay S. Hymowitz's "Tweens: Ten Going on Sixteen" (page 245), Leslie Savan's "Black Talk and Pop Culture" (page 258), Patricia Cohen's "Reality TV: Surprising Throwback to the Past?" (page 370), and Buzz Bissinger's "Innocents Afield" (page 407) present additional perspectives on this issue.

Writing Assignments Combining Patterns of Development

3. King advocates the horror movie precisely because "It deliberately appeals to all that is worst in us." Write an essay in which you rebut King. *Argue* instead that horror movies should be avoided precisely *because* they satisfy monstrous feelings in us. To refute King, provide strong *examples* drawn from your own and other people's experience. Consider supplementing your informal research with material gathered in the library and/or on the Internet.

4. Write an essay in which you *argue,* contrary to King, that humans are by nature essentially benevolent and kind. Brainstorm with others to generate vivid *examples* in support of your thesis.

Writing Assignment Using a Journal Entry as a Starting Point

5. King believes that horror movies involve "a very peculiar sort of fun." Review your pre-reading journal entry, and select *one* other form of popular entertainment that you think provides its own strange kind of enjoyment. Like King,

write an essay in which you analyze the causes of people's enjoyment of this type of entertainment. Brainstorm with others to identify convincing examples. You may, like King, endorse the phenomenon you examine—or you may condemn it. Patricia Cohen's "Reality TV: Surprising Throwback to the Past?" (page 370) provides another perspective on the issue of questionable popular entertainment.

BUZZ BISSINGER

H. G. "Buzz" Bissinger (1954–) worked as a newspaper reporter for fifteen years before moving his family from Philadelphia to Odessa, Texas, in order to write a book about high school football. In 1990, he published the best-selling *Friday Night Lights*, which was made into a movie starring Billy Bob Thornton in 2004 and into a television series in 2006. Bissinger is also the author of *Three Nights in August: Strategy, Heartbreak, and Joy Inside the Mind of a Manager* (2006) and *A Prayer for the City* (1991), and has written and produced episodes of the TV series *NYPD Blue*. Today he is a contributing editor for *Vanity Fair* and lives in Philadelphia. This essay was published in *The New York Times* on December 16, 2004.

Pre-Reading Journal Entry

Competitive sports play a large role in many high schools. What was your experience of sports in high school? Were you a high school athlete? Did you attend your school's games? How were athletes regarded in your school? How did being an athlete—or not being an athlete—affect your personal experience of high school sports? What memories do you have of your high school's athletes, teams, or coaches? Use your journal to answer these questions.

INNOCENTS AFIELD

1 Earlier this month, the high school football season ended around the country. There were the state championships and before that, the annual Thanksgiving Day games. There were the rose-colored images of innocence and valor and healthy competition, attributes that we continue to insist upon from sports in America even though such attributes have become extinct.

2 We are clinging to the supposed virtues of high school athletics with particular zeal. Everybody knows that pro sports is too far gone (take your pick of recent scandals). Everybody knows that college sports is too far gone (take your pick of recent scandals). But still there's high school sports, still the classic battle of one rival against the other in shaggy glory, what James Jones described in *From Here to Eternity*[1] as "the magnificent foolishness of youth as if the whole of life depended on this game." A half-century later, the depiction of noble sacrifice at the high school level still forms our baseline, gives us hope that something in sports is still unsullied, restores our faith in the family values fad that has overtaken the low-carb diet.

[1]A novel published in 1951 about World War II and its aftermath (editors' note).

Except that high school sports in America has become an epidemic of win-at-all-costs in too many places, just as corroded as college and the pros; actually more so because none of the ends can possibly justify the means when many of those involved are still too young to vote. No Super Bowl with television ratings through the roof. No Bowl Championship Series games with millions watching. Just millions of dollars spent by certain school districts that cannot possibly begin to explain the millions they are spending. Just booster clubs, like little Mafia families, filling in the gap between what the board of education is willing to cough up and what the athletic department claims that it needs to keep churning out those precious state championships. Just coaches in some places making close to $90,000 a year without teaching a class. Just further social stratification between the athlete and the nonathlete, those who are in and those who are out and feel humiliated and ridiculed with repercussions that can become deadly. Just steroid abuse, including a 17-year-old baseball player in a Dallas suburb who committed suicide because of what his parents believe was depression caused by stopping anabolic steroids. 3

Maybe I'm overselling the problem. But my point of reference is the late 1980's, when I moved to Odessa, Tex., to do research for my book. When [*Friday Night Lights*] was published in 1990, Permian High School in Odessa became a national symbol of everything that was wrong in high school sports—spending close to $70,000 on chartered jet trips to several away games, building a high school football stadium that seated nearly 20,000 and cost $5.6 million. 4

Over the past 14 years, I have had hundreds of conversations with parents about high school sports careening out of control. In virtually all of them, the reaction has been the same—approving nods of solidarity, followed by my own queasy sense that they weren't really listening to a word I said, their own private SportsCenter moment reeling in their heads for their sons and daughters. Over those 14 years, the excesses have only gotten worse. 5

As *USA Today* reported in October, millions upon millions of dollars are being spent on high school football stadiums and related buildings across the country. Texas, of course, leads the arms race with new or pending high school football stadium projects in the Dallas area alone costing close to $180 million. But in Jefferson, Ind., as part of a privately financed $8 million building project, there's a new 6,000-seat high school football stadium with an expensive video scoreboard. In Valdosta, Ga., $7.5 million was spent to renovate its football stadium, including building a museum to the glory of the Valdosta Wildcats. North Hills High, in the Pittsburgh region, spent $10 million to renovate the stadium and build a 13,000-square-foot field house. 6

The arguments for these sports centers are as familiar as they are wearying as they are transparent: the football programs not only are self-sustaining but also support other sports; these are stadiums the community wants so there's no harm, particularly when they are privately financed. 7

But no community, at least no community I would want my children to live in, can justify any of these monoliths. In an age where educational resources are dwindling, how can the building of a lavish new stadium or a field house possibly be justified, much less needed? What does it say to the rest of the student body, the giant-sized majority who do not play football, except that they are inferior, a sloppy second to the football stars who shine on Friday night. How can a community brag about its ability 8 to get financing for a multimillion-dollar football stadium when it can't conjure up the money to hire more teachers that would lead to the nirvana of smaller class sizes? If it's the desire of boosters to pour money into sports, and it usually is, then why not use these private funds for a physical education program to reduce obesity among teenagers?

9 It isn't simply money that has contributed to the professionalism of high school sports. As a reporter for *The Chicago Tribune*, I spent a year uncovering abuses in Illinois as disturbing as anything in Texas—high school coaches recruiting eighth-grade players with glossy pitches and come-ons straight out of the major-college mold, parents getting so many calls from high school recruiters that they simply had their phones turned off, high school basketball coaches siphoning off Chicago's best players just so they wouldn't compete against them. Jump a level down into that emotional hell known as travel team—there isn't a parent of a travel team player who can't recite at least one horror story of another parent going berserk or a coach flipping out in the name of providing 10– and 11– and 12–years-olds with a little extra competition.

10 In October, the National Association of State Boards of Education issued a report calling for greater oversight of high school athletics because of the alarming trickle-down of virtually every bad college practice. The list of concerns included steroid use, shady shoe agents, mercenary coaches, dubious recruiting tactics and extravagant gifts. Steroid abuse does exist in high schools. As many as 11 percent of the nation's youth have used them, according to a study by the Mayo Clinic. Based on other research, some of the most disturbing users are freshman high school girls, with a rate of abuse at a minimum of 7 percent. "We have a moral obligation to prevent the exploitation of high school students," the national association said.

11 Those are important words, but I'm afraid they are going to fall on deaf ears.

12 Sports as an institution is every bit as powerful in this country as corporate America or the Catholic Church. Yet sports are still considered a side light, ancillary to our daily experience. It's still too easy to put on those rose-colored glasses, . . . to get wrapped up in the supposed character-building elements of it, the false narratives of heroes and come-from-behind glory fed us by newspapers and television networks and cable networks in their ceaseless search for easy emotional aphrodisiacs.

13 Which means that high school sports will continue to fester into shameful overemphasis in too many places, will continue to emulate the college sports model that is America's educational shame. Which means that by the time we completely ruin the institution of sports for our teenagers, it will be too late to do anything except appoint a national commission to try to figure out how we could have missed so many warning signs.

Questions for Close Reading

1. What is the selection's thesis? Locate the sentence(s) in which Bissinger states his main idea. If he doesn't state his thesis explicitly, express it in your own words.

2. In paragraph 2, Bissinger describes the "supposed virtues" of high school sports. What are these "supposed virtues"?

3. What is the role of money in high school sports? What is Bissinger's opinion of the role of money in high school sports?

4. In paragraph 10, Bissinger describes a way to rein in the excesses of high school sports. What solution does he present? How effective does he think it would be?

5. Refer to your dictionary as needed to define the following words used in the selection: *valor* (paragraph 1), *zeal* (2), *unsullied* (2), *social stratification* (3), *repercussions* (3), *careening* (5), *queasy* (5), *monolith* (8), *conjure* (8), *nirvana* (8), *siphoning* (9), *ancillary* (12), and *emulate* (13).

Questions About the Writer's Craft

1. **The pattern.** Bissinger deals with both causes and effects in this essay. According to Bissinger, what has helped *cause* the professionalization of high school sports in recent years? What are the *effects* of this professionalization on athletes? What are the *effects* on nonathletes? Cite the paragraphs in which Bissinger discusses causes and effects.

2. **Other patterns.** In paragraph 3, Bissinger *contrasts* the imaginary purchases that might be made with high school sports money with the actual purchases. What words does he use repeatedly to signal the nonexistent and the actual purchases of high school sports? How effective is this use of repetition?

3. **Other patterns.** In paragraph 5, Bissinger *argues* that the excesses of high school sports have gotten worse since he published *Friday Night Lights* in 1990. What evidence does he cite for this claim? Is the evidence convincing?

4. Bissinger concludes his essay with a prediction (paragraph 13). What is his prediction? Why is he so pessimistic about the future of high school sports?

Writing Assignments Using Cause-Effect as a Pattern of Development

1. Bissinger's essay focuses mostly on the role of money in professionalizing high school sports, but he mentions other factors as well. These factors include recruitment practices, travel teams, and steroid abuse. Do research in the library or on the Internet about one of these other factors and write an essay about its *effect* on high school sports.

2. Bissinger's essay focuses on the negative aspects of high school sports, arguing that the worst aspects of professional and college sports have contaminated competition at the high school level. Write an essay in which you present the beneficial *effects* of high school sports on athletes, families, and communities. For example, you might discuss how playing a team sport teaches students

about working with others on a school assignment, a family project, or a community event.

Writing Assignments Combining Patterns of Development

3. *Friday Night Lights,* the movie based on Bissinger's book about high school football in Odessa, Texas, shows that the expectations of classmates, coaches, family, and community take a heavy toll on team members. Still, the film has many of the elements of the classic Hollywood underdog sports movie, in which a team battles great odds to make it to the playoffs or win a championship. These movies—such as *Bad News Bears* (baseball), *Hoosiers* (basketball), *Remember the Titans* (football), and *Miracle* (hockey)—are all inspriational in tone. Select a sports movie that you have seen and show how this movie *exemplifies* particular values of sports in America culture. Along the way, consider what is the message of the movie and what *causes* such movies to be so popular.

4. Bissinger contrasts James Jones's 1951 description of the nobility of high school athletics with the modern reality, which has been affected by money and fame. This contrast between an earlier, more innocent version of a present-day cultural practice underlies several of the essays in this book. For example, in "Family Counterculture" (page 6), Ellen Goodman contrasts the past influence of ministers, teachers, and societal leaders on children's development with the present influence of TV and advertising. And in "Tweens: Ten Going on Sixteen" (page 245), Kay S. Hymowitz describes how today's eight- to twelve-years-olds are more like teenagers than like children. Select a present-day cultural phenomenon, and write an essay in which you *compare* and *contrast* present-day practices with those of the past and explain how and why these practices have *affected* people's behavior. For example, you can write an essay comparing teens' social lives before and after the Internet and explain how the Internet has affected social behavior. Or you can contrast spending habits before and after credit cards became common and explain their effect on people's consumer behavior. Or you can compare modern indoor shopping malls to old-time main streets and describe the effect of malls on shopping habits.

Writing Assignment Using a Journal Entry as a Starting Point

5. Whether you were an athlete or not, sports probably had some effect on your high school experience. Review your pre-reading journal entry about high school sports. Select one of your experiences with high school sports, whether as an athlete, a spectator, or a fan, and write an essay *narrating* the experience. Was your experience good or bad, or both? How did this experience influence your overall experience of high school?

BRENT STAPLES

After earning a Ph.D. in psychology from the University of Chicago, Brent Staples (1951–) soon became a nationally recognized essayist. He has worked on numerous newspapers and is now an Editorial Board member of *The New York Times*. Staples's autobiography, *Parallel Time: Growing Up in Black and White*, was published in 1995. He is currently working on a history of the Negro Press and lives in Brooklyn, New York, with his wife. This selection first appeared in slightly different form in *Ms.* magazine (1986) and then in *Harper's* (1987).

Pre-Reading Journal Entry

In recent years, racial profiling—targeting people for investigation based on their race or ethnicity—has become a controversial issue. What is your opinion of this practice? Is racial profiling ever acceptable? Freewrite on these questions in your journal.

BLACK MEN AND PUBLIC SPACE

My first victim was a woman—white, well dressed, probably in her early twenties. 1 I came upon her late one evening on a deserted street in Hyde Park, a relatively affluent neighborhood in an otherwise mean, impoverished section of Chicago. As I swung onto the avenue behind her, there seemed to be a discreet, uninflammatory distance between us. Not so. She cast back a worried glance. To her, the youngish black man—a broad six feet two inches with a beard and billowing hair, both hands shoved into the pockets of a bulky military jacket—seemed menacingly close. After a few more quick glimpses, she picked up her pace and was soon running in earnest. Within seconds she disappeared into a cross street.

That was more than a decade ago. I was twenty-two years old, a graduate student 2 newly arrived at the University of Chicago. It was in the echo of that terrified woman's footfalls that I first began to know the unwieldy inheritance I'd come into—the ability to alter public space in ugly ways. It was clear that she thought herself the quarry of a mugger, a rapist, or worse. Suffering a bout of insomnia, however, I was stalking sleep, not defenseless wayfarers. As a softy who is scarcely able to take a knife to a raw chicken—let alone hold one to a person's throat—I was surprised, embarrassed, and dismayed all at once. Her flight made me feel like an accomplice in tyranny. It also made it clear that I was indistinguishable from the muggers who occasionally seeped into the area from the surrounding ghetto. That first encounter, and those that followed, signified that a vast, unnerving gulf lay between nighttime pedestrians—particularly women—and me. And I soon gathered that being perceived as dangerous is a hazard in itself. I only needed to turn a corner into a dicey situation, or crowd some frightened, armed person in a foyer somewhere, or make an errant move after being pulled over by a policeman. Where fear and weapons meet—and they often do in urban America—there is always the possibility of death.

3 In that first year, my first away from my hometown, I was to become thoroughly familiar with the language of fear. At dark, shadowy intersections, I could cross in front of a car stopped at a traffic light and elicit the *thunk, thunk, thunk, thunk* of the driver—black, white, male, or female—hammering down the door locks. On less traveled streets after dark, I grew accustomed to but never comfortable with people crossing to the other side of the street rather than pass me. Then there were the standard unpleasantries with policemen, doormen, bouncers, cabdrivers, and others whose business it is to screen out troublesome individuals *before* there is any nastiness.

4 I moved to New York nearly two years ago and I have remained an avid night walker. In central Manhattan, the near-constant crowd cover minimizes tense one-on-one street encounters. Elsewhere—in SoHo, for example, where sidewalks are narrow and tightly spaced buildings shut out the sky—things can get very taut indeed.

5 After dark, on the warrenlike streets of Brooklyn where I live, I often see women who fear the worst from me. They seem to have set their faces on neutral, and with their purse straps strung across their chests bandolier-style, they forge ahead as though bracing themselves against being tackled. I understand, of course, that the danger they perceive is not a hallucination. Women are particularly vulnerable to street violence, and young black males are drastically overrepresented among the perpetrators of that violence. Yet these truths are no solace against the kind of alienation that comes of being ever the suspect, a fearsome entity with whom pedestrians avoid making eye contact.

6 It is not altogether clear to me how I reached the ripe old age of twenty-two without being conscious of the lethality nighttime pedestrians attributed to me. Perhaps it was because in Chester, Pennsylvania, the small, angry industrial town where I came of age in the 1960s, I was scarcely noticeable against a backdrop of gang warfare, street knifings, and murders. I grew up one of the good boys, had perhaps a half-dozen fistfights. In retrospect, my shyness of combat has clear sources.

7 As a boy, I saw countless tough guys locked away; I have since buried several, too. They were babies, really—a teenage cousin, a brother of twenty-two, a childhood friend in his mid-twenties—all gone down in episodes of bravado played out in the streets. I came to doubt the virtues of intimidation early on. I chose, perhaps unconsciously, to remain a shadow—timid, but a survivor.

8 The fearsomeness mistakenly attributed to me in public places often has a perilous flavor. The most frightening of these confusions occurred in the late 1970s and early 1980s, when I worked as a journalist in Chicago. One day, rushing into the office of a magazine I was writing for with a deadline story in hand, I was mistaken for a burglar. The office manager called security and, with an ad hoc posse, pursued me through the labyrinthine halls, nearly to my editor's door. I had no way of proving who I was. I could only move briskly toward the company of someone who knew me.

Another time I was on assignment for a local paper and killing time before an interview. I entered a jewelry store on the city's affluent Near North Side. The proprietor excused herself and returned with an enormous red Doberman pinscher straining at the end of a leash. She stood, the dog extended toward me, silent to my questions, her eyes bulging nearly out of her head. I took a cursory look around, nodded, and bade her good night. 9

Relatively speaking, however, I never fared as badly as another black male journalist. He went to nearby Waukegan, Illinois, a couple of summers ago to work on a story about a murderer who was born there. Mistaking the reporter for the killer, police officers hauled him from his car at gunpoint and but for his press credentials would probably have tried to book him. Such episodes are not uncommon. Black men trade tales like this all the time. 10

Over the years, I learned to smother the rage I felt at so often being taken for a criminal. Not to do so would surely have led to madness. I now take precautions to make myself less threatening. I move about with care, particularly late in the evening. I give a wide berth to nervous people on subway platforms during the wee hours, particularly when I have exchanged business clothes for jeans. If I happen to be entering a building behind some people who appear skittish, I may walk by, letting them clear the lobby before I return, so as not to seem to be following them. I have been calm and extremely congenial on those rare occasions when I've been pulled over by the police. 11

And on late-evening constitutionals I employ what has proved to be an excellent tension-reducing measure: I whistle melodies from Beethoven and Vivaldi and the more popular classical composers. Even steely New Yorkers hunching toward nighttime destinations seem to relax, and occasionally they even join in the tune. Virtually everybody seems to sense that a mugger wouldn't be warbling bright, sunny selections from Vivaldi's *Four Seasons*. It is my equivalent of the cowbell that hikers wear when they know they are in bear country. 12

Questions for Close Reading

1. What is the selection's thesis? Locate the sentence(s) in which Staples states his main idea. If he doesn't state the thesis explicitly, express it in your own words.

2. How did Staples first learn that he was considered a threat by many people? How did this discovery make him feel?

3. What are some of the dangers that Staples has encountered because of his race? How has he handled each dangerous situation?

4. What "precautions" does Staples take to appear nonthreatening to others? Why do these precautions work?

5. Refer to your dictionary as needed to define the following words used in the selection: *uninflammatory* (paragraph 1), *dicey* (2), *bandolier* (5), *lethality* (6), *bravado* (7), *berth* (11), and *constitutionals* (12).

Questions About the Writer's Craft

1. **The pattern.** Brent Staples reveals both causes and effects of people's reacting with fear to a black male. Does the essay end with a discussion of causes or of effects? Why do you suppose Staples concludes the essay as he does?
2. **Other patterns.** Why do you think Staples opens the piece with such a dramatic, yet intentionally misleading, *narrative*? What *effect* does he achieve?
3. Is Staples writing primarily for whites, blacks, or both? How do you know?
4. What is Staples's tone? Why do you think he chose this tone?

Writing Assignments Using Cause-Effect as a Pattern of Development

1. Write an essay showing how your or someone else's entry into a specific public space (for example, a bus, party, elevator, or table at the library) influenced other people's behavior. Identify the possible reasons that others reacted as they did, and explain how their reactions, in turn, affected the newcomer. Use your analysis to reach some conclusions about human nature. For another example of an uncomfortable cultural intersection, read Charmie Gholson's "Charity Display?" (page 220).
2. Staples describes circumstances that often result in fear. Focusing on a more positive emotion, like admiration or contentment, illustrate the situations that tend to elicit that emotion in you. Discuss why these circumstances have the effect they do.

Writing Assignments Combining Patterns of Development

3. Staples describes how others' expectations oblige him to alter his behavior. *Narrate* an event during which you felt forced to conform to what others expected. What did you learn as a *result* of the experience? Audre Lorde's "The Fourth of July" (page 208), George Orwell's "Shooting an Elephant" (page 214), Charmie Gholson's "Charity Display?" (page 220), and Diane Cole's "Don't Just Stand There" (page 333) may prompt some interesting thoughts on the issue of conformity.

4. When he encounters a startled pedestrian, Staples feels some fear but manages to control it. Write an essay showing the *steps* you took one time when you felt afraid but, like Staples, remained in control and got through safely. *Illustrate* your initial fear, your later relief, and any self-discovery that *resulted* from the experience.

Writing Assignment Using a Journal Entry as a Starting Point

5. Though he doesn't say so explicitly, Staples has been the target of racial profiling. Review your pre-reading journal entry, and then research the topic of racial profiling in the library and/or on the Internet. Write an essay in which you argue that racial profiling is *or* is not a justifiable practice. In the course of your essay, be sure to cite examples of hypothetical or actual situations in order to reinforce your position. You should also acknowledge and, where appropriate, refute opposing points of view.

ADDITIONAL WRITING TOPICS: CAUSE-EFFECT

General Assignments

Write an essay that analyzes the causes and/or effects of one of the following topics. Determine your purpose before beginning to write: Will the essay be informative, persuasive, or speculative? As you prewrite, think rigorously about causes and effects; try to identify causal chains. Provide solid evidence for the thesis, and use either chronological or emphatic order to organize your supporting points.

1. Sleep deprivation
2. Having the parents you have
3. Lack of communication in a relationship
4. Overexercising or not exercising
5. A particular celebrity's popularity
6. Skill or ineptitude in sports
7. A major life decision
8. Changing attitudes toward the environment
9. Voter apathy
10. An act of violence or cruelty
11. A particular national crisis
12. Choosing to attend a particular college
13. The use of computers in the classroom

14. A bad habit

15. A fear of

16. Legalizing drugs

17. Abolishing the grading system

18. Joining a particular organization

19. Illegal digital music swapping

20. Reduced attention spans in children

Assignments with a Specific Purpose, Audience, and Point of View

On Campus

1. A debate about the prominence of athletics at colleges and universities is going to be broadcast on the local cable station. For this debate, prepare a speech pointing out either the harmful or the beneficial effects of "big-time" college athletic programs.

2. Why do students "flunk out" of college? Write an article for the campus newspaper outlining the main causes of failure. Your goal is to steer students away from dangerous habits and situations that lead to poor grades or dropping out.

At Home or in the Community

3. Write a letter to the editor of your favorite newspaper analyzing the causes of the country's current "trash crisis." Be sure to mention the nationwide love affair with disposable items and the general disregard of the idea of thrift. Conclude by offering brief suggestions for how people in your community can begin to remedy this problem.

4. Write a letter to the mayor of your town or city suggesting a "Turn Off the TV" public relations effort, convincing residents to stop watching television for a month. Cite the positive effects that "no TV" would have on parents, children, and the community in general.

On the Job

5. As the manager of a store or office, you've noticed that a number of employees have negative workplace habits and/or attitudes. Write a memo for your employees in which you identify these negative behaviors and show how they affect the workplace environment. Be sure to adopt a tone that will sound neither patronizing nor overly harsh.

6. Why do you think teenage suicide is on the rise? You're a respected psychologist. After performing some research, write a fact sheet for parents of teenagers and for high school guidance counselors describing the factors that could make a young person desperate enough to attempt suicide. At the end, suggest what parents and counselors can do to help confused, unhappy young people.

For additional writing, reading, and research resources, go to **www.mycomplab.com** and choose **Nadell/Langan/Comodromos'** ***The Longman Writer,*** **7/e**.

Definition

17

WHAT IS DEFINITION?

Donald Miralle/Getty Images

In Lewis Carroll's wise and whimsical tale *Through the Looking Glass,* Humpty Dumpty proclaims, "When I use a word . . . it means just what I choose it to mean—neither more nor less." If the world were filled with characters like Humpty Dumpty, all of them bending the meanings of words to their own purposes and accepting no challenges to their personal definitions, communication would creak to a halt.

For language to communicate, words must have accepted definitions. Dictionaries, the sourcebooks for definitions, are compilations of current word meanings, enabling speakers of a language to understand one another. But as you might suspect, things are not as simple as they first appear. We all know that a word like *discipline* has a standard dictionary definition. We also know that parents argue every day over the meaning of *discipline,* as do teachers and school administrators. Moreover, many of the wrenching moral debates of our time are attempts to resolve questions of definition. Much of the controversy over abortion, for instance, centers on what is meant by "life" and when it "begins."

Words can, in short, be slippery. Each of us has unique experiences, attitudes, and values that influence the way we use words and the way we interpret the words of others. Lewis Carroll may have been exaggerating, but to some degree Humpty Dumpty's attitude exists in all of us.

In addition to the idiosyncratic interpretations we may attach to words, some words shift in meaning over time. The word *pedagogue,* for instance, originally meant "a teacher or leader of children." However, with the passage of time, *pedagogue* has come to mean "a dogmatic, pedantic teacher." And, of course, we invent new words as the need arises. For example, *modem* and *byte* are just two of many new words created in response to recent breakthroughs in computer technology.

Writing a **definition,** then, is no simple task. Primarily, the writer tries to answer basic questions: "What does ___ mean?" and "What is the special or true nature of ___?" The word to be defined may be an object, a concept, a type of person, a place, or a phenomenon. Potential subjects might be the "user-friendly" computer, animal rights, a model teacher, cabin fever. As you will see, there are various strategies for expanding definitions far beyond the single-word synonyms or brief phrases that dictionaries provide.

HOW DEFINITION FITS YOUR PURPOSE AND AUDIENCE

Many times, short-answer exam questions call for definitions. Consider the following examples:

Define the term *mob psychology.*

What is the difference between a metaphor and a simile?

How would you explain what a religious cult is?

In such cases, a good response might involve a definition of several sentences or several paragraphs.

Other times, definition may be used in an essay organized mainly around another pattern of development. In this situation, all that's needed is a brief formal definition or a short definition given in your own words. For instance, a *process analysis* showing readers how computers have revolutionized the typical business office might start with a textbook definition of the term *artificial intelligence.* In an *argumentation-persuasion* paper urging students to support recent efforts to abolish fraternities and sororities, you could refer to the definitions of *blackballing* and *hazing* found in the university handbook. Or your personal definition of *hero* could be the starting point for a *causal analysis* that explains to readers why there are few real heroes in today's world.

But the most complex use of definition, and the one we focus on in this chapter, involves exploring a subject through an **extended definition.** Extended definition allows you to apply a personal interpretation to a word, to propose a revisionist view of a commonly accepted meaning, to analyze words representing complex or controversial issues. *Pornography, gun control, secular humanism,* and *right to privacy* would be good subjects for extended definition; each is multifaceted, often misunderstood, and fraught with emotion. *Junk food, anger, leadership,* and *anxiety* could also make interesting subjects, especially if the extended definition helped readers develop a new understanding of the word. You might, for example, define *anxiety* not as a negative state but as a positive force that propels us to take action.

An extended definition may run several paragraphs or a few pages. Keep in mind, however, that some definitions require a chapter or even an entire book to develop. Theologians, philosophers, and pop psychologists have devoted entire texts to concepts like *evil* and *love.*

At this point, you have a good sense of the way writers use definition to achieve their purpose and to connect with their readers. Now take a moment to look closely at the photograph at the beginning of this chapter. Imagine you're writing an essay, accompanied by the photo, for publication in your campus newspaper. Your purpose is to explain what it means to be an American in the twenty-first century. Jot down some ideas you might include in your *definition.*

PREWRITING STRATEGIES

The following checklist shows how you can apply to definition some of the prewriting techniques discussed in Chapter 2.

DEFINITION: A PREWRITING CHECKLIST

Choose Something to Define

- ☐ Is there something you're especially qualified to define? What about that thing do you hope to convey?
- ☐ Do any of your journal entries reflect an attempt to pinpoint something's essence: courage, pornography, a well-rounded education?
- ☐ Will you define a concept (energy), an object (the microchip), a type of person (the bigot), a place (the desert), a phenomenon (the rise in volunteerism), a complex or controversial issue (euthanasia)?
- ☐ Can your topic be meaningfully defined within the space and time allotted?

Identify Your Purpose, Audience, Tone, and Point of View

- ☐ Do you want simply to inform and explain—that is, to make meaning clear? Or do you want to persuade readers to accept your understanding of a term? Do you want to do both?

- ☐ Will you offer a personal interpretation? Propose a revised meaning? Explain an obscure or technical term? Discuss shifts in meaning over time? Distinguish one term from another, closely related term? Show conflicts in definition?
- ☐ Are your readers apt to be open to your interpretation of a term? What information will they need to understand your definition and to feel that it is correct and insightful?
- ☐ What tone and point of view will make your readers receptive to your definition?

Use Prewriting to Develop the Definition

- ☐ How might mapping, brainstorming, freewriting, and speaking with others generate material that develops your definition?
- ☐ Which of the prewriting questions below would generate the most details and, therefore, suggest patterns for developing your definition?

Question	*Pattern*
How does *X* look, taste, smell, feel, and sound?	Description
What does *X* do? When? Where?	Narration
What are some typical instances of *X*?	Illustration
What are *X*'s component parts? What different forms can *X* take?	Division-classification
How does *X* work?	Process analysis
What is *X* like or unlike?	Comparison-contrast
What leads to *X*? What are *X*'s consequences?	Cause-effect

STRATEGIES FOR USING DEFINITION IN AN ESSAY

After prewriting, you're ready to draft your essay. The following suggestions and Figure 17.1 (on page 423) will be helpful whether you use definition as a dominant or supportive pattern of development.

1. **Stay focused on the essay's purpose, audience, and tone.** Since your purpose for writing an extended definition shapes the entire paper, you need to keep that objective in mind when developing your definition. Suppose you decide to write an essay defining *jazz.* The essay could be purely *informative* and discuss the origins of jazz, its characteristic tonal patterns, and some of the great jazz musicians of the past. Or the essay could move beyond pure information and take on a *persuasive* edge. It might, for example, argue that jazz is the only contemporary form of music worth considering seriously.

   Just as your purpose in writing will vary, so will your tone. A strictly informative definition will generally assume a detached, objective tone

FIGURE 17.1
Development Diagram: Writing a Definition Essay

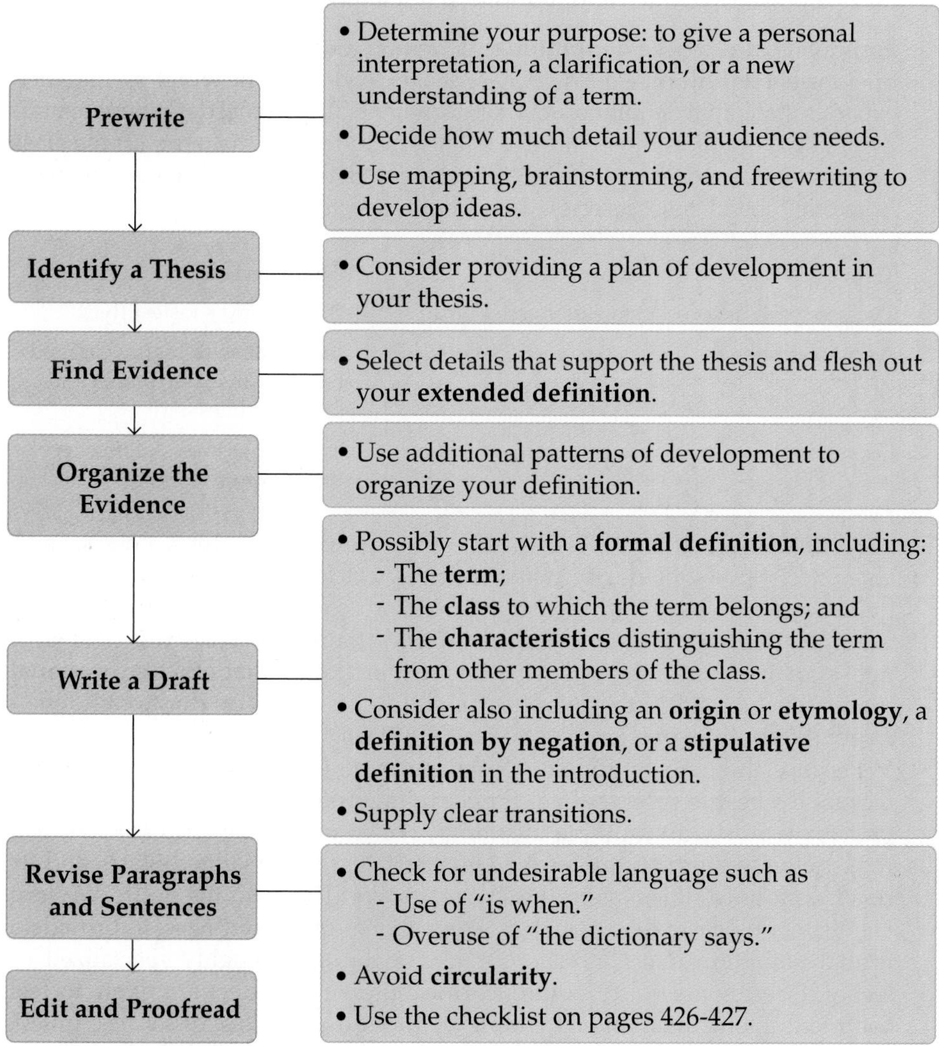

("Apathy is an emotional state characterized by listlessness and indifference"). By way of contrast, a definition essay with a persuasive slant might be urgent in tone ("To combat student apathy, we must design programs that engage students in campus life"), or it might take a satiric approach ("An apathetic stance is a wise choice for any thinking student").

As you write, keep thinking about your audience as well. Not only do your readers determine what terms need to be defined (and in how much detail), but they also keep you focused on the essay's purpose and tone. For instance, you probably wouldn't write a serious, informative piece for the college newspaper about the "mystery meat" served in the campus cafeteria. Instead, you would adopt a light tone as you defined the culinary horror and might even make a persuasive pitch about improving the food prepared on campus.

2. **Formulate an effective definition.** A definition essay sometimes begins with a brief **formal definition**—the dictionary's, a textbook's, or the writer's—and then expands that initial definition with supporting details. Formal definitions are traditionally worded as three-part statements, including (1) the **term,** (2) the **class** to which the term belongs, and (3) the **characteristics** that distinguish the term from other members of its class. Consider these examples of formal definition:

Term	Class	Characteristics
The peregrine falcon,	an endangered bird,	is the world's fastest flyer.
A bodice-ripper	is a paperback book	that deals with highly charged romance in exotic places and faraway times.
Back to basics	is a trend in education	that emphasizes skill mastery through rote learning.

A definition that meets these three guidelines—term, class, and characteristics—will clarify what your subject *is* and what it *is not.* These guidelines also establish the boundaries or scope of your definition. For example, defining *back to basics* as "a trend that emphasizes rote . . . learning" signals a certain boundary; it lets readers know that other educational trends (such as those that emphasize children's social or emotional development) won't be part of the essay's definition.

Because they are formulaic, formal definitions tend to be dull. For this reason, it's best to reserve them for clarifying potentially confusing words—perhaps words with multiple meanings. For example, the term *the West* can refer to the western section of the United States, to the United States and its non-Communist allies (as in the "Western world"), or to the entire Western Hemisphere. Before discussing the West, then, you would need to provide a formal definition that clarifies your use of the term. Highly specialized or technical terms may also require clarification. Few readers are likely to feel confident about their understanding of the term *cognitive dissonance* unless you supply them with a formal definition: "a conflict of thoughts arising when two or more ideas do not go together."

If you decide to include a formal definition in your essay, avoid tired openings like "the dictionary says" or "according to *Webster's.*" Such weak starts lack imagination. You should also keep in mind that a strict dictionary definition may actually confuse readers. Suppose you're writing a paper on the way people tend to absorb their ideas and values from the media. Likening this automatic response to the process of osmosis, you decide to open the paper with a dictionary definition. If you write, "Osmosis is the tendency of a solvent to disperse through a semipermeable membrane into a more concentrated medium," readers are apt to be baffled. *Remember:* The purpose of a definition is to clarify meaning, not obscure it.

You should also stay clear of ungrammatical "is when" definitions: "Blind ambition is when you want to get ahead, no matter how much other people are hurt." Instead, write "Blind ambition is wanting to get ahead, no matter how much other people are hurt." A final pitfall to avoid in writing formal definitions is **circularity,** saying the same thing twice and therefore defining nothing: "A campus tribunal is a tribunal composed of various members of the university community." Circular definitions like this often repeat the term being defined (*tribunal*) or use words having the same meaning (*campus; university community*). In this case, we learn nothing about what a campus tribunal is; the writer says only that "X is X."

3. **Develop the extended definition.** You can use the patterns of development when formulating an extended definition. Description, narration, process analysis, comparison-contrast, or any of the other patterns discussed in this book may be drawn upon—alone or in combination. Imagine you're planning to write an extended definition of *robotics.* You might develop the term by providing *examples* of the way robots are currently being used in scientific research; by *comparing* and *contrasting* human and robot capabilities; or by *classifying* robots, starting with the most basic and moving to the most advanced or futuristic models. (To deepen your understanding of which patterns to use when developing a particular extended definition, take a moment to review the last item in this chapter's Prewriting Checklist on pages 421–422.)

4. **Organize the material that develops the definition.** If you use a single pattern to develop the extended definition, apply the principles of organization suited to that pattern, as described in the appropriate chapter of this book. Assume that you're defining *fad* by means of *process analysis.* You might organize your paragraphs according to the steps in the process: a fad's slow start as something avant-garde or eccentric; its wildfire acceptance by the general public; the fad's demise as it becomes familiar or tiresome. If you want to define *character* by means of a single *narration,* you would probably organize paragraphs chronologically. In a definition essay using several methods of development, you should devote separate paragraphs to each pattern. A definition of *relaxation,* for instance, might start with a paragraph that *narrates* a particularly relaxing day; then it might move to a paragraph that presents several *examples* of people who find it difficult to unwind; finally, it might end with a paragraph that explains a *process* for relaxing the mind and body.

5. **Write an effective introduction.** It can be helpful to provide—near the beginning of a definition essay—a brief formal definition of the term you're going to develop in the rest of the paper. Beyond this basic element, the introduction might include a number of other features. You may explain the *origin* of the term being defined: "*Acid* rock is a term first coined in the 1960s to describe music that was written or listened to under the influence of the drug LSD."

Similarly, you could explain the *etymology,* or linguistic origin, of the key word that focuses the paper: "The term *vigilantism* is derived from a Latin word meaning 'to watch and be awake.'"

You may also use the introduction to clarify what your subject is *not.* Such **definition by negation** can be an effective strategy at a paper's beginning, especially if readers don't share your view of the subject. In such a case, you might write something like this: "The gorilla, far from being the vicious killer of jungle movies and popular imagination, is a sedentary, gentle creature living in a closely knit family group." Such a statement provides the special focus for your essay and signals some of the misconceptions or fallacies soon to be discussed.

In addition, you may include in the introduction a **stipulative definition,** one that puts special restrictions on a term: "Strictly defined, a mall refers to a one- or two-story enclosed building containing a variety of retail shops and at least two large anchor stores. Highway-strip shopping centers or downtown centers cannot be considered true malls." When a term has multiple meanings, or when its meaning has become fuzzy through misuse, a stipulative definition sets the record straight right at the start, so that readers know exactly what is, and is not, being defined.

Finally, the introduction may end with a *plan of development* that indicates how the essay will unfold. A student who returned to school after having raised a family decided to write a paper defining the mid-life crisis that had led to her enrollment in college. After providing a brief formal definition of *mid-life crisis,* the student rounded off her introduction with this sentence: "Such a mid-life crisis often starts with vague misgivings, turns into depression, and ends with a significant change in lifestyle."

REVISION STRATEGIES

Once you have a draft of the essay, you're ready to revise. The following checklist will help you and those giving you feedback apply to definition some of the revision techniques discussed in Chapters 7 and 8.

DEFINITION: A REVISION/PEER REVIEW CHECKLIST

Revise Overall Meaning and Structure

- ☐ Is the essay's purpose informative, persuasive, or both?
- ☐ Is the term being defined clearly distinguished from similar terms?
- ☐ Where does a circular definition cloud meaning? Where are technical, nonstandard, or ambiguous terms a source of confusion?
- ☐ Where would a word's historical or linguistic origin clarify meaning? Where would a formal definition, stipulative definition, or definition by negation help?

- ☐ Which patterns of development are used to develop the definition? How do these help the essay achieve its purpose?
- ☐ If the essay uses only one pattern, is the essay's method of organization suited to that pattern (step-by-step for process analysis, chronological for narration, and so on)?
- ☐ Where could a dry formal definition be deleted without sacrificing overall clarity?

Revise Paragraph Development

- ☐ If the essay uses several patterns of development, where would separate paragraphs for different patterns be appropriate?
- ☐ Which paragraphs are flat or unconvincing? How could they be made more compelling?

Revise Sentences and Words

- ☐ Which sentences and words are inconsistent with the essay's tone?
- ☐ Where should overused phrases, like "the dictionary says" and "according to Webster's," be replaced by more original wording?
- ☐ Have "is when" definitions been avoided?

STUDENT ESSAY: FROM PREWRITING THROUGH REVISION

The student essay that follows was written by Laura Chen in response to this assignment:

> In "Entropy," K. C. Cole takes a scientific term from physics and gives it a broader definition and a wider application. Choose another specialized term and define it in such a way that you reveal something significant about contemporary life.

Before writing her essay, Laura sat down at a computer and *brainstormed* material on the subject she decided to write about: inertia in everyday life. Later on, when she started shaping this material, she jotted down notes in the margin, starred important ideas, crossed out an item, added other ideas, drew connecting arrows, and used numbers and letters to sequence points. In the process, the essay's underlying structure began to emerge so clearly that an outline seemed unnecessary; Laura felt she could move directly from her brainstormed material to a first draft. Laura's original brainstormed list is reprinted on page 428. The handwritten marks indicate her later efforts to organize the preliminary material.

Now read Laura's paper, "Physics in Everyday Life," noting the similarities and differences between her prewriting and final essay. You'll see, for example, that Laura's decision to discuss national inertia *after* individual inertia makes the essay's sequence of points more emphatic. Similarly, by moving the mention of gravity to the essay's end, Laura creates a satisfying symmetry: The paper now opens and closes with principles of physics. As you read the essay, also consider how well it applies the principles of definition discussed in this chapter. (The commentary that follows the paper will help you look at Laura's essay more closely and will give you some sense of how she went about revising her first draft.)

Brainstorming

Entropy—an imp. term in physics. (Just like gravity. — Put in conclusion?)

Formal definition

Boulder sitting or rolling

*③ National inertia (save broadest for last)

3b We accept pollution

3a Accept shoddy products

~~Accept growing homelessness~~

3c Go ahead with genetic engineering even though uncomfortable

3d Keep producing nuclear arms

3e Watch too much TV, despite all the reports

1c Racial discrimination remains a problem Move to section on the individual

① Individual inertia, too

We resist change

1a Vote the same way all the time

1b Need jolts to change (a perfect teenage daughter becomes pregnant) Add example here

② But on TV—no inertia

2a Soap operas, commercials—everyone changes easily give specifics

2b In real life—wear same hairstyle, use same products, wars and national problems drag on

Commentary

Introduction

As the title of her essay suggests, Laura has taken a scientific term (*inertia*) from a specialized field and drawn on the term to help explain some everyday phenomena. Using the *simple-to-complex* approach to structure the introduction, she opens with a vivid *descriptive* example of inertia. This description is then followed by a *formal definition* of inertia: "the tendency of matter to remain at rest or, if moving, to keep moving in one direction unless affected by an outside force." Laura wisely begins the paper with the easy-to-understand description rather than with the more-difficult-to-grasp scientific definition. Had the order been reversed, the essay would not have gotten off to nearly as effective a start. She then ends her introductory paragraph with a *thesis,* "Inertia, an important factor in the world of physics, also plays a crucial role in the human world," and with a *plan of development,* "Inertia affects our individual lives as well as the direction taken by society as a whole."

Organization

To support her definition of inertia and her belief that it can rule our lives, Laura generates a number of compelling examples. She organizes these examples by grouping them into three major points, each point signaled by a *topic sentence* that opens each of the essay's three supporting paragraphs (2–4).

A definite organizational strategy determines the sequence of Laura's three central points. The essay moves from the way inertia affects the individual to the way it affects the nation. The phrase "most importantly" at the beginning of the fourth paragraph indicates that Laura has arranged her points emphatically, believing that inertia's impact on society is most critical.

A Problem with Organization and a Weak Example

When reading the fourth paragraph, you might have noticed that Laura's examples aren't sequenced as effectively as they could be. To show that we, as a nation, tend to keep moving in the same direction, Laura discusses our ongoing uneasiness about genetic engineering, nuclear arms, and excessive television viewing. The point about nuclear weapons is most significant, yet it gets lost in the middle. The paragraph would be stronger if it ended with the point about nuclear arms. Moreover, the example about excessive television viewing doesn't belong in this paragraph since, at best, it has limited bearing on the issue being discussed.

Combining Patterns of Development

In addition to using numerous *examples* to illustrate her points, Laura draws on several other patterns of development to show that inertia can be a powerful force. In the second and fourth paragraphs, she uses *causal analysis* to explain how inertia can paralyze people and nations. The second paragraph indicates that only "an outside force—a jolt of some sort—" can motivate inert people to change. To support this view, Laura provides two examples of parents who experience such jolts. Similarly, in the fourth paragraph, she contends that inertia causes the persistence of specific national problems: shoddy consumer goods and environmental pollution.

Another pattern, *comparison-contrast,* is used in the third paragraph to highlight the differences between television and real life: on television, people zoom into action, but in everyday life, people tend to stay put and muddle through. The essay also contains a distinct element of *argumentation-persuasion* since Laura clearly wants readers to accept her definition of inertia and her view that it often governs human behavior.

Conclusion

Laura's *conclusion* rounds off the essay nicely and brings it to a satisfying close. Laura refers to another law of physics, one with which we are all familiar—gravity. By creating an *analogy* between gravity and inertia, she suggests that our ability to defy gravity should encourage us to defy inertia. The analogy enlarges the scope of the essay; it allows Laura to reach out to her readers by challenging them to action. Such a challenge is, of course, appropriate in a definition essay having a persuasive bent.

Revising the First Draft

When it was time to rework her essay, Laura began by reading her paper out loud. Then, referring to the revision checklist on pages 426–427, she noted in the margin of her draft the problems she detected, numbering them in order of importance. After reviewing her notes, she started to revise in earnest, paying special attention to her third paragraph. The first draft of that paragraph, together with her annotations, is reprinted here:

Original Version of the Third Paragraph

Annotation	Draft
	The ordinary actions of daily life are, in part,
① Paragraph rambles	determined by inertia. To understand this, it is helpful to
④ First two sentences awkward	compare the world of television with real life, for, in the TV-land of ads and entertainment, inertia does not exist. For example, on television, people are often shown making all kinds of drastic changes. They switch brands of coffee or try a new hair color with no hesitation. In one car commercial, a young
⑦ Make more specific	accountant leaves her career and sets off for a cabin by the sea to write poetry. In a soap opera, a character may progress from homemaker to hooker to nun in a single year. In contrast, inertia rules in real life. People tend to stay where they are,
③ Delete part about annoyed wives and hairstyles	to keep their jobs, to be loyal to products (wives get annoyed if a husband brings home the wrong brand or color of bathroom tissue from the market). Middle-aged people wear the hairstyles

or makeup that suited them in high school. A second major difference between television and real life is that, on TV, everyone takes prompt and dramatic action to solve problems. (A woman finds the solution to dull clothes) at the end of a commercial; the police catch the murderer within an hour; the family learns to cope with a son's disturbing lifestyle by the time the movie is over. In contrast, the law of real-life inertia means that few problems are solved neatly or quickly. Things, once started, tend to stay as they are. Few crimes are actually solved. Medical problems are not easily diagnosed. Messy wars in foreign countries seem endless. National problems are identified, but Congress does not pass legislation to solve them.

⑤ Trite—replace

⑥ Point about lifestyle not clear

② Last two sentences don't belong

After rereading her draft, Laura realized that her third paragraph rambled. To give it more focus, she removed the last two sentences ("Messy wars in foreign countries seem endless," and "National problems are identified, but Congress does not pass legislation . . . ") because they referred to national affairs but were located in a section focusing on the individual. Further, she eliminated two flat, unconvincing examples: wives who get annoyed when their husbands bring home the wrong brand of bathroom tissue and middle-aged people whose hairstyles and makeup are outdated. Condensing the two disjointed sentences that originally opened the paragraph also helped tighten this section of the essay. Note how much crisper the revised sentences are: "To illustrate how inertia governs our lives, it is helpful to compare the world of television with real life. On TV, inertia does not exist."

Laura also worked to make the details and the language in the paragraph more specific and vigorous. The vague sentence, "A woman finds the solution to dull clothes at the end of the commercial," is replaced by the more dramatic, "The construction worker with a thudding headache is pain-free at the end of the sixty-second commercial." Similarly, Laura changed a "son's disturbing lifestyle" to a "son's life-threatening drug addiction"; "by the time the movie is over" became "by the time the made-for-TV movie ends at eleven"; and "a young accountant leaves her career and sets off for a cabin by the sea to write poetry" was changed to "an ambitious young accountant abandons her career with a flourish and is seen driving off into the sunset as she heads for a small cabin by the sea to write poetry."

After making these changes, Laura decided to round off the paragraph with a powerful summary statement highlighting how real life differs from television: "Illnesses drag on, few crimes are solved, and family conflicts last for years."

These third-paragraph revisions are similar to those that Laura made elsewhere in her first draft. Her astute changes enabled her to turn an already effective paper into an especially thoughtful analysis of human behavior.

ACTIVITIES: DEFINITION

Prewriting Activities

1. Imagine you're writing two essays: One explains an effective strategy for registering a complaint; the other contrasts the styles of two stand-up comics. Jot down ways you might use definition in each essay.

2. Use the prewriting questions for the patterns of development on pages 421–422 to generate material for an extended definition of *one* of the terms that follow. Then answer these questions about your prewriting material: What thesis does the prewriting suggest? Which pattern(s) yielded the most supporting material? In what order would you present this support when writing an essay?

a. popularity
b. cruelty
c. "dork"
d. self-esteem
e. "wimp"
f. loneliness

3. Select a term whose meaning varies from person to person or one for which you have a personal definition. Some possibilities include:

success	femininity	a liberal
patriotism	affirmative action	a housewife
individuality	pornography	intelligence

Brainstorm with others to identify variations in the term's meaning. Then examine your prewriting material. What thesis comes to mind? If you were writing an essay, would your purpose be informative, persuasive, or both? Finally, prepare a scratch list of the points you might cover.

Revising Activities

4. Explain why each of the following is an effective or ineffective definition. Rewrite those you consider ineffective.

a. *Passive aggression* is when people show their aggression passively.
b. A *terrorist* tries to terrorize people.
c. Being *assertive* means knowing how to express your wishes and goals in a positive, noncombative way.
d. *Pop music* refers to music that is popular.
e. *Loyalty* is when someone stays by another person during difficult times.

5. The following introductory paragraph is from the first draft of an essay contrasting walking and running as techniques for reducing tension. Although intended to be a definition paragraph, it actually doesn't tell us anything we don't already know. It also relies on the old-hat "*Webster's* says." Rewrite the paragraph so it is more imaginative. You might use a series of anecdotes or one extended example to define *tension* and introduce the essay's thesis more gracefully.

According to *Webster's*, *tension* is "mental or nervous strain, often accompanied by muscular tightness or tautness." Everyone feels tense at one time or another. It may occur when there's a deadline to meet. Or it could be caused by the stress of trying to fulfill academic, athletic, or social goals. Sometimes it comes from criticism by family, bosses, or teachers. Such tension puts wear and tear on our bodies and on our emotional well-being. Although some people run to relieve tension, research has found that walking is a more effective tension reducer.

PROFESSIONAL SELECTIONS: DEFINITION

K. C. COLE

K. C. Cole (1946–) has contributed articles on science to numerous national publications and has written a regular column for *Discovery* magazine. Her essays are collected in *Sympathetic Vibrations: Reflections on Physics as a Way of Life* (1985). She has written several books, including *Facets of Light: Color Images and Things That Glow in the Dark* (1980), *Order in the Universe: The Shape of Relative Motion* (1986), *The Universe and the Teacup* (1998), *The Hole in the Universe* (2000), and *Mind Over Matter* (2003). She is currently a science writer and editor at the *L. A. Times*. The selection that follows first appeared as a "Hers" column in *The New York Times* (1982).

Please note the essay structure diagram that appears following this selection (Figure 17.2 on page 438).

Pre-Reading Journal Entry

Do you consider yourself an orderly or a disorderly person? What about those around you? What are the benefits and the drawbacks of being orderly? Of being disorderly? Use your journal to reflect on these questions.

ENTROPY

It was about two months ago when I realized that entropy was getting the better of me. On the same day my car broke down (again), my refrigerator conked out and I learned that I needed root-canal work in my right rear tooth. The windows in the bedroom were still leaking every time it rained and my son's baby sitter was still failing to show up every time I really needed her. My hair was turning gray and my typewriter was wearing out. The house needed paint and I needed glasses. My son's sneakers were developing holes and I was developing a deep sense of futility. 1

After all, what was the point of spending half of Saturday at the Laundromat if the clothes were dirty all over again the following Friday? 2

Disorder, alas, is the natural order of things in the universe. There is even a precise measure of the amount of disorder, called entropy. Unlike almost every other physical property (motion, gravity, energy), entropy does not work both ways. It can only increase. Once it's created it can never be destroyed. The road to disorder is a one-way street. 3

Because of its unnerving irreversibility, entropy has been called the arrow of time. We all understand this instinctively. Children's rooms, left on their own, tend to get messy, not neat. Wood rots, metal rusts, people wrinkle and flowers wither. Even mountains wear down; even the nuclei of atoms decay. In the city we see entropy in the rundown subways and worn-out sidewalks and torn-down buildings, in the increasing disorder of our lives. We know, without asking, what is old. If we were suddenly to see the paint jump back on an old building, we would know that something was wrong. If we saw an egg unscramble itself and jump back into its shell, we would laugh in the same way we laugh at a movie run backward. 4

Entropy is no laughing matter, however, because with every increase in entropy energy is wasted and opportunity is lost. Water flowing down a mountainside can be made to do some useful work on its way. But once all the water is at the same level it can work no more. That is entropy. When my refrigerator was working, it kept all the cold air ordered in one part of the kitchen and warmer air in another. Once it broke down the warm and cold mixed into a lukewarm mess that allowed my butter to melt, my milk to rot and my frozen vegetables to decay. 5

Of course the energy is not really lost, but it has defused and dissipated into a chaotic caldron of randomness that can do us no possible good. Entropy is chaos. It is loss of purpose. 6

People are often upset by the entropy they seem to see in the haphazardness of their own lives. Buffeted about like so many molecules in my tepid kitchen, they feel that they have lost their sense of direction, that they are wasting youth and opportunity at every turn. It is easy to see entropy in marriages, when the partners are too preoccupied to patch small things up, almost guaranteeing that they will fall apart. There is much entropy in the state of our country, in the relationships between nations—lost opportunities to stop the avalanche of disorders that seems ready to swallow us all. 7

Entropy is not inevitable everywhere, however. Crystals and snowflakes and galaxies are islands of incredibly ordered beauty in the midst of random events. If it was not 8 for exceptions to entropy, the sky would be black and we would be able to see where the stars spend their days; it is only because air molecules in the atmosphere cluster in ordered groups that the sky is blue.

9 The most profound exception to entropy is the creation of life. A seed soaks up some soil and some carbon and some sunshine and some water and arranges it into a rose. A seed in the womb takes some oxygen and pizza and milk and transforms it into a baby.

10 The catch is that it takes a lot of energy to produce a baby. It also takes energy to make a tree. The road to disorder is all downhill but the road to creation takes work. Though combating entropy is possible, it also has its price. That's why it seems so hard to get ourselves together, so easy to let ourselves fall apart.

11 Worse, creating order in one corner of the universe always creates more disorder somewhere else. We create ordered energy from oil and coal at the price of the entropy of smog.

12 I recently took up playing the flute again after an absence of several months. As the uneven vibrations screeched through the house, my son covered his ears and said, "Mom, what's wrong with your flute?" Nothing was wrong with my flute, of course. It was my ability to play it that had atrophied, or entropied, as the case may be. The only way to stop that process was to practice every day, and sure enough my tone improved, though only at the price of constant work. Like anything else, abilities deteriorate when we stop applying our energies to them.

13 That's why entropy is depressing. It seems as if just breaking even is an uphill fight. There's a good reason that this should be so. The mechanics of entropy are a matter of chance. Take any ice-cold air molecule milling around my kitchen. The chances that it will wander in the direction of my refrigerator at any point are exactly 50–50. The chances that it will wander away from my refrigerator are also 50–50. But take billions of warm and cold molecules mixed together, and the chances that all the cold ones will wander toward the refrigerator and all the warm ones will wander away from it are virtually nil.

14 Entropy wins not because order is impossible but because there are always so many more paths toward disorder than toward order. There are so many more different ways to do a sloppy job than a good one, so many more ways to make a mess than to clean it up. The obstacles and accidents in our lives almost guarantee that constant collisions will bounce us on to random paths, get us off the track. Disorder is the path of least resistance, the easy but not the inevitable road.

15 Like so many others, I am distressed by the entropy I see around me today. I am afraid of the randomness of international events, of the lack of common purpose in the world; I am terrified that it will lead into the ultimate entropy of nuclear war. I am upset that I could not in the city where I live send my child to a public school; that people are unemployed and inflation is out of control; that tensions between sexes and races seem to be increasing again; that relationships everywhere seem to be falling apart.

16 Social institutions—like atoms and stars—decay if energy is not added to keep them ordered. Friendships and families and economies all fall apart unless we constantly make an effort to keep them working and well oiled. And far too few people, it seems to me, are willing to contribute consistently to those efforts.

Of course, the more complex things are, the harder it is. If there were only a dozen or so air molecules in my kitchen, it would be likely—if I waited a year or so—that at some point the six coldest ones would congregate inside the freezer. But the more factors in the equation—the more players in the game—the less likely it is that their paths will coincide in an orderly way. The more pieces in the puzzle, the harder it is to put back together once order is disturbed. "Irreversibility," said a physicist, "is the price we pay for complexity." 17

FIGURE 17.2
Essay Structure Diagram: "Entropy" by K. C. Cole

Introductory paragraphs **Thesis** **Formal definition** (paragraphs 1–3)	Examples of entropy from everyday life. **Thesis:** Disorder is the natural order of the universe. **Formal definition:** Entropy is a measure of the amount of disorder in the universe.
Extended definition through comparison-contrast (4–12)	**Extended definition:** Entropy is loss of purpose, haphazard chaos in people's lives. **Comparison:** As in nature, entropy in everyday life is irreversible. (Several examples follow.) **Comparison:** Entropy results in wasted energy and opportunities in life. (Examples follow.) **Comparison:** Entropy affects human relationships. (Examples follow.) **Contrast:** Entropy is not always inevitable. Creation of life is the most profound exception to entropy. (Examples follow.) **Contrast:** Creation takes harder work than entropy; there are more paths to disorder than to order. (Examples follow.)
Extended definition through cause-effect (13–15)	Entropy is depressing. Entropy creates distressing disorder in life.
Concluding paragraph (16–17)	Restatement of thesis and author's pessimistic feelings about entropy.

Questions for Close Reading

1. What is the selection's thesis? Locate the sentence(s) in which Cole states her main idea. If she doesn't state the thesis explicitly, express it in your own words.
2. How does entropy differ from the other properties of the physical world? Is the image "the arrow of time" helpful in establishing this difference?
3. Why is the creation of life an exception to entropy? What is the relationship between entropy and energy?
4. Why does Cole say that entropy "is no laughing matter"? What is so depressing about the entropy she describes?
5. Refer to your dictionary as needed to define the following words used in the selection: *futility* (paragraph 1), *dissipated* (6), *buffeted* (7), *tepid* (7), and *atrophied* (12).

Questions About the Writer's Craft

1. **The pattern.** What is Cole's underlying purpose in defining the scientific term *entropy?* What gives the essay its persuasive edge?
2. What tone does Cole adopt to make reading about a scientific concept more interesting? Identify places in the essay where her tone is especially prominent.
3. Cole uses such words as *futility, loss,* and *depressing*. How do these words affect you? Why do you suppose she chose such terms? Find similar words in the essay.
4. **Other patterns.** Many of Cole's sentences follow a two-part pattern involving a *contrast*: "The road to disorder is all downhill but the road to creation takes work" (paragraph 10). Find other examples of this pattern in the essay. Why do you think Cole uses it so often?

Writing Assignments Using Definition as a Pattern of Development

1. Define *order* or *disorder* by applying the term to a system that you know well—for example, your school, dorm, family, or workplace. Develop your definition through any combination of writing patterns: by supplying examples, by showing contrasts, by analyzing the process underlying the system, and so on.
2. Choose, as Cole does, a technical term that you think will be unfamiliar to most readers. In a humorous or serious paper, define the term as it is used

technically; then show how the term can shed light on some aspect of your life. For example, the concept in astronomy of a *supernova* could be used to explain your sudden emergence as a new star on the athletic field, in your schoolwork, or on the social scene. Here are a few suggested terms:

symbiosis	volatility	resonance
velocity	erosion	catalyst
neutralization	equilibrium	malleability

Writing Assignments Combining Patterns of Development

3. Can one person make much difference in the amount of entropy—disorder and chaos—in the world? *Argue* your position in an essay. Use *examples* of people who have tried to overcome the tendency of things to "fall apart." Make clear whether you think these people succeeded or failed in their attempts. To inform your perspective before writing, read James Gleick's "Life As Type A" (page 441), an evaluation of the factors that influence people's compulsion for order.

4. Cole claims that our lives contain a distressing amount of "haphazardness" (paragraph 7). Write an essay *arguing* that people either do or do not control their own fates. Support your point with a series of specific *examples*. For one author's reflections on life's unpredictability, read Beth Johnson's "Bombs Bursting in Air" (page 252).

Writing Assignment Using a Journal Entry as a Starting Point

5. Write an essay arguing that disorder can be liberating *or* that it can be stifling. Review your pre-reading journal entry, and select strong, compelling examples that support your position. Aim to refute as many opposing arguments as possible. Your essay may have a serious or a humorous tone.

JAMES GLEICK

After graduating from Harvard College in 1976, James Gleick helped found *Metropolis*, an alternative newspaper in Minneapolis. He then spent ten years as a reporter and editor with *The New York Times*, where he wrote a column about the impact of science and technology on modern life. His earlier books, *Chaos: Making a New Science* (1987) and *Genius: The Life and Science of Richard Feynman* (1992), were both finalists for the National Book Award and Pulitzer Prize. Most recently, he wrote the biography *Isaac Newton* (2003) and *What Just Happened: A Chronicle from the Information Frontier* (2002), a collection of previously published essays on the first ten years of the information revolution. Formerly McGraw Distinguished Lecturer at Princeton University, Gleick lives with his wife, writer Cynthia Crossen, in New York. The following piece is taken from Gleick's book *Faster: The Acceleration of Just About Everything* (1999).

Pre-Reading Journal Entry

Like many people, you may feel harried and under pressure at least some of the time. Use your journal to reflect on the sources of stress in your everyday life. List several examples. For each, consider the factors leading to this frenzied feeling.

LIFE AS TYPE A

1 Everyone knows about Type A. This magnificently bland coinage, put forward by a pair of California cardiologists in 1959, struck a collective nerve and entered the language. It is a token of our confusion: are we victims or perpetrators of the crime of haste? Are we living at high speed with athleticism and vigor, or are we stricken by hurry sickness?

2 The cardiologists, Meyer Friedman and Ray Rosenman, listed a set of personality traits which, they claimed, tend to go hand in hand with one another and also with heart disease. They described these traits rather unappealingly, as characteristics about and around the theme of impatience. Excessive competitiveness. Aggressiveness. "A harrying sense of time urgency." The Type A idea emerged in technical papers and then formed the basis of a popular book and made its way into dictionaries. The canonical Type A, as these doctors portrayed him, was "Paul":

> A very disproportionate amount of his emotional energy is consumed in struggling against the normal constraints of time. "How can I move faster, and do more and more things in less and less time?" is the question that never ceases to torment him.
>
> Paul hurries his thinking, his speech and his movements. He also strives to hurry the thinking, speech, and movements of those about him; they must communicate rapidly and relevantly if they wish to avoid creating impatience in him. Planes must arrive and depart precisely on time for Paul, cars ahead of him on the highway must maintain a speed he approves of, and there must never be a queue of persons standing between him and a bank clerk, a restaurant table, or the interior of a theater. In fact, he is infuriated whenever people talk slowly or circuitously, when planes are late, cars dawdle on the highway, and queues form.

Let's think . . . Do we know anyone like "Paul"?

3 This was the first clear declaration of *hurry sickness*—another coinage of Friedman's. It inspired new businesses: mind-body workshops; videotapes demonstrating deep breathing; anxiety-management retreats; seminars on and even institutes of stress medicine. "I drove all the way in the right-hand lane," a Pacific Gas and Electric Company executive said proudly one morning in 1987 to a group of self-confessed

hurriers, led by Friedman himself, by then seventy-six years old. In the battle against Type A jitters, patients tried anything and everything—the slow lane, yoga, meditation, visualization: "Direct your attention to your feet on the floor. . . . Be aware of the air going in your nostrils cool and going out warm. . . . Visualize a place you like to be. . . . Experience it and see the objects there, the forms and shadows. Take another deep breath and experience the sounds, the surf, the wind, leaves, a babbling brook." Some hospital television systems now feature a "relaxation channel," with hour after hour of surf, wind, leaves, and babbling brooks.

We believe in Type A—a triumph for a notion with no particular scientific validity. 4
The Friedman-Rosenman claim has turned out to be both obvious and false. Clearly some heart ailments do result from, or at least go along with, stress (itself an ill-defined term), both chronic and acute. Behavior surely affects physiology, at least once in a while. Sudden dashes for the train, laptop computer in one hand and takeout coffee in the other, can accelerate heartbeats and raise blood pressure. That haste makes coronaries was already a kind of folk wisdom—that is, standard medical knowledge untainted by research. "Hurry has a clearly debilitating effect upon the tissues and may in time injure the heart," admonished Dr. Cecil Webb-Johnson in *Nerve Troubles*, an English monograph of the early 1900s. "The great men of the centuries past were never in a hurry," he added sanctimoniously, "and that is why the world will never forget them in a hurry." It might be natural—even appealing—to expect certain less-great people to receive their cardiovascular comeuppance. But in reality, three decades of attention from cardiologists and psychologists have failed to produce any carefully specified and measurable set of character traits that predict heart disease—or to demonstrate that people who change their Type A behavior will actually lower their risk of heart disease.

Indeed, the study that started it all—Friedman and Rosenman's "Association of 5
Specific Overt Behavior Pattern with Blood and Cardiovascular Findings"—appears to have been a wildly flawed piece of research. It used a small sample—eighty-three people (all men) in what was then called "Group A." The selection process was neither random nor blind. White-collar male employees of large businesses were rounded up by acquaintances of Friedman and Rosenman on a subjective basis—they fit the type. The doctors further sorted the subjects by interviewing them personally and observing their appearance and behavior. Did a man gesture rapidly, clench his teeth, or exhibit a "general air of impatience"? If so, he was chosen. It seems never to have occurred to these experienced cardiologists that they might have been consciously or unconsciously selecting people whose physique indicated excess weight or other markers for incipient heart disease. The doctors' own data show that the final Group A drank more, smoked more, and weighed more than Group B. But the authors dismissed these factors, asserting, astonishingly, that there was no association between heart disease and cigarette smoking.

In the years since, researchers have never settled on a reliable method for identify- 6
ing Type A people, though not for want of trying. Humans are not reliable witnesses to their own impatience. Researchers have employed questionnaires like the Jenkins Activity Survey, and they have used catalogues of grimaces and frowns—Ekman and Friesen's Facial Action Coding System, for example, or the Cook-Medley Hostility Inventory. In the end, nothing conclusive emerges. Some studies have found Type A people to have *lower* blood pressure. The sedentary and obese have cardiac difficulties of their own.

7 The notion of Type A has expanded, shifted, and flexed to suit the varying needs of different researchers. V. A. Price adds *hypervigilance* to the list of traits. Some doctors lose patience with the inconclusive results and shift their focus to anger and hostility—mere subsets of the original Type A grab-bag. Cynthia Perry finds that Type A people have fewer daydreams. How does she know? She asks them to monitor lines flashing across a computer screen for forty painfully boring minutes and finds that, when interrupted by a beep (1000 hertz at 53 decibels), they are less likely to press a black button to confess that irrelevant thoughts had strayed into their minds. Studies have labeled as Type A not only children (those with a tendency to interrupt and to play competitively at games) but even babies (those who cry more). Meanwhile, researchers interested in pets link the Type A personality to petlessness; a National Institutes of Health panel reports: "The description of a 'coronary-prone behavior pattern,' or Type A behavior, and its link to the probability of developing overt disease provided hope that, with careful training, individuals could exercise additional control over somatic illness by altering their lifestyle. . . . Relaxation, meditation, and stress management have become recognized therapies. . . . It therefore seems reasonable that pets, who provide faithful companionship to many people, also might promote greater psychosocial stability for their owners, and thus a measure of protection from heart disease." This is sweet, but it is not science.

8 Typically a Type A study will begin with researchers who assume that there are some correlations to be found, look for a wide variety of associations, fail to find some and succeed in finding others. For example, a few dozen preschool children are sorted according to their game-playing styles and tested for blood pressure. No correlation is found. Later, however, when performing a certain "memory game," the supposed Type A children rank somewhat higher in, specifically, systolic pressure. Interesting? The authors of various published papers evidently think so, but they are wrong, because if their technique is to keep looking until they find some correlation, somewhere, they are bound to succeed. Such results are meaningless.

9 The categorizations are too variable and the prophecies too self-fulfilling. It is never quite clear which traits *define* Type A and which are fellow travelers. The "freefloating, but well-rationalized form of hostility"? The "deep-seated insecurity"? "Their restlessness, their tense facial muscles, their tics, or their strident-staccato manner of speaking"? If you are hard-driving yet friendly, chafing yet self-assured—if you race for the airport gate and then settle *happily* into your seat—are you Type A or not? If you are driven to walk briskly, briskly, all the time, isn't that good for your heart?

10 Most forget that there is also supposed to be a Type B, defined not by the personality traits its members possess but by the traits they lack. Type B people are the shadowy opposites of Type A people. They are those who are not so very Type A. They do *not* wear out their fingers punching that elevator button. They do *not* allow a slow car in the fast lane to drive their hearts to fatal distraction; in fact, they are at the wheel of that slow car. Type B played no real part in that mass societal gasp of recognition in the 1970's. Type B-ness was just a foil. Doctors Friedman and Rosenman actually claimed to have had trouble finding eighty men in all San Francisco who were not under any time pressure. They finally came up with a few, they wrote solemnly, "in the municipal clerks' and the embalmers' unions."

11 Even more bizarrely, that first Friedman-Rosenman study also included a Group C, comprising forty-six unemployed blind men. Not much haste in Group C. "The primary reason men of Group C exhibited little ambition, drive, or desire to compete,"

the doctors wrote, "was the presence of total blindness for ten or more years and the lack of occupational deadlines because none was gainfully employed." No wonder they omitted Type C from the subsequent publicity.

If the Type A phenomenon made for poor medical research, it stands nonetheless as a triumph of social criticism. Some of us yield more willingly to impatience than others, but on the whole Type A is who we are—not just the coronary-prone among us, but all of us, as a society and as an age. No wonder the concept has proven too rich a cultural totem to be dismissed. 12

Questions for Close Reading

1. What is the selection's thesis? Locate the sentence(s) in which Gleick states his main idea. If he doesn't state the thesis explicitly, express it in your own words.
2. What is Gleick's opinion of the study Friedman and Rosenman conducted? List at least two elements of the study that Gleick uses to support his assessment.
3. In paragraph 7, Gleick observes that the concept of Type A has changed since Friedman and Rosenman's study first chronicled it. How has it changed? What accounts for this change?
4. According to Gleick, how do Friedman and Rosenman define the Type B personality? Why does Gleick find fault with their definition of this personality type?
5. Refer to your dictionary as needed to define the following words used in the selection: *coinage* (paragraph 1), *harrying* (2), *canonical* (2), *circuitously* (2), *sanctimoniously* (4), *overt* (5), *incipient* (5), *sedentary* (6), *hypervigilance* (7), *correlations* (8), *strident* (9), *staccato* (9), *foil* (10), and *totem* (12).

Questions About the Writer's Craft

1. **The pattern.** In their work, Friedman and Rosenman use a description of Paul to define "canonical Type A" behavior (paragraph 2). Why do you suppose that Gleick, who criticizes Friedman and Rosenman's research, quotes their portrait of Paul at such length?
2. **The pattern.** Gleick uses a sequence of three fragments when discussing (in paragraph 2) how Type A has been defined. Identify these fragments. What effect do you think Gleick wanted the fragments to have?
3. Locate places where Gleick uses the first-person pronouns *we, us,* and *our.* What do you think Gleick's purpose is in using these pronouns?
4. In paragraph 1, Gleick sarcastically refers to the phrase *Type A* as "magnificently bland." Find other places in the essay where he uses sarcasm. Why might he have chosen to employ such language?

Writing Assignments Using Definition as a Pattern of Development

1. Write an essay offering a fuller definition of the Type B personality than Gleick's essay provides. Rather than defining Type B through negation, as Friedman and Rosenman do, marshal convincing evidence that illustrates the validity of the Type B phenomenon. Brainstorming with friends, family, and classmates will help you generate strong examples of this personality type. At some point in the essay, you might offer a brief personality sketch of the "canonical" Type B as well as discuss the factors that shape the Type B personality as you define it. You might find that K. C. Cole's "Entropy" (page 436) offers some useful insights into why people might be better off as Type B.

2. Gleick notes that, like *Type A*, *stress* is an ill-defined term. Brainstorm with others to identify as many examples of different kinds of stress as you can. Review the brainstormed material, and select a specific type of stress to focus on. Then write an essay providing a *clear* definition of that particular stress. Possibilities include "dating stress," "workplace stress," "online stress," "fitness stress." Near the end of the essay, you might provide concise hints for managing the stress you define. Your essay may have a humorous or a serious tone—whichever seems appropriate to your subject.

Writing Assignments Combining Patterns of Development

3. Write an essay *contrasting* situations in which being Type A would be beneficial with situations in which it would be counterproductive. Under what circumstances would Type A characteristics be desirable? Under what circumstances would they be undesirable? Drawing upon your own experiences and observations, reach some conclusions about the advantages and/or limitations of the Type A personality. Along the way, you should explore the *effects* of Type A behavior in the situations you're considering.

4. Gleick observes that "hurry sickness" is a trait induced by society at large. Identify a trait of yours that you think is also a reflection or *effect* of the society in which you live. You might discuss your tendency to be aggressive or non-assertive, materialistic or idealistic, studious or fun-loving. Write an essay *illustrating* this character trait at work in your everyday behavior. Explain whether you think this trait works to your advantage or disadvantage. For another "take" on how society helps determine and define a particular characteristic, read Natalie Angier's "The Cute Factor" (page 446).

Writing Assignment Using a Journal Entry as a Starting Point

5. Gleick claims that the Type A phenomenon is pervasive in our society. Write an essay of your own illustrating the extent to which your life reflects this phenomenon. Draw upon the most dramatic examples in your pre-reading journal entry. At the end of the essay, describe steps that you or anyone with similar pressures could take to slow down the frenetic pace of everyday life. Gathering information in the library and/or on the Internet might be helpful when you develop the final section of your paper.

NATALIE ANGIER

Natalie Angier was born in 1958 and was raised in the Bronx, New York, and in Michigan. She attended Barnard College, where she studied literature, astronomy, and physics. After working for *Discover* magazine, she became a reporter for the science section of *The New York Times* in 1990. The following year she won a Pulitzer Prize for her science reporting. In addition to reporting, Angier has written several books, including *The Beauty of the Beastly* (1995), *Natural Obsessions: Striving to Unlock the Deepest Secret of the Cancer Cell* (1999), and *Woman: An Intimate Geography* (1999). Angier has always been interested in bridging the gap between science and the humanities. This article, about the scientific basis of cuteness, was published in *The New York Times* on January 3, 2006.

Pre-Reading Journal Entry

Some concepts—like beauty, elegance, and cuteness—are hard to explain, although people usually believe they understand what those concepts are. Take a moment to reflect in your journal on what *you* mean when you say something is "cute." What qualities come to mind? Consider the kinds of things that you would deem cute, and list as many as you can think of in your journal.

THE CUTE FACTOR

If the mere sight of Tai Shan, the roly-poly, goofily gamboling masked bandit of a panda cub now on view at the National Zoo isn't enough to make you melt, then maybe the crush of his human onlookers, the furious flashing of their cameras and the heated gasps of their mass rapture will do the trick. 1

Awww. . . . Scientists who study the evolution of visual signaling have identified a wide and still-expanding assortment of features and behaviors that make something look cute. 2

Cute cues are those that indicate extreme youth, vulnerability, harmlessness and need, scientists say. 3

4 "Omigosh, look at him! He is too cute!"

5 "How adorable! I wish I could just reach in there and give him a big squeeze!"

6 "He's so fuzzy! I've never seen anything so cute in my life!"

7 A guard's sonorous voice rises above the burble. "OK, folks, five oohs and aahs per person, then it's time to let someone else step up front."

8 The 6-month-old, 25-pound Tai Shan—whose name is pronounced tie-SHON and means, for no obvious reason, "peaceful mountain"—is the first surviving giant panda cub ever born at the Smithsonian's zoo. And though the zoo's adult pandas have long been among Washington's top tourist attractions, the public debut of the baby in December has unleashed an almost bestial frenzy here. Some 13,000 timed tickets to see the cub were snapped up within two hours of being released, and almost immediately began trading on eBay for up to $200 a pair.

9 Panda mania is not the only reason that 2005 proved an exceptionally cute year. Last summer, a movie about another black-and-white charmer, the emperor penguin, became one of the highest-grossing documentaries of all time.[1] Sales of petite, willfully cute cars like the Toyota Prius and the Mini Cooper soared, while those of non-cute sport utility vehicles tanked.

10 Women's fashions opted for the cute over the sensible or glamorous, with low-slung slacks and skirts and abbreviated blouses contriving to present a customer's midriff as an adorable preschool bulge. Even the too big could be too cute. King Kong's newly reissued face has a squashed baby-doll appeal, and his passion for Naomi Watts ultimately feels like a serious case of puppy love—hopeless, heartbreaking, cute.[2]

11 Scientists who study the evolution of visual signaling have identified a wide and still expanding assortment of features and behaviors that make something look cute: bright forward-facing eyes set low on a big round face, a pair of big round ears, floppy limbs and a side-to-side, teeter-totter gait, among many others.

12 Cute cues are those that indicate extreme youth, vulnerability, harmlessness and need, scientists say, and attending to them closely makes good Darwinian sense. As a species whose youngest members are so pathetically helpless they can't lift their heads to suckle without adult supervision, human beings must be wired to respond quickly and gamely to any and all signs of infantile desire.

13 The human cuteness detector is set at such a low bar, researchers said, that it sweeps in and deems cute practically anything remotely resembling a human baby or a part thereof, and so ends up including the young of virtually every mammalian species, fuzzy-headed birds like Japanese cranes, woolly bear caterpillars, a bobbing balloon, a big round rock stacked on a smaller rock, a colon, a hyphen and a close parenthesis typed in succession.

14 The greater the number of cute cues that an animal or object happens to possess, or the more exaggerated the signals may be, the louder and more italicized are the squeals provoked.

15 Cuteness is distinct from beauty, researchers say, emphasizing rounded over sculptured, soft over refined, clumsy over quick. Beauty attracts admiration and demands a pedestal; cuteness attracks affection and demands a lap. Beauty is rare and brutal,

---

[1]A reference to *March of the Penguins* (2005), directed by Luc Jacquet (editors' note).

[2]A reference to the 2005 version of *King Kong*, directed by Peter Jackson and starring Naomi Watts as Ann Darrow, the oversized ape's female human ally (editors' note).

despoiled by a single pimple. Cuteness is commonplace and generous, content on occasion to cosegregate with homeliness.

Observing that many Floridians have an enormous affection for the manatee, which looks like an overfertilized potato with a sock puppet's face, Roger L. Reep of the University of Florida said it shone by grace of contrast. "People live hectic lives, and they may be feeling overwhelmed, but then they watch this soft and slow-moving animal, this gentle giant, and they see it turn on its back to get its belly scratched," said Dr. Reep, author with Robert K. Bonde of *The Florida Manatee: Biology and Conservation.* 16

"That's very endearing," said Dr. Reep. "So even though a manatee is 3 times your size and 20 times your weight, you want to get into the water beside it." 17

Even as they say a cute tooth has rational roots, scientists admit they are just beginning to map its subtleties and source. New studies suggest that cute images stimulate the same pleasure centers of the brain aroused by sex, a good meal or psychoactive drugs like cocaine, which could explain why everybody in the panda house wore a big grin. 18

At the same time, said Denis Dutton, a philosopher of art at the University of Canterbury in New Zealand, the rapidity and promiscuity of the cute response makes the impulse suspect, readily overridden by the angry sense that one is being exploited or deceived. 19

"Cute cuts through all layers of meaning and says, Let's not worry about complexities, just love me," said Dr. Dutton, who is writing a book about Darwinian aesthetics. "That's where the sense of cheapness can come from, and the feeling of being manipulated or taken for a sucker that leads many to reject cuteness as low or shallow." 20

Quick and cheap make cute appealing to those who want to catch the eye and please the crowd. Advertisers and product designers are forever toying with cute cues to lend their merchandise instant appeal, mixing and monkeying with the vocabulary of cute to keep the message fresh and fetching. 21

That market-driven exercise in cultural evolution can yield bizarre if endearing results, like the blatantly ugly Cabbage Patch dolls, Furbies, the figgy face of E.T., the froggy one of Yoda. As though the original Volkswagen Beetle wasn't considered cute enough, the updated edition was made rounder and shinier still. 22

"The new Beetle looks like a smiley face," said Miles Orvell, professor of American studies at Temple University in Philadelphia. "By this point its origins in Hitler's regime, and its intended resemblance to a German helmet, is totally forgotten." 23

Whatever needs pitching, cute can help. A recent study at the Veterans Affairs Medical Center at the University of Michigan showed that high school students were far more likely to believe antismoking messages accompanied by cute cartoon characters like a penguin in a red jacket or a smirking polar bear than when the warnings were delivered unadorned. 24

"It made a huge difference," said Sonia A. Duffy, the lead author of the report, which was published in *The Archives of Pediatrics and Adolescent Medicine*. "The kids expressed more confidence in the cartoons than in the warnings themselves." 25

Primal and widespread though the taste for cute may be, researchers say it varies in strength and significance across cultures and eras. They compare the cute response to the love of sugar: everybody has sweetness receptors on the tongue, but some people, and some countries, eat a lot more candy than others. 26

27 Experts point out that the cuteness craze is particularly acute in Japan, where it goes by the name "kawaii" and has infiltrated the most masculine of redoubts. Truck drivers display Hello Kitty–style figurines on their dash/boards. The police enliven safety billboards and wanted posters with two perky mouselike mascots, Pipo kun and Pipo chan.

28 Behind the kawaii phenomenon, according to Brian J. McVeigh, a scholar of East Asian studies at the University of Arizona, is the strongly hierarchical nature of Japanese culture. "Cuteness is used to soften up the vertical society," he said, "to soften power relations and present authority without being threatening."

29 In this country, the use of cute imagery is geared less toward blurring the line of command than toward celebrating America's favorite demographic: the young. Dr. Orvell traces contemporary cute chic to the 1960's, with its celebration of a perennial childhood, a refusal to dress in adult clothes, an inversion of adult values, a love of bright colors and bloopy, cartoony patterns, the Lava Lamp.

30 Today, it's not enough for a company to use cute graphics in its advertisements. It must have a really cute name as well. "Companies like Google and Yahoo leave no question in your mind about the youthfulness of their founders," said Dr. Orvell.

31 Madison Avenue may adapt its strategies for maximal tweaking of our inherent baby radar, but babies themselves, evolutionary scientists say, did not really evolve to be cute. Instead, most of their salient qualities stem from the demands of human anatomy and the human brain, and became appealing to a potential caretaker's eye only because infants wouldn't survive otherwise.

32 Human babies have unusually large heads because humans have unusually large brains. Their heads are round because their brains continue to grow throughout the first months of life, and the plates of the skull stay flexible and unfused to accommodate the development. Baby eyes and ears are situated comparatively far down the face and skull, and only later migrate upward in proportion to the development of bones in the cheek and jaw areas.

33 Baby eyes are also notably forward-facing, the binocular vision a likely legacy of our tree-dwelling ancestry, and all our favorite Disney characters also sport forward-facing eyes, including the ducks and mice, species that in reality have eyes on the sides of their heads.

34 The cartilage tissue in an infant's nose is comparatively soft and undeveloped, which is why most babies have button noses. Baby skin sits relatively loose on the body, rather than being taut, the better to stretch for growth spurts to come, said Paul H. Morris, an evolutionary scientist at the University of Portsmouth in England; that lax packaging accentuates the overall roundness of form.

35 Baby movements are notably clumsy, an amusing combination of jerky and delayed, because learning to coordinate the body's many bilateral sets of large and fine muscle groups requires years of practice. On starting to walk, toddlers struggle continuously to balance themselves between left foot and right, and so the toddler gait consists as much of lateral movement as of any forward momentum.

36 Researchers who study animals beloved by the public appreciate the human impulse to nurture anything even remotely babylike, though they are at times taken aback by people's efforts to identify with their preferred species. . . .

37 The giant panda offers . . . [a] case study in accidental cuteness. Although it is a member of the bear family, a highly carnivorous clan, the giant panda specializes in eating bamboo.

As it happens, many of the adaptations that allow it to get by on such a tough diet contribute to the panda's cute form, even in adulthood. Inside the bear's large, rounded head, said Lisa Stevens, assistant panda curator at the National Zoo, are the highly developed jaw muscles and the set of broad, grinding molars it needs to crush its way through some 40 pounds of fibrous bamboo plant a day. 38

When it sits up against a tree and starts picking apart a bamboo stalk with its distinguishing pseudo-thumb, a panda looks like nothing so much like Huckleberry Finn shucking corn. Yet the humanesque posture and paws again are adaptations to its menu. The bear must have its "hands" free and able to shred the bamboo leaves from their stalks. 39

The panda's distinctive markings further add to its appeal: the black patches around the eyes make them seem winsomely low on its face, while the black ears pop out cutely against the white fur of its temples. 40

As with the penguin's tuxedo, the panda's two-toned coat very likely serves a twofold purpose. On the one hand, it helps a feeding bear blend peacefully into the dappled backdrop of bamboo. On the other, the sharp contrast between light and dark may serve as a social signal, helping the solitary bears locate each other when the time has come to find the perfect, too-cute mate. 41

Questions for Close Reading

1. What is the selection's thesis? Locate the sentence(s) in which Angier states her main idea. If she doesn't state her thesis explicitly, express it in your own words.
2. Angier uses the scientific term *visual signaling* (paragraphs 2, 11). What is visual signaling? Give some examples from the article of the visual signaling of "cute."
3. In paragraph 13, Angier quotes researchers as saying that the "human cuteness detector is set at . . . a low bar." What does Angier assert is the underlying reason that people respond so strongly to cuteness?
4. In paragraph 26, Angier indicates that cute varies from culture to culture. How does the significance of cute in Japan differ from its significance in the United States? Give some examples of the differences between the two cultures.
5. Refer to your dictionary as needed to define the following words used in the selection: *gamboling* (paragraph 1), *rapture* (1), *sonorous* (7), *despoiled* (15), *cosegregate* (15), *homeliness* (15), *aesthetics* (20), *blatantly* (22), *unadorned* (24), *primal* (26), *redoubts* (27), *hierarchical* (28), *inherent* (31), *salient* (31), and *winsomely* (40).

Questions About the Writer's Craft

1. The opening of a newspaper article is called a *lead*, and its purpose is to hook the reader and set up a framework for the story. Analyze the lead of Angier's article (paragraphs 1–3). How does she try to engage your interest (the hook)?

How does this lead frame the contents of the remainder of the article? How are the lead and the thesis statement related in this article?

2. **The pattern.** What is the tone of Angier's article? Why did she adopt this tone? Do you think her tone is appropriate given her objective of defining the term *cuteness*? Explain your answer.

3. **Other patterns.** In paragraph 15, Angier contrasts cuteness with beauty. What are some transitional words and phrases that help sharpen this contrast?

4. **Other patterns.** Paragraphs 32 through 35 contain a lengthy description of a baby's appearance. What is the purpose of this description? Is the description mostly objective or subjective? Support your answer with examples.

Writing Assignments Using Definition as a Pattern of Development

1. In paragraph 15, Angier briefly characterizes beauty as sculptured, refined, and quick. She also contrasts beauty with cuteness. Do you agree with Angier's characterization of beauty? What are some words you would use to characterize beauty? Using Angier's characterization of beauty as a starting point, write an extended definition of beauty. Your essay can be serious, lighthearted, humorous, or satiric.

2. Angier indicates that the American view of cuteness is closely related to our celebration of youth (paragraph 29). Write an extended definition of youth in American culture. Consider actual youthfulness (children), the effort of mature adults to appear younger than they are, the efforts of young people to appear older than they are, youthful fashions, and other cultural manifestations of youth in America. For a view of changing youth culture you might read "Tweens: Ten Going on Sixteen" by Kay S. Hymowitz (page 245) and Buzz Bissinger's "Innocents Afield" (page 407).

Writing Assignments Combining Patterns of Development

3. Angier gives examples of cuteness in movies (*March of the Penguins*, the 2005 version of *King Kong*, the characters E.T. and Yoda), product design (the VW Beetle), and advertising (an antismoking campaign aimed at teens). Select one of these examples of cuteness—or another of your own choosing—and do some research on it. For example, if you choose a character in a movie or TV show, watch the movie or show; if you choose a product, do research on it and use it if possible; and if you choose an ad campaign, collect examples of the ads. Then write an essay in which you *describe* the item, explain how it is an *example* of cuteness, and recount the *effect* it has on you.

4. Angier's article suggests that all humans respond to cuteness, although there are cultural differences in these responses. Are there other differences as well? For example, do men and women respond differently to cuteness? Teenagers and senior citizens? Parents and nonparents? Reflect on your own experiences with cuteness, and inquire into the experiences of your friends, family members, and others. Then write an essay *comparing* and *contrasting* your responses with those of someone who differs from you in gender, age, or parental status. Explain the possible *causes* and *effects* of your different responses to cuteness. Before writing, consider reading Kay S. Hymowitz's "Tweens: Ten Going on Sixteen" (page 245) for an examination of the generation gap regarding the process of growing up.

Writing Assignment Using a Journal Entry as a Starting Point

5. Review the cute things you listed in your pre-reading journal. Do these things fall into categories, such as toys, cartoons, or animals? Which of them, if any, are cute according to the extended definition in Angier's article? Write an essay in which you *classify* your cute things and explain how they *exemplify* (or do not exemplify) Angier's definition of cute. If your items present different characteristics from those outlined by Angier, offer your own definition of cuteness.

ADDITIONAL WRITING TOPICS: DEFINITION

General Assignments

Using definition, write an essay on one of the following topics. Once you fix on a limited subject, decide if the essay has an informative or a persuasive purpose. The paper might begin with the etymology of the term, a stipulative definition, or a definition by negation. You may want to use a number of writing patterns—such as description, comparison, narration, process analysis—to develop the definition. Remember, too, that the paper doesn't have to be scholarly and serious. There is no reason it can't be a lighthearted discussion of the meaning of a term.

1. Fads
2. Helplessness
3. An epiphany
4. A workaholic
5. A Pollyanna

6. A con artist
7. A cheapskate
8. A Yiddish term such as *mensch, klutz, chutzpah,* or *dreck,* or a commonly used term imported from some other language
9. Empowerment
10. Hypocrisy
11. Inner peace
12. Obsession
13. Generosity
14. Depression
15. Greed
16. Exploitation
17. A double bind
18. A conflict of interest
19. An ethical quandary
20. A win-win situation

Assignments with a Specific Purpose, Audience, and Point of View

On Campus

1. You've been asked to write part of a pamphlet for students who come to the college health clinic. For this pamphlet, define *one* of the following conditions and its symptoms: *depression, stress, burnout, test anxiety, addiction* (to alcohol, drugs, or TV), *workaholism.* Part of the pamphlet should describe ways to cope with the condition described.

2. One of your responsibilities as a peer counselor in the student counseling center involves helping students communicate more effectively. To assist students, write a definition of some term that you think represents an essential component of a strong interpersonal relationship. You might, for example, define *respect, sharing, equality,* or *trust.* Part of the definition should employ definition by negation, a discussion of what the term is *not.*

At Home or in the Community

3. *Newsweek* magazine runs a popular column called "My Turn," consisting of readers' opinions on subjects of general interest. Write a piece for this column defining *today's college students.* Use the piece to dispel some negative

stereotypes (for example, that college students are apathetic, ill-informed, self-centered, and materialistic).

4. In your apartment building, several residents have complained about their neighbors' inconsiderate and rude behavior. You're president of the residents' association, and it's your responsibility to address this problem at your next meeting. Prepare a talk in which you define *courtesy,* the quality you consider most essential to neighborly relations. Use specific examples of what courtesy is and isn't to illustrate your definition.

On the Job

5. You're an attorney arguing a case of sexual harassment—a charge your client has leveled against an employer. To win the case, you must present to the jury a clear definition of exactly what *sexual harassment* is and isn't. Write such a definition for your opening remarks in court.

6. A new position has opened in your company. Write a job description to be sent to employment agencies that will screen candidates. Your description should define the job's purpose, state the duties involved, and outline essential qualifications.

For additional writing, reading, and research resources, go to **www.mycomplab.com** and choose **Nadell/Langan/Comodromos'** ***The Longman Writer,* 7/e.**

Argumentation-Persuasion

18

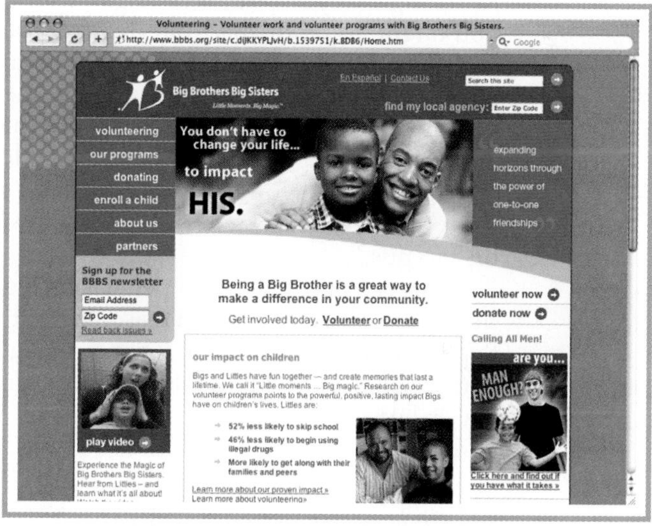

What Is Argumentation-Persuasion?

"You can't possibly believe what you're saying."

"Look, I know what I'm talking about, and that's that."

Does this heated exchange sound familiar? Probably. When we hear the word *argument*, most of us think of a verbal battle propelled by stubbornness and irrational thought, with one person pitted against the other.

Argumentation in writing, though, is a different matter. Using clear thinking and logic, the writer tries to convince readers of the soundness of a particular opinion on a controversial issue. If, while trying to convince, the writer uses emotional language and dramatic appeals to readers' concerns, beliefs, and values, then the piece is called **persuasion**. Besides encouraging acceptance of an opinion, persuasion often urges readers (or another group) to commit themselves to a course of action. Assume you're writing an essay protesting the federal government's policy of offering aid to those suffering from hunger in other countries while many Americans go hungry. If your purpose is to document, coolly and objectively, the presence of hunger in the United States, you would prepare an argumentation essay. Such an essay would be filled with statistics, report findings, and expert opinion to demonstrate how widespread hunger is nationwide. If, however, your purpose is to shake up readers, even motivate them to write letters to their congressional representatives and push for a change in policy, you would write a persuasive essay. In this case, your essay might contain emotional accounts of undernourished children, ill-fed pregnant women, and nearly starving elderly people.

Because people respond rationally *and* emotionally to situations, argumentation and persuasion are usually *combined*. Suppose you decide to write an article for the campus newspaper advocating a pre-Labor Day start for the school year. Your audience includes the college administration, students, and faculty. The article might begin by *arguing* that several schools starting the academic year earlier were able to close for the month of January and thus reduce heating and other maintenance expenses. Such an argument, supported by documented facts and figures, would help convince the administration. Realizing that you also have to gain student and faculty support for your idea, you might argue further that the proposed change would mean that students and faculty could leave for winter break with the semester behind them—papers written, exams taken, grades calculated and recorded. To make this part of your argument especially compelling, you could adopt a *persuasive* strategy by using emotional appeals and positively charged language: "Think how pleasant it would be to sleep late, spend time with family and friends, toast the New Year—without having to worry about work awaiting you back on campus."

When argumentation and persuasion blend in this way, emotion *supports* rather than *replaces* logic and sound reasoning. Although some writers resort to emotional appeals to the exclusion of rational thought, when you prepare argumentation-persuasion essays, you should advance your position through a balanced appeal to reason and emotion.

HOW ARGUMENTATION-PERSUASION FITS YOUR PURPOSE AND AUDIENCE

You probably realize that argumentation, persuasion, or a combination of the two is everywhere: an editorial urging the overhaul of an ill-managed literacy program; a commercial for a new shampoo; a scientific report advocating increased funding for AIDS research. Your own writing involves argumentation-persuasion as well. When you prepare a *causal analysis, descriptive piece, narrative*, or *definition essay*, you advance a specific point of view: MTV has a negative influence on teens' view of sex; Cape Cod in winter is imbued with a special kind of magic; a disillusioning experience can teach people much about themselves; *character* can be defined as the willingness to take unpopular positions on difficult issues. Indeed, an essay organized around any of the patterns of development described in this book may have a persuasive intent. You might, for example, encourage readers to try out a *process* you've explained, or to see one of the two movies you've *compared*.

Argumentation-persuasion, however, involves more than presenting a point of view and providing evidence. Unlike other forms of writing, it assumes controversy and addresses opposing viewpoints. Consider the following assignments, all of which require the writer to take a position on a controversial issue:

> In parts of the country, communities established for older citizens or childless couples have refused to rent to families with children. How do you feel about this situation? What do you think are the rights of the parties involved?
>
> Citing the fact that the highest percentage of automobile accidents involve young men, insurance companies consistently charge their highest rates to young males. Is this practice fair? Why or why not?
>
> Some colleges and universities have instituted a "no pass, no play" policy for athletes. Explain why this policy is or is not appropriate.

It's impossible to predict with absolute certainty what will make readers accept the view you advance or take the action you propose. But the ancient Greeks, who formulated our basic concepts of logic, isolated three factors crucial to the effectiveness of argumentation-persuasion: *logos*, *pathos*, and *ethos*.

Your main concern in an argumentation-persuasion essay should be with the *logos*, or **soundness**, of your argument: the facts, statistics, examples, and authoritative statements you gather to support your viewpoint. This supporting evidence must be unified, specific, sufficient, accurate, and representative (see pages 48–51 and 70–74). Imagine, for instance, you want to convince people that a popular charity misappropriates the money it receives from that public. Your readers, inclined to believe in the good works of the charity, will probably dismiss your argument unless you can substantiate your claim with valid, well-documented evidence that enhances the *logos* of your position.

Sensitivity to the *pathos*, or the **emotional power of language**, is another key consideration for writers of argumentation-persuasion essays. *Pathos* appeals to readers' needs, values, and attitudes, encouraging them to commit themselves to a viewpoint or course of action. The *pathos* of a piece derives partly from the writer's language. *Connotative* language—words with strong emotional overtones—can move readers to accept a point of view and may even spur them to act.

Advertising and propaganda generally rely on *pathos* to the exclusion of logic, using emotion to influence and manipulate. Consider the following pitches for a man's cologne and a woman's perfume. The language—and the attitudes to which it appeals—are different in each case:

> Brawn: Experience the power. Bold. Yet subtle. Clean. Masculine. The scent for the man who's in charge.
>
> Black Lace is for you—the woman who dresses for success but who dares to be provocative, slightly naughty. Black Lace. Perfect with pearls by day and with diamonds by night.

The appeal to men plays on the impact that the words *Brawn, bold, power*, and *in charge* may have for some males. Similarly, the charged words *Black Lace, provocative, naughty*, and *diamonds* are intended to appeal to business women who—in the advertiser's mind, at least—may be looking for ways to reconcile sensuality and professionalism. (For more on slanted language, read William Lutz's "Doublespeak," page 288.)

Like an advertising copywriter, you must select language that reinforces your message. In a paper supporting an expanded immigration policy, you might use evocative phrases like "land of liberty," "a nation of immigrants," and "America's open-door policy." However, if you were arguing for strict immigration quotas, you might use language like "save jobs for unemployed Americans," "flood of unskilled labor," and "illegal aliens." Remember, though: Such language should *support, not supplant,* clear thinking. (See pages 464–465 for additional information on persuasive language.)

Finally, whenever you write an argumentation-persuasion essay, you should establish your *ethos,* or **credibility** and **reliability**. You cannot expect readers to accept or act on your viewpoint unless you convince them that you know what you're talking about and that you're worth listening to. You will come across as knowledgeable and trustworthy if you present a logical, reasoned argument that takes opposing views into account. Make sure, too, that your appeals to emotion aren't excessive. Overwrought emotionalism undercuts credibility. (For more on general ethical considerations in writing, see "Characteristics of Evidence" on pages 47–52. For more on ethical considerations in conducting online research, see "Evaluating Online Materials" on page 555.)

Writing an effective argumentation-persuasion essay involves an interplay of *logos, pathos,* and *ethos*. The exact balance among these factors is determined by your audience and purpose (that is, whether you want the audience simply to agree with your view or whether you also want them to take action). More than any other kind of writing, argumentation-persuasion requires that you *analyze your readers* and tailor your approach to them. You need to determine how much they know about the issue, how they feel about you and your position, what their values and attitudes are, what motivates them.

In general, most readers will fall into one of three broad categories: supportive, wavering, or hostile. Each type of audience requires a different blend of *logos, pathos,* and *ethos* in an argumentation-persuasion essay.

1. **A supportive audience.** If your audience agrees with your position and trusts your credibility, you don't need a highly reasoned argument dense with facts, examples, and statistics. Although you may want to solidify support by providing additional information (*logos*), you can rely primarily on *pathos*—a strong emotional appeal—to reinforce readers' commitment to your shared viewpoint. Assume that you belong to a local fishing club and have volunteered to write an article encouraging members to support threatened fishing rights in state parks. You might begin by stating that fishing strengthens the fish population by thinning out overcrowded streams. Since your audience would certainly be familiar with this idea, you wouldn't need to devote much discussion to it. Instead, you would attempt to move them emotionally. You might evoke the camaraderie in the sport, the pleasure of a perfect cast, the beauty of the outdoors, and perhaps conclude with "If you want these enjoyments to continue, please make a generous contribution to our fund."

2. **A wavering audience.** At times, readers may be interested in what you have to say but may not be committed fully to your viewpoint. Or perhaps they're not as informed about the subject as they should be. In either case, because your readers need to be encouraged to give their complete support, you don't want to risk alienating them with a heavy-handed emotional appeal. Concentrate instead on *ethos* and *logos*, bolstering your image as a reliable source and providing the evidence needed to advance your position. If you want to convince an audience of high school seniors to take a year off to work between high school and college, you might establish your credibility by recounting the year you spent working and by showing the positive effects it had on your life (*ethos*). In addition, you could cite studies indicating that delayed entry into college is related to higher grade point averages. A year's savings, you would explain, allow students to study when they might otherwise need to hold down a job to earn money for tuition (*logos*).

3. **A hostile audience.** An apathetic, skeptical, or hostile audience is obviously most difficult to convince. With such an audience you should avoid emotional appeals because they might seem irrational, sentimental, or even comical. Instead, weigh the essay heavily in favor of logical reasoning and hard-to-dispute facts (*logos*). Assume your college administration is working to ban liquor from the student pub. You plan to submit to the campus newspaper an open letter supporting this generally unpopular effort. To sway other students, you cite the positive experiences of schools that have gone dry. Many colleges, you explain, have found their tavern revenues actually increase because all students—not just those of drinking age—can now support the pub. With the greater revenues, some schools have upgraded the food served in the pubs and have hired disc jockeys or musical groups to provide entertainment. Many schools have also seen a sharp reduction in alcohol-related vandalism. Readers may not be won over to your side, but your sound, logical argument may encourage them to be more tolerant of your viewpoint. Indeed, such increased receptivity may be all you can reasonably expect from a hostile audience. (*Note:* The checklists on pages 20 and 460 provide additional guidelines for analyzing your audience.)

At this point, you have a good sense of the way writers use argumentation-persuasion to achieve their purpose and to connect with their readers. Take a moment to look closely at the website screen shot at the beginning of this chapter. The sponsoring organization is Big Brothers Big Sisters, a mentoring organization for young people. Imagine you're writing an article, linked to this website, about the difficulties faced by young people who lack strong role models in their lives. Jot down some ideas you might cover when *arguing* the importance of volunteering one's time to make a difference in the lives of these young people.

PREWRITING STRATEGIES

The following checklist shows how you can apply to argumentation-persuasion some of the prewriting techniques discussed in Chapter 2.

ARGUMENTATION-PERSUASION: A PREWRITING CHECKLIST

Choose a Controversial Issue

- ☐ What issue (academic, social, political, moral, economic) do you feel strongly about? With what issues are your journal entries concerned? What issues discussed in recent newspaper, television, or magazine reports have piqued your interest?
- ☐ What is your view on the issue?

Determine Your Purpose, Audience, Tone, and Point of View

- ☐ Is your purpose limited to convincing readers to adopt your viewpoint, or do you also hope to spur them to action?
- ☐ Who is your audience? How much do your readers already know about the issue? Are they best characterized as supportive, wavering, or hostile? What values and needs may motivate readers to be responsive to your position?
- ☐ What tone is most likely to increase readers' commitment to your point of view? Should you convey strong emotion or cool objectivity?
- ☐ What point of view is most likely to enhance your credibility?

Use Prewriting to Generate Supporting Evidence

- ☐ How might brainstorming, journal entries, freewriting, or mapping help you identify personal experiences, observations, and examples to support your viewpoint?
- ☐ How might the various patterns of development help you generate supporting material? What about the issue can you describe? Narrate? Illustrate? Compare and contrast? Analyze in terms of process or cause-effect? Define or categorize in some especially revealing way?
- ☐ How might interviews or library research help you uncover relevant examples, facts, statistics, expert opinion?

STRATEGIES FOR USING ARGUMENTATION-PERSUASION IN AN ESSAY

After prewriting, you're ready to draft your essay. Figure 18.1 (on page 461) and the suggestions that follow will help you prepare a convincing and logical argument.

FIGURE 18.1
Development Diagram: Writing an Argumentation-Persuasion Essay

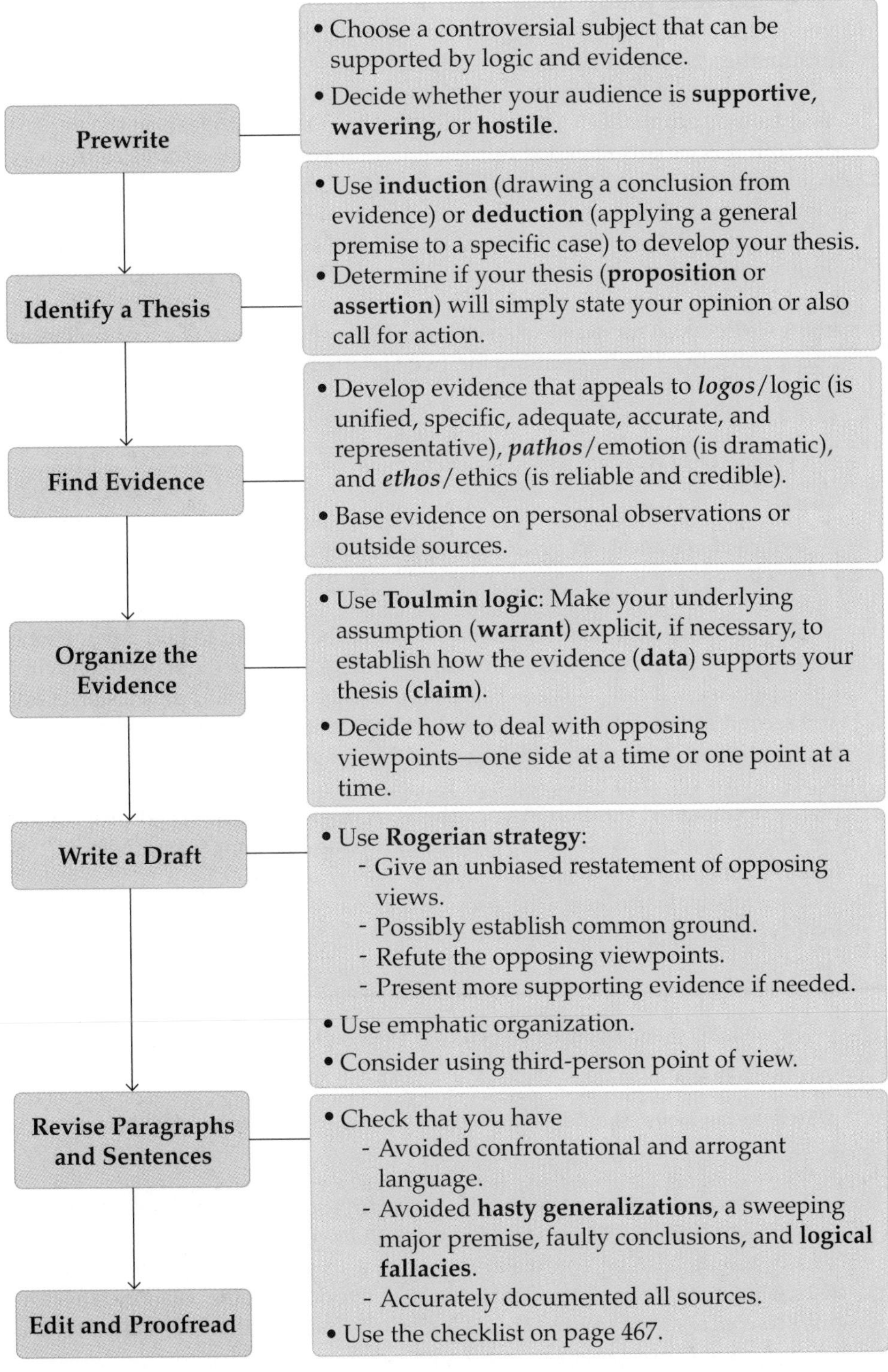

1. **At the beginning of the paper, identify the controversy surrounding the issue and state your position.** Your introduction should clarify the controversy about the issue. In addition, it should provide as much background information as your readers are likely to need.

   The thesis of an argumentation-persuasion paper is often called the **assertion** or **proposition**. Occasionally, the proposition appears at the paper's end, but it is usually stated at the beginning. If you state the thesis right away, your audience knows where you stand and is better able to evaluate the evidence presented.

   Remember: Argumentation-persuasion assumes conflicting viewpoints. Be sure your proposition focuses on a controversial issue and indicates your view. Avoid a proposition that is merely factual; what is demonstrably true allows little room for debate. To see the difference between a factual statement and an effective thesis, examine the two statements that follow.

   Fact

   > In the past few years, the nation's small farmers have suffered financial hardships.

   Thesis

   > Inefficient management, rather than competition from agricultural conglomerates, is responsible for the financial plight of the nation's small farmers.

   The first statement is certainly true. It would be difficult to find anyone who believes that these are easy times for small farmers. Because the statement invites little opposition, it can't serve as the focus of an argumentation-persuasion essay. The second statement, though, takes a controversial stance on a complex issue. Such a proposition is a valid starting point for a paper intended to argue and persuade. However, don't assume that this advice means that you should take a highly opinionated position in your thesis. A dogmatic, overstated proposition ("Campus security is staffed by overpaid, badge-flashing incompetents") is bound to alienate some readers.

   Remember also to keep the proposition narrow and specific, so you can focus your thoughts in a purposeful way. Consider the following statements:

   Broad Thesis

   > The welfare system has been abused over the years.

   Narrowed Thesis

   > Welfare payments should be denied to unmarried mothers under the age of eighteen.

   If you tried to write a paper based on the first statement, you would face an unmanageable task—showing all the ways that welfare has been abused. Your readers would also be confused about what to expect in the paper: Will it discuss unscrupulous bureaucrats, fraudulent bookkeeping, dishonest recipients? In contrast, the revised thesis is limited and specific. It signals that the paper will propose severe restrictions. Such a proposal will surely have opponents and is thus appropriate for argumentation-persuasion.

The thesis in an argumentation-persuasion essay can simply state your opinion about an issue, or it can go a step further and call for some action:

Opinion

The lack of affordable day-care centers discriminates against low-income families.

Call for Action

The federal government should support the creation of more day-care centers in low-income neighborhoods.

In either case, your stand on the issue must be clear to your readers.

2. **Offer readers strong support for your thesis.** Finding evidence that relates to your readers' needs, values, and experience (see pages 20 and 460) is a crucial part of writing an argumentation-persuasion essay. Readers will be responsive to evidence that is *unified, adequate, specific, accurate, dramatic,* and *representative* (see pages 48–51 and 70–74). The evidence might consist of personal experiences or observations. Or it could be gathered from outside sources—statistics; facts; examples; or expert opinion taken from books, articles, reports, interviews, and documentaries. A paper arguing that elderly Americans are better off than they used to be might incorporate the following kinds of evidence:

   - *Personal observation or experience:* A description of the writer's grandparents who are living comfortably on Social Security and pensions.
   - *Statistics from a report:* A statement that the per-capita after-tax income of older Americans is $335 greater than the national average.
   - *Fact from a newspaper article:* The point that the majority of elderly Americans do not live in nursing homes or on the streets; rather, they have their own houses or apartments.
   - *Examples from interviews:* Accounts of several elderly couples living comfortably in well-managed retirement villages in Florida.
   - *Expert opinion cited in a documentary:* A statement by Dr. Marie Sanchez, a specialist in geriatrics: "An over-sixty-five American today is likely to be healthier, and have a longer life expectancy, than a fifty-year-old living only a decade ago."

   You may wonder whether to use the *first-person (I)* or *third-person (he, she, they)* point of view when presenting evidence based on personal observation, experience, or interviews. The subjective immediacy typical of the first person often delivers a jolt of persuasive power; however, many writers arguing a point prefer to present personal evidence in an objective way, using the third person to keep the focus on the issue rather than on themselves. When you write an argumentation-persuasion essay, your purpose, audience, and tone will help you decide which point of view will be most effective. If you're not sure which point of view to use, check with your instructor. Some encourage a first-person approach; others expect a more objective stance.

As you seek outside evidence, you may—perhaps to your dismay—come across information that undercuts your argument. Resist the temptation to ignore such material; instead, use the evidence to arrive at a more balanced, perhaps somewhat qualified viewpoint. Conversely, don't blindly accept or disregard flaws in the arguments made by sources agreeing with you. Retain a healthy skepticism, analyzing the material as rigorously as if it were advanced by the opposing side.

Also, keep in mind that outside sources aren't infallible. They may have biases that cause them to skew evidence. So be sure to evaluate your sources. If you're writing an essay supporting a woman's right to abortion, the National Abortion Rights Action League (NARAL) can supply abundant statistics, case studies, and reports. But realize that NARAL won't give you the complete picture; it will probably present evidence that supports its "pro-choice" position only. To counteract such bias, you should review what those with differing opinions have to say. You should, for example, examine material published by such "pro-life" organizations as the National Right-to-Life Committee—keeping in mind, of course, that this material is also bound to present support for its viewpoint only. Remember, too, that there are more than two sides to a complex issue. To get as broad a perspective as possible, you should track down sources that have no axe to grind—that is, sources that make a deliberate effort to examine all sides of the issue. For example, published proceedings from a debate on abortion or an in-depth article that aims to synthesize various views on abortion would broaden your understanding of this controversial subject.

Whatever sources you use, be sure to *document* (give credit to) that material. Otherwise, readers may dismiss your evidence as nothing more than your subjective opinion, or they may conclude that you have *plagiarized*—tried to pass off someone else's ideas as your own. (Documentation isn't necessary when material is commonly known or is a matter of historical or scientific record.) In brief informal papers, documentation may consist of simple citations like, "Psychologist Aaron Beck believes depression is the result of distorted thoughts," or "*Newsweek* (December 10, 2001) observes that teens have embraced new technologies in their everyday lives." (For information about documenting sources in longer, more formal papers, see Chapters 19 and 20.)

3. **Seek to create goodwill.** Since your goal is to convince others of your position's soundness, you need to be careful about alienating readers—especially those who don't agree with you. Be careful, then, about using close-minded, morally superior language ("*Anyone* can see that . . . "). Exaggerated, overly emotional language can also antagonize readers. Consider an essay in which you argue that the speed limit shouldn't be raised from 55 m.p.h. to 65 m.p.h. Some readers may tune you out if you write, "Truckers, the beer-bellied bullies of the highways, have no respect for other drivers or for the speed limit. They roar along the highway, tailgating and driving at least 20 m.p.h. over the

speed limit. Now, with the new 65 m.p.h. speed limit, they're racing up on our bumpers at 80 m.p.h.—with disastrous consequences." Readers will probably be more receptive if you use less charged language: "The majority of truck drivers have more driving experience than anyone else on the road, and they handle their rigs responsibly. But when delivery deadlines encourage truckers to drive above the speed limit, an accident at 65 m.p.h. rather than at 55 m.p.h. will almost certainly be fatal." Last, guard against using confrontational language: "*My opponents* find the existing laws more effective than the proposed legislation" sounds adversarial, whereas" *Opponents* of the proposed legislation . . . ," "*Those opposed* to the proposed legislation . . . ," and "*Supporters* of the existing laws . . . ," seem more evenhanded and respectful. The last three statements also focus—as they should—on the issue, not on the people involved in the debate.

Goodwill can also be established by finding a *common ground*—some points on which all sides can agree, despite their differences. Assume a township council has voted to raise property taxes. The additional revenues will be used to preserve, as parkland, a wooded area that would otherwise be sold to developers. Before introducing its tax-hike proposal, the council would do well to remind homeowners of everyone's shared goals: maintaining the town's beauty and preventing the community's overdevelopment. This reminder of the common values shared by the town council and homeowners will probably make residents more receptive to the tax hike.

4. **Organize the supporting evidence.** The support for an argumentation-persuasion paper can be organized in a variety of ways. Any of the patterns of development described in this book (description, narration, definition, cause-effect, and so on) may be used—singly or in combination—to develop the essay's proposition. Imagine you're writing a paper arguing that car racing should be banned from television. Your essay might contain a *description* of a horrifying accident that was televised in graphic detail; you might devote part of the paper to a *causal analysis* showing that the broadcast of such races encourages teens to drive carelessly; you could include a *process analysis* to explain how young drivers "soup up" their cars in a dangerous attempt to imitate the racers seen on television. If your essay includes several patterns, you may need a separate paragraph for each.

When presenting evidence, arrange it so you create the strongest possible effect. In general, you should end with your most compelling point, leaving readers with dramatic evidence that underscores your proposition's validity.

5. **Use Rogerian strategy to acknowledge differing viewpoints.** If your essay has a clear thesis and strong, logical support, you've taken important steps toward winning readers over. However, because argumentation-persuasion focuses on controversial issues, you should also take opposing views into account. As you think about and perhaps research your subject, seek out conflicting viewpoints. As journalist Walter Lippman argued more than sixty years ago in an essay aptly titled "The Indispensable Opposition," it is through the "confrontation of opinion in debate" that we test our views.

A good argument seeks out contrary viewpoints, acknowledges them, perhaps even admits they have some merit. Such a strategy strengthens your argument in several ways. It helps you anticipate objections, alerts you to flaws in your own position, and makes you more aware of the other sides' weaknesses. Further, by acknowledging the dissenting views, you come across as reasonable and thorough—qualities that may disarm readers and leave them more receptive to your argument. You may not convince them to surrender their views, but you can enlarge their perspectives and encourage them to think about your position.

Psychologist Carl Rogers took the idea of acknowledging contrary viewpoints a step further. He believed that argumentation's goal should be to *reduce conflict*, rather than to produce a "winner" and a "loser." But he recognized that people identify so strongly with their opinions that they experience any challenge to those opinions as highly threatening. Such a challenge feels like an attack on their very identity. And what's the characteristic response to such a perceived attack? People become defensive; they dig in their heels and become more adamant than ever about their position. Indeed, when confronted with solid information that calls their opinion into question, they devalue that evidence rather than allow themselves to be persuaded. The old maxim about the power of first impressions demonstrates this point. Experiments show that after people form a first impression of another person, they are unlikely to let future conflicting information affect that impression. If, for example, they initially perceive someone to be unpleasant and disagreeable, they tend to reject subsequent evidence that casts the person in a more favorable light.

Taking into account this tendency to cling tenaciously to opinions in the face of a challenge, Rogerian strategy rejects the adversarial approach that often characterizes argumentation. It adopts, instead, a respectful, conciliatory posture—one that demonstrates a real understanding of opposing views, one that emphasizes shared interests and values. Such an approach makes it easier to negotiate differences and arrive at—ideally—a synthesis: a new position that both parties find at least as acceptable as their original positions.

How can you apply Rogerian strategy in your writing? Simply follow the steps in the following checklist.

☑ USING ROGERIAN STRATEGY: A CHECKLIST

- ☐ Begin by making a conscientious effort to *understand* the viewpoints of those with whom you disagree. As you listen to or read about their opinions, try to put yourself in their shoes; focus on *what they believe* and *why they believe it*, rather than on how you will challenge their beliefs.
- ☐ Open your essay with an unbiased, even-handed *restatement of opposing points of view*. Such an objective summary shows that you're

fair and open-minded—and not so blinded by the righteousness of your own position that you can't consider any other. Typically, people respond to such a respectful approach by lowering their defenses. Because they appreciate your ability to understand what they have to say, they become more open to your point of view.

- ☐ When appropriate, *acknowledge the validity* of some of the arguments raised by those with differing views. What should you do if they make a well-founded point? You'll enhance your credibility if you concede that point while continuing to maintain that, overall, your position is stronger.
- ☐ Point out areas of *common ground* (see page 000) by focusing on interests, values, and beliefs that you and those with opposing views share. When you say to them, "Look at the beliefs we share. Look at our common concerns," you communicate that you're not as unlike them as they first believed.
- ☐ Finally, *present evidence* for your position. Since those not agreeing with you have been "softened up" by your noncombative stance and disarmed by the realization that you and they share some values and beliefs, they're more ready to consider your point of view.

Let's consider, more specifically, how you might draw upon essentially Rogerian strategy when writing an argumentation-persuasion essay. In the following paragraphs, we discuss three basic strategies. As you read about each strategy, keep in mind this key point: The earlier you acknowledge alternate viewpoints, the more effective you will be. Establishing—right at the outset—your awareness of opposing positions shows you to be fair-minded and helps reduce resistance to what you have to say.

First, you may acknowledge the opposing viewpoint in a two-part proposition consisting of a subordinate clause followed by a main clause. The *first part of the proposition* (the subordinate clause) *acknowledges opposing opinions*; the *second part* (the main clause) *states your opinion* and implies that your view stands on more solid ground. (When using this kind of proposition, you may, but don't have to, discuss opposing opinions.) The following thesis illustrates this strategy (the opposing viewpoint is underlined once; the writer's position is underlined twice):

> Although some instructors think that standardized finals restrict academic freedom, such exams are preferable to those prepared by individual professors.

Second, *in the introduction*, you may provide—separate from the proposition—a *one-* or *two-sentence summary of the opposing viewpoint*. Suppose you're writing an essay advocating a ten-day waiting period before an individual can purchase a handgun. Before presenting your proposition at the end of the introductory paragraph, you might include sentences like these: "Opponents of the waiting period argue that the ten-day delay is worthless without a nationwide computer network that can perform background checks. Those opposed also point out that only a percentage of states with a waiting period have seen a reduction in gun-related crime."

Third, you can take *one or two body paragraphs* near the beginning of the essay to *present in greater detail arguments raised by opposing viewpoints*. After that, you *grant* (when appropriate) the validity of some of those points ("It may be true that . . . ," "Granted, . . . "). Then you go on to *present evidence* for your position ("Even so . . . ," "Nevertheless . . . "). Imagine you're preparing an editorial for your student newspaper arguing that fraternities and sororities on your campus should be banned. Realizing that many students don't agree with you, you "research" the opposing viewpoint by seeking out supporters of Greek organizations and listening respectfully to the points they raise. When it comes time to write the editorial, you decide not to begin with arguments for your position; instead, you start by summarizing the points made by those supporting fraternities and sororities. You might, for example, mention their argument that Greek organizations build college spirit, contribute to worthy community causes, and provide valuable contacts for entry into the business world. Following this summary of the opposing viewpoint, you might concede that the point about the Greeks' contributions to community causes is especially valid; you could then reinforce this conciliatory stance by stressing some common ground you share—perhaps you acknowledge that you share your detractors' belief that enjoyable social activities with like-minded people are an important part of campus life. Having done all that, you would be in a good position to present arguments why you nevertheless think fraternities and sororities should be banned. Because you prepared readers to listen to your opinion, they would tend to be more open to your argument.

6. **Refute differing viewpoint.** There will be times, though, that acknowledging opposing viewpoints and presenting your own case won't be enough. Particularly when an issue is complex and when readers strongly disagree with your position, you may have to *refute* all or part of the *dissenting view*. Refutation means pointing out the problems with opposing viewpoints, thereby highlighting your own position's superiority. You may focus on the opposing sides' inaccurate or inadequate evidence; or you may point to their faulty logic. (Some common types of illogical thinking are discussed on pages 470–473 and 475–477.)

   Let's consider how you could refute a competing position in an essay you're writing that supports sex education in public schools. Adapting the Rogerian approach to suit your purposes, you might start by acknowledging the opposing viewpoint's key argument: "Sex education should be the prerogative of parents." After granting the validity of this view in an ideal world, you might show that many parents don't provide such education. You could present statistics on the number of parents who avoid discussing sex with their children because the subject makes them uncomfortable; you could cite studies revealing that children in single-parent homes are apt to receive even less parental guidance about sex; and you could give examples of young people whose parents provided sketchy, even misleading information.

There are various ways to develop a paper's refutation section. The best method to use depends on the paper's length and the complexity of the issue. Two possible sequences are outlined here:

First Strategy

- State your proposition.
- Cite opposing viewpoints and the evidence for those views.
- Refute opposing viewpoints by presenting counterarguments.

Second Strategy

- State your proposition.
- Cite opposing viewpoints and the evidence for those views.
- Refute opposing viewpoints by presenting counterarguments.
- Present additional evidence for your proposition.

In the first strategy, you simply refute all or part of the opposing positions' arguments. The second strategy takes the first one a step further by presenting *additional evidence* to support your proposition. In such a case, the additional evidence *must be different* from the points made in the refutation. The additional evidence may appear at the essay's end (as in the preceding outline), or it may be given near the beginning (after the proposition); it may also be divided between the beginning and end.

No matter which strategy you select, you may refute opposing views *one side at a time* or *one point at a time*. When using the one-side-at-a-time approach, you cite all the points raised by the opposing side and then present your counterargument to each point. When using the one-point-at-a-time strategy, you mention the first point made by the opposing side, refute that point, then move on to the second point and refute that, and so on. (For more on comparing and contrasting the sides of an issue, see pages 349–354.) No matter which strategy you use, be sure to provide clear signals so that readers can distinguish your arguments from the other side's: "Despite the claims of those opposed to the plan, many think that . . ." and "Those not in agreement think that. . . . "

7. **Use induction or deduction to think logically about your argument.** The line of reasoning used to develop an argument is the surest indicator of how rigorously you have thought through your position. There are two basic ways to think about a subject: inductively and deductively. Though the following discussion treats induction and deduction as separate processes, the two often overlap and complement each other.

Inductive reasoning involves examination of specific cases, facts, or examples. Based on these specifics, you then draw a conclusion or make a generalization. This is the kind of thinking scientists use when they examine evidence (the results of experiments, for example) and then draw a *conclusion*: "Smoking increases the risk of cancer." All of us use inductive reasoning in everyday life. We might think the following: "My head is aching" (evidence); "My nose is stuffy" (evidence); "I'm coming down with a cold" (conclusion). Based on the conclusion, we might go a step further and take some action: "I'll take an aspirin."

With inductive reasoning, the conclusion reached can serve as the proposition for an argumentation-persuasion essay. If the paper advances a course of action, the proposition often mentions the action, signaling an essay with a distinctly persuasive purpose.

Let's suppose that you're writing a paper about a crime wave in the small town where you live. You might use inductive thinking to structure the essay's argument:

> Several people were mugged last month while shopping in the center of town. (*evidence*)
>
> Several homes and apartments were burglarized in the past few weeks. (*evidence*)
>
> Several cars were stolen from people's driveways over the weekend. (*evidence*)
>
> The police force hasn't adequately protected town residents. (*conclusion, or proposition, for an argumentation essay with probable elements of persuasion*)
>
> The police force should take steps to upgrade its protection of town residents. (*conclusion, or proposition, for an argumentation essay with a clearly persuasive intent*)

This inductive sequence highlights a possible structure for the essay. After providing a clear statement of your proposition, you might detail recent muggings, burglaries, and car thefts. Then you could move to the opposing viewpoint: a description of the steps the police say they have taken to protect town residents. At that point, you would refute the police's claim, citing additional evidence that shows the measures taken have not been sufficient. Finally, if you wanted your essay to have a decidedly persuasive purpose, you could end by recommending specific action the police should take to improve its protection of the community.

As in all essays, your evidence should be *unified, specific, accurate, dramatic, sufficient,* and *representative* (see pages 48–51 and 70–74). These last two characteristics are critical when you think inductively; they guarantee that your conclusion would be equally valid even if other evidence were presented. Insufficient or atypical evidence often leads to **hasty generalizations** that mar the essay's logic. For example, you might think the following: "Some elderly people are very wealthy and do not need Social Security checks" (evidence), and "Some Social Security recipients illegally collect several checks" (evidence). If you then conclude, "Social Security is a waste of taxpayers' money," your conclusion is invalid and hasty because it's based on only a few atypical examples. Millions of Social Security recipients aren't wealthy and don't abuse the system. If you've failed to consider the full range of evidence, any action you propose ("The Social Security system should be disbanded") will probably be considered suspect by thoughtful readers. It's possible, of course, that Social Security should be disbanded, but the evidence leading to such a conclusion must be sufficient and representative.

When reasoning inductively, you should also be careful that the evidence you collect is *recent* and *accurate*. No valid conclusion can result from dated or erroneous evidence. To ensure that your evidence is sound, you also need to evaluate the reliability of your sources. When a person who is legally drunk claims to have seen a flying saucer, the evidence is shaky, to say the least. But if two respected scientists, both with 20–20 vision, saw the saucer, their evidence is worth considering.

Finally, it's important to realize that there's always an element of uncertainty in inductive reasoning. The conclusion can never be more than an *inference*, involving what logicians call an **inductive leap**. There could be other explanations for the evidence cited and thus other positions to take and actions to advocate. For example, given a small town's crime wave, you might conclude not that the police force has been remiss but that residents are careless about protecting themselves and their property. In turn, you might call for a different kind of action—perhaps that the police conduct public workshops in self-defense and home security. In an inductive argument, your task is to weigh the evidence, consider alternative explanations, then choose the conclusion and course of action that seem most valid.

Unlike inductive reasoning, which starts with a specific case and moves toward a generalization or conclusion, **deductive reasoning** begins with a generalization that is then applied to a specific case. This movement from general to specific involves a three-step form of reasoning called a **syllogism**. The first part of a syllogism is called the **major premise**, a general statement about an entire group. The second part is the **minor premise**, a statement about an individual within that group. The syllogism ends with a **conclusion** about that individual.

Just as you use inductive thinking in everyday life, you use deductive thinking—often without being aware of it—to sort out your experiences. When trying to decide which car to buy, you might think as follows:

Major Premise	In an accident, large cars are safer than small cars.
Minor Premise	The Turbo Titan is a large car.
Conclusion	In an accident, the Turbo Titan will be safer than a small car.

Based on your conclusion, you might decide to take a specific action, buying the Turbo Titan rather than the smaller car you had first considered.

To create a valid syllogism and thus arrive at a sound conclusion, you need to avoid two major pitfalls of deductive reasoning. First, be sure not to start with a *sweeping* or *hasty generalization* (see pages 232–233 in Chapter 12) as your *major premise*. Second, don't accept as truth a *faulty conclusion*. Let's look at each problem.

Sweeping major premise. Perhaps you're concerned about a trash-to-steam incinerator scheduled to open near your home. Your thinking about the situation might follow these lines:

Major Premise	Trash-to-steam incinerators have had serious problems and posed significant threats to the well-being of people living near the plants.
Minor Premise	The proposed incinerator in my neighborhood will be a trash-to-steam plant.
Conclusion	The proposed trash-to-steam incinerator in my neighborhood will have serious problems and pose significant threats to the well-being of people living near the plant.

Having arrived at this conclusion, you might decide to join organized protests against the opening of the incinerator. But your thinking is somewhat illogical. Your *major premise* is a *sweeping* one because it indiscriminately groups all trash-to-steam plants into a single category. It's unlikely that you're familiar with all the trash-to-steam incinerators in this country and abroad; it's probably not true that *all* such plants have had serious difficulties that endangered the public. For your argument to reach a valid conclusion, the major premise must be based on repeated observations or verifiable facts. You would have a better argument, and thus reach a more valid conclusion, if you restricted or qualified the major premise, applying it to some, not all, of the group:

Major Premise	A *number* of trash-to-steam incinerators have had serious problems and posed significant threats to the well-being of people living near the plants.
Minor Premise	The proposed incinerator in my neighborhood will be a trash-to-steam plant.
Conclusion	*It's possible* that the proposed trash-to-steam incinerator in my neighborhood will run into serious problems and pose significant threats to the well-being of people living near the plant.

This new conclusion, the result of more careful reasoning, would probably encourage you to learn more about trash-to-steam incinerators in general and about the proposed plant in particular. If further research still left you feeling uncomfortable about the plant, you would probably decide to join the protest. On the other hand, your research might convince you that the plant has incorporated into its design a number of safeguards that have been successful at other plants. This added information could reassure you that your original fears were unfounded. In either case, the revised deductive process would lead to a more informed conclusion and course of action.

Faulty conclusion. Your syllogism—and thus your reasoning—would also be invalid if your *conclusion reverses the "if . . . then" relationship implied in the major premise*. Assume you plan to write a letter to the college newspaper urging the resignation of the student government president. Perhaps you pursue a line of reasoning that goes like this:

Major Premise	Students who plagiarize papers must appear before the Faculty Committee on Academic Policies and Procedures.
Minor Premise	Yesterday Jennifer Kramer, president of the student government, appeared before the Faculty Committee on Academic Policies and Procedures.
Conclusion	Jennifer must have plagiarized a paper.
Action	Jennifer should resign her position as student government president.

Such a chain of reasoning is illogical and unfair. Here's why. *If* students plagiarize their term papers and are caught, *then* they must appear before the committee. However, the converse isn't necessarily true—that *if* students appear before the committee, *then* they must have plagiarized. In other words, not *all* students appearing before the Faculty Committee have been called up on plagiarism charges. For instance, Jennifer could have been speaking on behalf of another student; she could have been protesting some action taken by the committee; she could have been seeking the committee's help on an article she plans to write about academic honesty. The conclusion doesn't allow for these other possible explanations.

Now that you're aware of the problems associated with deductive reasoning, let's look at the way you can use a syllogism to structure an argumentation-persuasion essay. Suppose you decide to write a paper advocating support for a projected space mission. You know that controversy surrounds the space program, especially since seven astronauts died in a 1986 launch. Confident that the tragedy has led to more rigorous controls, you want to argue that the benefits of an upcoming mission outweigh its risks. A deductive pattern could be used to develop your argument. In fact, outlining your thinking as a syllogism might help you formulate a proposition, organize your evidence, deal with the opposing viewpoint, and—if appropriate—propose a course of action:

Major Premise	Space programs in the past have led to important developments in technology, especially in medical science.
Minor Premise	The *Cosmos* Mission is the newest space program.
Proposition *(essay might be persuasive)*	The *Cosmos* Mission will most likely lead to important developments in technology, especially in medical science.
Proposition *(essay is clearly persuasive)*	Congress should continue its funding of the *Cosmos* Mission.

Having outlined the deductive pattern of your thinking, you might begin by stating your proposition and then discuss some new procedures developed to protect the astronauts and the rocket system's structural integrity. With that background established, you could detail the opposing claim that little of value has been produced by the space program so far. You could then move to your refutation, citing significant medical advances derived from former space missions. Finally, the paper might conclude on a persuasive note, with a plea to Congress to continue funding the latest space mission.

8. **Use Toulmin logic to establish a strong connection between your evidence and thesis.** Whether you use an essentially inductive or deductive approach, your argument depends on strong evidence. In *The Uses of Argument*, Stephen Toulmin describes a useful approach for strengthening the connection between evidence and thesis. Toulmin divides a typical argument into three parts:

   - **Claim**—the thesis, proposition, or conclusion
   - **Data**—the evidence (facts, statistics, examples, observations, expert opinion) used to convince readers of the claim's validity
   - **Warrant**—the underlying assumption that justifies moving from evidence to claim.

Here's a sample argument using Toulmin's terminology:

The train engineer was under the influence of drugs when the train crashed.

(Data)

Transportation employees entrusted with the public's safety should be tested for drug use.

(Claim)

Transportation employees entrusted with the public's safety should not be allowed on the job if they use drugs.

(Warrant)

As Toulmin explains in his book, readers are more apt to consider your argument valid if they know what your warrant is. Sometimes your warrant will be so obvious that you won't need to state it explicitly; an *implicit warrant* will be sufficient. Assume you want to argue that the use of live animals to test product toxicity should be outlawed. To support your claim, you cite the following evidence: first, current animal tests are painful and usually result in the animal's death; second, human cell cultures frequently offer more reliable information on how harmful a product may be to human tissue; and third, computer simulations often can more accurately rate a substance's toxicity. Your warrant, although not explicit, is nonetheless clear: "It is wrong to continue product testing on animals when more humane and valid test methods are available."

Other times, you'll do best to make your *warrant explicit*. Suppose you plan to argue that students should be involved in deciding which faculty members are granted tenure. To develop your claim, you present some evidence. You begin by noting that, currently, only faculty members and administrators review candidates for tenure. Next, you call attention to the controversy surrounding two professors, widely known by students to be poor teachers, who were nonetheless granted tenure. Finally, you cite a decision, made several years ago, to discontinue using student evaluations as part of the tenure process; you emphasize that since that time complaints about teachers' incompetence have risen dramatically. Some readers, though, still might wonder how you got from your evidence to your claim. In this case, your argument could be made stronger by stating your warrant explicitly: "Since students are as knowledgeable as the faculty and administrators about which professors are competent, they should be involved in the tenure process."

The more widely accepted your warrant, Toulmin explains, the more likely it is that readers will accept your argument. If there's no consensus about the warrant, you'll probably need to *back it up*. For the preceding example, you might mention several reports that found students evaluate faculty fairly (most students don't, for example, use the ratings to get back at professors against whom they have a personal grudge); further, students' ratings correlate strongly with those given by administrators and other faculty.

Toulmin describes another way to increase receptivity to an argument: *qualify the claim*—that is, explain under what circumstances it might be invalid or restricted. For instance, you might grant that most students know little about their instructors' research activities, scholarly publications, or participation in professional committees. You could, then, qualify your claim this way: "Because students don't have a comprehensive view of their instructors' professional activities, they should be involved in the tenure process but play a less prominent role than faculty and administrators."

As you can see, Toulmin's approach provides strategies for strengthening an argument. So, when prewriting or revising, take a few minutes to ask yourself the questions listed below.

QUESTIONS FOR USING TOULMIN LOGIC: A CHECKLIST

- ☐ What data (*evidence*) should I provide to support my claim (*thesis*)?
- ☐ Is my warrant clear? Should I state it explicitly? What backup can I provide to justify my warrant?
- ☐ Would qualifying my claim make my argument more convincing?

Your responses to these questions will help you structure a convincing and logical argument.

9. **Recognize logical fallacies.** When writing an argumentation-persuasion essay, you need to recognize **logical fallacies** both in your own argument and in points raised by the opposing side. Work to eliminate such gaps in logic from your own writing and, when they appear in the opposing argument, try to expose them in your refutation. Logicians have identified many logical fallacies—including the sweeping or hasty generalization and the faulty conclusion discussed earlier in this chapter. Other logical fallacies are described in the paragraphs that follow.

   The ***post hoc* fallacy** (short for a Latin phrase meaning "after this, therefore because of this") occurs when you conclude that a cause-effect relationship exists simply because one event preceded another. Let's say you note the growing number of immigrants settling in a nearby city, observe the city's economic decline, and conclude that the immigrants' arrival caused the decline. Such a chain of thinking is faulty because it assumes a cause-effect relationship based purely on co-occurrence. Perhaps the immigrants' arrival was a factor in the economic slump, but there could also be other reasons: the lack of financial incentives to attract business to the city, restrictions on the size of the city's manufacturing facilities, citywide labor disputes that make companies leery of settling in the area. Your argument should also consider these possibilities. (For more on the *post hoc* fallacy, see pages 388–389 in Chapter 16.)

The ***non sequitur* fallacy** (Latin for "it does not follow") is an even more blatant muddying of cause-effect relationships. In this case, a conclusion is drawn that has no logical connection to the evidence cited: "Millions of Americans own cars, so there is no need to fund public transportation." The faulty conclusion disregards the millions of Americans who don't own cars; it also ignores pollution and road congestion, both of which could be reduced if people had access to safe, reliable public transportation.

An ***ad hominem* argument** (from the Latin meaning "to the man") occurs when someone attacks a person rather than a point of view. Suppose your college plans to sponsor a physicians' symposium on the abortion controversy. You decide to write a letter to the school paper opposing the symposium. Taking swipes at two of the invited doctors who disapprove of abortion, you mention that one was recently involved in a messy divorce and that the other is alleged to have a drinking problem. By hurling personal invective, you avoid discussing the issue. Mudslinging is a poor substitute for reasoned argument. And as politician Adlai Stevenson once said, "He who slings mud generally loses ground."

Appeals to questionable or faulty authority also weaken an argument. Most of us have developed a healthy suspicion of phrases like *sources close to*, *an unidentified spokesperson states*, *experts claim*, and *studies show*. If these people and reports are so reliable, they should be clearly identified.

Begging the question involves failure to establish proof for a debatable point. The writer expects readers to accept as given a premise that's actually controversial. For instance, you would have trouble convincing readers that prayer should be banned from public schools if you based your argument on the premise that school prayer violates the U.S. Constitution. If the Constitution does, either explicitly or implicitly, prohibit prayer in public education, your essay must demonstrate that fact. You can't build a strong argument if you pretend there's no controversy surrounding your premise.

A **false analogy** disregards significant dissimilarities and wrongly implies that because two things share *some* characteristics, they are therefore *alike in all respects*. You might, for example, compare nicotine and marijuana. Both, you could mention, involve health risks and have addictive properties. If, however, you go on to conclude, "Driving while smoking a cigarette isn't illegal, so driving while smoking marijuana shouldn't be illegal either," you're employing a false analogy. You've overlooked a major difference between tobacco and marijuana: Marijuana impairs perception and coordination—important aspects of driving—while there's no evidence that tobacco does the same.

The ***either/or* fallacy** occurs when you assume that a particular viewpoint or course of action can have only one of two diametrically opposed outcomes—either totally this or totally that. Say you argue as follows: "Unless colleges continue to offer scholarships based solely on financial need, no one who is underprivileged will be able to attend college." Such a statement ignores the fact that bright, underprivileged students could receive scholarships based on their potential or their demonstrated academic excellence.

Finally, a **red herring** argument is an intentional digression from the issue—a ploy to deflect attention from the matter being discussed. Imagine you're arguing that condoms shouldn't be dispensed to high school students. You would introduce a red herring if you began to rail against parents who fail to provide their children with any information about sex. Most people would agree that parents *should* provide such information. However, the issue being discussed is not parents' irresponsibility but the pros and cons of schools' distributing condoms to students.

REVISION STRATEGIES

Once you have a draft of the essay, you're ready to revise. The following checklist will help you and those giving you feedback apply to argumentation-persuasion some of the revision techniques discussed in Chapters 7 and 8.

ARGUMENTATION-PERSUASION: A REVISION/PEER REVIEW CHECKLIST

Revise Overall Meaning and Structure

- ☐ What issue is being discussed? What is controversial about it?
- ☐ What is the essay's thesis? How does it differ from a generalization or mere statement of fact?
- ☐ What is the essay's purpose—to win readers over to a point of view, to spur readers to some type of action?
- ☐ For what audience is the essay written? What strategies are used to make readers receptive to the essay's thesis?
- ☐ What tone does the essay project? Is the tone likely to win readers over?
- ☐ If the essay's argument is essentially deductive, is the major premise sufficiently restricted? What evidence is the premise based on? Are the minor premise and conclusion valid? If not, how could these problems be corrected?
- ☐ Where is the essay weakened by hasty generalizations, a failure to weigh evidence honestly, or a failure to draw the most valid conclusion?
- ☐ Where does the essay commit any of the following logical fallacies: Concluding that a cause-effect relationship exists simply because one event preceded another? Attacking a person rather than an issue? Drawing a conclusion that isn't logically related to the evidence? Failing to establish proof for a debatable point? Relying on questionable or vaguely specified authority? Drawing a false analogy? Resorting to *either/or* thinking? Using a red herring argument?

Revise Paragraph Development

- ☐ How apparent is the link between the evidence (data) and the thesis (claim)? How could an explicit warrant clarify the connection?
- ☐ How would supporting the warrant or qualifying the claim strengthen the argument?
- ☐ Which paragraphs lack sufficient evidence (facts, examples, statistics, and expert opinion)?
- ☐ Which paragraphs lack unity? How could they be made more focused? In which paragraphs(s) does evidence seem bland, overly general, unrepresentative, or inaccurate?
- ☐ Which paragraphs take opposing views into account? Are these views refuted? How? Which counterarguments are ineffective?
- ☐ Where do outside sources require documentation?

Revise Sentences and Words

- ☐ What words and phrases help readers distinguish the essay's arguments from those advanced by the opposing side?
- ☐ Which words carry strong emotional overtones? Is this connotative language excessive? Where does emotional language replace rather than reinforce clear thinking?
- ☐ Where might dogmatic language ("Anyone can see that . . . " and "Obviously, . . . ") alienate readers?

STUDENT ESSAY: FROM PREWRITING THROUGH REVISION

The student essay that follows was written by Mark Simmons in response to this assignment:

> In "Rape: A Bigger Danger Than Feminists Know," Camille Paglia invites controversy by accusing feminism of having misled women regarding the subject of rape. Select another controversial issue, one that you feel strongly about. Using logic and solid evidence, convince readers that your viewpoint is valid.

Before writing his essay, Mark used the prewriting strategy of *group brainstorming* to generate material on the subject he decided to write about: compulsory national service. In a lively give-and-take with friends, Mark jotted down, as they occurred, ideas that seemed especially promising. Later on, he typed up his jottings so he could review them more easily. At that point, he began to organize the material.

Mark's typed version of the brainstormed list is on the next page. The handwritten marks indicate his later efforts to organize the material. As you can see, he started organizing the list by crossing out one item (the possibility of low morale) and adding several others (for example, that compulsory national service would be a relatively inexpensive way to repair bridges and roads). Then he labeled points raised by the opposing side and his counterarguments. In the process, the essay's underlying structure began to emerge so clearly that he had no trouble preparing an outline, which is presented on page 480.

Brainstorming

```
Compulsory service—ages 17-25                          Definition

Two years—military or public service
  Serve after high school or college

Israel has it, and it works well                       Example, where to use?

Nazi Germany had it, too                               Opposing position: Point 3
                                                       (potentially fascist)
Too authoritarian

Start of a dictatorship

Can choose what kind of service                        Refutation of point 3
                                                       (not fascist)
No uniforms

U.S. not a fascist country

Americans very lucky—economic opportunity, right to
vote, etc.
                                                       Introduction
Take without giving

Should have to give—program provides that chance

Program too expensive
                                                       Opposing position:
Pay—at least minimum wage                              Point 1 (too expensive)

Have to provide housing, too

Can live at home                                       Less costly way to repair
                                                       bridges and roads and
Payments from participating towns, cities, states      help elderly and
                                                       homeless
Could be like AmeriCorps's small budget   Refutation of point 1
                                          (not expensive)
~~Low morale because forced? (Unlike Volunteer peace corps)~~

Demoralizing                                           Opposing position: Point 2
                                                       (demoralizing)
Interfere with careers

Learn skills

Time to think about goals                              Refutation of point 2
                                                       (not demoralizing)
Make real contribution to society
  Feel good and worthwhile
```

Outline

Thesis: Compulsory national service would be good for both young people and the country.

I. Definition of compulsory national service

II. Cost of compulsory national service

  A. Would be expensive

    1. Would have high administrative costs

    2. Would have high salary and housing costs

  B. Wouldn't be expensive

    1. Could follow AmeriCorps model

    2. Would require the towns, cities, and states using the corps to pay salary and housing costs

    3. Would cut costs by having young people live at home

    4. Would provide a cost-efficient way to repair deteriorating bridges, roads, and neighborhoods

    5. Would provide a cost-efficient way to help the elderly and homeless

III. Effect of compulsory national service on young people

  A. Would be demoralizing

    1. Would interrupt career plans

    2. Would waste young people's time by making them do work that isn't personally meaningful

  B. Wouldn't be demoralizing

    1. Would give young people time to evaluate life and career goals

    2. Would equip young people with marketable skills

    3. Would make young people from different backgrounds feel good about coming together to contribute to society

IV. Effect of compulsory national service on American democracy

  A. Could encourage fascism, as it did in Germany

  B. Wouldn't encourage fascism

    1. Wouldn't undermine our present system of checks and balances

    2. Would offer young people choices about when they would serve and in which branch they would serve

    3. Wouldn't require uniforms or confinement in a barracks

    4. Wouldn't be that different from a regular nine-to-five job

Now read Mark's paper, "Compulsory National Service," noting the similarities and differences between his prewriting, outline, and final essay. One difference is especially striking: During prewriting, Mark and his friends tended to identify an objection to compulsory service, brainstorm an appropriate counterargument, then move to the next objection and its counterargument. Mark used the same *point-by-point* format in his outline. When drafting his paper, though, Mark decided to use the *one-side-at-a-time* format. He summarized all reservations first, then devoted the rest of the essay to a detailed refutation. This change in organization strengthened Mark's argument because his rebuttals acquired greater force when gathered together, instead of remaining scattered throughout the paper. As you read the essay, also consider how well it applies the principles of argumentation-persuasion discussed in this chapter. (The commentary that follows the paper will help you look at Mark's essay more closely and will give you some sense of how he went about revising his first draft.)

Compulsory National Service

by Mark Simmons

1 Our high school history class spent several weeks studying the events of the 1960s. The most interesting thing about that decade was the spirit of service and social commitment among young people. In the '60s, young people thought about issues beyond themselves; they joined the Peace Corps, worked in poverty-stricken Appalachian communities, and participated in freedom marches against segregation. Most young people today, despite their concern with careers and getting ahead, would also like an opportunity to make a worthwhile contribution to society.

Beginning of two-paragraph introduction

2 Convinced that many young adults are indeed eager for such an opportunity. President Bill Clinton implemented in 1994 a pilot program of voluntary national service. The following year, the program was formalized, placed under the management of the Corporation for National Service (CNS), and given the name AmeriCorps. In the years 1994–2007, approximately 400,000 AmeriCorps volunteers provided varied assistance in communities across the country ("AmeriCorps"). Such voluntary national service was also endorsed by President George W. Bush. Following the devastating terrorist attacks on September 11, 2001, President Bush urged Americans to volunteer as a way of assisting in the nation's recovery and of demonstrating a spirit of

Common knowledge: No need to document

Parenthetic citation of unpaged anonymous material obtained through the Internet national unity. He issued an executive order in early 2002 establishing USA Freedom Corps, an organization seeking to persuade Americans to perform 4,000 hours of volunteer service over a lifetime (Hutcheson A2). In general, programs such as USA Freedom Corps and the more established AmeriCorps hold out so much promise that it seems only natural to go one step further and make young people's participation in these programs or some kind of national service mandatory. By instituting a program of compulsory national service, the country could tap youth's idealistic desire to make a difference. Such a system would yield significant benefits.

Start of two-sentence thesis

Definition paragraph

What exactly is meant by compulsory national service? 3
Traditionally, it has tended to mean that everyone between the ages of seventeen and twenty-five would serve the country for two years. These young people could choose between two major options: military service or a public-service corps. They could serve their time at any point within an eight-year span. The unemployed or the uncertain could join immediately after high school; college-bound students could complete their education before joining the national service. Years ago, Senator Sam Nunn and Representative Dave McCurdy gave a new twist to the definition of compulsory national service. They proposed a plan that would require all high school graduates applying for federal aid for college tuition to serve either in the military or in a Citizens Corps. Anyone in the Citizens Corps would be required to work full-time at public-service duties for one or two years. During that time, participants would receive a weekly stipend, and, at the end, be given a voucher worth $10,000 for each year of civilian service. The voucher could then be applied toward college credit, employment training, or a down payment on a house (Sudo 9).

Beginning of summary of a source's ideas

Parenthetic citation—page number *and* author are given since the author is not cited earlier in the sentence

The traditional plan for compulsory national service and 4
the one proposed by Nunn and McCurdy are just two of many variations that have been discussed over the years. While this country debates the concept, some nations such as France have gone ahead and accepted it enthusiastically. The idea could be workable in this country too. Unfortunately, opponents are doing all they can to prevent the idea from taking hold. They

Topic sentence

contend, first of all, that the program would cost too much. A great deal of money, they argue, would be spent administering the program, paying young people's wages, and providing housing for participants. Another argument against compulsory national service is that it would demoralize young people; supposedly, the plan would prevent the young from moving ahead with their careers and would make them feel as though they were engaged in work that offered no personal satisfaction. A third argument is that compulsory service would lay the groundwork for a dictatorship. The picture is painted of an army of young people, controlled by the government, much like the Hitler Youth of World War II.

Beginning of summary of three points made by the opposing viewpoint

Topic sentence: Refutation of first point

5 Despite opponents' claims that compulsory national service would involve exorbitant costs, the program would not have to be that expensive to run. AmeriCorps has already provided an excellent model for achieving substantial benefits at reasonable cost. For example, a study conducted by universities in Iowa and Michigan showed that each dollar spent on AmeriCorps programs yielded $2.60 in reduced welfare costs, increased earnings, and other benefits (Garland 120). Also, the sums required for wages and housing could be reduced considerably through payments made by the towns, cities, and states using the corps's services. And the economic benefits of the program could be significant. AmeriCorps's official website gives an idea of the current scope of the program's activities. Volunteers provide crucial services including building affordable homes for families, improving health services, responding to natural disasters, and tutoring children. A compulsory national corps could also clean up litter, provide day care services, staff libraries, immunize children, and care for the country's growing elderly population ("AmeriCorps"; Clinton). All these projects would help solve many of the problems that plague our nation, and they would probably cost less than if they were handled by often inefficient government bureaucracies.

Information comes from two sources. Sources, separated by a semicolon, are given in the order they appear in the Works Cited list. Both sources are unpaged electronic texts.

Topic sentence: Refutation of second point

6 Also, rather than undermining the spirit of young people, as opponents contend, the program would probably boost their morale. Many young people feel enormous pressure and uncertainty; they

Attribution giving author's full name and area of expertise

Full-sentence quotation is preceded by a comma and begins with a capital letter

Where secondary source was quoted

Quotation is blended into the sentence (no comma and the quotation begins with a lowercased word)

Quotation with ellipsis

Just the page number is provided because the author's name is cited in the preceding attribution

Parenthetic citation for electronic source having two authors. No page given since electronic text is unpaged.

are not sure whether they want to find a job or further their education. Compulsory national service could give these young people much-needed breathing space. As Edward Lewis, president of St. Mary's College, says, "Many students are not ready for college at seventeen or eighteen. This kind of program responds to that need" (qtd. in Fowler 3). Robert Coles, psychiatrist and social activist, argues that a public service stint enriches participants' lives in yet another way. Coles points out that young people often have little sense of the job market. When they get involved in community service, though, they frequently "discover an area of interest . . . that launches them on a career" (93). Equally important, compulsory national service can provide an emotional boost for the young; all of them would experience the pride that comes from working hard, reaching goals, acquiring skills, and handling responsibilities (Waldman and Wofford). A positive mind-set would also result from the sense of community that would be created by serving in the national service. All young people--rich or poor, educated or not, regardless of sex and social class--would come together and perceive not their differences but their common interests and similarities (Waldman and Wofford). As President Clinton proclaimed at the Year 2000 swearing-in of AmeriCorps's recruits in Philadelphia, AmeriCorps gives volunteers a chance "to tear down barriers of distrust and misunderstanding and old-fashioned ignorance, and build a genuine American community" (Clinton).

Topic sentence: Refutation of third point

Finally, in contrast to what opponents claim, compulsory 7
national service would not signal the start of a dictatorship. Although the service would be required, young people would have complete freedom to choose any two years between the ages of seventeen and twenty-five. They would also have complete freedom to choose the branch of the military or public service corps that suits them best. And the corps would not need to be outfitted in military uniforms or to live in barrack-like camps. It could be set up like a regular job, with young people living at home as much as possible, following a nine-to-five schedule, enjoying all the personal freedoms that would ordinarily be theirs. Also, a dictatorship would no more likely emerge from compulsory national service than it has from our present military system. We would still have a series of checks and

balances to prohibit the taking of power by one group or individual. We should also keep in mind that our system is different from that of fascist regimes; our long tradition of personal liberty makes improbable the seizing of absolute power by one person or faction. A related but even more important point to remember is that freedom does not mean people are guaranteed the right to pursue only their individual needs. That is mistaking selfishness for freedom. And, as everyone knows, selfishness leads only to misery. The national service would not take away freedom. On the contrary, serving in the corps would help young people grasp this larger concept of freedom, a concept that is badly needed to counteract the deadly "look out for number one" attitude that is spreading like a poison across the nation. "We think that there's an inherent idealism in every person, especially young people, that if we give them the right structure and opportunity, we can call it out," says John Sarvey, who trains AmeriCorps participants for work in City Year San Jose, the program he directs ("Helping Hands").

Beginning of two-paragraph conclusion

8 Perhaps there will never be a time like the 1960s when so many young people were concerned with remaking the world. Still, a good many of today's young people want meaningful work. They want to feel that what they do makes a difference. A program of compulsory national service would harness this idealism and help young people realize the best in themselves. Such a program would also help resolve some of the country's most critical social problems.

Attribution leading to a long quotation. Attribution is followed by a colon since the lead-in is a full sentence. If the lead-in isn't a full sentence, use a comma after the attribution.

9 Almost two decades ago, political commentator Donald Eberly expressed his belief in the power of national service. Urging the inauguration of such a program, Eberly wrote the following:

> The promise of national service can be manifested in many ways: in cleaner air and fewer forest fires; in well-cared-for infants and old folks; in a better-educated citizenry and better-satisfied work force; perhaps in a more peaceful world. National service has a lot of promise. It's a promise well worth keeping. (651)

Long quotation is indented ten spaces. Don't leave any extra space within, above, or below the quotation.

Several years later, President Clinton took office, gave his support to the concept, and AmeriCorps was born. This advocacy of public service was then championed, at least in word, by

For an indented quotation, the period is placed *before* the parenthetic citation.

President Bush. During his administration, however, AmeriCorps was threatened by deep budget cuts advocated by opponents of the program and its Clintonian legacy. Fortunately, despite these measures, Congress voted in 2003 with overwhelming bipartisan support to save AmeriCorps and salvage a portion of its budget ("Timely Help"). In the words of a *Philadelphia Inquirer* editorial, "The civic yield from that investment is incalculable" ("Ill Served"). An efficient and successful program of voluntary service, AmeriCorps has paved the way. Now seems to be the perfect time to expand the concept and make compulsory national service a reality.

In *your* paper, the Works Cited list would be double-spaced like the rest of the paper, with no extra space after the heading or between entries. Also, in *your* paper, the Works Cited would start on a *separate* page.

Works Cited

Anonymous material obtained on the Internet. Names of website and of sponsoring organization appear. Electronic text is 10 paragraphs long.

"AmeriCorps: What Is AmeriCorps?" *AmeriCorps*. A Program for the Corporation of National and Community Service. 9 Apr. 2007: 10 pars. Web. 9 Apr. 2007.

Authored material on the Internet. Dates the material was published and accessed, respectively, are provided.

Clinton, William J. "Remarks by the President to AmeriCorps." Memorial Hall, Philadelphia. William J. Clinton Foundation. 11 Oct. 2000. Web. 6 Apr. 2007.

Book by one author

Coles, Robert. *The Call of Service*. Boston: Houghton, 1993. Print.

Published speech

Eberly, Donald. "What the President Should Do about National Service." *Vital Speeches of the Day* 15 Aug. 1989: 561-63. Print.

Newspaper article whose text is only one page

Fowler, Margaret. "New Interest in National Youth Corps." *New York Times* 16 May 1989, natl. ed.: A25. Print.

Article from weekly magazine

Garland, Susan B. "A Social Program CEOs Want to Save." *Business Week* 19 June 1996: 120-21. Print.

"Helping Hands." *Online NewsHour*. PBS. 19 July 2000. Print. Transcript.

Hutcheson, Ron. "Bush Moves to Establish His New Volunteer Program." *Philadelphia Inquirer* 31 Jan. 2002: A2. Print.

Internet article with unnumbered paragraphs or pages

"Ill Served." Editorial. *Philadelphia Inquirer Online* 27 June 2003. Web. 8 Apr. 2007.

Sudo, Phil. "Mandatory National Service?" *Scholastic Update* 23 Feb. 1990: 9. Print.

"Timely Help for AmeriCorps." Editorial. *New York Times Online* 17 July 2003: 4 pars. Web. 11 Apr. 2007.

Waldman, Steven, and Harris Wofford. "AmeriCorps the Beautiful? Habitat for Conservative Values." *Policy Review* Sept.–Oct. 1997: 49 pars. CD-ROM. EBSCOhost. 2000.

Article (by two authors) from scholarly journal on CD-ROM

Commentary

Blend of Argumentation and Persuasion

In his essay, Mark tackles a controversial issue. He takes the position that compulsory national service would benefit both the country as a whole and its young people in particular. Mark's essay is a good example of the way argumentation and persuasion often mix: Although the paper presents Mark's position in a logical, well-reasoned manner (argumentation), it also appeals to readers' personal values and suggests a course of action (persuasion).

Audience Analysis

When planning the essay, Mark realized that his audience—his composition class—would consist largely of two kinds of readers. Some, not sure of their views, would be inclined to agree with him if he presented his case well. Others would probably be reluctant to accept his view. Because of this mixed audience, Mark knew he couldn't depend on *pathos* (an appeal to emotion) to convince readers. Rather, his argument had to rely mainly on *logos* (reason) and *ethos* (credibility). So Mark organized his essay around a series of logical arguments—many of them backed by expert opinion—and he evoked his own authority by drawing on his knowledge of history and his "inside" knowledge of young people.

Introduction and Thesis

Mark introduces his subject by discussing an earlier decade when large numbers of young people worked for social change. Mark's references to the Peace Corps, community work, and freedom marches reinforce his image as a knowledgeable source and establish a context for his position. These historical references, combined with the comments about AmeriCorps, the program of voluntary national service, lead into the two-sentence thesis at the end of the two-paragraph introduction: "By instituting a program of compulsory national service, the country could tap youth's idealistic desire to make a difference. Such a system would yield significant benefits."

The second paragraph in the introduction also illustrates Mark's first use of outside sources. Because the assignment called for research in support of an argument, Mark went to the library and online and identified sources that helped him defend his position. If Mark's instructor had required extensive investigation of an issue, Mark would have been obligated both to dig more deeply into his subject and to use more scholarly and specialized sources. But given the instructor's requirements, Mark proceeded just as he should have: He searched out expert opinion that supported his viewpoint; he presented that evidence clearly; he documented his sources carefully.

Background Paragraph and Use of Outside Sources

The third paragraph provides a working *definition* of compulsory national service by presenting two common interpretations of the concept. Such background information guarantees that Mark's readers will share his understanding of the essay's central concept.

Acknowledging the Opposing Viewpoint

Having explained the meaning of compulsory national service, Mark is now in a good position to launch his argument. Even though he wasn't required to research the opposing viewpoint, Mark wisely decided to get together with some friends to brainstorm some issues that might be raised by the dissenting view. He acknowledges this position in the *topic sentence* of the essay's fourth paragraph: "Unfortunately, opponents are doing all they can to prevent the idea from taking hold." Next he summarizes the main points the dissenting opinion might advance: compulsory national service would be expensive, demoralizing to young people, and dangerously authoritarian. Mark uses the rest of the essay to counter these criticisms.

Refutation

The next three paragraphs (5–7) *refute* the opposing stance and present Mark's evidence for his position. Mark structures the essay so that against readers can follow his *counterargument* with ease. Each paragraph argues against one opposing point and begins with a *topic sentence* that serves as Mark's response to the dissenting view. Note the way the italicized portion of each topic sentence recalls a dissenting point cited earlier: "Despite opponents' claims that *compulsory national service would involve exorbitant costs*, the program would not have to be that expensive to run" (paragraph 5); "Also, rather than *undermining the spirit of young people*, as opponents contend, the program would probably boost their morale" (6); "Finally, in contrast to what opponents claim, *compulsory national service would not signal the start of a dictatorship*" (7). Mark also guides the reader through the various points in the refutation by using *transitions* within paragraphs: "*And* the economic benefits . . . could be significant" (5); "*Equally important*, compulsory national service could provide an emotional boost . . . " (6); "*Also*, a dictatorship would no more likely emerge . . . " (7).

Throughout the three-paragraph refutation, Mark uses outside sources to lend power to his argument. If the assignment had called for in-depth research, he would have cited facts, statistics, and case studies to develop this section of his essay. Given the nature of the assignment, though, Mark's reliance on expert opinion is perfectly acceptable.

Mark successfully incorporates material from these outside sources into his refutation. He doesn't, for example, string one quotation numbingly after another; instead he usually develops his refutation by *summarizing* expert opinion and saves *direct quotations* for points that deserve emphasis. Moreover, whenever Mark quotes or summarizes a source, he provides clear signals to indicate that the material is indeed borrowed. (For suggestions for citing outside sources in an essay of your own, see pages 463–464 and Chapter 19.)

Some Problems with the Refutation

Overall, Mark's three-paragraph refutation is strong, but it would have been even more effective if the paragraph had been resequenced. As it now stands, the last paragraph in the refutation (7) seems anticlimactic. Unlike the preceding two paragraphs, which are developed through fairly extensive reference to outside sources, paragraph 7 depends entirely on Mark's personal feelings and interpretations for its support. Of course, Mark was under no obligation to provide research in all sections of the paper. Even so, the refutation would have been more persuasive if Mark had placed the final paragraph in the refutation in a less emphatic position. He could, for example, have put it first or second in the sequence, saving for last either of the other two more convincing paragraphs.

You may also have felt that there's another problem with the third paragraph in the refutation. Here, Mark seems to lose control of his counterargument. Beginning with "And, as everyone knows, . . . " Mark falls into the *logical fallacy* called *begging the question*. He shouldn't assume that everyone agrees that a selfish life inevitably brings misery. He also indulges in charged emotionalism when he refers—somewhat melodramatically—to the "deadly 'look out for number one' attitude that is spreading like a poison across the nation."

Inductive Reasoning

In part, Mark arrived at his position *inductively*, through a series of *inferences* or *inductive leaps*. He started with some personal *observations* about the nation and its young people. Then, to support those observations, he added his friends' insights as well as information gathered through research. Combined, all this material led him to the general *conclusion* that compulsory national service would be both workable and beneficial.

Combining Patterns of Development

To develop his argument, Mark draws on several patterns of development. The third paragraph relies on *definition* to clarify what is meant by compulsory national service. The first paragraph of both the introduction and conclusion *compares* and *contrasts* young people of the 1960s with those of today. And, to support his position, Mark uses a kind of *causal analysis*; he both speculates on the likely consequences of compulsory national service and cites expert opinion to illustrate the validity of some of those speculations.

Conclusion

Despite some problems in the final section of his refutation, Mark comes up with an effective two-paragraph conclusion for his essay. In the first closing paragraph, he echoes the point made in the introduction about the 1960s and restates his thesis. That done, he moves to the second paragraph of his conclusion.

There, he quotes a dramatic statement from a knowledgeable source, cites efforts to undermine AmeriCorps, and ends by pointing out that AmeriCorps has earned the respect of some unlikely supporters. All that Mark does in this final paragraph lends credibility to the crisp assertion and suggested course of action at the very end of his essay.

Revising the First Draft

Given the complex nature of his argument, Mark found that he had to revise his essay several times. One way to illustrate some of the changes he made is to compare his final introduction with the original draft reprinted here:

Original Version of the Introduction

③ Choppy

① Focus right from start on young people—maybe mention youth of 1960s

② Need stronger link between early part of paragraph and thesis

"There's no free lunch." "You can't get something for nothing." "You have to earn your way." In America, these sayings are not really true. In America, we gladly take but give back little. In America, we receive economic opportunity, legal protection, the right to vote, and, most of all, a personal freedom unequaled throughout the world. How do we repay our country for such gifts? In most cases, we don't. This unfair relationship must be changed. The best way to make a start is to institute a system of national compulsory service for young people. This system would be of real benefit to the country and its citizens.

When Mark met with a classmate for a peer review session, he found that his partner had a number of helpful suggestions for revising various sections of the essay. But Mark's partner focused most of her comments on the essay's introduction because she felt it needed special attention. Following his classmate's suggestion, Mark deleted the original introduction's references to Americans in general. He made this change because he wanted readers to know—from the very start of the essay—that the paper would focus not on all Americans but on American youth. To reinforce this emphasis, he also added the point about the social commitment characteristic of young people in the 1960s. This reference to an earlier period gave the discussion an important historical perspective and lent a note of authority to Mark's argument. The decision to mention the '60s also helped Mark realize that his introduction should point out more recent developments—specifically, the promise of AmeriCorps. Mark was pleased to see that adding this new material not only gave the introduction a sharper focus, but it also provided a smoother lead-in to his thesis.

These are just a few of the many changes Mark made while reworking his essay. Because he budgeted his time carefully, he was able to revise thoroughly. With the exception of some weak spots in the refutation, Mark's essay is well reasoned and convincing.

ACTIVITIES: ARGUMENTATION-PERSUASION

Prewriting Activities

1. Imagine you're writing two essays: One defines hypocrisy; the other contrasts license and freedom. Identify an audience for each essay (college students, professors, teenagers, parents, employers, employees, or some other group). Then jot down how each essay might argue the merits of certain ways of behaving.

2. Following are several thesis statements for argumentation-persuasion essays. For each thesis, determine whether the three audiences indicated in parentheses are apt to be supportive, wavering, or hostile. Then select *one* thesis and use group brainstorming to identify, for each audience, general concerns on which you might successfully base your persuasive appeal (for example, the concern for approval, for financial well-being, for self-respect, for the welfare of others).

   a. The minimum wage should be raised every two years (*low-income employees, employers, congressional representatives*).

   b. Students should not graduate from college until they have passed a comprehensive exam in their majors (*college students, their parents, college officials*).

   c. Abandoned homes owned by the city should be sold to low-income residents for a nominal fee (*city officials, low-income residents, general citizens*).

   d. The town should pass a law prohibiting residents near the reservoir from using pesticides on their lawns (*environmentalists, homeowners, members of the town council*).

   e. Faculty advisers to college newspapers should have the authority to prohibit the publication of articles that reflect negatively on the school (*alumni, college officials, student journalists*).

3. Using the thesis you selected in activity 2, focus—for each group indicated in parentheses—on one or two of the general concerns you identified. Then brainstorm with others to determine the specific points you'd make to persuade each group. How would Rogerian argument (pages 465–468) and other techniques (page 459) help you disarm the most hostile audience?

4. Clip an effective advertisement from a magazine or newspaper. Through brainstorming, determine to what extent the ad depends on *logos*, *ethos*, and *pathos*. Consider the logical fallacies discussed in this chapter. After reviewing your brainstorming, devise a thesis that expresses your feelings about the ad's persuasive strategies. Are they responsible? Why or why not?

5. In a campus, local, or major newspaper, find an editorial with which you disagree. Using the patterns of development, freewriting, or another prewriting technique, generate points that refute the editorial. You may, for example, identify any logical fallacies in the editorial. Then, following one of the refutation strategies discussed in this chapter, organize your rebuttal, keeping in mind the power of Rogerian argument.

Revising Activities

6. Examine the following sets, each containing *data* (evidence) and a *claim* (thesis). For each set, identify the implied *warrant*. Which sets would benefit from an explicit warrant? Why? How might the warrant be expressed? In which sets would it be helpful to support the warrant or qualify the claim? Why? How might the warrant be supported or the claim qualified?

   a. *Data:* An increasing number of Americans are buying Japanese cars. The reason, they report, is that Japanese cars tend to have superior fuel efficiency and longevity. Japanese cars are currently manufactured under stricter quality control than American models.

      Claim: Implementing stricter quality controls is one way for the American auto industry to compete with Japanese imports.

   b. *Data:* Although laws guarantee learning-impaired children an education suitable to their needs, no laws safeguard the special needs of intellectually gifted children. There are, proportionately, far more programs that assist the slow learner than there are those that challenge the fast learner.

      Claim: Our educational system is unfair to gifted children.

   c. *Data:* To date, no woman or nonwhite and only one non-Protestant (John F. Kennedy) has ever been elected president of the United States.

      Claim: Until prejudicial attitudes change, American voters will not elect a president who is a female, a member of a racial minority, or a non-Protestant.

   d. *Data:* Minors aren't permitted to vote, marry without parental consent, or sign contracts. Nevertheless, the Supreme Court has ruled that a minor can receive the full penalty of the law—in some cases, even be executed—for a crime.

      Claim: Minors who engage in criminal acts should be treated with greater leniency than adults.

7. Examine the faulty chains of reasoning that follow. Which use essentially inductive logic? Which use essentially deductive logic? In each set, determine, in general terms, why the conclusion is invalid. (The next activity offers practice in identifying specific logical fallacies that render conclusions invalid.)

   a. Whenever I work in the college's computer lab, something goes wrong. The program crashes, the cursor freezes, the margins unset themselves.

      Conclusion: The college needs to allocate additional funds to repair and upgrade the computers in the lab.

   b. Many cars in the student parking lot are dented and look as though they have been in accidents.

      Conclusion: Students are careless drivers.

   c. Many researchers believe that children in families where both parents work develop confidence and independence. In a nearby community, the number of two-career families increased 15 percent over a two-year period.

Conclusion: Children in the nearby community will develop confidence and independence.

d. The local Chamber of Commerce elected a woman as president. The all-male Metropolitan Business Club approved a woman for membership.

Conclusion: Traditionally conservative male groups are starting to accept women's role in business.

e. Anyone found guilty of sexual harassment will be fired by XYZ Corporation. Curt A. was fired by XYZ Corporation.

Conclusion: Curt A. is guilty of sexual harassment.

8. Each set of statements that follows contains at least one of the logical fallacies described earlier in the chapter. Identify the fallacy or fallacies in each set and explain why the statements are invalid.

a. Grades are irrelevant to learning. Students are in college to get an education, not good grades. The university should eliminate grading altogether.

b. The best policy is to put juvenile offenders in jail so that they can get a taste of reality. Otherwise, they will repeat their crimes again and again.

c. Legal experts say that this bill will weaken consumers' rights. Based on their views, we should petition legislators not to sign the bill.

d. So-called sex education programs do nothing to decrease the rate of teenage pregnancy. Further expenditures on these programs should be curtailed.

e. This country should research environmentally sound ways to use coal as an energy source. If we don't, we will become enslaved to the oil-rich Middle East nations.

f. If we allow abortion, people will think it's acceptable to kill the homeless or pull the plug on sick people—two groups that are also weak and frail.

g. The curfews that some towns impose on teenagers are as repressive as the curfews in totalitarian countries.

h. Each day, Americans throw out ton after ton of edible food; it isn't true that some Americans suffer from hunger.

i. Two members of the state legislature have introduced gun-control legislation. Both have led sheltered, pampered lives that prevent them from seeing how ordinary people need guns to protect themselves.

j. Some say that auto insurance rates need to be more strictly regulated, but how strict are regulations on health insurance?

k. Last year, a few students managed to avoid paying for their parking decals. This year's increased student parking fees unfairly penalize everyone for the dishonesty of a few.

9. Following is the introduction from the first draft of an essay advocating the elimination of mandatory dress codes in public schools. Revise the paragraph, being sure to consider these questions: How effectively does the writer deal with the opposing viewpoint? Does the paragraph encourage those who might disagree with the writer to read on? Why or why not? Do you see any logical fallacies in the writer's thinking? Where? Does the writer introduce anything that veers away from the point being discussed? Where? Before revising, you may find it helpful to do some brainstorming—individually or in a group—to find ways to strengthen the paragraph.

After reworking the paragraph, take a few minutes to consider how the rest of the essay might unfold. What persuasive strategies could be used? How could Rogerian argument win over readers? What points could be made? What action could be urged in the effort to build a convincing argument?

In three nearby towns recently, high school administrators joined forces to take an outrageously strong stand against students' constitutional rights. Acting like Fascists, they issued an edict in the form of a preposterous dress code that prohibits students from wearing expensive jewelry, name-brand jeans, leather jackets—anything that the administrators, in their supposed wisdom, consider ostentatious. Perhaps the next thing they'll want to do is forbid students to play hip hop music at school dances. What prompted the administrators' dictatorial prohibition against certain kinds of clothing? Somehow or other, they got it into their heads that having no restrictions on the way students dress creates an unhealthy environment, where students vie with each other for the flashiest attire. Students and parents alike should protest this and any other dress code. If such codes go into effect, we might as well throw out the Constitution.

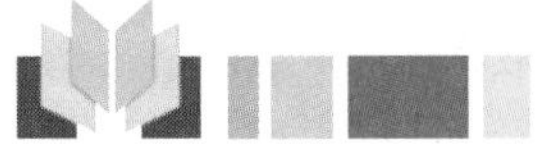

PROFESSIONAL SELECTIONS: ARGUMENTATION-PERSUASION

STANLEY FISH

Stanley Fish is best known as a scholar of the English poet John Milton and as a literary theorist. He was born in Providence, Rhode Island, in 1938, and grew up in Philadelphia, Pennsylvania. After earning his bachelor's degree from the University of Pennsylvania, he went on to receive a Ph.D. from Yale University in 1962. Fish has taught English at the University of California at Berkeley, Johns Hopkins University, and Duke University. From 1999 to 2004 he was dean of the College of Liberal Arts and Sciences at the University of Illinois at Chicago, and in 2005 he became a professor of humanities and law at Florida International University. His best-known work on Milton is *Surprised by Sin: The Reader in Paradise Lost* (1967). In addition to his distinguished academic career and many scholarly publications, Fish has also had a career as a public intellectual. He has written and lectured about many issues, including the politics of the university. His books on current political and cultural issues include *There's No Such Thing as Free Speech . . . and It's a Good Thing, Too* (1994) and *The Trouble With Principle* (1999). Currently, he blogs regularly for *The New York Times'* website on politics, education, and society. This article was published in *The Chronicle of Higher Education*, on June 13, 2003.

Please note the essay structure diagram that appears following the selection (Figure 18.2 on page 499).

Pre-Reading Journal Entry

The issue of freedom of speech on campus is a topic that never seems to go away, maintaining relevance from generation to generation of college students. How do you feel about freedom of speech on campus? In your journal, list several controversial issues that might be debated in a college setting. For each issue, indicate whether you feel that divergent, even inflammatory views should have an opportunity to be heard on campus—for example, in class, in the college newspaper, or in a lecture series. Reflect in your journal on why you feel as you do.

FREE-SPEECH FOLLIES

1 The modern American version of crying wolf is crying First Amendment.[1] If you want to burn a cross on a black family's lawn or buy an election by contributing millions to a candidate or vilify Jerry Falwell and his mother in a scurrilous "parody," and someone or some government agency tries to stop you, just yell "First Amendment rights" and you will stand a good chance of getting to do what you want to do.

2 In the academy,[2] the case is even worse: Not only is the First Amendment pressed into service at the drop of a hat (especially whenever anyone is disciplined for anything), it is invoked ritually when there are no First Amendment issues in sight.

3 Take the case of the editors of college newspapers who will always cry First Amendment when something they've published turns out to be the cause of outrage and controversy. These days the offending piece or editorial or advertisement usually involves (what is at least perceived to be) an attack on Jews. In January of this year, the *Daily Illini*, a student newspaper at the University of Illinois at Urbana-Champaign, printed a letter from a resident of Seattle with no university affiliation. The letter ran under the headline "Jews Manipulate America" and argued that because their true allegiance is to the state of Israel, the president should "separate Jews from all government advisory positions"; otherwise, the writer warned, "the Jews might face another Holocaust."

---

[1]The relevant part of the First Amendment of the U.S. Constitution reads: "Congress shall make no law . . . abridging the freedom of speech, or of the press; or the right of the people peaceably to assemble, and to petition the Government for a redress of grievances" (editors' note).

[2]Refers to institutions of higher learning (editors' note).

When the predictable firestorm of outrage erupted, the newspaper's editor responded by declaring, first, that "we are committed to giving all people a voice"; second, that, given this commitment, "we print the opinions of others with whom we do not agree"; third, that to do otherwise would involve the newspaper in the dangerous acts of "silencing" and "self-censorship"; and, fourth, that "what is hate speech to one member of a society is free speech to another." 4

Wrong four times. 5

I'll bet the *Daily Illini* is not committed to giving all people a voice—the KKK? man-boy love? advocates of slavery? would-be Unabombers? Nor do I believe that the editors sift through submissions looking for the ones they disagree with and then print those. No doubt they apply some principles of selection, asking questions like, Is it relevant, or Is it timely, or Does it get the facts right, or Does it present a coherent argument? 6

That is, they exercise judgment, which is quite a different thing from silencing or self-censorship. No one is silenced because a single outlet declines to publish him; silencing occurs when that outlet (or any other) is forbidden by the state to publish him on pain of legal action; and that is also what censorship is. 7

As for self-censoring, if it is anything, it is what we all do whenever we decide it would be better not to say something or cut a sentence that went just a little bit too far or leave a manuscript in the bottom drawer because it is not yet ready. Self-censorship, in short, is not a crime or a moral failing; it is a responsibility. 8

And, finally, whatever the merits of the argument by which all assertions are relativised—your hate speech is my free speech—this incident has nothing to do with either hate speech or free speech and everything to do with whether the editors are discharging or defaulting on their obligations when they foist them off on an inapplicable doctrine, saying in effect, "The First Amendment made us do it." 9

More recently, the same scenario played itself out at Santa Rosa Junior College. This time it was a student who wrote the offending article. Titled "Is Anti-Semitism Ever the Result of Jewish Behavior?" it answered the question in the affirmative, creating an uproar that included death threats, an avalanche of hate mail, and demands for just about everyone's resignation. The faculty adviser who had approved the piece said, "The First Amendment isn't there to protect agreeable stories." 10

He was alluding to the old saw that the First Amendment protects unpopular as well as popular speech. But what it protects unpopular speech *from* is abridgment by the government of its free expression; it does not protect unpopular speech from being rejected by a newspaper, and it confers no positive obligation to give your pages over to unpopular speech, or popular speech, or any speech. 11

Once again, there is no First Amendment issue here, just an issue of editorial judgment and the consequences of exercising it. (You can print anything you like; but if the heat comes, it's yours, not the Constitution's.) 12

In these controversies, student editors are sometimes portrayed, or portray themselves, as First Amendment heroes who bravely risk criticism and censure in order to uphold a cherished American value. But they are not heroes; they are merely confused and, in terms of their understanding of the doctrine they invoke, rather hapless. 13

Not as hapless, however, as the Harvard English department, which made a collective fool of itself three times when it invited, disinvited and then reinvited poet Tom Paulin to be the Morris Gray lecturer. Again the flash point was anti-Semitism. In his 14 poetry and in public comments, Paulin had said that Israel had no right to exist, that settlers on the West Bank "should be shot dead," and that Israeli police and military forces were the equivalent of the Nazi SS. When these and other statements came to light shortly before Paulin was to give his lecture, the department voted to rescind the invitation. When the inevitable cry of "censorship, censorship" was heard in the land, the department flip-flopped again, and a professor-spokesman declared, "This was a clear affirmation that the department stood strongly by the First Amendment."

15 It was of course nothing of the kind; it was a transparent effort of a bunch that had already put its foot in its mouth twice to wriggle out of trouble and regain the moral high ground by striking the pose of First Amendment defender. But, in fact, the department and its members were not First Amendment defenders (a religion they converted to a little late), but serial bunglers.

16 What should they have done? Well, it depends on what they wanted to do. If they wanted to invite this particular poet because they admired his poetry, they had a perfect right to do so. If they were aware ahead of time of Paulin's public pronouncements, they could have chosen either to say something by way of explanation or to remain silent and let the event speak for itself; either course of action would have been at once defensible and productive of risk. If they knew nothing of Paulin's anti-Israel sentiments (difficult to believe of a gang of world-class researchers) but found out about them after the fact, they might have said, "Oops, never mind" or toughed it out—again alternatives not without risk. But at each stage, whatever they did or didn't do would have had no relationship whatsoever to any First Amendment right—Paulin had no right to be invited—or obligation—there was no obligation either to invite or disinvite him, and certainly no obligation to reinvite him, unless you count the obligations imposed on yourself by a succession of ill-thought-through decisions. Whatever the successes or failures here, they were once again failures of judgment, not doctrine.

17 In another case, it looked for a moment that judgment of an appropriate kind was in fact being exercised. The University of California at Berkeley houses the Emma Goldman Papers Project, and each year the director sends out a fund-raising mailer that always features quotations from Goldman's work. But this January an associate vice chancellor edited the mailer and removed two quotations that in context read as a criticism of the Bush administration's plans for a war in Iraq. He explained that the quotations were not randomly chosen and were clearly intended to make a "political point, and that is inappropriate in an official university situation."

18 The project director (who acknowledged that the quotes were selected for their contemporary relevance) objected to what she saw as an act of censorship and a particularly egregious one given Goldman's strong advocacy of free expression.

19 But no one's expression was being censored. The Goldman quotations are readily available and had they appeared in the project's literature in a setting that did not mark them as political, no concerns would have been raised. It is just, said the associate vice chancellor, that they are inappropriate in this context, and, he added, "It is not a matter of the First Amendment."

20 Right, it's a matter of whether or not there is even the appearance of the university's taking sides on a partisan issue; that is, it is an empirical matter that requires just the exercise of judgment that associate vice chancellors are paid to perform. Of course he was pilloried by members of the Berkeley faculty and others who saw First Amendment violations everywhere.

But there were none. Goldman still speaks freely through her words. The project director can still make her political opinions known by writing letters to the editor or to everyone in the country, even if she cannot use the vehicle of a university flier to do so. Everyone's integrity is preserved. The project goes on unimpeded, and the university goes about its proper academic business. Or so it would have been had the administration stayed firm. But it folded and countermanded the associate vice chancellor's decision. 21

At least the chancellor had sense enough to acknowledge that no one's speech had been abridged. It was just, he said, an "error in judgment." Aren't they all? 22

Are there then no free-speech issues on campuses? Sure there are; there just aren't very many. When Toni Smith, a basketball player at Manhattanville College, turned her back to the flag during the playing of the national anthem in protest against her government's policies, she was truly exercising her First Amendment rights, rights that ensure that she cannot be compelled to an affirmation she does not endorse. . . . And as she stood by her principles in the face of hostility, she truly was (and is) a First Amendment hero, as the college newspaper editors, the members of the Harvard English department, and the head of the Emma Goldman Project are not. The category is a real one, and it would be good if it were occupied only by those who belong in it. 23

Questions for Close Reading

1. What is the selection's thesis? Locate the sentence(s) in which Fish states his main idea. If he doesn't state his thesis explicitly, express it in your own words.
2. What does Fish mean by "Self-censorship, in short, is not a crime or a moral failing; it is a responsibility" (paragraph 8)?
3. In paragraph 15, Fish refers to the Harvard English department as "serial bunglers." What does he mean by this?
4. According to Fish, why aren't the editors of student newspapers that publish inflammatory material First Amendment heroes? Who does he believe are the true First Amendment heroes?
5. Refer to your dictionary as needed to define the following words used in the selection: *vilify* (paragraph 1), *scurrilous* (1), *firestorm* (4), *coherent* (6), *abridgment* (11), *hapless* (13), *rescind* (14), *chancellor* (17), *egregious* (18), *partisan* (20), *empirical* (20), *pilloried* (20), *countermanded* (21).

Questions About the Writer's Craft

1. **The pattern.** Writing on a complex and controversial issue, Fish presents the opposing viewpoint—that self-censorship is not a violation of the First

FIGURE 18.2

Essay Structure Diagram: "Free-Speech Follies" by Stanley Fish

Introductory paragraphs Thesis (paragraphs 1–2)	Invoking the First Amendment has become a way of "crying wolf." **Thesis:** In the academy, the First Amendment is invoked often in situations that don't really concern free speech.
Opposing and supporting arguments illustrated by examples (3–22)	**Example:** Anti-Semitic letter in University of Illinois newspaper. **Opposing arguments:** (1) Editors have an obligation to give all people a voice. (2) Editors have an obligation to print views they don't agree with. (3) Not to publish is "silencing" and self-censorship. (4) Hate speech to one person is free speech to another. First Amendment protects all speech, not just agreeable speech. **Supporting arguments:** (1) Editors must use some selection criteria—for writing quality and content. (2) Exercising judgment is not the same as silencing because writers are free to publish elsewhere. (3) Self-censorship is not a crime; it's a responsibility. (4) The incident did not concern hate speech vs. free speech, but rather whether editors discharged their responsibilities. **Example:** Anti-Semitic article in a Santa Rosa Junior College newspaper. (Opposing and supporting arguments given.) **Example:** Harvard English department invites, then uninvites, then reinvites a poet who had expressed anti-Semitic views. (Opposing and supporting arguments given.) **Example:** Quotations critical of the Bush ad-ministration deleted from a University of California at Berkeley exhibit flyer. (Opposing and supporting arguments given.)
Concluding paragraph (23)	Example of a true First Amendment hero: College basketball player turning her back on the flag during the national anthem to protest government policies.

Amendment. What strategies does Fish use to deal with this view and to present his own argument?

2. **Other patterns.** All the examples that Fish uses to support his argument are related to anti-Semitism. If Fish had broadened the examples to include instances of speech that defamed groups other than Jews, would the essay have been more or less effective? Support your answer.
3. Paragraph 5 has only three words, "Wrong four times." What is the effect of this brevity?
4. Most readers of *The Chronicle of Higher Education*, where this essay was first published, are academics—administrators, faculty, and graduate students—or those with a professional interest in higher education. They are likely to know Fish by reputation, especially since he publishes a regular column. Given this, how would you assess Fish's *ethos*? How effective is his use of *logos* in this argument? How effective is his use of *pathos*?

Writing Assignments Using Argumentation-Persuasion as a Pattern of Development

1. Fish gives an example of a controversy surrounding an anti-Semitic letter to the editor published in a campus student newspaper. Since publications print letters to the editor to open up their pages to public opinion and dissent, one might argue that the criteria for printing letters to the editor should be quite broad—much broader than the criteria the publication uses for its own articles—in order to give members of the public an opportunity to air their views. Write an essay in which you *argue* that letters to the editor should (or should not) be printed with the aim of giving all readers an opportunity to state their opinions. Don't forget to acknowledge (and, if possible, to refute) opposing viewpoints—perhaps including Fish's—at some point in your paper.

2. Many colleges and universities have tried to compromise on the free-speech issue by limiting controversial speech to designated "free-speech zones," areas on campus where speeches, rallies, and pamphleteering are permitted. Elsewhere on such a campus, free speech is subject to tight administration control. Proponents of free-speech zones argue that universities have a right to control activities that interfere with their operation; opponents argue that free-speech zones are unconstitutional. Do some research about free-speech zones on the Internet or in the library. Write an essay *arguing* that free-speech zones are (or are not) a legitimate way to manage free-speech issues on campus. If your own campus has free-speech zones, use it as an example to support your argument. Use other colleges and universities as examples as well. Conclude your essay with a call to action.

Writing Assignments Combining Patterns of Development

3. What procedures has your college or university established so that people on campus—faculty, staff, and/or students—can file grievances if they feel they have been the targets of hate speech or have been discriminated against in some way? In an essay, describe this *process* and indicate whether you feel it is adequate and appropriate. If it isn't, explain what steps need to be taken to improve the procedures. No matter what position you take, you should provide *examples* to illustrate your point of view.

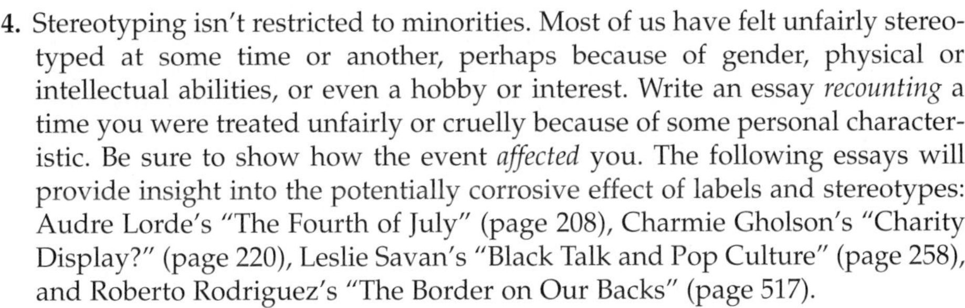

4. Stereotyping isn't restricted to minorities. Most of us have felt unfairly stereotyped at some time or another, perhaps because of gender, physical or intellectual abilities, or even a hobby or interest. Write an essay *recounting* a time you were treated unfairly or cruelly because of some personal characteristic. Be sure to show how the event *affected* you. The following essays will provide insight into the potentially corrosive effect of labels and stereotypes: Audre Lorde's "The Fourth of July" (page 208), Charmie Gholson's "Charity Display?" (page 220), Leslie Savan's "Black Talk and Pop Culture" (page 258), and Roberto Rodriguez's "The Border on Our Backs" (page 517).

Writing Assignment Using a Journal Entry as a Starting Point

5. Write an editorial for your college newspaper arguing that a college campus is *or* is not the place to air conflicting, even inflammatory views about *one* of the controversial issues listed in your pre-reading journal entry. Perhaps you feel that the issue warrants a public forum in one campus setting but not another. If so, explain why. To lend authority to your position, interview students who don't share your point of view. Be sure to acknowledge their position in your editorial.

MARY SHERRY

Following her graduation from Dominican University in 1962 with a degree in English, Mary Sherry (1940–) wrote freelance articles and advertising copy while raising her family. Over the years, a love of writing and an interest in education have been integral to all that Sherry does professionally. Founder and owner of a small research and publishing firm in Minnesota, she has taught creative and remedial writing to adults for more than sixteen years. The following selection first appeared as a 1991 "My Turn" column in *Newsweek*.

Pre-Reading Journal Entry

Imagine you had a son or daughter who didn't take school seriously. How would you go about motivating the child to value academic success? Would your strategies differ depending on the age and gender of the child? If so, how and why? What other factors might influence your approach? Use your journal to respond to these questions.

IN PRAISE OF THE "F" WORD

Tens of thousands of 18-year-olds will graduate this year and be handed meaningless diplomas. These diplomas won't look any different from those awarded their luckier classmates. Their validity will be questioned only when their employers discover that these graduates are semiliterate. 1

Eventually a fortunate few will find their way into educational repair shops—adult-literacy programs, such as the one where I teach basic grammar and writing. There, high-school graduates and high-school dropouts pursuing graduate-equivalency certificates will learn the skills they should have learned in school. They will also discover they have been cheated by our educational system. 2

As I teach, I learn a lot about our schools. Early in each session I ask my students to write about an unpleasant experience they had in school. No writers' block here! "I wish someone would have made me stop doing drugs and made me study." "I liked to party and no one seemed to care." "I was a good kid and didn't cause any trouble, so they just passed me along even though I didn't read well and couldn't write." And so on. 3

I am your basic do-gooder, and prior to teaching this class I blamed the poor academic skills our kids have today on drugs, divorce and other impediments to concentration necessary for doing well in school. But, as I rediscover each time I walk into the classroom, before a teacher can expect students to concentrate, he has to get their attention, no matter what distractions may be at hand. There are many ways to do this, and they have much to do with teaching style. However, if style alone won't do it, there is another way to show who holds the winning hand in the classroom. That is to reveal the trump card[1] of failure. 4

I will never forget a teacher who played that card to get the attention of one of my children. Our youngest, a world-class charmer, did little to develop his intellectual talents but always got by. Until Mrs. Stifter. 5

Our son was a high-school senior when he had her for English. "He sits in the back of the room talking to his friends," she told me. "Why don't you move him to the front row?" I urged, believing the embarrassment would get him to settle down. Mrs. Stifter looked at me steely-eyed over her glasses. "I don't move seniors," she said. "I flunk them." I was flustered. Our son's academic life flashed before my eyes. No teacher had ever threatened him with that before. I regained my composure and managed to say that I thought she was right. By the time I got home I was feeling pretty good about this. It was a radical approach for these times, but, well, why not? "She's going to flunk you," I told my son. I did not discuss it any further. Suddenly English became a priority in his life. He finished out the semester with an A. 6

I know one example doesn't make a case, but at night I see a parade of students who are angry and resentful for having been passed along until they could no longer 7

[1]In cards, an advantage held in reserve until it's needed (editors' note).

even pretend to keep up. Of average intelligence or better, they eventually quit school, concluding they were too dumb to finish. "I should have been held back" is a comment I hear frequently. Even sadder are those students who are high-school graduates who say to me after a few weeks of class, "I don't know how I even got a high-school diploma."

8 Passing students who have not mastered the work cheats them and the employers who expect graduates to have basic skills. We excuse this dishonest behavior by saying kids can't learn if they come from terrible environments. No one seems to stop to think that—no matter what environments they come from—most kids don't put school first on their list unless they perceive something is at stake. They'd rather be sailing.

9 Many students I see at night could give expert testimony on unemployment, chemical dependency, abusive relationships. In spite of these difficulties, they have decided to make education a priority. They are motivated by the desire for a better job or the need to hang on to the one they've got. They have a healthy fear of failure.

10 People of all ages can rise above their problems, but they need to have a reason to do so. Young people generally don't have the maturity to value education in the same way my adult students value it. But fear of failure, whether economic or academic, can motivate both.

11 Flunking as a regular policy has just as much merit today as it did two generations ago. We must review the threat of flunking and see it as it really is—a positive teaching tool. It is an expression of confidence by both teachers and parents that the students have the ability to learn the material presented to them. However, making it work again would take a dedicated, caring conspiracy between teachers and parents. It would mean facing the tough reality that passing kids who haven't learned the material—while it might save them grief for the short term—dooms them to long-term illiteracy. It would mean that teachers would have to follow through on their threats, and parents would have to stand behind them, knowing their children's best interests are indeed at stake. This means no more doing Scott's assignments for him because he might fail. No more passing Jodi because she's such a nice kid.

12 This is a policy that worked in the past and can work today. A wise teacher, with the support of his parents, gave our son the opportunity to succeed—or fail. It's time we return this choice to all students.

Questions for Close Reading

1. What is the selection's thesis? Locate the sentence(s) in which Sherry states her main idea. If she doesn't state the thesis explicitly, express it in your own words.

2. Sherry opens her essay with these words: "Tens of thousands of 18-year-olds will graduate this year and be handed meaningless diplomas." Why does Sherry consider these diplomas meaningless?

3. According to Sherry, what justification do many teachers give for "passing students who have not mastered the work" (paragraph 8)? Why does Sherry think that it is wrong to pass such students?

4. What does Sherry think teachers should do to motivate students to focus on school despite the many "distractions . . . at hand" (4)?

5. Refer to your dictionary as needed to define the following words used in the selection: *validity* (paragraph 1), *semiliterate* (1), *equivalency* (2), *impediments* (4), *composure* (6), *radical* (6), *priority* (6), *resentful* (7), *testimony* (9), *motivate* (10), *merit* (11), *conspiracy* (11), and *illiteracy* (11).

Questions About the Writer's Craft

1. **The pattern.** To write an effective argumentation-persuasion essay, writers need to establish their credibility. How does Sherry convince readers that she is qualified to write about her subject? What does this attempt to establish credibility say about Sherry's perception of her audience's point of view?

2. Sherry's title is deliberately misleading. What does her title lead you to believe the essay will be about? Why do you think Sherry chose this title?

3. Why do you suppose Sherry quotes her students rather than summarizing what they had to say? What effect do you think Sherry hopes the quotations will have on readers?

4. **Other patterns.** What *example* does Sherry provide to show that the threat of failure can work? How does this example reinforce her case?

Writing Assignments Using Argumentation-Persuasion as a Pattern of Development

1. Like Sherry, write an essay arguing your position on a controversial school-related issue. Possibilities include but need not be limited to the following: College students should *or* should not have to fulfill a physical education requirement; high school students should *or* should not have to demonstrate computer proficiency before graduating; elementary school students should *or* should not be grouped according to ability; a course in parenting should *or* should not be a required part of the high school curriculum. Once you select a topic, brainstorm with others to gather insight into varying points of view. When you write, restrict your argument to one level of education, and refute as many opposing arguments as you can. The following essays will help you identify educational issues worth writing about: Audre Lorde's "The Fourth of July" (page 208), Kay S. Hymowitz's "Tweens: Ten Going on Sixteen" (page 245), David Brooks's "Psst! Human Capital" (page 301), Clifford Stoll's "Cyberschool" (page 328), Buzz Bissinger's "Innocents Afield" (page 407), and Stanley Fish's "Free-Speech Follies" (page 495).

2. Sherry acknowledges that she used to blame students' poor academic skills on "drugs, divorce and other impediments." To what extent should teachers take these and similar "impediments" into account when grading students? Are there certain situations that call for leniency, or should out-of-school forces affecting students not be considered? To gain perspective on this issue, interview several friends, classmates, and instructors. Then write an essay in which you argue your position. Provide specific examples to support your argument, being sure to acknowledge and—when possible—to refute opposing viewpoints.

Writing Assignments Combining Patterns of Development

3. You probably feel, as Sherry does, that Mrs. Stifter is a strong, committed professional. Write an essay *illustrating* the qualities you think a teacher needs to have to be effective. Ask friends, classmates, family members, and instructors for their opinions; however, in your paper, focus on only those attributes you believe are most critical. To highlight the importance of these qualities, begin with a dramatic *contrasting* example of an ineffective teacher—someone who lacks the attributes you consider most important.

4. Where else, besides in the classroom, do you see people acting irresponsibly, expending little effort, and taking the easy way out? You might consider the workplace, a school-related club or activity, family life, or interpersonal relationships. Select *one* area and write an essay *illustrating the effects* of this behavior on everyone concerned. For a broader perspective on the issue of personal responsibility, read George Orwell's "Shooting an Elephant" (page 214), Diane Cole's "Don't Just Stand There" (page 333), Buzz Bissinger's "Innocents Afield" (page 407), Stanley Fish's "Free-Speech Follies" (page 495), Camille Paglia's "Rape: A Bigger Danger Than Feminists Know" (page 506), and Susan Jacoby's "Common Decency" (page 512).

Writing Assignment Using a Journal Entry as a Starting Point

5. Write the text for a brochure presenting parents with a step-by-step guide for dealing with academically unmotivated students. Focus your discussion on a specific level of schooling. From your pre-reading journal entry, select those strategies you consider most realistic and productive. When presenting your ideas, take into account children's likely resistance to the strategies described, and instruct parents how to deal with this resistance. Interviewing others (especially parents) and doing some research in

the library and/or on the Internet will broaden your understanding of the issues involved.

Debating the Issues: Date Rape

CAMILLE PAGLIA

Before 1990, Camille Paglia, professor of humanities at Philadelphia's University of the Arts, was known primarily for her electrifying performance in the classroom. Then came the publication of Paglia's *Sexual Personae: Art and Decadence from Nefertiti to Emily Dickinson,* a sweeping book that moves with dizzying speed from the days of cave art to the nineteenth century. *Sexual Personae* makes the case that man creates art as a defensive response to woman's terrifying cosmic power. Suddenly Paglia became an international celebrity and had many opportunities to express her controversial views. Born in 1947, Paglia earned her doctorate from Yale University, where her Ph.D. thesis was an early version of *Sexual Personae*. Other publications include *Sex, Art, and American Culture: Essays* (1992), *Vamps and Tramps: New Essays* (1994), *Alfred Hitchcock's "The Birds"* (1998), and, most recently, *Break, Blow, Burn: Camille Paglia Reads Forty-Three of the World's Best Poems* (2005). Formerly a columnist for *Salon* online magazine, she is a contributing editor to *Interview* magazine and appears frequently on television to provide commentary on pop culture and gender issues. The following selection first appeared in *New York Newsday* in 1991.

Pre-Reading Journal Entry

How would you define "date rape"? Use your journal to formulate a preliminary definition. Working as quickly as you can, jot down your preliminary thoughts about what it is and what it isn't.

RAPE: A BIGGER DANGER THAN FEMINISTS KNOW

Rape is an outrage that cannot be tolerated in civilized society. Yet feminism, which 1 has waged a crusade for rape to be taken more seriously, has put young women in danger by hiding the truth about sex from them.

In dramatizing the pervasiveness of rape, feminists have told young women that 2 before they have sex with a man, they must give consent as explicit as a legal contract's. In this way, young women have been convinced that they have been the victims of rape. On elite campuses in the Northeast and on the West Coast, they have held consciousness-raising sessions, petitioned administrations, demanded inquests. At Brown University, outraged, panicky "victims" have scrawled the names of alleged attackers on the walls of women's rest rooms. What marital rape was to the '70s, "date rape" is to the '90s.

The incidence and seriousness of rape do not require this kind of exaggeration. 3 Real acquaintance rape is nothing new. It has been a horrible problem for women for all of recorded history. Once, father and brothers protected women from rape. Once, the penalty for rape was death. I come from a fierce Italian tradition where, not so long ago in the motherland, a rapist would end up knifed, castrated, and hung out to dry.

4 But the old clans and small rural communities have broken down. In our cities, on our campuses far from home, young women are vulnerable and defenseless. Feminism has not prepared them for this. Feminism keeps saying the sexes are the same. It keeps telling women they can do anything, go anywhere, say anything, wear anything. No, they can't. Women will always be in sexual danger.

5 One of my male students recently slept overnight with a friend in a passageway of the Great Pyramid in Egypt. He described the moon and sand, the ancient silence and eerie echoes. I am a woman. I will never experience that. I am not stupid enough to believe I could ever be safe there. There is a world of solitary adventure I will never have. Women have always known these somber truths. But feminism, with its pie-in-the-sky fantasies about the perfect world, keeps young women from seeing life as it is.

6 We must remedy social injustice whenever we can. But there are some things we cannot change. There are sexual differences that are based in biology. Academic feminism is lost in a fog of social constructionism. It believes we are totally the product of our environment. This idea was invented by Rousseau.[1] He was wrong. Emboldened by dumb French language theory, academic feminists repeat the same hollow slogans over and over to each other. Their view of sex is naive and prudish. Leaving sex to the feminists is like letting your dog vacation at the taxidermist's.

7 The sexes are at war. Men must struggle for identity against the overwhelming power of their mothers. Women have menstruation to tell them they are women. Men must do or risk something to be men. Men become masculine only when other men say they are. Having sex with a woman is one way a boy becomes a man.

8 College men are at their hormonal peak. They have just left their mothers and are questing for their male identity. In groups, they are dangerous. A woman going to a fraternity party is walking into Testosterone Flats, full of prickly cacti and blazing guns. If she goes, she should be armed with resolute alertness. She should arrive with girlfriends and leave with them. A girl who lets herself get dead drunk at a fraternity party is a fool. A girl who goes upstairs alone with a brother at a fraternity party is an idiot. Feminists call this "blaming the victim." I call it common sense.

9 For a decade, feminists have drilled their disciples to say, "Rape is a crime of violence but not of sex." This sugar-coated Shirley Temple nonsense has exposed young women to disaster. Misled by feminism, they do not expect rape from the nice boys from good homes who sit next to them in class.

10 Aggression and eroticism, in fact, are deeply intertwined. Hunt, pursuit and capture are biologically programmed into male sexuality. Generation after generation, men must be educated, refined, and ethically persuaded away from their tendency toward anarchy and brutishness. Society is not the enemy, as feminism ignorantly claims. Society is woman's protection against rape. Feminism, with its solemn Carry Nation[2] repressiveness, does not see what is for men the eroticism or fun element in rape,

[1]A French political writer and philosopher (1712–78) (editors' note).

[2]A nineteenth-century reformer who advocated the abolition of alcohol (editors' note).

especially the wild, infectious delirium of gang rape. Women who do not understand rape cannot defend themselves against it.

The date-rape controversy shows feminism hitting the wall of its own broken promises. The women of my '60s generation were the first respectable girls in history to swear like sailors, get drunk, stay out all night—in short, to act like men. We sought total sexual freedom and equality. But as time passed, we woke up to cold reality. The old double standard protected women. When anything goes, it's women who lose. 11

Today's young women don't know what they want. They see that feminism has not brought sexual happiness. The theatrics of public rage over date rape are their way of restoring the old sexual rules that were shattered by my generation. Yet nothing about the sexes has really changed. The comic film *Where the Boys Are* (1960), the ultimate expression of '50s man-chasing, still speaks directly to our time. It shows smart, lively women skillfully anticipating and fending off the dozens of strategies with which horny men try to get them into bed. The agonizing date-rape subplot and climax are brilliantly done. The victim, Yvette Mimieux, makes mistake after mistake, obvious to the other girls. She allows herself to be lured away from her girlfriends and into isolation with boys whose character and intentions she misreads. *Where the Boys Are* tells the truth. It shows courtship as a dangerous game in which the signals are not verbal but subliminal. 12

Neither militant feminism, which is obsessed with politically correct language, nor academic feminism, which believes that knowledge and experience are "constituted by" language, can understand preverbal or nonverbal communication. Feminism, focusing on sexual politics, cannot see that sex exists in and through the body. Sexual desire and arousal cannot be fully translated into verbal terms. This is why men and women misunderstand each other. 13

Trying to remake the future, feminism cut itself off from sexual history. It discarded and suppressed the sexual myths of literature, art and religion. Those myths show us the turbulence, the mysteries and passions of sex. In mythology we see men's sexual anxiety, their fear of woman's dominance. Much sexual violence is rooted in men's sense of psychological weakness toward women. It takes many men to deal with one woman. Woman's voracity is a persistent motif. Clara Bow,[3] it was rumored, took on the USC[4] football team on weekends. Marilyn Monroe, singing "Diamonds Are a Girl's Best Friend," rules a conga line of men in tuxes. Half-clad Cher, in the video for "If I Could Turn Back Time," deranges a battleship of screaming sailors and straddles a pink-lit cannon. Feminism, coveting social power, is blind to woman's cosmic sexual power. 14

To understand rape, you must study the past. There never was and never will be sexual harmony. Every woman must be prudent and cautious about where she goes and with whom. When she makes a mistake, she must accept the consequences and, through self-criticism, resolve never to make that mistake again. Running to mommy and daddy on the campus grievance committee is unworthy of strong women. Posting lists of guilty men in the toilet is cowardly, infantile stuff. 15

[3]A movie star from the Roaring Twenties era (editors' note).

[4]University of Southern California (editors' note).

16 The Italian philosophy of life espouses high-energy confrontation. A male student makes a vulgar remark about your breasts? Don't slink off to whimper with the campus shrinking violets. Deal with it. On the spot. Say, "Shut up, you jerk! And crawl back to the barnyard where you belong!" In general, women who project this take-charge attitude toward life get harassed less often. I see too many dopey, immature, self-pitying women walking around like melting sticks of butter. It's the Yvette Mimieux syndrome: make me happy. And listen to me weep when I'm not.

17 The date-rape debate is already smothering in propaganda churned out by the expensive Northeastern colleges and universities, with their overconcentration of boring, uptight academic feminists and spoiled, affluent students. Beware of the deep manipulativeness of rich students who were neglected by their parents. They love to turn the campus into hysterical psychodramas of sexual transgression, followed by assertions of parental authority and concern. And don't look for sexual enlightenment from academe, which spews out mountains of books but never looks at life directly.

18 As a fan of football and rock music, I see in the simple, swaggering masculinity of the jock and in the noisy posturing of the heavy-metal guitarist certain fundamental, unchanging truths about sex. Masculinity is aggressive, unstable, combustible. It is also the most creative cultural force in history. Women must reorient themselves toward the elemental powers of sex, which can strengthen or destroy.

19 The only solution to date rape is female self-awareness and self-control. A woman's number-one line of defense against rape is herself. When a real rape occurs, she should report it to the police. Complaining to college committees because the courts "take too long" is ridiculous. College administrations are not a branch of the judiciary. They are not equipped or trained for legal inquiry. Colleges must alert incoming students to the problems and dangers of adulthood. Then colleges must stand back and get out of the sex game.

Questions for Close Reading

1. What is the selection's thesis? Locate the sentence(s) in which Paglia states her main idea. If she doesn't state the thesis explicitly, express it in your own words.
2. In Paglia's opinion, why are women more "vulnerable and defenseless" now than in the past?
3. According to Paglia, what "truth about sex" has feminism hidden from young women?
4. What does Paglia believe is "the only solution to date rape"?
5. Refer to your dictionary as needed to define the following words used in the selection: *inquests* (paragraph 2), *testosterone* (8), *constituted* (13), *grievance* (15), and *judiciary* (19).

Questions About the Writer's Craft

1. **The pattern.** Examine the way Paglia develops her argument in paragraphs 6 and 8. Which of her assertions in these paragraphs can be assumed to be true without further proof? Why do you think Paglia includes these essentially incontestable statements? Conversely, which of her assertions in paragraphs 6 and 8 require further proof before their truth can be demonstrated? Does Paglia provide such support? Explain.

2. **Other patterns.** How does Paglia use the *comparison-contrast* pattern to develop her argument?

3. Paglia's style is frequently characterized by short sentences strung together with few transitions. Locate some examples of this style. Why might Paglia have chosen this style? What is its effect?

4. Where does Paglia use emotional, highly connotative language? Where does she employ strongly worded absolute statements? Do you think that this use of pathos makes Paglia's argument more or less convincing? Explain.

Writing Assignments Using Argumentation-Persuasion as a Pattern of Development

1. Read Susan Jacoby's "Common Decency" (page 512), an essay that takes exception to Paglia's view of date rape. Decide which writer presents her case more convincingly. Then write an essay arguing that the *other writer* has trouble making a strong case for her position. Consider the merits and flaws (including any logical fallacies) in the argument, plus such issues as the writer's credibility, strategies for dealing with the opposing view, and use of emotional appeals. Throughout, support your opinion with specific examples drawn from the selection. Keep in mind that you're critiquing the effectiveness of the writer's argument. It's not appropriate, then, simply to explain why you agree or disagree with the writer's position or merely to summarize what the writer says.

2. Paglia criticizes those who claim that the environment, or social climate, is primarily responsible for shaping gender differences. She believes that such differences "are based in biology." Write an essay arguing your own position about the role that environment and biology play in determining sex-role attitudes and behavior. Remembering to acknowledge opposing views, defend your own viewpoint with plentiful examples based on your experiences and observations. You may also need to conduct some library research to gather support for your position. The following essays will provide insights that you may want to draw upon in your paper: Kay S. Hymowitz's "Tweens: Ten Going on Sixteen" (page 245), Scott Russell Sanders's "The Men We Carry in Our Minds" (page 295), Patricia Cohen's "Reality TV: Surprising Throwback to the Past?" (page 370), and Natalie Angier's "The Cute Factor" (page 446).

Writing Assignments Combining Patterns of Development

3. Paglia writes in paragraph 7 that "men become masculine only when other men say they are. Having sex with a woman is one way a boy becomes a man." Write an essay constructing your own *definition* of masculinity. Comment on the extent to which you feel being sexually active is an important criterion, but also include other hallmarks and *examples* of masculinity.

4. Date rape seems to be on the rise. Brainstorm with others to identify what may be leading to its growing occurrence. Focusing on several related *factors,* write an essay showing how these factors contribute to the problem. Possible factors include the following: the way males and females are depicted in the media (advertisements, movies, television, rock videos); young people's use of alcohol; the emergence of co-ed college dorms. At the end of the essay, offer some recommendations about *steps* that can be taken to create a safer climate for dating. You should consider supporting your speculations with information about date rape gathered in the library and/or on the Internet.

Writing Assignment Using a Journal Entry as a Starting Point

5. Drawing upon the material in your pre-reading journal entry, write an essay in which you present a carefully considered definition of the term *date rape.* Explain clearly what constitutes date rape and what doesn't. To deepen your understanding of this thorny issue, consider brainstorming with others as well as conducting research in the library and/or on the Internet. One issue to consider: Do males and females define the term differently? If so, how do they define it, and why might their definitions differ?

SUSAN JACOBY

In her first job as a newspaper reporter, Susan Jacoby (1945–) carefully avoided doing "women's stories," believing that such features weren't worthy of a serious journalist. However, Jacoby's opinion changed with the times, especially as women's issues began to gain increasing attention. Indeed, many of her essays—including those in *The New York Times* and *McCall's*—have dealt with women's concerns. Several of Jacoby's essays have been collected in *The Possible She* (1979) and *Money, Manner, and Morals* (1993). In 1994, she coauthored the biography *Soul to Soul: A Black Russian American Family 1865–1992*. Jacoby's most recent books include *Half-Jew: A Daughter's Search for Her Family's Buried Past* (2000) and *Freethinkers: A History of American Secularism* (2004). A contributor to *The Washington Post, The New York Times, Newsday*, and *Vogue*, Jacoby lives in New York City. The following selection, published in *The New York Times* in April 1991, was written in response to the book *Sexual Personae* by Camille Paglia (see page 506).

Pre-Reading Journal Entry

The phrase "boys will be boys" is often cited to explain certain types of male behavior. What kinds of actions typically fall into this category? List a few of these in your journal. Which behaviors are positive? Why? Which are negative? Why?

COMMON DECENCY

She was deeply in love with a man who was treating her badly. To assuage her wounded ego (and to prove to herself that she could get along nicely without him), she invited another man, an old boyfriend, to a dinner *à deux* in her apartment. They were on their way to the bedroom when, having realized that she wanted only the man who wasn't there, she changed her mind. Her ex-boyfriend was understandably angry. He left her apartment with a not-so-politely phrased request that she leave him out of any future plans. 1

And that is the end of the story—except for the fact that he was eventually kind enough to accept her apology for what was surely a classic case of "mixed signals." 2

I often recall this incident, in which I was the embarrassed female participant, as the controversy over "date rape"—intensified by the assault that William Kennedy Smith[1] has been accused of—heats up across the nation. What seems clear to me is that those who place acquaintance rape in a different category from "stranger rape"—those who excuse friendly social rapists on grounds that they are too dumb to understand when "no" means no—are being even more insulting to men than to women. 3

These apologists for date rape—and some of them are women—are really saying that the average man cannot be trusted to exercise any impulse control. Men are nasty and men are brutes—and a woman must be constantly on her guard to avoid giving a man any excuse to give way to his baser instincts. 4

If this view were accurate, few women would manage to get through life without being raped, and few men would fail to commit rape. For the reality is that all of us, men as well as women, send and receive innumerable mixed signals in the course of our sexual lives—and that is as true in marital beds at age fifty as in the back seats of cars at age fifteen. 5

Most men somehow manage to decode these signals without using superior physical strength to force themselves on their partners. And most women manage to handle conflicting male signals without, say, picking up carving knives to demonstrate their displeasure at sexual rejection. This is called civilization. 6

Civilized is exactly what my old boyfriend was being when he didn't use my muddleheaded emotional distress as an excuse to rape me. But I don't owe him excessive gratitude for his decent behavior—any more than he would have owed me special thanks for not stabbing him through the heart if our situations had been reversed. Most date rapes do not happen because a man honestly mistakes a woman's "no" for 7

[1]William Kennedy Smith, the nephew of John, Robert, and Edward Kennedy, was accused of raping a woman in 1991. Kennedy was acquitted, but the trial, broadcast on television, created a national furor and generated heated debate on the issue of date rape (editors' note).

a "yes" or a "maybe." They occur because a minority of men—an ugly minority, to be sure—can't stand to take "no" for an answer.

8 This minority behavior—and a culture that excuses it on grounds that boys will be boys—is the target of the movement against date rape that has surfaced on many campuses during the past year.

9 It's not surprising that date rape is an issue of particular importance to college-age women. The campus concentration of large numbers of young people, in an unsupervised environment that encourages drinking and partying, tends to promote sexual aggression and discourage inhibition. Drunken young men who rape a woman at a party can always claim they didn't know what they were doing—and a great many people will blame the victim for having been there in the first place.

10 That is the line adopted by antifeminists like Camille Paglia,[2] author of the controversial *Sexual Personae: Art and Decadence from Nefertiti to Emily Dickinson*. Paglia, whose views strongly resemble those expounded twenty years ago by Norman Mailer[3] in *The Prisoner of Sex*, argues that feminists have deluded women by telling them they can go anywhere and do anything without fear of rape. Feminism, in this view, is both naïve and antisexual because it ignores the power of women to incite uncontrollable male passions.

11 Just to make sure there is no doubt about a woman's place, Paglia also links the male sexual aggression that leads to rape with the creative energy of art. "There is no female Mozart," she has declared, "because there is no female Jack the Ripper." According to this "logic," one might expect to discover the next generation of composers in fraternity houses and dorms that have been singled out as sites of brutal gang rapes.

12 This type of unsubtle analysis makes no distinction between sex as an expression of the will to power and sex as a source of pleasure. When domination is seen as an inevitable component of sex, the act of rape is defined not by a man's actions but by a woman's signals.

13 It is true, of course, that some women (especially the young) initially resist sex not out of real conviction but as part of the elaborate persuasion and seduction rituals accompanying what was once called courtship. And it is true that many men (again, especially the young) take pride in the ability to coax a woman a step further than she intended to go.

14 But these mating rituals do not justify or even explain date rape. Even the most callow youth is capable of understanding the difference between resistance and genuine fear; between a halfhearted "no, we shouldn't" and tears or screams; between a woman who is physically free to leave a room and one who is being physically restrained.

15 The immorality and absurdity of using mixed signals as an excuse for rape is cast in high relief when the assault involves one woman and a group of men. In cases of gang rape in a social setting (usually during or after a party), the defendants and their lawyers frequently claim that group sex took place but no force was involved. These upright young men, so the defense invariably contends, were confused because the girl had voluntarily gone to a party with them. Why, she may have even displayed sexual

[2]For information on Camille Paglia, see page 506 (editors' note).

[3]An American essayist and novelist (editors' note).

interest in *one* of them. How could they have been expected to understand that she didn't wish to have sex with the whole group?

The very existence of the term "date rape" attests to a slow change in women's consciousness that began with the feminist movement of the late 1960s. Implicit in this consciousness is the conviction that a woman has the right to say no at any point in the process leading to sexual intercourse—and that a man who fails to respect her wishes should incur serious legal and social consequences. 16

The other, equally important half of the equation is respect for men. If mixed signals are the real cause of sexual assault, it behooves every woman to regard every man as a potential rapist. 17

In such a benighted universe, it would be impossible for a woman (and, let us not forget, for a man) to engage in the tentative emotional and physical exploration that eventually produces a mature erotic life. She would have to make up her mind right from the start in order to prevent a rampaging male from misreading her intentions. 18

Fortunately for everyone, neither the character of men nor the general quality of relations between the sexes is that crude. By censuring the minority of men who use ordinary socializing as an excuse for rape, feminists insist on sex as a source of pure pleasure rather than as a means of social control. Real men want an eager sexual partner—not a woman who is quaking with fear or even one who is ambivalent. Real men don't rape. 19

Questions for Close Reading

1. What is the selection's thesis? Locate the sentence(s) in which Jacoby states her main idea. If she doesn't state the thesis explicitly, express it in your own words.
2. Why does Jacoby feel that she doesn't owe her old boyfriend a great deal of gratitude, even though she sent mixed signals about what type of relationship she wanted?
3. What does Jacoby mean in paragraph 6 by her comment, "This is called civilization"? How does this comment support her thesis?
4. Why does Jacoby think that it's insulting to men to accept Paglia's notion that men are ruled by uncontrollable passions?
5. Refer to your dictionary as needed to define the following words used in the selection: *apologists* (paragraph 4), *deluded* (10), *unsubtle* (12), *implicit* (16), *benighted* (18), *erotic* (18), *rampaging* (18), and *ambivalent* (19).

Questions About the Writer's Craft

1. **The pattern.** One way to refute an idea is to carry it to its logical extreme, thus revealing its inherent falsity or absurdity. This technique is called *reduction ad absurdum*. Examine paragraphs 4–5 and 15 and explain how Jacoby uses this technique to refute Paglia's position on date rape.

2. **Other patterns.** Locate places in the essay where Jacoby *compares* and *contrasts* male and female behavior or the behavior of rapists and nonrapists. How does her use of comparison-contrast help her build her argument?

3. What introduction technique (see pages 79–82) does Jacoby use to begin the essay? How does this type of introduction help her achieve her persuasive goal?

4. How would you characterize Jacoby's tone? Identify specific sentences and words that convey this tone. What effect might Jacoby have hoped this tone would have on readers?

Writing Assignments Using Argumentation-Persuasion as a Pattern of Development

1. Jacoby feels that Camille Paglia and others "excuse . . . rapists." If you haven't already done so, read "Rape: A Bigger Danger Than Feminists Know" (page 506) to see what Paglia says about who bears primary responsibility for preventing rape. Then decide to what degree you feel men who commit date rape should be held accountable for their actions. Argue your position in an essay, making reference to both Jacoby's and Paglia's ideas to support your case. Also include reasons and evidence of your own.

2. Determine what your campus is doing about date rape. Does it have a formal policy defining date rape, a hearing process, ongoing workshops, discussions during orientation for incoming students? Write a paper explaining how your college deals with date rape. Then argue either that more attention should be devoted to this issue or that your college has adopted fair and comprehensive measures to deal with the problem. If you feel the college should do more, indicate what additional steps should be taken.

Writing Assignments Combining Patterns of Development

3. Jacoby acknowledges that males and females often send "mixed signals" and cause each other confusion. Select one time that you found "mixed signals" with a person of the opposite sex to be a problem. For example, you might have conflicted because of different ways of expressing anger or because of dissimilar styles in asking for support. *Recount* what happened and explore the *reason(s)* why you think such mixed signals occurred. Before writing the paper, you may want to read "The Men We Carry in Our Minds" (page 295) by Scott Russell Sanders to see what this author has to say about some basic differences between men and women.

4. Interview some people, both males and females, to determine their *definition* of date rape. In an essay, discuss any *differences* between the two sexes' perspectives. That done, present your own definition of date rape, explaining what it is and what it isn't.

Writing Assignment Using a Journal Entry as a Starting Point

5. Some people believe that "boys-will-be-boys" behavior is potentially dangerous and therefore not acceptable. Others argue that it is perfectly innocent and therefore permissible. What do you think? Drawing upon your pre-reading journal entry, write an essay taking a position on this issue. Provide persuasive examples to support your viewpoint, refuting as much of the opposing argument as you can. Discussing the topic with others and doing some research in the library and/or on the Internet will broaden your understanding of this complex issue.

Debating the Issues: Immigration

ROBERTO RODRIGUEZ

Roberto Rodriguez was born in 1954 in Aguacalientes, Mexico, and raised in East Los Angeles. In 1972, he began his journalism career at *La Gente*, a newspaper at the University of California, Los Angeles. He has written for many publications, including *Black Issues in Higher Education, Lowrider* magazine, the *Eastside Sun* (Los Angeles), and *La Opinion*, the largest Spanish-language daily newspaper in the United States. In addition, Rodriguez's columns have been syndicated in *The Washington Post, The Los Angeles Times*, and *USA Today*. Since 1994, he and his wife, Patrisia Gonzales, have written "Column of the Americas," a weblog that focuses on current issues from the perspective of indigenous peoples. Two books he wrote about police brutality were published under one title, *Justice: A Question of Race* (1997). In 2002, Rodriguez and Gonzales were named Distinguished Community Scholars at the Cesar Chavez Center at UCLA, where they are establishing the discipline of indigenous studies. The following article was posted on the "Column of the Americas" website, www.voznuestra.com/Americas, on April 17, 2006.

Pre-Reading Journal Entry

Do you think that schools should engage in discussions of immigration, ethnicity, and racism, which can be sensitive and painful topics? Why do you feel as you do? Would such discussions be appropriate at some levels of school but not at others? Take some time to explore these questions in your journal.

THE BORDER ON OUR BACKS

1 Look up the word *Mexican* or *Central American* in any U.S. political dictionary and you will find these definitions:

> 1) people who are illegal, or are treated as such, no matter how long they've been living in this country; 2) the nation's number one threat to homeland security; 3) people who do the jobs no Americans want and who threaten the American Way of Life; 4) as a result of extremist politicians, the nation's favorite scapegoats; and 5) people, who due to vicious anti-immigrant hysteria, are prone to become Democrats.

2 By next year, there may be two new entries: 6) Peoples who carry the border on their backs, and 7) peoples not afraid to stand up for their rights.

3 Who could have predicted that millions of peoples would be taking to the streets nationwide to protest draconian immigration bills that call for the building of Berlin-style walls, more *migra*,[1] massive repatriations, the criminalization of human beings and the creation of a new anti-family apartheid-style Bracero[2] or Guest Worker program? Beyond the bills, the protests are actually about asserting the right—virtually a cry—to be treated as full human beings.

4 How long was this community supposed to remain in silence?

5 Perhaps it is racial/cultural fatigue.

6 Let's not pretend that this hysteria is not about race, color and dehumanization. It's not even anti-immigrant or even anti-Latino/Hispanic bigotry. It's the exploitation of a deep-seated fear and loathing of Mexicans and Central Americans by shameless politicians. Why? Because of what our color represents. Otherwise, how and why do government agents single us out at lines, borders and internal checkpoints? Otherwise, why do dragnet immigrant raids always target brown peoples? Why is all the hate and vilification directed at brown peoples and the southern border? Otherwise, why are these politicians also not bothered by the millions of Canadians, Europeans or Russians who overstay their visas? (No one should hate them either.)

7 Just what does brown represent in this country? Shall we delude ourselves like the Census Bureau and pretend that we're actually White?

8 Or should we simply stop speaking our languages, stop eating our own foods . . . and stop identifying with our home countries of Mexico, El Salvador, Guatemala, Peru, Colombia, etc. In other words, we're OK if we stop being who we are—if we culturally deport ourselves and conduct auto ethnic cleansing campaigns (we're also OK if we fight their illegal permanent wars).

9 And yet, there's that small matter of our red-brown skin. Just what could it possibly represent? A reminder? Memory? Might it be our thousands-of-years old Indigenous cultures—the ones that were supposedly obliterated—the ones we were supposed to reject?

---

[1]Mexican term for "immigration police" (editors' note).

[2]Latin American migrant worker (editors' note).

We deny the nopal[3] no longer. We know full well we're not on foreign soil, but on 10
Indian lands. (Were we supposed to forget that too?) So there's no going back. If anything, we are back. The whole continent, the whole earth—which our ancestors have traversed for thousands of years—is our mother. Meanwhile, we watch Congress and the president do a dance about not pardoning or not granting amnesty to those who've been remanded to live in shadows. Sinverguenzas![4] Just who precisely needs to be pardoned? Those who are exploited and who've been here forever . . . or those who've been complicit in our dehumanization?

Through all this, we've been baited into fighting with African Americans, 11
American Indians, Asians, Mexican Americans, and poor and white middle class workers—because Mexicans supposedly steal their jobs and are ruining the quality of life.

The truth is, American Indians, African Americans and Asians should be at the 12
head of our protests—for it is they and their struggles against dehumanization that we draw inspiration from. But in the end, it is those who allow extremists to speak in their name, who must also step forward and tell their representatives that a society divided into legal and illegal human beings is no longer acceptable.

Every cell in our bodies tells us this. And the unprecedented protests have cre- 13
ated the consciousness that a two-tiered society—the definition of apartheid—is intolerable.

A flawed bill will pass—many bills will pass—yet some sectors of the population 14
will continue to view and treat Mexicans/Central Americans as illegal, unwanted and subhuman.

But enough. Ya Basta! IKUALI![5] As is said at the rallies: Nosotros no somos ilegales 15
ni inmigrantes. Somos de este continente.[6] We are neither illegal nor even immigrants. Tojuan Titehuaxkalo Panin Pacha Mama.[7]

---

[3]Literally, "prickly pear." There is a common Mexican expression, "Pareces que tienes el nopal en la frente," which literally translated means "It appears you have a prickly pear on your forehead." Idiomatically, the meaning is "You appear to be Indian, yet you deny it" (editors' note).

[4]Mexican expression meaning "Scoundrels!" (editors' note).

[5]*Ya basta* is Spanish and *ikuali* is Nahuatl (the Aztec language) for "enough" (editors' note).

[6]Spanish for "We are neither illegal nor immigrants. We are from this continent" (editors' note).

[7]Nahuatl for "We are from this earth" (editors' note).

Questions for Close Reading

1. What is the selection's thesis? Locate the sentence(s) in which Rodriguez states his main idea. If he doesn't state his thesis explicitly, express it in your own words.
2. What is the meaning of the essay's title, "The Border on Our Backs"?
3. According to Rodriguez, how are American policies on illegal immigrants similar to apartheid?

4. According to Rodriguez, who should be the inspiration for illegal Mexican and Central American immigrants in the United States? Why?

5. Refer to your dictionary as needed to define the following words used in the selection: *scapegoats* (paragraph 1), *draconian* (3), *repatriations* (3), *apartheid* (3), *bigotry* (6), *dragnet* (6), *vilification* (6), *delude* (7), *indigenous* (9), *obliterated* (9), *traversed* (10), *amnesty* (10), *remanded* (10), and *complicit* (10).

Questions About the Writer's Craft

1. Rodriguez opens his essay with some definitions of *Mexican* and *Central American* that he claims can be found in any U.S. political dictionary. How effective is this opening? What tone does it set for the remainder of the essay?

2. **The pattern.** What evidence does Rodriguez cite to support his claim that American attitudes toward immigrants from Mexico and Central America are fundamentally racist? How effective is this evidence and the way it is presented? What is the balance between *logos* and *pathos* here?

3. Rodriguez uses many words and phrases in Spanish and Nahuatl throughout the essay without translating them. How effective is this use of language? What does it suggest about the audience for which he is writing?

4. **The pattern.** What fallacies, if any, are in this argument? Explain the nature of the fallacy or fallacies.

Writing Assignments Using Argumentation-Persuasion as a Pattern of Development

1. Rodriguez argues that the struggle of illegal immigrants is similar to the struggle of American Indians, African Americans, Mexican Americans, and other American groups who have fought against dehumanization (paragraphs 11 and 12). Do you agree? Focusing on a specific group of disadvantaged Americans, write an essay in which you support or challenge Rodriguez's argument. To ensure that your position is more than a reflexive opinion, conduct some library research on the group in question, and read Star Parker's "Se Habla Entitlement" (page 521), an essay that is in sharp opposition to Rodriguez's. No matter which side you take, assume that some readers are opposed to your point of view. Acknowledge and try to dismantle as many of their objections as possible. Refer, whenever it's relevant, to Parker's argument in your paper.

2. Rodriguez suggests that racial profiling at the U.S. borders unfairly targets people of color and is used by politicians to exploit whites' fears (paragraph 6). In recent years, racial profiling has been used by many law enforcement agencies to identify suspected criminals and terrorists as well as illegal immigrants,

although many people dispute both the fairness and the effectiveness of the technique. Do some research on racial profiling and then write an essay arguing that racial profiling is (or is not) a fair and effective method of identifying people who are likely to be criminals. Your essay can focus on the issue of racial profiling in general, or it can focus on a particular use of racial profiling. In your essay, you should acknowledge and refute as many opposing arguments as possible.

Writing Assignments Combining Patterns of Development

3. Rodriguez believes that illegal immigrants should stand up for their right to be treated as "full human beings." Select a group that you believe is disadvantaged and should stand up for its rights. Possibilities include a specific racial, ethnic, or religious group; the disabled; the overweight; those in abusive relationships. Write an essay explaining some specific *steps* these groups could take to secure their rights. Conclude your paper by discussing the *effects* of winning such rights. What would be gained? What, if anything, would be lost? Before writing, read one or more of the following essays to sharpen your understanding of disadvantaged people and the struggle for human rights: "The Fourth of July" by Audre Lorde (page 208), "Charity Display?" by Charmie Gholson (page 220), Toni Morrison's "A Slow Walk of Trees" (page 364), and Brent Staples's "Black Men and Public Space" (page 412).

4. Rodriguez refers to Mexicans and Central Americans as threatening the American Way of Life (paragraph 1). Write an essay in which you *define* what the American Way of Life means to you. Along the way, *compare* and/or *contrast* your definition with what you think is the prevailing definition of this term. To illustrate your definition, provide *examples* and/or *stories*. Your essay can be serious, humorous, or satiric in tone.

Writing Assignment Using a Journal Entry as a Starting Point

5. Write an essay arguing that schools should or should not encourage students to discuss immigration, ethnicity, and racism. Review your pre-reading journal entry, and select a specific level of schooling to focus on before taking a position. Supplement the material in your journal by gathering the opinions, experiences, and observations of friends, family, and classmates. No matter which position you take, remember to cite opposing arguments, refuting as many of them as you can. Before writing, consider reading "Free-Speech Follies" (page 495), in which Stanley Fish forcefully argues that free speech in student publications must be balanced by good judgment.

STAR PARKER

Star Parker, born in 1957, is the founder and leader of the Coalition on Urban Renewal and Education, a nonprofit organization that advocates on issues of race, poverty, education, and inner-city neighborhoods. At one time a single mother living on welfare in Los Angeles, Parker eventually returned to college for a bachelor's degree in marketing. She went on to establish an urban Christian magazine and become a strong advocate for conservative Christian political views. In 1992, her business was destroyed in the Los Angeles riots. This experience intensified her focus on faith-based and free-market approaches to solving the problems of poverty. As a social policy consultant, Parker frequently appears on national television and radio stations, including CNN, MSNBC, and Fox, and she often testifies before Congress. Parker is a syndicated columnist and has published three books: *Pimps, Whores, and Welfare Brats: From Welfare Cheat to Conservative Messenger* (1998), *Uncle Sam's Plantation: How Big Government Enslaves American's Poor and What We Can Do About It* (2003), and *White Ghetto: How Middle Class America Reflects Inner City Decay* (2006). This opinion piece was published on WorldNetDaily.com, an independent news website, on April 18, 2006.

Pre-Reading Journal Entry

The issue of immigration—especially questions of who should be permitted into the country and who should be permitted to stay—has recently been hotly debated both by politicians and pundits and by everyday people. What do you think would happen if U.S. immigration laws were strictly enforced and those who were here illegally were sent back to their home countries? What positive effects would there be? What negative effects would there be? What do you think would happen if all immigrants who were here illegally were allowed to stay and start the process of becoming citizens? Take some time to respond to these questions in your journal.

SE HABLA[1] ENTITLEMENT

1 When it comes to matters of economy, I think of myself as libertarian. I believe in free markets, free trade and limited government. But I must confess, our Latino neighbors are challenging my libertarian instincts regarding our immigration conundrum.

2 The recent pro-immigration demonstrations around the country have been a major turnoff.

3 There is something not convincing about illegal immigrants demonstrating to claim they have inalienable rights to come here, be here, work here, become citizens here—and make all these claims in Spanish.

4 Hearing "We Shall Overcome" in Spanish just doesn't provoke my sympathies. I don't buy that, along with life, liberty and the pursuit of happiness, our Creator

[1]Spanish for "is spoken" (editors' note).

endowed anyone with the right to sneak into the United States, bypass our laws and set up shop. Maybe our immigration laws do need fixing. But this is a discussion for American citizens. In English.

This could be the finest hour for the political left if we really can be convinced that illegal immigration is a right, that those here illegally are innocent victims, and that the real guilt lies with U.S. citizens who believe our laws mean something and should be enforced. 5

Draping these bogus claims in the garb of the civil-rights movement is particularly annoying. 6

The civil-rights movement was about enforcing the law, not breaking it. The Civil War amendments to the Constitution were not getting the job done in what has been a long struggle in this country to treat blacks as human beings. If Americans were kidnapping Mexicans and selling them into slavery here, I might see the equivalence. But these are free people, who chose to come here and chose to do so illegally. 7

Just considering Mexicans, how can we understand their taking to the streets of our country to demand rights and freedom when they seem to have little interest in doing this where they do have rights, which is in Mexico? There is no reason why Mexico, a country rich in beauty and natural resources, cannot be every bit as prosperous as the United States. 8

It's not happening because of a long history of mismanagement, corruption and excessive government. Although Mexico is a democracy, for some reason Mexicans seem to need to be north of the Rio Grande to get politically active and demand the benefits of a free society. 9

Last year the Pew Hispanic Center surveyed adults in Mexico and asked them if they would come to the United States if they had the means and opportunity to do so. Forty-six percent responded yes. Almost half of Mexican adults said they'd rather live here! When asked if they would do it illegally, more than 20 percent said yes. 10

Yet in the contest for the Mexican presidency, the leading candidate is a leftist former mayor of Mexico City who is polling in the high 30s.[2] 11

Maybe you can figure out why almost half of Mexican adults say they would rather live in the United States, presumably because of the opportunities our free society affords, yet vote for a leftist candidate who will continue policies in Mexico that choke off any prospect for growth, prosperity and opportunity. 12

So forgive me for being a little suspicious of the wholesome picture being painted of these folks who are pouring across our border allegedly just to be free, work and maintain traditional families. 13

Anyone who lives in Southern California, as I do, knows that the Latino-immigrant community is far from the paragon of virtue that the forces who want to encourage open borders would have us believe. I see much of the same troubling behavior that blacks get tarred with. Much of the gang behavior in Los Angeles, unfortunately, is Latino-related. The L.A. Unified School District is over three-quarters Latino, who drop out at the same alarming 50 percent rate as inner-city blacks. Out-of-wedlock births among Hispanic women approach 50 percent. 14

---

[2]With a very narrow margin, the more conservative Felipe Calderon ultimately defeated the leftist Andres Manuel Lopez Obrador in the Mexican presidential election of 2006.

15 Those who want to hoist the banner of the Statue of Liberty, Ellis Island and the American tradition of immigration should remember that when immigrants were passing through Ellis Island at the early part of the last century, the federal government accounted for about 3 percent of the American economy. Today it is 25 percent.

16 Part of the package deal that comes with showing up in the United States today is our welfare state as well as our free economy. Illegal status is really a temporary situation, anyway. Illegal immigrants' children who are born here are U.S. citizens. Significant demands are being made on our tax dollars in the way of schools, health care and government services, including law enforcement.

17 Yes, let's encourage freedom. But freedom is a privilege and a responsibility.

18 We have enough people already here who think it's all about entitlement.

Questions for Close Reading

1. What is the selection's thesis? Locate the sentence(s) in which Parker states her main idea. If she doesn't state her thesis explicitly, express it in your own words.
2. Why does Parker object to pro-immigration demonstrators adopting the strategies of the American civil rights movement?
3. In paragraph 15, Parker contrasts the size of the federal government a hundred years ago with its size now. To what does she attribute its increase?
4. Why does Parker object to the feeling of entitlement that she claims immigrants have?
5. Refer to your dictionary as needed to define the following words used in the selection: *entitlement* (title), *libertarian* (paragraph 1), *conundrum* (1), *inalienable* (3), *provoke* (4), *bogus* (6), *garb* (6), and *paragon* (14).

Questions About the Writer's Craft

1. **The pattern.** Which of the two possible strategies for organizing a refutation (see pages 468–469 does Parker use in her essay? Do you consider the points she makes in the refutation sufficiently persuasive? Explain.
2. **Other patterns.** In paragraph 14, Parker compares and contrasts the Latino and African American communities of southern California. What is the purpose of this comparison? How effective is it?
3. The second paragraph of the Declaration of Independence begins: "We hold these truths to be self-evident, that all men are created equal, that they are endowed by their Creator with certain unalienable Rights, that among these are Life, Liberty and the pursuit of Happiness." There are echoes of this

sentence in paragraphs 3 and 4 of Parker's essay. What is the effect of her adopting this vocabulary?

4. Throughout the essay, Parker uses language that describes her reactions to pro-immigration demonstrations and arguments: "a major turnoff" (paragraph 2), "not convincing" (3), "doesn't provoke my sympathies" (4), "particularly annoying" (6), and "a little suspicious" (13). What do these phrases contribute to the tone of the essay? How do they help Parker communicate her argument more convincingly?

Writing Assignments Using Argumentation-Persuasion as a Pattern of Development

1. Parker, an African American, claims to have been "turned off" by the pro-immigration demonstrations that took place in spring of 2006 in an attempt to influence immigration legislation pending in Congress. She objects to the pro-immigration movement's adoption of the strategies of the American civil rights movement—the language, the demonstrations, and the songs sung in Spanish. In contrast, in "The Border on Our Backs" (page 517), Roberto Rodriguez, a Mexican American, is elated by these demonstrations, claiming that immigrants are finally asserting their human rights in the great tradition of the civil rights movement. What do you think of demonstrations in the United States by illegal immigrants? Do you sympathize with the immigrants' arguments? Do you think their demonstrations further the immigrants' cause, or set it back? Write an essay in which you argue that demonstrations by illegal immigrants are (or are not) justified and appropriate, citing at least two or three reasons for your position. Be sure to support your reasons with examples wherever possible.

2. Parker characterizes herself as a libertarian in matters of economics. Libertarians advocate that individuals should be free to do whatever they want with themselves and their property, as long as they do not infringe on the liberty of others. Libertarians also believe that people are responsible for their own actions. They strongly oppose welfare programs, which they believe force taxpayers to provide aid to others. In fact, Parker's final reason for opposing illegal immigrants is that they contribute to the growth of the welfare state (paragraphs 15 and 16). Write an essay supporting or opposing the libertarian position on the welfare state. Argue that government does (or does not) have the responsibility to help individuals in times of need (poor economic conditions, disability, and natural disasters, for example). Be sure to address whether the effect on individuals of such government assistance is empowering—or whether it perpetuates dependence. Use specific examples to support your position.

Writing Assignments Combining Patterns of Development

3. Imagine what your life would be like if you moved to another state or country alone or just with your immediate family. Then write an essay in which you provide *examples* showing how your life would or would not change if you moved to a strange place. Consider the language barrier, if any, in your education, your work, your friendships, and your family life. Reach some conclusions about the overall *effect* of making this move, including whether life would be easier or more difficult. Before writing, consider reading "Euromail and Amerimail" (page 375), in which Eric Weiner explores an important cultural difference.

4. Choose a social program or common practice that involves the concept of entitlement. For example, among social programs you could choose affirmative action, Medicaid, Medicare, welfare, or unemployment insurance. Among common practices you might select nepotism (favoring relatives or friends when hiring), legacy admissions to colleges (admitting the children of alumni), or illegal campaign contributions. Research the program or practice on the Internet or in the library. Write an essay in which you explain the *effects* of such a program or practice on recipients. *Compare* and *contrast* the benefits and drawbacks of receiving such an entitlement. Finally, *argue* that the program or practice should be continued or abolished.

Writing Assignment Using a Journal Entry as a Starting Point

5. Review your journal entries about the possible effects of deporting illegal immigrants or allowing them to stay, also called *amnesty*. The last amnesty in the United States took place in 1986 and was granted to immigrants who could prove they had resided here for five years or more. Amnesty is always controversial. Some argue that granting amnesty rewards illegal behavior and encourages more illegal immigration. Others argue that regularizing the status of long-time illegal residents simply provides them with a path for becoming full citizens, upholding the ideals of an open and democratic society. Write an essay in which you *argue* either in favor of or against an amnesty for current illegal immigrants who have resided in the United States for at least five years. In addition to discussing the *effects* of allowing immigrants to stay that you outlined in your journal entry, do some research on the 1986 amnesty to understand its *effects*. If they are still relevant today, use them to support your point of view about amnesty.

ADDITIONAL WRITING TOPICS: ARGUMENTATION-PERSUASION

General Assignments

Using argumentation-persuasion, develop one of the following topics in an essay. After choosing a topic, think about your purpose and audience. Remember that the paper's thesis should state the issue under discussion as well as your position on the issue. As you work on developing evidence, you might want to do some outside research. Keep in mind that effective argumentation-persuasion usually means that some time should be spent acknowledging and perhaps refuting opposing points of view. Be careful not to sabotage your argument by basing your case on a logical fallacy.

1. Hiring or college-education quotas
2. Giving birth control to teenagers
3. Prayer in the schools
4. Gay marriage
5. Reinstating the military draft
6. Penalties for plagiarism
7. Increasing the retirement age
8. Spouses sharing housework equally
9. Smoking in public places
10. Big-time sports in college
11. File-sharing on the Internet
12. Drugs and alcohol on campus
13. Requiring college students to pass a comprehensive exam in their majors before graduating
14. Putting elderly parents in nursing homes
15. Financial aid for college students
16. Stay-at-home dads
17. Telecommuting
18. Campaign finance reform
19. Removing term limits for elected officials
20. Voter apathy

Assignments with a Specific Purpose, Audience, and Point of View

On Campus

1. Your college's financial aid department has decided not to renew your scholarship for next year, citing a drop in your grades last semester and an unenthusiastic recommendation from one of your instructors. Write a letter to the Director of Financial Aid arguing for the renewal of your scholarship.

2. You strongly believe that a particular policy or regulation on campus is unreasonable or unjust. Write a letter to the Dean of Students (or other appropriate administrator) arguing that the policy needs to be, if not completely revoked, amended in some way. Support your contention with specific examples showing how the regulation has gone wrong. End by providing constructive suggestions for how the policy problem can be solved.

At Home or in the Community

3. You and one or more family members don't agree on some aspect of your romantic life (you want to live with your boyfriend/girlfriend and they don't approve; you want to get married and they want you to wait; they simply don't like your partner). Write a letter explaining why your preference is reasonable. Try hard to win your family member(s) over to your side.

4. Assume you're a member of a racial, ethnic, religious, or social minority. You might, for example, be a Native American, an elderly person, a female executive. On a recent television show or in a TV commercial, you saw something that depicts your group in an offensive way. Write a letter (to the network or the advertiser) expressing your feelings and explaining why you feel the material should be taken off the air.

On the Job

5. As a staff writer for an online pop-culture magazine, you've been asked to nominate the "Most Memorable TV Moment of the Last 50 Years" to be featured as the magazine's lead article. Write a letter to your supervising editor in support of your nominee.

6. As a high school teacher, you support some additional restriction on students. The restriction might be "no cell phones in school," "no T-shirts," "no food in class," "no smoking on school grounds." Write an article for the school newspaper justifying this new rule to the student body.

For additional writing, reading, and research resources, go to **www.mycomplab.com** and choose **Nadell/Langan/Comodromos'** ***The Longman Writer,*** **7/e**.

PART IV

THE RESEARCH PAPER

19

Locating, Evaluating, and Integrating Research Sources

"Go ask your search engine."

If you're like many of the students we know, **research papers** probably make you nervous. Why, you may wonder, do instructors assign them? Such projects take time, and the payoff, you may feel, doesn't seem worth the effort. If this *is* how you feel, we hope to show you that conducting research and writing up your findings can be rewarding, even fun.

Aside from enabling you to experience the joys of unearthing useful material during research, writing a research paper enlarges your perspective. As you test your own views against existing evidence, evaluate conflicting opinions, and learn how to detect other people's biases, you acquire analytic skills that will benefit you throughout life. In everyday conversation, most of us feel free to voice all kinds of opinions, even if they're based on nothing more than emotion and secondhand information. Researched opinions, though, are sounder and more logical. They're based on authoritative evidence rather than on limited personal experience, on fact rather than on hearsay. Simply put, researched opinions emerge from a careful consideration of the evidence.

All of this may sound intimidating, but keep in mind that writing a research paper essentially expands what you already know about writing essays; many of the steps are the same. The two major differences are the greater length of the research paper—usually five or more pages—and the kind of support you offer for your thesis. Rather than relying on your own experience or that of friends or family, you use published information and expert opinion to support your thesis. Even so, writing a research paper can be a challenge. One way to make the project more manageable is to view it as a process consisting of two major phases: (1) the **research stage,** when you find out all you can about your subject and identify a working thesis, and (2) the **writing stage,** when you present in an accepted format what you've discovered. This chapter focuses on the first stage; the next, Chapter 20, examines the second stage. Although we discuss the research process as a series of steps, we encourage you to modify the sequence to suit your subject, your personal approach to writing, and the requirements of a particular assignment.

During the first stage of the research process, you do the following:

- Plan the research
- Find sources in the library and on the Internet
- Prepare a working bibliography
- Take notes to support the thesis with evidence

PLAN THE RESEARCH

Understand the Paper's Boundaries

Your first step in planning the research is to *clarify the project's requirements.* How long is the paper supposed to be? How extensively should you deal with opposing viewpoints? Are there any restrictions about the number and type of sources? Are popular magazines, books, and websites acceptable, or should you use only scholarly sources? Has the instructor limited your subject choices?

Also, be sure you *understand the paper's overall purpose.* Unless you've been assigned a purely informative report ("explain several psychologists' theories of hostility"), your research paper shouldn't simply display all the information you have gathered. Instead of merely patching together ideas from a variety of sources, you should develop your own position, using outside sources to arrive at a balanced but definitive conclusion.

One more point: You should be aware that most instructors expect students to use the third-person point of view in research papers. If you plan to include any personal experiences, observations, or interviews (see the following page and page 581) along with your outside research, ask your instructor whether the use of the first-person point of view would be appropriate.

Understand Primary Versus Secondary Research

You should determine whether your instructor expects you to conduct any **primary research**—information gathered from firsthand observations, personal interviews, and the like. Most college research papers involve **library** or **secondary research**—information gathered secondhand from published print sources or from the Internet (see pages 547–556). Such material includes information derived from published accounts, including statistics, facts, case studies, expert opinion, critical interpretations, and experimental results. Occasionally, though, you may want or be asked to conduct primary research. You may, for example, run an experiment, visit an organization, observe a situation, schedule an interview, or conduct a survey. In such cases of primary research, you'll need to prepare carefully and establish a strict schedule for yourself. (See page 581 for hints on incorporating primary research into a paper.)

Conducting Interviews in Person, by Phone, and by E-Mail

If you plan to go on an information-gathering interview, put some careful thought into how you will proceed. If you use a letter or e-mail message rather than a telephone call to request an interview, get feedback on the message's overall effectiveness before sending it. When you set up your appointment, request enough time (30–60 minutes) to discuss your topic in depth; keep in mind, however, that the person may not be able to set aside as much time as you'd like. If you hope to record the interview, you must obtain permission to do so beforehand. (Some organizations don't permit employees to be recorded during interviews.) Also, when making the appointment, ask if you may quote the person directly; he or she is entitled to know that all comments will be "on the record."

Most important, plan the interview carefully. First, determine what you want to accomplish: Do you want to gather general background material or do you want to clear up confusion about a specific point? Then, well in advance of the interview, prepare a list of questions geared toward that goal. During the interview, though, remain flexible—follow up on interesting remarks even if they diverge somewhat from your original plan. (If you discover that your interviewee isn't as informed as you had hoped, graciously request the names of other people who might help you further.) Throughout the interview, take accurate and complete notes (even if you're recording—equipment sometimes fails!) If certain remarks seem especially quotable, make sure you get the statements down correctly. Finally, soon after the interview ends, be sure to fill in any gaps in your notes.

If a face-to-face interview isn't feasible, a phone interview often will provide the information you need. Don't, however, call the person and expect a phone interview on the spot. Instead, call, explain the kind of help you would like, and see if the person is willing to schedule time to talk at a later date.

Another way to conduct an interview is by e-mail. Your e-mail correspondence should describe the topic you're researching, explain your reasons for establishing contact, and list clearly and concisely the information you would like the interviewee to provide. It's also a good idea to give the date by which you hope he or she can get back to you.(For additional information about the Internet and e-mail interviews, see pages 547–556).

Conducting Surveys

A survey helps you gather a good deal of information from many people (called "respondents")—and in a much shorter period of time than would be needed to interview each person individually. Bear in mind, though, that designing, administering, and interpreting a survey questionnaire are time-consuming tasks that demand considerable skill. Be sure, then, to have someone knowledgeable about surveys evaluate both your questionnaire and the responses it evokes.

When you write your survey questions, make them as clear and precise as possible. For example, if your goal is to determine the frequency with which something occurs, do not ask for vague responses such as "seldom," "often," and "occasionally." Instead, ask the respondents to identify more specific time periods: "weekly," "1–3 times a week," "4–6 times a week," and "daily." Also, steer away from questions that favor one side of an issue or that restrict the range of responses. Consider the following survey questions:

> Should already overburdened college students be required to participate in a community-service activity before they can graduate?
>
> Yes___________ No___________ Maybe___________
>
> In your opinion, how knowledgeable are college students about jobs in their majors?
>
> Knowledgeable___________ Not knowledgeable___________

Both of the preceding questions need to be revised. The first, by assuming that students are "already overburdened," biases respondents to reply negatively. To make the question more neutral, you would have to eliminate the prejudicial words. The second question asks respondents to answer in terms of a simple contrast: "Knowledgeable" or "Not knowledgeable." It ignores the likelihood that some respondents may wish to reply "Very knowledgeable," "Somewhat knowledgeable," and so on.

You should include in your survey only those items that will yield useful information. For example, in a survey of students, you would ask respondents some questions about their age, college year, major, and so forth—as long as you planned to break responses into subgroups. But these questions would be unnecessary if you didn't intend to analyze responses in such a manner. In any case, be sure to limit the number of questions you ask. If you don't, you may find that sorting out the responses will be too time-consuming a task.

Unless you're able to survey every member of the group whose opinions you seek, you must poll a *representative subgroup*. By *representative*, we mean "having characteristics similar to the group as a whole." Imagine you're writing a research paper on unfair employment practices. As part of your data collection, you decide to poll students on campus about their job experiences. If you, a first-year student, give the questionnaire only to students in your introductory courses, your sample won't be representative of the student body as a whole. Upper-level students might have significantly different work experiences and thus quite different opinions about employer fairness. So, to gauge students' attitudes with accuracy, you'll have to hand out your survey in numerous places and on varied occasions on the campus. That way, your responses will be drawn from the whole spectrum of undergraduate backgrounds, majors, ages, and so forth.

This method of collecting student responses still wouldn't amount to what is called a *random sample*. To achieve a random sample, you must choose respondents by a scientific method—one that would, theoretically, give each person in the group to be studied the chance to respond. For example, to survey undergraduates on your campus, you would have to obtain a comprehensive list of all enrolled students. From this list, you would pick names at a regular interval, perhaps every tenth; to each tenth person, you would deliver (or mail or e-mail) a survey, or you would telephone to ask the questions orally. With this method, every enrolled student has the potential of being chosen as a respondent. Survey software such as SurveyMonkey (*www.surveymonkey.com*) makes it relatively easy to distribute a survey via e-mail and then to analyize the results.

Since there's so much time and, possibly, cost involved in doing a random sample, you'll most likely use an informal method of collecting responses. Using the "street corner" approach, you might hand your survey to passersby or to people seated in classes, in student lounges, and so on. Or, if you're collecting information about the service provided at a particular facility, you might (with permission) place a short questionnaire where respondents can pick it up, quickly fill it out, and return it. Because of your informal methods, your results would be an *approximate* portrait of the group polled; however, the more people you survey, the more accurate your profile of the larger population is likely to be. (See page 581 for hints on incorporating survey results into a research paper.)

Once you're sure of the paper's boundaries and understand your instructor's expectations regarding primary and secondary research, it's time for you to move on. At this point, you'll need to (1) choose a general subject, (2) limit that subject, (3) conduct preliminary research, (4) identify a working thesis, and (5) make a schedule.

CHOOSE A GENERAL SUBJECT

Your instructor may provide a list of acceptable topics for a research paper, or you may be free to select a topic on your own. In the latter case, your second step in planning the research is to *choose a general subject*. If you have an area of interest—say, Native American culture or animal rights—the subject might be suitable for a research paper. If you don't immediately know what you'd like to research, consider current events, journal entries, the courses you're taking, the reading you've done on your own, or some of the selections in this book. A sociology course may have piqued your interest in child abuse or the elderly. Current events might suggest research on immigration or business ethics. Several of your journal entries may focus on an issue that concerns you—maybe, for example, use of drugs in college athletics. Perhaps you've come across a provocative article on genetic engineering or the nation's health-care crisis. Maybe you find yourself disagreeing with what Clifford Stoll suggests about classroom computer use in "Cyberschool" on page 328 of this book. (In the activities at the end of this chapter, you'll find a list of suggested research topics derived from the readings in this text.)

If you're still not sure of what subject to research, do some background reading on several possible general subjects. Also try using one or more prewriting techniques to identify areas that interest or puzzle you. Brainstorming, questioning, freewriting, and mapping (see pages 26–29) should help you generate ideas worth exploring. As soon as you have a list of possible topics, use the following checklist to help you determine which of these subjects would or would not be appropriate for a research paper.

SELECTING AN APPROPRIATE SUBJECT TO RESEARCH: A CHECKLIST

- ☐ Will you enjoy learning about the subject for the substantial period of time you'll be working on the research paper? If you think you might get bored, select another subject.
- ☐ Can you obtain enough information on the subject? Recent developments (an ongoing government scandal or a controversial new program to help the homeless) can be investigated only through mass-circulation newspapers and magazines. Books as well as specialized or scholarly journal articles on recent events may not be available for some time.
- ☐ Has the topic been researched so often (the legalization of marijuana, violence in sports) that there's nothing new or interesting left to say about it?
- ☐ Is the topic surrounded by unreliable testimony (ESP, UFOs, the Bermuda Triangle), making it unsuitable for a research paper?
- ☐ Is the topic (a rock star's conflict with the recording industry, for example) too trivial for an academic project?
- ☐ Does the subject lend itself to or call for research? If it doesn't, think about selecting another topic. For example, the dangers of smoking are now almost universally acknowledged and so probably wouldn't make an appropriate topic for a research paper.
- ☐ Has the topic been written about by only one major source? If so, your research will be one-sided.
- ☐ Can you be objective about your topic? Researching both sides of an issue about which you feel strongly usually deepens your understanding of the issue's complexity. But if you feel so committed to a point of view that you'll have trouble considering opposing opinions, it's best to avoid that subject altogether.

Once you have a general topic in mind, you may want to clear it with your instructor. Or you can wait until the next stage to do so—after you've narrowed the topic further.

Prewrite to Limit the General Subject

The next step is to *limit* or *narrow your topic*. "Pollution" is too broad a topic, but "The Effect of Acid Rain on Urban Structures" poses a realistic challenge. Similarly, "Cable Television" is way too general, but "Trends in Cable Comedy" is manageable. Remember, you aren't writing a book but a paper of probably five to fifteen pages.

Sometimes you'll know the particular aspect of a subject you want to explore. Usually, though, you'll have to do some work to restrict your subject. In such cases, try using the prewriting techniques of questioning, mapping, freewriting, and brainstorming described in Chapter 2. Discussing the topic with other people and doing some background reading on your subject can also help focus your thinking. (For more on limiting general subjects, see pages 26–30).

Conduct Preliminary Research

Frequently, you won't be able to narrow your topic until you learn more about it. When that's the case, background reading, often called **preliminary research,** is necessary. Just as prewriting precedes a first draft, preliminary research precedes the in-depth research you conduct further along in the process.

At this point, you don't have to track down highly specialized material. Instead, you simply browse the Internet (see pages 547–556) and skim books and mass-market or newspaper articles on your topic to get an overview and to identify possible slants on your subject. If your broad subject is inspired by a class, you can check out the topic in your textbook. And, of course, you can consult library sources—the *computerized catalog, the reference section*, and *periodical indexes* such as the *Readers' Guide to Periodical Literature*. All of these sources break broad subjects into subtopics, thus helping you focus your research. These and other library resources, discussed in greater detail later in the chapter, are among the most valuable tools available to researchers.

After you locate several promising books or articles on your general subject, glance through the material rapidly to get a sense of issues and themes. Do the sources suggest a particular angle of inquiry? If you don't find much material on your subject, think about selecting another topic, one about which more has been written.

While conducting preliminary research, there's no need to take notes, unless you want to jot down possible limited topics. However, you should keep an informal record of the books and articles you skim. In a computer file, in a notebook, or on index cards (one for each source), note the following information: For each book, record the author, title, and call number; for each article, record the publication, date, and page numbers. Such basic information will help you relocate material later on, when you'll need to look at your sources more closely. Also, it's a good idea to jot down the authors and titles of other works mentioned in the sources you skim. You may decide to consult them at another point. All this information can help you start a working bibliography (see page 556) when you begin your actual research.

Once you arrive at your limited topic—or several possibilities—ask your instructor for feedback, listening carefully to any reservations he or she may have about your idea. Moreover, even though you've identified a limited subject, don't be surprised if it continues to shift and narrow further as you go along. Such reshaping is part of the research process.

Identify a Working Thesis

Once you have done some preliminary research on your limited topic and have determined there's sufficient material available, your next step is to form a **working thesis**—an idea of your own that is in some way original. Having a tentative thesis guides your research and helps you determine which sources will be appropriate. However, general statements like "Congress should not make further cuts in social programs," and "Prayer in public schools should not be allowed" are so broad that they fail to restrict the scope of research. Whole books have been written on welfare, just one of many social programs. Be sure, then, that your working thesis focuses on a *limited subject*. The thesis should also take a stand by *expressing your point of view, or attitude, about the subject.* Note the difference between the broad statements above and the effective limited thesis statements that follow (the limited subjects are underlined once, the attitudes twice):

> The Congressional decision to reduce funding of school lunch programs has had unfortunate consequences for disadvantaged children.

> A moment of silence in public schools does not violate the constitutional separation of church and state.

It's important for you to view your working thesis as tentative; you probably won't have a thesis until your research is almost complete and all the facts are in. Indeed, if your thesis *doesn't* shift as you investigate your topic, you may not be tapping a wide enough range of sources, or you may be resisting challenges to your original point of view. *Remember*: Gathering information with a closed mind undermines the purpose of a research project.

In its *final* form, your thesis should accomplish at least one of three things. First, it may offer your personal synthesis of multiple findings, your own interpretation of "what it all means." Second, it may refine or extend other people's theories or interpretations. Third, it may offer a perspective that differs from or opposes the one you find expressed in most of your sources. (For more on thesis statements, see pages 36–42).

Make a Schedule

Having identified your working thesis, you're nearly ready to begin the research stage of your project. Before you begin, though, *make a schedule*. First, list what you need to do. Then, working back from your paper's due date, set rough time limits for the different phases of the project. For a paper due December 4, you might create the following four-week schedule.

November 13	Locate relevant periodicals and books.
November 23	Read materials and take notes.
November 25	Locate additional information—interviews, and so on.
November 29	Write a first draft.
December 1	Revise the draft.
December 3	Edit, print, and proofread the paper.
December 4	Submit the paper.

FIND SOURCES IN THE LIBRARY

Now is the time to start your research in earnest. Always keep in mind that you're looking for material to support your working thesis. What should you do if you come across material that contradicts your thesis? Resist the temptation to disregard such material. Instead, evaluate it as objectively as you can, and use it to arrive at a more valid statement of your thesis.

Even if your paper contains some primary research, most of your information-gathering will take place in your college library. Most college libraries contain several floors of bookshelves (often called *stacks*), with fiction and nonfiction arranged according to the Dewey Decimal or Library of Congress system of classification (see pages 539–540). You'll also find sections for periodicals, microfilm and microfiche files, reference works, reserved books, government documents, rare books, and the like. Special collections may be housed in the main library or elsewhere; for example, an extensive music library may be located in the music department. In any case, the main library catalog lists all the material contained in such special collections.

The Computerized Catalog

Most college libraries have **computerized catalogs** of their book holdings, some of which can even be accessed online. You'll be pleased to learn that most computerized systems are equipped with on-screen prompts that make it easy to search for sources. Even so, don't wait until your paper is due to familiarize yourself with your college's online catalog system. It can be overwhelming to learn the system *and* conduct research at the same time. Instead, early in the academic year, spend an hour or so at the library. Take an orientation tour, read any handouts that are provided, speak to the librarian, and experiment with the system. The confidence you gain will make all the difference when you begin researching in earnest.

A typical online catalog search is by *author*, *title*, or *subject*. If you're searching by author or title, you type into the search box the author's first and last names or the title, respectively. If you're searching by subject, you type in a key word or phrase that summarizes your topic. You may have to try several key terms to discover under which term(s) the catalog lists sources on your topic. Assume you're conducting research to identify classroom strategies that undermine student success. You type the word *Education*. But that word would probably yield so many possibilities that you wouldn't know where to start. You might narrow your search by keying in "teaching techniques," "classroom practices," or "academic failure." For help in identifying appropriate key terms, speak with your college librarian. He or she will probably have you consult the *Library of Congress Subject Headings* or a bound or on-screen thesaurus of headings used in your library's database.

One other point: When you search for a book by subject, the screen will usually indicate narrower subheadings under that topic. As soon as one of those subheads is clicked, the screen provides a list of books on that subject. To get complete bibliographic information about a specific book, follow the computer's instructions. The book's publisher, publication date, call number, and so on will then appear on the screen. Most computerized catalogs also indicate the status of a book—whether it is out on loan, overdue, lost, or available.

A Sample Search

Figure 19.1 on the following page shows the steps in a search of the Library of Congress catalog found at *www.loc.gov*. As the largest library in the world, the Library of Congress catalogs more than 134 million items, including more than 20 million books. Many of these resources are made available to other libraries through interlibrary loans. The library also provides links to online resources. Your college library catalog search may be similar to this search in many respects.

Suppose you are researching the thesis "Public sentiment toward the military draft is determined primarily by whether a war is perceived to be just." You decide to explore the response to the draft during the Civil War. At the Library of Congress site, you would click on "Library Catalogs" and then on "Guided Search" to do a keyword search. A search for "Civil War" and "draft" yields 115 items dating back into the 1800s. You choose to display the items in descending order of date, in order to see the most recent items first. Scanning the list, you find this entry:

```
The New York City draft riots : their significance for American
society and politics in the age of the Civil War / Iver
Bernstein.
```

Clicking on the title produces a screen with a brief record for the book. You can click on a "Brief record" tab to get to the screen shown in Figure 19.2. For this particular book, you can click on "Publisher description" to get an idea of the scope of the book and on "Contributor biographical information" to find out that the

FIGURE 19.1
Sample Library Catalog Search

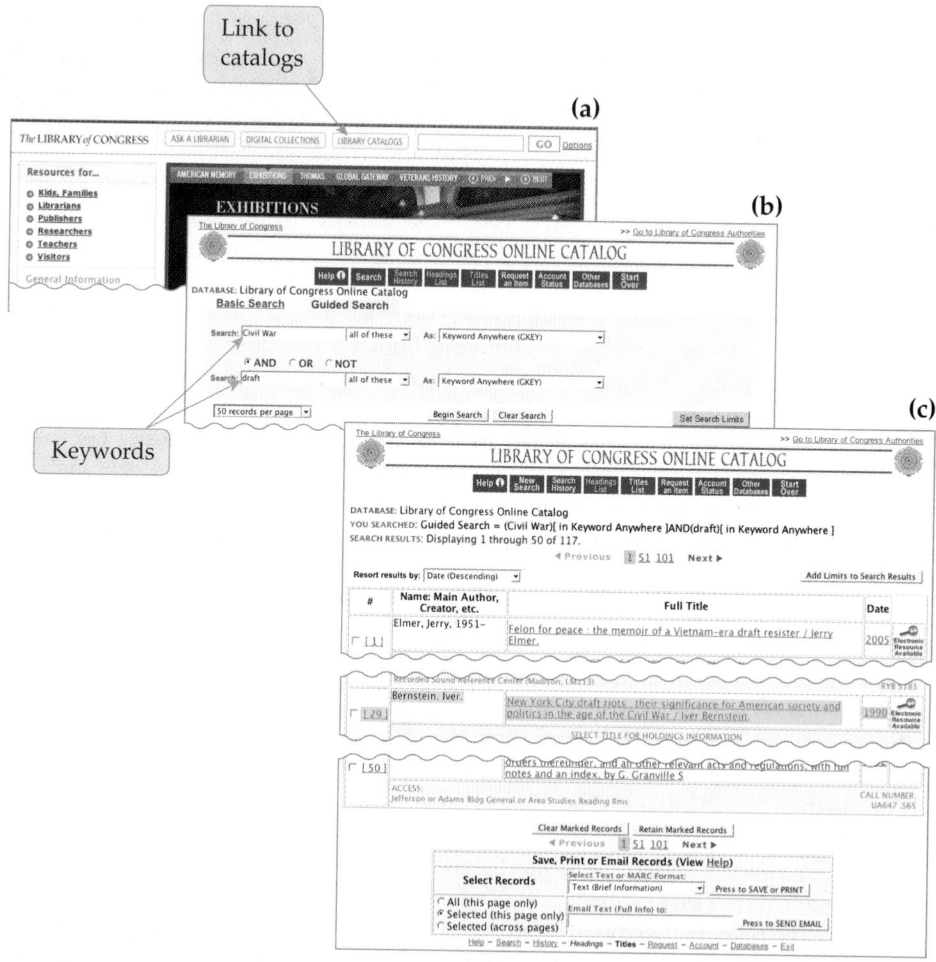

Most computerized library catalogs lead users step by step through the search process. (a) At the Library of Congress site, you would click on "Library Catalogs." (b) At the search page, you would enter your search terms. (c) This catalog also allows you to sort the items by descending date order so you can find the most recent materials. Most systems allow you to print selected information or e-mail it to yourself.

author is a noted academic author. You can also click on the "Call number" (see pages 539–540) and "Subject" links to get to more resources on the same topic. If you decide that you would like to examine the book, you can print the record or e-mail it to yourself, and then ask your librarian to help you get the book.

By mastering your library's computerized catalog, you'll find that it will take only minutes to identify a large number of sources. One caution, however, about computerized catalogs: Few libraries have their entire collections online.

FIGURE 19.2
Sample Catalog Source Record

Brief Record | Subjects/Content | Full Record | MARC Tags

The New York City draft riots : their significance for American society and...

LC Control No.: 89002858
Type of Material: Book (Print, Microform, Electronic, etc.)
Personal Name: Bernstein, Iver.
Main Title: The New York City draft riots : their significance for American society and politics in the age of the ***Civil War*** / Iver Bernstein.
Published/Created: New York : Oxford University Press, 1990.
Description: ix, 363 p., [8] p. of plates : ill. ; 25 cm.
ISBN: 0195050061 (alk. paper) :
Links: Publisher description
Contributor biographical information

CALL NUMBER: F128.44 .B47 1990
Copy 1
-- Request in: Jefferson or Adams Bldg General or Area Studies Reading Rms
-- Status: Not Charged

CALL NUMBER: F128.44 .B47 1990 FT MEADE
Copy 2
-- Request in: Main or Science/Business Reading Rms - STORED OFFSITE
-- Status: Not Charged

◀ Previous Next ▶

Save, Print or Email Records (View Help)
Select Download Format: Text (Brief Information) | Press to SAVE or PRINT
Email Text (Full Info) to: | Press to SEND EMAIL

The brief catalog record gives important information, including the call number. You can also click on the link at "Subjects" to get to more resources on the same topic.

Special collections and older books may not be included. You'll have to use the traditional card catalog to track down those sources not covered by the computerized catalog. Ask a librarian for help.

How to Find a Book

To locate a book on the shelves, use its **call number.** Besides appearing in the computerized catalog, the call number is printed on the spine of the book. There are two systems of call numbers in use in the United States: the **Dewey Decimal** and the **Library of Congress.** Most college libraries use the latter system, though some still reference older books by the Dewey Decimal system and more recent acquisitions by the Library of Congress. Check with the librarian to see which system(s) your library uses. Listed here are both systems' call numbers and the subjects they represent:

Dewey Decimal System

000–099	General Works
100–199	Philosophy and Psychology
200–299	Religion
300–399	Social Science
400–499	Language
500–599	Pure Science
600–699	Technology (Applied Sciences)
700–799	The Arts
800–899	Literature
900–999	History

Library of Congress System

A	General works—Polygraphy	M	Music
B	Philosophy—Religion	N	Fine Arts
C	History—Auxiliary Sciences	P	Language and Literature
D	History and Topography (except America)	Q	Science
E–F	America	R	Medicine
G	Geography—Anthropology	S	Agriculture—Plant and Animal Industry
H	Social Sciences	T	Technology
J	Political Science	U	Military Science
K	Law	V	Naval Science
L	Education	Z	Bibliography and Library Science

Once you have a book's call number, consult a map or list posted near the card catalog to determine the book's location in the stacks or ask the librarian. In libraries with closed stacks, make out a call slip so that a member of the staff can get the book for you.

If you can't find a book in the stacks, check the tables and shelves nearby. If you still can't locate the book, consult the person at the circulation desk. If the book has been checked out, you can usually fill out a form (by hand or online) to have the current borrower notified that you're waiting for the book, which will be held for you as soon as it is returned. You might also check with a librarian to see if the book has been put on reserve or moved to a special collection, or if it is available through an inter-library loan system. Sometimes, all you need to do is type the book's call number into the computerized system, and the computer screen will tell you whether the book has been checked out, moved to a special location, or lost.

The Reference Section

Some reference works (*Encyclopaedia Britannica* and the *World Almanac and Book of Facts*) cover a wide range of subjects. Others (*Mathematics Dictionary* and *Dance Encyclopedia*) are more specialized. Despite these differences, all reference volumes present significantly condensed information. They provide basic facts but not much interpretation. Explanations are brief. Most reference works are, then, unsuitable as sources for in-depth research. In fact, they're usually omitted from the list of Works Cited at the end of a paper. However, though they have limitations, reference volumes can sometimes be useful.

How do you track down reference works that might be helpful? Start by looking up your subject in your library's computerized catalog. Record the call numbers and titles of those books marked "Ref" (Reference). The Library of Congress call number for reference is "Z," but a library may keep only some of its "Z" books in the reference section and the rest in the stacks. Most libraries arrange reference shelves alphabetically by subject ("Art," "Economics," "History"), which makes it easy to browse for other useful references once you've identified one on a subject. Keep in mind that reference materials don't circulate; that is, they cannot be checked out, so you must consult them while in the library.

Listed here are some of the common reference books found in most college libraries:

Biography
International Who's Who
Who's Who in America

Business/Economics
Dictionary of Banking and Finance
Encyclopedia of Economics

Ethnic/Feminist Studies
Encyclopedia of Feminism
Harvard Encyclopedia of American Ethnic Groups

Fine Arts
New Grove Dictionary of American Music
The Harvard Dictionary of Music
The Oxford Dictionary of Art
The Thames & Hudson Dictionary of Art Terms

History/Political Science
Editorials on File
Encyclopedia of American Political History
Facts on File
Political Handbook of the World

Literature/Film
The Oxford Companion to American Literature
The Oxford Companion to English Literature
World Encyclopedia of Film

Philosophy/Religion
A Dictionary of Non-Christian Religions
Encyclopedia of American Religions
Encyclopedia of Philosophy

Psychology/Education
Encyclopedia of Education
Encyclopedia of Psychology
Encyclopedia of Special Education

Science/Technology/Mathematics
Dictionary of Mathematics
Encyclopedia of Medical History
McGraw-Hill Encyclopedia of Science & Technology
The Merck Index

Social Sciences
The Dictionary of Anthropology
Encyclopedia of Crime & Justice
International Encyclopedia of the Social Sciences

Periodicals

Periodicals are publications issued at periodic (regular or intermittent) intervals throughout the year. There are three broad types of periodicals: general, scholarly, and serious (see also Figure 19.3).

Periodical Indexes, Abstracts, and Bibliographies

Periodical indexes, updated anywhere from every week to once a year, are cumulative directories that list articles published in certain journals, newspapers, and magazines. In addition, major newspapers, including *The New York Times*,

FIGURE 19.3
Types of Periodicals

	General Periodicals	Scholarly Periodicals	Serious Periodicals
Intended audience	Average reader	Readers with specialized knowledge	Well-educated laypeople
Examples of publications	Daily newspapers and magazines such as *Time, Psychology Today*, and *The New York Times*	Academic journals such as *Journal of Experimental Child Psychology, Renaissance Drama*, and *Veterinary Medicine*	Newsstand publications such as *National Geographic, Scientific American*, and *Smithsonian*
Writing style	Personal or anecdotal	Objective	Generally objective
Types of articles	Easy-to-read overviews of subjects with some background information	In-depth analyses developed with facts, studies, and well-reasoned commentary	Articles with less depth than in scholarly periodicals but with a broader perspective
Authors	Usually generalists or journalists rather than experts	Authorities in the field	Authorities in the field or specialized journalists
Documentation	Inadequate: Poses difficulty tracking down sources and verifying information	Complete: Sources fully documented	Mostly adequate: Documentation often not as complete in scholarly publications

This chart describes the types of periodicals students are likely to encounter while researching topics for college papers.

publish annual subject directories. Most periodical indexes arrange listed articles under subject headings. Beneath the headings, individual articles are organized alphabetically by authors' last names.

A growing number of college libraries now offer computerized searches of many of the major indexes, abstracts, and bibliographies listed on pages 543–544. In most cases, libraries provide computer terminals with Internet connections, allowing users to access up-to-date online periodical index databases. In some libraries, a database that groups directories alphabetically by subject is maintained in the same system as the computerized catalog for books (see pages 536–539). In other libraries, there may be a separate bank of terminals for searching periodical directories. These terminals are usually connected to an online database or to a **CD-ROM** player containing compact discs on which periodical indexes are stored.

Your library may keep hard copies of some periodical indexes in a periodicals room; a separate, alphabetically arranged section in the reference room; or in closed stacks. Occasionally, you may find the periodical index to a highly specialized field shelved in the stacks near books in the same field of study. Check with the librarian for the right location.

You're probably familiar with two indexes—the *Readers' Guide to Periodical Literature* and *InfoTrac*. They list general-interest articles published by popular newsstand magazines, such as *U.S. News & World Report* and *Sports Illustrated.* When you were in high school, you probably used the *Readers' Guide* or *InfoTrac* because they index accessible, nontechnical publications. To locate articles appropriate for college-level research, you'll need to consult indexes that list articles from more academic, professional, and specialized publications. The college equivalents of the *Readers' Guide* and *InfoTrac* are the *Humanities Index* and the *Social Sciences Index*. You should become familiar with these indexes as well as with the main indexes for the field in which you plan to major.

Some specialized indexes provide brief descriptions of the articles they list. These indexes are usually called **abstracts.** Examples are *Abstracts of Folklore Studies, Criminal Justice Abstracts*, and *Biological Abstracts*. Abstracts usually contain fewer listings than other types of indexes and are restricted to a limited field. In contrast to indexes that list only articles, **bibliographies** like the *Modern Language Association International Bibliography* list books as well as articles.

Listed here are representative indexes, abstracts, and bibliographies found in most college libraries. To save time, check with the librarian to see which of these sources can be accessed electronically at your library or by Internet connection from your own computer (see page 544).

General

Academic Search FullTEXT
Biography Index
BSCOhost
Humanities Index
InfoTrac Academic Index
InfoTrac Magazine Index
InfoTrac National Newspaper Index
Magazine Index Plus
The New York Times Index
News Bank
Readers' Guide to Periodical Literature
Social Sciences Index
Speech Index

Arts/Literature

Art Index
Book Review Digest
Film International Index
Modern Language Association (MLA) International Bibliography
Music Catalogue
The New York Times Book Review Index
Play Index

Business/Economics

Business Periodicals Index
The Economist Index
Wall Street Journal Index

History, Political Science, Government

Historical Abstracts
Government Publications Index
Political Science Abstracts
Public Affairs Information Service
Vertical File Index

Education

Education Index

ERIC (Educational Resources Information Center)

Philosophy/Religion

Philosopher's Index

Religion Index

Psychology/Religion

PsychArticles

SocioFile

Sciences

Applied Science and Technology Index

Biological Abstracts

Computer Database

Engineering & Applied Science Index

Environment Index

Health Index

Medline

Women's and Ethnic Studies

Bibliography on Women

Black Studies Database

Ethnic Newswatch

Hispanic American Periodicals Index

Women's Studies

More and more libraries offer Internet access to databases located off campus. These Internet-access databases not only list the titles of specific journal articles but also print out the articles themselves. Some major online databases are Dialog, Wilsonline, LexisNexis, and EBSCOhost.

As you no doubt realize, library technology is changing rapidly. At some colleges, book catalogs and major reference works—as well as periodical indexes, abstracts, and bibliographies—are available not just on the library's computer terminals but also remotely via the Internet. With remote access, students can conduct much of their research from their bedrooms at any time of the day or night. (For more information on accessing electronic information, see pages 547–556.)

Using Computerized and Printed Indexes

Besides saving time, computerized directories have the advantage of being current. Most are updated monthly (unlike print volumes, which are generally updated quarterly or annually). Plus, in many libraries the computer terminals at which you view database listings are connected to printers, so you can print out the listings or send them to your e-mail address. Some online databases offer access to the full text of selected articles or books. You may read these on the screen, e-mail them to yourself, or print them out. Even when the full text isn't available, you may have the option of accessing the abstract of a work that seems promising. Remember, though, that an abstract is simply a summary. Although it can help you decide whether you should track down the original complete text, an abstract can't be cited as a source in your paper.

Being able to print out the computerized text of work that originally appeared in print form is, of course, a real time-saver. However, computerized text can have drawbacks. Unless articles are shown in PDF (personal document format), original page breaks may not be noted. (PDF shows documents as facsimiles of the printed page.) So, you may have no way of knowing where one page ends and another begins and consequently won't be able to provide exact page numbers of specific passages for your readers.

In addition, many computerized databases catalog only recent material, from the past few years or decades. When researching a topic with a historical component, you may find computerized indexes inadequate. For instance, to discover how J. D. Salinger's novel *The Catcher in the Rye* was received when it first appeared in 1951, you would need to identify articles and reviews written in that year. Bound volumes of the *Modern Language Association International Bibliography*, *Book Review Index*, and *The New York Times Book Review Index* would provide you with the needed information.

Whether a periodicals directory is in computerized or print form, you can search by subject (or keywords) to uncover titles of relevant articles. If you don't find your subject listed in a printed index, or if a computerized database yields no titles when you type in keywords, try alternate terms for your topic. Suppose you're researching the subject of business ethics. In addition to using "Business ethics" as your subject heading or keywords, you might try "Bribery" or "Fraud" to find relevant articles. Both computerized and print indexes also show cross-references. By looking under "Business ethics," you might see suggested search terms such as "Advertising ethics," "Banking, ethical aspects," and "Commercial crime."

Periodical directories in print form list articles alphabetically, both by subject and by author. Under each subject, articles are listed alphabetically by title. When using a computerized guide to articles in periodicals, type in either an author's name or your subject. The database will then list appropriate articles, usually in reverse chronological order (most recent first). The precise procedures for searching computerized databases vary; libraries usually post instructions for the particular databases they offer.

Figure 19.4 on the following page shows an entry from the computerized database EBSCOhost. The entry gives an abstract of the article and a link to a replica (PDF version) of the article as it originally appeared in the journal. It also gives, under "Source," all the information you need to track down the article in the print journal in a library if the text is not available online. By clicking on "Subject Terms" links, you can get to additional resources.

If you see puzzling abbreviations or symbols in computerized guides, ask your librarian either to explain their meaning or to direct you to a printed key for an explanation.

Be sure not to end your search for appropriate material until you've consulted the most pertinent indexes and bibliographies. For a paper on the psychology of child abuse, you might start with *The New York Times Index* and then move to more specialized volumes, such as *Psychological Abstracts, Child Development Abstracts*, and *Mental Health Book Review Index*. To ensure that you don't miss current developments in your subject area, always start with the most recent years and work your way back.

Locating Specific Issues of Periodicals

If you can't print out computerized text of relevant articles, you'll need to obtain the original text. To do so, you first have to determine whether your library owns the specific periodicals and the issues you want. If your library

FIGURE 19.4
Sample Database Search

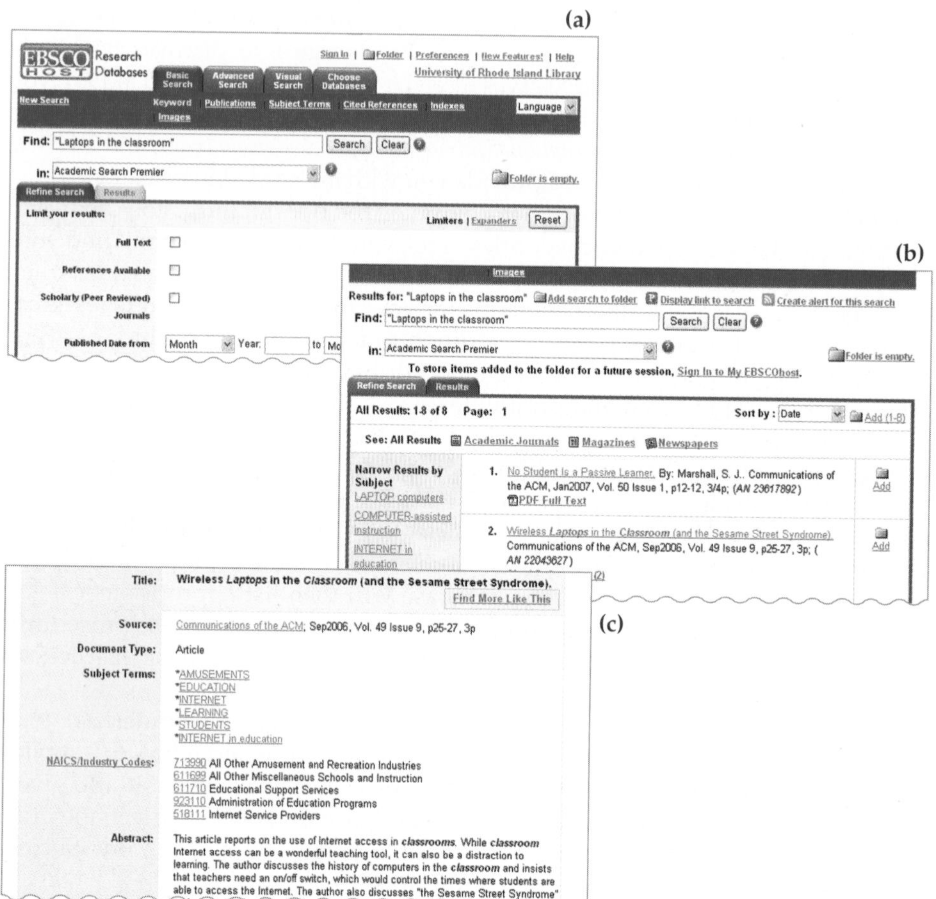

Databases such as EBSCOhost function similarly to your library's catalog. (a) At the home page for EBSCOhost, you would type in your search terms. (b) The results of the search would be listed. (c) From the results page, you would click on the item you are interested in. The listing for an item found on EBSCOhost allows you to view the full text as it appeared in the journal (PDF file), find more items by the same author, find more items on similar subjects, and print or e-mail the record. The accession number (labeled "AN" on the results page) enables you to easily find the article on EBSCOhost again.

catalogs its periodicals online, search for a periodical by typing in its name. Does that particular name appear on screen? If it does, your library owns issues of that publication. With a few additional keystrokes, you can obtain more detailed information—such as the specific volumes held by your library and the periodical's call number and location in the library.

If your library doesn't catalog its periodicals online, check with your librarian. He or she will direct you to a card catalog, a computer printout, a spiral-bound volume, or some other source that lists the library's periodicals.

Recent issues of magazines, newspapers, and journals are kept in the library's current periodicals section, where they are arranged alphabetically by name. Less current issues can be found in the periodicals room, in the stacks, or on microfilm. Bound volumes of periodicals don't circulate. Back issues of major newspapers are usually stored on microfilm filed in cabinets in a separate location.

USE THE INTERNET

Nothing demonstrates the staggering impact of the computer revolution more powerfully than the growth of the **Internet.** This global network of interlinked computer systems puts a massive storehouse of information within the reach of anyone with access to a personal computer and an Internet connection. Such a wealth of material presents obvious research benefits to you as a student. However, when faced with the task of using the Internet, you may feel overwhelmed and unsure of how to proceed. The following pages will show you how to access and evaluate Internet resources.

The Internet and the World Wide Web

The Internet is the global electronic network that links individual computer networks at tens of thousands of educational, scientific, state, federal, and commercial agencies in more than 250 countries and regions around the world. While the **World Wide Web** exists on the Internet, the two are not synonymous. The Internet is the nuts-and-bolts of the network: the cables and computers. The World Wide Web is one of several information-sharing systems existing on the Internet. The Web consists of uncounted millions of **websites.** Some websites feature text only; others contain graphics; still others contain audio and video components. Although there's great variation in the content and design of websites, nearly all contain a *home page* (generally modeled after the contents page of a book) that provides the site's title, introductory descriptive material about the site, and a menu consisting of **links** to other pages on the site or to related websites. (For more on links, see page 551.)

What the Web Offers

While often compared to a library, the Web is more accurately thought of as an enormous storage shed, piled to the ceiling with boxes and crates and items of every description. Because it's not subject to a central system of organization, and because anyone—from preteens to Nobel Prize winners to representatives of the most extreme fringe groups—can post material on it at any time, the Web is in a state of constant flux. The quality of information found online ranges from authoritative to speculative to fraudulent. It's impossible to say with certainty even how large the Web is. Billions of pages of data may appear on the millions of websites in operation.

What can be stated with confidence is that the World Wide Web offers a collection of data that surpasses anything the world has ever seen. With the click of a mouse, you can read electronic versions of *The Washington Post* or *The London Times*; you can search thousands of documents published by federal, state, and local governments and agencies throughout the world; you can check the temperature in Moscow or get up-to-the-minute stock quotes in Hong Kong; you can scan breaking news from the Associated Press or learn the latest information on alternative treatments for arthritis.

The Advantages and Limitations of the Library and the Web

The availability of the Web makes doing research over the computer an attractive option. But that doesn't mean that libraries have become obsolete. Both the library and the Web have strengths and weaknesses. Depending upon your topic and its focus, one may be a better starting point than the other. Here are some issues to consider:

- The library is *consistently organized*. With some guidance from the catalog system and the reference librarian, you can quickly locate materials that are relevant to your topic.
- Because the Web *doesn't have a centralized organizational structure*, you are automatically—and somewhat haphazardly—exposed to a staggering array of material. If you're not sure how to focus your topic, browsing the Web may help you narrow your topic by identifying directions you wouldn't have thought of on your own. Conversely, the sheer volume of material on your subject may leave you stunned and glassy-eyed, the information overload making you feel all the more confused about how to proceed.
- Some sources in the library may be dated or even no longer accurate. By contrast, online material is usually up-to-date because it can be posted on the Web as soon as it's created. (See page 555 for hints on evaluating the currency of electronic data.)
- The instantaneous nature of Web postings can create problems, though. Library materials certainly aren't infallible, but most have gone through a process of editorial review before being published. This is often *not* the case with material on the Web. Most of us realize that the claim "I saw it in the newspaper!" doesn't ensure that information is accurate or valid. "I saw it on the Web!" is even less of a guarantee. Given this basic limitation, it's a

good idea not to rely solely on the Web when you research your topic. Consider using it as a supplement to, rather than a substitute for, library research. (For more about evaluating the validity of material on the Web, see page 555.)

Using Online Time Efficiently

The Internet is known as the "information superhighway," and the analogy is a good one. Like any superhighway, the Internet has its rush hours and even its periods of gridlock. The checklist that follows offers some suggestions to keep you cruising in the express lane.

USING ONLINE TIME EFFICIENTLY: A CHECKLIST

- ☐ Experiment with logging on at different times of day and evening. Typically, evening hours (approximately 6 p.m. to 10 p.m.) are times of peak Internet traffic. If you have trouble getting through to particular sites, you may have more success earlier in the day or later at night.
- ☐ If it takes more than a couple of minutes to retrieve files from a website, hit the "Stop" or "Cancel" button and try again later.
- ☐ If you don't need to see the graphics (illustrations, photographs, charts, and so on) included in a website, check if your browser offers a "text only" option. If it does, activate that option. Waiting for graphics to download can increase your online time substantially.
- ☐ Just as you do when conducting library research, be sure to record sufficient information about your online source so you can provide full documentation when it comes time to write your paper. Specifically, when you print information from the Web, make sure your browser is set so that the material's title, date, and page as well as the date of your retrieval appear on the printed copy. You also need to check that the **URL** (*uniform resource locator*), or **Internet address,** appears clearly on the copy. Having the address makes it possible for you to return to the site in the future.

It's critical that you type in an address exactly as it appears on the website's home page. Keying in even slight changes in the address usually makes it impossible to access the site. The easiest way to ensure that you get the address correct is to electronically highlight and copy it directly from the address line on the Web page.

Here is an address—broken down into elements—for an editorial column by Fouad Ajami in the May 13, 2007, edition of the news magazine *U.S. News & World Report*:

http://www.usnews.com/usnews/news/articles/070513/21fouad.htm

http:	For "hypertext transfer protocol": tells computers how to transfer the information.
www.	Indicates the site is located on the World Wide Web.
usnews.com	Internet address of the organization (in this case, *U.S. News & World Report*). The *.com* portion, or domain name, indicates the type of organization. The primary domains are as follows: *.com*—commercial *.edu*—educational institutions *.gov*—government *.mil*—military *.net*—Internet service providers *.org*—nonprofit organizations
usnews/news/articles/ 070513/21fouad.htm	Indicates where the site's files are stored, the path to those files, and the name of the particular file being retrieved. (The *.htm*—often written as *html*—stands for *hypertext mark-up language*, the language in which these particular Web pages are written.)

When you find a website that you like and may want to visit again, use your browser's **Bookmark** or **Favorite Places** option to save the address in your personal file. This way, you can click on its name and instantly return to the site.

Using the Net to Find Materials on Your Topic

What do you do if you want to go online to track down articles, speeches, legislation, TV transcripts, and so on about your subject? How, given the overwhelming array of online material, can you identify sources that will be pertinent? Search directories and search engines will help.

Search Directories

A **search directory,** a service that organizes websites by categories, will begin pointing you in the right direction. If you're not sure how to narrow your topic, the search directory's categories may help you by identifying directions you wouldn't have thought of on your own. New search directories crop up regularly, but one of the most popular and user-friendly is Yahoo (*http://www.yahoo.com*). You can get to Yahoo's directory from the Yahoo home page by clicking on "More" and then "Directory."

Making Use of Links on the Web. Yahoo divides websites into fourteen categories: Arts & Humanities, Business & Economy, and so on. Each category is presented as a **link** (see page 547). Typically, a link shows up as an underlined word or phrase that may be a different color from the type elsewhere on the page. When you click on a link, you're transported to a more focused list of websites to choose from. As you move from link to link, you move from the general topic to more specific aspects of the topic. For example, say you're researching athletes' use of drugs. Clicking on "Recreation & Sports" takes you to the directory, where you can click on "Sports" and then "Drugs in Sports." You're then presented with a screen that gives links to a number of sites relevant to your topic (see Figure 19.5 on the following page).

General Search Engines

Search directories like Yahoo are wonderful tools when you begin exploring your topic. But when you're refining your investigation, you'll want to use another kind of resource: **search engines.** Search engines—the most popular of which is Google—comb through the vast amount of information on the Web for sites or documents that match your research needs. You activate a search engine by typing in key words or phrases that tell the engine what to look for. Increasingly, search engines and search directories are combined, making it possible to access both from one site's home page. Some popular search engines and search directories, and their Web addresses, follow.

About at *www.about.com*
AltaVista at *www.altavista.com*
Excite! at *www.excite.com*
Google at *www.google.com*
Lycos at *www.lycos.com*
Refdesk at *www.refdesk.com*
Yahoo! at *www.yahoo.com*

Tips for Using Search Engines. When you reach the home page of a search engine, it's a good idea to click on the "Help" or "Tips" button to receive specific guidelines for using that particular search engine efficiently. As you proceed, don't forget to "bookmark" (see page 550) the search engines you use so you can return to them easily at a later date.

On a search engine's home page look for the empty box where you type in the keyword(s) describing your research topic. After you click on the "search" command, the engine scans the Web for your keyword(s). It then provides you with a list of "hits," or links, to websites where your keyword is found. Most search engines also provide a brief description of each site.

How to Limit Your Search. The success of your search depends on how carefully you follow your search engine's guidelines and on how specific and descriptive your search terms are. For example, say you're doing research on

FIGURE 19.5
Sample Internet Directory Search

Subdirectories get increasingly detailed and specific. (a) At the "Recreation & Sports" subdirectory, you can click on "Sports" to get access to thousands of sites about that subject. (b) The extensive "Sports" directory indicates that the "Drugs in Sports" link will provide links to thirteen sites. (c) On the "Drugs in Sports" page, you can link directly to relevant sites.

college financial aid. Depending upon your search engine, if you simply enter the words *college financial aid* in the search box, the engine may provide a list of every document that contains the word *college* or *financial* or *aid*—hundreds of thousands of hits. Again, the most efficient way to limit the number of hits you get is to follow with great care your search engine's specific guidelines. If no guidelines are provided or if the guidelines are confusing, try the following suggestions.

FOCUSING A WEB SEARCH: A CHECKLIST

- ☐ Put quotation marks around the phrase you are searching for—in this case, "college financial aid." Many search engines interpret the quotation marks to mean you want only those documents that include the complete phrase *college financial aid*. If you don't include the quotation marks, you may receive listings for each word.
- ☐ To focus your search further, use the plus (+) and minus (−) signs, leaving no space before or after the signs. Say you're interested in college financial aid as it applies to tuition grants. Try typing this in the search box:

  "college financial aid"+grants

- ☐ The + sign between *college financial aid* and *grants* instructs the search engine to locate items that contain both sets of keywords. A minus (−) sign has the opposite effect. If you want information about college financial aid, *excluding* information about grants, you would type your search phrase like this:

  "college financial aid"−grants

- ☐ Use the Boolean operative words AND, OR, and NOT to limit your search. (Boolean logic is named for the nineteenth-century mathematician George Boole.) For some sites, using these words between key terms broadens or narrows the range of your search. For example, assume you typed the following: reggae music AND Rastafarians AND Jamaica. Using the operative *AND* instructs the search engine to return only those documents containing all three search terms.

Suppose you plan to write about the costs and benefits of urbanized, low-density land use (urban sprawl). A search on Google for selected keywords will turn up lists of sites that may be more or less useful to your research. Even slight changes in keywords (*"urban sprawl" advantages* or *"benefits of urban sprawl"*) can produce different lists. Clicking on the links takes you to the relevant page—not necessarily the home page—of each site.

Specialized Search Engines

Search engines that specialize in a particular field may be able to provide more in-depth resources to researchers. For example, FindLaw (*www.findlaw.com*) could help you find out about international adoptions and MedlinePlus (*www.medlineplus.gov*) will take you to a medical encyclopedia, among other sites. Many specialized search engines are also search directories.

Using Discussion Groups and Blogs

Thousands of groups operate on the Web, focusing on every topic imaginable. You can find addresses for these groups in various ways: in computer publications and special-interest magazines, or by conducting a search through a search engine.

An online **discussion group** consists of individuals who share a similar interest, with members of the group communicating with one another in a variety of ways, depending on the technical structure of the group. Some groups enable participants to communicate through e-mail. Each e-mail message is automatically distributed to everyone on the discussion group's membership list. In some groups, people post messages on a central "bulletin board," where anyone can read and respond to a message. In a moderated group, contributions are reviewed by a group facilitator before being posted to the group at large. In unmoderated groups, there is no such review. Membership in some groups may be restricted to people with qualifying credentials or to subscribers. Not surprisingly, unmoderated newsgroups tend to have a high ratio of junk mail. (To browse through categories of online groups, go to *http://groups.google.com.)*

Blogs (short for weblogs) could be compared to online diaries or journals. The blog's owner posts entries that readers can read and then respond to online. Blogs can be on a particular topic (say, politics) or not, depending on the owner's interest. A number of sites, including Technorati (*http://technorati.com*) and Google Blog Search (*http://blogsearch.google.com/*), offer ways to locate specific blogs.

Keep in mind that anyone—scholar, fraud, con artist, or saint—can voice an opinion online. Also, be careful not to assume that a talkative member of a group or a blog owner is necessarily an expert: any self-styled "authority" can contribute to most online discussions. Despite these problems, discussion groups and blogs *can* be helpful sources of information and provide valuable leads as you do your research. They may also put you in e-mail touch with respected authorities in your field of research.

Using Wikis

Wikis are Web pages that can be modified by any Internet user; no special software is needed. They can be useful tools for groups constructing a document together online. Perhaps the best-known wiki is Wikipedia (*www.wikipedia.org*), an online encyclopedia hosted by the nonprofit Wikimedia Foundation. Viewers can contribute to and modify articles on Wikipedia, and all content is available for use free of charge. Although anyone can contribute to Wikipedia, the site operators do exercise editorial oversight.

Because of how Wikipedia entries are created and edited, viewers can't be sure that information in the articles is accurate and unbiased. That means you must use Wikipedia content with great caution. While you might read a Wikipedia entry to acquire some background information, as you would a regular encyclopedia article, you should take care to verify any specific facts in more conventional sources. Individual articles often end with lists of resources and links to other sources. The bottom line: Avoid quoting from, summarizing, or paraphrasing Wikipedia articles in a college paper.

Evaluating Online Materials

As noted in the preceding section and on pages 547–549, you need to take special care to evaluate the worth of material you find on the Web. Electronic documents may appear seemingly out of nowhere and can disappear without a trace. And anyone with access to a computer can create a webpage or state a position in a discussion group. How, then, do you know if a source found on the Net is credible? The following checklist provides some questions to ask when you work with online material.

☑ EVALUATING ONLINE MATERIALS: A CHECKLIST

- ☐ Who is the author of the material? Does the author offer his or her credentials in the form of a résumé or biographical information? Do these credentials qualify the author to provide information on the topic? Does the author provide an e-mail address so you can request more information? The less you know about an author, the more suspicious you should be about using the data.
- ☐ Can you verify the accuracy of the information presented? Does the author refer to studies or to other authors you can investigate? If the author doesn't cite other works or other points of view, that may suggest the document is opinionated and one-sided. In such a case, it's important to track down material addressing alternative points of view.
- ☐ Who is sponsoring the website? Check for an "About Us" link on the home page, which may tell you the site's sponsorship and goals. Many sites are published by organizations—businesses, agencies, lobby groups—as well as by individuals who are advocating a single point of view. Even organizations with the *.org* domain name may have a specific bias on an issue. You should use the material with great caution. And once again, make an extra effort to locate material addressing other sides of the issue.
- ☐ Is the information cited recent and up-to-date? Being on the Internet doesn't guarantee that information is current. To assess the timeliness of Internet materials, check at the top or bottom of the document for copyright date, publication date, and/or revision date. Those dates will help you determine whether the material is recent enough for your purposes.
- ☐ Is the information original or taken from another source? Is quoted material accurate? Some Web pages may reproduce material from other sources without identifying them. Watch out for possible plagiarism. Nonoriginal material should be accurately quoted and acknowledged on the site.

Using Other Online Tools

The World Wide Web is not the only portion of the Internet that you'll find interesting or useful. Other aspects of the Net include Telnet, a software networking tool that allows you to log onto another computer and access its files; FTPs (file transfer protocols), through which you download files from remote computers and upload files to computers to which you have access; and Gopher, a comprehensive menu-based program. If you become interested in the workings of the Net beyond the World Wide Web and want to investigate further, your favorite search engine—and your college librarian—should provide the help you need.

Prepare a Working Bibliography

As you gather promising books, reference volumes, print articles, and online material about your subject, prepare a **working bibliography**—a master list of potential sources. Having such a list means you won't have to waste time later tracking down a source whose title you remember only vaguely.

Since you want to read as much as you can about your subject, the working bibliography will contain more sources than your instructor requires for the final paper. In the long run, you probably won't use all the sources in your working bibliography. Some will turn out to be less helpful than you thought they would be; others may focus on an aspect of your topic you decide not to cover after all.

The working bibliography may be compiled in a computer file, on standard notebook paper, or on index cards. You might find it easiest to use a computer file, since you can often e-mail library catalog information and journal articles to yourself and copy and paste Web addresses right into the bibliography. Both these options can help you avoid transcription errors. A computer document can also be sorted and re-sorted alphabetically as you develop your list. (Check the Help feature on your word processing program for instructions on sorting.) And you can add comments to the individual items as you work.

Some researchers prefer to use a notebook. A notebook keeps all your writing in one place, but it's hard to make changes to items you have already entered. Another useful approach is to use large (4- x 6-inch) note cards, one card for each source. Unlike a notebook, index cards can be arranged in alphabetical order quickly, which makes it easy to prepare your Works Cited list (see page 593). And the larger index cards give you room to comment on a source's value ("Good discussion of landfill regulations") or availability ("See if book is on reserve"). Finally, note cards are very portable.

However you prepare your working bibliography, take time to record the information listed in the checklist on page 557.

Recording this basic information helps you locate these potentially useful sources later on. In the next stage, as you start taking notes, you'll refine the information in your working bibliography.

PREPARING A WORKING BIBLIOGRAPHY: A CHECKLIST

- ☐ For a book, write down the title, author, and call number.
- ☐ For an article in a printed reference volume, note the titles of both the article and the reference work, the article's author, and the reference work's call number.
- ☐ For an article in a printed periodical, note the titles of both the article and periodical, the article's author, and the article's date and pages.
- ☐ If you obtain an article title electronically, write down the same information you would if you were using a print directory. If you don't expect to locate the article in print form (because a print version is either nonexistent or difficult to obtain), then also note any information essential for accessing the article electronically. For example, if later on you want to locate the article's text on the same CD-ROM you are using as an index, write down "CD-ROM" and the database (for example, *ERIC*). For an online source, note the database (for example, *Magazine Database Plus*); the computer network or service through which you access the database (for example, Earthlink); and any keyboard commands you need to access the material, especially the online address).

TAKE NOTES TO SUPPORT THE THESIS WITH EVIDENCE

Now that you've formed a working thesis, identified promising sources, and compiled a working bibliography, it's almost time to take notes. Your goal at this point is to find support for your preliminary thesis—*and* to pay close attention to material suggesting alternative viewpoints. Sifting through this conflicting information will enable you to refine your working thesis with more precision. (For more about evaluating contrasting positions, see pages 558–559). At this point you may be wondering why you should take notes at all. Why not simply read the sources and then draft the research paper, referring to the sources when you need to check a fact or quote something?

Such an approach is bound to create problems. For one thing, you may have to return a source to the library before you're ready to start writing. Taking the time to go back to the library to retrieve the source later on can slow you down considerably—and, in fact, someone else could have checked out the only copy of the source. With notes, though, you'll have all the necessary information at hand without having to return to the original source.

Moreover, if you have your sources in front of you as you write, you'll be tempted to move large chunks of material directly from your sources to your paper, without first evaluating and distilling the material. Writing directly from your sources also aggravates any tendency you may have to string together one quotation after another, without providing many ideas of your own. Worst of all, such an approach often leads to **plagiarism:** passing off someone else's work as your own. (For more on plagiarism, see pages 565–566, 570–572, and 581–590.)

Note-taking can eliminate such problems. When done well, it encourages you to assess, synthesize, and react to your sources. Keeping your working thesis firmly in mind, you examine what others have to say about your subject. Some authors will support your working thesis; others will serve as "devil's advocates," prodding you to consider opposing viewpoints. In either case, note-taking helps you refine your position and develop a sound basis for your conclusions.

Before Note-Taking: Evaluate Sources

You shouldn't take notes on a source until after you've evaluated its *relevance, timeliness, seriousness of approach*, and *objectivity*. Titles can be misleading. If a source turns out to be irrelevant, skip note-taking; just indicate on your working bibliography that you consulted the source and found it didn't relate to your topic. Next, consider the source's age. To some extent, the topic and kind of research you're doing determine whether a work is outdated. If you're researching a historical topic such as the internment of Japanese Americans during World War II, you would most likely consult sources published in the 1940s and 1950s, as well as more up-to-date sources. In contrast, if you're investigating a recent scientific development—cloning, for example—it would make sense to restrict your search to current material. For most college research, a source older than ten years is considered outdated unless it was the first to present key concepts in a field.

You should also ask yourself if each source is serious and scholarly enough for your purpose and your instructor's requirements. Finally, examine your sources for possible bias, keeping in mind that a strong conclusion or opinion is *not in itself* a sign of bias. As long as a writer doesn't ignore opposing positions or distort evidence, a source can't be considered biased. A biased source presents only those facts that fit the writer's predetermined conclusions. Such a source is often marked by emotionally charged language (see page 21). Publications sponsored by special interest groups—a particular industry, religious association, advocacy group, or political party—are usually biased. Reading such materials *does* familiarize you with a specific point of view, but remember that contrary evidence has probably been ignored or skewed.

A special problem occurs when you find a source that takes a position contrary to the one that you had previously considered credible. When you come across such conflicting material, you can be sure you've identified a pivotal issue within your topic. To decide which position is more valid, you need to take good notes from both sources (see pages 562–573) or carefully annotate your photocopies or printed documents (see pages 565–566). Then evaluate each source for bias. On this basis alone, you might discover serious flaws in one or both sources. Also compare the key points and supporting evidence in the two sources. Where do they agree? Where do they disagree? Does one source argue against the other's position, perhaps even discrediting some of the opposing view's evidence? The answers to these questions may very well cause you to question the quality, completeness, or fairness of one or both sources. To resolve such a conflict of sources, you can also research your subject more fully. For example, if your conflicting sources are at the general or serious level (see pages 541–544), you should probably turn to more scholarly sources. By referring to more authoritative material, you may be able to determine which of the conflicting sources is more valid.

When you try to resolve discrepancies among sources, be sure not to let your own bias come into play. Try not to favor one position over the other simply because it supports your working thesis. Remember, your goal is to arrive at the most well-founded position you can. In fact, researching a topic may lead you to change your original viewpoint. In this case, you shouldn't hesitate to revise your working thesis to accord with the evidence you gather.

Before Note-Taking: Refine Your Working Bibliography

After determining the sources from which you will take notes, spend some time refining the relevant entries in your working bibliography. With the sources in front of you, use the guidelines listed in the following checklist to fill in any missing information. (At times, the guidelines include a bit more information than MLA requires. This precision will often be helpful if you use a format other than MLA.)

☑ REFINING YOUR WORKING BIBLIOGRAPHY: A CHECKLIST

- ☐ Take down the authors' names exactly as they appear on the title pages of the original works and in the order shown there. The author listed first is considered the primary author, so don't rearrange the names alphabetically. Occasionally, a work will be attributed to an organization, university, or institute rather than to a person. If so, consider that organization the author.
- ☐ For a *book*, record:
  - The full title (including any subtitle) on the title page
  - The publisher's name from the title page
  - The publisher's location from the title page. If the publisher is international, use the publishing location in your country, if there is one. If several locations within your country are listed, use as the city of publication the one that's listed first on the title page.
  - The volume number for multivolume books, from the title page.
  - The copyright year, the most recent year in which the text was registered, from the copyright page. (For example, for the copyright line "Copyright © 2003, 2007 by Pearson Education, Inc." use "2007" as the year of publication.) If you have doubts

whether your edition is the most recent, check the online catalog to see if the library has a later one. Remember, the number of editions in which a book has appeared is not the same as the number of printings the book has gone through. A book may say "ninth printing," yet be only the second edition.
- The book's call number.

□ For a *mass-publication magazine*, note:
- The author's name (if any)
- The article or column title
- The magazine title
- The date (usually month and year)
- The pages on which the article appears.
- Any special explanation, such as "Editorial" or "Letter to the editor."

□ For a *newspaper article*, take down:
- The author's name (if any)
- The article or column title
- The newspaper title
- The date (month, day, and year)
- The edition, if specified
- The section and pages where the article appears.
- Any special explanation, such as "Editorial" or "Letter to the editor."

□ For an *article or essay in a book-length collection*, record:
- The authors of the article
- The article title
- The book title
- The book's editor
- The publisher and its location
- The copyright date
- The specific book pages on which the article appears.

□ For an *article in a scholarly or serious journal*, note:
- The article's author(s)
- The article title
- The journal title
- The date (including month and year)
- The volume and issue (if any)
- The pages on which the article appears. Also indicate whether the journal is paginated continuously from issue to issue throughout a given year or whether each issue is paginated separately.

□ For all periodicals, note the library location of relevant issues.

- ☐ For *text obtained on CD-ROM or online*, note:
  - The identical information you would for a printed source in the same category (for example, a magazine article)
  - The page numbers. If the database doesn't specify an article's precise page numbers (see page 544), write down the page number (if available) on which the article began in the original, plus the number of pages or number of paragraphs in the article.
  - For CD-ROMs, the database (for instance, *The New York Times Ondisc*), CD-ROM publisher (for example, UMI-ProQuest), and CD-ROM publication date.
  - For text accessed online, note the database (for instance, *The New York Times Online*), the computer service or network (for example, EBSCOhost), your date of access, and any other information someone would need to retrieve the text (such as the online address).
- ☐ For other electronic sources, record:
  - The creator's name (interviewer, blogger).
  - The name of the item.
  - The title of the website hosting the item.
  - The date the item was posted or last updated.
  - The date you retrieved the item.
  - The web page address.
  - Any special explanation, such as "Podcast" or "E-mail."
- ☐ For non-text material, write down:
  - The creator's name (documentary film director, artist, composer).
  - The title of the piece (song title) and of the larger work it is part of (CD title).
  - The producer (recording company, film company, television network).
  - The place of performance or exhibit (concert hall, museum).
  - The relevant dates (performance date, release date).

Be sure to include any information you might need for your paper's Works Cited or References page. If your working bibliography is accurate and complete, you won't need to refer to your sources later on when preparing your paper's final reference list.

Before Note-Taking: Read Your Sources

At this point, you should spend some time analyzing each source for its *central ideas, main supporting points*, and *key details*. As you read, keep asking yourself how the source's content meshes with your working thesis and with what you know about your subject. Does the source repeat what you already know? If so, you may not need any notes. But if a source provides detailed support for important ideas, plan to take full notes.

When Note-Taking: What to Select

What, specifically, should you take notes on? Your notes might include any of the following: facts, statistics, anecdotal accounts, expert opinion, case studies, surveys, reports, results of experiments. If a source suggests a new angle on your subject, thoughtful and extensive notes are in order. As you begin taking notes, you may not be able to judge how helpful a source will be. In that case, you probably should take fairly detailed notes. After a while, you'll become more selective.

As you go along, you may come across material that challenges your working thesis and forces you to think differently about your subject. Indeed, the more you learn, the more difficult it may be to state anything conclusively. This is a sign that you're synthesizing and weighing all the evidence. In time, the confusion will lessen, and you'll emerge with a clearer understanding of your subject.

When Note-Taking: How to Record Statistics

As you read your sources, you'll probably come across statistics that reinforce points you want to make. Follow the guidelines listed in the following checklist when taking notes on statistics.

☑ RECORDING STATISTICS: A CHECKLIST

- ☐ Check that you record the figures accurately. Also note how and by whom the statistics were gathered, as well as where and when they were first reported.
- ☐ Take down your source's interpretation of the statistics, but be sure to scrutinize the interpretation. Although the source's figures may be correct, they could have been given a "spin" that distorts them. For example, if 80 percent of Americans think violent crime is our number one national problem, that doesn't mean that violent crime *is* our main problem; it simply means that 80 percent of the people polled *think* it is. And if a "majority" of people think that homelessness should be among our top national priorities, it may be that a mere 51 percent—a bare majority—feels that way. In short, make sure the statistics mean what your sources say they mean.
- ☐ Examine each source for possible bias. If a source takes a highly impassioned stance, you should regard its statistics with healthy

skepticism. Indeed, it's a good idea to corroborate such figures elsewhere; tracking down the original source of a statistic is the best way to ensure that numbers are being reported fairly.

- ☐ Be suspicious of statistics that fail to indicate the number of respondents or that are based on a small, nonrepresentative sample (see pages 531–532). For instance, assume the claim is made that 90 percent of the people sampled wouldn't vote for a candidate who had an extramarital affair. However, if only ten people were polled one Sunday as they left church, then the 90 percent statistic is misleading. (For hints on using statistics in a paper, see page 590.)

When Note-Taking: Recording Information

With your sources (books and printouts of articles) and working bibliography close at hand, you're ready to begin taking notes. You may want to use a computer. For a short paper, you may find it convenient to keep the notes from all sources in a single file. For longer papers, where you are consulting many sources, it will be more useful to create a separate file for each source.

Taking notes on computer files allows for easy manipulation of material. You can cut and paste text as you work with it. You also don't have to write information twice—once in longhand and then again by typing it into your draft. The danger of using a computer file, however, is the temptation to copy and paste text without taking the time to identify its origin, which can lead to inadvertent plagiarism. Another problem with having notes on computer files is the difficulty of seeing more than one file at a time as you write your first draft. If the split-screen function on your software is not easy to use, you may have to print your notes in order to work with them.

Your instructor may ask you to take notes on 4- x 6-inch (or larger) index cards. If so, on each card, record notes from only *one source* and on only *one subtopic* of your subject. *Note cards* have several advantages. First, cards help you break information into small, easy-to-manage chunks. Second, they allow you to rearrange information since they can be piled and sorted. You can also delete information easily by simply removing a card. Last, you can create some note cards from printed excerpts of computer files you are using.

For every computer file or note card, follow the guidelines in the checklist given here.

☑ TAKING NOTES: A CHECKLIST

- ☐ *Key* each file or card *to the appropriate source* in your working bibliography. For a computer file, copy the bibliographic entry onto the top of the document and insert an identifier (Jones, p. 31) before each separate note. For note cards, write the author's last name on each note card. If you have more than one source by the same author, also record the source's title.

- ☐ Make sure each source file has a name that identifies the source.
- ☐ Record the *page* or *pages* in the source that the note refers to. If the material is drawn from several pages, indicate clearly where the page breaks occur in the source. That way, if you use only a portion of the material later, you will know its exact page number.
- ☐ Write a key word or phrase at the top of each note card, or at the beginning of each note on a computer file, indicating the gist of the note and the aspect of your topic the note focuses on. Often your key terms will themselves develop subtopics. For example, suppose you are writing a paper on erosion If you are using note cards, you may have two major stacks of cards: "Beach erosion" and "Mountain erosion," with beach erosion being divided into "Dune" and "Shoreline" erosion. If you are taking notes on a computer, you might label each note on a source file by topic: "Beach erosion—dune," "Beach erosion—shoreline," "Mountain erosion."
- ☐ Finally, write down the actual note. Pages 566–570 describe specific kinds of notes to take. In the meantime, here's some general advice. Some notes will be only a line or two; others will be quite full. If you are using cards and you run out of space on a card, don't use the other side; this makes it hard to see at a glance what the note is about. Instead, use a second card, being sure to record the source, page, and so on. Also label successive cards carefully (1 of 2, 2 of 2) and clip them to the first card in the series. If you print computer documents to work with them, make sure to print on only one side of the sheet.

The sample card in Figure 19.6 illustrates one way to identify information on a note card. But whichever way you choose, be consistent. When you scan your cards or file before finishing with a source, you'll be more inclined to notice any missing information if you've prepared the notes in some consistent style. You'll also find it easier to retrieve information later on from well-organized cards or files.

If you are using a computer, once you finish taking notes on a source and labeling the notes by topic, you may want to collate your notes by topic and subtopic. One way to do this is to copy and paste notes from the "source" files into a fresh "topic" file, so that all notes on a specific topic are gathered in the same place and can be reviewed together. If you do so, make sure to copy the source identifier with the note itself. Another method is to print the source files and annotate them as you work, first circling all the notes on dune erosion, say, and then all the notes on shoreline erosion as you draft those parts of your essay.

Notes may also include your comments about a source. Enclosing your observations in square brackets—"[helpful summary]" or "[controversial interpretation]"—keeps these interpretive remarks separate from your notes on a source. If taking notes sparks new ways of looking at your subject, get down such

FIGURE 19.6
Sample Note Card

Unethical business behavior: causes Etzioni, p. 22
Economists suggest that people's desire for profit causes them to cheat—cheat to stay ahead.
But recent studies by social scientists show otherwise—"social ties" and other non-economic factors cause ethical or noneth. behav.
Most important "social ties"—family mores and the culture of one's business peers.

Take notes on only one side of a card, making sure to identify the source in the same way on each card.

thoughts, carefully separating them from your source material. Write "Me" or "My idea" next to the note, or highlight the comment in color on a computer file, or enclose your observations in a box on a note card. If your own comments become extensive, use separate files or cards, clearly labeling them as your own ideas.

If you prefer to handwrite notes but can't get the hang of the note-card system, try using *sheets of paper in much the same way that you would set up computer files*. Head each sheet with a key to the source. Then enter all notes from that source, along with page numbers, on the same sheet. If you run out of space, don't take notes on the other side. Instead, start a new sheet, entering on each a key to the source, and continue to keep track of the pages in the source from which you're taking notes. Mark each sheet in the sequence clearly (1 of 3, 2 of 3, and so on). Using key phrases to signal subtopics will also make it easier to organize your notes later.

When Note-Taking: Photocopies and Printouts

Photocopying or **printing** material is another way to gather information. Many journal articles can be printed in the library or e-mailed to your address for printing later on. You have the right to duplicate published work as long as you use it for your own research and give credit for borrowed material. Using copies *does* have advantages. It allows unhurried analysis and reconsideration of research material at home. It can also be a way of ensuring accuracy since sources can be checked so easily. Duplicating can be especially useful if you need to retrieve a detail that initially seemed unimportant. It may also be a good idea to photocopy the title and copyright pages of books you use so that you can double-check source information later on.

However, using printed documents is not without its dangers, especially if you're an inexperienced researcher. You may get a false sense of security if you convince yourself that once you've photocopied or printed material, you've done most of the work. *Remember*: You still have to evaluate and synthesize your source material, figuring out what evidence supports your working thesis. That means you should dig into the material, underlining or boxing sections you might use, jotting subtopics in the margins, and recording your reaction to the material.

There's one more pitfall to consider: Working with duplicated material can encourage *plagiarism*. Instead of recasting material in your own words, you may be tempted to copy others' language and ideas. If that is the case, you'd be better off steering clear of duplicating altogether. (For more on plagiarism, see pages 565–566, 570–572, and 581–590.)

If you do photocopy or print materials, don't forget to include the duplicated sources in your working bibliography and to write complete source information on the photocopy itself.

Kinds of Notes

There are four broad kinds of notes: direct quotations, summaries, paraphrases, and combined notes. Knowing how and when to use each type is an important part of the research process.

Direct Quotations

A **quotation note** reproduces, word for word, that which is stated in a source. Although quoting can demonstrate the thoroughness with which you reviewed relevant sources, don't take one direct quote note card after another; such a string of quotations means you haven't evaluated and synthesized your sources sufficiently. When should you quote? If a source's ideas are unusual or controversial, record a representative quotation in your notes so you can include it in your paper to show you have accurately conveyed the source's viewpoint. Also record a quotation if a source's wording is so eloquent or convincing that it would lose its power if you restated the material in your own words. And, of course, you should take down a quotation if a source's ideas reinforce your own conclusions. If the source is a respected authority, such a quotation will lend authority to your own ideas. When taking notes, you might aim for one to three quotations from each major source. More than that can create a problem when you write the paper.

A note containing a direct quotation from a source should be clearly indicated by quotation marks, perhaps even a notation like "Direct Quotation" or "DQ." Whenever your source quotes someone else (a secondary source) and you want to take notes on what that other person said, put the statement in quotes and indicate its original source. (See page 589 for more on quoting secondary sources.)

When copying a quotation, you must record the author's statement *exactly* as it appears in the original work, right down to the punctuation. As long as you don't change the meaning of the original, you may delete a phrase or sentence from a quotation if it's not pertinent to the point you're making. In such cases, insert three spaced periods, called an **ellipsis** (...), in place of the deleted words.

Original Passage

> The plot, with one exciting event after another, was representative of the usual historical novel. But *Gone with the Wind* placed its emphasis as much on the private individual as on the panorama.

Ellipsis Used to Show Material Omitted

When omitting material *in or near the middle* of the original sentence, proceed as follows: Leave a space before the first period of the ellipsis and leave a space after the third period of the ellipsis before continuing with the quoted matter:

> "The plot . . . was representative of the usual historical novel. But *Gone with the Wind* placed its emphasis as much on the private individual as on the panorama."

Ellipsis at the End

When deleting material *at the end* of the original sentence, proceed as above, but insert a period before the first ellipsis period and provide the closing quotation mark:

> "The plot, with one exciting event after another, was representative of the usual historical novel. . . . "

No Ellipsis Needed

You don't need an ellipsis if you omit material at the start of a quotation. Simply place the quotation marks where you begin quoting directly. Also, don't capitalize the first word in the quotation unless it ordinarily requires capitalization:

> *Gone with the Wind*'s piling up of "one exciting event after another" was typical of the historical potboiler.

This example also illustrates that you can omit the ellipsis if all you quote is a key term or short phrase. In such cases, just enclose the borrowed material in quotation marks. (For more examples of the ellipsis, see pages 582–583.)

Additions to a Quotation

If, for the sake of clarity or grammar, you need to add a word or short phrase to a quotation (for example, by changing a verb tense or replacing a vague pronoun with a noun), enclose your insertion in **brackets:**

> "Not only did it [*Gone with the Wind*] for a short time become America's speediest-selling novel, but over the long haul, it became the nation's largest-selling novel."

Quotation Within a Quotation

When a source you're quoting quotes another source, place single quotation marks around the words of the secondary source:

> "Despite its massive scope, *Gone with the Wind* sustained, according to one reviewer, 'remarkable continuity in its plot and character development.'"

Summaries

By **summaries,** we mean *condensing* someone else's ideas and restating them *in your own words*. Skim the source; then, using your own language, condense the material to its central idea, main supporting points, and key details. Summary note cards may be written as lists, brief paragraphs, or both. You may use abbreviations and phrases as well as complete sentences. *A caution*: When summarizing, don't use the ellipsis to signal that you have omitted some ideas. The ellipsis is used only when quoting.

The length of the summary depends on your topic and purpose. Read the following excerpt from page 8 of Julian Stamp's book *The Homeless and History*. Then look at the subsequent summary note cards. (Although the summaries here are shown on cards, you may prefer to type your summaries in your source files or topic files. Just make sure that each summary is clearly labeled as such.)

> The key to any successful homeless policy requires a clear understanding of just who are the homeless. Since fifty percent of shelter residents have drug and alcohol addictions, programs need to provide not only a place to sleep but also comprehensive treatment for addicts and their families. Since roughly one-third of the homeless population is mentally ill, programs need to offer psychiatric care, perhaps even institutionalization, and not just housing subsidies. Since the typical head of a homeless family (a young woman with fewer than six months' working experience) usually lacks the know-how needed to maintain a job and a home, programs need to supply employment and life skills training; low-cost housing alone will not ensure the family's stability.
>
> However, if we switch our focus from the single person to the larger *economic* issues, we begin to see that homelessness cannot be resolved solely at the level of individual treatment. Beginning in the 1980s and through the 1990s, the gap between the rich and the poor has widened, buying power has stagnated, industrial jobs have fled overseas, and federal funding for low-cost housing has been almost eliminated. Given these developments, homelessness begins to look like a product of history, our recent history, and only by addressing shifts in the American economy can we begin to find effective solutions for people lacking homes. Moreover, these solutions—ranging from renewed federal spending to tax laws favoring job-creating companies—will require a sustained national commitment that transcends partisan politics.

The summary notes shown in Figures 19.7 (a) and (b) were taken by two students writing on related but different topics. Although both students eventually used more scholarly and detailed sources in their papers, they found—in the early stages of their research—that Stamp's book provided helpful background and perspective. The first student, planning to write on the causes of homelessness, prepared an in-depth summary card labeled "Personal and Economic Causes of Homelessness." The second student, planning to write on the day-to-day experience of homeless families, took a much shorter note under the heading "Profile: Heads of Homeless Families."

Problems Writing a Summary. The sample note cards in Figure 19.7 were prepared by students who were careful about translating ideas into their own language. The note cards shown in Figure 19.8, however, were prepared by students

FIGURE 19.7
Sample Summary Notes

Personal and Economic Causes of Homelessness — Stamp, p. 8

Point: As individuals, homeless have personal problems.
- 50% in shelters are substance abusers.
- 33% of all homeless suffer mental illnesses.
- Head of homeless family usually has little or no job experience.
- Treatment program needed to solve these problems.

Stamp, p. 8

Point: As a nation, homelessness is an economic problem. Since 1980:
- Growing gulf between rich and poor.
- Decline in industrial jobs.
- Loss of federal money for housing.
- Only economic treatment—from government spending to new tax laws—can permanently solve the homeless problem.

2 of 2

(a)

(b)

Profile: Heads of Homeless Families — Stamp, p. 8

Most homeless families are led by young women who haven't held a job for longer than six months. Without training in work skills and household management, these women can't maintain their families or any housing that might be available.

The length of a summary depends on the usefulness of the source for your essay. (a) The first student wrote a detailed summary that required two cards. (b) The second student needed only a brief summary of the source.

who had difficulty recasting ideas from the Stamp passage. In the first example, the student was so determined to put things her way that she added her own ideas and ended up *distorting* Stamp's meaning. For instance, note the way she emphasizes personal problems over economic issues, making the former the cause of the latter. Stamp does just the opposite and highlights economic solutions

FIGURE 19.8
Problematic Summary Notes

(a)

Who Are the Homeless? Stamp, p. 8

The homeless are people with big problems like addiction, mental illness, and poor job skills. Because they haven't been provided with proper treatment and training, the homeless haven't been able to adapt to a changing economy. So their numbers soared in the 1990s.

(b)

Effective Homeless Programs Stamp, p. 8

Homeless need economic—not psychiatric—treatment and solutions.

Writing a summary requires thoughtfulness. (a) In this summary, the source's original meaning is altered. (b) This summary is so condensed that it is unlikely to be useful.

rather than individual treatment. In the second example, the student worked so hard to compress material that he prepared an *overly condensed* note card. His excessively terse statement, lacking detail and explanation, renders the summary almost meaningless.

Paraphrases

Unlike a summary, which condenses the original, a paraphrase recasts material by using roughly the same number of words, retaining the same level of detail, and adopting the same style as the original. Since the research process requires you to distill information, you'll probably find summary note cards much more helpful than paraphrases.

Plagiarism

Plagiarism occurs when a writer borrows someone else's ideas, facts, or language but doesn't properly credit that source. Summarizing and paraphrasing, in particular, can lead to plagiarism. Look, for example, at the note card in Figure 19.9 (a). When preparing his paraphrase, the student stayed too close to the source and borrowed much of Stamp's language *word for word*. Note, for example, the underlined words, which are taken directly from Stamp. If the student transferred this phrasing to his paper without supplying quotation marks, he'd be guilty of plagiarism. Indeed, even if this student acknowledged Stamp in the paper, he'd still be plagiarizing—the lack of quotation marks implies that the language is the student's when, in fact, it is Stamp's.

As the sample card in Figure 19.9 (b) shows, another student believed, erroneously, that if she changed a word here and omitted a word there, she'd be preparing an effective paraphrase. Note that the language is all Stamp's *except* for the underlined words, which signal the student's slight rephrasings of Stamp. Notice, too, that the student occasionally deleted a word from Stamp, thinking that such changes would constitute a legitimate paraphrase. For instance, Stamp's "only

FIGURE 19.9
Plagiarized Paraphrase Notes

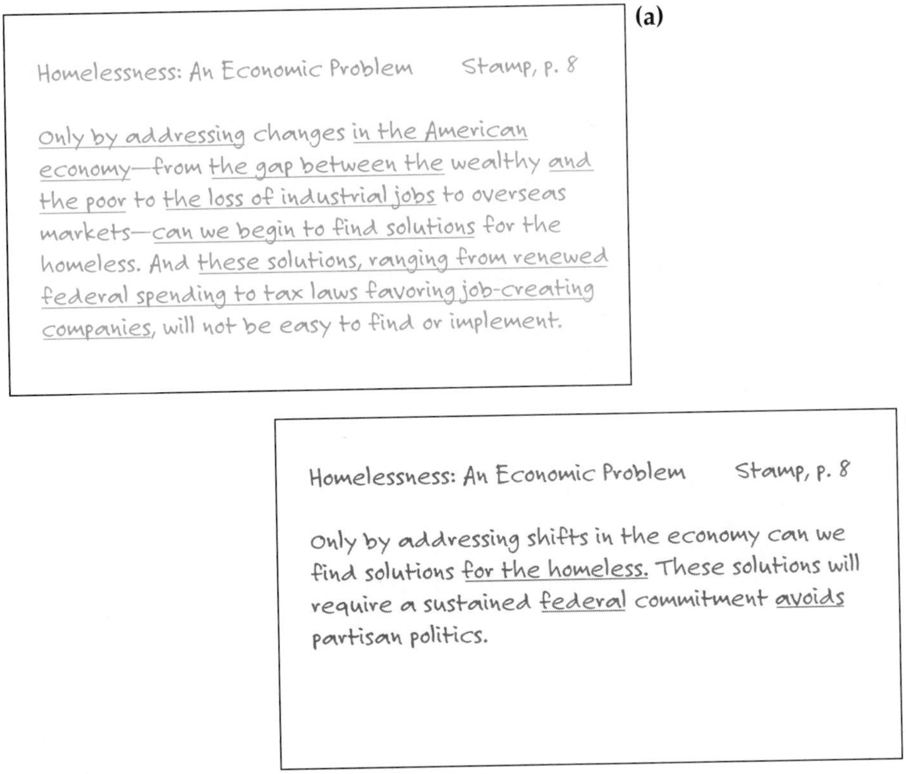

(a)

Homelessness: An Economic Problem Stamp, p. 8

Only by addressing changes in the American economy—from the gap between the wealthy and the poor to the loss of industrial jobs to overseas markets—can we begin to find solutions for the homeless. And these solutions, ranging from renewed federal spending to tax laws favoring job-creating companies, will not be easy to find or implement.

(b)

Homelessness: An Economic Problem Stamp, p. 8

Only by addressing shifts in the economy can we find solutions for the homeless. These solutions will require a sustained federal commitment avoids partisan politics.

Careless paraphrasing can easily lead to plagiarism. (a) In this plagiarized paraphrase, the underlined portions are taken word-for-word from the source. (b) This plagiarized paraphrase is a near-quote because the student has simply changed a few words (underlined) in the original quotation.

by addressing shifts in the American economy can we begin to find effective solutions" became "only by addressing shifts in the economy can we find solutions." The student couldn't place quotation marks around these *near-quotes* because her wording isn't identical to that of the source. Yet to place the near-quotes in a paper without quotation marks would be deceptive; the lack of quotation marks would suggest that the language is the student's when actually it's substantially (but not exactly) Stamp's. Such near-quotes are also considered plagiarism, even if, when writing the paper, the student supplied a note citing the source. (For hints on steering clear of plagiarism when you actually write a research paper, see the discussion of documentation on pages 581–590.)

Combining Notes

When taking notes, you may summarize someone else's ideas in your own words but also include some of the source's exact wording. The result, a **combined note,** is legitimate as long as you put quotation marks around the source's language. The combined note cards in Figure 19.10 are based on the same passage from Stamp's book.

FIGURE 19.10
Sample Combined Notes

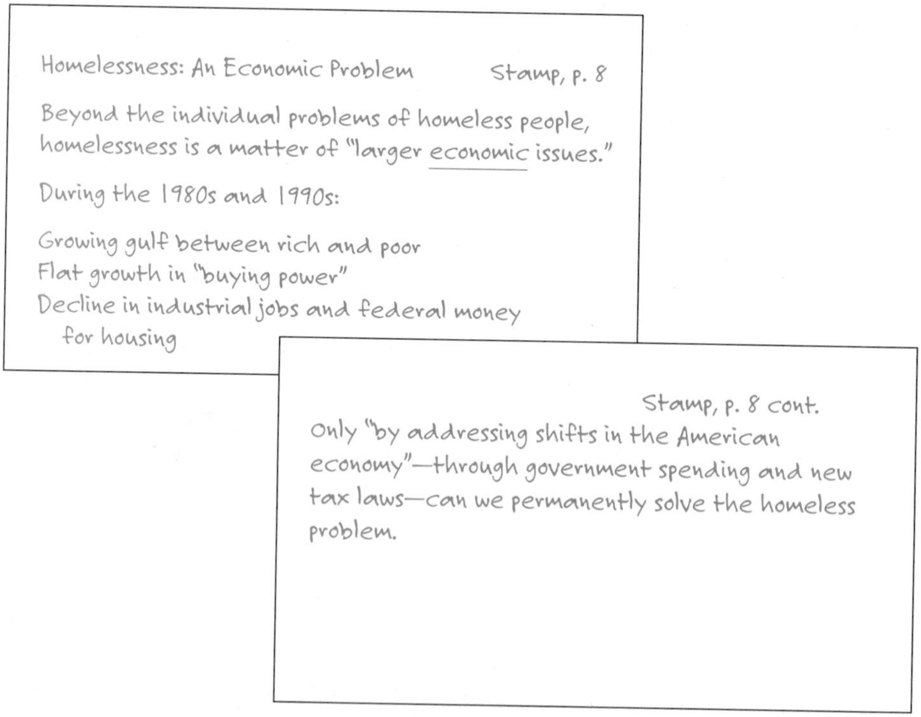

Homelessness: An Economic Problem Stamp, p. 8

Beyond the individual problems of homeless people, homelessness is a matter of "larger economic issues."

During the 1980s and 1990s:

Growing gulf between rich and poor
Flat growth in "buying power"
Decline in industrial jobs and federal money for housing

Stamp, p. 8 cont.

Only "by addressing shifts in the American economy"—through government spending and new tax laws—can we permanently solve the homeless problem.

Combining summary and quotation in a single note can be very useful if you take care to clearly identify quotations.

Combination note cards are effective. They allow you to retain key phrases as well as eloquent or controversial statements from your source; you don't have to spend time recasting material that resists translation into your own words. At the same time, combined notes indicate that you're actively involved with your research material, that you're continually asking yourself, "What should I state in my own words? What is so informative, so interesting, so provocative that I want to use it exactly as it is, word for word?" Such questions prompt discipline and careful thought, two qualities that will serve you well as you move ahead to the next phase of your research—organizing and writing the paper, our focus in Chapter 20.

ACTIVITIES: LOCATING, EVALUATING, AND INTEGRATING RESEARCH SOURCES

1. Use the computer catalog to answer the following questions:
   a. What are three books dealing with the subject of adoption? Of the Internet? Of urban violence? Of genetic research?
   b. What is the title of a book by Betty Friedan? By John Kenneth Galbraith?
   c. Who is the author of *The Invisible Man*? Of *A Swiftly Tilting Planet*?
2. Examine the computerized catalog entry below and then use it to answer the questions that follow.
   a. Which catalog system does this library use?
   b. What is the title of the book?
   c. How many authors does the book have? What are their names?
   d. Under what subjects is this book listed in the catalog?
   e. When was the book published?
   f. Assume you're writing a paper about the ways computers are being used in the education of deaf preschoolers. Considering the information on the card, would you try to locate this book? Why or why not?
3. Prepare a bibliography entry for each of the following books. Gather all the information necessary at the library so that you can write an accurate and complete bibliography entry:
   a. Barbara Tuchman, *Practicing History*
   b. L. Jacobs, *The Documentary Tradition*
   c. Margaret Mead, *Coming of Age in Samoa*
   d. Stephen Bank, *The Sibling Bond*
   e. Ronald Gross, *The New Old*
   f. Matthew Arnold, *Culture and Anarchy*

AUTHOR(S):	Dominique Monolescu, Catherine Schifter, Linda Greenwood
TITLE:	The Distance Education Evolution: Issues and Case Studies
PUBLICATION INFO:	Hershey, PA: Information Science Pub., 2004
PHYSICAL DESCRIP:	xiv, 326 p.; 27 cm.
SUBJECTS:	Distance education–Computer-assisted instruction. Higher Education–Computer-assisted instruction. Educational technology.

1. CALL NUMBER: LC5803.C65D545 2004—STACKS—Checked Out

4. Using reference works available in your library, find the answers to the following questions:

   a. When was the Persian Gulf War fought?
   b. Who invented Kodachrome film, and when?
   c. What is the medical condition *rosacea*?
   d. What television show won the Emmy in 2003 for Outstanding Comedy Series?
   e. What was artist John Sartain known for?
   f. When was an African American first elected to Congress?
   g. In economics, what is Pareto's Law?
   h. In art, what is *écorché*?
   i. Give two other names for a *mbira*, a musical instrument.
   j. In the religion of the Hopi Native Americans, what are *kachinas*?

5. Select one of the following limited topics. Then, using the appropriate periodical indexes and bibliographies (see pages 543–544), locate three periodicals that would be helpful in researching the topic. Examine each periodical to determine whether it is aimed at a general, serious, or scholarly audience.

   a. Drug abuse among health-care professionals
   b. Ethical considerations in organ-transplant surgery
   c. Women in prison
   d. Deforestation of the Amazon rain forest
   e. The difference between *Cold Mountain* as a novel and as a film

6. Select one of the following limited topics. Then, using the Internet, locate at least three relevant articles on the topic: one from a general-interest magazine,

one from a newspaper, *and* one from a serious or scholarly journal. Make a bibliography card for each article.

a. Ordaining women in American churches
b. Attempts to regulate Internet pornography
c. The popularity of novelist and essayist Isak Dinesen
d. The growing interest in painter David Hockney
e. AIDS education programs
f. The global economy

7. Listed here are some of this book's professional essays, along with broad research topics that they suggest. Choose *one* of these general subjects and, using the Internet and/or the library's resources, do some background reading. (You should find helpful some of the sources listed on pages 540–541 and 543–544.) Keep an informal record of the works you consult. As you read, jot down potential limited topics. After doing some further reading on *one* of the limited topics, devise a working thesis. (Don't, by the way, feel constrained by the point of view expressed in the essay[s] that initially prompted your research.)

a. "Sister Flowers" (page 167); "The Fourth of July" (page 208); "A Slow Walk of Trees" (page 364); "Black Men and Public Space" (page 412)

- Preservation of cultural differences
- Teaching about diversity
- Relations between different racial or ethnic groups

b. "Family Counterculture" (page 6); "The Fourth of July" (page 208); "Shooting an Elephant" (page 213); "Charity Display?" (page 220); "Tweens: Ten Going on Sixteen" (page 245); "Doublespeak" (page 288); "Don't Just Stand There" (page 333)

- Teaching morality to children
- Morality in the mass media
- Morality in the workplace
- Sexual morality

c. "Psst! Human Capital" (page 301); "Cyberschool" (page 328); "Life as Type A" (page 441)

- The impact of technology on everyday life
- The increasingly fast pace of modern life
- Technology and education
- Technology and the workplace

8. Referring to paragraphs 7–10 in Scott Russell Sanders's "The Men We Carry in Our Minds" (page 295), prepare three note cards: a direct quotation, a summary, and a combined note. Assume you're using the Sanders essay to research equality of opportunity for different economic sectors of American society.

Writing the Research Paper

20

After you complete your note-taking, you're ready to begin the writing phase of the research project. When writing the paper, you'll probably find it helpful to follow these steps:

- Refine your working thesis.
- Sort the note cards.
- Organize the evidence by outlining.
- Write the first draft.
- Document borrowed material.
- Revise, edit, and proofread.
- Prepare the Works Cited list.

REFINE YOUR WORKING THESIS

This is a good time to *reexamine your working thesis*; it's undoubtedly evolved since you first started your research. Indeed, now that you're more informed about the topic, you may feel that your original thesis oversimplifies the issue. To clarify your position, begin by sifting through your note cards; your goal is to formulate a position that makes the most sense in light of the research you've done and the information you've gathered. Then, revise your working thesis, keeping in mind the evidence on your note cards. This refined version of your thesis will serve as the starting point for your first draft. Remember, though—as you write the paper, new thoughts may emerge that will cause you to modify your thesis even further. (For more on thesis statements, see Chapter 3 and the writing process diagrams in Chapters 10–18.)

SORT YOUR NOTES

Keeping your refined thesis in mind, *sort your notes by topic*. If you are using note cards, make separate piles of cards for different topics. Suppose, for example, your thesis is "Lotteries are an inefficient means of raising money for state programs." You might form one pile of note cards on administrative costs, another on types of state programs, a third on the way money is allocated, and so on. Although you can sort by the key terms or headings you previously placed at the tops of cards, it's a good idea to reread the cards. You may find, for example, that a heading needs to be changed because its information better suits some other category. If some cards don't fit into any pile—and this is likely—put them aside. You don't need to use every note card.

If you have been taking notes on the computer, you probably started with a separate file for each source. During the research process, you may have identified each note by topic and collated the notes into separate topic files. You can now create one file out of these topic files to use for your draft.

If you have not yet collated your notes by topic, you can do so now. Print each source file on one side of a sheet. Read through the notes and label them by topic. Using the printed sheets as a guide, copy and paste a note from a source file into your draft file. Make sure to circle or cross out the note on your printout so that you don't find yourself using the same notes more than once. One caution: For every note you copy into your draft, make sure you also copy the source of the note. You now have all your notes roughly sorted by topic in a file that will become your first draft.

At this point, you should consider which organizational approach will help you sequence your material. (See pages 55–58) and the development diagrams in Chapters 10–18 for tips on using specific patterns of development.) Arrange your topics to reflect the organizational pattern you have chosen.

Once you've arranged your notes cards according to the topic headings, sort each topic pile by *subtopic*. For example, notes about types of state programs might be divided into these three subtopics: programs for the elderly, programs for preschool children, programs for the physically disabled. Next, using the patterns of development and organizational approaches discussed, respectively, on pages 46–47 and 55–58, order each set of subtopics to match the sequence in which you think you'll discuss those subtopics in your paper. This sorting will make your next step—preparing an outline—much easier.

ORGANIZE THE EVIDENCE BY OUTLINING

Whether or not your instructor requires an *outline*, it's a good idea to prepare one before you begin writing the paper. Because an outline groups and sequences points, it provides a blueprint you can follow when writing. Outlining clarifies what your main ideas are, what your supporting evidence is, and how everything fits together. It reveals where your argument is well supported and where it is weak.

To design your outline, focus first on the paper's body. How can you best explain and support your thesis? For now, don't worry about your introduction or conclusion. General guidelines on outlining are discussed in Chapter 5 (page 59). To apply those guidelines to a research paper, keep in mind the points listed in the checklist that follows.

OUTLINING RESEARCH EVIDENCE: A CHECKLIST

- ☐ Base the outline on your organized notes.
- ☐ Label your main topic headings with roman numerals (I, II, III, and so on) to indicate the order in which you plan to discuss each topic in the paper.
- ☐ Label the subtopics grouped under each main topic heading with capital letters (A, B, C). Indent the subtopic entries under their respective main topics, listing them in the order you plan to discuss them.
- ☐ Label supporting points (ideas noted on your cards) with arabic numerals (1, 2, 3) and indent them under the appropriate subtopics.
- ☐ Label specific details (facts, quotations, statistics, examples, expert opinion) with lowercase letters (a, b, c) and indent them under the appropriate supporting points. Use shorthand for details. For example, write "Bitner quote here" instead of copying the entire quotation into your outline.
- ☐ Where appropriate, map out sections of the paper that will provide background information or define key terms.
- ☐ You may want to use the Outline feature of your word processing software. Or you can type outline headings directly into the draft file and then copy and paste the headings into a separate file to see the outline clearly. The Clipboard feature of your software may make this easy to do.

Here's how the various outline elements look when they're properly labeled and indented:

```
I. Main topic
   A. Subtopic
      1. Supporting point
      2. Supporting point
```

```
      a. Specific detail
      b. Specific detail
  B. Subtopic
    1. Supporting point
    2. Supporting point
II. Main topic
  A. Subtopic
    1. Supporting point
    2. Supporting point
      a. Specific detail
      b. Specific detail
  B. Subtopic
```

Even if you've been taking notes by hand, you may find it useful to outline on the computer. It's far easier to revise an outline done on a computer, and you can then actually write your first draft by filling in the outline with text. As you revise your outline, take care to save each revision as a separate file: "Lotteries_outline1," "Lotteries_outline2," and so forth. That way, if you decide a revision is not working, you can retrieve earlier work.

Your first outline probably won't be a formal full-sentence one; rather, it's more likely to be a *topic* (or phrase) *outline*, like those on pages 318, 356–357, and 480–481. A topic outline helps you clarify a paper's overall structure. A *full-sentence outline* (see pages 237 and 614–616) or a *combined topic and sentence outline* (see pages 390–391) is better suited to mapping out in detail the development of a paper's ideas. If you're preparing an outline that will be submitted with the paper, find out in advance which kind your instructor prefers.

Before you go any further, it's a good idea to get some feedback on your outline—from an instructor or a critical friend—to make sure others agree that your meaning and organization are logical and clear. Then, using your readers' reactions, make whatever changes seem necessary.

WRITE THE FIRST DRAFT

Once you've refined your working thesis, sorted your notes, and constructed an outline, you're ready to write your first draft. As with the early versions of an essay, don't worry at this stage about grammar, spelling, or style. Just try to get down as much of the paper's basic content and structure as you can.

Chapter 6 offers general guidelines for writing a first draft. (See page 65 and the development diagrams for the different patterns of development in Chapter 10–18.) When applying those guidelines to a research paper, keep in mind the points discussed in the following checklist.

WRITING THE FIRST DRAFT OF A RESEARCH PAPER: A CHECKLIST

- ☐ As you write, use your note cards, source files, and outline. Don't rely on your memory for the information you've gathered.
- ☐ Feel free to deviate from your outline if, as you write, you discover a more effective sequence, realize some material doesn't fit, or see new merit in previously discarded information.
- ☐ Include any quotations and summaries in the draft by copying and pasting material from your computer files or typing in material from your note cards.
- ☐ Provide rough documentation (see pages 581–590) for all material borrowed from your sources.
- ☐ Use the present tense when quoting or summarizing a source ("Stamp reports that . . . " rather than "Stamp reported that . . . ").
- ☐ Use the third-person point of view throughout, unless your instructor has indicated that you may use the first person when presenting primary research (see page 529).
- ☐ Give your first draft and subsequent drafts different file names: "Lotteries_draft1," "Lotteries_draft2," etc.

There are two contrasting strategies for generating a first draft. One is to *overwrite,* explaining each point as fully as possible, even including alternative explanations and wordings. The other strategy is to *underwrite.* In this approach, you jot down your ideas quickly, leaving gaps where points need to be expanded, making notations like "Insert a quote here." The disadvantage of this latter strategy is that it simply defers filling in the gaps until a later time, when it might be difficult to recapture your original train of thought. The advantage is that generating material quickly can make a long piece of writing more manageable and less forbidding. Some writers combine the two strategies—writing out parts of the paper fully but only sketching out those sections where getting down all the details would interrupt the flow of thought. If you have been using collated notes as the basis for your draft, you may find that a lot of the "filling in" work has largely been done.

Whichever strategy you use, keep in mind that your draft shouldn't merely string together other people's words and ideas. Rather than simply presenting fact after fact or quotation after quotation, you must *analyze* and *comment on* your research, clearly showing how it supports your thesis. Similarly, when drafting the paper, be sure your language doesn't stay too close to that of your sources. To avoid overreliance on your sources' language, refer to your notes as you write, not to the sources themselves. Remember, too, that taking source material and merely changing a word here and there still constitutes *plagiarism*—passing off someone else's thoughts or language as your own. In such a situation, it's important that you acknowledge your source. (For more pointers on steering clear of plagiarism, see pages 565–566, 570–572, and 581–590.)

Presenting the Results of Primary Research

If your instructor requires you to conduct primary research (see pages 530–531), you might be tempted to include in the draft every bit of information you gathered through any surveys, experiments, or interviews you conducted. Remember, though, your primary purpose is to provide evidence for your thesis, so include only that material that furthers your goal. To preserve the draft's overall unity, you should also avoid the temptation to mass, without commentary, all your primary research in one section of the paper. Instead, insert the material at those places where it supports the points you want to make. Sometimes instructors will ask you to devote one part of the paper to a detailed discussion of the process you used to conduct primary research—everything from your methodology to a detailed interpretation of your results. In such a case, before writing your draft, ask your instructor where you should cover that information. Perhaps it should be placed in a separate introductory section or in an appendix.

DOCUMENT BORROWED MATERIAL TO AVOID PLAGIARISM: MLA FORMAT

Copyright law and the ethics of research require that you give credit to those whose words and ideas you borrow; that is, you must provide full and accurate **documentation**. A lack of such documentation results in *plagiarism*—borrowing someone's ideas, facts, and words without properly crediting your source. Faulty documentation undermines your credibility. For one thing, readers may suspect that you're hiding something if you fail to identify your sources clearly. Further, readers planning follow-up research of their own will be perturbed if they have trouble locating your sources. Finally, weak documentation makes it difficult for readers to distinguish your ideas from those of your sources.

To avoid plagiarizing, you must provide documentation in the following situations:

- When you include a *word-for-word quotation* from a source
- When you *paraphrase* or *summarize* (restate in your own words) ideas or information from a source, *unless* that material is *commonly known* and *accepted* (whether or not you yourself were previously aware of it) *or* is a *matter* of historical or scientific *record*
- When you *combine* a *summary* and a *quotation*

One exception to formal documentation occurs in writing for the general public. For example, you may have noticed that the authors of this book's essays don't use full documentation when they borrow ideas. *Academic writers*, though, *must provide full documentation* for all borrowed information. The next section explains how to do this.

The following discussion focuses on the MLA—Modern Language Association—format for documenting borrowed material. The **MLA format**, based on the *MLA Handbook for Writers of Research Papers*, is used widely in the liberal arts. (The system used in the social sciences—that of the American Psychological Association [APA]—is described on pages 604–611. On page 614, you'll also find a description of the format commonly used in the hard sciences and in technical fields.) For a sample paper that uses MLA documentation, turn to the student essay on pages 612–628. For an exerpt showing APA documentation, see pages 630–631.

Indicate Author and Page

Both the MLA documentation system described here and the APA system described later in the chapter use the **parenthetic reference**, a brief note in parentheses inserted into the text after borrowed material. The parenthetic reference doesn't provide full bibliographic information, but it provides enough so that readers can turn to the Works Cited list (or bibliography) for complete information. If the method of documentation you learned in high school involved footnotes or endnotes, you'll be happy to know that parenthetic documentation is much easier to use and is usually preferred by professors. To be on the safe side, though, check with your professors to determine their documentation preferences.

Whenever you use borrowed material, you must, within your paper's text, do two things. First, you must *identify the author*. (Since the Works Cited page is arranged according to authors' last names, readers can refer to that listing for title, publisher, and so on.) Second, you must *specify the page(s)* in your source on which the material appears.

Using Parentheses Only

The simplest way to provide documentation involves the use of *parentheses* for both *author* and *page* references. The examples that follow, based on references to Julian Stamp's *The Homeless and History*, illustrate this method. (If you like, turn to page 568 for the extract from Stamp's book and compare the original there with the documentation here. And turn to pages 566–567 if you would like to review the use of ellipsis and brackets when deleting material from a source.)

```
Counseling and other support services are not enough to solve
the problem of homelessness; proposed solutions must address the
complex economic issues at the heart of homelessness (Stamp 8).
```

It is no coincidence that as "the gap between the rich and the poor has widened . . ." (Stamp 8), homelessness has emerged as a social ill.

If we look beyond the problems of homeless people "to the larger economic issues, we . . . see that homelessness cannot be resolved solely at the level of individual treatment" (Stamp 8).

Because half of those taking refuge in shelters have substance-abuse problems, "programs need to provide not only a place to sleep but also comprehensive treatment for addicts . . ." (Stamp 8).

Take a moment to look again at the preceding examples. Note the following:

What to Provide Within the Parentheses

- Give the author's last name only, even when the author is cited for the first time. If there is no author, use a shortened version of the title or whatever element is given first in the Works Cited entry for the item.
- Write the page number immediately after the author's last name, with no punctuation between. (If the source is only one page, only the author's name is needed.) Provide a full page range of the summary or quotation if it spans more than one page. Don't use the designation *p.* or *page*.

Where to Place the Parentheses

- At the end of the sentence or immediately *after* the borrowed material, at a natural pause in the sentence
- Before any terminal punctuation (period, question mark) or internal punctuation (comma, semicolon)
- After an ellipsis and bracket at the end of a quotation but before the final period

Using Parentheses and Attributions

Skilled writers indicate clearly where their ideas stop and those of their sources begin. So, besides providing careful parenthetic documentation, writers often provide **attributions**—nonparenthetical source identifiers like those (underlined) in the following two *summary* statements:

Julian Stamp argues that homelessness must be addressed in terms of economics—and not simply in terms of individual counseling, addiction therapy, or job training (8).

According to statistics, one-half of the homeless individuals in shelters are substance abusers (Stamp 8).

A *quotation* should also be inserted smoothly with an attribution. Don't just drop a quotation into your text, as in this example:

Incorrect

"The key to any successful homeless policy requires a clear understanding of just who are the homeless" (Stamp 8).

Instead, provide an attribution for the quoted statement:

Correct

As Stamp explains, "The key to any successful homeless policy requires a clear understanding of just who are the homeless" (8).

One social scientist points out that "the key to any successful homeless policy requires a clear understanding of just who are the homeless" (Stamp 8).

In *The Homeless and History*, Stamp maintains that "the key to any successful homeless policy requires a clear understanding of just who are the homeless" (8).

Glance back at the examples on this page and note the following:

- An attribution may specify the author's name (*Julian Stamp argues that; As Stamp explains*), or it may refer to a source more generally (*According to statistics; One social scientist points out*). If you want to call attention to a specific author, use an attribution indicating the author's name. Otherwise, use a more general attribution with a parenthetic citation that includes the name along with the page number.
- The first time an author is referred to in the text, the author's full name is provided; afterward, only the last name is given.
- When the author's name is provided in the text, the name is *not* repeated in the parentheses. (Later nonparenthetic references to the same author give only the last name.)

Sometimes, to inform readers of an author's area of expertise, you may identify that person by profession (*The social scientist Julian Stamp*). Don't, however, use such personal titles as *Mr.* or *Ms.* Finally, as part of an attribution, you may mention your source's title (*In* The Homeless and History, *Stamp maintains that . . .*).

When providing the necessary information, try to avoid such awkward constructions as these: "According to Julian Stamp, he says that . . . " and "In the book by Julian Stamp, he argues that . . . " Instead, follow these hints for writing smooth, graceful attributions.

1. Aim for variety. Don't always place attributions at the beginning of the sentence; experiment by placing them in the middle (*The key to any successful*

homeless policy, ***Stamp explains,*** *"requires a clear understanding of just who are the homeless"*) or at the end (*Half of homeless individuals living in shelters are substance abusers,* ***according to statistics.***)

2. Try not to use a predictable subject-verb sequence (*Stamp argues that, Stamp explains that*) in all your attributions. Aim for variations like the following:

```
The information compiled by Stamp shows . . .
In Stamp's opinion, . . .
Stamp's study reveals that . . .
```

3. Rather than repeatedly using the verbs *says* or *writes* in your attributions, seek out more vigorous verbs, making sure the verbs you select are appropriate to the tone and content of the piece you're quoting. The list that follows offers a number of options.

acknowledges	compares	grants	questions	shows
adds	confirms	implies	reasons	speculates
admits	contends	insists	reports	states
argues	declares	maintains	responds	suggests
asserts	demonstrates	notes	reveals	wonders
believes	endorses	points out	says	writes

Special Cases of Authorship

In some situations, providing authorship in the attribution or in the parenthetic citation becomes slightly more complicated. The guidelines that follow will help you deal with special types of authorship.

More Than One Source by the Same Author. When your paper includes references to more than one work by the same author, you must specify the particular work being cited. You do this by providing the *title,* as well as the author's name and the page(s). As with the author's name, the title may be given in *either* the attribution *or* the parenthetic citation. Here are some examples:

In *The Language and Thought of the Child*, Jean Piaget states that "discussion forms the basis for a logical point of view" (240).

Piaget considers dialog essential to the development of logical thinking (*Language* 240).

The Child's Conception of the World shows that young children think that the name of something can never change (Piaget 81).

Young children assume that everything has only one name and that no others are possible (Piaget, *Child's* 81).

Notice that when a work is named in the attribution, the full title appears; when a title is given in the parenthetic citation, only the first few significant words appear. (However, don't use the ellipsis to indicate that some words have been omitted from a title; the ellipsis is used only when quoting a source.) In the preceding examples, the work is a book, so its title is *italicized* (or it may be underlined, if that is your instructor's preference). If the source is an article or a selection from a compilation, the title is placed in quotation marks.

Two or Three Authors. Supply all the authors' last names in either the attribution or parentheses.

More Than Three Authors. In either the attribution or parentheses, give the last name of the first author followed by et al. (which means "and others").

Two or More Authors with the Same Last Name. When you use two or more sources written by authors with the same last name, you must include (in either the attribution or parentheses) each author's first name or initial(s).

A Source with No Author. For a source without a named author, use, in your attribution or parenthetic reference, the title of the work *or* the name of the issuing organization—whichever you used to alphabetize the source on the Works Cited list.

Common Knowledge During your research, you may come across several sources that cite the same *general* information or share the same *widely accepted* opinion. Such material is considered *common knowledge* and *doesn't* need to be documented. Some examples of common knowledge are well-known historical facts and dates (the Magna Carta was first issued in 1215), geographical facts (Rhodesia is the former name of Zimbabwe), and commonly accepted views (the separation of church and state is an important principle in American politics).

Information Found in Two or More Sources. When you come across several sources who cite the same *highly specialized* information or who share the same *controversial* opinion, that material *does* need to be documented. In such a case, state the material in your own words. Then present in the parenthetic citation each source, listed in the order in which it appears on the Works Cited list. Here's an example:

A number of educators agree that an overall feeling of competence—rather than innate intelligence—is a key factor in determining which students do well the first year in college (Smith 465; Jones 72; Greene 208).

If you use a quotation to express an idea that occurs in several sources, provide an attribution for the quoted source and, in the parentheses, give the source's page number followed by a note that other sources make the same point:

The educator Henry Schneider argues that "students with low self-esteem tend to disregard the academic success they achieve" (23; also pointed out in Rabb 401).

Special Cases of Pagination

Occasionally, a source will have unusual pagination. Here's how to deal with such situations.

A Source with No Page Numbers, Such as a Website. The parenthetic citation simply lacks a page number.

Each Volume of a Multivolume Source Paged Separately. Indicate the volume number, then the page number, with a colon between the two (Kahn 3: 246). Do not use *vol.* or *v.*

A Nonprint Source (Television Show, Lecture, Interview). In a parenthetic citation, give only the item (title, speaker, person interviewed) you used to alphabetize the source on your Works Cited list. Or provide the identifying information in the attribution, thus eliminating the need for parenthetic information:

In the documentary *Financing a College Education*, Cheryl Snyder states that . . .

Blending Quotations into Your Text

On the whole, your paper should be written in your own words. A string of quotations signals that you haven't sufficiently evaluated and distilled your sources. Use quotations sparingly; draw upon them only when they dramatically illustrate key points you want to make or when they lend authority to your own conclusions. Also, keep in mind that supplying the appropriate citation may not be enough to blend the quotation smoothly into your own writing; additional wording may be needed to achieve a smooth transition. Finally, don't forget that a quotation, by itself, won't always make your case for you; it may be necessary to interpret the quotation, showing why it's significant and explaining how it supports your central points. Indeed, such commentary is often precisely what's needed to blend quoted material gracefully into your discussion.

Consider the following examples, noting how the first quotation is dropped awkwardly into the text, without any transition or commentary. In contrast, brief interpretive remarks in the second example provide a transition that allows the quotation to merge easily with the surrounding material:

Awkward

Recent studies of parenting styles are designed to control researcher bias. "Recent studies screen out researchers whose strongly held attitudes make objectivity difficult" (Layden 10).

Revised

Recent studies of parenting styles are designed to control researcher bias. Psychologist Marsha Layden, a harsh critic of earlier studies, acknowledges that nowadays most investigations "screen out researchers whose strongly held beliefs make objectivity difficult" (10).

Besides following the guidelines on pages 566–567 for using ellipsis and brackets, you should be familiar with the following capitalization and punctuation conventions when quoting.

Capitalization and Punctuation of Short Quotations

The way a short quotation is used in a sentence determines whether it begins or doesn't begin with a capital letter and whether it is or isn't preceded by a comma.

1. When an attribution introduces a short quotation that can stand alone as a sentence, *do capitalize* the quotation's *first word*. Also, *precede the quotation with a comma*:

   According to Stamp, "Beginning in the 1980s and through the 1990s, the gap between the rich and the poor has widened, buying power has stagnated, industrial jobs have fled overseas, and federal funding for low-cost housing has been almost eliminated" (8).

   Stamp observes, "Beginning in the 1980s and through the 1990s, the gap between the rich and the poor has widened, buying power has stagnated, industrial jobs have fled overseas, and federal funding for low-cost housing has been almost eliminated" (8).

2. When blending a short quotation into the structure of your own sentence, *don't capitalize* the quotation's *first word* and *don't precede it with a comma*:

   Stamp observes that "beginning in the 1980s and through the 1990s, the gap between the rich and the poor has widened, buying power has stagnated, industrial jobs have fled overseas, and federal funding for low-cost housing has been almost eliminated" (8).

   Even if—as in this case—the material being quoted originally started with a capital letter, you still use lowercase when incorporating the quotation into your own sentence. Quotations often merge with your own words in this way when they are introduced, as in the preceding example, by a pronoun (*that, which, who*)—either stated or implied.

3. If, for variety, you *interrupt a full-sentence quotation* with an attribution, *place commas on both sides of the attribution*, and *resume* the quotation with a *lowercase* letter:

   "The key to any successful homeless policy," Stamp comments, "requires a clear understanding of just who are the homeless" (8).

Long Quotations

A quotation longer than four lines starts on a new line and is indented, throughout, ten spaces from the left margin. Since this **block format** indicates a quotation, quotation marks are unnecessary. Double-space the block quotation, as you do the rest of your paper. Don't leave extra space above or below the quotation. Long quotations, always used sparingly, require a lead-in. A lead-in that *isn't* a full sentence is followed by a comma; a lead-in that *is* a full sentence (see below) is followed by a colon:

```
Stamp cites changing economic conditions as the key to a national
homeless policy:
        Beginning in the 1980s and through the 1990s, the gap
        between the rich and the poor has widened, buying power
        has stagnated, industrial jobs have fled overseas, and
        federal funding for low-cost housing has been almost
        eliminated. Given these developments, homelessness begins
        to look like a product of history, our recent history,
        and only by addressing shifts in the American economy
        can we begin to find effective solutions for people
        lacking homes. (8)
```

Notice that the page number in parentheses appears *after* the period, not before as it would with a short quotation.

Quoting or Summarizing a Source Within a Source

If you quote or summarize a *secondary source* (someone whose ideas come to you only through another source), you need to make this clear. The parenthetic documentation should indicate "as quoted in" with the abbreviation *qtd. in*:

```
According to Sherman, "Recycling has, in several communities,
created unanticipated expenses" (qtd. in Pratt 3).

Sherman explains that recycling can be surprisingly costly (qtd.
in Pratt 3).
```

If the material you're quoting includes a quotation, place single quotation marks around the secondary quotation:

```
Pratt believes that "recycling efforts will be successful if, as
Sherman argues, 'communities launch effective public-education
campaigns'" (2).
```

Note: Your Works Cited list should include the source you actually read (Pratt), rather than the source you refer to secondhand (Sherman).

Presenting Statistics

Citing statistics can be an effective strategy for supporting your ideas. Be careful, though, not to misinterpret the data or twist its significance, and remember to provide an attribution indicating the source. Also, be sure not to overwhelm readers with too many statistics; include only those that support your central points in compelling ways. Keep in mind, too, that statistics won't speak for themselves. You need to interpret them for readers, showing how the figures cited reinforce your key ideas. Suppose you're writing a paper showing that Medicare reform is needed to control increasing costs. It wouldn't be effective if you simply provided an attribution, then present one statistic after the other, without explanatory commentary:

Ineffective

> The Centers for Medicaid and Medicare Services reports that 1992 revenues ($185 billion) exceeded spending ($120 billion). But in 1997, revenues ($204 billion) and spending ($208 billion) were almost the same. It is projected that by the year 2010, revenues will be $310 billion and spending $410 billion (Mohr 14).

Instead, after providing an attribution, present only the most telling statistics, being sure to explain their significance:

Effective

> The Centers for Medicaid and Medicare Services reports that in 1992, Medicare revenues actually exceeded spending by about $65 billion. But five years later, costs had increased so much that they exceeded revenues by about $4 billion. This trend toward escalated costs is expected to continue. It's projected that by the year 2010, revenues will be only $310 billion, while spending—if not controlled—will climb to at least $410 billion (Mohr 14).

(For more on statistics, see pages 562–563.)

REVISE, EDIT, AND PROOFREAD THE FIRST DRAFT

After completing your first draft, reward yourself with a break. Set the paper aside for a while, as least for a few hours. When you pick up the draft later, you'll have a fresh, more objective point of view on it. Then, referring to the checklist on page 104 and the first section of the revision checklist that follows, reread your entire draft to get a general sense of how well the paper works. Outlining the draft (see page 103)—*without* referring to the outline that guided the draft's preparation—is a good way to evaluate the paper's overall meaning and structure.

Despite all the work you've done, you may find when you reread the paper that a main point in support of your thesis seems weak. Sometimes a review of your note cards—including those you didn't use for your draft—will uncover appropriate material that you can add to the paper. Other times, though, you may need another trip to the library to gather additional information. Once you're confident that the paper's overall meaning and structure are strong, go ahead and write your introduction and conclusion—if you haven't already done so.

That done, move ahead and evaluate your paper's paragraph development. To focus your revision, use the checklist on page 105, as well as the second section of the revision checklist that follows. Also consult the development diagrams for each pattern of development (Chapters 10–18) for more tips on revision specific to each pattern. As you work, it's a good idea to pay special attention to the way you present evidence in the paragraphs. Does your evidence consist of one quotation after another, or do you express borrowed ideas in your own words? Do you simply insert borrowed material without commentary, or do you interpret the material and show its relevance to the points you want to make?

Before moving to the next stage in the revision process, look closely at the way you introduce borrowed material. If you prepared the draft without providing many attributions, now is the time to supply them. Then, consulting the checklists on pages 124 and 134, as well as the third section of the revision checklist that follows, go ahead and refine your draft's words and sentences.

Finally, when you start editing and proofreading, allow enough time to verify the accuracy of quoted and summarized material. Check such material against your note cards, and check your documentation against both your bibliography cards and Works Cited list (pages 593–604), making sure everything matches. When preparing the final copy of your paper, follow the format guidelines on pages 141–142, using the sample research paper (pages 613–628) as a model. Note that the research paper, when accompanied by an outline, has a separate title page. For a research paper without an outline, the title and other identifying information are usually placed at the top of the paper's first page.

Chapters 7, 8, and 9 discuss techniques for revising and editing an essay draft. The following checklist will help you and those giving you feedback apply those techniques to the research paper.

☑ REVISING THE RESEARCH PAPER: A CHECKLIST

Revise Overall Meaning and Structure

- ☐ What is the thesis of the research paper? Where is it stated? How could the thesis be expressed more clearly?
- ☐ Where would background material or a definition of terms clarify overall meaning?
- ☐ Where does research evidence (facts, statistics, expert opinion, surveys, and experimental results) seem irrelevant or contradict the thesis? What can be done to correct these problems?

- ☐ Which principle of organization (chronological, spatial, emphatic, simple-to-complex) does the paper use? How does this organizing principle reinforce the paper's thesis and make it easy for readers to follow the paper's line of reasoning?

Revise Paragraph Development

- ☐ In which paragraphs is evidence solid and compelling? Where is it confusing, insufficient, irrelevant, too abstract, inaccurate, nonrepresentative, or predictable? How can these problems be remedied?
- ☐ Which paragraphs merely present research, without analyzing and relating it to the thesis? How can the research material be better incorporated into the paper's point of view?
- ☐ Which paragraphs simply string together quotations, without interpretive commentary? Where is commentary needed? Which quotations could be eliminated?

Revise Sentences and Words

- ☐ Where is more documentation needed to avoid plagiarism? Where do another author's words appear but without quotation marks? Where is a source's language only slightly modified? Which borrowed ideas are summarized but not credited?
- ☐ Where would attributions help signal more clearly where a source's ideas begin and stop?
- ☐ How could attributions be made more graceful and varied?

Edit and Proofread

- ☐ Where is parenthetic documentation lacking required information? Where must an author's name, a title, publication data, or page numbers be added?
- ☐ Which parenthetic citations contain punctuation errors? Where should a title be underlined or placed in quotation marks? Where should a comma be added or deleted?
- ☐ Where are quotations punctuated incorrectly? Which should start with a capital letter? Which should begin in lowercase? Which should be preceded by a comma? Which should not? Where should a capital letter be deleted? Where is a comma needed to connect the quotation to the text? Where should a comma be deleted?
- ☐ Where is the format for long quotations incorrect? How can it be corrected?
- ☐ Where is the format for the Works Cited list incorrect (pages 593–604)? Which entries are out of alphabetical order? Which titles should be underlined or placed in quotation marks? Where should commas or periods be added or deleted? Where should page numbers be added?

PREPARE THE WORKS CITED LIST: MLA FORMAT

At this point, you need to assemble your paper's **Works Cited list** (or bibliography). As a first step in preparing your Works Cited list, pull out the bibliography cards (or working bibliography) for the sources you referred to in your paper. Alphabetize them by the authors' last names. For now, put any anonymous works at the end.

The Works Cited list, which will appear at the end of your paper, should include only those works you actually quote, summarize, or otherwise directly refer to in your paper. Don't list other sources, no matter how many you may have read. Placed on its own page, the Works Cited list provides readers with full bibliographic information about the sources you cite in the paper.

Double-space the entries on the Works Cited list, and *don't* add extra space between entries. The first line of each new entry should start at the left margin; if an entry extends beyond one line of type, all subsequent lines should be indented five spaces. The major items in a bibliographic entry (the author's full name, the title, all the information on publication) are separated with periods. (See the sample Works Cited list on pages 626–628.)

The following sample entries will help you prepare an accurate Works Cited list.

Citing Book Sources

Here is the basic format for listing a book in Works Cited:

- Start with the author's name, last name first, then first name and any initial, with a comma between the first and last names. Put a period after the first name or initial. Leave one space between the period and the next item.
- Give the complete book title. If the book has a subtitle, separate it from the title with a colon. Leave a space after the colon. Underline the full title and follow it with a period. Leave one space between the period and the next item. (*Important note:* According to MLA guidelines, underlining titles is generally preferred to italicizing them because of the greater visibility of underlines; if you'd like to use italics instead, check with your instructor.)
- Next, give the city of publication, followed by a colon. Leave a space between the colon and the next item. If the publisher has more than one location, use the city listed first on the book's title page. If the book is published in the United States, give only the city. If it is published in a foreign city that may be unfamiliar to readers, give the city as well as an abbreviation of the country, separating them with a comma.
- Supply the publisher's name, giving only key words and omitting the words *Company, Press, Publishers, Inc.*, and the like. (For example, write *Rodale* for Rodale Press and *Norton* for W. W. Norton and Company.) In addition, use *UP* to abbreviate the names of university presses (as in *Columbia UP* and *U of California P*). Place a comma and a space after the publisher's name.
- End with the publication date and a period. Supply the most recent year of copyright. Don't use the year of the most recent printing. Conclude with the medium, *Print*.

Book by One Author

Neckerman, Kathryn M. *Schools Betrayed: Roots of Failure in Inner-City Education*. Chicago: U of Chicago P, 2007. Print.

For books varying from this basic entry, consult the examples that follow. If you don't spot a sample entry for the type of source you need to document, consult the latest edition of the *MLA Handbook for Writers of Research Papers* for more comprehensive examples.

Multiple Works by the Same Author

McChesney, Robert W. *The Problem of the Media: U.S. Communication Politics in the 21st Century*. New York: Monthly Review, 2004. Print.

---. *Rich Media, Poor Democracy: Communication Politics in Dubious Times*. Champaign: U of Illinois P, 1999. Print.

If you use more than one work by the same author, list each book separately. Give the author's name in the first entry only; begin the entries for other books by that author with three hyphens followed by a period. Arrange the works alphabetically by title. The words *A, An,* and *The* are ignored when alphabetizing by title.

Book by Two or Three Authors

Douglas, Susan, and Meredith Michaels. *The Mommy Myth: The Idealization of Motherhood and How It Has Undermined Women*. New York: Free Press, 2004. Print.

Gunningham, Neil A., Robert Kagan, and Dorothy Thornton. *Shades of Green: Business, Regulation, and Environment*. Palo Alto: Stanford UP, 2003. Print.

For a book with two or three authors, give all the authors' names but reverse only the first name. List the names in the order shown on the title page.

Book by Four or More Authors

Brown, Michael K., et al. *Whitewashing Race: The Myth of a Color-Blind Society*. Berkeley: U of California P, 2003. Print.

For a work with four or more authors, give only the first author's name followed by a comma and *et al.* (Latin for "and others").

Revised Edition

Weiss, Thomas G., David P. Forsythe, and Roger A. Coate. *The United Nations and Changing World Politics*. 3rd ed. Boulder: Westview, 2001. Print.

Zinn, Howard. *A People's History of the United States: 1492-Present.* Rev. ed. New York: Perennial, 2003. Print.

Follow the title with the edition, identified either by number (for example, *2nd*) or by the abbreviation *Rev.* (for *Revised*), depending on how the book itself indicates edition.

Book with an Author and Editor or Translator

Douglass, Frederick. *My Bondage and My Freedom.* Ed. John David Smith. New York: Penguin, 2003. Print.

Place the editor's or translator's name after the title, with the identifying abbreviation *Ed.* or *Trans.* before the person's name. Don't reverse the first and last names of the editor or translator. Figure 20.1 (on page 596) shows where to find the elements you need to compile this type of citation.

Anthology or Compilation of Works by Different Authors

Kasser, Tim, and Allen D. Kanner, eds. *Psychology and Consumer Culture: The Struggle for a Good Life in a Materialistic World.* Washington: American Psychological Association, 2004. Print.

If you refer in general to an edited book—rather than to the individual authors whose work it contains—give the editor's name in the author position, followed by a comma and the abbreviation *ed.* or *eds.* for two or more editors.

Section of an Anthology or Compilation

Levin, Diane E., and Susan Linn. "The Commercialization of Childhood: Understanding the Problem and Finding Solutions." *Psychology and Consumer Culture: The Struggle for a Good Life in a Materialistic World.* Eds. Tim Kasser and Allen D. Kanner. Washington: American Psychological Association, 2004. 212-28. Print.

If you use only a section from an anthology, list first the author of that particular selection or chapter. The remaining information should be presented in this order: selection title (in quotation marks), book title (italicized), editor's name (preceded by the abbreviation *Ed.*), publication data, selection's page numbers (don't use *p.* or *page*), and the medium "*Print.*"

Section or Chapter in a Book by One Author

Wolfson, Evan. "Is Marriage Equality a Question of Civil Rights?" *Why Marriage Matters: America, Equality, and Gay People's Right to Marry.* New York: Simon, 2004. 242-69. Print.

FIGURE 20.1
Book with an Author and Editor

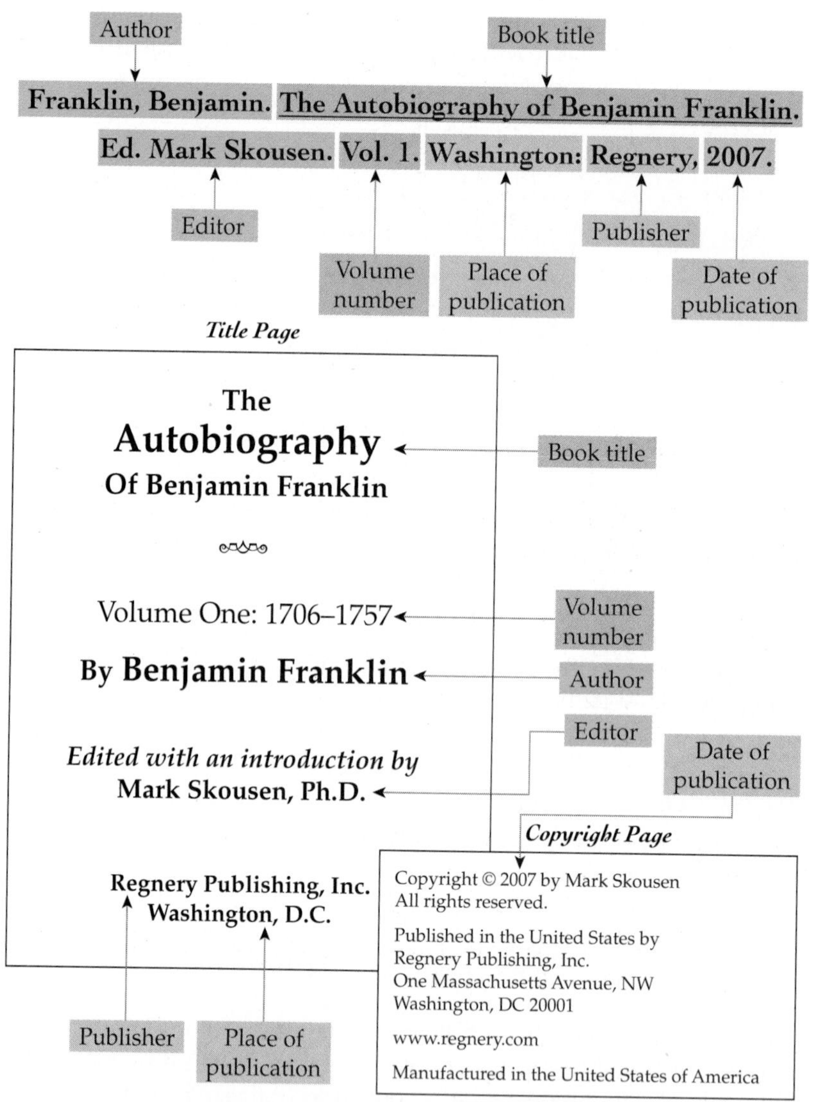

The MLA citation information for this book comes from its title and copyright pages. The copyright page is usually located on the back of the title page.

If you use only one named section or chapter of a book, give the section's title in quotation marks before the title of the book. At the end, give the section's page numbers. Don't use *p.* or *page.* If you use several sections, don't name each of them; just put the page numbers for all the sections at the end of the entry, before the medium of publication, *Print*.

Reference Work

"Temperance Movements." *Columbia Encyclopedia*. 6th ed. New York: Columbia UP, 2000. Print.

Book by an Institution or Corporation

United Nations. Department of Economic and Social Affairs. *Human Development, Health, and Education: Dialogues at the Economic and Social Council*. New York: United Nations, 2004. Print.

Give the name of the institution or corporation in the author position, even if the same institution is the publisher.

Citing Periodical Sources

For a periodical in print form, you'll need to consult the page with the journal title and copyright information and the first and last pages of the article. If you find the article through a database, the database will have identified and organized the information for you as a citation record. Here is the basic format for listing periodical articles in Works Cited:

- Start with the author's last name, following the guidelines for a book author. If the article is unsigned, begin with its title.
- Give the article's complete title followed by a period, all of which is enclosed in quotation marks. Leave one space between the terminal quotation mark and the next item in the entry.
- Supply the periodical's name, italicizing it. Don't place any punctuation after it.
- Give the date of publication. For newspapers and weekly magazines, include the day, month, and year—in that order. Abbreviate the month (using the first three to four letters) if it is five letters or longer. For scholarly journals, give the volume number, issue number (if appropriate), and year. In both cases, follow the date with a colon. Leave a space between the colon and the next item.
- Provide page number(s) without using *p.*, *pp.*, *page*, or *pages* before the numbers. If the pages in an article are continuous, give the page range (for example, 67–72 or 427–32). If the pages in an article aren't continuous (for example, 67–68, 70, 72), write the first page number and a plus sign (67+). Place a period after the page-number information. Conclude with the medium, "*Print*."

The following sample entries for articles in periodicals are formatted in the MLA style. If you don't spot an entry for the type of source you need to document, consult the *MLA Handbook* (see page 582) for more comprehensive examples.

Article in a Weekly or Biweekly Magazine

Kliff, Sarah. "A Stem-Cell Surprise." *Newsweek* 30 July 2007: 46-47. Print.

Article in a Monthly or Bimonthly Magazine

Wheeler, Jacob. "Outsourcing the Public Good." *Utne* Sept.-Oct. 2004: 13-14. Print.

Article in a Daily Newspaper

Doolin, Joseph. "Immigrants Deserve a Fair Deal." *Boston Globe* 19 Aug. 2003: A19+. Print.

Use the newspaper's name as it appears on the masthead, but delete any initial *The*. If the title doesn't specify the paper's location and the paper lacks nationwide recognition, put the town or city and (if necessary) the state in brackets after the title: *Today's Sunbeam* [Salem, NJ]. If the paper is a large daily, add a comma after the date and then indicate the particular edition (late, early, national, and so on), abbreviating longer words such as *national* (*natl.*) and *edition* (*ed.*).

For a newspaper with sections, if the section letter is part of each page number (see the example above), provide the section designation and page exactly as they appear (for example, *A15* or *10C*). However, if the section designation isn't part of the page number, use the abbreviation *sec.* followed by the section number or letter, a colon, and then the page number (for example, *sec. 3: 5* or *sec. C: 2+*). For a newspaper without sections, simply provide the page number. If the article is printed on multiple, nonconsecutive pages, simply list the first page (including both section and page numbers or letters) followed by a plus sign (+).

Editorial, Letter to the Editor, or Reply to a Letter

"Playing Fair with Nuclear Cleanup." Editorial. *Seattle Times* 5 Oct. 2003: D2. Print.

Johnson, Paul. "Want to Prosper? Then Be Tolerant." Editorial. *Forbes* 21 June 2004: 41. Print.

List as you would any signed or unsigned article, but indicate the nature of the piece by adding *Editorial, Letter,* or *Reply to letter of [letter writer's name]* after the article's title.

Article in a Scholarly Journal

Manning, Wendy D. "Children and the Stability of Cohabiting Couples." *Journal of Marriage and the Family* 66 (2004): 674-89. Print.

Chew, Cassie. "Achieving Unity Through Diversity." *Black Issues in Higher Education* 21.5 (2004): 8-11. Print.

Some journals are paged continuously (the first example): the first issue of each year starts with page 1, and each subsequent issue picks up where the previous one left off. For such journals, use numerals to indicate the volume number after the title, and then indicate the year in parentheses. Note that neither *volume* nor *vol.* is used. The article's page or pages appear at the end, separated from the year by a colon.

For a journal that pages each issue separately (the second example), use numerals to indicate the volume *and issue* numbers; separate the two with a period, leaving no space after the period.

Citing Electronic Sources

In general, include as much information as readers would need to locate the source for themselves.

Article in an Online Periodical

Orecklin, Michele. "Stress and the Superdad." *Time Online*. 16 Aug. 2004. Web. 19 May 2005.

Nachtigal, Jeff. "We Own What You Think." *Salon* 18 Aug. 2004. Web. 17 Mar. 2005.

Figure 20.2 (on page 600) shows where to find the elements you need to compile this type of citation. For an article obtained online, supply the same information you would for printed text: author's name, selection's title, source, and (when available) publication date. Add the medium of publication ("Web"), followed by a period, and the date you accessed the source, followed by a final period. Include the URL only if your instructor requires it or if readers may have trouble locating the source without one. Note that URLs should be broken only after slashes.

Article from a Library Subscription Service

Weiler, Angela M. "Using Technology to Take Down Plagiarism." *Community College Week* 16.16 (2004): 4-6. *MasterFILE Premier*. EBSCOhost. Web. 17 Apr. 2005.

For full-text articles accessed through an online database (generally only available to libraries by subscription), begin with the same information as for online periodicals. After the publication information (issue and date), list the title of the subscription service (italicized), the database, the medium of publication (Web) and the date you accessed the index. (*Note:* Because online material can be revised or updated at any time, providing the date on which you accessed the material is critical since that date is the only way to identify the version you retrieved.) Figure 20.3 (on page 601) shows where to find the elements you need to compile this type of citation.

FIGURE 20.2
Article in an Online Periodical

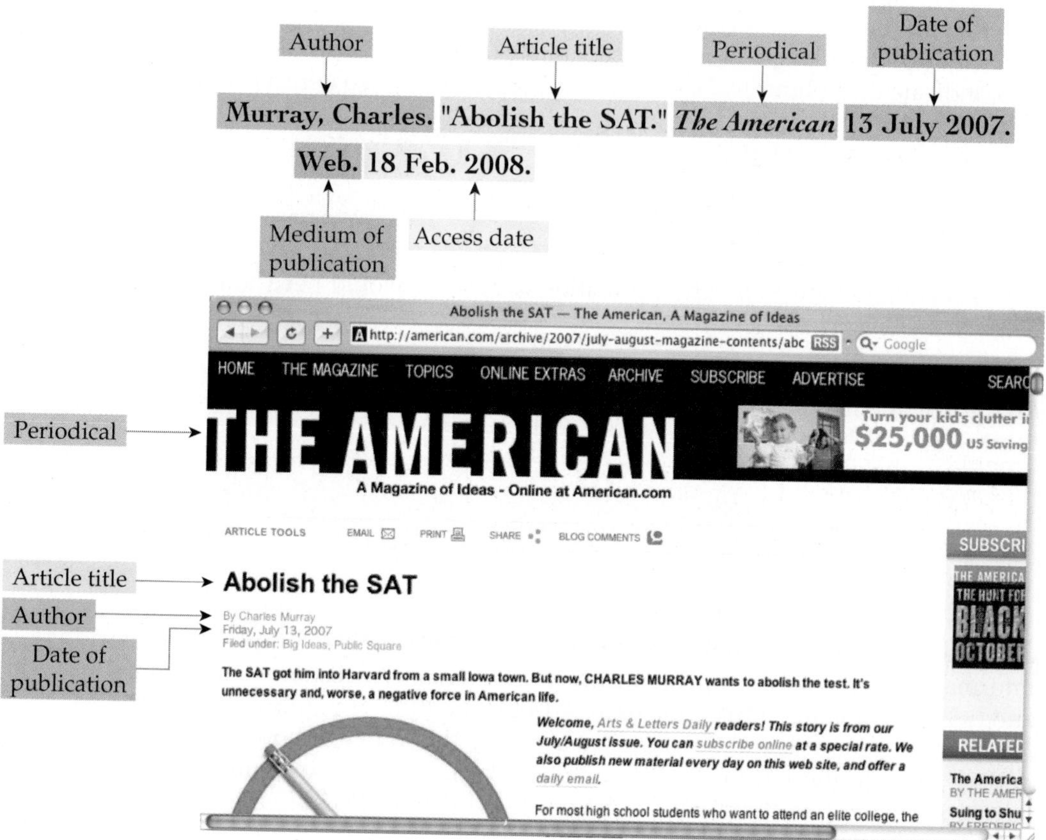

In this online article, the date of access is the date the student first visited the source.

Online Book

Franklin, Benjamin. *The Autobiography of Benjamin Franklin.* London, 1793. *Electronic Text Center*. Ed. Judy Boss. 1995. Web. 16 Jan. 2005.

When it's available, include the book's original publication information between the book's title and the italicized database name. Also include (when available) the name of the site's editor, its electronic publication date, its sponsoring organization, the medium "*Web*" (followed by a period), and your date of access.

FIGURE 20.3
Full-Text Article from a Library Subscription Service

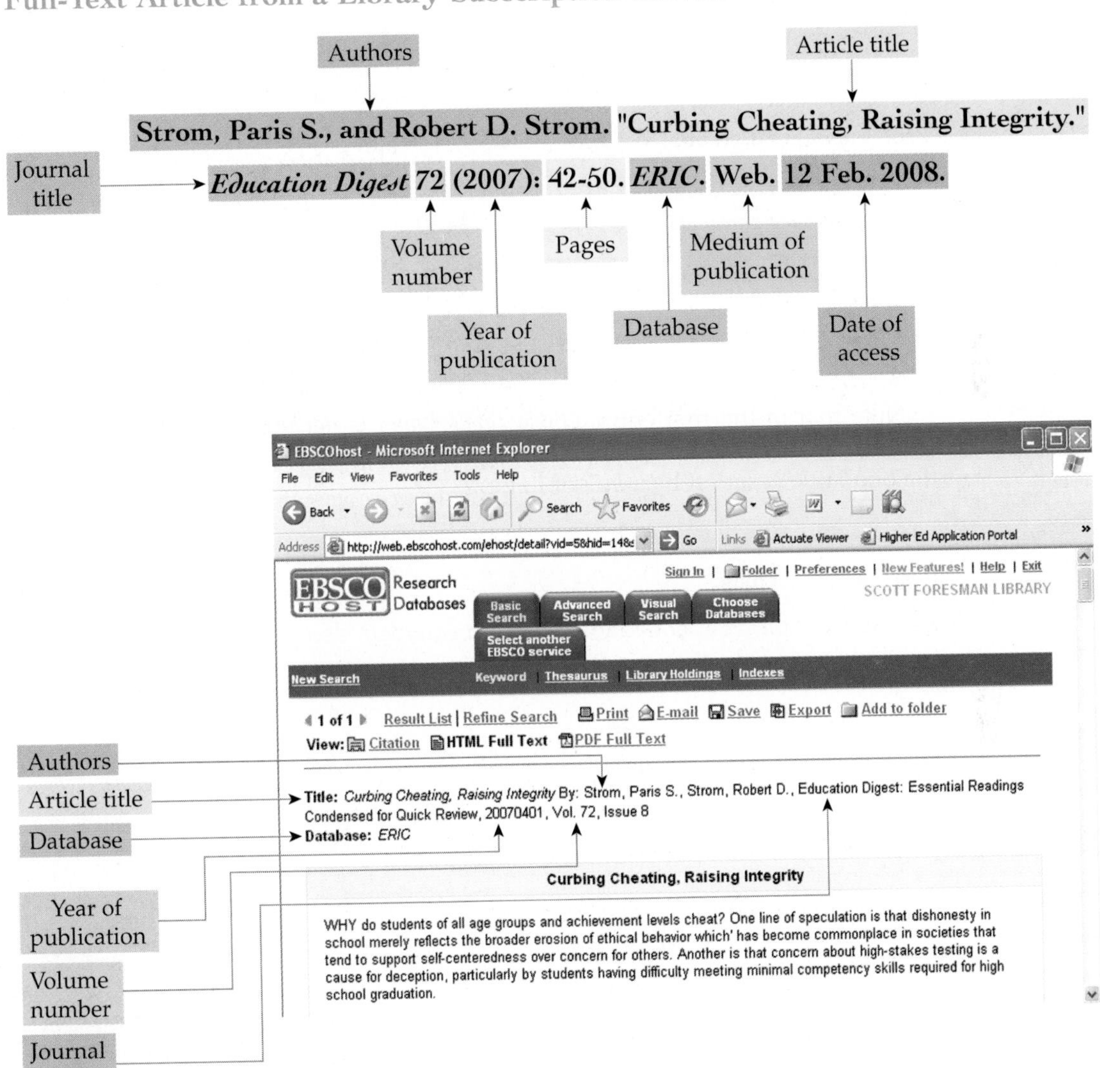

Because the above article was accessed in full-text HTML format, page numbers do not appear on screen. But page numbers are an integral piece of the citation and can be obtained from the PDF version of the article, the search results screen, or the article's detail screen (where you will also find additional information about the article, including an abstract.) In this example, the date of access is the date the student first visited the source.

Online Reference Work

"Salem Witch Trials." *Encyclopaedia Britannica Online*. 2007. Encyclopaedia Britannica. Web. 8 June 2007.

Professional or Personal Website

Railton, Stephen, ed. *Harriet Beecher Stowe's* Uncle Tom's Cabin *& American Culture: A Multi-Media Archive*. Dept. of English, U of Virginia, 20 Jan. 2003. Web. 2 Apr. 2005.

Finney, Dee. *Native American Culture*. 18 Jan. 2007. Web. 17 Feb. 2007.

Note that in the first entry, *Uncle Tom's Cabin* is *not* italicized. It's a title that would ordinarily be italicized, but since the rest of the website title is italicized, the book title is set off by a *lack* of italics.

Posting to a Weblog

TexasDemO. Online posting. *The Huffington Post*. 21 Apr. 2007. Web. 12 May 2007.

Postings to an Online Group

Zoutron. "Re: Geometry of sound." Online posting. 30 Mar. 2007. Web. 21 Apr. 2007.

Podcast

"Eban Goodstein, Global Warming Expert." Interview. *New Horizons in Education with Bob Kustra*. News 91 FM. Boise State Radio. 16 Feb. 2007. Web. 31 Mar. 2007.

Computer Software

World Book Encyclopedia 2004 Premiere Edition. 2004 ed. Renton: Topics Entertainment, 2004. CD-ROM.

Cite the following information (when available): author of the software, title (italicized), version, publication city, publisher, year of publication, and medium (CD-ROM or DVD-ROM).

E-Mail Message

Mack, Lynn. "New Developments in Early Childhood Education." Message to the author. 21 Mar. 2007. E-mail.

To cite e-mail, provide the name of the writer; the title of the message (if any), taken from the subject line of the posting and enclosed in quotation marks; a description of the message that includes the recipient (for example, "Message to the author"), the date of the message, and the medium *"E-mail."*

Citing Other Nonprint Sources

Television or Radio Program

"A Matter of Choice? Gay Life in America." *Nightline*. Narr. Ted Koppel. Part 4 of 5. ABC. WPVI-TV, Philadelphia. 23 May 2002. Television.

List, at a minimum, the program's title (italicized), the network that carried the program, the local station on which the program was seen or heard, and the city and date of the broadcast. If, as in the example above, the program is an episode in a continuing series, give the episode title first (in quotation marks), then the program title (italicized), then the series title, if any (neither italicized nor in quotation marks) and the medium ("Television"). You might also include additional information such as the director or narrator before the series title.

Movie, Recording, Videotape, DVD, Filmstrip, or Slide Program

Pan's Labyrinth. Dir. Guillermo del Toro. 2006. New Line Home Video, 2007. DVD.

List the title (italicized), director, distribution company, and year. The writer, main performers, or producers may be listed after the director and before the company. If the work is a videotape, filmstrip, or slide program, indicate the original release date (if applicable) and the medium (for example, *videotape, filmstrip,* etc.). If you use the source to discuss the work of a particular individual, begin with that person's name followed by his or her position (as in the second example above).

Personal or Phone Interview

Langdon, Paul. Personal interview. 26 Jan. 2007.

Como, Anna. Telephone interview. 1 Oct. 2006.

Lecture

Blacksmith, James. "Urban Design in the New Millennium." *Cityscapes Lecture Series*. Urban Studies Institute. Metropolitan College, Washington, 18 Apr. 2007. Address.

Papa, Andrea. "Reforming the Nation's Tax Structure." Lecture. Accounting 302, Cypress College. Astoria, New York. 3 Dec. 2007.

Start with the speaker's name, followed by the lecture's title (in quotation marks) if there is one. If not, identify the lecture with an appropriate label such as *Keynote address* or *Lecture*. Then provide the sponsoring organization's name, the site of the lecture, and the date.

DOCUMENT BORROWED MATERIAL TO AVOID PLAGIARISM: APA FORMAT

MLA documentation style is appropriate for research papers written for courses in the humanities, such as your composition course. Researchers in the social sciences and in education use a different citation format, one developed by the American Psychological Association (APA) and explained in the *Publication Manual of the American Psychological Association,* Sixth Edition. If you're writing a paper for a course in sociology, psychology, anthropology, economics, or political science, your professor will probably expect **APA-style documentation**. History, philosophy, and religion are sometimes considered humanities, sometimes social sciences, depending on your approach to the topic.

Parenthetic Citations

As in the MLA format, APA citations are enclosed in parentheses within the text and provide the author's last name. The main difference between the two formats is that the APA parenthetic note *always includes the year* of publication but *may not include the page number*. Specifically, the page number is *required* when a source is *quoted* or when *specific parts* of a source are *paraphrased* or *summarized.* (A citation without a page number refers to the source as a whole.) Also, APA citations are punctuated with commas between the author's name and the year and between the year and the page. Finally, *p.* or *pp.* appears before the page number(s).

Here are some examples of APA parenthetic citations:

Education experts have observed that "as arts education funding dwindles in school systems, theatres of all sizes have assumed more and more of the burden of training young people and exposing them to the arts" (Cameron, 2004, p. 6).

Today, theaters are increasingly playing the crucial role of cultivating the arts in youngsters, whose schools have been victimized by shrinking arts education budgets (Cameron, 2004, p. 6).

In APA format, if you lead into a quotation, paraphrase, or summary with an attribution that gives the author's name, the publication year follows the author's name in parentheses, and the page number appears at the end:

The social commentator Bob Herbert (2004) argues that middle-class Americans "are caught in a squeeze between corporations bent on extracting every last ounce of productivity from U.S. employees and a vast new globalized work force that is eager . . . to do the jobs of American workers at a fraction of the pay" (p. 20).

Bob Herbert (2004) believes that because of the pressures posed by globalization, middle-class Americans are increasingly under pressure by corporations to increase their work productivity (p. 20).

If a work has two authors, cite both. Join their names by *and* within the attribution and by an ampersand (&) within a parenthetic reference:

Dawn Newman-Carlson and Arthur M. Horne (2004) assert that schools must "explore the implementation not only of programs that assist bullies and aid their victims but also of those that strengthen the positive relationships between teachers, bullies, victims, and . . . bystanders to bullying" (p. 259).

Schools need to develop programs that work on improving the relationships between all parties to school bullying . . . bullies, their victims, bystanders, and teachers (Newman-Carlson & Horne, 2004, p. 259).

If a work has three to five authors, name all authors in the first citation. In subsequent citations, name only the first author followed by *et al.* If there are six or more authors, cite the first author followed by *et al.*

References List

As in the MLA style, a double-spaced alphabetical list of sources appears at the end of a research paper using APA documentation style. However, whereas the MLA titles this list *Works Cited*, the APA gives it the heading *References*.

The MLA and APA formats for listing sources include the same basic information, but they present it in different ways. Here are some of the distinguishing features of APA-style entries:

- The first line of each entry should start at the left margin; subsequent lines are indented one-half inch.
- The publication date is placed in parentheses directly after the author's name and is followed by a period.
- Two or more works by the same author are arranged according to publication date, with the earliest appearing first.
- Two or more works written by the same author and published in the same year are differentiated by lowercase letters—(1996a), (1996b)—and are alphabetized by title.
- All author names, numbering up to six, are given in the reference. When there are seven or more authors, write the name of the first, followed by *et al.* Use the ampersand (&) instead of *and*.
- All author names are inverted. In addition, an author's first and middle names are represented by initials only.
- Only the first letter of a book or article title (and subtitle) and any proper names contained within it are capitalized.
- Book titles should be *italicized* rather than underlined. Titles of chapters, which are placed within quotation marks in MLA style, appear *without* quotation marks in APA style.
- All titles appear *with* any initial *A*, *An*, or *The*.
- Include the city and state of publication; also, include the word *Press* when it's part of a publisher's name. The same applies to the word *University*.

Citing Book Sources

Here are sample APA-style citations for the most commonly used book references. (To illustrate the differences between MLA and APA formats, we have included here the same sources cited in the MLA documentation section [pages 594–604] but formatted them according to APA style. More information about APA documentation can be found in the latest edition of the *Publication Manual of the American Psychological Association.*)

Book by One Author

Neckerman, K. M. (2007). *Schools betrayed: Roots of failure in inner-city education*. Chicago, IL: University of Chicago Press.

Multiple Works by the Same Author

McChesney, R. W. (1999). *Rich media, poor democracy: Communication politics in dubious times*. Champaign, IL: University of Illinois Press.

McChesney, R. W. (2004). *The problem of the media: U.S. communication politics in the 21st century*. New York, NY: Monthly Review.

Book by Multiple Authors

Gunningham, N. A., Kagan, R., & Thornton, D. (2003). *Shades of green: Business, regulation, and environment*. Palo Alto, CA: Stanford University Press.

APA style lists the names of up to seven authors, with an ampersand (&) between the last two names. For eight or more authors, list the first six authors, insert an ellipsis (. . .), and give the last author's name.

Revised Edition

Weiss, T. G., Forsythe, D. P., & Coate, R. A. (2001). *The United Nations and changing world politics* (3rd ed.). Boulder, CO: Westview.

Book with an Author and Editor

Douglass, F. (2003). *My bondage and my freedom* (J. D. Smith, Ed.). New York, NY: Penguin. (Original work published 1855.)

Anthology or Compilation of Works by Different Authors

Kasser, T., & Kanner, A. D. (Eds.). (2004). *Psychology and consumer culture: The struggle for a good life in a materialistic world*. Washington, DC: American Psychological Association.

Section of an Anthology or Compilation

Levin, D. E., & Linn, S. (2004). The commercialization of childhood: Understanding the problem and finding solutions. In T. Kasser & A. D. Kanner (Eds.), *Psychology and consumer culture: The struggle for a good life in a materialistic world* (pp. 212-228). Washington, DC: American Psychological Association.

Section or Chapter in a Book by One Author

Wolfson, E. (2004). Is marriage equality a question of civil rights? In E. Wolfson, *Why marriage matters: America, equality, and gay people's right to marry* (pp. 242-269). New York, NY: Simon & Schuster.

Wolfson, E. (2004). *Why marriage matters: America, equality, and gay people's right to marry* (pp. 242-269). New York, NY: Simon & Schuster.

Reference Work

Temperance Movements. (2000). In *Columbia encyclopedia* (6th ed.). New York, NY: Columbia University Press.

Book by an Institution or Corporation

United Nations Department of Economic and Social Affairs. (2004). *Human development, health and education: Dialogues at the Economic and Social Council*. New York, NY: United Nations.

Citing Periodical Sources

Unlike the MLA, the APA uses no quotation marks around article titles. And, as noted, only the first word of an article's title and subtitle is capitalized. However, a periodical's name is italicized and all major words within it are capitalized. Include any initial *A, An* or *The* in a periodical's name. For both print and online sources, the APA recommends the addition of a Digital Object Identifier (DOI) at the end of the entry, when one is available. One source that can be used to locate a DOI is http://www.crossref.org.

Here are sample APA listings for articles in print periodicals:

Article in a Weekly or Biweekly Magazine

Kliff, S. (2007, July 30). A stem-cell surprise. *Newsweek*, 150, 46-47.

Article in a Monthly or Bimonthly Magazine

Wheeler, J. (2004, September/October). Outsourcing the public good. *Utne, 125*, 13-14.

Article in a Daily Newspaper

Doolin, J. (2003, August 19). Immigrants deserve a fair deal. *The Boston Globe*, pp. A19, A25.

Editorial, Writter to the Editor, or Unsigned Article in a Daily Newspaper

Playing fair with nuclear cleanup. (2003, 5 October). [Editorial]. *The Seattle Times*, p. D2.

Article in a Continuously Paginated Scholarly Journal

Manning, W. D. (2004). Children and the stability of cohabiting couples. *Journal of Marriage & Family, 66*, 674-689. doi: 10.1111/j.0022-2445.2004.00046.x

Article in a Scholarly Journal That Paginates Each Issue Separately

Chew, C. (2004). Achieving unity through diversity. *Black Issues in Higher Education, 21*(5), 8-11.

Citing Electronic Sources

Include the source's DOI at the end of the entry. If no DOI is assigned, provide the home page URL for the source. In general, do the same for sources that are accessed through an online database. If you cannot find the source's home page, simply cite the database (Retrieved from XXX database.).

Article in a Journal

Menjivar, Cecilia. (2009). Who belongs and why. *Society,* 46(5), 416-418. doi: 10.1007/s12115-009-9248-z

Article in an Online Periodical

Orecklin, M. (2004, August 16). Stress and the superdad. *Time Online*. Retrieved from http://www.time.com

Nachtigal, J. (2004, August 18). We own what you think. *Salon.com*. Retrieved from http://www.salon.com

Article in an Online Database

Weiler, A. M. (2004). Using technology to take down plagiarism. *Community College Week,* 16(16), 4-6. Retrieved from http://www.ccweek.com

Online Book

Franklin, B. (1995). *The autobiography of Benjamin Franklin*. Charlottesville: University of Virginia Library. (Original work published 1793). Retrieved from http://etext.lib .virginia.edu/toc/modeng/public/Fra2Aut.html

Online Reference Work

Salem Witch Trials. (2004). In *Encyclopaedia Britannica Online*. Retrieved from http://www.britannica.com/ebc /article-9065052/Salem-witch-trials

Professional or Personal Website

Railton, S. (Ed.). (2003, January 20). *Harriet Beecher Stowe's* Uncle Tom's Cabin *and American culture: A multi-media archive*. Retrieved from http://www.iath.virginia.edu/utc/

Finney, D. (2007, January 18). *Native American culture*. Retrieved from http://www.greatdreams.com/native.htm

Posting to a Weblog

Huffington, A. (2007, April 21). Tom DeLay has the solution to gun violence: More guns! [Weblog message]. Retrieved from http://www.huffingtonpost.com/arianna-huffington/tom-delay-has-the-solutio_b_46426.html

Posting to an Online Group

Zoutron. (2007, March 30). Re: Geometry of sound. [Online forum comment]. Retrieved from http://groups.google.com/group/geometry.research, archived at http://groups.google.com/group/geometry.research/browse_frm/month/2007-03

Podcast

Brown, J. (Producer). (2007, February 16). *Eban Goodstein, global warming expert.* [Audio podcast]. Retrieved from http://radio.boisestate.edu/NewHorizons.html

Computer Software

World Book Encyclopedia 2004 Premiere Edition. (2004). [Computer software]. Renton, WA: Topics Entertainment.

E-mail Message

According to APA style, personal correspondence, such as e-mail, is not included in the References list. Instead, cite such communications parenthetically in the text.

Citing Other Nonprint Sources

Television or Radio Program

Koppel, T. (Narrator). (2002, May 23). A matter of choice? Gay life in America. (Television series episode). In L. Sievers (Executive Producer), *Nightline*. Philadelphia, PA: WPVI.

Movie, Recording, Videotape, DVD, Filmstrip, or Slide Program

del Toro, G. (Writer/Director). (2007). *Pan's labyrinth* [Motion picture DVD]. Culver City, CA: New Line Home Video.

Personal Interview, Phone Interview, or Lecture

As with e-mail messages, these personal communications should not be noted in the References list but, rather, parenthetically within the text.

A NOTE ABOUT OTHER DOCUMENTATION SYSTEMS

Generally, professionals in the hard sciences (biology, chemistry, medicine, physics) and technical fields (computer science and electrical engineering) use neither the MLA nor the APA system of documentation. Rather, using bracketed or superscripted (raised) reference numbers, they key each item of borrowed material to an entry on the References page. The References list, therefore, isn't alphabetized; instead, the numbered sources simply appear in the order in which they are mentioned in the paper.

When you write a paper for a science course, ask your professor whether you should use MLA style, APA style, or the system found in most science and technical journals. If your instructor prefers the last, find out which publication can serve as your model. That way, you won't be unpleasantly surprised by any criticism that you've used an inappropriate system of documentation.

STUDENT RESEARCH PAPER: MLA-STYLE DOCUMENTATION

The sample outline and research paper that follow were written by Brian Courtney for a composition class. In his paper, Brian uses the MLA documentation system. (On pages 630–631, excerpts from the research paper are formatted in APA style.) To help you spot various types of sources, quotations, and attributions, we've annotated the paper. Our marginal comments also flag key elements, such as the paper's thesis statement, plan of development, and concluding summary.

Note that the main headings in Brian's outline parallel, to a large degree, the topic sentences of the paper's paragraphs; subheadings generally represent the points that develop those paragraphs. The outline contains no sections corresponding to Brian's introduction and conclusion because he wrote those only after completing the body of his paper. As you read the paper, pay special attention to the way Brian incorporates source material and uses it to support his own ideas.

As you'll see, Brian provided a title page because his paper was preceded by an outline. For a paper submitted without an outline, use a top heading rather than a title page. Here is the format for a first page with a top heading.

Commentary

Brian begins his introduction with an evocative description of a typical street person's struggle to survive. These descriptive passages prepare readers for a general statement of the problem of homelessness. This two-sentence statement, starting with "'They' are the homeless" and ending with "the private sector and local governments can't possibly cope," leads the way to Brian's *thesis*: "To help homeless people toward independence, the federal government must support rehabilitation and job training programs, raise the minimum wage, and fund more low-cost housing."

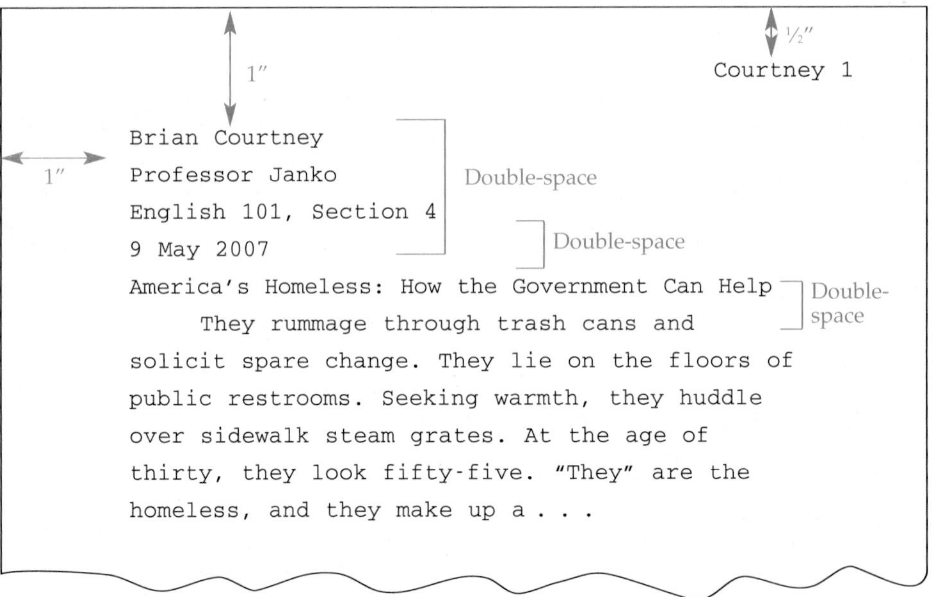

Courtney 1

Brian Courtney
Professor Janko
English 101, Section 4
9 May 2007

America's Homeless: How the Government Can Help

They rummage through trash cans and solicit spare change. They lie on the floors of public restrooms. Seeking warmth, they huddle over sidewalk steam grates. At the age of thirty, they look fifty-five. "They" are the homeless, and they make up a . . .

America's Homeless:
How the Government Can Help
by
Brian Courtney
English 101, Section 4
Professor Janko
9 May 2007

Although a title page isn't necessary, you may be asked to provide one.

A paper *with* an outline often has a separate title page.

Title begins about one-third of the way down the page.

Center the title. Double-space between lines of the title and your name.

Course and section, instructor's name, and date, on separate lines, are double-spaced and centered.

½″

1″

Courtney i

After the title page, number all pages in upper-right corner—a half-inch from the top. Place your name before the page number. Use small roman numerals on outline pages. Use Arabic numbers on pages following the outline.

The word *Outline* (without underlining or quotation marks) is centered one inch from the top. Double-space to first line of outline.

Double-space both outline and text. Leave one-inch margins at top, bottom, and sides.

Outline

Thesis: The federal government should do more to help the homeless toward independence.

I. Homelessness is a major problem in the United States.
   A. Experts disagree about the number of Americans who are homeless.
   B. Experts agree that the number of homeless, particularly homeless families, is growing.

II. Finding ways to help the homeless is difficult.
   A. Even if the homeless find shelter, they still often wander the street.
      1. Some homeless people are addicted to alcohol or drugs.
      2. Some have serious psychiatric problems.
      3. Others lack basic survival skills.
   B. Comprehensive programs are needed to address the complex problems that many homeless people have.

III. Some programs offer exactly this kind of broad assistance to the homeless.
   A. Bloomberg's "supportive housing" model ensures needed services are located near the housing of formerly homeless tenants.
   B. Project Renewal and Pine Street Inn offer substance-abuse programs.
   C. Lenox Hill Neighborhood House and CANP also offer psychological-support programs for the homeless.
      1. Counseling sessions are attended by those with substance-abuse problems.

1″ 1″

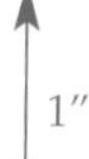

Courtney ii

2. Counseling sessions are attended by runaway teens.
3. Counseling sessions are attended by those overwhelmed by personal difficulties.

IV. Some broad-assistance programs provide training in everyday survival skills.
   A. Homes for the Homeless offers workshops on everything from nutrition to interview techniques.
   B. Project Hope shows clients how to apply for food stamps and other benefits to which they are entitled.
   C. House of Hope provides instruction in household budgeting and home maintenance.

V. Some broad-assistance programs help the homeless get a job.
   A. Many of the homeless have no jobs or have never worked more than six months.
   B. CANP provides training in résumé writing and interviewing.
   C. CANP's job training has a high success rate.

VI. The federal government should help such broad-assistance programs.
   A. CANP'S funding has slipped.
   B. Project Hope doesn't have the resources needed to meet the growing demands on its services.

VII. The government should also raise the minimum wage.
   A. Some of the homeless have jobs, but their low incomes put most housing out of their reach.

Courtney iii

B. The last two decades have seen a dramatic drop in minimum-wage buying power.

VIII. A lack of affordable housing is at the center of the homeless problem.

A. One magazine argues that people's deep disturbance--in addition to the unavailability of inexpensive housing--are another source of the homeless problem.

B. Numerous studies and many experts refute this viewpoint and show that recent trends in housing are the real culprit.

IX. The federal government should finance more low-cost housing.

A. Affordable private housing is almost non-existent.

1. Gentrification increases the price of previously low-cost housing units, putting them beyond the reach of poor people.

2. Even rundown SRO hotels charge more than the poor can afford.

B. Public housing can accommodate only a small percentage of those seeking relief from high costs in the private housing market.

1. The federal government has cut funding of public housing and housing subsidies.

2. Cities have slashed funding for the construction of public housing and shelters.

Courtney 1

1 America's Homeless: How the Government Can Help

They rummage through trash cans and solicit spare change. They lie on the floors of public restrooms. Seeking warmth, they huddle over sidewalk steam grates. At the age of thirty, they look fifty-five. "They" are the homeless, and they make up a growing percentage of America's population. Indeed, homelessness has reached such proportions that the private sector and local governments can't possibly cope. To help homeless people toward independence, the federal government must support rehabilitation and job training programs, raise the minimum wage, and fund more low-cost housing.

2 Not everyone agrees on the number of Americans who are homeless. Estimates range anywhere from 600,000 to 2.3 million at any given time (Link et al. 353; "Millions Still Face"). According to *The Economist*, a study in the mid 1990s estimated that twelve million Americans "have been homeless at some point in their lives" ("Out of Sight"). Although the figures may vary, analysts agree on another matter: that the number of homeless, particularly of homeless families, is increasing. According to the National Alliance to End Homelessness, families with children are the "fastest growing group of homeless people," comprising about 40% of the homeless population. A U.S. Conference of Mayors survey in 2003 found that requests for shelter access by homeless families increased in 88% of twenty-five major U.S. cities, an increase of 15% over the previous year ("U.S. Conference" i-ii).

3 Finding ways to assist this growing and changing homeless population has become increasingly difficult. Even when homeless individuals or families manage to find a shelter that will give them three

For a paper with a separate title page, you may repeat the paper's title, centered, on the first page of the text. Double-space between the title and text.

Introduction

Thesis, with plan of development

Parenthetic citation for information that appears in two sources. Sources given in order they appear on Works Cited list. First citation indicates a work with more than three authors; page number *and* first author's name given since author is not cited earlier in the sentence. No author or page number given for the second source since it is an anonymous online article.

Common Knowledge is not documented.

Courtney 2

Attribution gives author's name and area of expertise. Parenthetical reference at end of sentence gives just the page number since the author is cited in the attribution.

Parenthetic reference gives page but not author since author is cited in the paper.

meals a day and a place to sleep at night, a good number have trouble moving beyond the shelter system and securing a more stable lifestyle. Part of the problem, explains sociologist Christopher Jencks in his now classic study, is that many homeless adults are addicted to alcohol and drugs (41-42). And psychiatrist E. Fuller Torrey adds that nearly one-third of the homeless have serious psychiatric disorders (17). Individuals suffering from such disorders and from addiction often lack the ability to seek and obtain jobs and homes, and therefore remain homeless for a longer period of time ("Mental Illness"). While not addicted or mentally ill, many others simply lack the everyday survival skills needed to turn their lives around. Reporter Lynette Holloway notes that New York City officials believe the situation will improve only when shelters provide comprehensive programs that address the many needs of the homeless (B1). As Catherine Howard, director of the Bronx-based Paradise Transitional Housing Program, wrote in a letter to *The New York Times*, "Identifying the needs of the homeless and linking them with services in the community is as important as finding suitable housing. Many homeless people return to the . . . shelter system and eventually to the street because of the lack of such support services" (A26). Far from seeking to assist the homeless, Leonard C. Feldman observes in *Citizens Without Shelter*, many U.S. cities have "turned to a more punitive approach," passing legislation outlawing the homeless lifestyle (2).

Full-sentence quotation is preceded by a comma and begins with a capital letter.

Quotation blends into rest of the sentence (no comma; quotation's first word is not capitalized).

Luckily, a number of agencies are beginning to 4
act on the belief that the homeless need "more

Courtney 3

than a key and a lease" if they are to acquire the attitudes, skills, and behaviors needed to stay off the street (Howard A26). In an effort to reduce homelessness in New York City, Mayor Michael R. Bloomberg sought in 2004 to implement more widely a "supportive housing" model. Originally applied to single homeless people, supportive housing was expanded to include families, "keeping the services tenants need close to their apartments"--often in shared buildings (Kaufman, "City Is Gambling" B1). Such a government initiative follows the lead of many nonprofit agencies. Besides providing shelter, nonprofit agencies such as New York City's Project Renewal and Boston's Pine Street Inn offer substance-abuse programs and intensive follow-ups to ensure that clients remain sober and drug-free (Holloway B1; United States 29). To help the homeless cope with psychological problems, New York City's Lenox Hill Neighborhood House and Boston's Community Action Now Program (CANP) provide in-house social workers and psychiatric care (Holloway B1; Van Meder). Joan Van Meder, CANP's cofounder and director, explained in an e-mail interview that her organization offers one-on-one and group sessions helping not only recovering substance abusers but also runaway teenagers (some of whom are pregnant) as well as individuals overwhelmed by personal traumas like divorce, death of a family member, or loss of a job. Staff counselors refer individuals with more severe psychological disturbances to community health agencies.

For one of multiple works by the same author, include all or part of title, preceded by a comma, between author's name and page number.

Second source is a government publication.

No page number given for second source in parenthetic citation because source is an e-mail interview.

E-mail interview source is identified.

In addition to providing psychological support, 5
many organizations instruct the homeless in basic survival skills. Adapting the principles of

"Continuum of Care," a project sponsored by the Department of Housing and Urban Development, such agencies provide training in the everyday skills that clients need to live independently (Halper and McCrummen 26). New York City's Homes for the Homeless has established facilities called "American Family Inns." Functioning as "residential, literacy, employment, and training centers for entire families," these centers emphasize good nutrition, effective parenting, education, household-management skills, and job-search and interview techniques (Nunez 72). Boston's Project Hope also works to guide the homeless toward self-sufficiency, showing them how to apply for jobs and how to obtain disability compensation and veterans' benefits (Leonard 12-13). At St. Martin de Porres House of Hope, a Chicago shelter, homeless women and their children are assigned household jobs upon their arrival and learn the basics of domestic budgeting and home maintenance (Driscoll 46). Such increased responsibility teaches the homeless how to cope with life's everyday challenges--and prepares them for the demands of working life.

Parenthetic citation for a work with two authors

Parenthetic citation for a single-author source. Page number *and* author are given since the author is not cited earlier in the sentence.

Since many of the homeless have little work experience, it is not surprising that vocational training is a key service provided by broad-based agencies. According to Jencks's often-cited survey, 94% of the homeless lack steady work (50). The same survey shows that most heads of homeless families have never worked longer than six months (Nunez 28). Through challenging instruction that includes practice in writing a résumé and interviewing for a position, CANP and other agencies coach the homeless in getting and keeping a job. As a result 6

Courtney 5

of such intensive training, CANP has an outstanding job placement rate, with 75% of those completing its job-training program moving on to self-sufficiency (Van Meder).

E-mail interview source provided in parentheses since no attribution given in the sentence.

7 Unfortunately, organizations like CANP are struggling to survive on dwindling allocations. Boston's Project Hope, for example, served as a short-term way-station for homeless families through the late 1980s, until the recession of the early '90s. Then welfare and public-assistance policies of the mid 1990s reduced the program's operating budget. Fewer families now meet the tighter eligibility requirements to stay at the shelter, and those who do are forced to stay longer because so few housing subsidies are available (Leonard 11-12). It's apparent that government aid is necessary if suppliers of comprehensive assistance--like CANP and Project Hope--are to meet the needs of a growing population.

Besides funding local programs for the homeless, the government also needs to raise the minimum wage. Some homeless people are employed, but their limited education locks them into minimum-wage positions that make it nearly impossible for them to afford housing. According to the Economic Policy Institute, "real pay for the bottom 10 percent of wage earners rose less than 1 percent in adjusted dollars from 1979 to 2003"; meanwhile, housing costs tripled in the same period (Kaufman, "Surge in Homeless" A18). Dennis Culhane, professor of Social Welfare Policy at the University of Pennsylvania, explains that employed homeless individuals--who typically receive the minimum wage--pay such a high percentage of their salary on housing 8

Second title by author of multiple works cited in this paper.

Courtney 6

Where a secondary source is quoted—in a government publication

that "their income doesn't cover their housing costs" (qtd. in United States 12). For instance, researchers studying the economics of Baltimore, MD, determined that, per hour, the actual living wage is approximately $2.50 *more than* the minimum wage earned by workers in that city Hess). Patrick Markee also points to this disastrous decline in minimum-wage buying power:

Attribution leading to a long quotation. Attribution is followed by a colon since the lead-in is a full sentence. If the lead-in isn't a full sentence, use a comma after the attribution.

> Indeed, the causes of modern mass homelessness are a matter of little debate, and reside in what many academics and advocates call the affordability gap: the distance between the affordability (and availability) of secure, stable housing and the income levels of poor Americans.... The other side of the affordability gap has two elements, one of which is by now familiar to most Americans: the steep decline in real wages since the mid-seventies; the steady erosion of the minimum wage; the widening gulf between rich and poor during the past two decades; and the growing severity of poverty. (27)

Long quotation indented ten spaces. Double-space the quotation, as you do the rest of the paper. Don't leave extra space above or below the quotation.

The word *Americans* is followed by an ellipsis plus a period, indicating that some material has been deleted from the end of the original sentence.

The Economist concurs that this escalating 9
affordability gap makes it difficult for poor people to find suitable housing. Even so, the magazine argues, eroding incomes and a lack of affordable housing aren't the only culprits in the homeless problem. For *The Economist*, homelessness owes to a variety of social problems, including single-parenting, substance abuse, and mental illness—and a combination thereof ("Out of Sight").

No author or page number is given since source is an anonymous one-page article.

Courtney 7

Numerous studies dispute such an interpretation; 10
they conclude, as does one urban researcher, that a lack of affordable housing—not "an enduring internal state" like addiction or mental illness—plays the critical role in putting people on the street (Shinn). In *Making Room: The Economics of Homelessness*, Brendan O'Flaherty points out that large-scale deinstitutionalization of the mentally ill occurred between 1960 and 1975; however, it wasn't until the 1980s—a period marked by sharp cuts in subsidized housing—that large numbers of the mentally ill wound up living on the streets (235). Shinn cites a study that supports the view that a lack of affordable housing is at the center of the homelessness problem. She conducted a longitudinal study of homeless families who received subsidized housing in New York City and found that "whatever other problems families may have had, an average of 5 years after entering shelter, 61% were stably housed in their own apartments for at least a year and an average of 3 years. Only 4% were in shelter." Shinn concludes, "Receipt of subsidized housing was both a necessity and a sufficient condition for achieving stability." Even Jencks, whose views are similar to those of *The Economist*, believes that more affordable "housing is still the first step in dealing with the homeless problem. Regardless of why people are on the streets, giving them a place to live...is usually the most important thing we can do to improve their lives" (qtd. in United States 7).

Clearly, the federal government must increase 11
its funding of low-cost housing. Such a commitment is essential given recent developments in both the

Parenthetic citation for article obtained online; author provided but no page given since electronic text does not follow the pagination of the original

Attribution naming book and its author

Quotation preceded by *that* blends into the rest of the sentence (no comma; quotation's first word is not capitalized).

No parenthetic citation is needed because author's name appears in text and because electronic text does not follow pagination of the original.

Courtney 8

private and public housing markets. As Markee explains, affordable private housing has become increasingly scarce in the last several decades (27). The major problem affecting the private market is gentrification, a process by which low-cost units are transformed into high-cost housing for affluent professionals. Following the economic boom of the late 1990s, rents have risen across America, tempting landlords to gentrify their low-income housing ("Out of Sight"). As neighborhoods gentrify, housing that formerly trickled down to the poor is taken off the low-cost market, increasing homelessness (O'Flaherty 117). Also, in gentrified areas, many of the tenements and SRO (single-room occupancy) hotels in which the desperately poor used to live have been gutted and replaced by high-priced condominiums. And the tenements and SROs that remain generally demand more rent than the poor can pay (Halper and McCrummen 29).

Where can people turn to seek relief from these 12
inflated costs in the private housing market? What remains of public housing can hardly answer the problem. As Markee notes, the 1980s saw the federal government cut spending on public housing and housing subsidies by 75%. In 1980, for example, federal agencies helped build 183,000 housing units. By the mid-1980s, that number had fallen to 20,000 (27). To counteract these reductions, many cities invested heavily in new housing in the late 1980s. In the 1990s, though, city budgets slashed such investments in half (Halper and McCrummen 28). Municipal money now goes to constructing temporary shelters that can

house only 2% of the cities' homeless population (Halper and McCrummen 27).

In light of all these problems, one conclusion seems inevitable: the federal government must take a more active role in helping America's homeless. While debate may continue about the extent and the causes of homelessness, we know which approaches work and which do not. The government must increase its support of programs that make a demonstrable difference. Such programs do more than provide food and shelter; they also offer substance-abuse counseling, psychological support, instruction in basic survival skills, and job training. Finally, unless the government guarantees a decent minimum wage and affordable housing, even skilled, well-adjusted individuals may be forced to live on the street. The government can't continue to walk past the homeless, face averted. In doing so, it walks past millions in need.

13 Conclusion provides a summary and restates the thesis.

Courtney 10

Interview published in a weekly magazine—interview's pages are consecutive

Book by one author—publisher's name is abbreviated

Article by two authors, in a monthly magazine; pages are consecutive

Article in a full-text online periodicals index. The title of the index, its vendor, the medium, and the access date are listed after the publication information.

Article in a daily newspaper—section indicated along with pages; pages are not consecutive

Letter to a daily newspaper, obtained from a CD-ROM

Second work by the same author, listed alphabetically. Three hyphens and a period appear in place of author's name.

Works Cited

Driscoll, Connie. "Responsibility 101: A Chat with Sister Connie Driscoll." Interview with Bruce Upbin. *Forbes* 19 May 1997: 46-47. Print.

Feldman, Leonard C. *Citizens Without Shelter: Homelessness, Democracy, and Political Exclusion*. Ithaca: Cornell UP, 2004. Print.

Halper, Evan, and Stephanie McCrummen. "Out of Sight, Out of Mind: New York City's New Homeless Policy." *Washington Monthly* Apr. 1998: 26-29. Print.

Hess, Robert V. "Helping People Off the Streets: Real Solutions to Urban Homelessness." *USA Today Magazine* Jan. 2000: 18-20. *MasterFILE Premier*. EBSCOhost. Web. 6 Feb. 2007.

Holloway, Lynette. "Shelters Improve under Private Groups, Raising a New Worry." *New York Times* 12 Nov. 1997, late ed.: B1+. Print.

Howard, Catherine. Letter. *New York Times*. 18 Nov. 1997, late ed.: A26. *New York Times Ondisc*. UMI-ProQuest. Oct. 1998. CD-ROM.

Jencks, Christopher. *The Homeless*. Cambridge: Harvard UP, 1994. Print.

Kaufman, Leslie. "City Is Gambling on an Old Program to Cure Homelessness." *New York Times* 19 July 2004: B1+. Print.

---. "Surge in Homeless Familes Sets Off Debate on Cause." *New York Times* 29 June 2004: A18. Print.

Leonard, Margaret A. "Project Hope: An Interview with Margaret A. Leonard." Interview with George Anderson. *America* 2 Nov. 1996: 10-14. Print.

Courtney 11

Link, Bruce, et al. "Lifetime and Five-Year Prevalence of Homelessness in the United States: New Evidence on an Old Debate." *American Journal of Orthopsychiatry* 65 (1995): 347-54. Print.

Markee, Patrick. "The New Poverty: Homeless Families in America." Rev. of *The New Poverty*, by Ralph Nunez. *The Nation* 14 Oct. 1996: 27-28. Print.

"Mental Illness and Homelessness." *National Coalition for the Homeless*. 18 Apr. 2001. Web. 27 Nov. 2007.

"Millions Still Face Homelessness in a Booming Economy." *The Urban Institute*. 1 Feb. 2000. Web. 2 May 2007.

Nunez, Ralph da Costa. *The New Poverty: Homeless Families in America*. New York: Insight, 1996. Print.

O'Flaherty, Brendan. *Making Room: The Economics of Homelessness*. Cambridge: Harvard UP, 1998. Print.

"Out of Sight, Out of Mind." Editorial. *Economist* 20 May 2000: 27. *MasterFILE Premier*. EBSCOhost. Web. 27 Mar. 2007.

Shinn, Marybeth. "Family Homelessness: State or Trait?" *American Journal of Community Psychology* 25.6 (1997): 36-42. *Expanded Academic Index ASAP*. InfoTrac Search Bank. Web. 30 Mar. 2007.

Torrey, E. Fuller. *Out of the Shadows: Confronting America's Mental Illness Crisis*. New York: Wiley, 1997. Print.

Article, by more than three authors, in a scholarly journal with continuous pagination

Book review in a monthly magazine

Anonymous material obtained on the Internet. Name of website, publication, and access dates appear.

Anonymous editorial in a weekly magazine obtained through an online database

Article in a scholarly journal obtained through an online database

Courtney 12

Government publication

United States. Cong. House. Subcommittee on Housing and Community Opportunity of the Committee on Banking and Financial Services. *Hearing on Homeless Housing Programs Consolidation and Flexibility Act*. 105th Cong., 1st sess. Washington: GPO, 1997. Print.

"U.S. Conference of Mayors-Sodexho Hunger and Homelessness Survey." *National Alliance to End Homelessness*. Dec. 2003. Web. 3 May 2007.

E-mail interview

Van Meder, Joan. Correspondence with the author. 18 Apr. 2007. E-mail.

Commentary

Brian begins his introduction with an evocative description of a typical street person's struggle to survive. These descriptive passages prepare readers for a general statement of the problem of homelessness. This two-sentence statement, starting with "'They' are the homeless" and ending with "the private sector and local governments can't possibly cope," leads the way to Brian's *thesis*: "To help homeless people toward independence, the federal government must support rehabilitation and job training programs, raise the minimum wage, and fund more low-cost housing."

By researching his subject thoroughly, Brian was able to marshal many compelling facts and opinions. He sorted through this complex web of material and arrived at a logical structure that reinforces his thesis. He describes the extent of the problem (paragraph 2), analyzes some of the causes of the problem (3, 4, 8–12), and points to solutions (4–6, 8, 11–12). He draws upon *statistics* to establish the severity of the problem and quotes *expert opinion* to demonstrate the need for particular types of programs. Note, too, that Brian writes in the *present tense* and uses the *third-person point of view*.

Beyond being clearly organized and maintaining a consistent point of view, the paper is *unified* and *coherent*. For one thing, Brian makes it easy for readers to follow his line of thought. He often uses *transitions*: "In addition" (5), "Besides" (8), and so forth. In other places, he asks a *question* (for example, at the beginning of the twelfth paragraph), or he uses a *bridging sentence* (for instance, at the beginning of the fifth, sixth, and eighth paragraphs). Moreover, he always provides clear attributions and parenthetic references so that readers know at every point along the way whose idea is being presented. Brian has, in short, prepared a well-written, carefully documented paper.

STUDENT RESEARCH PAPER: APA-STYLE DOCUMENTATION

To give you an idea of how a research paper in APA style would look, we've excerpted Brian Courtney's research paper (pages 617–628) and reformatted those pages in APA style. APA papers may also require a title page and an abstract. The pages are numbered continuously, starting with the title page, and the References list starts on a new page. For additional specifics, see the APA *Publication Manual* or ask your instructor.

½″

1″

America's Homeless 3

Center, bold, and double-space the title. Indent the first line of every paragraph 5 spaces. Double-space the text.

America's Homeless: How the Government Can Help

They rummage through trash cans and solicit spare change. They lie on the floors of public restrooms. Seeking warmth, they huddle over side-walk steam grates. At the age of 30, they look 55. "They" are the homeless, and they make up a growing percentage of America's population. Indeed, homelessness has reached such proportions that the private sector and local governments can't possibly cope. To help homeless people toward independence, the federal government must support rehabilitation and job training programs, raise the minimum wage, and fund more low-cost housing.

In general, use numerals for 10 and above.

1″

1″

For a source with five or more authors, give the first author's surname and "et al." followed by a comma and the year. Alphabetize two sources given in the same citation and separate them with a semicolon.

Not everyone agrees on the number of Americans who are homeless. Estimates range anywhere from 600,000 to 2.3 million at any given time (Link et al. 1995; Urban Institute, 2000). According to *The Economist*, a study in the mid 1990s estimated that 12 million Americans "have been homeless at some point in their lives" (Out of Sight, 2000). Although the figures may vary, analysts agree on another matter: that the number of homeless, particularly of homeless families, is increasing. According to the National Alliance to End Homelessness, families with children are the "fastest growing group of homeless people," comprising about 40% of the homeless population. A U.S. Conference of Mayors survey in 2003 found that requests for shelter access by homeless families increased in 88% of twenty-five major U.S. cities, an increase of 15% over the previous year (*U.S. Conference*, 2003).

For a source listed by title in the References list, abbreviate the title in the text citation.

For a source listed by organization in the References list, give a shortened form of the organization name.

1″

America's Homeless 10

References

Anderson, G. (Interviewer) & Leonard, M. A. (Interviewee). (1996, November 2). Project Hope: An interview with Margaret A. Leonard [Interview transcript]. *America*, 10–14.

Feldman, L. C. (2004). *Citizens without shelter: Homelessness, democracy, and political exclusion*. Ithaca, NY: Cornell University Press.

Halper, E., & McCrummen, S. (1998, April). Out of sight, out of mind: New York City's new homeless policy. *Washington Monthly*, 26–29.

Hess, R. V. (2000, January). Helping people off the streets: Real solutions to urban homelessness. *USA Today Magazine*, 18–20. Retrieved from http://www.usatoday.com

Kaufman, L. (2004, June 29). Surge in homeless families sets off debate on cause. *New York Times*, p. A18.

Kaufman, L. (2004, July 19). City is gambling on an old program to cure homelessness. *New York Times*, pp. B1, B3.

Center "References" at the top of a new page and double-space to the first line. Start each entry flush left and indent subsequent lines 5 spaces. Double-space throughout.

Spell out names of months.

Give the author's last name and first initial, followed by the date.

For books, give the city and state (Postal Service abbreviation) for place of publication.

For two authors, use an ampersand (&) between names and invert the second author's name.

For names of periodicals, capitalize and use italics.

Place the date in parentheses right after the author's name.

Retrieval date is no longer required for texts in their final (archived) forms, such as published articles. For an item accessed electronically, add the home page URL of the database and any retrieval number, if necessary.

For journal, magazine, and newspaper articles, capitalize the first word of the title and subtitle and proper nouns. Use regular type.

Give all page numbers on which an article appears.

Items by the same author are listed in chronological order—earliest first.

ACTIVITIES: WRITING THE RESEARCH PAPER

1. Imagine that you've just written a research paper exploring how parents can ease their children's passage through adolescence. Prepare a Works Cited list for the following sources, putting all information in the correct MLA format. When you are finished, reformat the list as a References list in APA style.

   a. "The Emotional Life of the Adolescent," a chapter in Ralph I. Lopez, M.D.'s *The Teen Health Book: A Parent's Guide to Adolescent Health and Well-Being*. The chapter runs from page 55 to page 70. The book was published by W.W. Norton & Company (New York, NY) in 2002.

   b. One radio broadcast within a series called *Voices in the Family*, hosted by Dr. Daniel Gottlieb and produced by Laura Jackson. The broadcast, titled "Adolescents, TV, and Sex," aired on 27 September 2004, on WHYY-FM of Philadelphia, PA.

   c. An article titled "Transmission of Values from Adolescents to Their Parents," by Martin Pinquart and Rainer K. Silbereisen. The article appeared in Spring 2004 in volume 39, issue 153 of *Adolescence* (which paginates each issue separately). The article runs from page 83 to page 100.

   d. A book and an article by Laurence Steinberg. The book, *You and Your Adolescent: A Parent's Guide for Ages 10–20*, was published in 1997 by HarperCollins Publishing (PA). The article, "Ethnicity and Adolescent Achievement," appeared on pages 28 to 35 and 44 to 48 in the Summer 1996 issue of *American Educator*.

   e. An unpaginated article, titled "Normal Adolescent Development," on the website *Adolescence Directory On-Line*, published by the Center for Adolescent Studies at Indiana University. The article appeared on 29 September 1998 and was accessed on 27 March 2002. The URL is <http://education.indiana.edu/cas/adol/development.html>.

   f. An article from pages 1 and 4, section B, of the July 21, 2001, issue of *The Wall Street Journal*. Written by Tara Parker-Pope, the article is titled, "Rise in Early Puberty Causes Parents to Ask, 'When Is It Too Soon?'" and has nine paragraphs. The article was found on the *ERIC Database* CD-ROM, published by the U.S. Department of Education in 2001.

2. Assume you're writing a research paper on "type A" personalities. You decide to incorporate into your paper points made by James Gleick in "Life As Type A" (page 441). To practice using attributions, parenthetic citations, and correct punctuation with quoted material, do the following:

   a. Choose a statement from the essay to quote. Then write one or more sentences that include the quotation, a specific attribution, and the appropriate parenthetic citation.

b. Choose an idea to summarize from the essay. Then write one or more sentences that include the summary and the appropriate parenthetic documentation.

c. Find a place in the essay where the author quotes an expert or experts. Use this quotation to write one or more sentences in which you:
   - first, quote the expert(s) quoted by Gleick
   - second, summarize the ideas of the expert(s) quoted by Gleick

Each of the above should include the appropriate attribution and parenthetic citation.

For additional writing, reading, and research resources, go to **www.mycomplab.com** and choose **Nadell/Langan/Comodromos'** ***The Longman Writer, 7/e***.

PART V

THE LITERARY PAPER AND EXAM ESSAY

21

Writing About Literature

PEANUTS reprinted by permission of United Feature Syndicate, Inc.

Does the idea of writing a **literary analysis** make you anxious? If it does, we'd like to reassure you that in some ways writing a literary analysis is easier than writing other kinds of essays. For one thing, you don't have to root around, trying to figure out what you want to accomplish: Your purpose in any literary analysis is simply to share with readers some insights about an aspect of a poem, play, story, or novel.[1] Second, in a literary analysis, your thesis and supporting evidence grow directly out of your reading of the text. All you have to do is select the textual evidence that supports your thesis.

By examining both *what* the author says and *how* he or she expresses it, you increase your readers' understanding and appreciation of the work. And, of course, literary analysis rewards you as well. Close textual analysis develops your ability to think critically and independently. Studying literature also strengthens your own writing. As you examine literary works, you become familiar with the strategies that skilled writers use to convey meaning with eloquence and power. Finally, since literature deals with the largest, most timeless issues, literary analysis is one way to learn more about yourself, others, and life in general.

[1]For the sake of simplifying a complex subject, we discuss literary analysis as though it focuses on a single work. In practice, though, a literary analysis often examines two or more works.

ELEMENTS OF LITERARY WORKS

Before you can analyze a literary text, you need to become familiar with literature's key elements. The following list of literary terms will help you understand what to look for when reading and writing about literature.

Literary Terms

Theme: a work's controlling idea, the main issue the work addresses (for example, loyalty to an individual versus loyalty to a cause; the destructive power of a lie). Most literary analyses deal with theme, even if the analysis focuses on the methods by which that theme is conveyed.

Plot: the series of events that occurs within the work. Typically, plays and stories hinge on plot much more heavily than poetry, which is often constructed around images and ideas rather than actions.

Structure: a work's form, as determined by plot construction, act and scene divisions, stanza and line breaks, repeated images, patterns of meter and rhyme, and other elements that create discernible patterns. (See also *image, meter, rhyme,* and *stanza.*)

Setting: the time and place in which events unfold (the present, on a hot New York City subway car; a nineteenth-century sailing vessel in the South Pacific).

Character: an individual within a poem, play, story, or novel (Tom Sawyer, Ophelia, Oliver Twist, Bigger Thomas).

Characterization: the way in which the author develops an individual within the work.

Conflict: a struggle between individuals, between an individual and some social or environmental force, or within an individual.

Climax: the most dramatic point in the action, usually near the end of a work and usually involving the resolution of conflict.

Foreshadowing: hints, within the work, of events to come.

Narrator or **speaker:** the individual in the work who relates the story. It's important to remember that the narrator is not the same as the author. The opening of Mark Twain's *Huckleberry Finn* makes this distinction especially clear: "You don't know me, without you have read a book by the name of *The Adventures of Tom Sawyer,* but that ain't no matter. That book was made by Mr. Mark Twain, and he told the truth, mainly." A poorly educated boy named Huck Finn is the narrator; it is *his* captivating but ungrammatical voice that we hear. In contrast, Twain, the author, was a sophisticated middle-aged man whose command of the language was impeccable.

Point of view: the perspective from which a story is told. In the **first-person** (*I*) point of view, the narrator tells the story as he or she experienced it ("*I* saw the bird flap its wings"). The first-person narrator either participates in or observes the action. In the **third-person** point of view, the narrator tells the story the way someone else experienced it ("*Dave* saw the bird flap its wings"). The third-person narrator is not involved in the action. He or she may simply report outwardly observable behavior or events, enter the mind of only one character, or enter the minds of several characters. Such a third-person narrator may be *omniscient* (all-knowing) or have only *limited knowledge* of characters and events.

Irony: a discrepancy or incongruity of some kind. *Verbal irony,* which is often tongue-in-cheek, involves a discrepancy between the literal words and what is actually meant ("Here's some news that will make you sad. You received the highest grade in the course"). If the ironic comment is designed to be hurtful or insulting, it qualifies as *sarcasm* ("Congratulations! You failed the final exam"). In *dramatic irony,* the discrepancy is between what the speaker says and what the author means or what the audience knows. The wider the gap between the speaker's words and what can be inferred about the author's attitudes and values, the more ironic the point of view.

Satire: ridicule (either harsh or gentle) of vice or folly, with the purpose of developing awareness—even bringing about reform. Besides using wit, satire often employs irony to attack absurdity, injustice, and evil.

Figure of speech: a non-literal comparison of dissimilar things. The most common figures of speech are **similes,** which use the word *like* or *as* ("*Like* a lightning bolt, the hawk streaked across the sky"); **metaphors,** which state or imply that one thing *is* another ("All the world's a stage"); and **personification,** which gives human attributes to something nonhuman ("The angry clouds unleashed their fury").

Image: a short, vivid description that creates a strong sensory impression ("A black flag writhed in the wind").

Imagery: a combination of images.

Symbol: an object, place, characteristic, or phenomenon that suggests one or more things (usually abstract) in addition to itself (rain as mourning; a lost wedding ring as betrayal). Usually, though, symbols don't convey meaning in pat, unambiguous ways. Rain, for example, may suggest purification as well as mourning; a lost wedding ring may suggest a life-affirming break from a destructive marriage as well as betrayal.

Motif: a recurring word, phrase, image, figure of speech, or symbol that has particular significance.

Meter: a basic, fixed rhythm of accented and unaccented syllables that the lines of a particular poem follow.

Rhyme: a match between two or more words' final sounds (*Cupid, stupid; mark, park*).

Stanza: two or more lines of a poem that are grouped together. A stanza is preceded and followed by some blank space.

Alliteration: repetition of initial consonant sounds (such as the "b" sounds in "A *b*utterfly *b*looms on a *b*uttercup").

Assonance: repetition of vowel sounds (like the "a" sounds in "m*a*d *a*s *a* h*a*tter").

Sonnet: a fourteen-line, single-stanza poem following a strict pattern of meter and rhyme. The Italian, or *Petrarchan,* sonnet consists of two main parts: eight lines in the rhyme pattern *a b b a, a b b a,* followed by six lines in the pattern *c d c, c d c* or *c d e, c d e.* The English, or *Shakespearean,* sonnet consists of twelve lines in the rhyme scheme *a b a b, c d c d, e f e f,* followed by two rhymed lines *g g* (called a *couplet*). Traditionally, sonnets are love poems that involve some change in tone or outlook near the end.

HOW TO READ A LITERARY WORK

Read to Form a General Impression

The first step in analyzing a literary work is to read it through for an overall impression. Do you like the work? What does the writer seem to be saying? Do you have a strong reaction to the work? Why or why not?

Ask Questions About the Work

One way to focus your initial impressions is to ask yourself questions about the literary work. You could, for example, select from the following checklist those items that interest you the most or those that seem most relevant to the work you're analyzing.

ANALYZING A LITERARY WORK: A CHECKLIST

- ☐ What *themes* appear in the work? How do *structure, plot, characterization, imagery,* and other literary strategies reinforce theme?
- ☐ What gives the work its *structure* or shape? Why might the author have chosen this form? If the work is a poem, how do *meter, rhyme, alliteration, assonance,* and *line breaks* emphasize key ideas? Where does the work divide into parts? What words and images are repeated? What patterns do they form?
- ☐ How is the *plot* developed? Where is there any *foreshadowing?* What are the points of greatest suspense? Which *conflicts* add tension? How are they resolved? Where does the *climax* occur? What does the *resolution* accomplish?
- ☐ What do the various *characters* represent? What motivates them? How is character revealed through dialog, action, commentary, and physical description? In what ways do major characters change? What events and interactions bring about the changes?
- ☐ What is the relationship between *setting* and *action*? To what extent does setting mirror the characters' psychological states?

- ☐ Who is the *narrator*? Is the story told in the *first* or the *third person*? Is the narrator omniscient or limited in his or her knowledge of characters and events? Is the narrator recalling the past or reporting events as they happen?
- ☐ What is the author's own *point of view*? What are the author's implied *values* and *attitudes*? Does the author show any religious, racial, sexual, or other biases? Is there any discrepancy between the author's values and attitudes and those of the narrator? To whom in the work does the author grant the most status and consideration? Who is presented as less worthy of consideration?
- ☐ What about the work is *ironic* or surprising? Where is there a discrepancy between what is said and what is meant?
- ☐ What role do *figures of speech* play? What *metaphors*, if any, are sustained and developed? Why might the author have used these metaphors?
- ☐ What functions as a *symbol*? How can you tell?
- ☐ What *flaws* do you find in the work? Which elements fail to contribute to thematic development? Where does the work lose impact because ideas are stated directly rather than implied? Do any of the characters seem lifeless or inconsistent? Are any of them unnecessary to the work's key events and themes?

Reread and Annotate

Focusing on what you consider the most critical questions from the preceding checklist, begin a second, closer reading of the literary work. With pen or pencil in hand, look for answers to your questions, being sure to note telling details and patterns. Underline striking words, images, and ideas. Draw connecting lines between related items. Jot down questions, answers, and comments in the margins. Of course, if you don't own the work, then you can't write in it. In this case, make notes on a sheet of paper or on index cards.

We've marked the accompanying poem to give you an idea of just what annotation involves. The poem is Shakespeare's Sonnet 29, first published in 1609. Notice that the annotations reveal patterns crucial to an interpretation. For example, jotting down the *rhyme scheme* (*a b a b, c d c d,* and so on) leads to the discovery that one change in rhyme corresponds to a turning point in the narrator's thoughts (see line 9). Similarly, the circling or underlining of repeated or contrasting words highlights ideas developed throughout the poem. The words, *I, my,* and *state,* for instance, are emphasized by repetition. The marginal comments also capture possible *themes,* such as love's healing, redemptive power and the futility of self-absorption and envy.

a When, in disgrace with Fortune and men's eyes,
b I all alone beweep my outcast state,
a And trouble deaf heaven with my bootless (useless) cries,
b And look upon myself and curse my fate,
c Wishing me like to one more rich in hope,
d Featur'd (good looks) like him, like him with friends possess'd,
c Desiring this man's art (talent), and that man's scope (knowledge),
d With what I most enjoy contented least;
e Yet in these thoughts myself almost despising
b Haply I think on thee (First time lover is mentioned.), and then my state,
e Like to the lark at break of day arising
b From sullen earth, sings hymns at heaven's gate;
f For thy sweet love rememb'red such wealth brings
f That then I scorn to change my state (don't want to trade places) with kings.

Envy

Contrast between unhappy self-absorption ("beweep") and joyous love ("haply"), between "outcast state" and "scorn to change my state."

Changes to increasing joy. Turns away from self-absorption.

Joyous images. New beginning. Healing power of love.

Modify Your Annotations

Your annotations will help you begin to clarify your thoughts about the work. With these ideas in mind, try to read the work again; make further annotations on anything that seems relevant and modify earlier annotations in light of your greater understanding of the work. At this point, you're ready to move on to the actual analysis.

WRITE THE LITERARY ANALYSIS

When you prepare a literary analysis, the steps you follow are the same as those for writing an essay. You start with prewriting; next, you identify your thesis, gather evidence, write the draft, and revise; finally, you edit and proofread your paper.

Prewrite

Early in the prewriting stage, you should take a moment to think about your purpose, audience, point of view, and tone. Your **purpose** in writing a literary analysis is to share your insights about the work. Even if your paper criticizes some aspect of the work (perhaps it finds fault with the author's insensitive depiction of the poor), your primary purpose is still to convey your interpretation of the work's meaning and methods. When writing literary analysis, you customarily assume that your **audience** is composed of readers already familiar with the work. This makes your task easier. In the case of a play or story, for example, there's no need to rehash the plot.

As you write, you should adopt an objective, **third-person point of view.** Even though you're expressing your own interpretation of the work, guard against veering off into first-person statements like "In my opinion" and "I feel that." The **tone** of a literary analysis is generally serious and straightforward. However, if your aim is to point out that an author's perspective is narrow or biased or that a work is artistically unworthy of high regard, your tone may also have a critical edge. Be careful, though, to concentrate on the textual evidence in support of your view; don't simply state your objections.

Prewriting actually begins when you annotate the work in light of several key questions you pose about it (see pages 637–639). After refining your initial annotations (see page 639), try to impose a tentative order on your annotations. Ask yourself, "What points do my annotations suggest?" List the most promising of these points on a separate sheet; then link these points to your annotations. There are a number of ways to proceed. You could, for instance, simply list the annotations under the points they support. Or you can number each point and give relevant annotations the same number as that point. Another possibility is to color-code your annotations: Give each point a color; then underline or circle in the same color any annotation related to that point. Finally, prepare a scratch outline of the main points you plan to cover, inserting your annotations in the appropriate spots. (For more on scratch outlines, see pages 31–33 in Chapter 2.)

If you have trouble generating and focusing ideas in this way, experiment with other prewriting strategies. You might, for example, *freewrite* a page or two on what you have highlighted in the literary text, *brainstorm* a list of ideas, or *map out* the work's overall structure (see pages 25–26 in Chapter 2). Mapping is especially helpful when analyzing a poem.

If the work still puzzles you, it may be helpful to consult outside sources. Encyclopedias, biographies of the author, and history books can clarify the context in which the work was written. Such reference books as *The Oxford Companion to American Literature* and *The Oxford Companion to English Literature* offer brief biographies of authors and summaries of their major works. In addition, *Twentieth-Century Short Story Explication: Interpretations, 1900–1975, of Short Fiction* lists books and articles on particular stories; and *Poetry Explication: A Checklist of Interpretation Since 1925 of British and American Poems Past and Present* does the same for individual poems.

Identify Your Thesis

Looking over your scratch list and any supplementary prewriting material or research notes you've collected, try to formulate a **working thesis.** As in other kinds of writing, your thesis statement for a literary analysis should include both your *limited subject* (the literary work you'll analyze and what aspect of the work you'll focus on), as well as your *attitude* toward that subject (the claim you'll make about the work's themes, the author's methods, the author's attitudes, and so on).

Here are some effective thesis statements for literary analysis:

In the poem "The Garden of Love," William Blake uses sound and imagery to depict what he considers the deadening effect of organized religion.

The characters in the novel *Judgment Day* illustrate James Farrell's belief that psychology, not sociology, determines fate.

The figurative language in Marge Piercy's poem "The Longings of Women" reveals much about women's feelings and their struggle for power.

If your instructor asks you to include commentary from professional critics, or if you explore such sources at your own initiative, proceed with caution. To avoid merely adopting others' ideas, try to formulate your thesis about the work *before* you read anyone else's interpretation. Then use others' opinions as added evidence in support of your thesis or as opposing viewpoints that you can counter. (For more on thesis statements, see pages 36–42 in Chapter 3.)

Thesis Statements to Avoid

Guard against a *simplistic* thesis. A statement like "The author shows that people are often hypocritical" doesn't say anything surprising and fails to get at a work's complexity. More likely, the author shares insights about the *nature* of hypocrisy, the *reasons* underlying it, the *forms* it can take, or its immediate and long-term *effects.*

An *overly narrow* thesis is equally misguided. Don't limit your thesis to the time and place in which the work is set. You shouldn't, for example, sum up the theme of Hawthorne's *The Scarlet Letter* with the thesis "Hawthorne examines the intolerance of seventeenth-century Puritan New England." Hawthorne's novel probes the general, or universal, nature of communal intolerance. Puritan New England is simply the setting in which the work's themes are dramatized.

Also, make sure your thesis is *about the work.* Discussion of a particular *social* or *political issue* is relevant only if it sheds light on the work. If you feel a work has a strong feminist theme, it's fine to say so. It's a mistake, however, to stray to a nonliterary thesis such as "Feminism liberates both men and women."

A *biographical thesis* is just as inappropriate as a sociopolitical one. By all means, point out the way a particular work embodies an author's prejudices or beliefs ("Through a series of striking symbols, Yeats pays tribute in 'Easter, 1916' to the valiant struggle for Irish independence"). Don't, however, devise a thesis that passes judgment on the author's personal or psychological shortcomings ("Poe's neurotic attraction to inappropriate women is reflected in the poem 'To Helen'"). It's usually impossible to infer such personal flaws from the text alone. Perhaps the author had a mother fixation, but that determination belongs in the domain of psychoanalysis, not literary analysis.

Support the Thesis with Evidence

Once you've identified a working thesis, return to the text to make sure that nothing in the text contradicts your theory. Also, keeping your thesis in mind, search for previously overlooked **evidence** (*quotations* and *examples*) that develops your thesis. Consider, too, how *summaries* of portions of the work might support your interpretation.

If you don't find solid textual evidence for your thesis, either drop or modify it. Don't—in an effort to support your thesis—cook up possible relationships among characters, twist metaphors out of shape, or concoct elaborate patterns of symbolism. As Sigmund Freud once remarked, "Sometimes a cigar is just a cigar." Be sure there's plentiful evidence in the work to support your interpretation. The text of Shakespeare's *Romeo and Juliet,* for instance, doesn't support the view that the feud between the lovers' two families represents a power struggle between right-wing and left-wing politics.

Organize the Evidence

When it comes time to **organize your evidence,** look over your scratch list and evaluate the main points, textual evidence, and outside research it contains. Focusing on your thesis, decide which points should be deleted and which new ones should be added. Then identify an effective sequence for your points. That done, check to see if you've placed textual evidence and outside research under the appropriate points. If you plan to refute what others have said about the work, the discussion on pages 468–469 will help you block out the outline's refutation section. What you're aiming for is a solid, well-developed outline that will guide your writing of the first draft. (For more on outlining, see page 59 in Chapter 5.)

When preparing your outline, remember that the patterns of development can help you sequence material. If you're writing in response to an assignment, the assignment itself may suggest certain patterns. Consider these examples:

Comparison-Contrast

In Mark Twain's *Huckleberry Finn,* what traits do the Duke and the Dauphin have in common? In what ways do the two characters differ?

Definition

How does Ralph Waldo Emerson define "forbearance" in his poem of that name?

Process Analysis

Discuss the stages by which Morgan Evans is transformed into a scholar in Emlyn Williams's play *The Corn Is Green.*

Notice that, in these assignments, certain words and phrases (*have in common; in what ways . . . differ; define;* and *discuss the stages*) signal which pattern would be particularly appropriate. Often, though, you'll write on a topic of your own choice. For help in deciding which pattern(s) of development you might use in such circumstances, turn to pages 69–70 in Chapter 6.

Write the First Draft

At this point, you're all set to write. As you rough out your first draft, try to include textual evidence (quotations, examples, summaries), as well as any outside commentary you may have gathered. However, if you get bogged down either incorporating all the evidence or making it blend smoothly with your own points, move on. You can go back and smooth out any rough spots later. In general, proceed as you would in a research paper when blending quotations and summaries with your own words (see pages 587–589 in Chapter 21).

When preparing the draft, you should also take into account the following four conventions of literary analysis.

Use the Present Tense

Literary analysis is written in the **present,** not the past, tense:

In "Arrangement in Black and White," Dorothy Parker depicts the self-deception of a racist who is not conscious of her own racism.

The present tense is used because the literary work continues to exist after its completion. Use of the past tense is appropriate only when you refer to a time earlier than that in which the narrator speaks.

Identify Your Text

Even if your only source is the literary work itself, some instructors may want you to identify it by author, title, and publication data in a formal bibliographic note. In such a case, the first time you refer to the work in the paper, place a superscripted number after its title. Then, at the bottom of the page, type the same superscripted number, and, after it, provide full bibliographic information. Here's an example of such a bibliographic footnote:

[1]Marianne Moore, "To a Steam Roller," *The Voice That Is Great within Us: American Poetry of the Twentieth Century*, ed. Hayden Carruth (New York: Bantam, 1985) 126.

(For more about bibliographic footnotes, consult the most recent edition of the *MLA Handbook for Writers of Research Papers.*)

Use Parenthetic References

If you're writing about a very short literary work, your instructor may not require documentation. Usually, however, documentation is expected.

Fiction quotations are followed by the page number(s) in parentheses (89); poetry quotations, by the line number(s) (12–14); and drama quotations, by act, scene, and line numbers (2.1.34–37). The parenthetic reference goes right after the quotation, even if your own sentence continues. When your sentence concludes with the quotation, the final period belongs *after* the parenthetic reference. If you use sources other than the literary text itself, document these as you would quotations or borrowed ideas in a research paper, and provide a Works Cited page. In this case, the literary work you're writing about should also be listed on the Works Cited page, rather than in a bibliographic footnote. (For more on parenthetic documentation and Works Cited listings, see Chapter 20.)

Quote Poetry Appropriately

If you're writing about a short poem, it's a good idea to include the poem's entire text in your paper. When you need to quote fewer than four lines from a poem, you can enclose them in quotation marks and indicate each line break with a slash (/): "But at my back I always hear / Time's winged chariot hurrying near." (Notice that space appears before and after the slash.) Verse quotations of four or more lines should be indented ten spaces from the left margin of your paper and should appear line for line, as in the original source—without slashes to indicate line breaks.

Revise Overall Meaning, Structure, and Paragraph Development

After completing your first draft, you'll gain helpful advice by showing it to others. The checklist that follows will help you and your readers apply to literary analysis some of the revision techniques discussed in Chapters 7 and 8.

☑ REVISING A LITERARY ANALYSIS: A CHECKLIST

Revise Overall Meaning and Structure

- ☐ What is the thesis of the analysis? According to the thesis, which elements of the work (such as theme and structure) will be discussed? In what ways, if any, is the thesis simplistic or too narrow? In what ways, if any, does it introduce extraneous social, political, or biographical issues?
- ☐ What main points support the thesis? If any points stray from or contradict the thesis, what changes should be made?
- ☐ How well supported by textual evidence is the essay's thesis? What evidence, crucial to the thesis, needs more attention? What other interpretation, if any, seems better supported by the evidence?
- ☐ Which patterns of development (comparison-contrast, process analysis, and so on) help shape the analysis? How do these patterns support the thesis?

- ☐ What purpose does the analysis fulfill? Does it simply present a straightforward interpretation of some aspect of the work? Does it point out some flaw in the work? Does it try to convince readers to accept an unconventional interpretation?
- ☐ How well does the analysis suit an audience already familiar with the work? How well does it suit an audience that may or may not share the interpretation expressed?
- ☐ What tone does the analysis project? Is it too critical or too admiring? Where does the tone come across as insufficiently serious?

Revise Paragraph Development

- ☐ What method of organization underlies the sequence of paragraphs? How effective is the sequence?
- ☐ Which paragraphs lack sufficient or sufficiently developed textual evidence? Where does textual evidence fail to develop a paragraph's central point? What important evidence, if any, has been overlooked?
- ☐ Which paragraphs contain too much textual evidence? Which quotations are longer than necessary?
- ☐ Where could textual evidence in a paragraph be more smoothly incorporated into the analysis?
- ☐ If any of the paragraphs include outside research (expert commentary, biographical data, historical information), how does this material strengthen the analysis? If any of the paragraphs consider alternative interpretations, are these opposing views refuted? Should they be?

Revise Sentences and Words

- ☐ Which words and phrases wrongly suggest that there is only one correct interpretation of the work ("Everyone must agree . . ." "Obviously . . .")?

- ☐ What words give the false impression that it is possible to read an author's mind ("Clearly, Dickinson intends us to see the flowers as . . ." "With Willy Loman's suicide, Miller wants to show that . . .")
- ☐ Where does the analysis fail to maintain the present tense? Which uses of past tense aren't justified—that is, which don't refer to something that occurred earlier than the narrator's present?
- ☐ Where is there inadequate or incorrect documentation?
- ☐ Where does language lapse into needless literary jargon?
- ☐ If poetry is quoted, where should slash marks indicate line breaks? Where should lines be indented?

Edit and Proofread

When editing and proofreading your literary analysis, you should proceed as you would with any other type of essay (see pages 140–143 in Chapter 9). Be sure, though, to check textual quotations with special care. Make sure you quote correctly, use ellipses appropriately, and follow punctuation and capitalization conventions.

PULLING IT ALL TOGETHER

Read to Form a General Impression

By this time, you're familiar with the steps involved in writing a literary analysis, so you're probably ready to apply what you've learned. The following short story was written by Langston Hughes (1902–1967), a poet and fiction writer who emerged as a major literary figure during the Harlem Renaissance of the 1920s. Published in 1963, the story first appeared in *Something in Common,* a collection of Hughes's work. Read the story and gather your first impressions. Then follow the suggestions after the story.

LANGSTON HUGHES

EARLY AUTUMN

When Bill was very young, they had been in love. Many nights they had spent walk- 1
ing, talking together. Then something not very important had come between them, and they didn't speak. Impulsively, she had married a man she thought she loved. Bill went away, bitter about women.

Yesterday, walking across Washington Square, she saw him for the first time in years.

"Bill Walker," she said.

He stopped. At first he did not recognize her, to him she looked so old.

"Mary! Where did you come from?" 5

Unconsciously, she lifted her face as though wanting a kiss, but he held out his hand. She took it.

"I live in New York now," she said.

"Oh"—smiling politely. Then a little frown came quickly between his eyes.

"Always wondered what happened to you, Bill."

"I'm a lawyer. Nice firm, way downtown." 10

"Married yet?"

"Sure. Two kids."

"Oh," she said.

A great many people went past them through the park. People they didn't know. It was late afternoon. Nearly sunset. Cold.

"And your husband?" he asked her. 15

"We have three children. I work in the bursar's office at Columbia."

"You're looking very . . . " (he wanted to say *old*) " . . . well," he said.

She understood. Under the trees in Washington Square, she found herself desperately reaching back into the past. She had been older than he then in Ohio. Now she was not young at all. Bill was still young.

"We live on Central Park West," she said. "Come and see us sometime."

"Sure," he replied. "You and your husband must have dinner with my family some night. Any night. Lucille and I'd love to have you."

The leaves fell slowly from the trees in the Square. Fell without wind. Autumn dusk. She felt a little sick.

"We'd love it," she answered.

"You ought to see my kids." He grinned.

Suddenly the lights came on up the whole length of Fifth Avenue, chains of misty brilliance in the blue air.

"There's my bus," she said.

He held out his hand, "Good-by."

"When . . . " she wanted to say, but the bus was ready to pull off. The lights on the avenue blurred, twinkled, blurred. And she was afraid to open her mouth as she entered the bus. Afraid it would be impossible to utter a word.

Suddenly she shrieked very loudly, "Good-by!" But the bus door had closed.

The bus started. People came between them outside, people crossing the street, people they didn't know. Space and people. She lost sight of Bill. Then she remembered she had forgotten to give him her address—or to ask him for his—or tell him that her youngest boy was named Bill, too.

Ask Questions About the Work

Now that you've read Hughes's story, consult the questions on pages 637–638 so you can devise your own set of questions to solidify your first impressions. Here are some questions you might consider:

1. How does *setting* help bring out the theme?

Answer: Both the time of year, "early autumn," and the time of day, "nearly sunset" suggest that time is running out. The place, a crowded walkway in a big city, highlights the idea of all the people with whom we never make contact—that is, of life's missed connections.

2. From what *point of view* is the story told? How does this relate to the story's meaning?

Answer: The point of view is the third-person omniscient. This enables the author to show the discrepancy between what characters are thinking and what they are willing or able to communicate.

3. What *words* and *images* are repeated in the course of the story? How do these *motifs* reflect the story's theme?

Answer: The words *young* and *old* appear a number of times. This repetition helps bring out the theme of aging, of time running out. *Walking* is another repeated word that gives the reader the sense of people's uninterrupted movement through life. The repeated phrase *people they don't know* emphasizes how hard it is for people to genuinely communicate and connect with one another. *Love,* another repeated word, underscores the tragedy of love lost or unfulfilled.

Reread and Annotate

In light of the questions you develop, reread and annotate Hughes's story. Then consider the writing assignments that follow.

1. Analyze how Hughes develops the theme that it is urgently important for people to "take time out" to communicate with one another.
2. Discuss some strategies that Hughes uses to achieve universality. You might, for example, call attention to the story's impersonal point of view, the lack of descriptive detail about the characters' appearances, and the generality of the information about the characters' lives.
3. Explain how Hughes uses setting to reveal the characters' psychological states and to convey their sense of loss.

STUDENT ESSAY

Which of the preceding assignments appeals to you most? Student Karen Vais decided to write in response to the first assignment. After using questions to focus her initial impressions and guide her annotations, Karen organized her prewriting and began to draft her literary analysis. The final version of her analysis follows. As you read the essay, consider how well Karen addresses both *what* Hughes expresses and *how* he expresses it. What literary devices does Karen discuss? How are these related to the story's theme? Also note that Karen doesn't identify "Early Autumn" with a bibliographic footnote. Because the story was assigned in class and everyone used the same text, she didn't need to provide such a footnote. Similarly, her instructor didn't require parenthetic documentation of quoted material because the story is so brief.

Stopping to Talk

by Karen Vais

Introduction

Thesis with plan of development

In his short story "Early Autumn," Langston Hughes dramatizes the idea that hurried movement through life prevents people from forming or maintaining meaningful relationships. Hughes develops his theme of "walking" versus "talking" through such devices as setting, plot construction, and dialog. 1

2 The story's setting continually reminds the reader that time is running out; it is urgent for people to stop and communicate before it is too late. The meeting between the two characters takes place on a busy walkway, where strangers hurry past one another. The season is autumn, the time is "late afternoon," the temperature is "cold." The end of the renewed connection between Mary and Bill coincides with the blurring of the streetlights. The chilly, dark setting suggests the coming of winter, of night, even of death.

First supporting paragraph: focus on setting

3 In keeping with the setting, the plot is a series of lost chances for intimacy. When they were young and in love, Bill and Mary used to "walk . . . [and] talk . . . together," but that was years ago. Then "something not very important . . . [came] between them, and they didn't speak." When she says Bill's name, Mary halts Bill's movement through the park, and, for a short time, Bill "Walker" stops walking. But when Mary hurries onto the bus, the renewed connection snaps. Moreover, even their brief meeting in the park is already a thing of the past, having taken place "yesterday."

Second supporting paragraph: focus on plot

4 Like their actions, the characters' words illustrate a reluctance to communicate openly. The dialog consists of little more than platitudes: "I live in New York now. . . . We have three kids. . . . You and your husband must have dinner with my family some night." The narrator's telling comments about what remains *unspoken* ("he *wanted* to say . . . ," "she *wanted* to say . . . ") underscore Bill and Mary's separateness. Indeed, Mary fails to share the one piece of information that would have revealed her feelings for Bill Walker—that her youngest son is also named Bill.

Third supporting paragraph: focus on dialog

5 The theme of walking vs. talking runs throughout "Early Autumn." "Space and people," Hughes writes, once again come between Bill and Mary, and, as in the past, they go their separate ways. Through the two characters, Hughes seems to be urging each of us to speak—to slow our steps long enough to make emotional contact.

Conclusion

Commentary

Note that Karen states her *thesis* in the opening paragraph; this first sentence addresses the *what* of the story: "the idea that hurried movement through life prevents . . . meaningful relationships." The next sentence addresses the *how*: "Hughes develops his theme . . . through such devices as setting, plot construction, and dialog." This second sentence also announces the essay's *plan of development*. Karen will discuss setting, then plot, then dialog, with one paragraph devoted to each of these literary elements. In the body of the analysis, Karen backs up her thesis with *textual evidence* in the form of summaries and quotations. The quotations are no longer than is necessary to support her points. In the concluding paragraph, Karen repeats her thesis, reinforcing it with Hughes's own words. She ends by pointing out the relevance of the story's theme to the reader's own life.

Writing Assignment on "Early Autumn"

Having seen what one student did with "Early Autumn," look back at the second and third writing assignments on page 648 and select one for your own analysis of Hughes's story. Then, in light of the assignment you select, read the story again, making any adjustments in your annotations. Next, organize your prewriting annotations into a scratch list, identify a working thesis, and organize your ideas into an outline. That done, write your first draft. Before submitting your analysis, take time to revise, edit, and proofread it carefully.

ADDITIONAL SELECTIONS AND WRITING ASSIGNMENTS

The two selections that follow—a poem by Robert Frost and a short story by Kate Chopin—will give you further practice in analyzing literary texts. No matter which selection you decide to write on, the following guidelines should help you approach the literary analysis with confidence.

Start by reading the text once to gain an overall impression. Then, draw on any of the questions on pages 637–638 to help you focus your first impressions and guide your annotations. When deciding what to write about, you may select a topic of your own, a subject proposed by your instructor, or one of the assignments suggested after the readings. With your topic in mind, reread the selection and evaluate the appropriateness of your earlier annotations. Make whatever changes are needed before moving your annotations into an informal scratch list. Next, review the scratch list so you can formulate a working thesis and prepare an outline of your ideas. Then go ahead and write your first draft, making sure you revise, edit, and proofread thoroughly before handing in your analysis.

ROBERT FROST

Best known for his poetry about New England life, Robert Frost (1874–1963) was born in San Francisco and moved to Massachusetts in 1885. After briefly attending Dartmouth and Harvard Universities, Frost worked several jobs, including farming for five years. His first two collections of poetry, *A Boy's Will* (1913) and *North of Boston* (1914), were published in England, where he went after failing to be published in the United States. These collections—and the distinctly American voice shaping them—eventually won Frost recognition back home, where he returned to publish *Mountain Interval* (1916), a volume containing some of his most recognized poems. The recipient of numerous awards and honors, Frost received four Pulitzer Prizes and presented the poem "The Gift Outright" at President John F. Kennedy's inauguration in 1961. The following poem first appeared in Mountain Interval.

"OUT, OUT—"[1]

The buzz-saw snarled and rattled in the yard
And made dust and dropped stove-length sticks of wood,
Sweet-scented stuff when the breeze drew across it.
And from there those that lifted eyes could count
Five mountain ranges one behind the other
Under the sunset far into Vermont.
And the saw snarled and rattled, snarled and rattled,
As it ran light, or had to bear a load.
And nothing happened: day was all but done.
Call it a day, I wish they might have said
To please the boy by giving him the half hour
That a boy counts so much when saved from work.
His sister stood beside them in her apron
To tell them "Supper." At the word, the saw,
As if to prove saws knew what supper meant,
Leaped out at the boy's hand, or seemed to leap—
He must have given the hand. However it was,
Neither refused the meeting. But the hand!
The boy's first outcry was a rueful laugh,
As he swung toward them holding up the hand
Half in appeal, but half as if to keep
The life from spilling. Then the boy saw all—
Since he was old enough to know, big boy
Doing a man's work, though a child at heart—
He saw all spoiled. "Don't let him cut my hand off—
The doctor, when he comes. Don't let him, sister!"
So. But the hand was gone already.
The doctor put him in the dark of ether.
He lay and puffed his lips out with his breath.
And then—the watcher at his pulse took fright.
No one believed. They listened at his heart.
Little—less—nothing—and that ended it.
No more to build on there. And they, since they
Were not the one dead, turned to their affairs.

---

[1]This title alludes to the words of Shakespeare's Macbeth on receiving news that his queen is dead: "Out, out, brief candle! / Life's but a walking shadow, a poor player/That struts and frets his hour upon the stage/And then is heard no more. It is a tale/Told by an idiot, full of sound and fury, /Signifying nothing" (*Macbeth* 5.5.23–28).

Writing Assignments on "Out, Out—"

1. Because it tells a story, "Out, Out—" can be described as a narrative poem. Discuss the poem's various narrative elements, including its setting, plot, characters, conflict, climax, and resolution. Analyze how these narrative elements work to convey what you think is the poem's main theme.
2. Despite the concise language of the poem, Frost manages to provide clear descriptions of the boy and the men in the timber mill and of what each of them represents. Looking closely at how Frost depicts the boy and the men—known as *they* in the poem—write a paper analyzing the different views of human nature Frost conveys.
3. The buzz-saw plays a central role in Frost's poem—to such an extent that it can be considered a character in its own right. Analyze the ways in which the buzz-saw is characterized in the poem. Be sure to discuss what commentary Frost might be making about the relationship between people and their objects of labor in his depiction of the buzz-saw.

KATE CHOPIN

Fiction writer Kate Chopin (1851–1904) is best known for her novel *The Awakening* (1899). When first published, the novel shocked readers with its frank sensuality and the independent spirit of its female protagonist. The story that follows, first published in *Vogue* in 1894, shows a similar defiance of socially prescribed expectations and norms.

THE STORY OF AN HOUR

Knowing that Mrs. Mallard was afflicted with heart trouble, great care was taken to break to her as gently as possible the news of her husband's death. 1

It was her sister Josephine who told her, in broken sentences, veiled hints that revealed in half concealing. Her husband's friend Richards was there, too, near her. It was he who had been in the newspaper office when intelligence of the railroad disaster was received, with Brently Mallard's name leading the list of "killed." He had only taken the time to assure himself of its truth by a second telegram, and had hastened to forestall any less careful, less tender friend in bearing the sad message. 2

She did not hear the story as many women have heard the same, with a paralyzed inability to accept its significance. She wept at once, with sudden, wild abandonment, in her sister's arms. When the storm of grief had spent itself she went away to her room alone. She would have no one follow her. 3

There stood, facing the open window, a comfortable, roomy armchair. Into this she sank, pressed down by a physical exhaustion that haunted her body and seemed to reach into her soul. 4

She could see in the open square before her house the tops of trees that were all aquiver with the new spring life. The delicious breath of rain was in the air. In the street below a peddler was crying his wares. The notes of a distant song which 5 someone was singing reached her faintly, and countless sparrows were twittering in the eaves.

6 There were patches of blue sky showing here and there through the clouds that had met and piled one above the other in the west facing her window.

7 She sat with her head thrown back upon the cushion of the chair, quite motionless, except when a sob came up into her throat and shook her, as a child who has cried itself to sleep continues to sob in its dreams.

8 She was young, with a fair, calm face, whose lines bespoke repression and even a certain strength. But now there was a dull stare in her eyes, whose gaze was fixed away off yonder on one of those patches of blue sky. It was not a glance of reflection, but rather indicated a suspension of intelligent thought.

9 There was something coming to her and she was waiting for it, fearfully. What was it? She did not know, it was too subtle and elusive to name. But she felt it, creeping out of the sky, reaching toward her through the sounds, the scents, the color that filled the air.

10 Now her bosom rose and fell tumultuously. She was beginning to recognize this thing that was approaching to possess her, and she was striving to beat it back with her will—as powerless as her two white slender hands would have been.

11 When she abandoned herself a little whispered word escaped her slightly parted lips. She said it over and over under her breath: "Free, free, free!" The vacant stare and the look of terror that had followed it went from her eyes. They stayed keen and bright. Her pulses beat fast, and the coursing blood warmed and relaxed every inch of her body.

12 She did not stop to ask if it were not a monstrous joy that held her. A clear and exalted perception enabled her to dismiss the suggestion as trivial.

13 She knew that she would weep again when she saw the kind, tender hands folded in death; the face that had never looked save with love upon her, fixed and gray and dead. But she saw beyond that bitter moment a long procession of years to come that would belong to her absolutely. And she opened and spread her arms out to them in welcome.

14 There would be no one to live for during those coming years; she would live for herself. There would be no powerful will bending her in that blind persistence with which men and women believe they have a right to impose a private will upon a fellow creature. A kind intention or a cruel intention made the act seem no less a crime as she looked upon it in that brief moment of illumination.

15 And yet she had loved him—sometimes. Often she had not. What did it matter! What could love, the unsolved mystery, count for in face of this possession of self-assertion which she suddenly recognized as the strongest impulse of her being.

16 "Free! Body and soul free!" she kept whispering.

17 Josephine was kneeling before the closed door with her lips to the keyhole, imploring for admission. "Louise, open the door! I beg; open the door—you will make yourself ill. What are you doing, Louise? For heaven's sake open the door."

18 "Go away. I am not making myself ill." No; she was drinking in a very elixir of life through that open window.

19 Her fancy was running riot along those days ahead of her. Spring days, and summer days, and all sorts of days that would be her own. She breathed a quick prayer that life might be long. It was only yesterday she had thought with a shudder that life might be long.

She arose at length and opened the door to her sister's importunities. There was a feverish triumph in her eyes, and she carried herself unwittingly like a goddess of Victory. She clasped her sister's waist, and together they descended the stairs. Richards stood waiting for them at the bottom. 20

Some one was opening the front door with a latchkey. It was Brently Mallard who entered, a little travel-stained, composedly carrying his gripsack and umbrella. He had been far from the scene of the accident, and did not even know there had been one. He stood amazed at Josephine's piercing cry; at Richards' quick motion to screen him from the view of his wife. 21

But Richards was too late. 22

When the doctors came they said she had died of heart disease—of joy that kills. 23

Writing Assignments on "The Story of an Hour"

1. Show how Chopin uses imagery and descriptive detail to contrast the rich possibilities for which Mrs. Mallard yearns with the drab reality of her everyday life.
2. Argue that "The Story of an Hour" dramatizes the theme that domesticity saps a woman's spirit and physical strength.
3. Does Chopin's characterization of Mrs. Mallard justify the story's unexpected and ironic climax? Explain your response.

For additional writing, reading, and research resources, go to **www.mycomplab.com** and choose **Nadell/Langan/Comodromos'** ***The Longman Writer,*** **7/e**.

Writing Exam Essays

22

You may never consider **exam essays** fun, but once you develop the knack, writing an essay as part of an exam can be as much of a learning experience as writing an essay or report out of class. There are differences, of course. At home, you can "hatch" your essay over several hours, days, or even weeks; you can write and rewrite; you can produce an impressively typed final copy.

Exam essays, though, are different. Time pressure is the name of the game. If you have trouble writing essays at home, the idea of preparing one in a test situation may throw you into a kind of panic. How, you may wonder, can you show what you know in such a short time? Indeed, you may feel that such tests are designed to show you at your worst.

Befuddling students and causing anxiety are not, however, the goals that instructors have in mind when they prepare essay exams. Instructors intend such exams to reveal your understanding of the subject—and to stimulate you to interpret course material in perceptive, new ways. They realize that the writing done under time pressure won't result in a masterpiece; such writing may include misspellings and awkward sentences. However, they *do* expect reasonably complete essay answers: no brief outlines, no rambling lists of unconnected points. Focused, developed, coherent responses are what instructors are looking for. Such expectations are not as unrealistic as they may first seem when you realize that all the writing techniques discussed in this book are applicable to taking essay tests.

THREE FORMS OF WRITTEN ANSWERS

There are three general types of questions that require written answers—some as short as one or two sentences, others as long as a full, several-paragraph essay.

Short Answers

One kind of question calls for a **short answer** of only a few sentences. Always read the instructions carefully to determine exactly what's expected. Such questions often ask you to identify (or define) a term *and* explain its importance. An instructor may give full credit only if you answer *both* parts of the question. Also, unless the directions indicate that fragmentary responses are acceptable, be prepared to write one to three full sentences.

Here are several examples of short answers for an exam in modern art history.

Directions: Identify and explain the significance of the following:

1. *Composition with Red, Yellow, and Blue*, 1921: Like most of Piet Mondrian's "compositions," this painting consists of horizontal and vertical lines and the primary colors, red, yellow, and blue. The painting also shows Matisse's influence on Mondrian since Matisse believed that art should express a person's spirit through pure form and color rather than depict real objects or scenes.
2. "Concerning the Spiritual in Art": This is an essay written by Wassily Kandinsky in 1912 to justify the abstract painting style he used. Showing Matisse's influence, the essay maintains that pure forms and basic colors convey reality more accurately than true-to-life depictions.
3. The Eiffel Tower Series: Done around 1910 by Robert Delaunay, this is a series of paintings having the Eiffel Tower as subject. Delaunay used a cubist approach, analyzing surface, space, and interesting planes.

Paragraph-Length Answers

Questions requiring a **paragraph-length answer** may signal—directly or indirectly—the length of response expected. For example, such questions may indicate "answer in a few sentences," or they may be followed by a paragraph-sized space on the answer sheet. In any case, a successful answer should address the question as completely yet as concisely as possible. Beginning with a strong topic sentence will help you focus your response.

Following is a paragraph-length answer to a question on a political science exam:

> Directions: Discuss the meaning of the term *interest group* and comment briefly on the role such groups play in the governing of democratic societies.

An interest group is an "informal" type of political organization; its goal is to influence government policy and see legislation enacted that favors its members. An interest group differs from a political party; the interest group doesn't want to control the government or have an actual share in governing (the whole purpose of a political party). Interest groups are considered "informal" because they are not officially part of the governing process. Still, they exert tremendous power. Democratic governments constantly respond to interest groups by passing new laws and policies. Some examples of interest groups are institutions (the military, the Catholic Church), associations (the American Medical Association, Mothers Against Drunk Driving), and nonassociational groups (car owners, television viewers).

Essay-Length Answers

You will frequently be asked to write an **essay-length answer** as part of a longer examination. Occasionally, an exam may consist of a single essay, as in a "test-out" exam at the end of a writing course.

Here is a typical essay question from an exam in an introductory course in linguistics. A response to this question can be found on pages 663–664.

> Account for the differences in American and British English by describing at least three major influences that affected the way this country's settlers spoke English. Give as many examples as you can of words derived from these influences.

The rest of this chapter discusses the features of a strong essay response and shows how the writing process can be adapted to a test-taking situation.

How to Prepare for Exam Essays

Being able to write a good exam essay is the result of a certain type of studying. There are times when cramming is probably unavoidable, but you should try to avoid this last-minute crunch whenever possible. It prevents you from gaining a clear overview of a course and a real understanding of a course's main issues.

In contrast, spaced study throughout the semester gives you a sense of the *whys* of the subject, not just the *who, what, where*, and *when*.

As you prepare for an exam essay, you should try to follow the guidelines listed in the checklist below.

PREPARING FOR AN EXAM ESSAY: A CHECKLIST

- ☐ In light of the main concepts covered in the course, identify key issues that the exam might logically address.
- ☐ With these issues in mind, design several exam essay questions.
- ☐ Draft an answer for each anticipated question.
- ☐ Commit to memory any facts, quotations, data, lists of reasons, and so forth that you would include in your answers.

Although you may not anticipate the exam's actual questions, preparing some questions and answers can give you practice analyzing and working with the course material. In the process, you'll probably allay some pre-exam jitters as well.

AT THE EXAMINATION

Survey the Entire Test

Look over the entire written-answer section of a test before working on any part of it. Note which sections are worth the highest point value and plan to spend the longest time on those sections. Follow any guidelines that the directions may provide about the length of the response. When "a brief paragraph" is all that is required, don't launch into a full-scale essay.

If you're given a choice about which exam questions to answer, read them all before choosing. Of course, select those you feel best equipped to answer. If it's a toss-up between two, you might quickly sketch out answers to both (see page 660) before deciding which to do. To avoid mistakes, circle questions you plan to answer and cross out those you'll skip. Then give yourself a time limit for writing each response and, within reason, stick with your plan.

Understand the Essay Question

Once you've selected the question on which you're going to write, you need to make sure you know what the question is looking for. Examine the question carefully to determine its slant or emphasis. Most essay questions ask you to focus on a specific issue or to bring together material from different parts of a course.

Many questions use **key directional words** that suggest an answer developed according to a particular pattern of development. Here are some key directional words and the patterns they suggest:

Key Directional Words	Pattern of Development
Provide details about . . .	Description
Give the history of . . . Trace the development of . . .	Narration
Explain . . . List . . . Provide examples of . . .	Illustration
Analyze the parts of . . . Discuss the types of . . .	Division-classification
Analyze . . . Explain how . . . Show how . . .	Process analysis
Discuss advantages and disadvantages of . . . Show similarities and differences between . . .	Comparison-contrast
Account for . . . Analyze . . . Discuss the consequences of . . . Explain the reasons for . . . Explain why . . . Show the influence of . . .	Cause-effect
Clarify . . . Explain the meaning of . . . Identify . . .	Definition
Argue . . . Defend . . . Evaluate . . . Justify . . . Show the failings or merits of . . . Support . . .	Argumentation-persuasion

The following sample questions show the way key directional words imply the approach to take. In each example, the key words are italicized. Note that some essay questions call for two or more patterns of development. The key terms could, for example, indicate that you should *contrast* two things before *arguing* the merits of one.

1. Galileo, now recognized as having made valuable contributions to our understanding of the universe, was twice tried by the Vatican. *Explain the factors* that *caused* the church and the astronomer to fall into what one historian has termed a "fatal collision of opposite philosophies." [Cause-effect]
2. *Define* the superego and *explain how*, according to Freud, the superego develops. [Definition; process analysis]
3. *Explain the difference* between "educational objectives" and "instructional objectives." *Provide specific examples* of each, focusing on the distinction between students' immediate and long-term needs. [Comparison-contrast; illustration]

WRITE THE ESSAY

The steps in the writing process are the same, whether you compose an essay at home or prepare an essay response in a classroom test situation. The main difference is that during a test the process is streamlined. Following are some helpful guidelines for handling each writing stage when you prepare an essay as part of an exam.

Prewrite

Prewriting begins when you analyze the essay question and determine your essay's basic approach (see pages 658–659). We suggest that you do your analysis of the question on the exam sheet: Underline key directional terms, circle other crucial words, and put numbers next to points that the question indicates you should cover.

Then, still using your exam page or a piece of scratch paper, make notes for an answer. (Writing on the exam sheet means you won't have several pieces of paper to keep track of.) Jot down main points as well as facts and examples. If you feel blocked, try brainstorming, freewriting, mapping, or another prewriting technique (see pages 25–30) to get yourself going.

What to Avoid. Don't get overinvolved in the prewriting stage; you won't have time to generate pages of notes. Try using words and phrases, not full sentences or paragraphs. Also, don't spend time analyzing your audience (you know it's your instructor) or choosing a tone (exams obviously require a serious, analytic approach).

Identify Your Thesis

Like essays written at home, exam essays should have a **thesis.** Often, the thesis is a statement answering the exam question. For example, in response to a question asking you to "Discuss the origins of apartheid," your thesis might begin, "The South African law of 'separateness,' or apartheid, originated in 1948, a result of a series of factors that. . . ." Similarly, the essay answer to a question asking you to "Discuss the process by which nations are admitted to the European Community . . ." might start, "Nations are admitted to the European Community through the process of. . . ." Note that these thesis statements are somewhat informal. They state the *subject* of the essay but *not* the writer's *attitude* toward the subject. In a test-taking situation, these less-structured thesis statements are perfectly acceptable. (For more on thesis statements, see Chapter 3.)

Support the Thesis with Evidence

In the prewriting stage, you jotted down material needed to answer the question. At this point, you should review the **evidence** quickly to make sure it's *adequate*. Does it provide sufficient support for your thesis? If not, make some additional quick notes. Also, check that support for your thesis is *unified, specific, accurate*, and *representative* (see pages 47–52 and 70–75).

Organize the Evidence

Before you start writing, devise some kind of **outline.** You may simply sequence your prewriting jottings by placing numbers or letters beside them. Or you can quickly translate the jottings into a brief, informal outline.

However you proceed, go back and review the essay question one more time. If the question has two or three parts, your outline should tackle each one in turn. Suppose a question asks you to "Consider the effects of oil spills on wildlife, ocean ecology, and oil reserves." Your answer should address each of these three areas, with separate paragraphs for each area.

Also, focus again on the question's key *directional words*. If the question asks you to discuss similarities and differences, your outline should draw on one of the two basic *comparison-contrast* formats (see pages 349–354). Since many exam questions call for more than one task (for example, you may be asked both to *define* a theory and to *argue* its merits), you should make sure your outline reflects the appropriate patterns of development.

Many outlines use an *emphatic* approach to organize material ("Discuss which factors are most critical in determining whether a wildlife species will become extinct"). However, when discussing historical or developmental issues (for example, in psychology), you often structure material *chronologically*. In some fields (art history is one) you may choose a *spatial* approach—for instance, if you describe a work of art. Quickly assess the situation to determine which approach would work best, and keep it in mind as you sequence the points in your outline. (Turn to pages 58–61 and 55–58 for more on, respectively, outlining and emphatic, chronological, spatial, and simple-to-complex plans.)

What to Avoid. Don't prepare a formal or many-leveled outline; you'll waste valuable time. A phrase outline with two levels of support should be sufficient in most cases.

Write the Draft

Generally, you won't have time to write a formal introduction, so it's fine to begin the essay with your thesis, perhaps followed by a plan of development (see pages 39–40). Write as many paragraphs as you need to show you have command of the concepts and facts taught in the course. Refer to your outline as you write, but, if inspiration strikes, feel free to add material or deal with a point in a different order.

As you draft your response, you may want to write on every other line or leave several blank spaces at the bottom of the page. That way, you can easily slot in any changes you need to make along the way. Indeed, you shouldn't feet hesitant about crossing out material—a quotation you didn't get quite right, a sentence that reads awkwardly, a fact that should be placed elsewhere. *Do* make these changes, but make them neatly.

When preparing the draft, remember that you'll be graded in part on how *specific, accurate*, and *representative* your evidence is (see pages 49–51 and 71–75). Provide concrete, correct, true-to-type evidence. Make sure, too, that your response is *unified* (see pages 48–49 and 70–71). Don't include interesting but basically irrelevant information. Stay focused on the question. Using topic sentences to structure your paragraphs will help you stay on track.

Your instructor will need transitions and other markers to understand fully how your points connect to one another. Try to show how your ideas relate by using *signal devices*, such as *first, second, however, for instance*, and *most important* (see pages 76–77).

As you near the end of the essay, check the original question. Have you covered everything? Does the question call for a final judgment or evaluative comment? If so, provide it. Also, if you have time, you may want to close with a brief, one- or two-sentence summary.

What to Avoid. Don't write your essay on scrap paper and plan to recopy. You probably won't have enough time. Even if you do, you may, in your haste, leave out words, phrases, or whole sentences. Your first and only draft should be the one written on the exam booklet or paper. Also, unless your instructor specifically requests it, don't waste time recopying the question in your exam booklet.

Instructors find it easier to evaluate what you know if you've used paragraphs. Don't, then, cast your answer as one long paragraph spanning three pages. If you've outlined your ideas, you'll have a clear idea where paragraph breaks should occur. Finally, don't cram your response with everything you know about the subject. Most instructors can detect padded answers in a second. Give focused, intelligent responses, not one rambling paragraph after another.

Revise, Edit, and Proofread

If you've budgeted your time, you should have a few minutes left to review your essay answer. (Don't skip rereading it just so you can leave the room a few minutes early.) Above all, read your response to be sure it answers the question fully. Make any changes that will improve the answer—perhaps add a fact, correct a quotation, tighten a sentence. If you want to add a whole sentence or more, write the material in some nearby blank space and use an arrow to show where it goes. If something is in the wrong place, use an arrow and a brief note to indicate where it should go.

Instructors will accept insertions and deletions—as long as such changes are made with consideration for their sanity. Use a few bold strokes, not wild spidery scribbles, to cross out text. Use the standard editing marks such as the caret (see page 143) to indicate additions and other changes.

As you reread, check grammar and spelling. Obvious grammatical errors and spelling mistakes—especially if they involve the subject's key terms—may affect your grade. If spelling is a problem for you, request permission to have your dictionary at hand.

Sample Essay Answer

The essay that follows was written by Andrew Kahan in response to this take-home exam question:

> Account for the differences in American and British English by describing at least three major influences that affected the way this country's settlers spoke English. Give as many examples as you can of words derived from these influences.

① Maritime pidgin (Portug. influ.)
② African pidgin (Slaves comm. with each other and with owners)
③ Native American pidgin (words for native plants and animals)

Andrew started by underlining the question's key words. Then he listed in the margin the main points and some of the supporting evidence he planned to include in his answer. That done, he formulated a thesis and began writing his essay. The handwritten annotations reflect the changes Andrew made when he refined his answer before handing in his exam.

American English diverged from British English because those who settled the New World had contact with people that those back in England generally did not. As a result of ^this contact, several pidgin languages developed. A pidgin language, which has its own grammar and vocabulary, comes about when the speakers of two or more unrelated languages communicate ~~for a while~~ over a period of time. Maritime pidgin, African pidgin, and Indian pidgin were three influences that helped shape American English.

By the time the New World began to be settled, sailors and sea merchants of ^all the European nations had traveled widely. A maritime pidgin thus ~~immerged~~ emerged that enabled diverse groups to communicate.* Since Portugal controlled the seas around the time the colonies were settled, maritime pidgin was largely influenced by the Portuguese. Such Portuguese-derived words as "cavort," "palaver," and "savvy" first entered American English in this way.

*and trade with each other

The New World's trade with Africa also ~~effec~~ affected American English. The slave trade, in particular, took American sailors and merchants all over the African continent. Since the traders mixed up slaves of many tribes to prevent them from becoming unified, the Africans had to rely on their own pidgin to communicate with each other. Moreover, slave owners relied on this African-based pidgin to communicate with their slaves.** Since slaves tended to be settled in the heavily populated American coastal areas, elements of the African pidgin readily worked their way into the language of the New World. Words and phrases derived from African pidgins include "caboodle" and "kick the bucket." Other African-based words include "buckaroo" and "goobers," plus words known only in the Deep South, like "cooter" for turtle. African-based slang terms and constructions ("uptight," "put-on," and "hip," meaning "cool" or "in") continue to enter mainstream English from black English even today.

Another important influence on American English, in the nation's early days, was contact with Native American culture. As settlers moved inland from coastal areas, they confronted Native Americans, and new pidgins grew up, melding English and Native American terms. Native American words like "squaw," "tomahawk," and "papoose" entered English. Also, many words for Native American plants and animals have Native American roots: "squash," "raccoon," and "skunk" are just a few. Another possible effect of Native American languages on American English may be the tendency to form noun-noun compounds ("apple butter" and "shade tree"). While such constructions do occur in British English, they are much more frequent in American English.

British and American English differ because the latter has been shaped by contact with European languages like Portuguese, as well as by contact with non-European languages--especially those spoken by Africans and Native Americans.

**until they mastered English.

Commentary

Alert to such phrases as *account for* and *influences that affected* in the question, Andrew wrote an essay that describes three *causes* for the divergence of American from British English. The three causes are organized roughly chronologically, beginning with the influence of maritime exploration, moving to the effect of contact with African culture, and concluding with the influence of Native Americans.

Although the essay is developed mainly through a decision of causes, other patterns of development come into play. The first paragraph *defines* the term *pidgin*, while the second, third, and fourth paragraphs draw on *process analysis*; they describe how pidgins developed, as well as how they affected the language spoken by early settlers. Finally, the essay includes numerous *examples*, as the exam question requested. Andrew's response shows a solid knowledge of the material taught in the course and demonstrates his ability to organize the material into a clear, coherent statement.

ACTIVITY: WRITING EXAM ESSAYS

In preparation for an exam with essay questions, devise four possible essay questions on the material in one of your courses. For each, do some quick prewriting, determine a thesis, and jot down an outline. Then, for one of the questions, write a full essay answer, giving yourself a time limit of fifteen to twenty-five minutes, whatever is appropriate for the question. Don't forget to edit and proofread your answer.

For additional writing, reading, and research resources, go to **www.mycomplab.com** and choose **Nadell/Langan/Comodromos'** ***The Longman Writer*****, 7/e**.

A Guide to Avoiding Plagiarism*

What is Plagiarism?

Plagiarism is using someone else's work—words, ideas, or illustrations that are published or unpublished—without giving the creator of that work sufficient credit. A serious breach of scholarly ethics, plagiarism can have severe consequences. Students risk a failing grade or disciplinary action ranging from suspension to expulsion. A record of such action can adversely affect professional opportunities in the future as well as graduate school admission. (See also pages 570–572 for more on plagiarism.)

Documentation: The Key to Avoiding Unintentional Plagiarism

It can be difficult to tell when you have unintentionally plagiarized something. The legal doctrine of **fair use** allows writers to use a limited amount of another's work in their own papers and books. However, to make sure that they are not plagiarizing that work, writers need to take care to accurately and clearly credit the source for *every* use. **Documentation** is the method writers employ to give credit to the creators of material they use. It involves providing essential information about the source of the material, enabling readers to find the material for themselves. It requires two elements: (1) a separate list of sources used in the paper and (2) citations in the text to items in that list. To use documentation and avoid unintentionally plagiarizing from a source, you need to know how to:

- Identify sources and information that need to be documented.
- Document sources in a Works Cited list.
- Use material gathered from sources: summary, paraphrase, quotation.
- Create in-text references.
- Use correct grammar and punctuation to blend quotations into a paper.

Identifying Sources and Information That Need to Be Documented

Whenever you use information from **outside sources**, you need to identify the source of that material. Some major outside sources include: books, newspapers, magazines, government sources, radio or television programs, material from electronic databases, correspondence, films, plays, interviews, speeches, or information from websites. Virtually all the information you find in outside sources requires documentation. The one major exception to this guideline is that you do not have to document common knowledge. **Common knowledge** is widely known information about current events, famous people, geographical facts, or familiar history. However, when in doubt, the safest strategy is to provide documentation.

---

*By Linda Stern, Publishing School of Continuing and Professional Studies, New York University

DOCUMENTING SOURCES IN A WORKS CITED LIST

You need to choose the documentation style that is dominant in your field or is required by your instructor. (See pages 581–611 for more on documentation.) Take care to use only one documentation style in any one paper and to follow the documentation formats consistently for the chosen style. The most widely used style manuals are ***MLA Handbook for Writers of Research Papers,*** published by the **Modern Language Association (MLA)**, which is popular in the fields of English language and literature; the ***Publication Manual of the American Psychological Association* (*APA*)**, which is favored in the social sciences; and ***The Chicago Manual of Style,*** published by the **University of Chicago Press (CMS)**, which is preferred in other humanities and sometimes business. Other, more specialized style manuals are used in various fields. Certain elements are common to all citation formats in all styles:

- Author or other creative individual or entity
- Source of the work
- Relevant identifying numbers or letters
- Title of the work
- Publisher or distributor
- Relevant dates

Constructing a Works Cited List in MLA Style

As an accompaniment to your English text, this guide will explore MLA style. MLA lists are alphabetized by authors' last names. If no author is given, however, an individual item can also be alphabetized by article title, by editor, or by the sponsoring organization. Generally, for MLA style, spell out names in full, invert only the first author's name, and separate elements with a period. In the MLA Works Cited list below, note the use of punctuation such as commas, colons, and angle brackets to separate and introduce material within elements.

Books

Chernow, Ron. *Alexander Hamilton*. New York: Penguin, 2004. Print.

Maupassant, Guy de. "The Necklace." Trans. Marjorie Laurie. *An Introduction to Fiction*. Ed. X. J. Kennedy and Dana Gioia. 7th ed. New York: Longman, 1999. 160–66. Print.

Claiborne, Robert. *Our Marvelous Native Tongue: The Life and Times of the English Language*. New York: New York Times, 1983. Print.

Periodicals

"Living on Borrowed Time." *Economist* 25 Feb.–3 Mar. 2006: 34–37. Print.

"Restoring the Right to Vote." Editorial. *New York Times* 10 Jan. 2006, late ed., sec. A: 24. Print.

Ulrich, Lars. "It's Our Property." *Newsweek* 5 June 2000: 54. Print.

Williams, N. R., M. Davey, and K. Klock-Powell. "Rising from the Ashes: Stories of Recovery, Adaptation, and Resiliency in Burn Survivors." *Social Work Health Care* 36.4 (2003): 53–77. Print.

Zobenica, Jon. "You Might As Well Live." Rev. of *A Long Way Down* by Nick Hornby. *Atlantic*. July–Aug. 2005: 148. Print.

Electronic Sources

Glanz, William. "Colleges Offer Students Music Downloads." *Washington Times*. 25 Aug. 2004. Web. 17 Oct. 2004.

McNichol, Elizabeth C., and Iris J. Lav. "State Revenues and Services Remain below Pre-Recession Levels." *Center on Budget Policy Priorites*. 6 Dec. 2005. Web. 10 Mar. 2006.

Reporters Without Borders. "Worldwide Press Freedom Index 2005." *Reporters Without Borders*. 2005. Web. 28 Feb. 2006.

USING MATERIAL GATHERED FROM SOURCES: SUMMARY, PARAPHRASE, QUOTATION

Essentially, you can integrate material into your paper in three ways—by summarizing, paraphrasing, or quoting. A quotation, paraphrase, or summary must be used in a way that accurately conveys the meaning of the source. (See pages 566–570 for more on these topics.)

A **summary** is a brief restatement in your own words of the source's main ideas. Summary is used to convey the general meaning of the ideas in a source, without specific details or examples that may appear in the original. A summary is always much shorter than the work it treats. Take care to give the essential information as clearly and succinctly as possible in your own language.

Rules to Remember

1. Write the summary using your own words.
2. Indicate clearly where the summary begins and ends.
3. Use attribution and parenthetical reference to tell the reader where the material came from.
4. Make sure your summary is an accurate restatement of the source's main ideas.
5. Check that the summary is clearly separated from your own contribution.

A **paraphrase** is a restatement, in your own words and using your own sentence structure, of specific ideas or information from a source. The chief purpose of a paraphrase is *to maintain your own writing style* throughout your paper. A paraphrase can be about as long as the original passage.

Rules to Remember

1. Use your own words and sentence structure. Do not duplicate the source's words or phrases.
2. Use quotation marks within your paraphrase to indicate quoted material.
3. Make sure your readers know when the paraphrase begins and ends.
4. Check that your paraphrase is an accurate and objective restatement of the source's specific ideas.
5. Immediately follow your paraphrase with a parenthetical reference indicating the source.

A **quotation** reproduces an actual part of a source, word for word, to support a statement or idea, to provide an example, to advance an argument, or to add interest or color to a discussion. The length of a quotation can range from a word or phrase to several paragraphs. In general, quote the least amount possible that gets your point across to the reader.

Rules to Remember

1. Copy the material from your source to your paper exactly as it appears in the original. Do not alter the spelling, capitalization, or punctuation of the original. If a quotation contains an obvious error, you may insert [sic], which is Latin for "so" or "thus," to show that the error is in the original.
2. Enclose short quotations (four or fewer lines of text) in quotation marks, and set off longer quotations as block quotations.
3. Immediately follow each quotation with a parenthetical reference indicating the specific source information required.

Creating In-Text References

In-text references need to supply enough information to enable a reader to find the correct source listing in the Works Cited list. (See also pages 593–604.) To properly cite a source in the text of your report, you generally need to provide some or all of the following information for each use of the source:

- Name of the person or organization that authored the source
- Title of the source, if there is more than one source by the same author
- Page, paragraph, or line number, if the source has one

These items can appear as an attribution in the text ("According to Smith . . . ") or in a parenthetical reference placed directly after the summary, paraphrase, or quotation. The examples that follow are in MLA style.

Using an Introductory Attribution and a Parenthetical Reference

The author, the publication, or a generalized reference can introduce source material. Remaining identifiers (title, page number) can go in the parenthetical reference at the end, as in the first sentence of the example below. If a source, such as a website, does not have page numbers, it may be possible to put all the information into the in-text attribution, as in the second sentence of the example below.

> Recently, *The Economist* noted that since 2004, "state tax revenues have come roaring back across the country" ("Living" 34). However, McNichol and Lav, writing for the Center on Budget and Policy Priorities, claim that recent gains are not sufficient to make up for the losses suffered.

Identifying Material by an Author of More than One Work Used in Your Paper

The attribution and the parenthetical reference combined must provide the title of the work, as well as the author and the page number of the citation.

> Describing the testing of the first atom bomb, Jennet Conant says, "The test had originally been scheduled for 4:00 A.M. on July 16, when most of the surrounding population would be sound asleep and there would be the least number of witnesses" (*109 East Palace* 304–05).

Identifying Material That the Source Is Quoting

To use material that has been quoted in your cited source, add *qtd. in,* for "quoted in."

> The weather was worrisome, but procrastination was even more problematic. General Groves was concerned that "every hour of delay would increase the possibility of someone's attempting to sabotage the tests" (qtd. in Conant, *109 East Palace* 305).

USING CORRECT GRAMMAR AND PUNCTUATION TO BLEND QUOTATIONS INTO A PAPER

Quotations must blend seamlessly into the writer's original sentence so the resulting sentence is neither ungrammatical nor awkward, and punctuation must be handled properly.

Using a Full-Sentence Quotation of Fewer than Four Lines

A quotation of one or more complete sentences can be enclosed in double quotation marks and introduced with a verb, usually in the present tense and followed by a comma. Omit any periods at the close of quoted sentences, but keep any question or exclamation marks. Insert the parenthetical reference and then a period.

> One commentator asks, "What accounts for the government's ineptitude in safeguarding our privacy rights?" (Spinello 9).
>
> "The test had originally been scheduled for 4:00 A.M. on July 16," Jennet Conant writes, "when most of the surrounding population would be sound asleep" (*109 East Palace* 304–05).

Introducing a Quotation with a Full Sentence

Use a colon after a full sentence that introduces a quotation.

> Spinello asks an important question: "What accounts for the government's ineptitude in safeguarding our privacy rights?" (9).

Introducing a Quotation with "That"

A single complete sentence can be introduced with a *that* construction.

> Chernow suggests that "the creation of New York's first bank was a formative moment in the city's rise as a world financial center" (199–200).

Quoting Part of a Sentence

Make sure the quoted material is blended grammatically into the new sentence.

> McNichol and Lav assert that during that period, state governments were helped by "an array of fiscal gimmicks" (372).

Using a Quotation That Contains Another Quotation

Replace the internal double quotation marks with single quotation marks.

Lowell was "famous as a 'confessional' writer, but he scorned the term," according to Bidart (vii).

Adding Information to a Quotation

Any addition for clarity or any change for grammatical reasons should be placed in square brackets.

Describing how the weather would affect the testing of the first atom bomb, Jennet Conant said, "The test had originally been scheduled for 4:00 A.M. on July 16, [1945,] when most of the surrounding population would be sound asleep" (*109 East Palace* 304–05).

Omitting Information from Source Sentences

Indicate the omission with ellipsis marks (three spaced dots).

Describing how the weather would affect the testing of the first atom bomb, Jennet Conant says, "The test had originally been scheduled for 4:00 A.M. on July 16, when . . . there would be the least number of witnesses" (304–05).

Using a Quotation of More than Four Lines

Begin on a new line and set off the quote by indenting it one inch from the left margin and double spacing throughout. Put the parenthetical reference *after* the period at the end of the quotation. Do not enclose in quotation marks.

Human Rights Watch recently documented the repression of women's rights in Libya:

> The government of Libya is arbitrarily detaining women and girls in "social rehabilitation" facilities, . . . locking them up indefinitely without due process. Portrayed as "protective" homes for wayward women and girls, . . . these facilities are de facto prisons . . . [where] the government routinely violates women's and girls' human rights, including those to due process, liberty, freedom of movement, personal dignity, and privacy. (Human 132–133)

Is it Plagiarism? Test Yourself on In-Text References

Read the excerpt marked "Original Source." Can you spot the plagiarism in the examples that follow?

Original Source

To begin with, language is a system of communication. I make this rather obvious point because to some people nowadays it isn't obvious: they see language as above all a means of "self-expression." Of course, language is one way that we express our personal feelings and thoughts—but so, if it comes to that, are dancing, cooking and making music. Language does much more: it enables us to convey to others what we think, feel and want. Language-as-communication is the prime means of organizing the cooperative activities that enable us to accomplish as groups things we could not possibly do as individuals. Some other species also engage in cooperative activities, but these are either quite simple (as among baboons and wolves) or exceedingly stereotyped (as among bees, ants and termites). Not surprisingly, the communicative systems used by these animals are also simple or stereotypes. Language, our uniquely flexible and intricate system of communication, makes possible our equally flexible and intricate ways of coping with the world around us: in a very real sense, it is what makes us human (Claiborne 8).

Works Cited entry:

Claiborne, Robert. *Our Marvelous Native Tongue: The Life and Times of the English Language.* New York: New York Times, 1983. Print.

Plagiarism Example 1

One commentator makes a distinction between language used as **a means of self-expression** and **language-as-communication**. It is the latter that distinguishes human interaction from that of other species and allows humans to work cooperatively on complex tasks (8).

What's wrong? The source's name is not given, and there are no quotation marks around words taken directly from the source (in **boldface** in the example).

Plagiarism Example 2

Claiborne notes that language "is the prime means of organizing the cooperative activities." Without language, we would, consequently, not have civilization.

What's wrong? The page number of the source is missing. Parenthetical references should immediately follow the material being quoted, paraphrased, or summarized. You may omit a parenthetical reference only if the information that you have included in your attribution is sufficient to identify the source in your Works Cited list and no page number is needed.

Plagiarism Example 3

Other animals also **engage in cooperative activities**. However, these actions are not very complex. Rather, they are either the very **simple** activities of, for example, **baboons and wolves** or the **stereotyped** activities of animals such as **bees, ants and termites** (Claiborne 8).

What's wrong? A paraphrase should capture a specific idea from a source but must not duplicate the writer's phrases and words (in **boldface** in the example). In the example, the wording and sentence structure follow the source too closely.

(For more practice in avoiding plagiarism, see pages 565–573.)

Evaluating Sources

It's very important to critically evaluate every source you consult, especially on the Internet, where it may be difficult to separate reliable sources from questionable ones. Ask these questions to help evaluate your sources:

- Is the material relevant to your topic?
- Is the source well respected?
- Is the material accurate?
- Is the information current?
- Is the material from a primary source or a secondary source?

Avoiding Plagiarism: Note-Taking Tips

The most effective way to avoid unintentional plagiarism is to follow a systematic method of note taking and writing.

- **Keep copies of your documentation information.** For all sources that you use, keep photocopies of the title and copyright pages and the pages with quotations you need. Highlight the relevant citation information in color. Keep these materials until you've completed your paper.
- **Quotation or paraphrase?** Assume that all the material in your notes is direct quotation, unless you indicated otherwise. Double-check any paraphrases for quoted phrases and insert the necessary quotation marks.
- **Create the Works Cited or References list** ***first***. Before you begin writing your paper, you can start out with a **working bibliography**, a list of possible sources to which you add source entries as you discover them. As you finalize your list, you can delete items that you've decided not to use in your paper.

Acknowledgments

American.com screen capture. Reprinted by permission of *American.com*.

Angelou, Maya. "Sister Flowers." Copyright © 1969 and renewed 1997 by Maya Angelou, from *I Know Why The Caged Bird Sings* by Maya Angelou. Used with permission of Random House, Inc.

Angier, Natalie. "The Cute Factor" from *The New York Times,* January 3, 2006. Copyright © 2006 The New York Times. Reprinted with permission.

Big Brothers Big Sisters screen capture, BigBrothersBigSisters.org. Used by permission.

Bissinger, Buzz. 'Innocents Afield' from *The New York Times,* December 16, 2004. Copyright © 2004 The New York Times. Reprinted by permission.

Brooks, David. 'Psst! Human Capital' from *The New York Times,* November 13, 2005. Copyright © 2005 The New York Times. Reprinted by permission.

Cohen, Patricia. "Reality TV: Surprising Throwback to the Past?" Reprinted by permission of the author.

Cole, Diane. "Don't Just Stand There," from *The New York Times,* 1982. Reprinted by permission of the author.

Cole, K. C. "Entropy" from *The New York Times,* March 18, 1982. Reprinted by permission of the author.

EBSCO screen captures. Reprinted by permission of EBSCO Publishing Inc.

Education Digest screen captures. Reprinted by permission of *Education Digest*.

Fish, Stanley. "Free-Speech Follies" from *The Chronicle of Higher Education,* March 13, 2003. © 2003, Stanley Fish, Davidson-Kahn Distinguished University Professor of Humanities and Law, Florida International University, College of Law. Reprinted with permission.

Gholson, Charmie. "Charity Display?" from *The New York Times,* January 2, 2005. Copyright © 2005 Charmie Gholson. Reprinted by permission.

Gleick, James. From *Faster* by James Gleick, copyright © 1999 by James Gleick. Used by permission of Pantheon Books, a division of Random House, Inc.

Goodman, Ellen. "Family Counterculture." Copyright © 1991 The Washington Post Writers Group. Reprinted with permission.

Greenpeace screen capture. Reprinted by permission of www.greenpeace.org.

Helvarg, David. "The Storm This Time." Copyright © 2005 by David Helvarg. First appeared in *Multinational Monitor*. Reprinted by permission of the author and the Sandra Dijkstra Literary Agency.

Hughes, Langston. "Early Autumn" from *Short Stories* by Langston Hughes. Copyright © 1996 by Romona Bass and Arnold Rampersad. Reprinted by permission of Hill and Wang, a division of Farrar, Straus and Giroux, LLC.

Hymowitz, Kay S. "Tweens: Ten Going on Sixteen." Reprinted with the permission of Manhattan Institute's *City Journal.*

Jacoby, Susan. "Common Decency." Copyright © 1991 by Susan Jacoby. Originally appeared in *The New York Times* (1991). Reprinted by permission of Georges Borchardt, Inc. on behalf of the author.

Johnson, Beth. "Bombs Bursting in Air." Reprinted by permission of the author.

King, Stephen. "Why We Crave Horror Movies." Reprinted With Permission. © Stephen King. All rights reserved. Originally appeared in *Playboy* (1982).

Library of Congress screen captures. Reprinted by permission of the Library of Congress.

Lorde, Audre. "The Fourth of July." Reprinted with permission from *Zami: A New Spelling of My Name* by Audre Lorde. Copyright © 1982 by Audre Lorde, Crossing Press, an imprint of Ten Speed Press, Berkeley, CA. www.tenspeed.com.

Lutz, William. "Doublespeak" from Doublespeak by William Lutz. Copyright © 1989 by Blond Bear, Inc. Reprinted by permission of the author and his agency, Jean V. Naggar Literary Agency Inc.

Morrison, Toni. "A Slow Walk of Trees" by Toni Morrison. Reprinted by permission of International Creative Management, Inc. Copyright © 1976 by Toni Morrison.

Orwell, George. "Shooting an Elephant" from *Shooting an Elephant and Other Essays* by George Orwell, copyright © 1950 by Sonia Brownell Orwell and renewed 1978 by Sonia Pitt-Rivers, reprinted with permission of Harcourt, Inc. Copyright © George Orwell, 1936, by pemission of Bill Hamilton as the Literary Executor of the Estate of the Late Sonia Brownell Orwell and Secker.

Paglia, Camille. "Rape: A Bigger Danger Than Feminists Know." Reprinted by permission of the author.

Parks, Gordon. "Flavio's Home" from *Voices in the Mirror* by Gordon Parks, Copyright © 1990 by Gordon Parks. Used by permission of Doubleday, a division of Random House, Inc.

Parker, Star. "*Se Habla* Entitlement," posted on Coalition on Urban Renewal and Education, April 18, 2006. Reprinted by permission of the author.

Rodriguez, Roberto. "The Border on Our Backs" from *Column of the Americas*. Reprinted by permission of the author.

Sanders, Scott Russell. "The Men We Carry in Our Minds." Copyright © 1984 by Scott Russell Sanders; first appeared in *Milkweed Chronicle;* from *The Paradise of Bombs*; reprinted by permission of the author and the author's agents, the Virginia Kidd Agency, Inc.

Savan, Leslie. "Black Talk and Pop Culture" from *Slam Dunks and No-Brainers* by Leslie Savan, copyright © 2005 by Leslie Savan. Used by permission of Alfred A. Knopf, a division of Random House, Inc.

Sherry, Mary. "In Praise of the 'F' Word" from *Newsweek,* May 6, 1991. Reprinted by permission of the author.

Shipley, David. "What We Talk About When We Talk About Editing" from *The New York Times,* July 31, 2005. Copyright © 2005 The New York Times. Reprinted by permission.

Staples, Brent. "Black Men and Public Space" from *Ms Magazine,* 1986. Copyright © 1986 by Brent Staples. Reprinted by permission of the author.

Stoll, Clifford. "Cyberschool" from *High Tech Heretic* by Clifford Stoll, © 1999 by Clifford Stoll. Used by permission of Doubleday, a division of Random House, Inc.

Weiner, Eric. "Euromail and Amerimail." Reprinted by permission of the author.

Yahoo! screen captures. Reproduced with permission of Yahoo! Inc. © 2007 by Yahoo! Inc. *Yahoo!* and the *Yahoo!* logo are trademarks of Yahoo! Inc.

Index